Mazda 626 and MX-6 Automotive Repair Manual

by Larry Warren
and John H Haynes
Member of the Guild of Motoring Writers

Models covered:

Mazda 626 and MX-6

1.6, 2.0 and 2.2 liter 4-cylinder engines with 4 or 5-speed manual or 3-speed automatic transaxle

1983 through 1992

Does not include diesel engine information

(4E14 - 61041)
(1082)

ABCDE
FGHIJ
KLMNO
PQRST 3

Haynes Publishing Group
Sparkford Nr Yeovil
Somerset BA22 7JJ England

Haynes North America, Inc
861 Lawrence Drive
Newbury Park
California 91320 USA

Acknowledgements
We are grateful for the help and cooperation of the Mazda Motor Company for their assistance with technical information, certain illustrations and vehicle photos.

A book in the Haynes Automotive Repair Manual Series

Printed in the U.S.A.

ISBN 1 56392 373 4

Library of Congress Catalog Card Number 00-100879

00-288

Contents

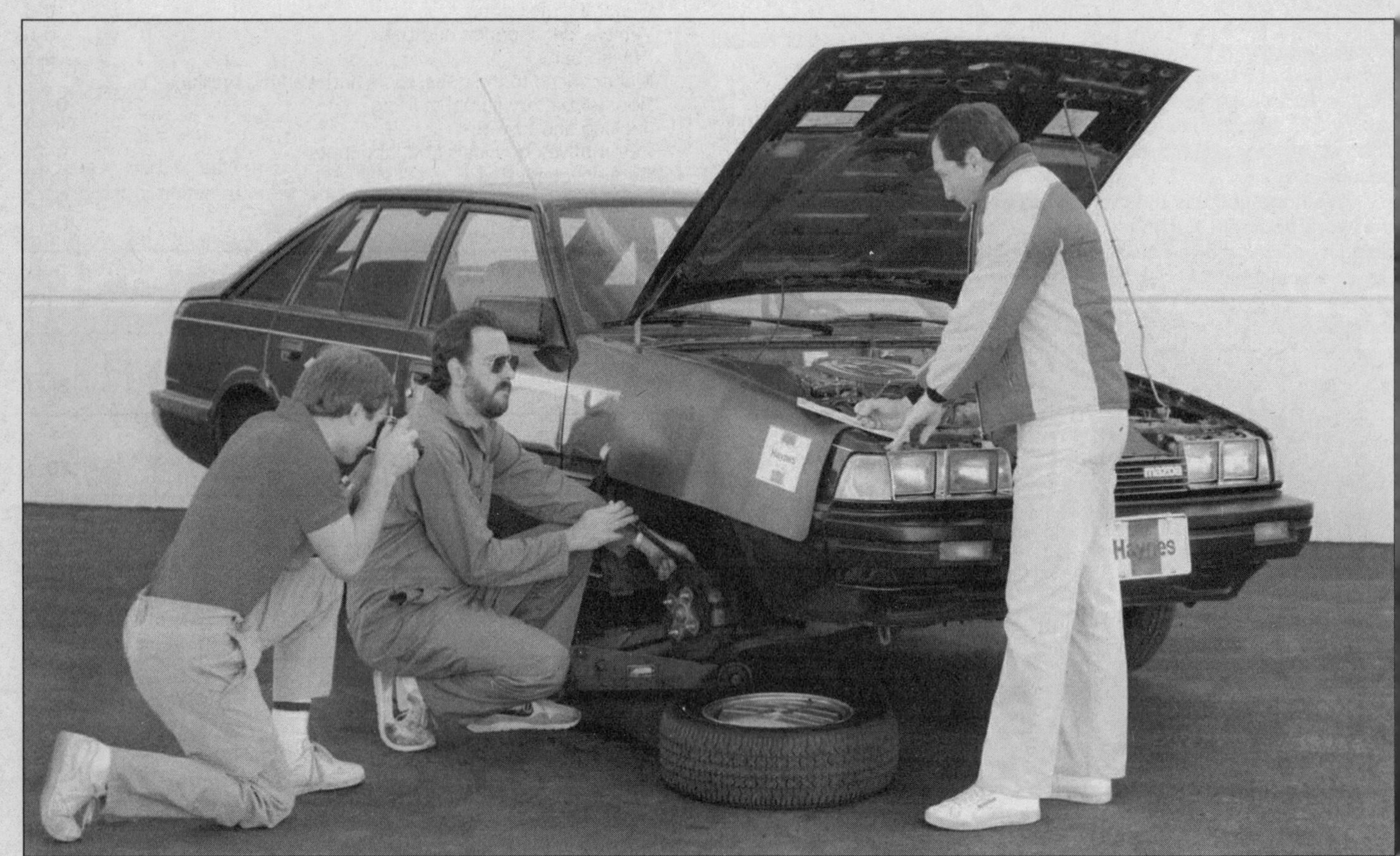

Haynes mechanic, author and photographer with Mazda 626

About this manual

Its purpose

The purpose of this manual is to help you get the best value from your vehicle. It can do so in several ways. It can help you decide what work must be done, even if you choose to have it done by a dealer service department or a repair shop; it provides information and procedures for routine maintenance and servicing; and it offers diagnostic and repair procedures to follow when trouble occurs.

We hope you use the manual to tackle the work yourself. For many simpler jobs, doing it yourself may be quicker than arranging an appointment to get the vehicle into a shop and making the trips to leave it and pick it up. More importantly, a lot of money can be saved by avoiding the expense the shop must pass on to you to cover its labor and overhead costs. An added benefit is the sense of satisfaction and accomplishment that you feel after doing the job yourself.

Using the manual

The manual is divided into Chapters. Each Chapter is divided into numbered Sections, which are headed in bold type between horizontal lines. Each Section consists of consecutively numbered paragraphs.

At the beginning of each numbered Section you will be referred to any illustrations which apply to the procedures in that Section. The reference numbers used in illustration captions pinpoint the pertinent Section and the Step within that Section. That is, illustration 3.2 means the illustration refers to Section 3 and Step (or paragraph) 2 within that Section.

Procedures, once described in the text, are not normally repeated. When it's necessary to refer to another Chapter, the reference will be given as Chapter and Section number. Cross references given without use of the word "Chapter" apply to Sections and/or paragraphs in the same Chapter. For example, "see Section 8" means in the same Chapter.

References to the left or right side of the vehicle assume you are sitting in the driver's seat, facing forward.

Even though we have prepared this manual with extreme care, neither the publisher nor the author can accept responsibility for any errors in, or omissions from, the information given.

NOTE

A **Note** provides information necessary to properly complete a procedure or information which will make the procedure easier to understand.

CAUTION

A **Caution** provides a special procedure or special steps which must be taken while completing the procedure where the Caution is found. Not heeding a Caution can result in damage to the assembly being worked on.

WARNING

A **Warning** provides a special procedure or special steps which must be taken while completing the procedure where the Warning is found. Not heeding a Warning can result in personal injury.

Introduction to the Mazda 626 and MX-6

These models are available in 2-door coupe, 4-door sedan and 4-door liftback body styles and feature four coil suspension and front wheel drive.

The cross-mounted four-cylinder engine is equipped with a conventional carburetor. The engine drives the front wheels through a choice of either a 4-speed or 5-speed manual transaxle or a 3-speed automatic transaxle. The rack and pinion steering gear is mounted behind the engine.

The brakes are disc at the front and either drum-type or disc at the rear, with vacuum servo assist as standard equipment.

General dimensions

Overall length	177 in
Overall width	66.5 in
Overall height	
4-door	55.7 in
2-door	53.7 in

Vehicle identification numbers

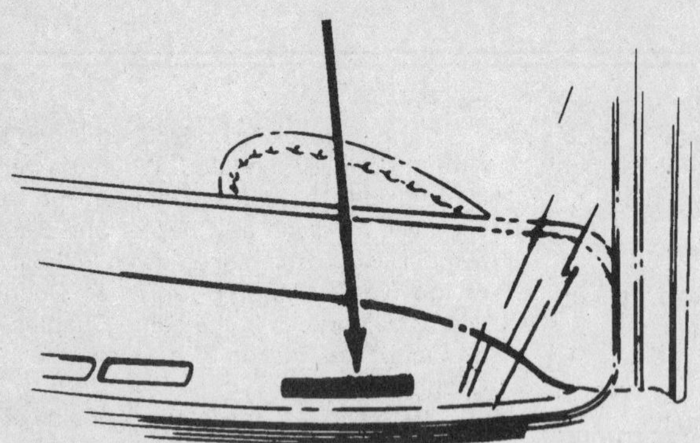

The Vehicle Identification Number (VIN) is located on the driver's side of the dashboard and is visible through the windshield

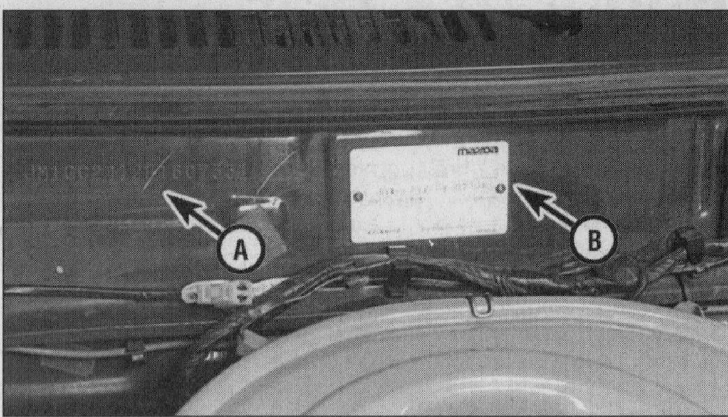

The VIN number can also be found stamped on the engine compartment firewall (A) and the body identification plate (B)

Modifications are a continuing and unpublicized process in vehicle manufacturing. Since spare parts manuals and lists are compiled on a numerical basis, the individual vehicle numbers are essential to correctly identify the component required.

Vehicle identification number (VIN)

This very important identification number is located on a plate attached to the top left corner of the dashboard of all U.S. vehicles. The VIN is also stamped on the firewall in the engine compartment and on the adjacent body identification tag. The VIN also appears on the Vehicle Certificate of Title and Registration. It contains valuable information such as where and when the vehicle was manufactured, the model year and the body style.

Engine identification numbers

The engine identification numbers are stamped on the cylinder block below the number one spark plug, adjacent to the alternator.

Transaxle number

The transaxle ID numbers are stamped on a label affixed to the bellhousing, below the rear of the cylinder head.

Alternator numbers

The alternator numbers are located on a tag affixed to the housing

Vehicle Emissions Control Information numbers

The Emissions Control Information label is attached to the underside of the hood.

Engine information labels

The vacuum hose routing, recommended lubricant and drivebelt checking adjustment procedure diagram labels are all located on the underside of the hood (photo).

Body identification

The body identification tag is attached to the engine compartment firewall.

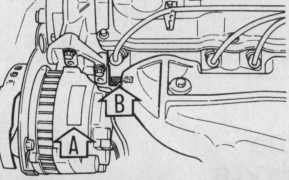

The alternator serial number (A) and engine number (B) locations

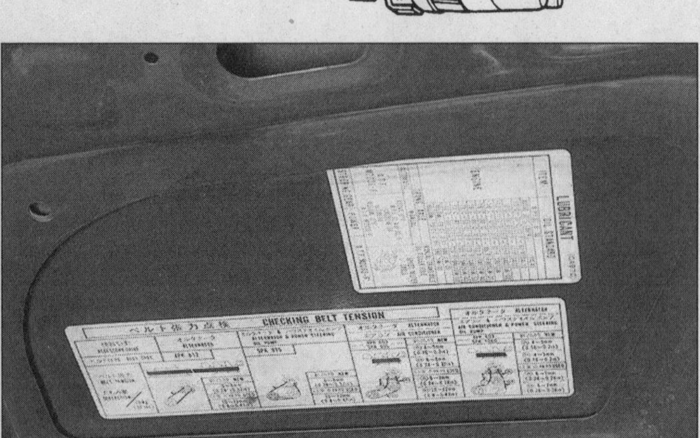

The recommended lubricant and engine drivebelt information labels can be found on the underside of the hood (U.S. models only)

The Vehicle Emissions Control Information label (U.S. models only) is located on the hood near the latch hook

Buying parts

Replacement parts are available from many sources, which generally fall into one of two categories - authorized dealer parts departments and independent retail auto parts stores. Our advice concerning these parts is as follows:

Retail auto parts stores: Good auto parts stores will stock frequently needed components which wear out relatively fast, such as clutch components, exhaust systems, brake parts, tune-up parts, etc. These stores often supply new or reconditioned parts on an exchange basis, which can save a considerable amount of money. Discount auto parts stores are often very good places to buy materials and parts needed for general vehicle maintenance such as oil, grease, filters, spark plugs, belts, touch-up paint, bulbs, etc. They also usually sell tools and general accessories, have convenient hours, charge lower prices and can often be found not far from home.

Authorized dealer parts department: This is the best source for parts which are unique to the vehicle and not generally available elsewhere (such as major engine parts, transmission parts, trim pieces, etc.).

Warranty information: If the vehicle is still covered under warranty, be sure that any replacement parts purchased - regardless of the source - do not invalidate the warranty!

To be sure of obtaining the correct parts, have engine and chassis numbers available and, if possible, take the old parts along for positive identification.

Maintenance techniques, tools and working facilities

Maintenance techniques

There are a number of techniques involved in maintenance and repair that will be referred to throughout this manual. Application of these techniques will enable the home mechanic to be more efficient, better organized and capable of performing the various tasks properly, which will ensure that the repair job is thorough and complete.

Fasteners

Fasteners are nuts, bolts, studs and screws used to hold two or more parts together. There are a few things to keep in mind when working with fasteners. Almost all of them use a locking device of some type, either a lockwasher, locknut, locking tab or thread adhesive. All threaded fasteners should be clean and straight, with undamaged threads and undamaged corners on the hex head where the wrench fits. Develop the habit of replacing all damaged nuts and bolts with new ones. Special locknuts with nylon or fiber inserts can only be used once. If they are removed, they lose their locking ability and must be replaced with new ones.

Rusted nuts and bolts should be treated with a penetrating fluid to ease removal and prevent breakage. Some mechanics use turpentine in a spout-type oil can, which works quite well. After applying the rust penetrant, let it work for a few minutes before trying to loosen the nut or bolt. Badly rusted fasteners may have to be chiseled or sawed off or removed with a special nut breaker, available at tool stores.

If a bolt or stud breaks off in an assembly, it can be drilled and removed with a special tool commonly available for this purpose. Most automotive machine shops can perform this task, as well as other repair procedures, such as the repair of threaded holes that have been stripped out.

Flat washers and lockwashers, when removed from an assembly, should always be replaced exactly as removed. Replace any damaged washers with new ones. Never use a lockwasher on any soft metal surface (such as aluminum), thin sheet metal or plastic.

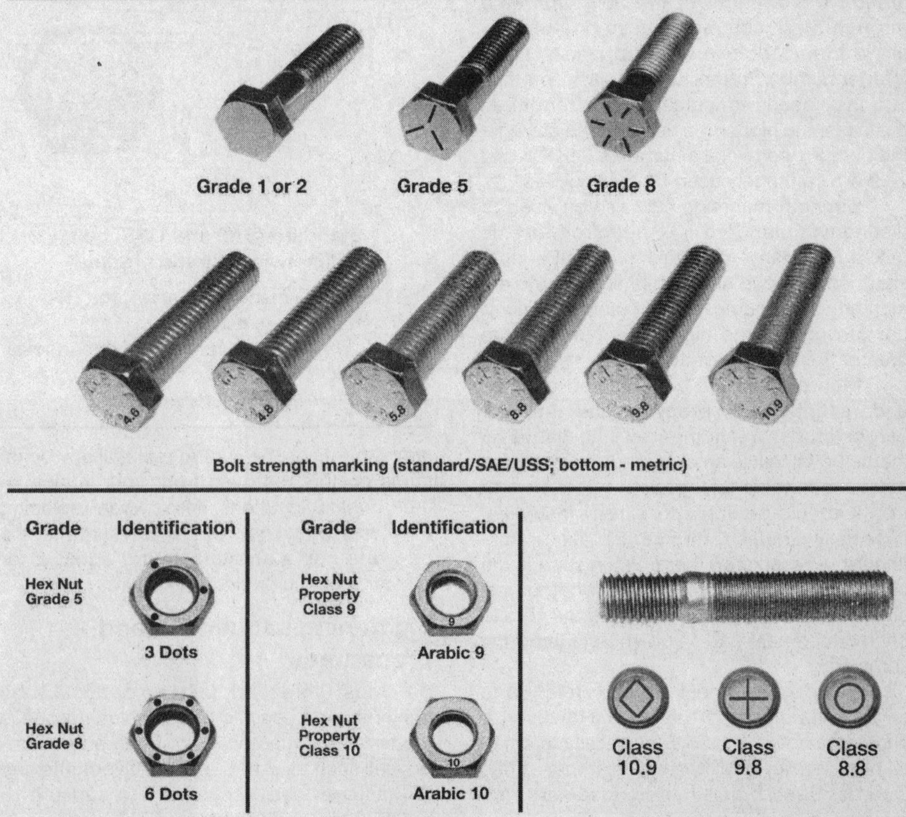

Fastener sizes

For a number of reasons, automobile manufacturers are making wider and wider use of metric fasteners. Therefore, it is important to be able to tell the difference between standard (sometimes called U.S. or SAE) and metric hardware, since they cannot be interchanged.

All bolts, whether standard or metric, are sized according to diameter, thread pitch and length. For example, a standard 1/2 - 13 x 1 bolt is 1/2 inch in diameter, has 13 threads per inch and is 1 inch long. An M12 - 1.75 x 25 metric bolt is 12 mm in diameter, has a thread pitch of 1.75 mm (the distance between threads) and is 25 mm long. The two bolts are nearly identical, and easily confused, but they are not interchangeable.

In addition to the differences in diameter, thread pitch and length, metric and standard bolts can also be distinguished by examining the bolt heads. To begin with, the distance across the flats on a standard bolt head is measured in inches, while the same dimension on a metric bolt is sized in millimeters (the same is true for nuts). As a result, a standard wrench should not be used on a metric bolt and a metric wrench should not be used on a standard bolt. Also, most standard bolts have slashes radiating out from the center of the head to denote the grade or strength of the bolt, which is an indication of the amount of torque that can be applied to it. The greater the number of slashes, the greater the strength of the bolt. Grades 0 through 5 are commonly used on automobiles. Metric bolts have a property class (grade) number, rather than a slash, molded into their heads to indicate bolt strength. In this case, the higher the number, the stronger the bolt. Property class numbers 8.8, 9.8 and 10.9 are commonly used on automobiles.

Strength markings can also be used to distinguish standard hex nuts from metric hex nuts. Many standard nuts have dots stamped into one side, while metric nuts are marked with a number. The greater the number of dots, or the higher the number, the greater the strength of the nut.

Metric studs are also marked on their ends according to property class (grade). Larger studs are numbered (the same as metric bolts), while smaller studs carry a geometric code to denote grade.

It should be noted that many fasteners, especially Grades 0 through 2, have no distinguishing marks on them. When such is the case, the only way to determine whether it is standard or metric is to measure the thread pitch or compare it to a known fastener of the same size.

Standard fasteners are often referred to as SAE, as opposed to metric. However, it should be noted that SAE technically refers to a non-metric fine thread fastener only. Coarse thread non-metric fasteners are referred to as USS sizes.

Since fasteners of the same size (both standard and metric) may have different strength ratings, be sure to reinstall any bolts, studs or nuts removed from your vehicle in their original locations. Also, when replacing a fastener with a new one, make sure that the new one has a strength rating equal to or greater than the original.

Metric thread sizes	**Ft-lbs**	**Nm**
M-6	6 to 9	9 to 12
M-8	14 to 21	19 to 28
M-10	28 to 40	38 to 54
M-12	50 to 71	68 to 96
M-14	80 to 140	109 to 154
Pipe thread sizes		
1/8	5 to 8	7 to 10
1/4	12 to 18	17 to 24
3/8	22 to 33	30 to 44
1/2	25 to 35	34 to 47
U.S. thread sizes		
1/4 - 20	6 to 9	9 to 12
5/16 - 18	12 to 18	17 to 24
5/16 - 24	14 to 20	19 to 27
3/8 - 16	22 to 32	30 to 43
3/8 - 24	27 to 38	37 to 51
7/16 - 14	40 to 55	55 to 74
7/16 - 20	40 to 60	55 to 81
1/2 - 13	55 to 80	75 to 108

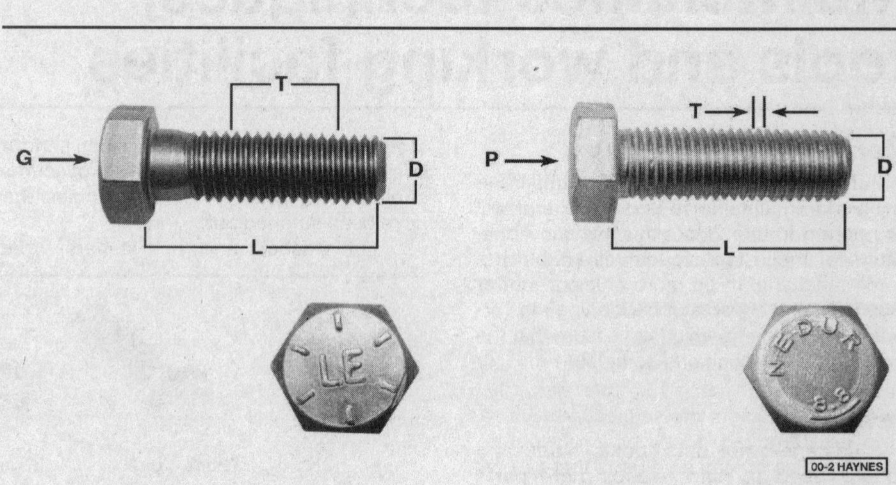

Standard (SAE and USS) bolt dimensions/grade marks

G *Grade marks (bolt strength)*
L *Length (in inches)*
T *Thread pitch (number of threads per inch)*
D *Nominal diameter (in inches)*

Metric bolt dimensions/grade marks

P *Property class (bolt strength)*
L *Length (in millimeters)*
T *Thread pitch (distance between threads in millimeters)*
D *Diameter*

Tightening sequences and procedures

Most threaded fasteners should be tightened to a specific torque value (torque is the twisting force applied to a threaded component such as a nut or bolt). Overtightening the fastener can weaken it and cause it to break, while undertightening can cause it to eventually come loose. Bolts, screws and studs, depending on the material they are made of and their thread diameters, have specific torque values, many of which are noted in the Specifications at the beginning of each Chapter. Be sure to follow the torque recommendations closely. For fasteners not assigned a specific torque, a general torque value chart is presented here as a guide. These torque values are for dry (unlubricated) fasteners threaded into steel or cast iron (not aluminum). As was previously mentioned, the size and grade of a fastener determine the amount of torque that can safely be applied to it. The figures listed here are approximate for Grade 2 and Grade 3 fasteners. Higher grades can tolerate higher torque values.

Fasteners laid out in a pattern, such as cylinder head bolts, oil pan bolts, differential cover bolts, etc., must be loosened or tight-

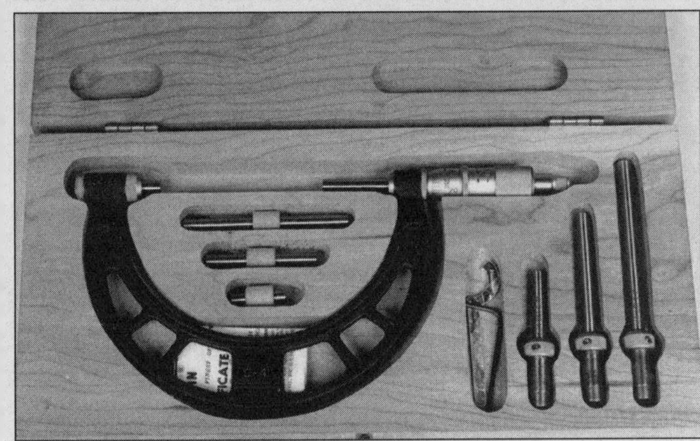
Micrometer set

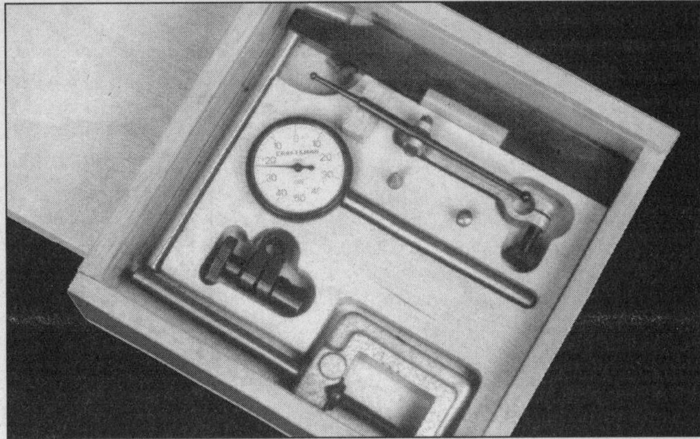
Dial indicator set

ened in sequence to avoid warping the component. This sequence will normally be shown in the appropriate Chapter. If a specific pattern is not given, the following procedures can be used to prevent warping.

Initially, the bolts or nuts should be assembled finger-tight only. Next, they should be tightened one full turn each, in a criss-cross or diagonal pattern. After each one has been tightened one full turn, return to the first one and tighten them all one-half turn, following the same pattern. Finally, tighten each of them one-quarter turn at a time until each fastener has been tightened to the proper torque. To loosen and remove the fasteners, the procedure would be reversed.

Component disassembly

Component disassembly should be done with care and purpose to help ensure that the parts go back together properly. Always keep track of the sequence in which parts are removed. Make note of special characteristics or marks on parts that can be installed more than one way, such as a grooved thrust washer on a shaft. It is a good idea to lay the disassembled parts out on a clean surface in the order that they were removed. It may also be helpful to make sketches or take instant photos of components before removal.

When removing fasteners from a component, keep track of their locations. Sometimes threading a bolt back in a part, or putting the washers and nut back on a stud, can prevent mix-ups later. If nuts and bolts cannot be returned to their original locations, they should be kept in a compartmented box or a series of small boxes. A cupcake or muffin tin is ideal for this purpose, since each cavity can hold the bolts and nuts from a particular area (i.e. oil pan bolts, valve cover bolts, engine mount bolts, etc.). A pan of this type is especially helpful when working on assemblies with very small parts, such as the carburetor, alternator, valve train or interior dash and trim pieces. The cavities can be marked with paint or tape to identify the contents.

Whenever wiring looms, harnesses or connectors are separated, it is a good idea to identify the two halves with numbered pieces of masking tape so they can be easily reconnected.

Gasket sealing surfaces

Throughout any vehicle, gaskets are used to seal the mating surfaces between two parts and keep lubricants, fluids, vacuum or pressure contained in an assembly.

Many times these gaskets are coated with a liquid or paste-type gasket sealing compound before assembly. Age, heat and pressure can sometimes cause the two parts to stick together so tightly that they are very difficult to separate. Often, the assembly can be loosened by striking it with a soft-face hammer near the mating surfaces. A regular hammer can be used if a block of wood is placed between the hammer and the part. Do not hammer on cast parts or parts that could be easily damaged. With any particularly stubborn part, always recheck to make sure that every fastener has been removed.

Avoid using a screwdriver or bar to pry apart an assembly, as they can easily mar the gasket sealing surfaces of the parts, which must remain smooth. If prying is absolutely necessary, use an old broom handle, but keep in mind that extra clean up will be necessary if the wood splinters.

After the parts are separated, the old gasket must be carefully scraped off and the gasket surfaces cleaned. Stubborn gasket material can be soaked with rust penetrant or treated with a special chemical to soften it so it can be easily scraped off. A scraper can be fashioned from a piece of copper tubing by flattening and sharpening one end. Copper is recommended because it is usually softer than the surfaces to be scraped, which reduces the chance of gouging the part. Some gaskets can be removed with a wire brush, but regardless of the method used, the mating surfaces must be left clean and smooth. If for some reason the gasket surface is gouged, then a gasket sealer thick enough to fill scratches will have to be used during reassembly of the components. For most applications, a non-drying (or semi-drying) gasket sealer should be used.

Hose removal tips

Warning: *If the vehicle is equipped with air conditioning, do not disconnect any of the A/C hoses without first having the system depressurized by a dealer service department or a service station.*

Hose removal precautions closely parallel gasket removal precautions. Avoid scratching or gouging the surface that the hose mates against or the connection may leak. This is especially true for radiator hoses. Because of various chemical reactions, the rubber in hoses can bond itself to the metal spigot that the hose fits over. To remove a hose, first loosen the hose clamps that secure it to the spigot. Then, with slip-joint pliers, grab the hose at the clamp and rotate it around the spigot. Work it back and forth until it is completely free, then pull it off. Silicone or other lubricants will ease removal if they can be applied between the hose and the outside of the spigot. Apply the same lubricant to the inside of the hose and the outside of the spigot to simplify installation.

As a last resort (and if the hose is to be replaced with a new one anyway), the rubber can be slit with a knife and the hose peeled from the spigot. If this must be done, be careful that the metal connection is not damaged.

If a hose clamp is broken or damaged, do not reuse it. Wire-type clamps usually weaken with age, so it is a good idea to replace them with screw-type clamps whenever a hose is removed.

Tools

A selection of good tools is a basic requirement for anyone who plans to maintain and repair his or her own vehicle. For the owner who has few tools, the initial investment might seem high, but when compared to the spiraling costs of professional auto maintenance and repair, it is a wise one.

To help the owner decide which tools are needed to perform the tasks detailed in this manual, the following tool lists are offered: *Maintenance and minor repair, Repair/overhaul* and *Special.*

The newcomer to practical mechanics

Dial caliper

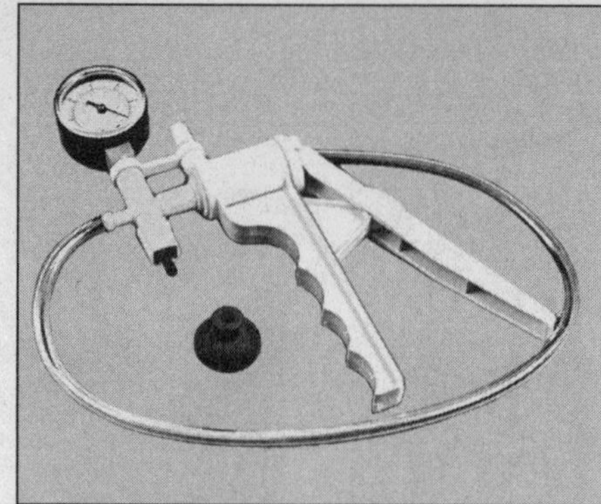
Hand-operated vacuum pump

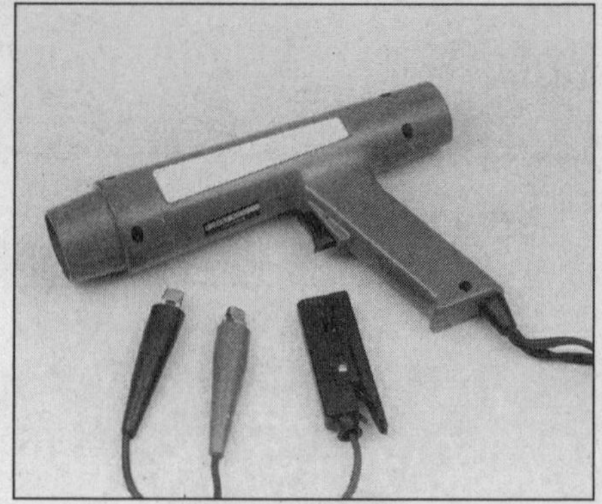
Timing light

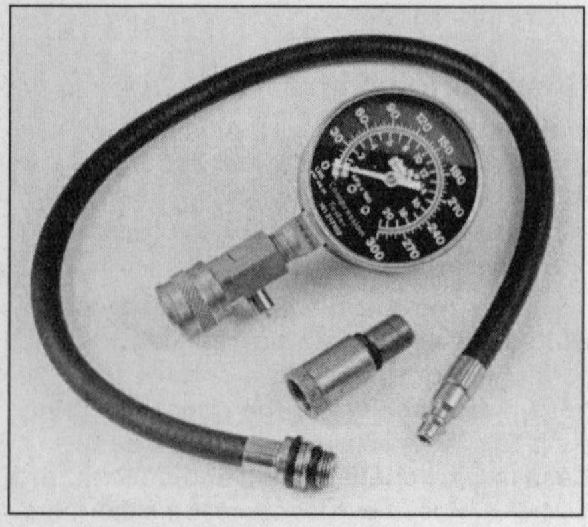
Compression gauge with spark plug hole adapter

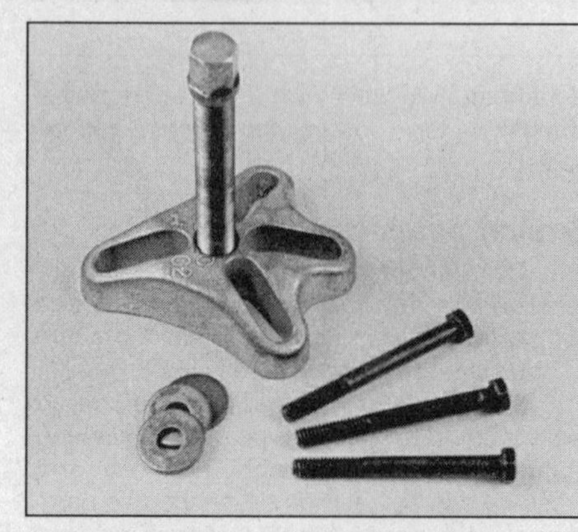
Damper/steering wheel puller

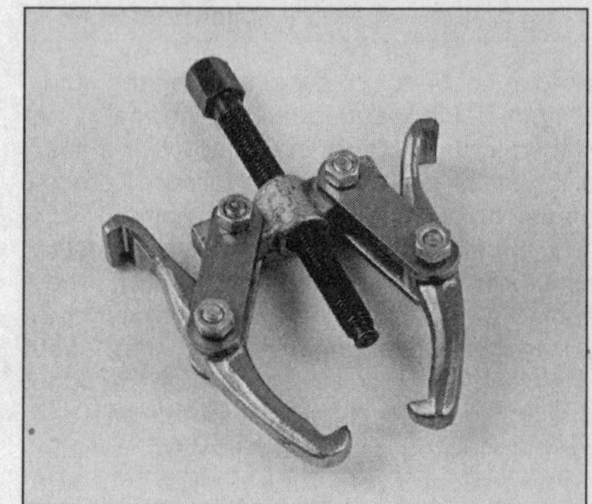
General purpose puller

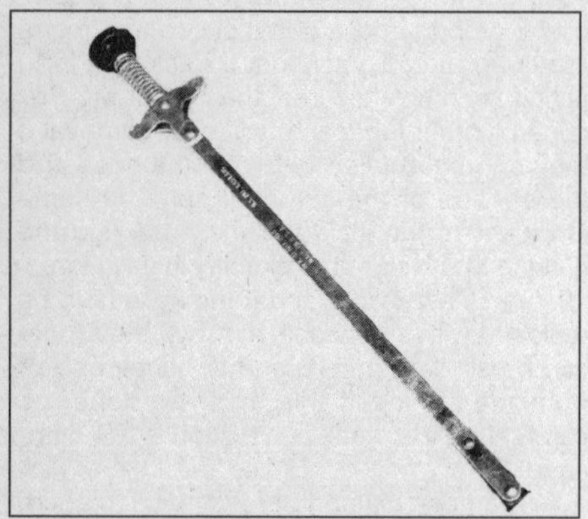
Hydraulic lifter removal tool

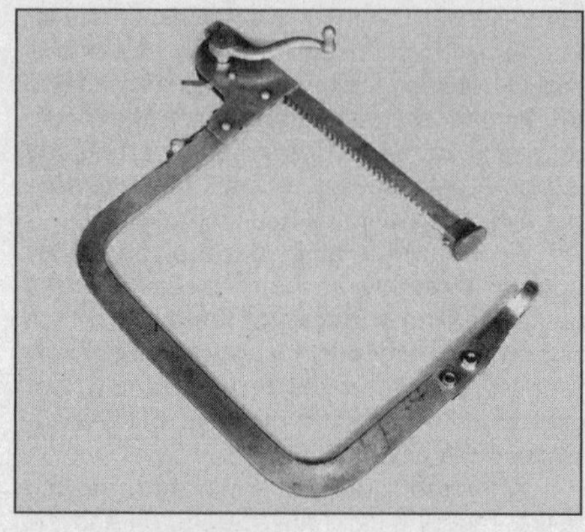
Valve spring compressor

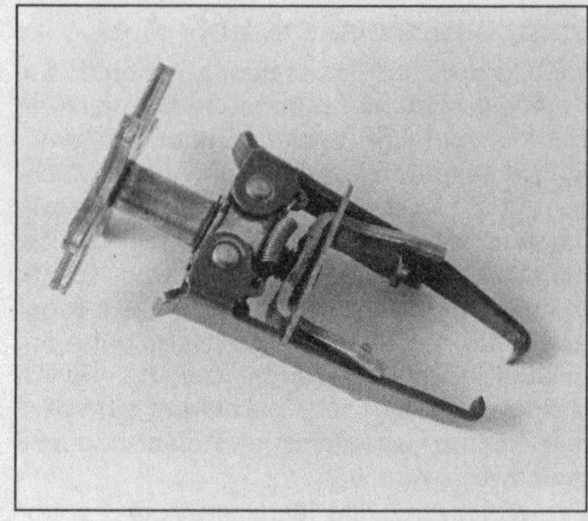
Valve spring compressor

Ridge reamer

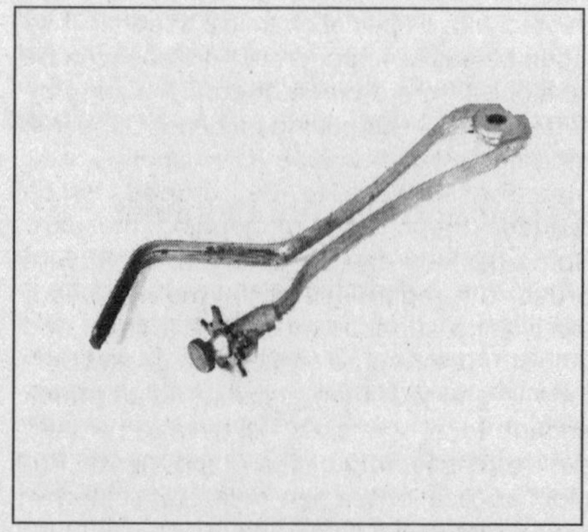
Piston ring groove cleaning tool

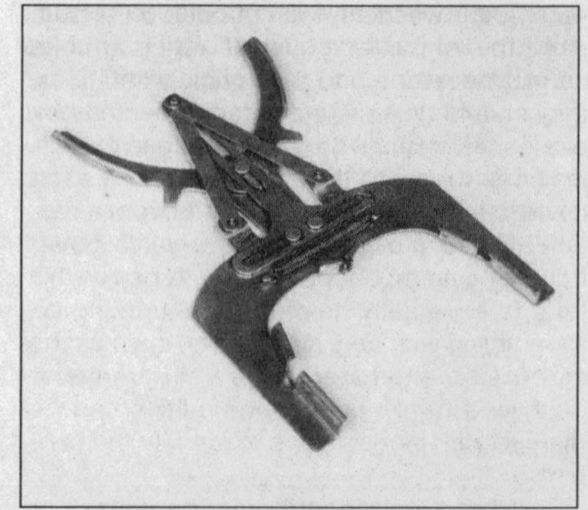
Ring removal/installation tool

Ring compressor

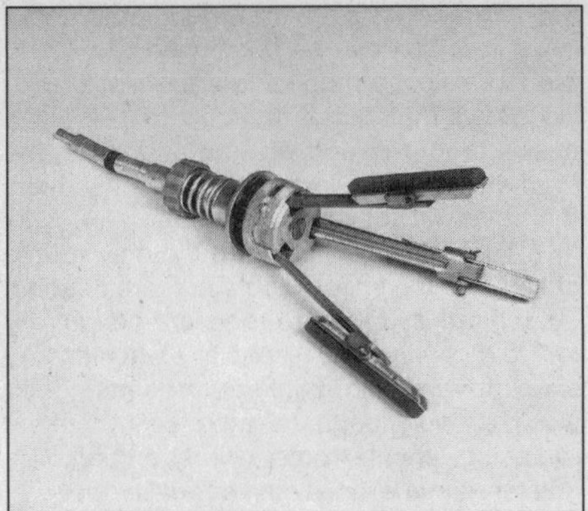

Cylinder hone

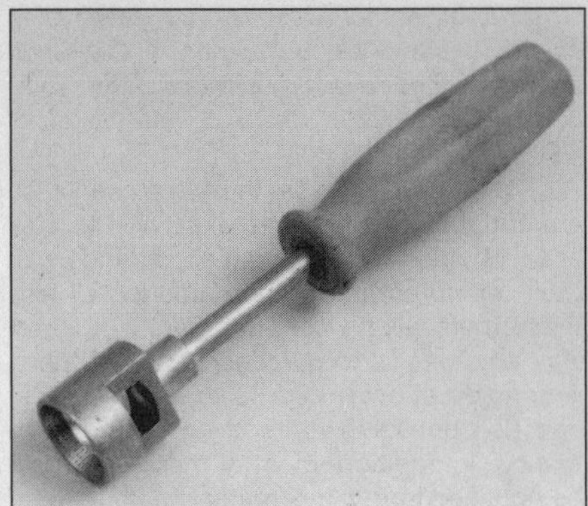

Brake hold-down spring tool

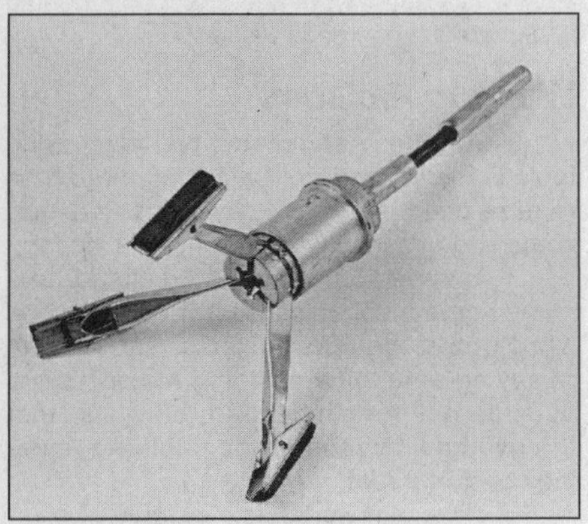

Brake cylinder hone

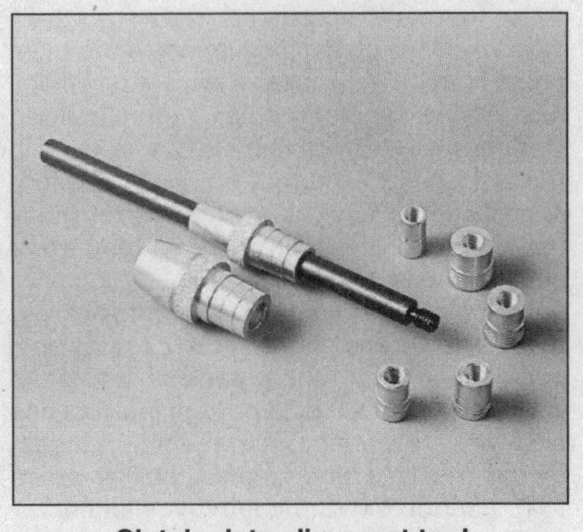

Clutch plate alignment tool

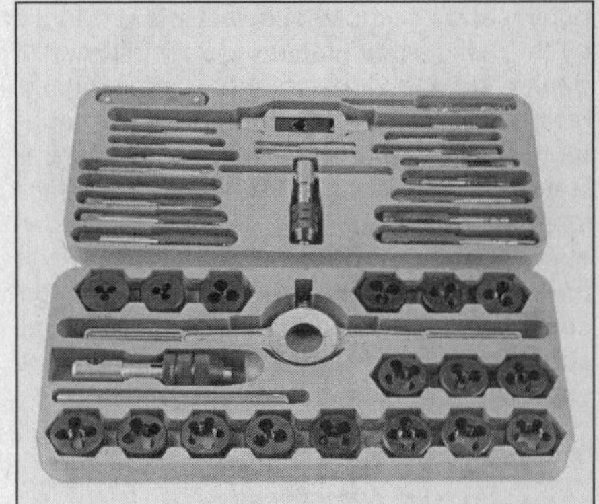

Tap and die set

should start off with the *maintenance and minor repair* tool kit, which is adequate for the simpler jobs performed on a vehicle. Then, as confidence and experience grow, the owner can tackle more difficult tasks, buying additional tools as they are needed. Eventually the basic kit will be expanded into the *repair and overhaul* tool set. Over a period of time, the experienced do-it-yourselfer will assemble a tool set complete enough for most repair and overhaul procedures and will add tools from the special category when it is felt that the expense is justified by the frequency of use.

Maintenance and minor repair tool kit

The tools in this list should be considered the minimum required for performance of routine maintenance, servicing and minor repair work. We recommend the purchase of combination wrenches (box-end and open-end combined in one wrench). While more expensive than open end wrenches, they offer the advantages of both types of wrench.

Combination wrench set (1/4-inch to 1 inch or 6 mm to 19 mm)
Adjustable wrench, 8 inch
Spark plug wrench with rubber insert
Spark plug gap adjusting tool
Feeler gauge set
Brake bleeder wrench
Standard screwdriver (5/16-inch x 6 inch)
Phillips screwdriver (No. 2 x 6 inch)
Combination pliers - 6 inch
Hacksaw and assortment of blades
Tire pressure gauge
Grease gun
Oil can
Fine emery cloth
Wire brush
Battery post and cable cleaning tool
Oil filter wrench
Funnel (medium size)
Safety goggles
Jackstands (2)
Drain pan

Note: *If basic tune-ups are going to be part of routine maintenance, it will be necessary to purchase a good quality stroboscopic timing light and combination tachometer/dwell meter. Although they are included in the list of special tools, it is mentioned here because they are absolutely necessary for tuning most vehicles properly.*

Repair and overhaul tool set

These tools are essential for anyone who plans to perform major repairs and are in addition to those in the maintenance and minor repair tool kit. Included is a comprehensive set of sockets which, though expensive, are invaluable because of their versatility, especially when various extensions and drives are available. We recommend the 1/2-inch drive over the 3/8-inch drive. Although the larger drive is bulky and more expensive, it has the capacity of accepting a very wide range of large sockets. Ideally, however, the mechanic should have a 3/8-inch drive set and a 1/2-inch drive set.

Socket set(s)
Reversible ratchet
Extension - 10 inch
Universal joint
Torque wrench (same size drive as sockets)
Ball peen hammer - 8 ounce
Soft-face hammer (plastic/rubber)
Standard screwdriver (1/4-inch x 6 inch)
Standard screwdriver (stubby - 5/16-inch)
Phillips screwdriver (No. 3 x 8 inch)
Phillips screwdriver (stubby - No. 2)
Pliers - vise grip
Pliers - lineman's
Pliers - needle nose
Pliers - snap-ring (internal and external)
Cold chisel - 1/2-inch
Scribe
Scraper (made from flattened copper tubing)
Centerpunch
Pin punches (1/16, 1/8, 3/16-inch)
Steel rule/straightedge - 12 inch
Allen wrench set (1/8 to 3/8-inch or 4 mm to 10 mm)
A selection of files
Wire brush (large)
Jackstands (second set)
Jack (scissor or hydraulic type)

Note: *Another tool which is often useful is an electric drill with a chuck capacity of 3/8-inch and a set of good quality drill bits.*

Special tools

The tools in this list include those which are not used regularly, are expensive to buy, or which need to be used in accordance with their manufacturer's instructions. Unless these tools will be used frequently, it is not very economical to purchase many of them. A consideration would be to split the cost and use between yourself and a friend or friends. In addition, most of these tools can be obtained from a tool rental shop on a temporary basis.

This list primarily contains only those tools and instruments widely available to the public, and not those special tools produced by the vehicle manufacturer for distribution to dealer service departments. Occasionally, references to the manufacturer's special tools are included in the text of this manual. Generally, an alternative method of doing the job without the special tool is offered. However, sometimes there is no alternative to their use. Where this is the case, and the tool cannot be purchased or borrowed, the work should be turned over to the dealer service department or an automotive repair shop.

Valve spring compressor
Piston ring groove cleaning tool
Piston ring compressor
Piston ring installation tool
Cylinder compression gauge
Cylinder ridge reamer
Cylinder surfacing hone
Cylinder bore gauge
Micrometers and/or dial calipers
Hydraulic lifter removal tool
Balljoint separator
Universal-type puller
Impact screwdriver
Dial indicator set
Stroboscopic timing light (inductive pick-up)
Hand operated vacuum/pressure pump
Tachometer/dwell meter
Universal electrical multimeter
Cable hoist
Brake spring removal and installation tools
Floor jack

Buying tools

For the do-it-yourselfer who is just starting to get involved in vehicle maintenance and repair, there are a number of options available when purchasing tools. If maintenance and minor repair is the extent of the work to be done, the purchase of individual tools is satisfactory. If, on the other hand, extensive work is planned, it would be a good idea to purchase a modest tool set from one of the large retail chain stores. A set can usually be bought at a substantial savings over the individual tool prices, and they often come with a tool box. As additional tools are needed, add-on sets, individual tools and a larger tool box can be purchased to expand the tool selection. Building a tool set gradually allows the cost of the tools to be spread over a longer period of time and gives the mechanic the freedom to choose only those tools that will actually be used.

Tool stores will often be the only source of some of the special tools that are needed, but regardless of where tools are bought, try to avoid cheap ones, especially when buying screwdrivers and sockets, because they won't last very long. The expense involved in replacing cheap tools will eventually be greater than the initial cost of quality tools.

Care and maintenance of tools

Good tools are expensive, so it makes sense to treat them with respect. Keep them clean and in usable condition and store them properly when not in use. Always wipe off any dirt, grease or metal chips before putting them away. Never leave tools lying around in the work area. Upon completion of a job, always check closely under the hood for tools that may have been left there so they won't get lost during a test drive.

Some tools, such as screwdrivers, pliers, wrenches and sockets, can be hung on a panel mounted on the garage or workshop wall, while others should be kept in a tool box or tray. Measuring instruments, gauges, meters, etc. must be carefully stored where they cannot be damaged by weather or impact from other tools.

When tools are used with care and stored properly, they will last a very long time. Even with the best of care, though, tools will wear out if used frequently. When a tool is damaged or worn out, replace it. Subsequent jobs will be safer and more enjoyable if you do.

How to repair damaged threads

Sometimes, the internal threads of a nut or bolt hole can become stripped, usually from overtightening. Stripping threads is an all-too-common occurrence, especially when working with aluminum parts, because aluminum is so soft that it easily strips out.

Usually, external or internal threads are only partially stripped. After they've been cleaned up with a tap or die, they'll still work. Sometimes, however, threads are badly damaged. When this happens, you've got three choices:

1) *Drill and tap the hole to the next suitable oversize and install a larger diameter bolt, screw or stud.*
2) *Drill and tap the hole to accept a threaded plug, then drill and tap the plug to the original screw size. You can also buy a plug already threaded to the original size. Then you simply drill a hole to the specified size, then run the threaded plug into the hole with a bolt and jam nut. Once the plug is fully seated, remove the jam nut and bolt.*
3) *The third method uses a patented thread repair kit like Heli-Coil or Slimsert. These easy-to-use kits are designed to repair damaged threads in straight-through holes and blind holes. Both are available as kits which can handle a variety of sizes and thread patterns. Drill the hole, then tap it with the special included tap. Install the Heli-Coil and the hole is back to its original diameter and thread pitch.*

Regardless of which method you use, be sure to proceed calmly and carefully. A little impatience or carelessness during one of these relatively simple procedures can ruin your whole day's work and cost you a bundle if you wreck an expensive part.

Working facilities

Not to be overlooked when discussing tools is the workshop. If anything more than routine maintenance is to be carried out, some sort of suitable work area is essential.

It is understood, and appreciated, that many home mechanics do not have a good workshop or garage available, and end up removing an engine or doing major repairs outside. It is recommended, however, that the overhaul or repair be completed under the cover of a roof.

A clean, flat workbench or table of comfortable working height is an absolute necessity. The workbench should be equipped with a vise that has a jaw opening of at least four inches.

As mentioned previously, some clean, dry storage space is also required for tools, as well as the lubricants, fluids, cleaning solvents, etc. which soon become necessary.

Sometimes waste oil and fluids, drained from the engine or cooling system during normal maintenance or repairs, present a disposal problem. To avoid pouring them on the ground or into a sewage system, pour the used fluids into large containers, seal them with caps and take them to an authorized disposal site or recycling center. Plastic jugs, such as old antifreeze containers, are ideal for this purpose.

Always keep a supply of old newspapers and clean rags available. Old towels are excellent for mopping up spills. Many mechanics use rolls of paper towels for most work because they are readily available and disposable. To help keep the area under the vehicle clean, a large cardboard box can be cut open and flattened to protect the garage or shop floor.

Whenever working over a painted surface, such as when leaning over a fender to service something under the hood, always cover it with an old blanket or bedspread to protect the finish. Vinyl covered pads, made especially for this purpose, are available at auto parts stores.

Booster battery (jump) starting

Observe the following precautions when using a booster battery to start a vehicle:

a) *Before connecting the booster battery, make sure the ignition switch is in the Off position.*
b) *Ensure that all electrical equipment (lights, heater, wipers etc.) are switched off.*
c) *Make sure that the booster battery is the same voltage as the discharged battery in the vehicle.*
d) *If the battery is being jump started from the battery in another vehicle, the two vehicles MUST NOT TOUCH each other.*
e) *Make sure the transaxle is in Neutral (manual transaxle) or Park (automatic transaxle).*
f) *Wear eye protection when jump starting a vehicle.*

Connect one jumper lead between the positive (+) terminals of the two batteries. Connect the other jumper lead first to the negative (-) terminal of the booster battery, then to a good engine ground on the vehicle to be started **(see illustration)**. Attach the lead at least 18 inches from the battery, if possible. Make sure that the jumper leads will not contact the fan, drivebelt of other moving parts of the engine.

Start the engine using the booster battery and allow the engine idle speed to stabilize. Disconnect the jumper leads in the reverse order of connection.

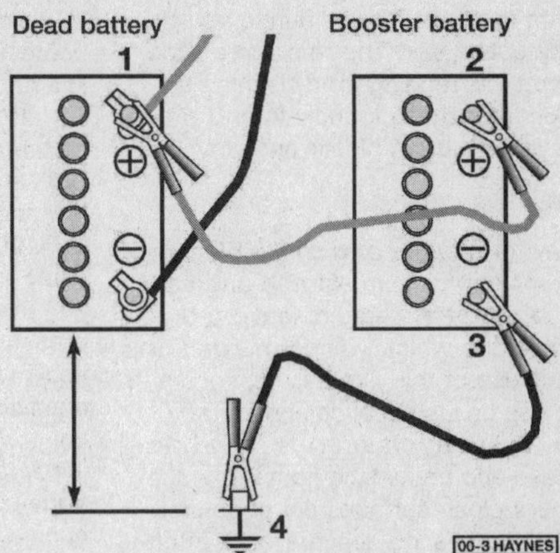

Make the booster battery cable connections in the numerical order shown (note that the negative cable of the booster battery is NOT attached to the negative terminal of the dead battery)

Jacking and towing

Jacking

The jack supplied with the vehicle should only be used for raising the vehicle when changing a tire or placing jackstands under the frame. **Warning**: *Never work under the vehicle or start the engine while this jack is being used as the only means of support.*

The vehicle should be on level ground with the wheels blocked and the transaxle in Park (automatic) or Reverse (manual). On 4WD models, the transfer case must be in the 2H, 4H or 4L position (never in Neutral). If the wheel is being changed, loosen the lug nuts one–half turn and leave them in place until the wheel is raised off the ground.

Place the jack under the side of the vehicle in the indicated position and raise it until the jack head groove fits into the rocker flange notch. Operate the jack with a slow, smooth motion until the wheel is raised off the ground.

Lower the vehicle, remove the jack and tighten the nuts (if loosened or removed) in a criss–cross sequence by turning the wrench clockwise. Replace the hub cap (if equipped) by placing it in position and using the heel of your hand or a rubber mallet to seat it.

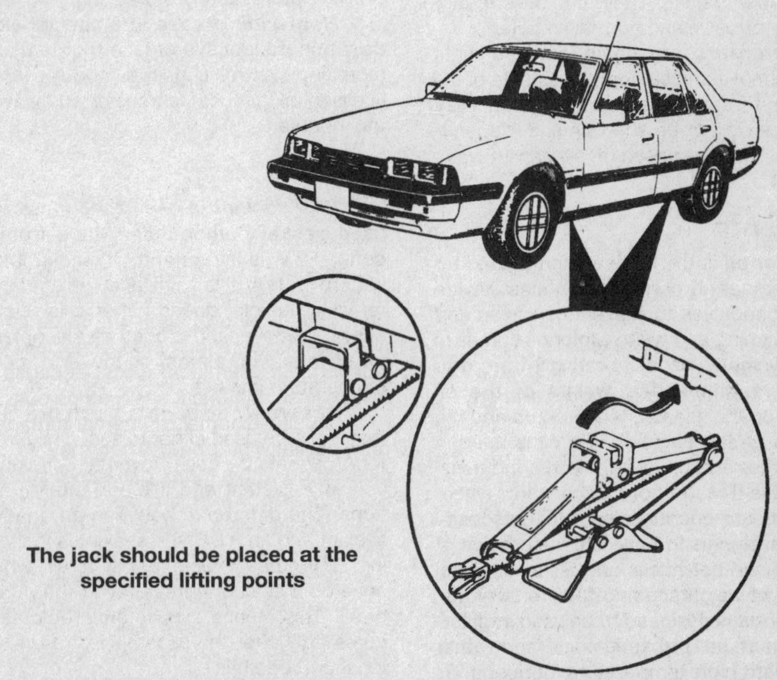

The jack should be placed at the specified lifting points

Towing

The vehicle can be towed with all four wheels on the ground, provided that speeds do not exceed 35 mph and the distance is not over 50 miles, otherwise transaxle damage can result.

Towing equipment specifically designed for this purpose should be used and should be attached to the main structural members of the vehicle, not the bumper or brackets.

Safety is a major consideration when towing and all applicable state and local laws must be obeyed. A safety chain system must be used for all towing.

While towing, the parking brake should be released and the transaxle must be in Neutral. The steering must be unlocked (ignition switch in the Acc position). Remember that power steering and power brakes will not work with the engine off.

Automotive chemicals and lubricants

A number of automotive chemicals and lubricants are available for use during vehicle maintenance and repair. They include a wide variety of products ranging from cleaning solvents and degreasers to lubricants and protective sprays for rubber, plastic and vinyl.

Cleaners

Carburetor cleaner and choke cleaner is a strong solvent for gum, varnish and carbon. Most carburetor cleaners leave a dry-type lubricant film which will not harden or gum up. Because of this film it is not recommended for use on electrical components.

Brake system cleaner is used to remove grease and brake fluid from the brake system, where clean surfaces are absolutely necessary. It leaves no residue and often eliminates brake squeal caused by contaminants.

Electrical cleaner removes oxidation, corrosion and carbon deposits from electrical contacts, restoring full current flow. It can also be used to clean spark plugs, carburetor jets, voltage regulators and other parts where an oil-free surface is desired.

Demoisturants remove water and moisture from electrical components such as alternators, voltage regulators, electrical connectors and fuse blocks. They are non-conductive, non-corrosive and non-flammable.

Degreasers are heavy-duty solvents used to remove grease from the outside of the engine and from chassis components. They can be sprayed or brushed on and, depending on the type, are rinsed off either with water or solvent.

Lubricants

Motor oil is the lubricant formulated for use in engines. It normally contains a wide variety of additives to prevent corrosion and reduce foaming and wear. Motor oil comes in various weights (viscosity ratings) from 0 to 50. The recommended weight of the oil depends on the season, temperature and the demands on the engine. Light oil is used in cold climates and under light load conditions. Heavy oil is used in hot climates and where high loads are encountered. Multi-viscosity oils are designed to have characteristics of both light and heavy oils and are available in a number of weights from 5W-20 to 20W-50.

Gear oil is designed to be used in differentials, manual transmissions and other areas where high-temperature lubrication is required.

Chassis and wheel bearing grease is a heavy grease used where increased loads and friction are encountered, such as for wheel bearings, balljoints, tie-rod ends and universal joints.

High-temperature wheel bearing grease is designed to withstand the extreme temperatures encountered by wheel bearings in disc brake equipped vehicles. It usually contains molybdenum disulfide (moly), which is a dry-type lubricant.

White grease is a heavy grease for metal-to-metal applications where water is a problem. White grease stays soft under both low and high temperatures (usually from -100 to +190-degrees F), and will not wash off or dilute in the presence of water.

Assembly lube is a special extreme pressure lubricant, usually containing moly, used to lubricate high-load parts (such as main and rod bearings and cam lobes) for initial start-up of a new engine. The assembly lube lubricates the parts without being squeezed out or washed away until the engine oiling system begins to function.

Silicone lubricants are used to protect rubber, plastic, vinyl and nylon parts.

Graphite lubricants are used where oils cannot be used due to contamination problems, such as in locks. The dry graphite will lubricate metal parts while remaining uncontaminated by dirt, water, oil or acids. It is electrically conductive and will not foul electrical contacts in locks such as the ignition switch.

Moly penetrants loosen and lubricate frozen, rusted and corroded fasteners and prevent future rusting or freezing.

Heat-sink grease is a special electrically non-conductive grease that is used for mounting electronic ignition modules where it is essential that heat is transferred away from the module.

Sealants

RTV sealant is one of the most widely used gasket compounds. Made from silicone, RTV is air curing, it seals, bonds, waterproofs, fills surface irregularities, remains flexible, doesn't shrink, is relatively easy to remove, and is used as a supplementary sealer with almost all low and medium temperature gaskets.

Anaerobic sealant is much like RTV in that it can be used either to seal gaskets or to form gaskets by itself. It remains flexible, is solvent resistant and fills surface imperfections. The difference between an anaerobic sealant and an RTV-type sealant is in the curing. RTV cures when exposed to air, while an anaerobic sealant cures only in the absence of air. This means that an anaerobic sealant cures only after the assembly of parts, sealing them together.

Thread and pipe sealant is used for sealing hydraulic and pneumatic fittings and vacuum lines. It is usually made from a Teflon compound, and comes in a spray, a paint-on liquid and as a wrap-around tape.

Chemicals

Anti-seize compound prevents seizing, galling, cold welding, rust and corrosion in fasteners. High-temperature ant-seize, usually made with copper and graphite lubricants, is used for exhaust system and exhaust manifold bolts.

Anaerobic locking compounds are used to keep fasteners from vibrating or working loose and cure only after installation, in the absence of air. Medium strength locking compound is used for small nuts, bolts and screws that may be removed later. High-strength locking compound is for large nuts, bolts and studs which aren't removed on a regular basis.

Oil additives range from viscosity index improvers to chemical treatments that claim to reduce internal engine friction. It should be noted that most oil manufacturers caution against using additives with their oils.

Gas additives perform several functions, depending on their chemical makeup. They usually contain solvents that help dissolve gum and varnish that build up on carburetor, fuel injection and intake parts. They also serve to break down carbon deposits that form on the inside surfaces of the combustion chambers. Some additives contain upper cylinder lubricants for valves and piston rings, and others contain chemicals to remove condensation from the gas tank.

Miscellaneous

Brake fluid is specially formulated hydraulic fluid that can withstand the heat and pressure encountered in brake systems. Care must be taken so this fluid does not come in contact with painted surfaces or plastics. An opened container should always be resealed to prevent contamination by water or dirt.

Weatherstrip adhesive is used to bond weatherstripping around doors, windows and trunk lids. It is sometimes used to attach trim pieces.

Undercoating is a petroleum-based, tar-like substance that is designed to protect metal surfaces on the underside of the vehicle from corrosion. It also acts as a sound-deadening agent by insulating the bottom of the vehicle.

Waxes and polishes are used to help protect painted and plated surfaces from the weather. Different types of paint may require the use of different types of wax and polish. Some polishes utilize a chemical or abrasive cleaner to help remove the top layer of oxidized (dull) paint on older vehicles. In recent years many non-wax polishes that contain a wide variety of chemicals such as polymers and silicones have been introduced. These non-wax polishes are usually easier to apply and last longer than conventional waxes and polishes.

Conversion factors

Length (distance)					
Inches (in)	X 25.4	= Millimetres (mm)	X 0.0394	= Inches (in)
Feet (ft)	X 0.305	= Metres (m)	X 3.281	= Feet (ft)
Miles	X 1.609	= Kilometres (km)	X 0.621	= Miles
Volume (capacity)				
Cubic inches (cu in; in^3)	X 16.387	= Cubic centimetres (cc; cm^3)	X 0.061	= Cubic inches (cu in; in^3)
Imperial pints (Imp pt)	X 0.568	= Litres (l)	X 1.76	= Imperial pints (Imp pt)
Imperial quarts (Imp qt)	X 1.137	= Litres (l)	X 0.88	= Imperial quarts (Imp qt)
Imperial quarts (Imp qt)	X 1.201	= US quarts (US qt)	X 0.833	= Imperial quarts (Imp qt)
US quarts (US qt)	X 0.946	= Litres (l)	X 1.057	= US quarts (US qt)
Imperial gallons (Imp gal)	X 4.546	= Litres (l)	X 0.22	= Imperial gallons (Imp gal)
Imperial gallons (Imp gal)	X 1.201	= US gallons (US gal)	X 0.833	= Imperial gallons (Imp gal)
US gallons (US gal)	X 3.785	= Litres (l)	X 0.264	= US gallons (US gal)
Mass (weight)				
Ounces (oz)	X 28.35	= Grams (g)	X 0.035	= Ounces (oz)
Pounds (lb)	X 0.454	= Kilograms (kg)	X 2.205	= Pounds (lb)
Force				
Ounces-force (ozf; oz)	X 0.278	= Newtons (N)	X 3.6	= Ounces-force (ozf; oz)
Pounds-force (lbf; lb)	X 4.448	= Newtons (N)	X 0.225	= Pounds-force (lbf; lb)
Newtons (N)	X 0.1	= Kilograms-force (kgf; kg)	X 9.81	= Newtons (N)
Pressure				
Pounds-force per square inch (psi; lbf/in^2; lb/in^2)	X 0.070	= Kilograms-force per square centimetre (kgf/cm^2; kg/cm^2)	X 14.223	= Pounds-force per square inch (psi; lbf/in^2; lb/in^2)
Pounds-force per square inch (psi; lbf/in^2; lb/in^2)	X 0.068	= Atmospheres (atm)	X 14.696	= Pounds-force per square inch (psi; lbf/in^2; lb/in^2)
Pounds-force per square inch (psi; lbf/in^2; lb/in^2)	X 0.069	= Bars	X 14.5	= Pounds-force per square inch (psi; lbf/in^2; lb/in^2)
Pounds-force per square inch (psi; lbf/in^2; lb/in^2)	X 6.895	= Kilopascals (kPa)	X 0.145	= Pounds-force per square inch (psi; lbf/in^2; lb/in^2)
Kilopascals (kPa)	X 0.01	= Kilograms-force per square centimetre (kgf/cm^2; kg/cm^2)	X 98.1	= Kilopascals (kPa)
Torque (moment of force)				
Pounds-force inches (lbf in; lb in)	X 1.152	= Kilograms-force centimetre (kgf cm; kg cm)	X 0.868	= Pounds-force inches (lbf in; lb in)
Pounds-force inches (lbf in; lb in)	X 0.113	= Newton metres (Nm)	X 8.85	= Pounds-force inches (lbf in; lb in)
Pounds-force inches (lbf in; lb in)	X 0.083	= Pounds-force feet (lbf ft; lb ft)	X 12	= Pounds-force inches (lbf in; lb in)
Pounds-force feet (lbf ft; lb ft)	X 0.138	= Kilograms-force metres (kgf m; kg m)	X 7.233	= Pounds-force feet (lbf ft; lb ft)
Pounds-force feet (lbf ft; lb ft)	X 1.356	= Newton metres (Nm)	X 0.738	= Pounds-force feet (lbf ft; lb ft)
Newton metres (Nm)	X 0.102	= Kilograms-force metres (kgf m; kg m)	X 9.804	= Newton metres (Nm)
Vacuum				
Inches mercury (in. Hg)	X 3.377	= Kilopascals (kPa)	X 0.2961	= Inches mercury
Inches mercury (in. Hg)	X 25.4	= Millimeters mercury (mm Hg)	X 0.0394	= Inches mercury
Power				
Horsepower (hp)	X 745.7	= Watts (W)	X 0.0013	= Horsepower (hp)
Velocity (speed)				
Miles per hour (miles/hr; mph)	X 1.609	= Kilometres per hour (km/hr; kph)	X 0.621	= Miles per hour (miles/hr; mph)
Fuel consumption*				
Miles per gallon, Imperial (mpg)	X 0.354	= Kilometres per litre (km/l)	X 2.825	= Miles per gallon, Imperial (mpg)
Miles per gallon, US (mpg)	X 0.425	= Kilometres per litre (km/l)	X 2.352	= Miles per gallon, US (mpg)

Temperature

Degrees Fahrenheit = (°C x 1.8) + 32

Degrees Celsius (Degrees Centigrade; °C) = (°F - 32) x 0.56

****It is common practice to convert from miles per gallon (mpg) to litres/100 kilometres (l/100km), where mpg (Imperial) x l/100 km = 282 and mpg (US) x l/100 km = 235***

Safety first!

Regardless of how enthusiastic you may be about getting on with the job at hand, take the time to ensure that your safety is not jeopardized. A moment's lack of attention can result in an accident, as can failure to observe certain simple safety precautions. The possibility of an accident will always exist, and the following points should not be considered a comprehensive list of all dangers. Rather, they are intended to make you aware of the risks and to encourage a safety conscious approach to all work you carry out on your vehicle.

Essential DOs and DON'Ts

DON'T rely on a jack when working under the vehicle. Always use approved jackstands to support the weight of the vehicle and place them under the recommended lift or support points.

DON'T attempt to loosen extremely tight fasteners (i.e. wheel lug nuts) while the vehicle is on a jack - it may fall.

DON'T start the engine without first making sure that the transmission is in Neutral (or Park where applicable) and the parking brake is set.

DON'T remove the radiator cap from a hot cooling system - let it cool or cover it with a cloth and release the pressure gradually.

DON'T attempt to drain the engine oil until you are sure it has cooled to the point that it will not burn you.

DON'T touch any part of the engine or exhaust system until it has cooled sufficiently to avoid burns.

DON'T siphon toxic liquids such as gasoline, antifreeze and brake fluid by mouth, or allow them to remain on your skin.

DON'T inhale brake lining dust - it is potentially hazardous (see *Asbestos* below).

DON'T allow spilled oil or grease to remain on the floor - wipe it up before someone slips on it.

DON'T use loose fitting wrenches or other tools which may slip and cause injury.

DON'T push on wrenches when loosening or tightening nuts or bolts. Always try to pull the wrench toward you. If the situation calls for pushing the wrench away, push with an open hand to avoid scraped knuckles if the wrench should slip.

DON'T attempt to lift a heavy component alone - get someone to help you.

DON'T rush or take unsafe shortcuts to finish a job.

DON'T allow children or animals in or around the vehicle while you are working on it.

DO wear eye protection when using power tools such as a drill, sander, bench grinder, etc. and when working under a vehicle.

DO keep loose clothing and long hair well out of the way of moving parts.

DO make sure that any hoist used has a safe working load rating adequate for the job.

DO get someone to check on you periodically when working alone on a vehicle.

DO carry out work in a logical sequence and make sure that everything is correctly assembled and tightened.

DO keep chemicals and fluids tightly capped and out of the reach of children and pets.

DO remember that your vehicle's safety affects that of yourself and others. If in doubt on any point, get professional advice.

Asbestos

Certain friction, insulating, sealing, and other products - such as brake linings, brake bands, clutch linings, torque converters, gaskets, etc. - may contain asbestos. Extreme care must be taken to avoid inhalation of dust from such products, since it is hazardous to health. If in doubt, assume that they do contain asbestos.

Fire

Remember at all times that gasoline is highly flammable. Never smoke or have any kind of open flame around when working on a vehicle. But the risk does not end there. A spark caused by an electrical short circuit, by two metal surfaces contacting each other, or even by static electricity built up in your body under certain conditions, can ignite gasoline vapors, which in a confined space are highly explosive. Do not, under any circumstances, use gasoline for cleaning parts. Use an approved safety solvent.

Always disconnect the battery ground (-) cable at the battery before working on any part of the fuel system or electrical system. Never risk spilling fuel on a hot engine or exhaust component. It is strongly recommended that a fire extinguisher suitable for use on fuel and electrical fires be kept handy in the garage or workshop at all times. Never try to extinguish a fuel or electrical fire with water.

Fumes

Certain fumes are highly toxic and can quickly cause unconsciousness and even death if inhaled to any extent. Gasoline vapor falls into this category, as do the vapors from some cleaning solvents. Any draining or pouring of such volatile fluids should be done in a well ventilated area.

When using cleaning fluids and solvents, read the instructions on the container carefully. Never use materials from unmarked containers.

Never run the engine in an enclosed space, such as a garage. Exhaust fumes contain carbon monoxide, which is extremely poisonous. If you need to run the engine, always do so in the open air, or at least have the rear of the vehicle outside the work area.

If you are fortunate enough to have the use of an inspection pit, never drain or pour gasoline and never run the engine while the vehicle is over the pit. The fumes, being heavier than air, will concentrate in the pit with possibly lethal results.

The battery

Never create a spark or allow a bare light bulb near a battery. They normally give off a certain amount of hydrogen gas, which is highly explosive.

Always disconnect the battery ground (-) cable at the battery before working on the fuel or electrical systems.

If possible, loosen the filler caps or cover when charging the battery from an external source (this does not apply to sealed or maintenance-free batteries). Do not charge at an excessive rate or the battery may burst.

Take care when adding water to a non maintenance-free battery and when carrying a battery. The electrolyte, even when diluted, is very corrosive and should not be allowed to contact clothing or skin.

Always wear eye protection when cleaning the battery to prevent the caustic deposits from entering your eyes.

Household current

When using an electric power tool, inspection light, etc., which operates on household current, always make sure that the tool is correctly connected to its plug and that, where necessary, it is properly grounded. Do not use such items in damp conditions and, again, do not create a spark or apply excessive heat in the vicinity of fuel or fuel vapor.

Secondary ignition system voltage

A severe electric shock can result from touching certain parts of the ignition system (such as the spark plug wires) when the engine is running or being cranked, particularly if components are damp or the insulation is defective. In the case of an electronic ignition system, the secondary system voltage is much higher and could prove fatal.

Troubleshooting

Contents

Engine

1 Engine will not rotate when attempting to start

1 Battery terminal connections loose or corroded. Check the cable terminals at the battery. Tighten the cable or remove corrosion as necessary.
2 Battery discharged or faulty. If the cable connections are clean and tight on the battery posts, turn the key to the On position and switch on the headlights and/or windshield wipers. If they fail to function, the battery is discharged.
3 Automatic transmission not completely engaged in Park or clutch not completely depressed.
4 Broken, loose or disconnected wiring in the starting circuit. Inspect all wiring and connectors at the battery, starter solenoid and ignition switch.
5 Starter motor pinion jammed in flywheel ring gear. If manual transmission, place transmission in gear and rock the vehicle to manually turn the engine. Remove starter and inspect pinion and flywheel at earliest convenience.
6 Starter solenoid faulty (Chapter 5).
7 Starter motor faulty (Chapter 5).
8 Ignition switch faulty (Chapter 12).

2 Engine rotates but will not start

1 Fuel tank empty.
2 Battery discharged (engine rotates slowly). Check the operation of electrical components as described in previous Section.
3 Battery terminal connections loose or corroded. See previous Section.
4 Carburetor flooded and/or fuel level in carburetor incorrect. This will usually be accompanied by a strong fuel odor from under the hood. Wait a few minutes, depress the accelerator pedal all the way to the floor and attempt to start the engine.
5 Choke control inoperative (Chapter 1).
6 Fuel not reaching carburetor. With ignition switch in Off position, open hood, remove the top plate of air cleaner assembly and observe the top of the carburetor (manually move the choke plate back if necessary). Have an assistant depress the accelerator pedal and check that fuel spurts into the carburetor. If not, check the fuel filter (Chapter 1), fuel lines and fuel pump (Chapter 4).
7 Fuel injector or fuel pump faulty (fuel injected vehicles) (Chapter 4).
8 Excessive moisture on, or damage to, ignition components (Chapter 5).
9 Worn, faulty or incorrectly gapped spark plugs (Chapter 1).
10 Broken, loose or disconnected wiring in the starting circuit (see previous Section).
11 Distributor loose, causing ignition timing to change. Turn the distributor as necessary to start engine, then set ignition timing as soon as possible (Chapter 1).
12 Broken, loose or disconnected wires at the ignition coil or faulty coil (Chapter 5).

3 Starter motor operates without rotating engine

1 Starter pinion sticking. Remove the starter (Chapter 5) and inspect.
2 Starter pinion or flywheel teeth worn or broken. Remove the cover at the rear of the engine and inspect.

4 Engine hard to start when cold

1 Battery discharged or low. Check as described in Section 1.
2 Choke control inoperative or out of adjustment (Chapter 4).
3 Carburetor flooded (see Section 2).
4 Fuel supply not reaching the carburetor (see Section 2).
5 Carburetor/fuel injection system in need of overhaul (Chapter 4).
6 Distributor rotor carbon tracked and/or mechanical advance mechanism rusted (Chapter 5).
7 Fuel injection system malfunction (Chapter 4).

5 Engine hard to start when hot

1 Choke sticking in the closed position (Chapter 1).
2 Carburetor flooded (see Section 2).
3 Air filter clogged (Chapter 1).
4 Fuel not reaching the carburetor (see Section 2).
5 Fuel injection system malfunction (Chapter 4).

6 Starter motor noisy or excessively rough in engagement

1 Pinion or flywheel gear teeth worn or broken. Remove the cover at the rear of the engine (if so equipped) and inspect.
2 Starter motor mounting bolts loose or missing.

7 Engine starts but stops immediately

1 Loose or faulty electrical connections at distributor, coil or alternator.
2 Insufficient fuel reaching the carburetor. Disconnect the fuel line at the carburetor and remove the filter (Chapter 1). Place a container under the disconnected fuel line. Turn the engine over with the starter and observe the flow of fuel from the line. If little or none at all, check for blockage in the lines and/or replace the fuel pump (Chapter 4).
3 Vacuum leak at the gasket surfaces of the intake manifold and/or carburetor. Make sure that all mounting bolts/nuts are tightened securely and that all vacuum hoses connected to the carburetor and manifold are positioned properly and in good condition.
4 Fuel injection system malfunction (Chapter 4).

8 Engine lopes while idling or idles erratically

1 Vacuum leakage. Check mounting bolts/nuts at the carburetor and intake manifold for tightness. Make sure that all vacuum hoses are connected and in good condition. Use a stethoscope or a length of fuel hose held against your ear to listen for vacuum leaks while the engine is running. A hissing sound will be heard. A soapy water solution will also detect leaks. Check the carburetor and intake manifold gasket surfaces.
2 Leaking EGR valve or plugged PCV valve (see Chapters 1 and 6).
3 Air filter clogged (Chapter 1).
4 Fuel pump not delivering sufficient fuel to the carburetor (see Section 7).
5 Carburetor out of adjustment (Chapter 4).
6 Fuel injection system malfunction (Chapter 4).
7 Leaking head gasket. If this is suspected, take the vehicle to a repair shop or dealer where the engine can be pressure checked.
8 Timing chain and/or gears worn (Chapter 2).
9 Camshaft lobes worn (Chapter 2).
10 Fuel injection system malfunction (Chapter 4).

9 Engine misses at idle speed

1 Spark plugs worn or not gapped properly (Chapter 1).
2 Faulty spark plug wires (Chapter 1).
3 Choke not operating properly (Chapter 1).
4 Fuel injection system malfunction (Chapter 4).

10 Engine misses throughout driving speed range

1 Fuel filter clogged and/or impurities in the fuel system (Chapter 1). Also check fuel output at the carburetor or fuel injection (see Section 7).
2 Faulty or incorrectly gapped spark plugs (Chapter 1).
3 Incorrect ignition timing (Chapter 1).

4 Check for cracked distributor cap, disconnected distributor wires and damaged distributor components (Chapter 1).
5 Leaking spark plug wires (Chapter 1).
6 Faulty emissions system components (Chapter 6).
7 Low or uneven cylinder compression pressures. Remove spark plugs and test compression with gauge (Chapter 1).
8 Weak or faulty ignition system (Chapter 5).
9 Vacuum leaks at carburetor, fuel injection unit, intake manifold or vacuum hoses (see Section 8).
10 Fuel injection system malfunction (Chapter 4).

11 Engine stalls

1 Idle speed incorrect (Chapter 1).
2 Fuel filter clogged and/or water and impurities in the fuel system (Chapter 1).
3 Choke improperly adjusted or sticking (Chapter 1).
4 Distributor components damp or damaged (Chapter 5).
5 Faulty emissions system components (Chapter 6).
6 Faulty or incorrectly gapped spark plugs (Chapter 1). Also check spark plug wires (Chapter 1).
7 Vacuum leak at the carburetor/fuel injection unit, intake manifold or vacuum hoses. Check as described in Section 8.
8 Valve clearances incorrectly set (Chapter 2).
9 Fuel injection system malfunction (Chapter 4).

12 Engine lacks power

1 Incorrect ignition timing (Chapter 1).
2 Excessive play in distributor shaft. At the same time, check for worn rotor, faulty distributor cap, wires, etc. (Chapters 1 and 5).
3 Faulty or incorrectly gapped spark plugs (Chapter 1).
4 Carburetor not adjusted properly or excessively worn (Chapter 4).
5 Faulty coil (Chapter 5).
6 Brakes binding (Chapter 1).
7 Automatic transaxle fluid level incorrect (Chapter 1).
8 Clutch slipping (Chapter 8).
9 Fuel filter clogged and/or impurities in the fuel system (Chapter 1).
10 Emissions control system not functioning properly (Chapter 6).
11 Use of substandard fuel. Fill tank with proper octane fuel.
12 Low or uneven cylinder compression pressures. Test with compression tester, which will detect leaking valves and/or blown head gasket (Chapter 1).
13 Fuel injection system malfunction (Chapter 4).

13 Engine backfires

1 Emissions system not functioning properly (Chapter 6).
2 Ignition timing incorrect (Chapter 1).
3 Faulty secondary ignition system (cracked spark plug insulator, faulty plug wires, distributor cap and/or rotor) (Chapters 1 and 5).
4 Carburetor in need of adjustment or worn excessively (Chapter 4).
5 Vacuum leak at carburetor, intake manifold or vacuum hoses. Check as described in Section 8.
6 Valve clearances incorrectly set, and/or valves sticking (Chapter 2).
7 Fuel injection system malfunction (Chapter 4).

14 Pinging or knocking engine sounds during acceleration or uphill

1 Incorrect grade of fuel. Fill tank with fuel of the proper octane rating.
2 Ignition timing incorrect (Chapter 1).
3 Carburetor in need of adjustment (Chapter 4).
4 Improper spark plugs. Check plug type against Emissions Control Information label located in engine compartment. Also check plugs and wires for damage (Chapter 1).
5 Worn or damaged distributor components (Chapter 5).
6 Faulty emissions system (Chapter 6).
7 Fuel injection system malfunction (Chapter 4).
8 Vacuum leak. Check as described in Section 8.

15 Engine diesels (continues to run) after switching off

1 Idle speed too high (Chapter 1).
2 Idle system malfunction (Chapter 4).
3 Ignition timing incorrectly adjusted (Chapter 1).
4 Thermo-controlled air cleaner heat valve not operating properly (Chapter 6).
5 Excessive engine operating temperature. Probable causes of this are malfunctioning thermostat, clogged radiator, faulty water pump (Chapter 3).

Engine electrical system

16 Battery will not hold a charge

1 Alternator drivebelt defective or not adjusted properly (Chapter 1).
2 Electrolyte level low or battery discharged (Chapter 1).
3 Battery terminals loose or corroded (Chapter 1).
4 Alternator not charging properly (Chapter 5).
5 Loose, broken or faulty wiring in the charging circuit (Chapter 5).
6 Short in vehicle wiring causing a continual drain on battery.
7 Battery defective internally.

17 Ignition light fails to go out

1 Fault in alternator or charging circuit (Chapter 5).
2 Alternator drivebelt defective or not properly adjusted (Chapter 1).

18 Ignition light fails to come on when key is turned on

1 Warning light bulb defective (Chapter 12).
2 Alternator faulty (Chapter 5).
3 Fault in the printed circuit, dash wiring or bulb holder (Chapter 12).

Fuel system

19 Excessive fuel consumption

1 Dirty or clogged air filter element (Chapter 1).
2 Incorrectly set ignition timing (Chapter 1).
3 Choke sticking or improperly adjusted (Chapter 1).
4 Emissions system not functioning properly (not all vehicles, see Chapter 6).
5 Carburetor idle speed and/or mixture not adjusted properly (Chapter 1).
6 Carburetor internal parts excessively worn or damaged (Chapter 4).
7 Low tire pressure or incorrect tire size (Chapter 1).
8 Fuel injection system malfunction (Chapter 4).

20 Fuel leakage and/or fuel odor

1 Leak in a fuel feed or vent line (Chapter 4).
2 Tank overfilled. Fill only to automatic shut-off.
3 Emissions system filter clogged (Chapter 1).
4 Vapor leaks from system lines (Chapter 4).
5 Carburetor internal parts excessively worn or out of adjustment (Chapter 4).

Cooling system

21 Overheating

1 Insufficient coolant in system (Chapter 1).
2 Water pump drivebelt defective or not adjusted properly (Chapter 1).
3 Radiator core blocked or radiator grille dirty and restricted (Chapter 3).
4 Thermostat faulty (Chapter 3).
5 Fan blades broken or cracked (Chapter 3).
6 Radiator cap not maintaining proper pressure. Have cap pressure tested by gas station or repair shop.
7 Ignition timing incorrect (Chapter 1).

22 Overcooling

1 Thermostat faulty (Chapter 3).
2 Inaccurate temperature gauge (Chapter 12)

23 External coolant leakage

1 Deteriorated or damaged hoses or loose clamps. Replace hoses and/or tighten clamps at hose connections (Chapter 1).
2 Water pump seals defective. If this is the case, water will drip from the weep hole in the water pump body (Chapter 1).
3 Leakage from radiator core or header tank. This will require the radiator to be professionally repaired (see Chapter 3 for removal procedures).
4 Engine drain plugs or water jacket core plugs leaking (see Chapter 2).

24 Internal coolant leakage

Note: *Internal coolant leaks can usually be detected by examining the oil. Check the dipstick and inside of the camshaft cover for water deposits and an oil consistency like that of a milkshake.*
1 Leaking cylinder head gasket. Have the cooling system pressure tested.
2 Cracked cylinder bore or cylinder head. Dismantle engine and inspect (Chapter 2).

25 Coolant loss

1 Too much coolant in system (Chapter 1).
2 Coolant boiling away due to overheating (see Section 16).
3 Internal or external leakage (see Sections 23 and 24).
4 Faulty radiator cap. Have the cap pressure tested.

26 Poor coolant circulation

1 Inoperative water pump. A quick test is to pinch the top radiator hose closed with your hand while the engine is idling, then let it loose. You should feel the surge of coolant if the pump is working properly (Chapter 1).
2 Restriction in cooling system. Drain, flush and refill the system (Chapter 1). If necessary, remove the radiator (Chapter 3) and have it reverse flushed.
3 Water pump drivebelt defective or not adjusted properly (Chapter 1).
4 Thermostat sticking (Chapter 3).

Clutch

27 Fails to release (pedal pressed to the floor - shift lever does not move freely in and out of Reverse)

1 Improper linkage free play adjustment (Chapter 8).
2 Clutch fork off ball stud.
3 Clutch plate warped or damaged (Chapter 8).
4 Insufficient clutch fluid.
5 Leakage of clutch fluid.
6 Malfunction of clutch master cylinder or clutch release cylinder.

28 Clutch slips (engine speed increases with no increase in vehicle speed)

1 Linkage out of adjustment (Chapter 8).
2 Clutch plate oil soaked or lining worn. Remove clutch (Chapter 8) and inspect.
3 Clutch plate not seated. It may take 30 or 40 normal starts for a new one to seat.
4 Weak or damaged diaphragm spring.

29 Grabbing (chattering) as clutch is engaged

1 Oil on clutch plate lining. Remove (Chapter 8) and inspect. Correct any leakage source.
2 Worn or loose engine or transaxle mounts. These units move slightly when clutch is released. Inspect mounts and bolts.
3 Worn splines on clutch plate hub. Remove clutch components (Chapter 8) and inspect.
4 Warped pressure plate or flywheel. Remove clutch components and inspect.

30 Squeal or rumble with clutch fully engaged (pedal released)

1 Improper adjustment; no free play (Chapter 1).
2 Release bearing binding on transmission bearing retainer. Remove clutch components (Chapter 8) and check bearing. Remove any burrs or nicks, clean and relubricate before reinstallation.
3 Weak linkage return spring. Replace the spring.

31 Squeal or rumble with clutch fully disengaged (pedal depressed)

1 Worn, defective or broken release bearing (Chapter 8).
2 Worn or broken pressure plate springs (or diaphragm fingers) (Chapter 8).

32 Clutch pedal stays on floor when disengaged

1 Bind in linkage or release bearing. Inspect linkage or remove clutch components as necessary.
2 Linkage springs being over-extended. Adjust linkage for proper free play.

Manual transaxle

33 Noisy in neutral with engine running

1 Excessive gear backlash.
2 Damaged main drive gear bearing.
3 Worn bearings.

34 Noisy in all gears

1 Any of the above causes, and/or:
2 Insufficient lubricant (see checking procedures in Chapter 1).

35 Noisy in one particular gear

1 Worn, damaged or chipped gear teeth for that particular gear.
2 Worn or damaged synchronizer for that particular gear.

36 Slips out of high gear

1 Transaxle loose on clutch housing (Chapter 7).
2 Improperly installed engine mount (Chapter 2).
3 Shift rods not working freely (Chapter 7).
4 Worn shift fork.
5 Dirt between transaxle case and engine or misalignment of transaxle (Chapter 7).
6 Worn or improperly adjusted linkage (Chapter 7).

37 Difficulty in engaging gears

1 Clutch not releasing completely (see clutch adjustment in Chapter 8).
2 Loose, damaged or out-of-adjustment shift linkage. Make a thorough inspection, replacing parts as necessary (Chapter 7).

38 Oil leakage

1 Excessive amount of lubricant in transaxle (see Chapter 1 for correct checking procedures). Drain lubricant as required.
2 Rear oil seal or speedometer oil seal in need of replacement (Chapter 7).

Automatic transaxle

Note: *Due to the complexity of the automatic transaxle, it is difficult for the home mechanic to properly diagnose and service this component. For problems other than the following, the vehicle should be taken to a dealer or reputable mechanic.*

39 General shift mechanism problems

1 Chapter 7 deals with checking and adjusting the shift linkage on automatic transaxles. Common problems which may be attributed to poorly adjusted linkage are:

Engine starting in gears other than Park or Neutral.

Indicator on shifter pointing to a gear other than the one actually being used.

Vehicle moves when in Park.

2 Refer to Chapter 7 to adjust the linkage.

40 Transaxle will not downshift with accelerator pedal pressed to the floor

Chapter 7 deals with adjusting the kick-down switch cable to enable the transaxle to downshift properly.

41 Transaxle slips, shifts rough, is noisy or has no drive in forward or reverse gears

1 There are many probable causes for the above problems, but the home mechanic should be concerned with only one possibility - fluid level.
2 Before taking the vehicle to a repair shop, check the level and condition of the fluid as described in Chapter 1. Correct fluid level as necessary or change the fluid if needed. If the problem persists, have a professional diagnose the probable cause.

42 Fluid leakage

1 Automatic transmission fluid is a deep red color. Fluid leaks should not be confused with engine oil, which can easily be blown by air flow to the transaxle.
2 To pinpoint a leak, first remove all built-up dirt and grime from around the transaxle. Degreasing agents and/or steam cleaning will achieve this. With the underside clean, drive the vehicle at low speeds so air flow will not blow the leak far from its source. Raise the vehicle and determine where the leak is coming from. Common areas of leakage are:

a) *Pan: Tighten mounting bolts and/or replace pan gasket as necessary (see Chapters 1 and 7).*
b) *Filler pipe: Replace the rubber seal where pipe enters transaxle case.*
c) *Transaxle oil lines: Tighten connectors where lines enter transaxle case and/or replace lines.*
d) *Vent pipe: Transaxle overfilled and/or water in fluid (see checking procedures, Chapter 1).*
e) *Speedometer connector: Replace the O-ring where speedometer cable enters transaxle case (Chapter 7).*

Driveaxles

43 Clicking noise in turns

Worn or damaged outboard joint. Check for cut or damaged seals. Repair as necessary (Chapter 8).

44 Knock or clunk when accelerating from a coast

Worn or damaged inboard joint. Check for cut or damaged seals. Repair as necessary (Chapter 8).

45 Shudder or vibration during acceleration

1 Excessive joint angle. Have checked and correct as necessary (Chapter 8).
2 Worn or damaged inboard or outboard joints. Repair or replace as necessary (Chapter 8).
3 Sticking inboard joint assembly. Correct or replace as necessary (Chapter 8).

Rear axle

46 Noise

1 Road noise. No corrective procedures available.
2 Tire noise. Inspect tires and check tire pressures (Chapter 1).
3 Rear wheel bearings loose, worn or damaged (Chapter 10).

Brakes

Note: *Before assuming that a brake problem exists, make sure that the tires are in good condition and inflated properly (see Chapter 1), that the front end alignment is correct and that the vehicle is not loaded with weight in an unequal manner.*

47 Vehicle pulls to one side during braking

1 Defective, damaged or oil contaminated disc brake pads on one side. Inspect as described in Chapter 9.
2 Excessive wear of brake pad material or disc on one side. Inspect and correct as necessary.
3 Loose or disconnected front suspension components. Inspect and tighten all bolts to the specified torque (Chapter 10).
4 Defective caliper assembly. Remove caliper and inspect for stuck piston or other damage (Chapter 9).

48 Noise (high-pitched squeal without the brakes applied)

Disc brake pads worn out. The noise comes from the wear sensor rubbing against the disc (does not apply to all vehicles). Replace pads with new ones immediately (Chapter 9).

49 Excessive brake pedal travel

1 Partial brake system failure. Inspect entire system (Chapter 9) and correct as required.
2 Insufficient fluid in master cylinder. Check (Chapter 1), add fluid and bleed system if necessary (Chapter 9).
3 Rear brakes not adjusting properly. Make a series of starts and stops while the vehicle is in Reverse. If this does not correct the situation, remove drums and inspect self-adjusters (Chapter 9).

50 Brake pedal feels spongy when depressed

1 Air in hydraulic lines. Bleed the brake system (Chapter 9).
2 Faulty flexible hoses. Inspect all system hoses and lines. Replace parts as necessary.
3 Master cylinder mounting bolts/nuts loose.
4 Master cylinder defective (Chapter 9).

51 Excessive effort required to stop vehicle

1 Power brake booster not operating properly (Chapter 9).
2 Excessively worn linings or pads. Inspect and replace if necessary (Chapter 9).
3 One or more caliper pistons or wheel cylinders seized or sticking. Inspect and rebuild as required (Chapter 9).
4 Brake linings or pads contaminated with oil or grease. Inspect and replace as required (Chapter 9).
5 New pads or shoes installed and not yet seated. It will take a while for the new material to seat against the drum (or rotor).

52 Pedal travels to the floor with little resistance

Little or no fluid in the master cylinder reservoir caused by leaking wheel cylinder(s), leaking caliper piston(s), loose, damaged or disconnected brake lines. Inspect entire system and correct as necessary.

53 Brake pedal pulsates during brake application

1 Wheel bearings not adjusted properly or in need of replacement (Chapter 1).
2 Caliper not sliding properly due to improper installation or obstructions. Remove and inspect (Chapter 9).
3 Rotor defective. Remove the rotor (Chapter 9) and check for excessive lateral runout and parallelism. Have the rotor resurfaced or replace it with a new one.

Suspension and steering systems

54 Vehicle pulls to one side

1 Tire pressures uneven (Chapter 1).
2 Defective tire (Chapter 1).
3 Excessive wear in suspension or steering components (Chapter 10).
4 Front end in need of alignment.
5 Front brakes dragging. Inspect brakes as described in Chapter 9.

55 Shimmy, shake or vibration

1 Tire or wheel out-of-balance or out-of-round. Have professionally balanced.
2 Loose, worn or out-of-adjustment wheel bearings (Chapters 1 and 8).
3 Shock absorbers and/or suspension components worn or damaged (Chapter 10).

56 Excessive pitching and/or rolling around corners or during braking

1 Defective shock absorbers. Replace as a set (Chapter 10).
2 Broken or weak springs and/or suspension components. Inspect as described in Chapter 10.

57 Excessively stiff steering

1 Lack of fluid in power steering fluid reservoir (Chapter 1).
2 Incorrect tire pressures (Chapter 1).
3 Lack of lubrication at steering joints (Chapter 1).
4 Front end out of alignment.
5 See also section titled Lack of power assistance.

58 Excessive play in steering

1 Loose front wheel bearings (Chapter 1).
2 Excessive wear in suspension or steering components (Chapter 10).
3 Steering gearbox out of adjustment (Chapter 10).

59 Lack of power assistance

1 Steering pump drivebelt faulty or not adjusted properly (Chapter 1).
2 Fluid level low (Chapter 1).
3 Hoses or lines restricted. Inspect and replace parts as necessary.
4 Air in power steering system. Bleed system (Chapter 10).

60 Excessive tire wear (not specific to one area)

1 Incorrect tire pressures (Chapter 1).
2 Tires out of balance. Have professionally balanced.
3 Wheels damaged. Inspect and replace as necessary.
4 Suspension or steering components excessively worn (Chapter 10).

61 Excessive tire wear on outside edge

1 Inflation pressures incorrect (Chapter 1).
2 Excessive speed in turns.
3 Front end alignment incorrect (excessive toe-in). Have professionally aligned.
4 Suspension arm bent or twisted (Chapter 10).

62 Excessive tire wear on inside edge

1 Inflation pressures incorrect (Chapter 1).
2 Front end alignment incorrect (toe-out). Have professionally aligned.
3 Loose or damaged steering components (Chapter 10).

63 Tire tread worn in one place

1 Tires out of balance.
2 Damaged or buckled wheel. Inspect and replace if necessary.
3 Defective tire (Chapter 1).

Chapter 1
Tune-up and routine maintenance

Contents

Specifications

Recommended lubricants and fluids

Note: *Listed here are manufacturer recommendations at the time this manual was written. Manufacturers occasionally upgrade their fluid and lubricant specifications, so check with your local auto parts store for current recommendations.*

Engine oil	
Type	API grade SG or SG/CC multigrade
Viscosity	See accompanying chart
Engine oil capacity (including filter)	4 qts

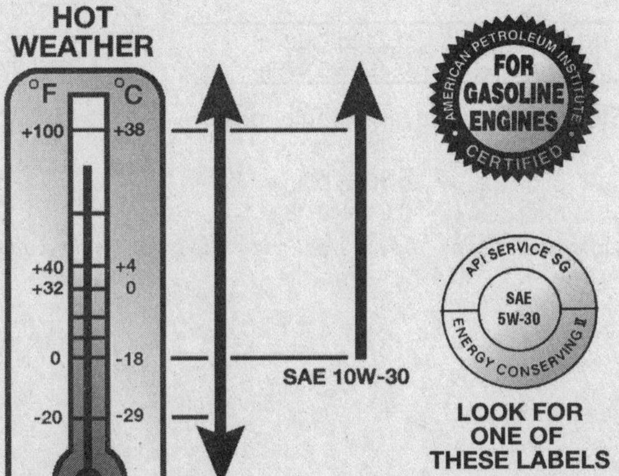

ENGINE OIL VISCOSITY CHART

For best fuel economy and cold starting, select the lowest SAE viscosity grade for the expected temperature range

Recommended lubricants, fluids and capacities (continued)

Cooling system capacity (approximate)	
Including heater	7.3 qts
Not including heater	6.9 qts
Coolant type	50/50 mix of ethylene glycol antifreeze and water
Manual transaxle oil type	
Above 0-degrees F (-18-degrees C)	API GL-5 SAE 80W-90 or 90 gear oil
Below 0-degrees F (-18-degrees C)	ATF Type F
Manual transaxle oil capacity	3.5 qts
Automatic transaxle fluid	
Type	Dexron II ATF
Capacity*	6 qts
Brake fluid type	DOT 3 or 4
Power steering fluid type	ATF Type F
Rear wheel bearing lubricant	NLGI No. 2 lithium base wheel bearing grease

** Capacity (dry). For refill after draining for routine maintenance, actual capacity should be measured on the transaxle dipstick as discussed in Section 28.*

General engine

Radiator cap opening pressure	15 psi
Thermostat	
Starts to open	188° to 193°F
Fully open	212°F
Engine idle speed*	
1983 through 1985	
Automatic transaxle	700 rpm
Manual transaxle	750 rpm
1986	
Manual transaxle and turbo	750 to 800 rpm
Automatic transaxle	900 to 950 rpm
1987	
Manual transaxle and turbo	800 to 850 rpm
Automatic transaxle	900 to 950 rpm
1988 and later (computer controlled)	750 rpm
Valve clearance	0.012 in
Engine compression pressure	Lowest reading should not be less than 70% of the highest cylinder reading with no cylinder below 100 psi
Drivebelt deflection (refer to Section 6)	
Type 1	
Alternator and power steering pump	
New	0.24 to 0.32 in
Used	0.40 to 0.47 in
Type 2	
Alternator and power steering pump	
New	0.16 to 0.20 in
Used	0.24 to 0.28 in
Air conditioner	
New	0.24 to 0.32 in
Used	0.40 to 0.47 in
Drivebelt deflection (refer to Section 6)	
Type 3	
All	
New	0.16 to 0.20 in
Used	0.24 to 0.28 in

**Refer to the Emission Control label in the engine compartment and follow the information on the label if it differs from that shown here.*

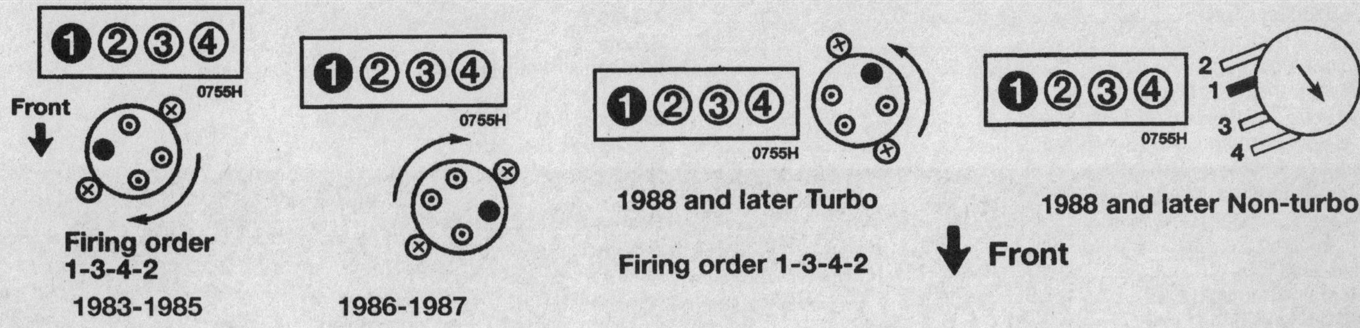

Engine cylinder numbering and distributor cap terminal locations

The blackened terminal shown on the distributor cap indicates the Number One spark plug wire position

Ignition system

Distributor direction of rotation	See accompanying diagrams
Firing order	1-3-4-2
Spark plug type*	
NGK	BPR-5ES, BPR-6ES
Motorcraft	AGR-32, AGR-22
Spark plug gap*	
1987 and earlier	0.030 to 0.033
1988 and later	0.039 to .043 (1.0 to 1.1mm)
Ignition timing (BTDC)*	
1983 through 1987	6°
1988 and later	
Turbo	9°
Non-turbo	6°

**Refer to the Emission Control Label in the engine compartment and follow the information on the label if it differs from that shown here.*

Brakes

Pad and shoe lining minimum thickness	0.04 in
Parking brake engagement	7 to 9 notches

Clutch

Clutch pedal	
Cable-operated	
Free play at pedal	0.43 to 0.67 in
Release lever clearance	0.08 to 0.12 in
Engaged height	8.5 in
Disengaged height	3.2 in
Hydraulic clutch	
Pedal height	8.5 to 8.7 in
Pedal freeplay	0.20 to 0.51 in
Minimum disengagement height	2.7 in

Torque specifications

	Ft-lbs
Rocker arm cover bolt	2 to 3
Spark plugs	10.8 to 16.6
Cylinder head bolts	69 to 72
Rear wheel bearing spindle nut initial preload	18 to 22
Rear wheel bearing spring scale torque (preload)	14.1 to 35.3 oz
Fuel filter banjo fitting bolts	18 to 15
Automatic transaxle drain plug	12
Brake caliper mounting bolts	2 to 5 in-lb
Wheel lug nuts	65 to 87

Typical engine compartment component layout

1 *Air injection housing (Chapter 9)*
2 *Windshield wiper arm and blade (Section 12)*
3 *Air cleaner wing nut (Section 21)*
4 *Thermostatically controlled air cleaner valve (Section 4)*
5 *Power brake vacuum reservoir (Chapter 9)*
6 *Windshield wiper motor (Chapter 12)*
7 *Brake master cylinder reservoir (Section 4)*
8 *Ignition coil (Chapter 5)*
9 *Fusible links (Chapter 12)*
10 *Battery (Section 5)*
11 *Headlight (Chapter 12)*
12 *Radiator hose (Section 7)*
13 *Distributor (Section 34 and 36)*
14 *Hood latch (Section 10)*
15 *Oxygen sensor (Section 30)*
16 *Radiator cap (Section 26)*
17 *Spark plug (Section 35)*
18 *Engine oil dipstick (Section 4)*
19 *Power steering dipstick (Section 4)*
20 *Oil filler cap (Section 4)*
21 *Alternator (Chapter 5)*
22 *Drivebelt (Section 6)*
23 *Radiator coolant reservoir (Section 4)*
24 *Windshield washer reservoir (Section 4)*
25 *PCV valve (Section 31)*
26 *Evaporative emissions canister location (Section 33)*

Typical of the underside of the front of the vehicle

1. *Driveaxle boot (Section 26)*
2. *Fuel and vapor lines (Section 17)*
3. *Automatic transaxle drain plug (Section 28)*
4. *Exhaust system heat shield (Section 11)*
5. *Exhaust system hanger (Section 11)*
6. *Steering gear boot (Section 12)*
7. *Engine oil drain plug (Section 16)*
8. *Front disc brake (Section 13)*
9. *Tire tread (Section 3 and 23)*

Typical view of the underside of the rear of the vehicle

1 *Fuel tank (Section 17)*
2 *Sway bar link (Section 12)*
3 *Muffler (Section 11)*
4 *Lower suspension arm (Section 12)*

1 Introduction and routine maintenance

This Chapter is designed to help the home mechanic maintain his or her vehicle for peak performance, economy, safety and long life.

On the following pages you will find a maintenance schedule along with Sections which deal specifically with each item on the schedule. Included are visual checks, adjustments and item replacements.

Servicing your vehicle using the time/mileage maintenance schedule and the sequenced Sections will give you a planned program of maintenance. Keep in mind that it is a full plan, and maintaining only a few items at the specified intervals will not give you the same results.

You will find as you service your vehicle that many of the procedures can, and should, be grouped together, due to the nature of the job at hand. Examples of this are as follows:

If the vehicle is raised for chassis lubrication, for example, it is an ideal time for the following checks: exhaust system, suspension, steering and fuel system.

If the tires and wheels are removed, as during a routine tire rotation, check the brakes and wheel bearings at the same time.

If you must borrow or rent a torque wrench, service the spark plugs and check the carburetor torque all in the same day to save time and money.

The first step of the maintenance plan is to prepare before the actual work begins. Read through the appropriate Sections for all work that is to be performed before you begin. Gather together all the necessary parts and tools. If it appears that you could have a problem during a particular job, don't hesitate to seek advice from your local parts man or dealer service department.

Routine maintenance intervals

The following recommendations are given with the assumption that the vehicle owner will be doing the maintenance or service work, as opposed to having a dealer service department do the work. The following are factory maintenance recommendations. However, the owner, interested in keeping his or her vehicle in peak condition at all times and with the vehicle's ultimate resale in mind, may want to perform many of these operations more often. We encourage such owner initiative.

When the vehicle is new it should be serviced initially by a factory authorized dealer service department to protect the factory warranty. In many cases the initial maintenance check is done at no cost to the owner. **Note:** *The following maintenance intervals are recommended by the manufacturer. In the interest of vehicle longevity, we recommend shorter intervals on certain operations, such as fluid and filter replacement.*

Every 250 miles or weekly, whichever comes first

Check the engine oil level (Section 4)
Check the engine coolant level (Section 4)
Check the windshield washer fluid level (Section 4)
Check the tires and tire pressures (Section 3)
Check the automatic transaxle fluid level (Section 4)
Check the operation of all lights (Chapter 10)
Check the horn operation (Chapter 10)

Every 3750 miles or sooner, if uneven wear develops

Rotate the tires (Chapter 10)

Every 7500 miles or 7.5 months, whichever comes first

Check the power steering fluid level (Section 4)
Change the engine oil and oil filter (Section 16)
Check the tightness of the carburetor mounting bolts (Section 21)
Check and lubricate the chassis components (Section 10)
Check the cooling system (Section 7)
Check and replace (if necessary) the underhood hoses (Section 8)
Check the exhaust system (Section 11)
Check the steering and suspension components (Section 12)
Check the brake master cylinder fluid level (Section 4)
Check the automatic transaxle oil level (Section 4)
Check the driveaxle boots (Section 22)
Check the disc brake pads (Section 13)
Check the brake system (Section 13)
Check and service the battery (Section 5)
Check and replace (if necessary) the windshield wiper blades (Section 9)

Every 15,000 miles or 15 months, whichever comes first

Check the manual transaxle fluid level (Section 4)
Check and adjust (if necessary) the engine valve clearances (Section 37)
Check and adjust (if necessary) the engine drivebelts (Section 6)
Check the drum brake linings (Section 13)
Check and adjust (if necessary) the engine idle speed (Section 15 or 39)
Check the operation of the choke (Section 14)
Check the parking brake (Section 13)
Rotate the tires (Section 23)
Check the thermostatically controlled air cleaner for proper operation (Section 20)
Check the fuel system components (Section 17)
Check the throttle linkage (Section 19)
Check and adjust (if necessary) the idle speed (1986 and 1987 models) (Section 40)
Check and adjust (if necessary) the ignition timing (Section 34)
Check the clutch pedal free play (Section 24)

Every 22,500 miles or 22.5 months, whichever comes first

Check the EGR system (Section 32)
Check the evaporative emissions system (Section 33)
Check the engine compression (Section 37)

Every 30,000 miles or 30 months, whichever comes first

Drain, flush and refill the cooling system (Section 26)
Drain and refill the manual transaxle oil (Section 25)
Lubricate and adjust the rear wheel bearings (Section 27)
Check the operation of the EGR valve (Section 32)
Inspect and replace, if necessary, the PCV valve (Section 31)
Replace the air filter and PCV filter (Section 29)
Replace the spark plugs (Section 35)
Inspect and replace, if necessary, the spark plug wires, distributor cap and rotor (Section 36)
Inspect the fuel system hoses, lines and filler cap (Section 17)
Replace the fuel filter (Section 18)
Check the oxygen sensor (Chapter 6) and replace if necessary (Section 30)
Replace the brake fluid (Chapter 9)

Every 48,000 miles or 48 months, whichever comes first

Drain and refill the automatic transaxle (Section 28)

Every 60,000 or 60 months, whichever comes first

Replace the engine timing belt (Chapter 2)

Severe operating conditions

Severe operating conditions are defined as:
Frequent short trips or long periods of idling
Driving at sustained high speeds during hot weather (over 90°F, 32°C)
Driving in severe dust conditions
Driving in temperatures below 10°F (-12°C) for 60 or more days
Driving 2000 miles or more per month
Driving in extremely humid conditions
Mountain driving or where the brakes are used extensively

If the vehicle has been operated under severe conditions, follow these maintenance intervals:
Change the air and fuel filters more frequently
Change the engine oil and oil filter every 2000 miles or two months
Drain and refill the automatic transaxle every 22,500 miles

2 Tune-up sequence

The term tune-up is used for any general operation that puts the engine back in its proper running condition. A tune-up is not a specific operation, but rather a combination of individual operations, such as replacing the spark plugs, adjusting the idle speed, setting the ignition timing, etc.

If, from the time the vehicle is new, the routine maintenance schedule (Section 1) is followed closely and frequent checks are made of fluid levels and high wear items, as suggested throughout this manual, the engine will be kept in relatively good running condition and the need for additional tune-ups will be minimized.

More likely than not, however, there will be times when the engine is running poorly due to lack of regular maintenance. This is even more likely if a used vehicle, which has not received regular and frequent maintenance checks, is purchased. In such cases, an engine tune-up will be needed outside of the regular routine maintenance intervals.

The following series of operations are those most often needed to bring a generally poor running engine back into a proper state of tune.

Minor tune-up

Clean, inspect and test battery (Section 5)
Check all engine related fluids (Section 4)
Check engine compression (Section 37)
Check and adjust drivebelts (Section 6)
Replace spark plugs (Section 35)
Inspect distributor cap and rotor (Section 36)
Inspect spark plug and coil wires (Section 36)
Check and adjust the engine idle speed (Section 15 or 39)
Check and adjust timing (Section 34)
Check and adjust fuel/air mixture (see underhood VECI label)
Replace fuel filter (Section 18)
Check PCV valve (Section 31)
Check cooling system (Section 7)

Major tune-up

All items listed under Minor tune-up, plus . . .

Check EGR system (Chapter 6)
Check ignition system (Chapter 5)
Check charging system (Chapter 5)
Check fuel system (Section 17)

3 Tire and tire pressure checks

Refer to illustrations 3.2, 3.3, 3.4a, 3.4b and 3.8

1 Periodic inspection of the tires may spare you the inconvenience of being stranded with a flat tire. It can also provide you with vital information regarding possible problems in the steering and suspension systems before major damage occurs.

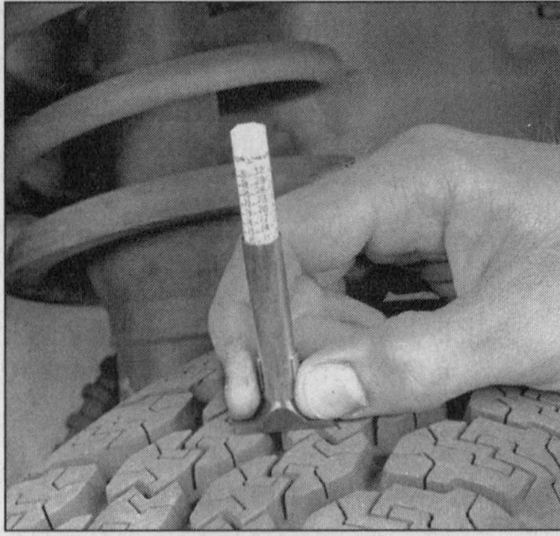

3.2 Use a tire tread depth indicator to monitor tire wear - they are available at auto parts stores and service stations and cost very little

2 The original tires on this vehicle are equipped with 1/2-inch side bands that will appear when tread depth reaches 1/16-inch, but they don't appear until the tires are worn out. Tread wear can be monitored with a simple, inexpensive device known as a tread depth indicator **(see illustration)**.

3 Note any abnormal tread wear **(see illustration)**. Tread pattern irregularities such as cupping, flat spots and more wear on one

UNDERINFLATION

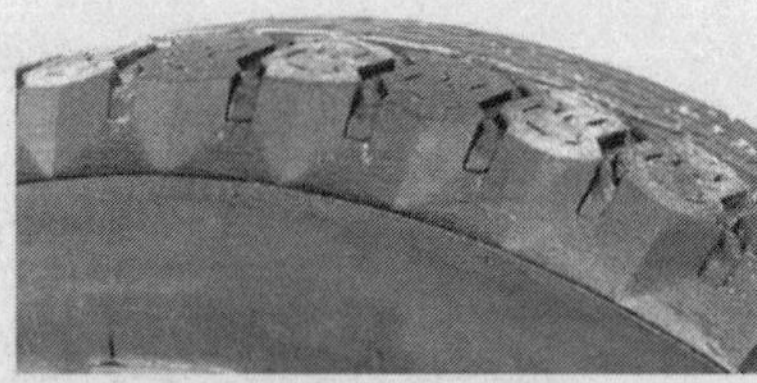

CUPPING

OVERINFLATION

Cupping may be caused by:

- **Underinflation and/or mechanical irregularities such as out-of-balance condition of wheel and/or tire, and bent or damaged wheel.**
- **Loose or worn steering tie-rod or steering idler arm.**
- **Loose, damaged or worn front suspension parts.**

INCORRECT TOE-IN OR EXTREME CAMBER

FEATHERING DUE TO MISALIGNMENT

3.3 This chart will help you determine the condition of the tires, the probable cause(s) of abnormal wear and the corrective action necessary

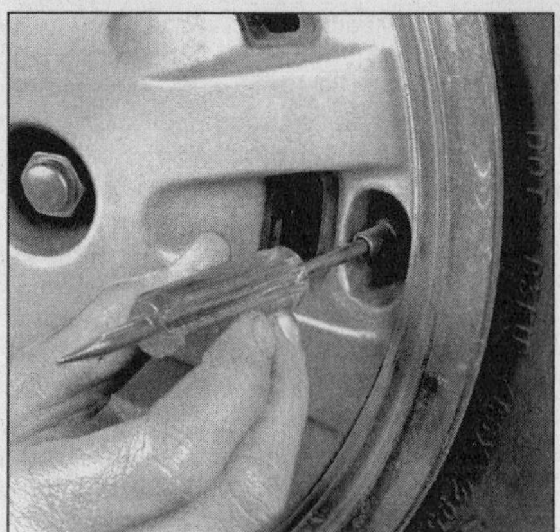

3.4a If a tire loses air on a steady basis, check the valve stem core first to make sure it's snug (special inexpensive wrenches are commonly available at auto parts stores)

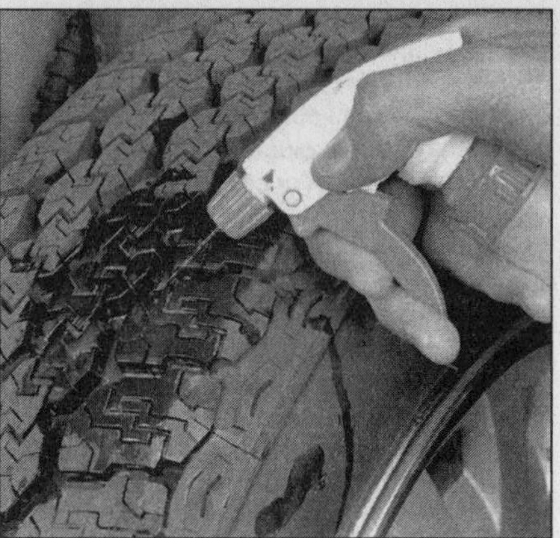

3.4b If the valve stem core is tight, raise the corner of the vehicle with the low tire and spray a soapy water solution onto the tread as the tire is turned slowly - leaks will cause small bubbles to appear

side than the other are indications of front end alignment and/or balance problems. If any of these conditions are noted, take the vehicle to a tire shop or service station to correct the problem.

4 Look closely for cuts, punctures and embedded nails or tacks. Sometimes a tire will hold air pressure for a short time or leak down very slowly after a nail has embedded itself in the tread. If a slow leak persists, check the valve stem core to make sure it is tight **(see illustration)**. Examine the tread for an object that may have embedded itself in the tire or for a "plug" that may have begun to leak (radial tire punctures are repaired with a plug that is installed in a puncture). If a puncture is suspected, it can be easily verified by spraying a solution of soapy water onto the puncture area **(see illustration)**. The soapy solution will bubble if there is a leak. Unless the puncture is unusually large, a tire shop or service station can usually repair the tire.

5 Carefully inspect the inner sidewall of each tire for evidence of brake fluid leakage. If you see any, inspect the brakes immediately.

6 Correct air pressure adds miles to the lifespan of the tires, improves mileage and enhances overall ride quality. Tire pressure cannot be accurately estimated by looking at a tire, especially if it's a radial. A tire pressure gauge is essential. Keep an accurate gauge in the glove compartment. The pressure gauges attached to the nozzles of air hoses at gas stations are often inaccurate.

7 Always check tire pressure when the tires are cold. Cold, in this case, means the vehicle has not been driven over a mile in the three hours preceding a tire pressure check. A pressure rise of four to eight pounds is not uncommon once the tires are warm.

8 Unscrew the valve cap protruding from the wheel or hubcap and push the gauge firmly onto the valve stem **(see illustration)**. Note the reading on the gauge and compare the figure to the recommended tire pressure shown on the tire placard on the driver's side door. Be sure to reinstall the valve cap to keep dirt and moisture out of the valve stem mechanism. Check all four tires and, if necessary, add enough air to bring them up to the recommended pressure.

9 Don't forget to keep the spare tire inflated to the specified pressure (refer to your owner's manual or the decal attached to the right door pillar). Note that the pressure recommended for the temporary (mini) spare is higher than for the tires on the vehicle.

4 Fluid level checks

1 A number of components on a vehicle rely on the use of fluids to perform their job. During normal operation of the vehicle, these fluids are used up and must be replenished before damage occurs. See *Recommended lubricants and fluids* at the front of this Chapter for the specific fluid to be used when addition is required. When checking fluid levels, it is important to have the vehicle on a level surface.

Engine oil

Refer to illustrations 4.4a and 4.4b

2 Engine oil level is checked with a dipstick. The dipstick travels through a tube and into the oil pan to the bottom of the engine.

3 The oil level should be checked before the vehicle has been driven, or about 15 minutes after the engine has been shut off. If the oil is checked immediately after driving the vehicle, some of the oil will remain in the upper engine components, producing an inaccurate reading on the dipstick.

4 Pull the dipstick from the tube **(see illustration)** and wipe all the oil from the end with a clean rag or paper towel. Insert the clean dipstick all the way back into the oil pan and pull it out again. Observe the oil at the end of the dipstick. At its highest point, the level should be between the L and F marks **(see illustration)**.

5 It takes one quart of oil to raise the level from the L mark to the F mark on the dipstick. Do not allow the level to drop below the L mark as engine damage due to oil starvation may occur. On the other hand, do not overfill the engine by adding oil above the F mark since it may result in oil fouled spark plugs, oil leaks or oil seal failures.

3.8 To extend the life of the tires, check the air pressure at least once a week with an accurate gauge (don't forget the spare!)

4.4a The oil dipstick is located on the front (radiator) side of the engine

4.4b The oil level should be at or near the Full mark on the dipstick - if it isn't, add enough oil to bring the level near the Full mark

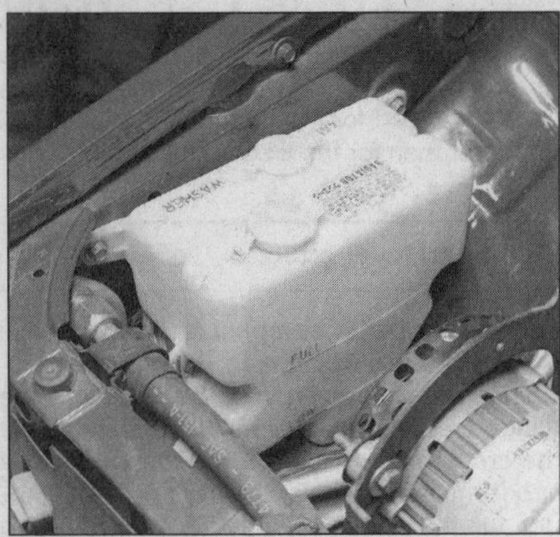

4.9 The coolant and windshield washer reservoir reservoirs are located next to each other but use different fluids, so don't mix them up

6 Oil is added to the engine after removing a twist off cap located on the rocker arm cover. A funnel will reduce spills.

7 Checking the oil level can be an important preventative maintenance step. If you find the oil level dropping abnormally, it is an indication of oil leakage or internal engine wear that should be corrected. If there are water droplets in the oil, or if it is milky looking, component failure is indicated and the engine should be checked immediately. The condition of the oil can also be checked along with the level. With the dipstick removed from the engine, take your thumb and index finger and wipe the oil up the dipstick, looking for small dirt or metal particles which will cling to the dipstick. This is an indication that the oil should be drained and fresh oil added (Section 16).

Engine coolant

Refer to illustration 4.9

8 All vehicles covered by this manual are equipped with a pressurized coolant recovery system. A hose to the radiator cap connects a white coolant reservoir attached to the inner fender panel. As the engine heats up during operation, coolant is forced from the radiator, through the connecting tube and into the reservoir. As the engine cools, the coolant is automatically drawn back into the radiator to keep the level correct.

9 Coolant level should be checked when the engine is hot. Observe the level of fluid in the reservoir, which should be at or near the Full mark on the side of the reservoir **(see illustration)**. If the system is completely cool, also check the level in the radiator by removing the cap.

10 **Warning:** *Under no circumstances should the radiator cap or the coolant recovery reservoir cap be removed when the system is hot, because escaping steam and scalding liquid could cause serious personal injury. In the case of the radiator, wait until the system has cooled completely, then wrap a thick cloth around the cap and turn it to the first stop. If any steam escapes, wait until the system has cooled further, then remove the cap. The coolant recovery cap may be removed carefully after it is apparent that no further boiling is occurring in the recovery tank.*

11 If only a small amount of coolant is required to bring the system up to the proper level, regular water can be used. However, to maintain the proper antifreeze/water mixture in the system, both should be mixed together to replenish a low level. High quality antifreeze offering protection to -20°F should be mixed with water in the proportion specified on the container. Do not allow antifreeze to come in contact with your skin or painted surfaces of the vehicle. Flush contacted areas immediately with plenty of water.

12 Coolant should be added to the reservoir until it reaches the Full mark.

13 As the coolant level is checked, note the condition of the coolant. It should be relatively clear. If it is brown or a rust color, the system should be drained, flushed and refilled (Section 26).

14 If the cooling system requires repeated additions to maintain the proper level, have the radiator cap checked for proper sealing ability. Also check for leaks in the system from cracked hoses, loose hose connections, leaking gaskets, etc.

Windshield washer fluid

Refer to illustration 4.15

15 Fluid for the windshield washer system is located in a plastic reservoir located next to the coolant reservoir **(see illustration)**. The reservoir should be kept no more than 2/3 full to allow for expansion should the fluid freeze. The use of an additive such as windshield washer fluid, available at auto parts stores, will help lower the freezing point of the fluid and will result in better cleaning of the windshield surface. Do not use antifreeze because it will cause damage to the vehicle's paint.

16 To help prevent icing in cold weather, warm the windshield with the defroster before using the washer.

Rear window washer

17 On models equipped with rear window washers, the reservoir is accessible behind a panel in the rear compartment and should also be kept at the 2/3 full level using the same fluid as in the windshield washer.

Headlight washer

18 Some models are equipped with headlight washers, the reservoir for which is located in the engine compartment. Because of the variety of reservoir configurations used, trace the tubes leading from the washers to the reservoir to determine its location. The reservoir should be kept at the 2/3 full level with the same fluid used in the windshield and rear window washer reservoirs.

Battery electrolyte

Refer to illustration 4.19

19 All vehicles with which this manual is concerned are equipped with a battery which is permanently sealed (except for vent holes) and has no filler caps. Water does not have to be added to these batteries at any time **(see illustration)**.

Brake and clutch fluid

Refer to illustration 4.21

20 The brake master cylinder is mounted on the front of the power booster unit in the engine compartment. The clutch cylinder used on manual transaxles is mounted adjacent to the master cylinder.

21 The master cylinder and clutch cylinder reservoirs incorporate two windows, which allow checking the fluid level without removal of the reservoir cover. The level should be maintained at the Max marking on the reservoir **(see illustration)**.

22 If a low level is indicated, be sure to

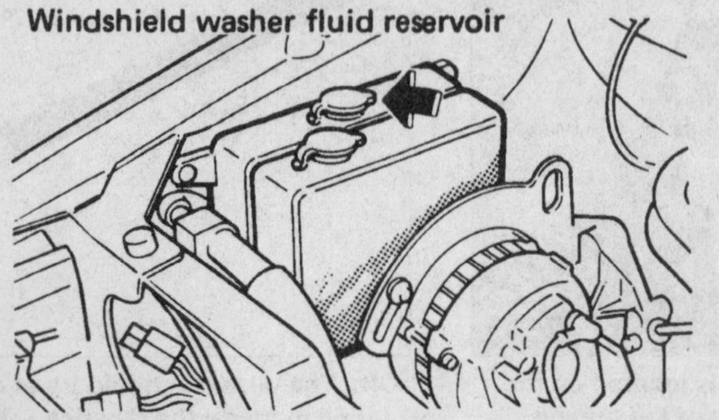

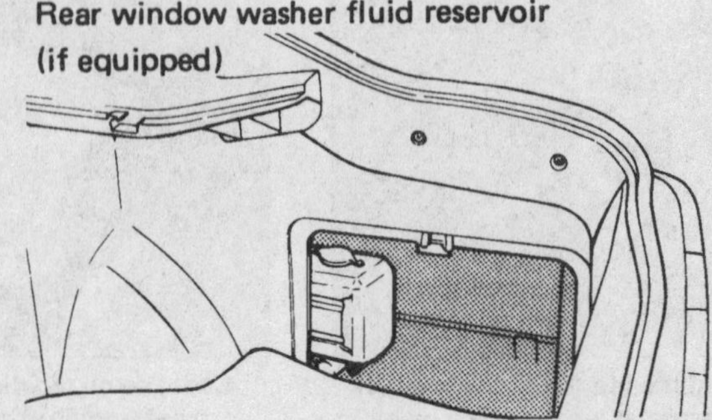

4.15 Windshield and rear window washer reservoir locations

4.19 This type of battery never requires the addition of water, but normal maintenance should be performed

4.21 The brake fluid level can be checked without removing the cap

wipe the top of the reservoir cover with a clean rag, to prevent contamination of the brake and/or clutch system, before lifting the cover.

23 When adding fluid, pour it carefully into the reservoir, taking care not to spill any onto surrounding painted surfaces. Be sure the specified fluid is used, since mixing different types of brake fluid can cause damage to the system. See Recommended lubricants and fluids or your owner's manual.

24 At this time the fluid and cylinder can be inspected for contamination. The manufacturer recommends that the brake system be drained and refilled at the specified intervals (Chapter 9). The system should also be drained and refilled if deposits, dirt particles or water droplets are seen in the fluid.

25 After filling the reservoir to the proper level, make sure the lid is properly seated to prevent fluid leakage and/or system pressure loss.

26 The brake fluid in the master cylinder will drop slightly as the brake shoes or pads at each wheel wear down during normal operation. If the master cylinder requires repeated replenishing to keep it at the proper level, this is an indication of leakage in the brake system, which should be corrected immediately. Check all brake lines and connections, along with the wheel cylinders and booster (see Section 13 for more information).

27 If, upon checking the master cylinder fluid level, you discover one or both reservoirs empty or nearly empty, the brake system should be bled (Chapter 9).

Manual transaxle oil

Refer to illustration 4.29

28 Manual transaxles do not have a dipstick. The fluid level is checked by removing the speedometer driven gear.

29 Remove the retaining bolt, withdraw the gear, wipe the driven gear clean and reinsert it. Pull the gear out again and check that the oil level is between the F and L level **(see illustration)**.

30 If the transaxle needs more oil, use a syringe to squeeze the appropriate lubricant into the speedometer gear hole.

31 Install the gear, thread the attaching bolt into the transaxle and tighten it securely. Drive the vehicle a short distance, then check for leaks.

Automatic transaxle fluid

Refer to illustrations 4.34 and 4.37

32 The level of the automatic transaxle fluid should be carefully maintained. Low fluid level can lead to slipping or loss of drive, while overfilling can cause foaming and loss of fluid.

33 With the parking brake set, start the engine, then move the shift lever through all the gear ranges, ending in Park. The fluid level must be checked with the vehicle level and the engine running at idle. **Note:** *Incorrect fluid level readings will result if the vehicle has just been driven at high speeds for an extended period, in hot weather in city traffic, or if it has been pulling a trailer. If any of these conditions apply, wait until the fluid has cooled (about 30 minutes).*

34 With the transaxle at normal operating temperature, remove the dipstick from the filler tube **(see illustration)**.

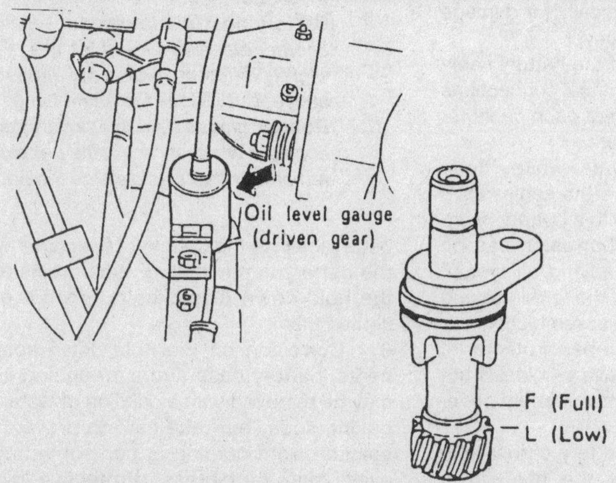

4.29 Manual transaxle driven gear and oil level gauge

4.34 The automatic transaxle dipstick is located at the rear of the transaxle

4.37 The automatic transaxle fluid level should be kept within the hatched area on the dipstick (arrow) - do not overfill

35 Wipe the fluid from the dipstick with a clean rag and push it back into the filler tube until the cap seats.

36 Pull the dipstick out again and note the fluid level.

37 The level should be in the area between the L and F mark **(see illustration)**.

38 Add just enough of the recommended fluid to fill the transmission to the proper level. It takes about one pint to raise the level from the L mark to the F mark with a hot transaxle, so add the fluid a little at a time and keep checking the level until it is correct.

39 The condition of the fluid should also be checked along with the level. If the fluid at the end of the dipstick is a dark reddish-brown color, or if the fluid has a burned smell, the transaxle fluid should be changed. If you are in doubt about the condition of the fluid, purchase some new fluid and compare the two for color and smell.

Power steering fluid

Refer to illustration 4.41

40 Unlike manual steering, the power steering system relies on fluid which may, over a period of time, require replenishing.

41 The fluid reservoir for the power steering pump is located behind the radiator near the front of the engine **(see illustration)**.

42 For the check, the front wheels should be pointed straight ahead and the engine should be off.

43 Use a clean rag to wipe off the reservoir cap and the area around the cap. This will help prevent any foreign matter from entering the reservoir during the check.

44 Run the engine until it is at normal operating temperature.

45 Remove the dipstick, wipe it off with a clean rag, reinsert it, then withdraw it and read the fluid level. The level should be between the Add and Full Hot marks.

46 If additional fluid is required, pour the specified type directly into the reservoir, using a funnel to prevent spills.

47 The dipstick must be reinstalled with the arrow on the cap pointing forward, toward the radiator.

4.41 The power steering reservoir is located near the engine oil dipstick

48 If the reservoir requires frequent fluid additions, all power steering hoses, hose connections, the power steering pump and the rack and pinion assembly should be carefully checked for leaks.

5 Battery check and maintenance

Refer to illustration 5.1

1 Tools and materials required for battery maintenance include eye and hand protection, baking soda, petroleum jelly, a battery cable puller and a cable/terminal post cleaning tool **(see illustration)**.

2 A sealed battery is standard equipment on all vehicles with which this manual is concerned. Although this type of battery has many advantages over the older, capped cell type, and never requires the addition of water, it should nevertheless be routinely maintained according to the procedures which follow. **Warning:** *Hydrogen gas in small quantities is present in the area of the side vents on sealed batteries, so keep lighted tobacco and open flames or sparks away from them.*

3 The external condition of the battery should be monitored periodically for damage such as a cracked case or cover.

4 Check the tightness of the battery cable clamps to ensure good electrical connections and check the entire length of each cable for cracks and frayed conductors.

5 If corrosion (visible as white, fluffy deposits) is evident, remove the cables from the terminals, clean them with a battery brush and reinstall the cables. Corrosion can be kept to a minimum by applying a layer of petroleum jelly or grease to the terminals and cable clamps after they are assembled.

6 Make sure that the rubber protector (if so equipped) over the positive terminal is not torn or missing. It should completely cover the terminal.

7 Make sure that the battery carrier is in good condition and that the hold-down clamp bolts are tight. If the battery is removed from the carrier, make sure that no parts remain in the bottom of the carrier when the battery is reinstalled. When reinstalling the hold-down clamp bolts, do not overtighten them.

8 Corrosion on the hold-down components, battery case and surrounding areas may be removed with a solution of water and baking soda, but take care to prevent any solution from coming in contact with your eyes, skin or clothes. Protective gloves should be worn. Thoroughly wash all cleaned areas with plain water.

5.1 Tools and materials required for battery maintenance

1 ***Face shield/safety goggles*** *- When removing corrosion with a brush, the acidic particles can easily fly up into your eyes*

2 ***Baking soda*** *- A solution of baking soda and water can be used to neutralize corrosion*

3 ***Petroleum jelly*** *- A layer of this on the battery posts will help prevent corrosion*

4 ***Battery post/cable cleaner*** *- This wire brush cleaning tool will remove all traces of corrosion from the battery posts and cable clamps*

5 ***Treated felt washers*** *- Placing one of these on each post, directly under the cable clamps, will help prevent corrosion*

6 ***Puller*** *- Sometimes the cable clamps are very difficult to pull off the posts, even after the nut/bolt has been completely loosened. This tool pulls the clamp straight up and off the post without damage*

7 ***Battery post/cable cleaner*** *- Here is another cleaning tool which is a slightly different version of Number 4 above, but it does the same thing*

8 ***Rubber gloves*** *- Another safety item to consider when servicing the battery; remember that's acid inside the battery!*

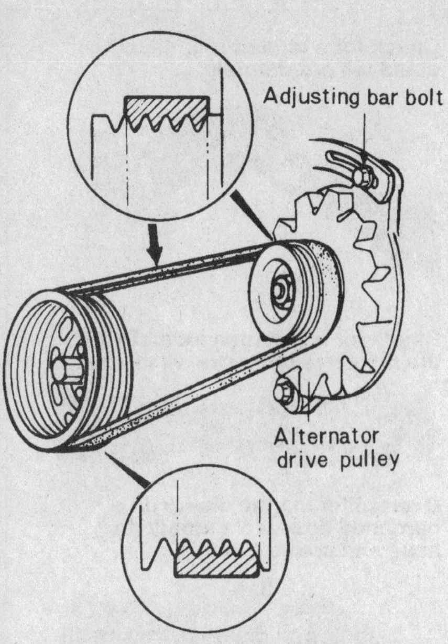

6.4a Type 1 ribbed belt installation and deflection testing point (arrow)

9 Any metal parts of the vehicle damaged by corrosion should be covered with a zinc-based primer then painted.

10 Further information on the battery, charging and jumpstarting can be found in Chapter 5 and at the front of this manual.

6 Drivebelt check and adjustment

Refer to illustrations 6.4a, 6.4b, 6.4c, 6.6 and 6.8

1 The drivebelts, or V-belts as they are more often called, are located at the front of the engine and play an important role in the overall operation of the vehicle and its components. Due to their function and material make up, the belts are prone to failure after a period of time and should be inspected and adjusted periodically to prevent major engine damage.

2 These vehicles use ribbed belts of a special design which must always be replaced with belts of the same design.

3 The number of belts used on a particular vehicle depends on the accessories installed. Drivebelts are used to turn the generator/alternator, power steering pump, water pump and air conditioning compressor. Depending on the pulley arrangement, a single belt may be used to drive more than one of these components.

4 There are three basic belt configurations **(see illustrations)**. The Type 1 belt is used for driving the alternator, Type 2 for power steering pump and alternator and Type 3 is a serpentine type using an idler pulley to maintain tension.

5 With the engine off, open the hood and locate the various belts at the front of the engine. Using your fingers (and a flashlight, if necessary), move along the belts checking for cracks and separation of the belt plies. Also check for fraying and glazing, which gives the belt a shiny appearance. Both sides of the belt should be inspected, which means you will have to twist the belt to check the underside.

6 The tension of each belt is checked by pushing on the belt at a distance halfway between the pulleys (at the points indicated by arrows in the illustrations). Push firmly with your thumb and see how much the belt moves (deflects). Measure the deflection with a ruler and compare the amount of deflection with Specifications **(see illustration)**.

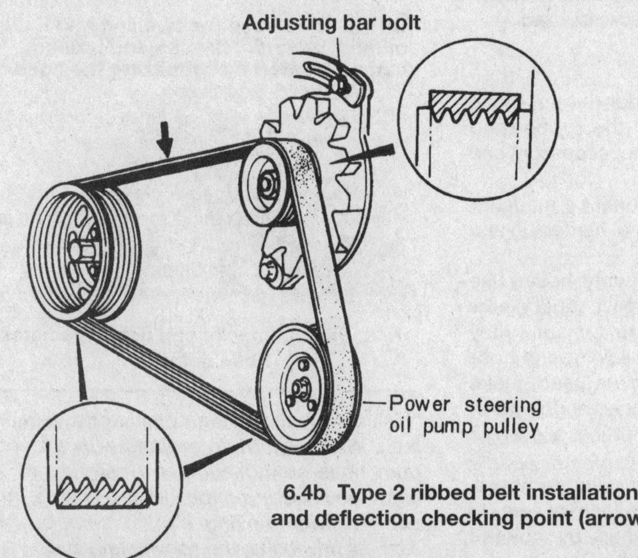

6.4b Type 2 ribbed belt installation and deflection checking point (arrow)

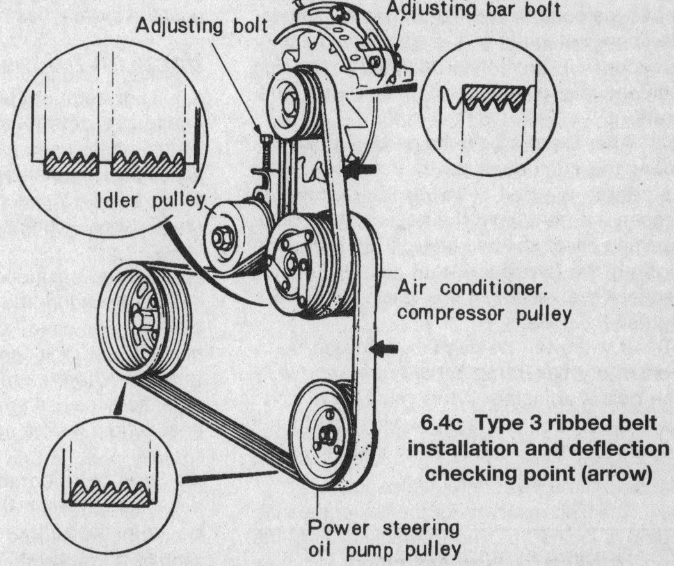

6.4c Type 3 ribbed belt installation and deflection checking point (arrow)

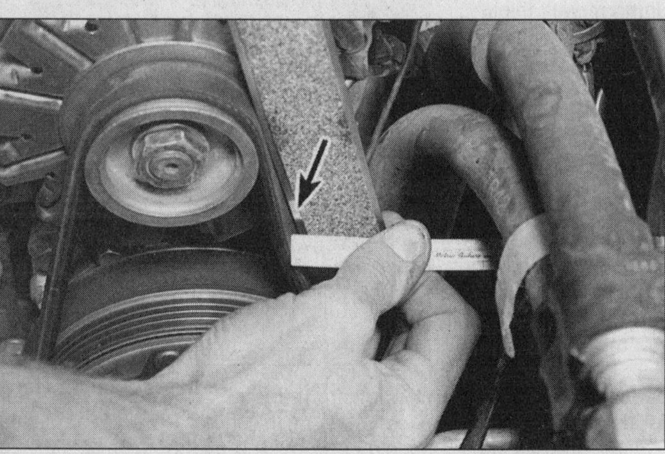

6.6 Measuring the drivebelt deflection (arrow)

6.8 The serpentine belt adjustment bolt location (arrow)

7.3 Never remove the radiator cap while the engine is hot. Inspect the gasket sealing surfaces (arrows) for corrosion and damage

7 If it is necessary to adjust the belt tension, either to make the belt tighter or looser, it is done by moving the belt-driven accessory on the bracket.

8 For each component there will be an adjusting bolt and a pivot bolt. Both bolts must be loosened slightly to enable you to move the component. On the Type 3 serpentine power steering and air conditioning compressor belt, tension is adjusted by turning only the idler pulley adjusting bolt **(see illustration)**.

9 After the two bolts have been loosened, move the component away from the engine to tighten the belt or toward the engine to loosen the belt. Hold the accessory in position and check the belt tension. If it is correct, tighten the two bolts until just snug, then recheck the tension. If the tension is correct, tighten the bolts.

10 It will often be necessary to use some sort of pry bar to move the accessory while the belt is adjusted. If this must be done to gain the proper leverage, be very careful not to damage the component being moved or the part being pried against.

7 Cooling system check

Refer to illustrations 7.3, 7.4a and 7.4b

1 Many major engine failures can be attributed to a faulty cooling system. If the vehicle is equipped with an automatic transmission, the cooling system also plays an important role in prolonging transmission life.

2 The cooling system should be checked with the engine cold. Do this before the vehicle is driven for the day or after it has been shut off for at least three hours.

3 Remove the radiator cap and thoroughly clean the cap, inside and out, with clean water. Also clean the filler neck on the radiator. All traces of corrosion should be removed **(see illustration)**.

4 Carefully check the upper and lower radiator hoses along with the smaller diameter heater hoses. Inspect each hose along its entire length, replacing any hose which is cracked, swollen or shows signs of deterioration **(see illustration)**. Cracks may become more apparent if the hose is squeezed **(see illustration)**.

5 Make sure that all hose connections are tight. A leak in the cooling system will usually show up as white or rust colored deposits on the areas adjoining the leak.

6 Use compressed air or a soft brush to remove bugs, leaves, etc. from the front of the radiator or air conditioning condenser. Be careful not to damage the delicate cooling fins or cut yourself on them.

7 Finally, have the cap and system pressure tested. If you do not have a pressure tester, most gas stations and repair shops will do this for a minimal charge.

8 Underhood hose check and replacement

Warning: *Replacement of air conditioning hoses must be left to a dealer or air conditioning specialist who has the proper equipment to depressurize the system safely. Never remove air conditioning components or hoses until the system has been depressurized.*

Vacuum hoses

1 High temperatures under the hood can cause the deterioration of the rubber and plastic hoses used for engine, accessory and emission systems operation.

2 Periodic inspection should be made for cracks, loose clamps, material hardening and leaks.

3 Some, but not all, vacuum hoses use clamps to secure the hoses to fittings. Where clamps are used, check to be sure they haven't lost their tension, allowing the hose to leak. Where clamps are not used, make sure the hose has not expanded and/or hardened where it slips over the fitting, allowing it to leak.

4 It is quite common for vacuum hoses, especially those in the emissions system, to be color coded or identified by colored stripes molded into the hose. Various systems require hoses with different wall thicknesses, collapse resistance and temperature resistance. When replacing hoses be sure to use the same hose material on the new hose.

5 Often the only effective way to check a hose is to remove it completely from the vehicle. Where more than one hose is removed, be sure to label the hoses and their attaching points to insure proper reattachment.

6 When checking vacuum hoses, be sure to include any plastic T-fittings in the check. Check the fittings for cracks and the hose where it fits over the fitting for enlargement, which could cause leakage.

7 A small piece of vacuum hose (1/4-inch inside diameter) can be used as a stethoscope to detect vacuum leaks. Hold one end of the hose to your ear and probe around vacuum hoses and fittings, listening for the "hissing'' sound characteristic of a vacuum leak. **Warning:** *When probing with the vacuum hose stethoscope, be careful not to allow your body or the hose to come into contact with moving engine components such as drivebelts, the cooling fan, etc.*

Check for a chafed area that could fail prematurely.

Check for a soft area indicating the hose has deteriorated inside.

Overtightening the clamp on a hardened hose will damage the hose and cause a leak.

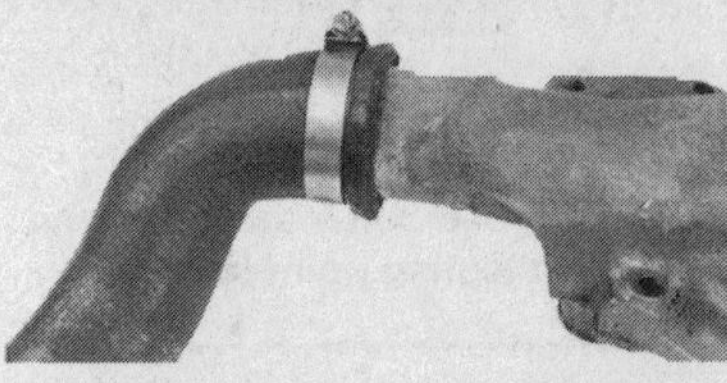

Check each hose for swelling and oil-soaked ends. Cracks and breaks can be located by squeezing the hose.

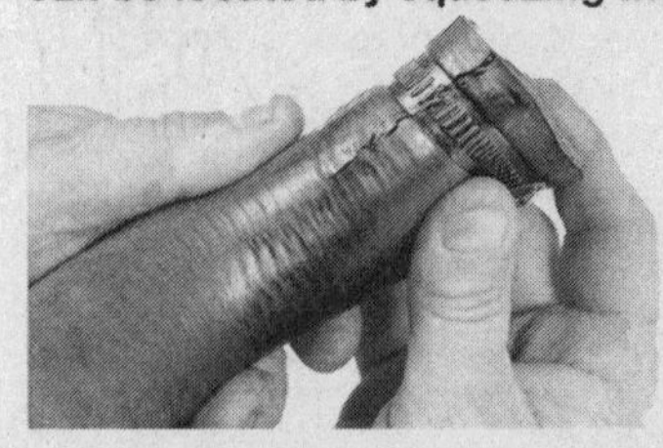

7.4a Simple checks can detect radiator hose defects

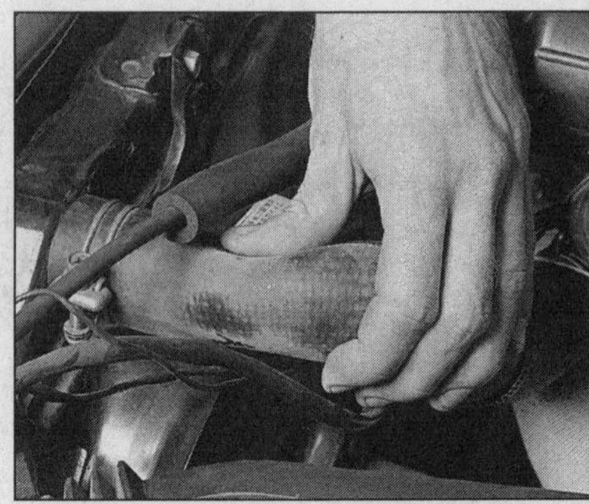
7.4b Although this radiator hose appears to be in good condition, it should be periodically checked for cracks, which are more easily revealed when squeezed

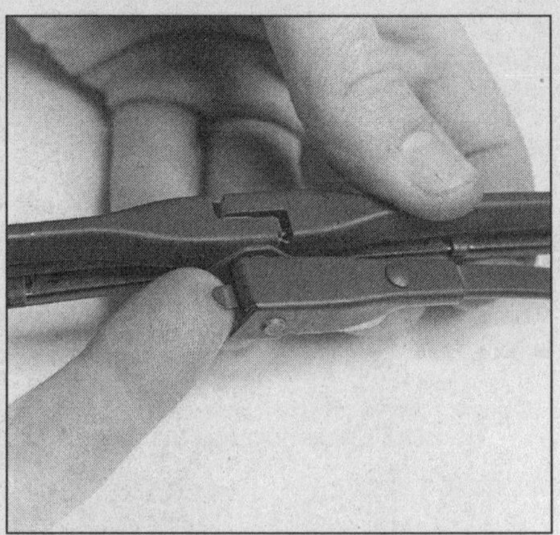

9.5a Press up on the wiper release lever and . . .

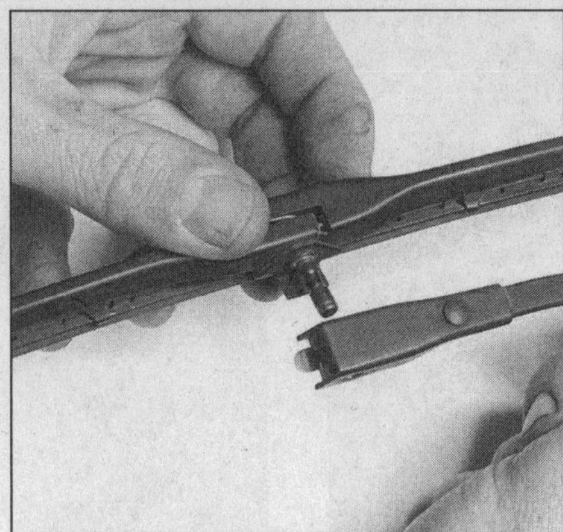

9.5b . . . slide the wiper off the pin

9.6 Squeeze the wiper tabs together and slide the wiper out of the arm

Fuel hose

8 **Warning:** *There are certain precautions which must be taken when inspecting or servicing fuel system components. Work in a well ventilated area and do not allow open flames (cigarettes, appliance pilot lights, etc.) or bare light bulbs near the work area. Mop up any spills immediately and do not store fuel soaked rags where they could ignite.*

9 The fuel lines are usually under a small amount of pressure, so if any fuel lines are to be disconnected be prepared to catch fuel spillage.

10 Check all rubber fuel lines for deterioration and chafing. Check especially for cracking in areas where the hose bends and just before clamping points, such as where a hose attaches to the fuel pump, fuel filter and carburetor or fuel injection unit.

11 High quality fuel line, usually identified by the word Fluroelastomer printed on the hose, should be used for fuel line replacement. Under no circumstances should unreinforced vacuum line, clear plastic tubing or water hose be used for fuel line replacement.

12 Spring-type clamps are commonly used on fuel lines. These clamps often lose their tension over a period of time, and can be "sprung" during the removal process. Therefore it is recommended that all spring-type clamps be replaced with screw clamps whenever a hose is replaced.

Metal lines

13 Sections of metal line are often used for fuel line between the fuel pump and carburetor or fuel injection unit. Check carefully to be sure the line has not been bent and crimped and that cracks have not started in the line in the area of bends.

14 If a section of metal fuel line must be replaced, only seamless steel tubing should be used, since copper and aluminum tubing do not have the strength necessary to withstand normal engine operating vibration.

15 Check the metal brake lines where they enter the master cylinder and brake proportioning unit (if used) for cracks in the lines or loose fittings. Any sign of brake fluid leakage calls for an immediate thorough inspection of the brake system.

9 Wiper blade inspection and replacement

Refer to illustrations 9.5a, 9.5b, 9.6 and 9.9

1 The windshield and rear window (if equipped) wiper and blade assembly should be inspected periodically for damage, loose components and cracked or worn blade elements.

2 Road film can build up on the wiper blades and affect their efficiency, so they should be washed regularly with a mild detergent solution.

3 The action of the wiping mechanism can loosen the bolts, nuts and fasteners, so they should be checked and tightened, as necessary, at the same time the wiper blades are checked.

4 If the wiper blade elements are cracked, worn or warped, they should be replaced with new ones.

5 Lift the arm assembly away from the glass for clearance and remove the blade by lifting the release lever **(see illustrations)**.

6 Remove the retaining clip with needle nose pliers and slide the blade element out **(see illustration)**.

7 Insert the new blade element and snap the retaining clip in place.

8 Lift the release lever and insert the blade element pin until it snaps securely in position.

9 Check the wiper arm nut to make sure it is securely tightened **(see illustration)**.

10 Chassis lubrication

Refer to illustration 10.3

1 There is no provision for lubrication of chassis or steering components on these models. Only the rear wheel bearings (Section 27) require periodic lubrication.

2 Lubricate all the hinges (door, hood, hatch) with a few drops of light engine oil to keep them in proper working order.

3 Open the hood and lubricate the latch mechanism with lithium base white grease **(see illustration)**.

4 Lubricate the door and trunk or liftgate weather-stripping with silicone spray. This will reduce chafing and retard wear.

5 The key lock cylinders can be lubricated with spray-on graphite, which is available at auto parts stores.

9.9 Rotate the trim cap up for access to the wiper arm nut

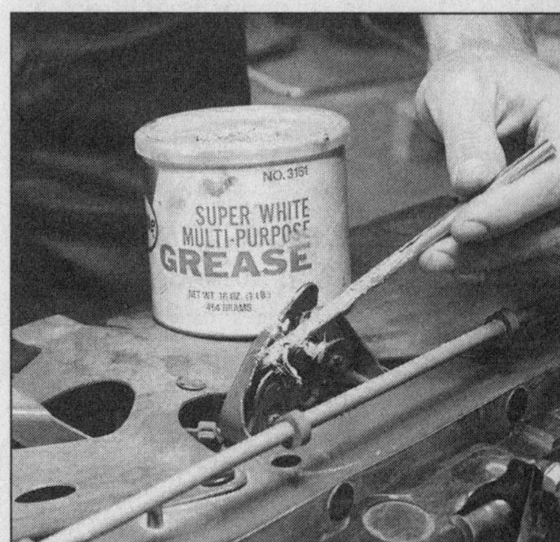

10.3 Multi-purpose grease is used to lubricate the hood latch mechanism

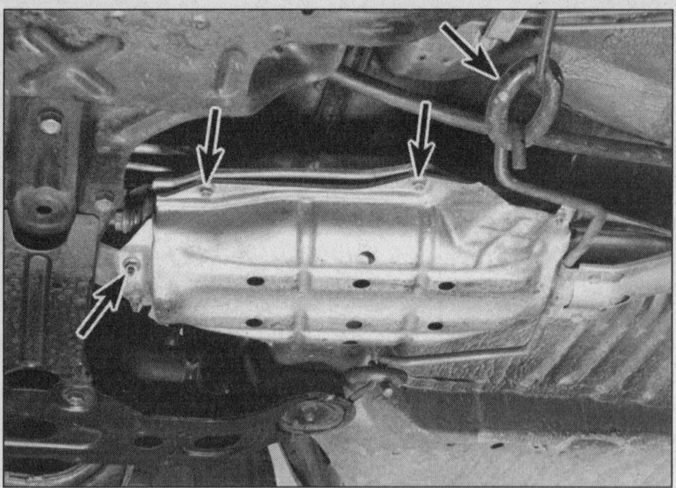

11.4 Check the exhaust system rubber hangers for cracks and the heat shield bolts for looseness

13.5 The amount of disc pad material (arrows) remaining can be checked by looking through the hole in the caliper

11 Exhaust system check

Refer to illustration 11.4

1 With the engine cold (at least three hours after the vehicle has been driven), check the complete exhaust system from its starting point at the engine to the end of the tailpipe. This should be done on a hoist where unrestricted access is available.

2 Check the pipes and connections for signs of leakage and/or corrosion indicating a potential failure. Make sure that all brackets and hangers are in good condition and tight.

3 At the same time, inspect the underside of the body for holes, corrosion, open seams, etc. which may allow exhaust gases to enter the passenger compartment. Seal all body openings with silicone or body putty.

4 Rattles and other noises can often be traced to the exhaust system, especially the mounts and hangers. Try to move the pipes, muffler and catalytic converter. If the components can come in contact with the body or suspension parts, secure the exhaust system with new mounts **(see illustration)**.

5 Check the running condition of the engine by inspecting inside the end of the tailpipe. The exhaust deposits here are an indication of engine state-of-tune. If the pipe is black and sooty or coated with white deposits, the engine is in need of a tune-up, including a thorough carburetor inspection and adjustment.

12 Suspension and steering check

1 Raise the front of the vehicle periodically and visually check the suspension and steering components for wear.

2 Indications of a fault in these systems are excessive play in the steering wheel before the front wheels react, excessive sway around corners, body movement over rough roads or binding at some point as the steering wheel is turned.

3 Before the vehicle is raised for inspection, test the shock absorbers by pushing down to rock the vehicle at each corner. If you push down and the vehicle does not come back to a level position within one or two bounces, the shocks/struts are worn and must be replaced. As this is done, check for squeaks and noises coming from the suspension components. Information on suspension components can be found in Chapter 10.

4 Raise the front end of the vehicle and support it securely on jackstands placed under the frame rails. Because of the work to be done, make sure the vehicle cannot fall from the stands.

5 Check the wheel bearings (see Section 27).

6 From under the vehicle check for loose bolts, broken or disconnected parts and deteriorated rubber bushings on all suspension and steering components. Look for grease or fluid leaking from the rack and pinion steering assembly. Check the power steering hoses and connections for leaks. Check the balljoints for wear.

7 Have an assistant turn the steering wheel from side-to-side and check the steering components for free movement, chafing and binding. If the steering does not react with the movement of the steering wheel, try to determine where the slack is located.

13 Brake check

Refer to illustration 13.5

Note: *For detailed photographs of the brake system, refer to Chapter 9.*

1 The brakes should be inspected every time the wheels are removed or whenever a defect is suspected. Indications of a potential brake system defect are: the vehicle pulls to one side when the brake pedal is depressed; noises coming from the brakes when they are applied; excessive brake pedal travel; pulsating pedal; leakage of fluid, usually seen on the inside of the tire or wheel.

Disc brakes

2 The front disc brakes can be visually checked without removing any parts except the wheels.

3 Raise the vehicle and place it securely on jackstands. Remove the wheels (see Jacking and towing at the front of the manual, if necessary).

4 The disc brake calipers, which contain the pads, are now visible. There is an outer pad and an inner pad in each caliper. All pads should be inspected.

5 Check the pad thickness by looking at each end of the caliper and through the inspection hole in the caliper body **(see illustration)**. If the lining material is 1/16-inch or less in thickness, the pads should be replaced. Keep in mind that the lining material is riveted or bonded to a metal backing shoe and the metal portion is not included in this measurement.

6 If it is difficult to measure the exact thickness of the remaining lining material, remove the pads for further inspection or replacement if you are in doubt as to the quality of the pad.

7 Before installing the wheels, check for leakage around the brake hose connections leading to the caliper and damage (cracking, splitting, etc.) to the brake hose. Replace the hose or fittings as necessary, referring to Chapter 9.

8 Check the condition of the rotor. Look for scoring, gouging and burned spots. If these conditions exist, the hub/rotor assembly should be removed for servicing (Chapter 9).

Drum brakes - rear

Refer to illustration 13.11

9 Remove the brake drum/hub assembly (Section 26). If this proves difficult, make sure the parking brake is released.

10 With the drum removed, carefully brush away any accumulations of dirt and dust. **Warning:** *Do not blow the dust out with compressed air. Make an effort not to inhale the*

13.11 After removing the brake drum, the remaining shoe lining can be measured

dust, as it contains asbestos and is harmful to your health.

11 Note the thickness of the lining material on the rear brake shoes **(see illustration)**. If the material is within 1/16-inch of the recessed rivets or metal backing, the shoes should be replaced. If the linings look worn, but you are unable to determine their exact thickness, compare them with a new set at an auto parts store. The shoes should also be replaced if they are cracked, glazed (shiny surface) or contaminated with brake fluid.

12 Check to see that all the brake assembly springs are connected and in good condition.

13 Check the brake components for signs of fluid leakage. With your finger, carefully pry back the rubber cups on the wheel cylinder located at the top of the brake shoes. Any leakage is an indication that the wheel cylinders should be overhauled immediately (Chapter 9). Also check the hoses and connections for signs of leakage.

14 Wipe the inside of the drum with a clean rag and denatured alcohol. Again, be careful not to breathe the dangerous asbestos dust.

15 Check the inside of the drum for cracks, scores, deep scratches and hard spots, which will appear as small discolored areas. If imperfections cannot be removed with fine emery cloth, the drum must be taken to a machine shop for resurfacing.

16 After the inspection process, if all parts are found to be in good condition, reinstall the hub/brake drum. Install the wheel and lower the vehicle to the ground.

Parking brake

17 Pull up on the parking brake handle with a force of approximately 22 ft-lbs to check that the handle moves the specified number of clicks. If it does not, adjust the parking brake (Chapter 9).

18 The easiest way to check the operation of the parking brake is to park the vehicle on a steep hill with the parking brake set and the transmission in Neutral. If the parking brake cannot prevent the vehicle from rolling, it is in need of adjustment (see Chapter 9).

14 Carburetor choke check

Refer to illustrations 14.3 and 14.7

1 A choke only operates when the engine is cold, so this check should be performed before the engine has been started for the day.

2 Open the hood and remove the top plate of the air cleaner assembly. It is held in place by a wing nut and three clips. Place the top plate and nut aside, out of the way of moving engine components.

3 Look at the top of the carburetor at the center of the air cleaner housing. You will notice a flat plate at the carburetor opening **(see illustration)**.

4 Have an assistant press the accelerator pedal to the floor. The plate should close completely. Start the engine while you observe the plate at the carburetor. **Warning:** *Do not position your face directly over the carburetor, because the engine could backfire and cause serious burns. When the engine starts, the choke plate should open slightly.*

5 Allow the engine to continue running at an idle speed. As the engine warms up to operating temperature, the plate should slowly open, allowing more air to enter through the top of the carburetor.

6 After a few minutes, the choke plate should be all the way open to the vertical position.

7 With the engine off, inspect the contact areas of the choke plate shaft for deposits which could cause binding. Use a spray choke cleaner, available at auto parts stores, to clean the choke shaft in the areas shown while working the choke linkage by hand **(see illustration)**.

8 Use a spray lubricant, also available at parts stores, on the contact surfaces while working the linkage to make sure the choke works freely.

9 If a malfunction is detected during the above checks, refer to Chapter 4 for specific information related to adjusting and servicing choke components.

15 Engine idle speed check and adjustment (carbureted models)

Refer to illustration 15.4

Note: *Refer to Section 39 for fuel-injected models).*

1 Engine idle speed is the speed at which the engine operates when no accelerator pedal pressure is applied. This speed is critical to the performance of the engine itself, as well as many engine subsystems.

2 A hand held tachometer must be used when adjusting idle speed to get an accurate reading. The exact hook-up for these meters varies with the manufacturer, so follow the particular directions included.

3 All vehicles covered in this manual should have a tune-up decal located on the inside of the hood. The printed instructions for setting idle speed can be found on this decal, and should be followed since they are for your particular engine. To plug a vacuum hose, insert a suitable size metal rod or thread a bolt into the opening to prevent any vacuum loss through the hose.

14.3 With the air cleaner removed, the choke plate can be checked

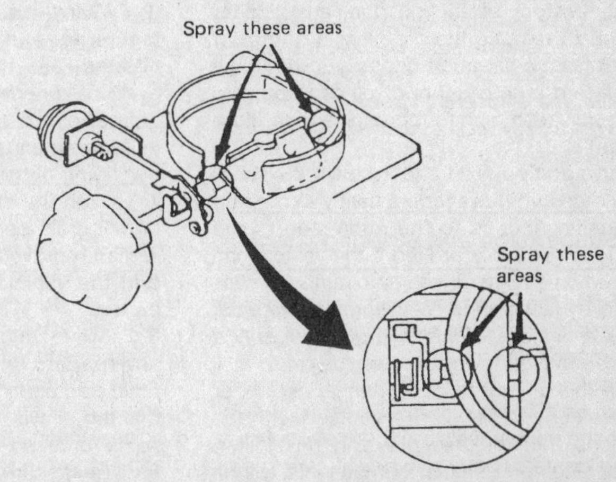

14.7 Details of carburetor choke shaft cleaning

15.4 The idle speed adjustment screw (arrow) is not easy to reach. The air cleaner has been removed here for clarity

4 With the engine at normal operating temperature, the parking brake firmly set and the wheels blocked to prevent the car from rolling, check the engine idle speed, following the instructions on the decal. Turn off all lights and accessories and disconnect the cooling fan motor. Adjustment of the idle speed is made by turning the throttle adjusting screw on the carburetor **(see illustration)**.

16 Engine oil and filter change

Refer to illustrations 16.3, 16.9, 16.14 and 16.22

1 Frequent oil changes may be the best form of preventative maintenance available to the home mechanic. When engine oil ages, it becomes diluted and contaminated and that leads to premature engine wear.

2 Although some sources recommend oil filter changes every other oil change, we feel that the minimal cost of an oil filter and the relative ease with which it is installed dictate that a new filter be used whenever the oil is changed.

3 The tools necessary for a normal oil and filter change are a wrench to fit the drain plug at the bottom of the oil pan, an oil filter wrench to remove the old filter, a container with at least a six-quart capacity to drain the old oil into and a funnel or oil can spout to help pour fresh oil into the engine **(see illustration)**.

4 In addition, you should have plenty of clean rags and newspapers handy to mop up any spills. Access to the underside of the vehicle is greatly improved if the vehicle can be lifted on a hoist, driven onto ramps or supported by jackstands. **Warning:** *Do not work under a vehicle which is supported only a bumper, hydraulic or scissors-type jack.*

5 If this is your first oil change, get under the vehicle and familiarize yourself with the locations of the oil drain plug and the oil filter. The engine and exhaust components will be warm during the actual work, so figure out any potential problems before the engine and accessories are hot.

6 Warm the engine to normal operating temperature. If the new oil or any tools are needed, use this warm-up time to gather everything necessary for the job. The correct type of oil for your application can be found in Recommended lubricants and fluids at the beginning of this Chapter.

7 With the engine oil warm (warm engine oil will drain better and more built-up sludge will be removed with the oil), raise and support the vehicle. Make sure it is firmly supported.

8 Move all necessary tools, rags and newspapers under the vehicle. Position the drain pan under the drain plug. Keep in mind that the oil will initially flow from the pan with some force, so place the pan accordingly.

9 Being careful not to touch any of the hot exhaust components, use the wrench to remove the drain plug near the bottom of the oil pan **(see illustration)**. Depending on how hot the oil has become, you may want to wear gloves while unscrewing the plug the final few turns.

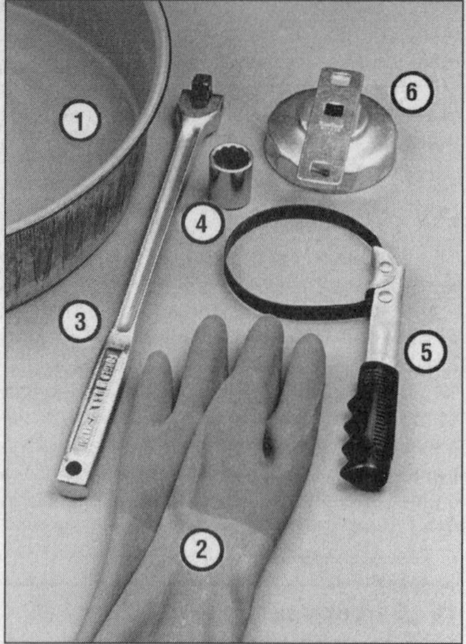

16.3 These tools are required when changing the engine oil and filter

1 ***Drain pan*** *- It should be fairly shallow in depth, but wide to prevent spills*
2 ***Rubber gloves*** *- When removing the drain plug and filter, you will get oil on your hands (the gloves will prevent burns)*
3 ***Breaker bar*** *- Sometimes the oil drain plug is tight, and a long breaker bar is needed to loosen it*
4 ***Socket*** *- To be used with the breaker bar or a ratchet (must be the correct size to fit the drain plug - six-point preferred)*
5 ***Filter wrench*** *- This is a metal band-type wrench, which requires clearance around the filter to be effective*
6 ***Filter wrench*** *- This type fits on the bottom of the filter and can be turned with a ratchet or breaker bar (different-size wrenches are available for different types of filters)*

16.9 Oil drain plug location (arrow)

16.14 A strap-type oil filter wrench works well in hard-to-reach locations

10 Allow the old oil to drain into the pan. It may be necessary to move the pan farther under the engine as the oil flow slows to a trickle.

11 After all the oil has drained, wipe off the drain plug with a clean rag. Small metal particles may cling to the plug which would immediately contaminate the new oil.

12 Clean the area around the drain plug opening and reinstall the plug. Tighten the plug securely with the wrench. If a torque wrench is available, use it to tighten the plug.

13 Move the drain pan into position under the oil filter.

14 Use the filter wrench to loosen the oil filter. Chain or metal band filter wrenches may distort the filter canister, but this is of no concern as the filter will be discarded anyway **(see illustration)**.

15 Sometimes the oil filter is on so tight it cannot be loosened, or it is positioned in an area which is inaccessible with a filter wrench. As a last resort, you can punch a metal bar or long screwdriver directly through the side of the canister and use it as a T-bar to turn the filter. If so, be prepared for oil to spurt out of the canister as it is punctured.

16 Completely unscrew the old filter. Be

16.22 Oil is added through a filler opening in the rocker arm cover

careful, it is full of oil. Empty the oil inside the filter into the drain pan.

17 Compare the old filter with the new one to make sure they are the same type.

18 Use a clean rag to remove all oil, dirt and sludge from the area where the oil filter mounts to the engine. Check the old filter to make sure the rubber gasket is not stuck to the engine mounting surface. If the gasket is stuck to the engine (use a flashlight if necessary), remove it.

19 Apply a light coat of oil around the full circumference of the rubber gasket of the new oil filter.

20 Attach the new filter to the engine, following the tightening directions printed on the filter canister or packing box. Most filter manufacturers recommend against using a filter wrench due to the possibility of overtightening and damage to the seal.

21 Remove all tools, rags, etc. from under the vehicle, being careful not to spill the oil in the drain pan, then lower the vehicle.

22 Move to the engine compartment and locate the oil filler cap on the engine camshaft cover **(see illustration)**.

23 If an oil can spout is used, push the spout into the top of the oil can and pour the fresh oil through the filler opening. A funnel may also be used.

24 Pour three quarts of fresh oil into the engine. Wait a few minutes to allow the oil to drain into the pan, then check the level on the oil dipstick (see Section 4 if necessary). If the oil level is at or near the F mark, start the engine and allow the new oil to circulate.

25 Run the engine for only about a minute and then shut it off. Immediately look under the vehicle and check for leaks at the oil pan drain plug and around the oil filter. If either is leaking, tighten with a bit more force.

26 With the new oil circulated and the filter now completely full, recheck the level on the dipstick and add enough oil to bring the level to the F mark on the dipstick.

27 During the first few trips after an oil change, make it a point to check frequently for leaks and proper oil level.

28 The old oil drained from the engine cannot be reused in its present state and should be disposed of. Oil reclamation centers, auto repair shops and gas stations will normally accept the oil, which can be refined and used again. After the oil has cooled, it can be drained into a suitable container (capped plastic jugs, topped bottles, milk cartons, etc.) for transport to one of these disposal sites.

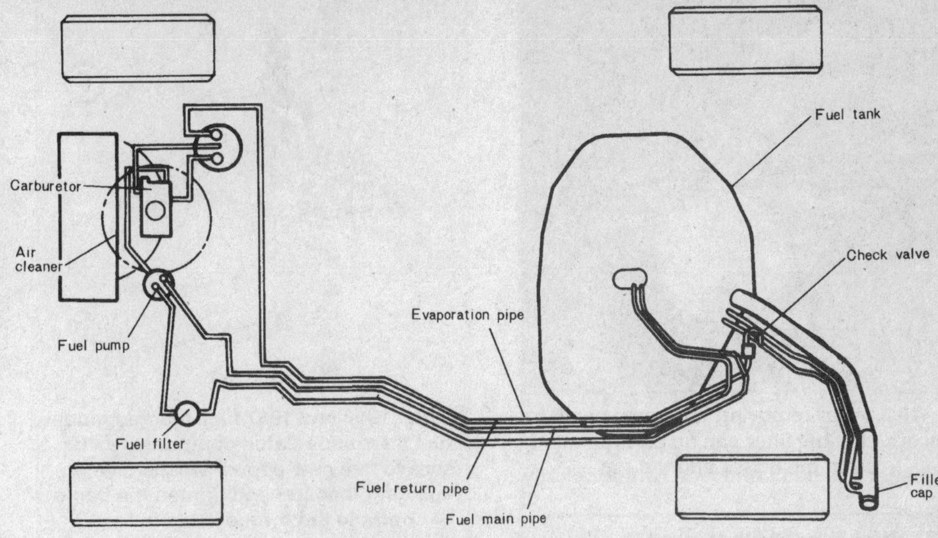

17.2 Fuel system layout

17 Fuel system check

Refer to illustrations 17.2 and 17.4

Warning: *There are certain precautions to take when inspecting or servicing the fuel system components. Work in a well ventilated area and do not allow open flames (cigarettes, appliance pilot lights, etc.) to get near the work area. Mop up spills immediately and do not store fuel soaked rags where they could ignite. On fuel injected models, refer to Chapter 4 and depressurize the system before disconnecting any fuel lines.*

1 The fuel system on carbureted models is under a small amount of pressure and on fuel injected models under considerable pressure. On all models, if any fuel lines are disconnected for servicing, be prepared to catch the fuel as it spurts out. Plug all disconnected fuel lines immediately after disconnection to prevent the tank from emptying itself.

2 The fuel system is most easily checked with the vehicle raised on a hoist so the components underneath the vehicle are readily visible and accessible **(see illustration)**.

3 If the smell of gasoline is noticed while driving or after the vehicle has been in the sun, the system should be thoroughly inspected immediately.

4 Remove the gas filler cap and check for damage, corrosion and an unbroken sealing imprint on the gasket **(see illustration)**. Replace the cap with a new one if necessary.

17.4 With today's sophisticated emissions systems, it is essential that seals (arrow) in the gas tank cap be checked regularly

5 With the vehicle raised, inspect the gas tank and filler neck for punctures, cracks and other damage. The connection between the filler neck and the tank is especially critical. Sometimes a rubber filler neck will leak due to loose clamps or deteriorated rubber, problems a home mechanic can usually rectify. **Warning:** Do not, under any circumstances, try to repair a fuel tank yourself (except rubber components) unless you have had considerable experience. A welding torch or any open flame can easily cause the fuel vapors to explode if the proper precautions are not taken.

6 Carefully check all rubber hoses and metal lines leading away from the fuel tank. Check for loose connections, deteriorated hoses, crimped lines and other damage. Follow the lines to the front of the vehicle, carefully inspecting them all the way. Repair or replace damaged sections as necessary.

7 If a fuel odor is still evident after the inspection, refer to Section 33.

18.3 After removing the clamps with pliers, the fuel filter can be disconnected from the hoses and the clip

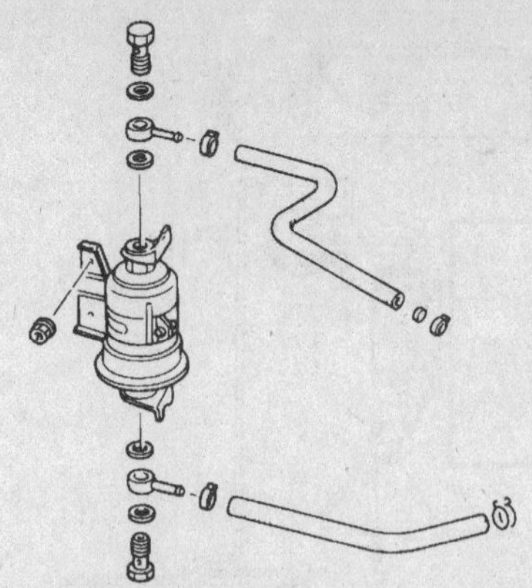

18.10a 1986 and 1987 fuel injected model fuel filter and related components - be sure to use new copper washers when replacing the filter and tighten the banjo bolts to the torque listed in the Specifications section

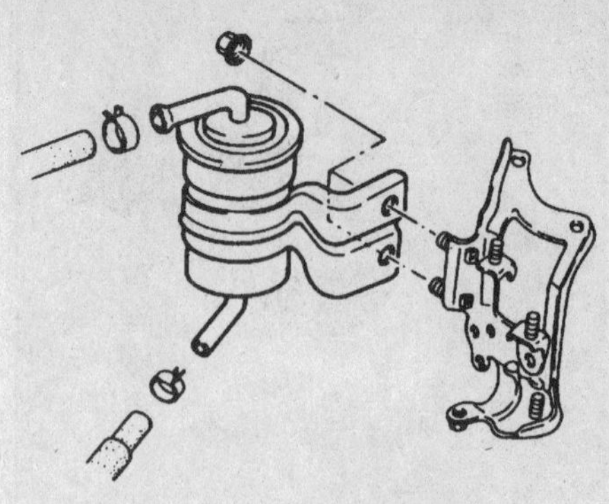

18.10b 1988 and later fuel injected model fuel filter details

18 Fuel filter replacement

Carbureted models

Refer to illustration 18.3

1 The fuel filter is located on the left side of the engine compartment on a spring clip mount. It is of the disposable type and should be replaced at the specified intervals.

2 Place some rags or newspapers under the fuel filter to catch spilled fuel as the hoses are disconnected.

3 Use pliers to slide the clips back on the fuel line hoses and disconnect the hoses from the filter **(see illustration)**.

4 Note the direction of flow arrow on the filter and unsnap the filter from the mounting clip.

5 Snap the new filter in place in the clip with the arrow pointing in the correct direction and connect the hoses and clamps.

Fuel injected models

Refer to illustrations 18.10a and 18.10b

Warning: *Gasoline is extremely flammable, so extra precautions must be taken when working on any part of the fuel system. DO NOT smoke or allow open flames or bare light bulbs near the work area. Also, don't work in a garage if a natural gas appliance (such as a water heater or clothes dryer) is present.*

6 The factory recommends fuel filter replacement every 30,000 miles on fuel injected models.

7 Depressurize the fuel injection system (Chapter 4)

8 Disconnect the cable from the negative battery terminal.

9 Locate the fuel filter, which is mounted on the left front shock tower near the brake master cylinder reservoir.

10 Have plenty of rags ready to absorb spilled gasoline. Remove the two banjo fitting bolts (one at each end of the filter) or detach the clamps and slide the hoses off **(see illustrations)**. Allow the fuel to drain out of the filter.

11 Remove the filter bracket nuts from the shock tower and detach the filter.

12 Position the new filter and bracket and install the nuts.

13 On models so equipped, install NEW copper washers on BOTH sides of each banjo fitting and tighten the fitting bolts to the specified torque.

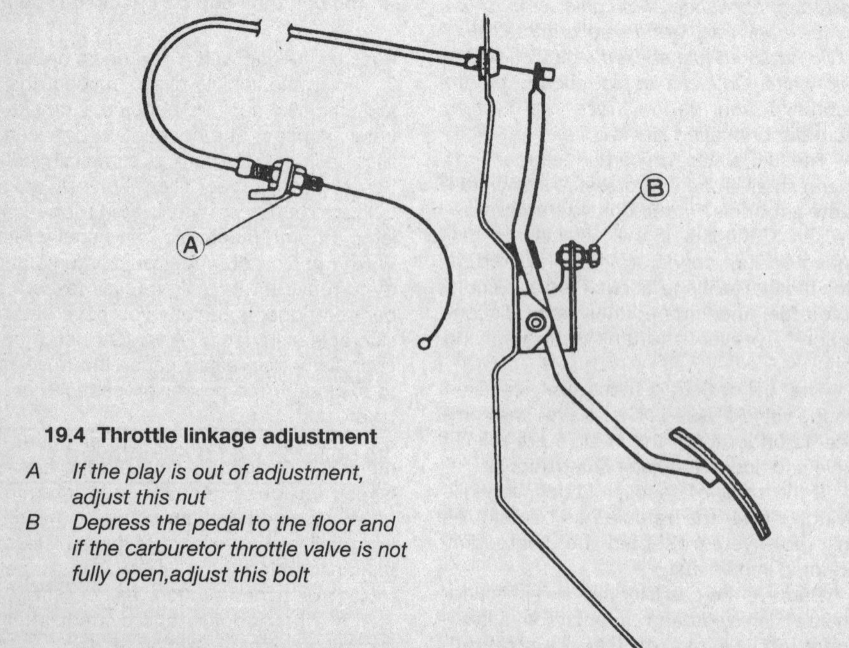

19.4 Throttle linkage adjustment

A *If the play is out of adjustment, adjust this nut*

B *Depress the pedal to the floor and if the carburetor throttle valve is not fully open,adjust this bolt*

19 Throttle linkage check and adjustment

Refer to illustration 19.4

1 The throttle linkage is a cable type and should be checked and adjusted periodically to assure proper function.

2 Check the entire length of the cable to make sure that it is not binding.

3 With the engine at normal operating temperature, make sure the choke plate is fully open (Section 14) and correctly adjusted (Chapter 4).

4 Measure the amount of play in the cable at the carburetor and adjust as necessary **(see illustration)**.

20 Carburetor mounting torque check

1 The carburetor is attached to the top of the intake manifold by four nuts. These fasteners can sometimes work loose from vibration and temperature changes during normal engine operation and cause a vacuum leak.

2 If you suspect that a vacuum leak exists at the bottom of the carburetor, obtain a length of hose about the diameter of fuel hose. Start the engine and place one end of the hose next to your ear as you probe

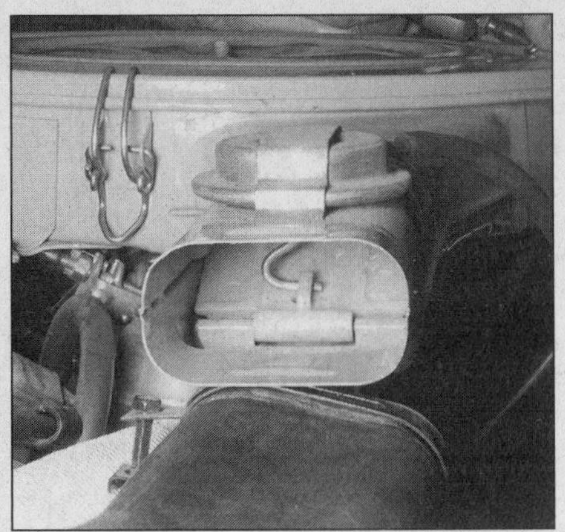

21.6 The thermostatically controlled damper door can be seen after removing the air inlet pipe

22.4 Check the driveaxle boot to make sure it is not cracked or loose

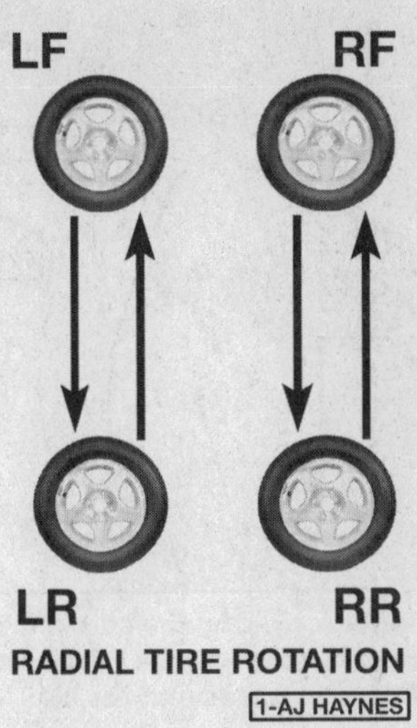

23.2 Tire rotation diagram

around the base with the other end. You will hear a hissing sound if a leak exists.

3 Remove the air cleaner assembly, tagging each hose to be disconnected with a piece of numbered tape to make reassembly easier.

4 Locate the mounting nuts at the base of the carburetor. Decide what special tools or adapters will be necessary, if any, to tighten the fasteners with a socket and the torque wrench.

5 Tighten the nuts securely and evenly. Do not overtighten them, as the threads could strip.

6 If, after the nuts are properly tightened, a vacuum leak still exists, the carburetor must be removed and a new gasket installed. See Chapter 4 for more information.

7 After tightening the fasteners, reinstall the air cleaner and return all hoses to their original positions.

21 Thermostatically controlled air cleaner check

Refer to illustration 21.6

1 All engines are equipped with a thermostatically controlled air cleaner which draws air to the carburetor from different locations, depending upon engine temperature.

2 This is a simple visual check. If access is limited, however, a small mirror may have to be used.

3 Open the hood and locate the damper door inside the air cleaner assembly. It will be located inside the long snorkel of the metal air cleaner housing. Make sure that the flexible air hose(s) are securely attached and undamaged.

4 If there is a flexible air duct attached to the end of the snorkel, leading to an area behind the grille, disconnect it at the snorkel. This will enable you to look through the end of the snorkel and see the damper inside.

5 The check should be done when the engine and outside air are cold. Start the engine and look through the snorkel at the damper, which should move to a closed position. With the damper closed, air cannot enter through the end of the snorkel, but instead enters the air cleaner through the flexible duct attached to the exhaust manifold and the heat stove passage.

6 As the engine warms up to operating temperature, the damper should open to allow air through the snorkel end. Depending on ambient temperature, this may take 10 to 15 minutes. To speed up this check you can reconnect the snorkel air duct, drive the vehicle and then check to see if the damper is completely open **(see illustration)**.

7 If the thermo-controlled air cleaner is not operating properly, see Chapter 6 for more information.

22 Transaxle output shaft seal and driveaxle boot check

Refer to illustration 22.4

1 At the recommended intervals the transaxle output shaft seals and driveaxle boots should be inspected for leaks and damage.

2 Raise the front of the vehicle and support it securely on jackstands.

3 Check the transaxle output shaft seals located at the point where the driveaxles exit from the transaxle. It may be necessary to clean this area before inspection. If there is any oil leaking from either of the driveaxle/transaxle junctions, the output shaft seals must be replaced. Refer to Chapter 7.

4 The driveaxle boots are very important because they prevent dirt, water and other foreign material from entering and damaging the constant velocity (CV) joints. Inspect the condition of all four boots (two on each axleshaft). It is a good idea to clean the boots using soap and water, as oil or grease will cause the boot material to deteriorate prematurely. If there is any damage or evidence of leaking lubricant, they must be replaced as described in Chapter 8. Check the tightness of the boot clamps. If they are loose and can't be tightened, the clamp must be replaced **(see illustration)**.

23 Tire rotation

Refer to illustration 23.2

1 Tires should be rotated at the specified intervals and whenever uneven wear is noticed. Since the vehicle will be raised and the tires removed anyway, check the brakes (Section 13) and the wheel bearings (Section 27).

2 Refer to the accompanying illustration for the preferred tire rotation pattern **(see illustration)**.

3 Refer to the information in Jacking and towing at the front of this manual for the proper procedures to follow when raising the vehicle and changing a tire. If the brakes are to be checked, do not apply the parking brake as stated. Make sure the tires are blocked to prevent the vehicle from rolling.

4 Preferably, the entire vehicle should be raised at the same time. This can be done on a hoist or by jacking up each corner and then lowering the vehicle onto jackstands placed under the frame rails. Always use four jackstands and make sure the vehicle is firmly supported.

5 After rotation, check and adjust the tire pressures as necessary and be sure to check the lug nut tightness.

6 For further information on the wheels and tires, refer to Chapter 10.

24 Clutch pedal adjustment

Cable-actuated

Refer to illustrations 24.1 and 24.2

1 If equipped with a manual shift transaxle, it is important to have the clutch pedal free play as well as engaged and disen-

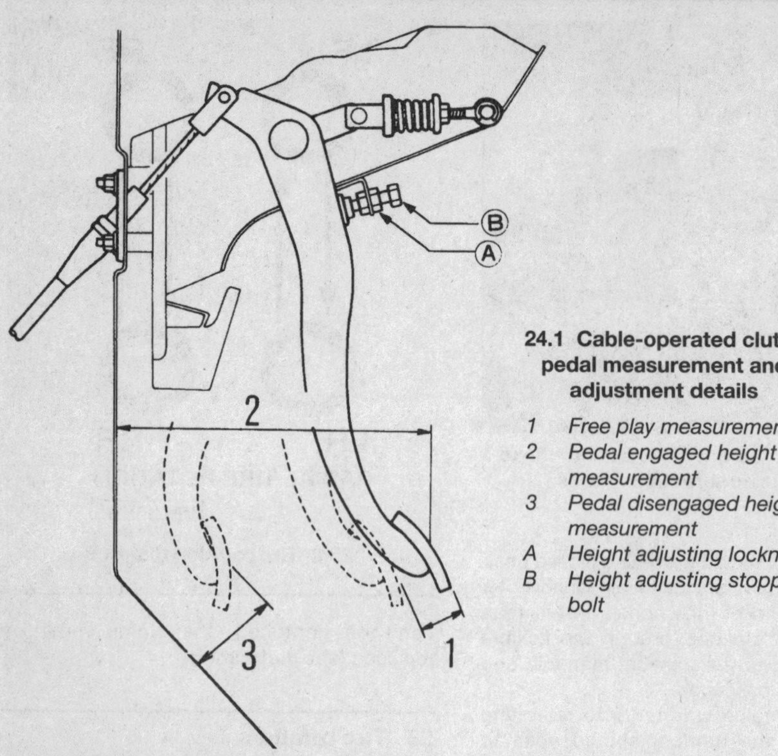

24.1 Cable-operated clutch pedal measurement and adjustment details

1 *Free play measurement*
2 *Pedal engaged height measurement*
3 *Pedal disengaged height measurement*
A *Height adjusting locknut*
B *Height adjusting stopper bolt*

gaged heights at the proper points. Free play at the clutch pedal is the distance the pedal moves from the full-up position to where resistance is felt as the clutch begins to disengage. Clutch pedal height is the measurement from the pedal pad to the firewall when the clutch is engaged (fully up). Clutch pedal disengaged height is the distance from the pedal pad to the floor with the clutch fully disengaged so shift lever can move between first and reverse with the engine running **(see illustration)**.

2 To check the free play, depress the clutch pedal until resistance is felt. Measure the distance traveled by the pedal and compare this measurement to the Specifications **(see illustration)**.

3 To check the clutch pedal height, measure from the top of the pedal to the firewall and compare this measurement to the Specifications.

4 Check the pedal fully disengaged height by measuring between the pedal pad and the floor and comparing the measurement to the Specifications.

5 To adjust the pedal height, first remove the heater air duct under the dash for clearance (Chapter 12). Loosen the locknut (A in the illustration) and adjust the pedal height by turning the stopper bolt (B in the illustration). Tighten the locknut securely after adjustment.

6 To adjust the pedal free play, press on the clutch release lever in the engine compartment while pulling on the roller and check the clearance (A in the accompanying illustration). Loosen the locknut and adjust the clearance by turning the adjusting nut (B). Check the pedal free play and clutch lever clearance again before tightening the locknut.

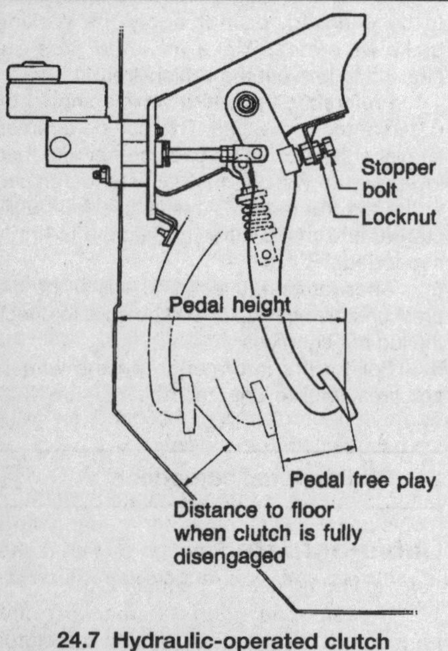

24.7 Hydraulic-operated clutch pedal details

Hydraulic-operated clutch

Clutch pedal height

Refer to illustration 24.7

7 Measure the distance from the upper surface of the pedal pad to the floor **(see illustration)**.

8 If this measurement is not within specifications, loosen the stopper locknut and adjust the stopper bolt until the height is correct (on later models the stopper bolt may be the clutch switch).

9 Tighten the lock-nut.

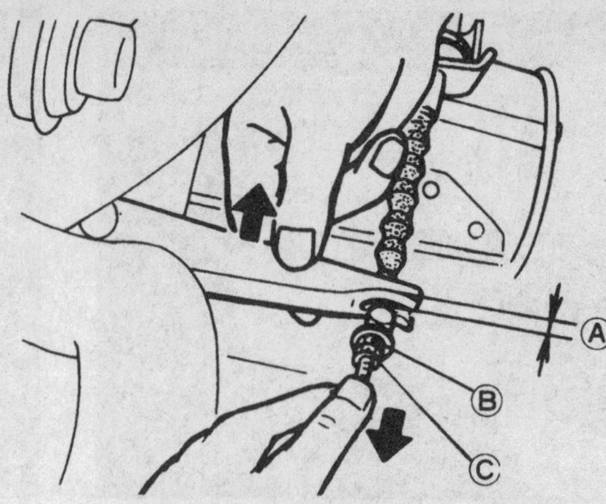

24.2 Cable-operated clutch pedal free play adjustment at the release lever

A *Clutch release lever clearance*
B *Adjusting nut*
C *Locknut*

Clutch pedal free-play and disengagement height

10 Depress the clutch pedal lightly by hand and measure the free-play (distance from the pedal height to the point where resistance is first felt).

11 If this measurement is not within specifications, loosen the lock-nut on the push-rod to the clutch master cylinder and turn the push-rod until the free-play is correct.

12 Check that the disengagement height from the upper surface of the pedal to the floor is correct when the pedal is fully depressed.

13 Tighten the lock-nut.

25 Manual transaxle oil change

Refer to illustration 25.3

1 Raise the vehicle and support it securely on jackstands.

2 Move a drain pan, rags, newspapers and wrenches under the transaxle.

3 Remove the transaxle drain plug at the bottom of the case and allow the oil to drain into the pan **(see illustration)**.

4 After the oil has drained completely, reinstall the plug and tighten it securely.

5 Remove the speedometer driven gear. Using a hand pump, syringe or funnel, fill the transaxle with the correct amount of the specified lubricant (Section 4). Reinstall the driven gear and tighten the bolt securely.

6 Lower the vehicle.

26 Cooling system servicing (draining, flushing and refilling)

Refer to illustration 26.6

1 Periodically, the cooling system should be drained, flushed and refilled to replenish the antifreeze mixture and prevent formation of rust and corrosion, which can impair the performance of the cooling system and cause engine damage.

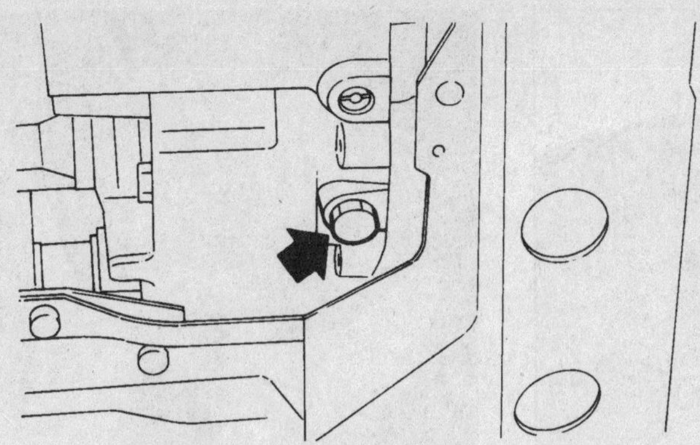

25.3 Manual transaxle drain plug location

26.6 The drain plug is located at the bottom of the radiator

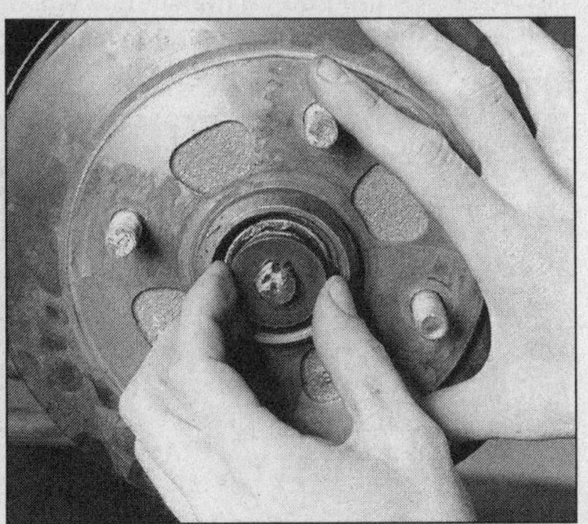

27.7a Pull the hub out to dislodge and remove the washer . . .

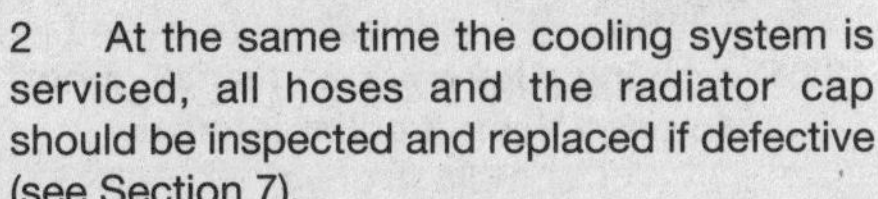

27.7b . . . and the outer bearing

27.8 Prying the bearing seal out of the hub

2 At the same time the cooling system is serviced, all hoses and the radiator cap should be inspected and replaced if defective (see Section 7).

3 Since antifreeze is a corrosive and poisonous solution, be careful not to spill any of the coolant mixture on the vehicle's paint or your skin. If this happens, rinse immediately with plenty of clean water. Consult your local authorities about the dumping of antifreeze before draining the cooling system. In many areas, reclamation centers have been set up to collect automobile oil and drained antifreeze/water mixtures, rather than allowing them to be added to the sewage system.

4 With the engine cold, remove the radiator cap.

5 Move a large container under the radiator to catch the coolant as it is drained.

6 Drain the radiator by removing the drain plug at the bottom **(see illustration)**. If this drain has excessive corrosion and cannot be turned easily, or if the radiator is not equipped with a drain, disconnect the lower radiator hose to allow the coolant to drain. Be careful that none of the solution is splashed on your skin or into your eyes.

7 Disconnect the hose from the coolant reservoir and remove the reservoir. Flush it out with clean water.

8 Place a garden hose in the radiator filler neck and flush the system until the water runs clear at all drain points.

9 In severe cases of contamination or clogging of the radiator, remove it (see Chapter 3) and reverse flush it. This involves inserting the hose in the bottom radiator outlet to allow the water to run against the normal flow, draining through the top. A radiator repair shop should be consulted if further cleaning or repair is necessary.

10 When the coolant is regularly drained and the system refilled with the correct antifreeze/water mixture, there should be no need to use chemical cleaners or descalers.

11 To refill the system, reconnect the radiator hoses and install the reservoir and the overflow hose.

12 Fill the radiator to the base of the filler neck and then add more coolant to the reservoir until it reaches the lower mark.

13 Run the engine until normal operating temperature is reached and, with the engine idling, add coolant up to the Full level. Install the radiator and reservoir caps.

14 Keep a close watch on the coolant level and the cooling system hoses during the first few miles of driving. Tighten the hose clamps and/or add more coolant as necessary.

27 Rear wheel bearing check and repack

Check

1 With the vehicle securely supported on jackstands, spin the rear wheels and check for noise, rolling resistance and free play. Now grab the top of the tire with one hand and the bottom of the tire with the other. Move the tire in-and-out. If it moves more than 0.005-inch, the bearings should be checked and replaced if necessary.

2 The front wheel bearings on these models require disassembly of the front hub for servicing (Chapter 11) but the rear wheel bearings can be serviced as a routine maintenance procedure.

1987 and earlier models

Repack

Refer to illustrations 27.7a, 27.7b, 27.8, 27.11, 27.15, 27.16, 27.17a, 27.17b and 27.17c

3 Raise the rear of the vehicle and support it securely on jackstands.

4 Remove the wheels.

5 Use a chisel and hammer to remove the grease cap, working around the circumference until it is dislodged and can be removed.

6 Remove the hub nut. The manufacturer recommends discarding the nut. New nuts can be obtained from a dealer.

7 Pull the hub assembly out slightly and then push it back into its original position. This should force the outer bearing and washer off the spindle enough so that it can be removed with your fingers **(see illustrations)**.

8 Remove the hub, place it on a suitable working surface and pry the inner bearing seal out with a screwdriver **(see illustration)**.

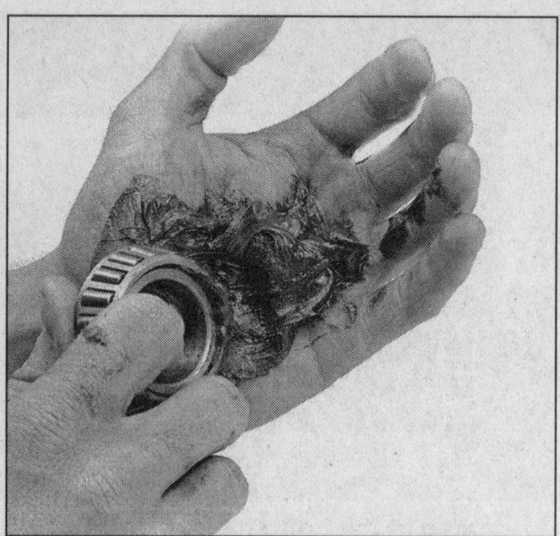
27.11 Packing a bearing with high-temperature wheel bearing grease. Work it well into the rollers

27.15 Installing a new seal over the inner bearing using a soft-face hammer

27.16 Place the hub on the spindle while holding the outer bearing and washer in place with your thumbs

27.17a Tightening the spindle nut with a torque wrench

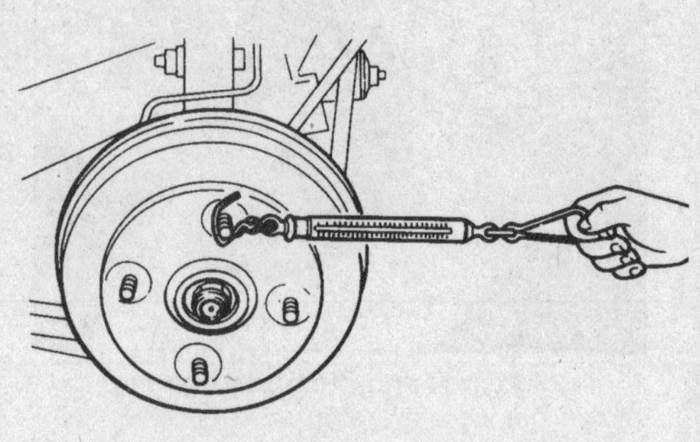
27.17b Checking the rear wheel bearing preload with a spring scale

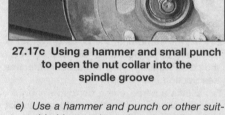

27.17c Using a hammer and small punch to peen the nut collar into the spindle groove

9 Use solvent to remove all traces of the old grease from the bearings, hub and spindle. A small brush may prove useful. Make sure no bristles from the brush embed themselves inside the bearing rollers. Allow the parts to air dry.

10 Carefully inspect the bearings for cracks, scoring and uneven surfaces. If the bearing races are defective, the hubs should be taken to a machine shop with the facilities to remove the old races and press in new ones. Bearings and races come in matched sets, and new races require new bearings. Likewise, replacement of the bearings requires that new races be installed in the hub.

11 Use an approved high temperature wheel bearing grease to pack the bearings. Work the grease completely into the bearings, forcing it between the rollers, cone and cage **(see illustration)**.

12 Apply a thin coat of grease to the spindle at the outer bearing seat, inner bearing seat, shoulder and seal seat.

13 Put a small quantity of grease inboard of each bearing race inside the hub. Using your finger, form a dam at these points to provide extra grease availability and to keep thinned grease from flowing out of the bearing.

14 Install the grease-packed inner bearing into the rear of the hub and put a little more grease outboard of the bearing.

15 Place a new seal over the inner bearing and press or tap the seal evenly into place **(see illustration)**.

16 Lubricate the lip of the seal with a light coat of grease, carefully place the hub assembly onto the spindle and push the grease-packed outer bearing and washer into position **(see illustration)**.

17 Install a new spindle nut and set the bearing preload using the following procedure.

a) *Tighten the spindle nut to the initial specified torque* **(see illustrations)**.
b) *Rotate the hub two or three times to seat the bearings, then loosen the spindle nut one turn (make sure the brakes are not dragging).*
c) *Attach a spring scale to the top wheel stud and measure the torque at which the hub starts to turn (this is the oil seal resistance).*
d) *Tighten the spindle nut until the resistance (point at which the hub starts to turn) is approximately 35 oz more than the oil seal resistance reading obtained in Step C.*
e) *Use a hammer and punch or other suitable blunt tool to crimp the collar of the nut into the spindle groove* **(see illustration)**.

18 Pack the cap with grease and install it, tapping around the outer circumference with a hammer and punch to seat it.

19 Install the wheels and lower the vehicle.

1988 and later models

Refer to illustration 27.22

20 1988 and later models use a sealed rear wheel bearing which does not require adjustment. To replace, raise the vehicle and support it securely on jackstands.

21 On disc brake equipped models, remove the rear caliper. **Caution:** *On ABS models, take care not to damage the wheel speed sensors.*

22 Remove the hub cap and the locknut **(see illustration)**.

23 Remove the brake drum or disc.

24 If the bearing is damaged, take the hub to a dealer to have it pressed out and a new one pressed in.

25 Place the hub in position on the spindle and install a new locknut. Tighten the locknut to the specified torque.

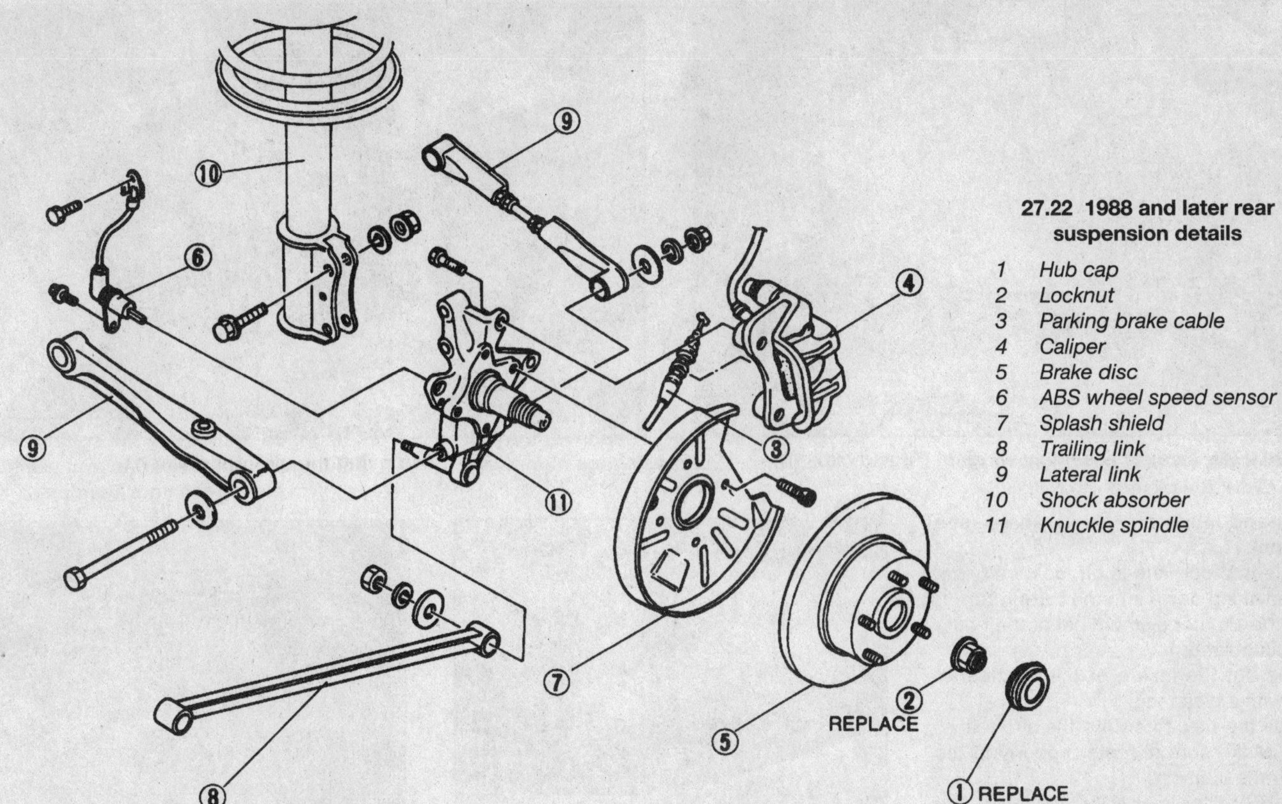

27.22 1988 and later rear suspension details

1. Hub cap
2. Locknut
3. Parking brake cable
4. Caliper
5. Brake disc
6. ABS wheel speed sensor
7. Splash shield
8. Trailing link
9. Lateral link
10. Shock absorber
11. Knuckle spindle

28 Automatic transaxle fluid change

Refer to illustration 28.7

1 At the specified time intervals, the transaxle fluid should be drained and replaced.

2 Before beginning work, purchase the specified transmission fluid (see Recommended fluids and lubricants at the front of this Chapter).

3 Other tools necessary for this job include jackstands to support the vehicle in a raised position, a drain pan capable of holding at least 8 pints, newspapers and clean rags.

28.7 Automatic transaxle drain plug location

4 The fluid should be drained immediately after the vehicle has been driven. This will remove any built up sediment better than if the fluid were cold. Because of this, it may be wise to wear protective gloves. Fluid temperature can exceed 350° in a hot transaxle.

5 After the vehicle has been driven to warm up the fluid, raise it and place it on the jackstands for access underneath.

6 Move the necessary equipment under the vehicle, being careful not to touch any of the hot exhaust components.

7 Place the drain pan under the lower part of the transaxle differential and remove the drain plug **(see illustration)**. Be sure the drain pan is in position, as fluid will come out with some force.

8 After the fluid has drained completely, clean the transaxle drain plug and reinstall it. Tighten the plug securely.

9 Lower the vehicle.

10 Open the hood and remove the transaxle fluid dipstick.

11 Add the specified type of fluid to the transaxle through the filler tube (use a funnel to prevent spills). It is best to add a little fluid at a time, continually checking the level with the dipstick (Section 4). Allow the fluid time to drain into the pan.

12 With the selector lever in Park, apply the parking brake and start the engine without depressing the accelerator pedal (if possible). Do not race the engine at high speed; run at slow idle only.

13 With the engine still idling, check the level on the dipstick. Look under the vehicle for leaks around the transaxle oil drain plug.

14 Check the fluid level to make sure it is just below the F mark on the dipstick. Do no allow the fluid level to go above this point, as the transaxle would then be overfilled, necessitating the draining of the excess fluid.

15 Push the dipstick firmly back into its tube and drive the vehicle to reach normal operating temperature. Park the vehicle on a level surface and check the fluid level on the dipstick with the engine idling and the transaxle in Park. The level should now be at the F mark on the dipstick. If not, add more fluid to bring the level up to this point. Again, do not overfill.

29 Air filter and PCV filter replacement

Refer to illustrations 29.2, 29.4 and 29.8

1 At the specified intervals, the air filter and PCV filter should be replaced with new ones. A thorough program of preventative maintenance would call for the two filters to be inspected between changes.

Carbureted models

2 The air filter is located inside the air cleaner housing on the top of the engine. The filter is replaced by removing the wing nut at the top of the air cleaner assembly, releasing

29.2 Air cleaner assembly wingnut (A) and clips (B)

29.4 Removing the air filter element

the clips and lifting off the top plate **(see illustration)**.

3 While the top plate is off, be careful not to drop anything down into the carburetor.

4 Lift the air filter element out of the housing **(see illustration)**.

5 Wipe out the inside of the air cleaner housing with a clean rag.

6 Place the new filter into the air cleaner housing. Make sure it seats properly in the bottom of the housing.

7 The PCV filter is also located inside the air cleaner housing. Remove the top plate and air filter as described previously, then locate the PCV filter on the side of the housing.

8 Use a screwdriver to pry the filter up an then pull it from the housing **(see illustration)**.

9 Install a new PCV filter and the air filter.

10 Install the top plate, making sure the arrow aligns with the arrow on the air intake.

Fuel injected models

11 Release the air cleaner cover clips.

12 Lift the cover up.

13 Lift the air filter element out of the housing and wipe out the inside of the air cleaner housing with a clean rag.

14 While the air cleaner cover is off, be careful not to drop anything down into the air cleaner assembly.

15 Place the new filter in the air cleaner housing. Make sure it seats properly in the lower half of the housing.

16 Install the air cleaner housing and secure the clips.

30 Oxygen sensor - check and replacement

Note: *Special care must be taken when handling the sensitive oxygen sensor:*

a) The oxygen sensor has a permanently attached pigtail and connector, which should not be removed from the sensor. Damage or removal of the pigtail or connector can adversely affect its operation.

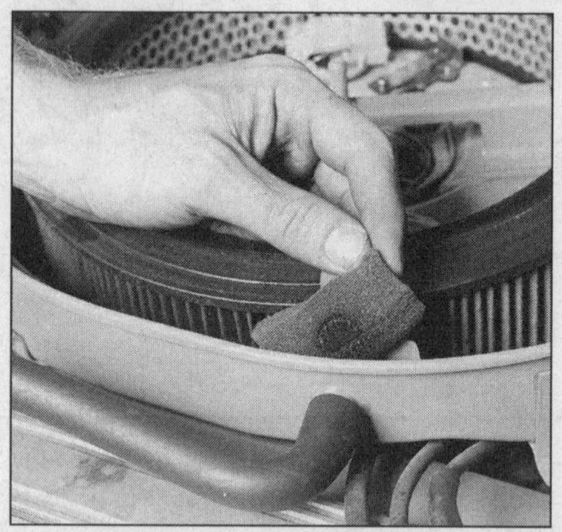
29.8 Removing the PCV filter

30.3 The oxygen sensor (arrow) threads into the exhaust manifold

b) Grease, dirt and other contaminants should be kept away from the electrical connector and the louvered end of the sensor.

c) Do not use cleaning solvents of any kind on the oxygen sensor.

d) Do not drop or roughly handle the sensor.

e) The silicone boot must be installed in the correct position to prevent the boot from being melted and to allow the sensor to operate properly.

Check

1 To check the oxygen sensor, start the engine and allow it to reach normal operating temperature. Unplug the sensor connector and attach a voltmeter to the oxygen sensor side of the connector. Increase the engine speed to 4000 RPM until the voltmeter indicates approximately 0.55-volt. Rev the engine several times and read the indicated voltage. When the speed is increased, the meter should read between 0.5-volt and 1.0-volt. When the speed is decreased, the reading should be between 0 and 0.4-volt. If the voltages are not as specified, replace the oxygen sensor.

2 To replace the sensor, unplug the sensor connector and unscrew the sensor from the exhaust manifold. Before installation, install a new sealing washer and coat the threads with anti-seize compound. Tighten the sensor securely.

Replacement

Refer to illustration 30.3

3 The sensor is located in the exhaust manifold and is accessible in the engine compartment **(see illustration)**.

4 Since the oxygen sensor may be difficult to remove with the engine cold, begin by operating the engine until it has warmed to at least 120 degrees F (48 degrees C).

5 Disconnect the electrical wire from the oxygen sensor.

6 Note the position of the silicone boot and carefully back out the oxygen sensor from the exhaust manifold. Be advised that excessive force may damage the threads. Inspect the oxygen sensor for damage.

7 A special anti-seize compound must be used on the threads of the oxygen sensor to aid in future removal. New or service sensors will have this compound already applied, but if for any reason an oxygen sensor is removed and then reinstalled, the threads must be coated before reinstallation.

8 Install the sensor and tighten it securely.

9 Connect the electrical wire.

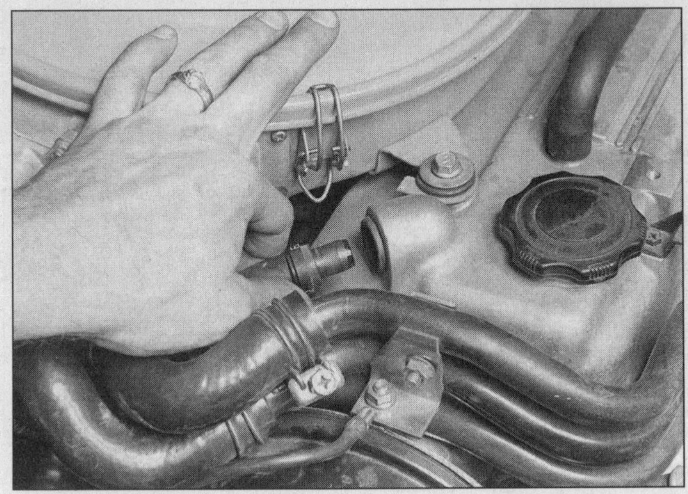

31.2 Removing the PCV valve from the camshaft cover

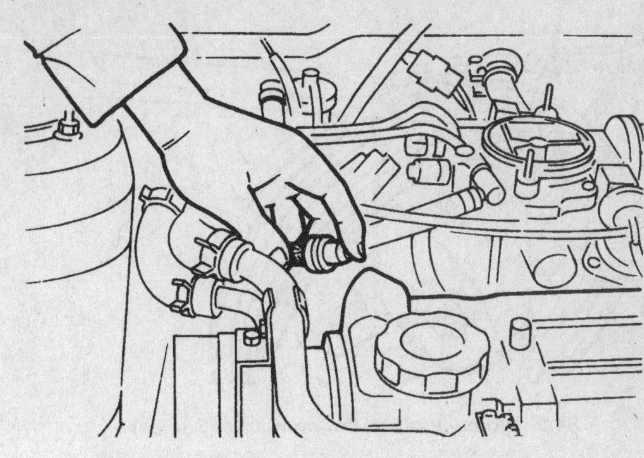

31.3 Checking the PCV valve

31 Positive Crankcase Ventilation (PCV) valve check and replacement

Refer to illustrations 31.2, 31.3 and 31.4

1 The PCV valve is located in the camshaft cover.

2 With the engine idling at normal operating temperature, pull the valve (with hose attached) from the rubber grommet in the camshaft cover **(see illustration)**.

3 Place your finger over the end of the valve **(see illustration)**. If the engine speed drops, the valve is working properly. If engine speed doesn't drop the valve is faulty and should be replaced with a new one.

4 To replace the valve, pull it from the end of the hose, noting its installed position and direction **(see illustration)**.

5 When purchasing a replacement PCV valve, make sure it is for your particular vehicle, model year and engine size. Compare the old valve with the new one to make sure they are the same.

6 Push the valve into the end of the hose until it is seated.

7 Inspect the rubber grommet for damage and replace it with a new one, if necessary.

8 Push the PCV valve and hose securely into position.

9 More information on the PCV system can be found in Chapter 6.

32 Exhaust Gas Recirculation (EGR) valve check

1 The EGR valve is located on the intake manifold, adjacent to the carburetor. Most of the time when a problem develops in this emissions system, it is due to a stuck or corroded EGR valve.

2 With the engine cold to prevent burns, reach under the EGR valve and manually push on the diaphragm. Using moderate pressure, you should be able to press the diaphragm up and down within the housing.

3 If the diaphragm does not move or moves only with much effort, replace the EGR valve with a new one. If in doubt about the condition of the valve, compare the free movement of your EGR valve with a new valve.

4 Refer to Chapter 6 for more information on the EGR system.

33 Evaporative emissions control system check

Refer to illustration 33.2

1 The function of the Evaporative Emissions Control System is to draw fuel vapors from the tank and carburetor, store them in a charcoal canister and then burn them during normal engine operation.

2 The most common symptom of a fault in the evaporative emissions system is a strong fuel odor in the engine compartment. If a fuel odor is detected, inspect the charcoal canister, located on the engine compartment firewall **(see illustration)**, and system hoses.

3 A simple check of system operation is to place your hand under the canister with the engine at normal operating temperature and slowly increase engine speed. If air can be felt being sucked into the bottom of the canister the system is operating properly.

4 The evaporative emissions control system is explained in more detail in Chapter 6.

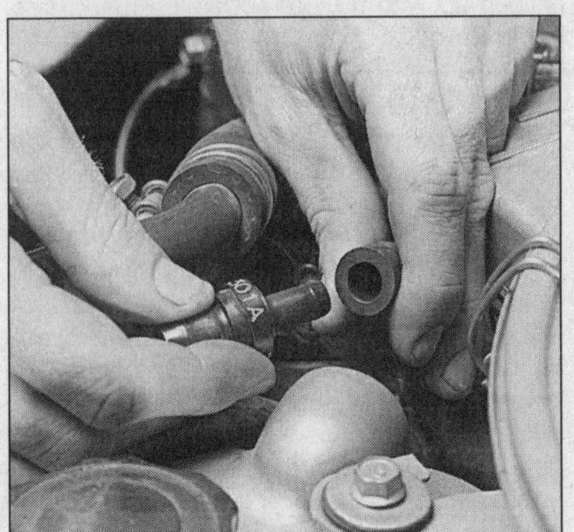

31.4 Removing the PCV valve from the hose

34 Ignition timing check and adjustment

Refer to illustrations 34.2, 34.3, 34.5a, 34.5b, 34.6 and 34.7

Note: *It is imperative that the procedures included on the Vehicle Emissions Control Information label be followed when adjusting the ignition timing. The label will include all information concerning preliminary steps to be performed before adjusting the timing, as well as the timing specifications.*

1 Locate the VECI label under the hood and read through and perform all preliminary instructions concerning ignition timing.

2 Locate the timing mark pointer plate located beside the crankshaft pulley. The T mark represents top dead center (TDC). The pointer plate will be marked in two degree increments, and should have the proper timing mark for your particular vehicle noted. If not, count back from the T mark the correct

33.2 The evaporative canister is located on the firewall

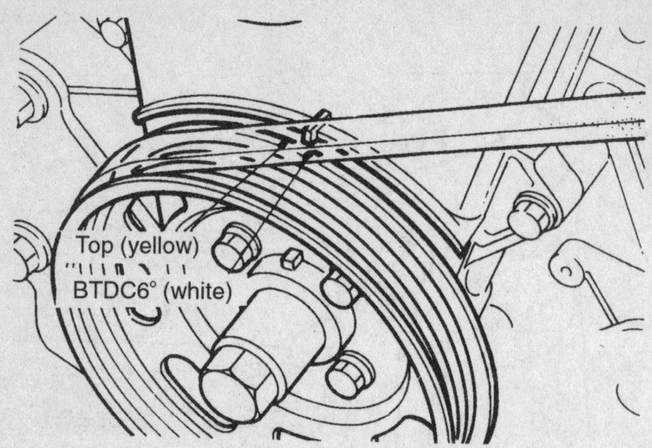

34.2 Typical ignition timing marks (Sec 34)

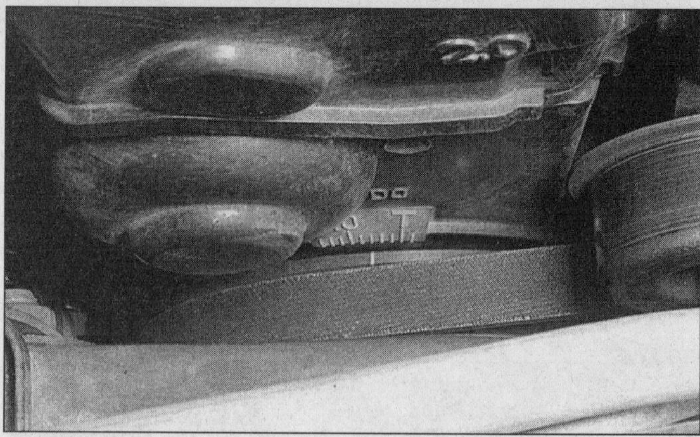

34.3 The engine timing marks are rather difficult to see so they should be marked with white paint

34.5a Connecting the timing light to the number one spark plug wire

34.5b Connecting the timing light to the battery

34.6 Aiming the timing light at the timing marks

number of degrees BTDC, as noted on the VECI label, and mark the plate **(see illustration)**.

3 Locate the notch on the crankshaft balancer or pulley and mark it with chalk or a dab of paint so it will be visible under the timing light **(see illustration)**.

4 Start the engine, warm it to normal operating temperature and shut it off. Turn off all lights and other electrical loads and unplug the engine cooling fan electrical connector.

5 With the ignition off, connect the pick up lead of the timing light to the number one spark plug **(see illustration)**. Use either a jumper lead between the wire and plug or an inductive-type pick up. Do not pierce the wire or attempt to insert a wire between the boot and wire. Connect the timing light power leads according to the manufacturer's instructions.

6 Start the engine, aim the timing light at the timing mark by the crankshaft pulley and note which timing mark the notch on the pulley is lining up with **(see illustration)**.

7 If the notch is not lining up with the correct mark, loosen the distributor hold-down bolt and rotate the distributor until the notch is lined up with the correct timing mark **(see illustration)**.

8 Retighten the hold-down bolt and recheck the timing.

9 Turn off the engine and disconnect the timing light. Reconnect the number one spark plug wire, if removed, and any other components which were disconnected.

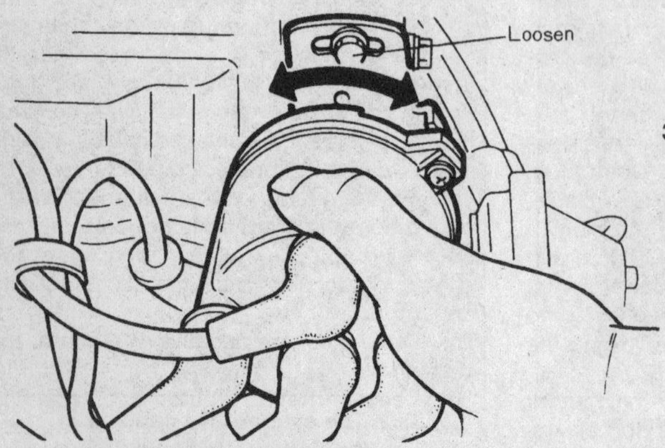

34.7 Adjust the ignition timing by turning the distributor

35 Spark plug replacement

Refer to illustrations 35.1, 35.6a, 35.6b and 35.11

1 In most cases, tools necessary for a spark plug replacement include a spark plug socket, which fits onto a ratchet wrench. This socket will be insulated inside to protect the porcelain insulator and hold the plug while you direct it to the spark plug hole. Also necessary will be a wire-type feeler gauge to check and adjust the spark plug gap **(see illustration)**.

2 The spark plugs are located on the front (radiator) side of the engine.

3 The best procedure to follow when replacing the spark plugs is to purchase the new spark plugs beforehand, adjust them to the proper gap, and then replace each plug one at a time.

4 When buying the new spark plugs it is important to obtain the correct plugs for your specific engine. This information can be

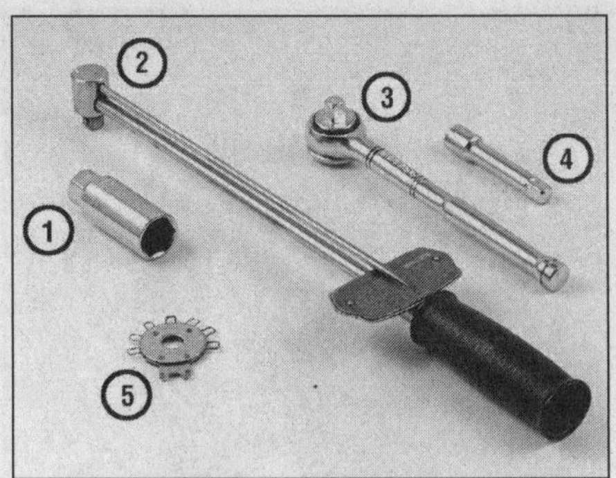

35.1 Tools required for changing spark plugs

1 ***Spark plug socket*** *- This will have special padding inside to protect the spark plug's porcelain insulator*
2 ***Torque wrench*** *- Although not mandatory, using this tool is the best way to ensure the plugs are tightened properly*
3 ***Ratchet*** *- Standard hand tool to fit the spark plug socket*
4 ***Extension*** *- Depending on model and accessories, you may need special extensions and universal joints to reach one or more of the plugs*
5 ***Spark plug gap gauge*** *- This gauge for checking the gap comes in a variety of styles. Make sure the gap for your engine is included*

35.6a Spark plug manufacturers recommend using a wire-type gauge when checking the gap. If the wire does not slide between the electrodes with a slight drag, adjustment is required

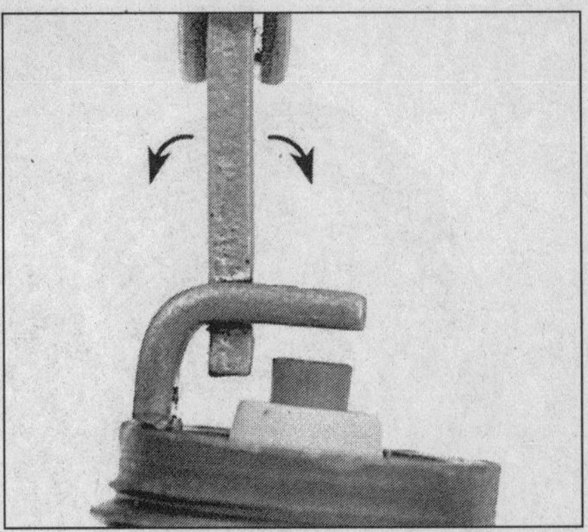

35.6b To change the gap, bend the side electrode only, as indicated by the arrows, and be very careful not to chip or crack the porcelain insulator around the center electrode

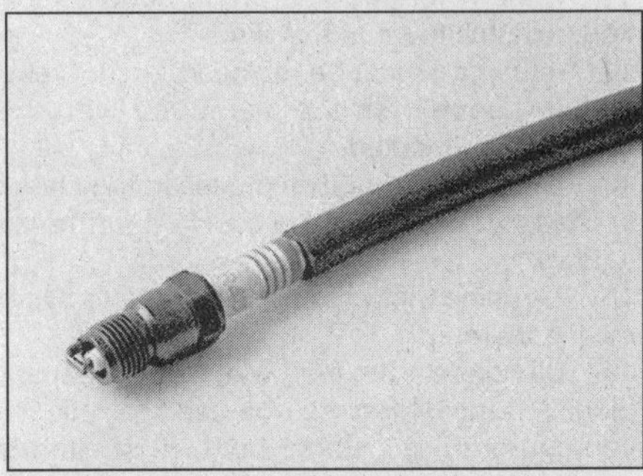

35.11 A length of 3/8-inch rubber hose will save time and prevent damaged threads when installing the spark plugs

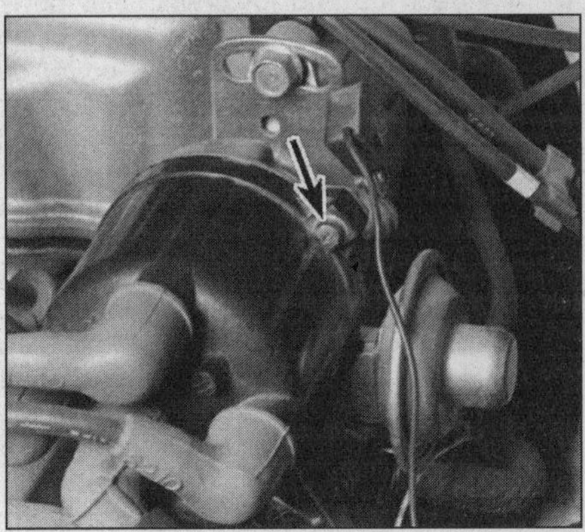

36.3 Loosen the distributor cap hold-down screws

found on the Vehicle Emissions Control Information label located under the hood or in the owner's manual. If differences exist between these sources, purchase the spark plug type specified on the Emissions Control label, because the information was printed for your specific engine.

5 With the new spark plugs at hand, allow the engine to cool completely before attempting plug removal. During this time, each of the new spark plugs can be inspected for defects and the gaps can be checked.

6 The gap is checked by inserting the proper thickness gauge between the electrodes at the tip of the plug **(see illustration)**. The gap between the electrodes should be the same as that given in the Specifications or on the Emissions Control label. The wire should just touch each of the electrodes. If the gap is incorrect, use the notched adjuster on the feeler gauge body to bend the curved side electrode slightly until the proper gap is achieved. If the side electrode is not exactly over the center electrode, use the notched adjuster to align the two **(see illustration)**. Check for cracks in the porcelain insulator, indicating the spark plug should not be used.

7 With the engine cool, remove the spark plug wire from one spark plug. Do this by grabbing the boot at the end of the wire, not the wire itself. Sometimes it is necessary to use a twisting motion while the boot and plug wire are pulled free.

8 If compressed air is available, use it to blow any dirt or foreign material away from the spark plug area. A common bicycle pump will also work. The idea here is to eliminate the possibility of debris falling into the cylinder as the spark plug is removed.

9 Place the spark plug socket over the plug and remove it from the engine by turning in a counterclockwise direction.

10 Compare the spark plug with those shown in the accompanying photos to get an indication of the overall running condition of the engine.

11 Thread the plug into the head until you can no longer turn it with your fingers, then tighten it with the socket. Where there might be difficulty in inserting the spark plugs into the spark plug holes, or the possibility of cross-threading them into the head, a short piece of 3/8-inch rubber tubing can be fitted over the end of the spark plug **(see illustration)**. The flexible tubing will act as a universal joint to help align the plug with the plug hole, and should the plug begin to cross-thread, the hose will slip on the spark plug, preventing thread damage. If one is available, use a torque wrench to tighten the plug to ensure that it is seated correctly. The correct torque figure is included in the Specifications.

12 Before pushing the spark plug wire onto the end of the plug, inspect it following the procedures outlined in Section 36.

13 Attach the plug wire to the new spark plug, again using a twisting motion on the boot until it is firmly seated on the spark plug. Make sure the wire is routed away from the exhaust manifold.

14 Follow the above procedure for the remaining spark plugs, replacing them one at a time to prevent mixing up the spark plug wires.

36 Spark plug wires, distributor cap and rotor check and replacement

Refer to illustrations 36.3, 36.4, 36.6, 36.9 and 36.14

1 Begin this procedure by making a visual check of the spark plug wires while the engine is running. In a darkened garage (make sure there is ventilation) start the engine and observe each plug wire. Be careful not to come into contact with any moving engine parts. If there is a break in the wire, you will see arcing or a small spark at the damaged area. If arcing is noticed, make a note to obtain new wires, then allow the engine to cool and check the distributor cap and rotor.

2 Disconnect the negative cable from the battery.

3 Loosen the distributor cap retaining screws. The screws are held in the cap with retainers. Lift off the cap **(see illustration)**.

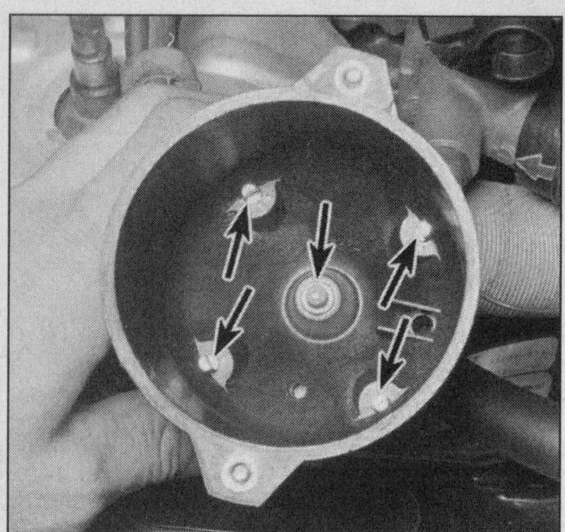

36.4 Inspect the distributor cap contacts (arrows) for corrosion and damage

36.6 The distributor rotor screws (A) and contact (B)

36.9 Push on the centrifugal advance weights to make sure the springs offer resistance and the weights are not stuck

4 Inspect the cap for cracks and other damage. Closely examine the contacts on the inside of the cap for excessive corrosion **(see illustration)**. Slight scoring is normal. Deposits on the contacts may be removed with a small file.

5 If the inspection reveals damage to the cap, make a note to obtain a replacement for your particular engine, then examine the rotor.

6 The rotor is visible, with the cap removed, at the top of the distributor shaft. It is held in place by two screws. Remove the screws and the rotor and inspect the rotor for cracks and other damage **(see illustration)**.

7 Carefully check the condition of the metal contact at the top of the rotor for excessive burning and pitting.

8 If it is determined that a new rotor is required, make a note to that effect.

9 Inspect the centrifugal advance assembly for damage, corrosion and broken springs. Push on the assembly to make sure it moves easily in one direction with the springs pulling it the other **(see illustration)**. Lubricate the contact surfaces of the assembly with a light coat of silicone grease.

10 If the rotor and cap are in good condition, reinstall them at this time.

11 If the cap must be replaced, do not reinstall it. Leave it off the distributor with the wires still connected.

12 If the spark plug wires passed the check in Step 1, they should be checked further as follows.

13 Examine the wires one at a time to avoid mixing them up.

14 Disconnect the plug wire from the spark plug. A removal tool can be used for this, or you can grab the rubber boot, twist slightly and then pull the wire free. Do not pull on the wire itself, only on the rubber boot **(see illustration)**.

15 Inspect inside the boot for corrosion, which will look like a white crusty powder. Some models use a conductive white silicone lubricant that should not be mistaken for corrosion.

16 Push the wire and boot back onto the end of the spark plug. It should be a tight fit on the plug end. If not, remove the wire and use pliers to carefully crimp the metal connector inside the wire boot until the fit is snug.

17 Using a clean rag, clean the entire length of the wire. Remove all built up dirt and grease. As this is done, check for burns, cracks and any other form of damage. Bend the wires in several places to ensure that the conductive wire inside has not hardened.

18 The wires should be checked at the distributor cap in the same manner. Remove the wire from the cap by pulling on the boot, again examining the wires one at a time, and reinstalling each one after examination.

19 If the wires appear to be in good condition, make sure that all wires are secure at both ends. If the cap and rotor are also in good condition, the check is finished. Reconnect the battery cable.

20 If it was determined in Steps 14 through 19 that new wires are required, obtain them at this time, along with a new cap and rotor if so determined in the checks above.

21 If new wires are being installed, replace them one at a time. **Note:** *It is important to replace the wires one at a time, noting the routing as each wire is removed and installed, to maintain the correct firing order.*

22 Attach the cap to the distributor, then reconnect the battery cable.

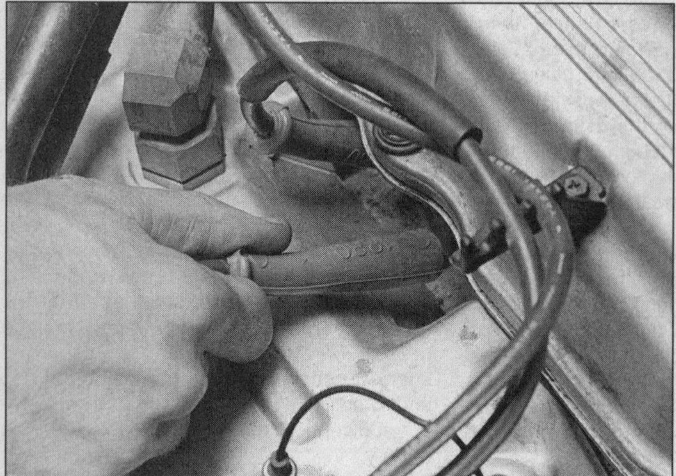

36.14 Pull on the spark plug boot, not the wire

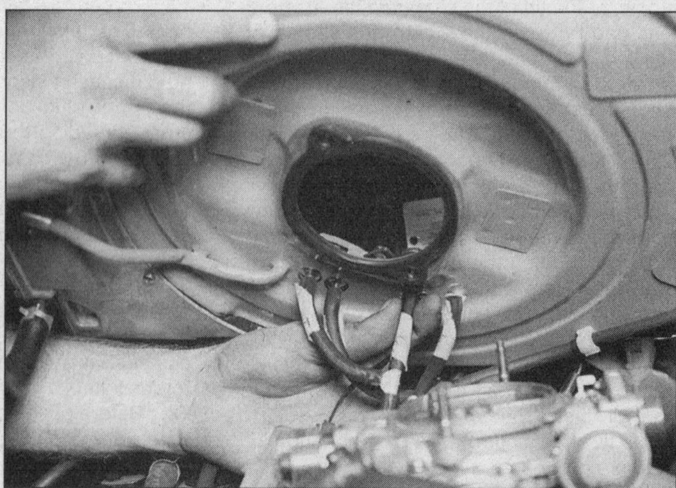

37.2 Mark the vacuum hoses which connect to the air cleaner with tape so they can be reinstalled in their original positions

37.4a Removing the camshaft cover bolts

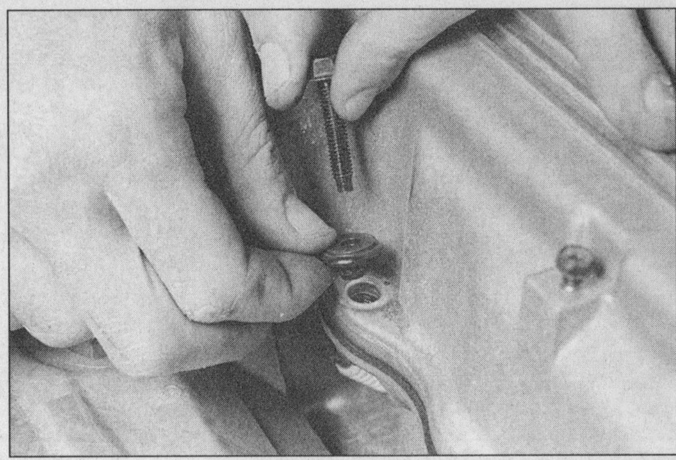
37.4b Be sure to keep the washers with the camshaft cover bolts

37 Valve adjustment (1987 and earlier models)

Refer to illustrations 37.2, 37.4a, 37.4b, 37.5, 37.6a, 37.6b, 37.7a, 37.7b, 37.7c, 37.9, 37.10 and 37.12

1 Run the engine until normal operating temperature is reached.

2 Stop the engine and remove the air cleaner assembly from the engine. Label all the hoses and electrical wiring leading to air cleaner for ease of installation **(see illustration)**.

3 Remove the PCV valve and spark plug wire mount from the camshaft cover. Use a piece of wire to hold the throttle cable out of the way.

4 Remove the camshaft cover bolts, taking care not to lose the washers **(see illustrations)**.

5 Use a large screwdriver with a rag wrapped around the end to carefully pry the camshaft cover free of the engine **(see illustration)**. Lift the cover from the engine and remove the gasket.

6 Position the number 1 piston at top dead center (TDC) on the compression stroke. To do this, first number each the spark plug wires, then remove all of the spark plugs from the engine. Locate the number 1 cylinder spark plug wire and trace it back to the distributor. Write a number 1 on the distributor body directly under the terminal where the number one spark plug wire attaches to the distributor cap. Do this for the other cylinders (using numbers 2, 3, 4) as well, then remove the cap and wires from the distributor **(see illustrations)**.

7 Slowly turn the engine over in a clockwise direction by slipping a wrench or socket over the large bolt at the front of the

37.5 Pry the camshaft cover up to break the gasket seal, using a screwdriver and a rag so the aluminum housing won't be damaged

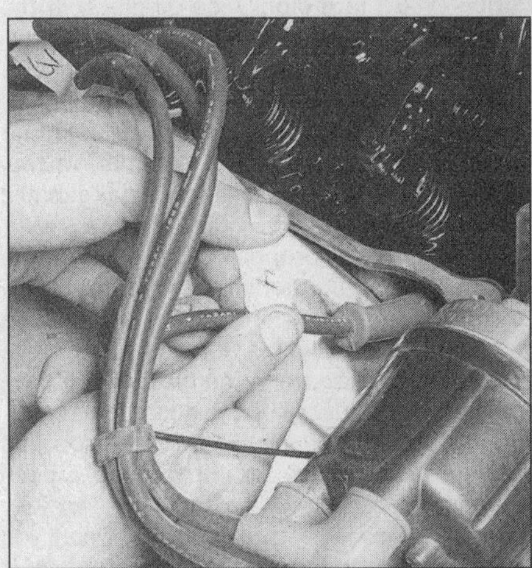
37.6a Marking the distributor wires with tape

37.6b Marking the distributor wire location on the housing

37.7a With the spark plugs removed and the drivebelt tight, the engine can be rotated using a socket or wrench on the alternator nut

37.7b The crankshaft notch aligned with the Top Dead Center (TDC) mark

37.7c The distributor rotor contact aligned with the number 1 spark plug wire mark (arrow) on the housing, indicating the number 1 cylinder is at TDC

37.9 Adjusting the valve clearance with a feeler gauge and screwdriver

crankshaft or (if the drivebelt is tight enough) the alternator, until the notch on the crankshaft pulley is aligned with the pointer **(see illustrations)**. The rotor should be pointing directly at the number 1 you made on the distributor body **(see illustration)**. If it is not, turn the crankshaft one more complete revolution (360°) in a clockwise direction. If the rotor is now pointing at the 1 on the distributor body, then the number 1 piston is at TDC on the compression stroke and the valve clearances can be checked and adjusted for the number 1 intake and exhaust valves, number 2 intake valve and number 3 exhaust valve.

8 Insert an appropriate size feeler gauge (refer to Specifications) between the valve stem and the rocker arm. If the feeler gauge fits between the valve and the rocker arm with a slight drag, then the clearance is correct and no adjustment is required.

9 If the feeler gauge will not fit between the valve and the screw, or if it is loose, loosen the adjusting screw locknut and carefully tighten or loosen the adjusting screw until you can feel a slight drag on the feeler gauge as it is withdrawn from between the valve stem and adjusting screw **(see illustration)**.

10 Hold the adjusting screw with a screwdriver, to keep it from turning, and tighten the locknut securely **(see illustration)**. Recheck the clearance to make sure it hasn't changed.

11 Turn the crankshaft one complete turn (360°), which will bring the number 4 piston to top dead center on the compression stroke. Verify this by checking to see that the rotor is pointing to the number 4 spark plug wire position. The valve clearance for the number 2 exhaust, number 3 intake and number 4 intake and exhaust can now be checked and adjusted.

12 With the camshaft cover removed and the engine warmed up, the cylinder head bolt torques can also be checked, using a torque wrench. Tighten the bolts in the sequence shown **(see illustration)**.

13 Install the camshaft cover (use new a gasket) and tighten the mounting bolts evenly and securely to the specified torque.

14 Install the spark plugs, distributor cap and spark plug wires. Install the air cleaner and hook up the various hoses, electrical connections and vacuum lines.

15 Start the engine and check for oil leakage between the camshaft cover and the cylinder head.

38 Compression check

Refer to illustration 38.5

1 A compression check will tell you what mechanical condition the engine is in. Specifically, it can tell you if the compression is down due to leakage caused by worn piston rings, defective valves and seats or a blown head gasket.

2 Warm the engine to normal operating temperature, shut it off and allow it to sit for ten minutes to allow the catalytic converter temperature to drop.

3 Begin by cleaning the area around the spark plugs before you remove them. This will keep dirt from falling into the cylinders while you are performing the compression test. Remove the spark plugs.

4 Disconnect the coil wire from the distributor. Block the throttle and choke valves open.

5 With the compression gauge in the number one spark plug hole, crank the engine over at least four compression strokes and observe the gauge. The compression should build up quickly **(see illustration)**. Low compression on the first stroke, which

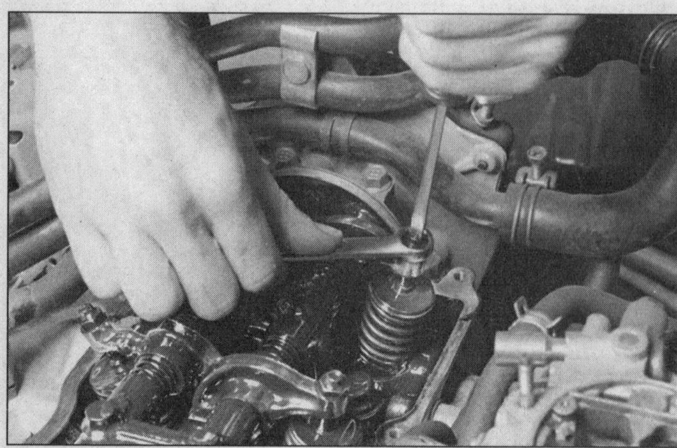

37.10 Hold the adjusting screw so that it can't move while tightening the locknut

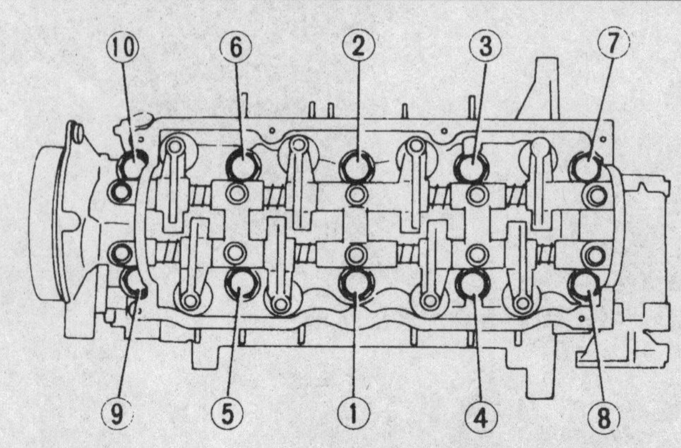

37.12 Cylinder head bolt tightening sequence

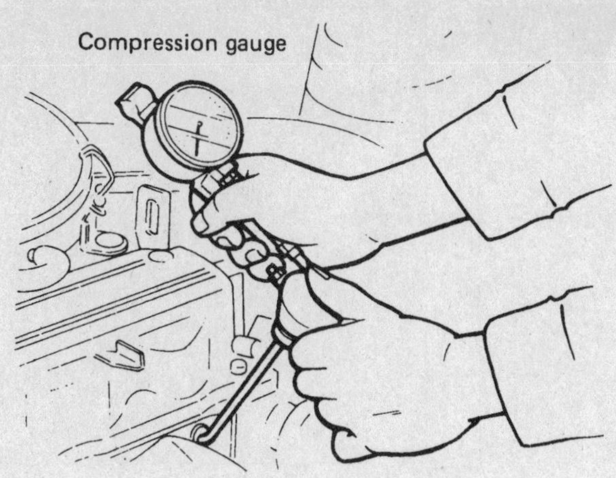

38.5 Checking engine compression

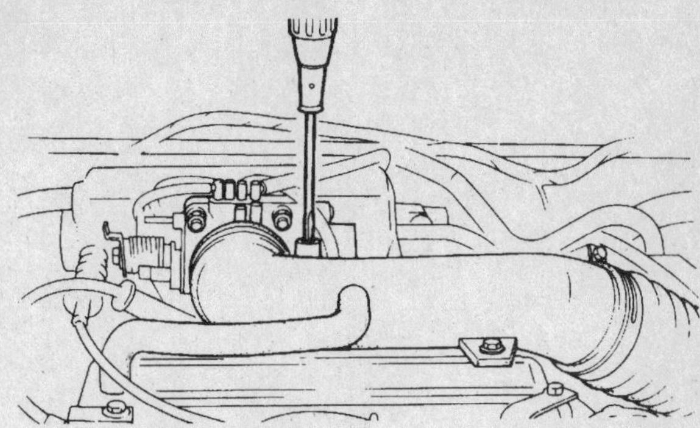

39.5 On 1986 and 1987 fuel injected models, adjust the idle speed by turning the air adjusting screw on the top of the throttle body

does not build up during successive strokes, indicates leaking valves, a blown head gasket or a cracked head. Record the highest gauge reading obtained and check this against Specifications.

6 Repeat the procedure for the remaining cylinders. The lowest compression reading should not be less than 70% of the highest reading. No reading should be less than 100 lbs.

7 Pour a couple of teaspoons of engine oil (a squirt can works great for this) into each cylinder, through the spark plug hole, and repeat the test.

8 If the compression increases after the oil is added, the piston rings are definitely worn. If the compression does not increase significantly, the leakage is occurring at the valves or head gasket. Leakage past the valves may be caused by burned valve seats or faces or warped, cracked or bent valves.

9 If two adjacent cylinders have equally low compression, there is a strong possibility that the head gasket between them is blown. The appearance of coolant in the combustion chambers or the crankcase would verify this condition.

10 If the compression is higher than normal, the combustion chambers are probably coated with carbon deposits. If that it the case, the cylinder head should be removed and decarbonized.

11 If compression is way down or varies greatly between cylinders, it would be a good idea to have a leakdown test performed by an automotive repair shop. This test will pinpoint exactly where the leakage is occurring and how severe it is.

39 Idle speed check and adjustment (1986 and 1987 fuel injected models)

Refer to illustration 39.5

Note 1: *On 1988 and later models the idle speed is computer controlled and not adjustable.*

Note 2: *Refer to Section 15 for carbureted models.*

1 Connect a tachometer to the engine. With the engine at normal operating temperature and the transmission in Park or Neutral, raise the engine speed to 2500 to 3000 RPM for three minutes.

2 Check the initial ignition timing and adjust it if necessary. Refer to the Vehicle Emission Control Information label for the proper ignition timing adjustment procedure.

3 Disconnect the air bypass solenoid valve connector if the altitude where the vehicle is being worked on is between sea level and 3280 feet (see Chapter 4 for the air bypass solenoid valve location).

4 If the cooling fan is operating, allow the engine to idle until it stops.

5 Check the idle speed. If it isn't within the idle speed range listed in the Specifications, adjust it by turning the air adjusting screw on the throttle body **(see illustration)**.

6 Reconnect the air bypass solenoid valve, if previously disconnected.

Notes

Chapter 2 Part A Engine

Contents

Specifications

Timing belt deflection	
1987 and earlier	0.47 to 0.55 in
1988 and later	
New	0.31 to 0.35 in (8 to 9 mm)
Used	0.35 to 0.39 in (9 to 10 mm)
Oil pump	
Outer gear tooth-to-crescent clearance limit	0.013 in
Inner gear tooth-to-crescent clearance limit	0.016 in
Outer gear-to-pump body clearance	0.008 in
Gear-to-pump cover clearance	0.008 in

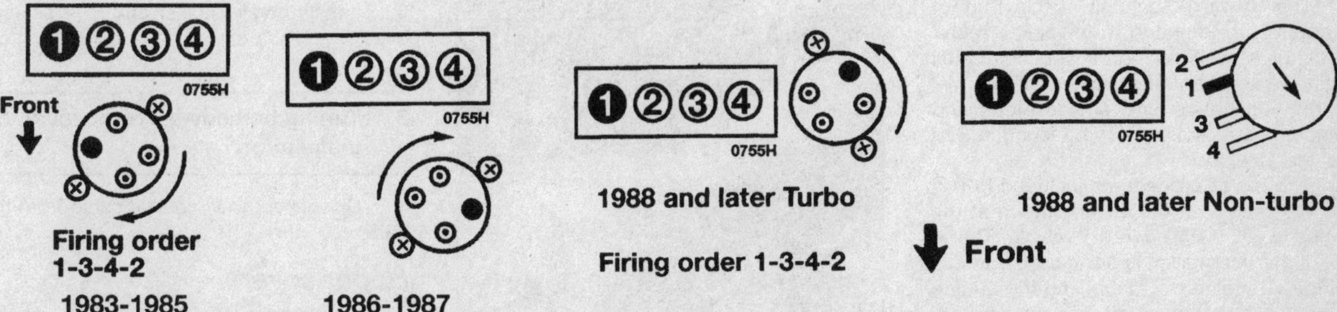

Engine cylinder numbering and distributor cap terminal locations

The blackened terminal shown on the distributor cap indicates the Number One spark plug wire position

Torque specifications

	Ft-lbs	M-kg
Alternator bracket to engine bolt	27 to 46	3.7 to 6.3
Alternator adjusting bolt	14 to 25	1.9 to 3.5
Cylinder head bolt		
Engine warm	69 to 80	9.5 to 11.0
Engine cold	59 to 64	8.2 to 8.8
Clutch plate bolt	71 to 96	9.8 to 13.2
Camshaft pulley bolt	35 to 48	4.8 to 6.6
Camshaft cap bolt	13 to 20	1.8 to 2.8
Camshaft cover bolts	2 to 3	0.28 to 0.41
Crankshaft pulley bolt	8 to 11	1.1 to 1.5
Exhaust manifold bolt	16 to 21	2.2 to 2.9
Engine mount bolts		
Number 1 engine mount-to-transaxle	27 to 38	3.7 to 5.2
Number 1 engine mount-to-body	32 to 40	4.4 to 5.5
Number 2 engine mount-to-transaxle	27 to 38	3.7 to 5.2
Number 2 engine mount-to-body	32 to 40	4.4 to 5.5
Number 3 engine mount-to-body	32 to 40	4.4 to 5.5
Number 3 engine mount-to-engine	41 to 59	5.7 to 8.1
Flywheel bolt	71 to 76	9.8 to 10.5
Intake manifold bolt	14 to 19	1.9 to 2.6
Oil pan bolt	5 to 9	0.7 to 1.2
Rocker arm shaft assembly bolts	13 to 20	1.8 to 2.7
Timing belt cover bolt	5 to 7	0.7 to 1.0
Timing belt pulley bolt (1983 through 1984)	108 to 116	14.9 to 16
Timing belt pulley bolt (1985)	80 to 87	11.0 to 12.0
Timing belt tensioner lockbolt	27.5 to 38.3	3.8 to 5.3
Torque stopper-to-engine bolt	49 to 56	6.8 to 7.7
Torque stopper-to-body bolt	40 to 50	5.5 to 6.9
Oil pressure switch	9 to 13	1.2 to 1.8
Water bypass hose clamp	14 to 25	1.9 to 3.5
Water inlet pipe assembly-to-water pump bolt	14 to 19	1.9 to 2.6
Water inlet pipe bracket-to-engine bolt	28 to 38	3.9 to 5.2

1 General information

The engine block is made of cast iron and the removable head is cast aluminum. The camshaft is located in the cylinder head and actuates the valves via shaft mounted rocker arms. 1987 and earlier engines use an 8-valve cylinder head. 1988 and later models have a 12-valve cylinder head which differs from earlier models in that it uses three valves per cylinder (two intake and one exhaust) instead of two. The valves are actuated by Hydraulic Lash Adjuster (HLA) units which do not require periodic valve adjustment.

The forward Sections in this Part of Chapter 2 are devoted to in-vehicle repair procedures, while the latter Sections detail engine removal and installation procedures. Information concerning engine block and cylinder head servicing can be found in Part B of this Chapter.

The repair procedures included in this part are based on the assumption that the engine is still installed in the vehicle. Therefore, if this information is being used during a complete engine overhaul, with the engine already out of the vehicle and on a stand, many of the steps included here will not apply.

The Specifications included in this part of Chapter 2 apply only to the procedures found here. Part B of Chapter 2 contains the specifications necessary for engine block and cylinder head rebuilding.

2 Camshaft cover - removal and installation

Refer to illustration 2.5

Removal

1 Remove the air cleaner assembly.

2.5 Use a torque wrench whenever possible, particularly when working on cylinder head components because they are made of aluminum

2 Remove the PCV valve and hose.

3 Remove the retaining bolts and separate the cover from the engine. It may be necessary to break the gasket seal by either tapping the cover with a soft faced hammer or inserting a very thin blade scraper or screwdriver at the corner.

4 Clean all traces of gasket material from the camshaft cover gasket mating surfaces. Be careful not to nick or gouge the soft aluminum.

Installation

5 Place the cover and new gasket in position. Install the attaching bolts and tighten to the specified torque **(see illustration)**.

6 Install the air cleaner and PCV assemblies.

3 Timing belt cover - removal and installation

1 Disconnect the negative cable from the battery.

Upper cover

Refer to illustrations 3.3a and 3.3b

2 Loosen the accessory drivebelt adjuster bolt and move the belt out of the way.

3 Remove all of the accessible timing belt cover bolts **(see illustrations)**.

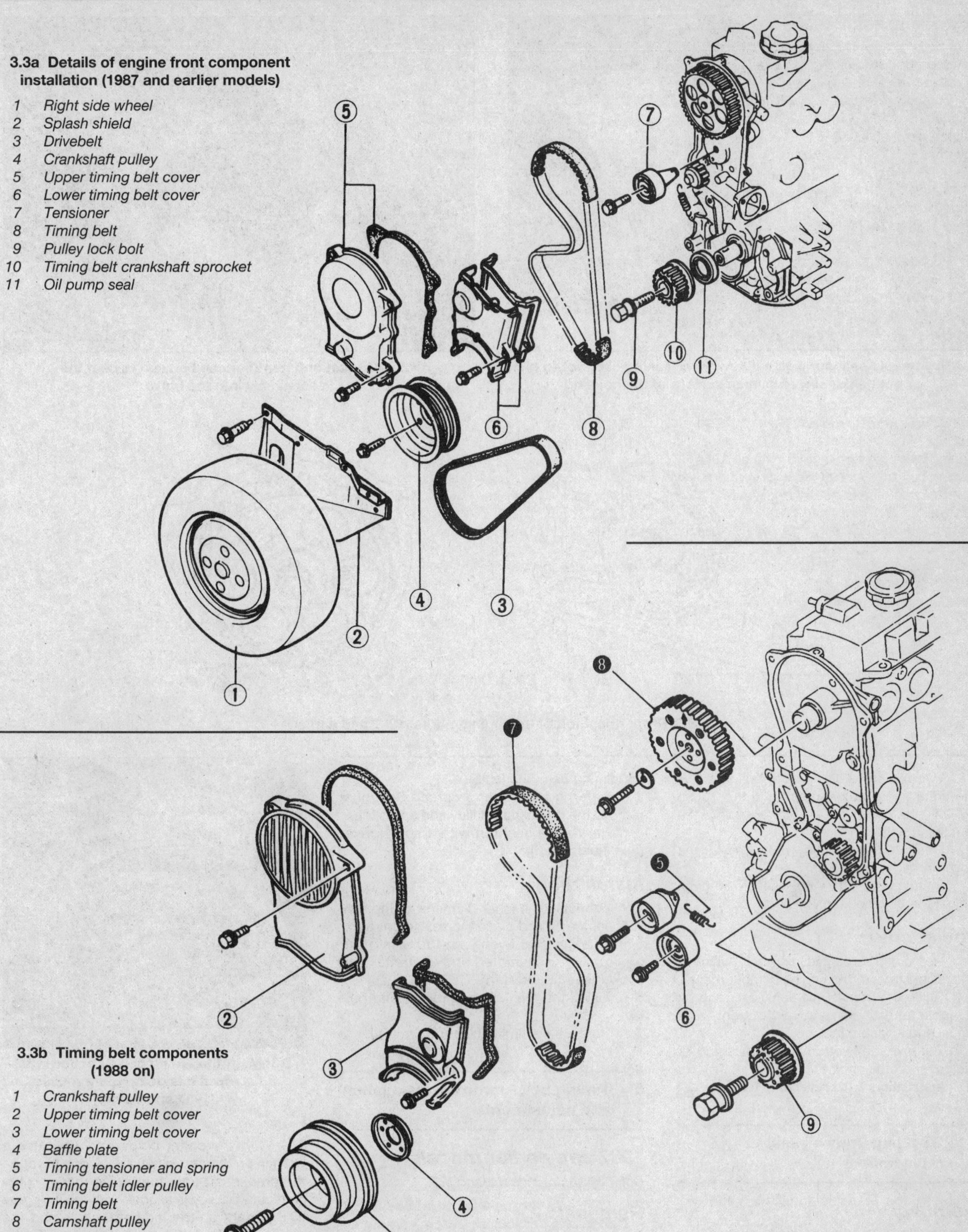

3.3a Details of engine front component installation (1987 and earlier models)

1 *Right side wheel*
2 *Splash shield*
3 *Drivebelt*
4 *Crankshaft pulley*
5 *Upper timing belt cover*
6 *Lower timing belt cover*
7 *Tensioner*
8 *Timing belt*
9 *Pulley lock bolt*
10 *Timing belt crankshaft sprocket*
11 *Oil pump seal*

3.3b Timing belt components (1988 on)

1 *Crankshaft pulley*
2 *Upper timing belt cover*
3 *Lower timing belt cover*
4 *Baffle plate*
5 *Timing tensioner and spring*
6 *Timing belt idler pulley*
7 *Timing belt*
8 *Camshaft pulley*
9 *Timing belt pulley*

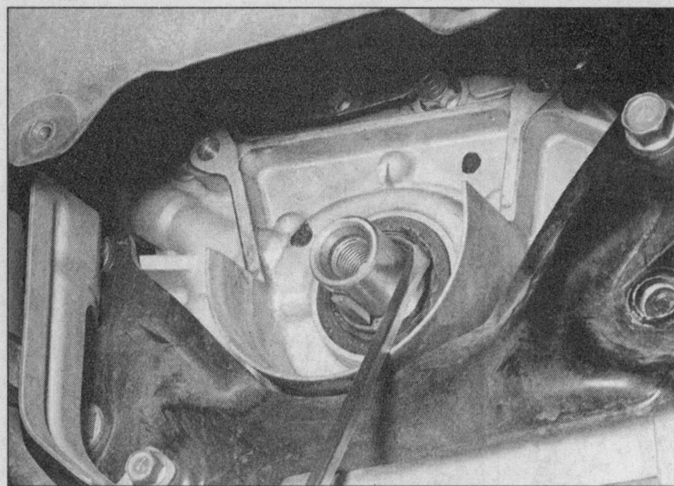

4.3 Pry the old seal out with a screwdriver, taking care not to nick or gouge the soft aluminum surface of the housing

4.5 A socket and hammer can be used to seat the seal evenly into the bore

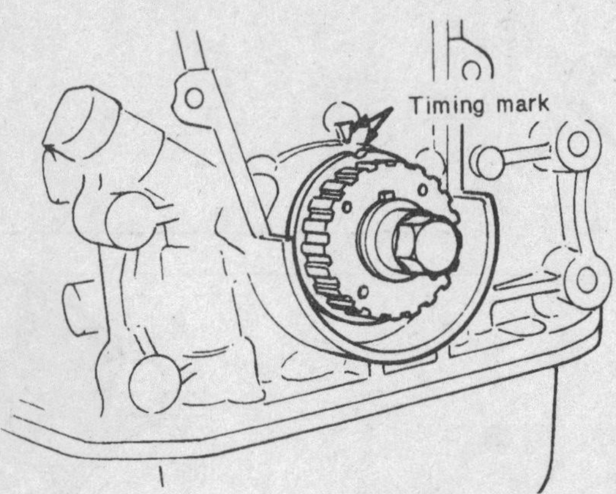

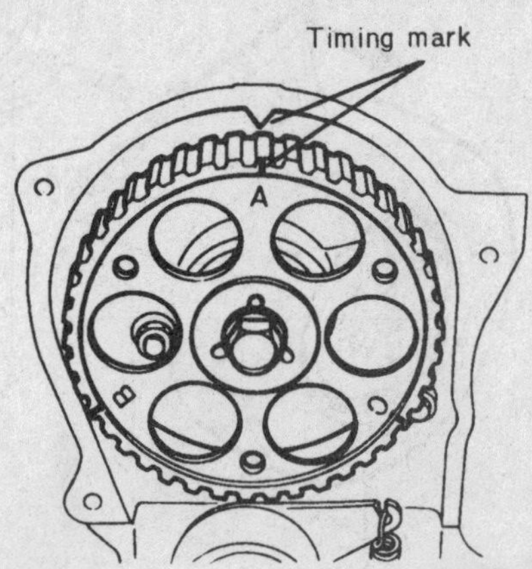

5.2 Proper position of the timing marks (1987 and earlier)

4 Use the drivebelt adjuster bolt to move the adjustment pulley down and then push the adjuster out of the way for access to the remaining bolts.

5 Remove the retaining bolts and lift the cover from the engine.

6 Installation is the reverse of removal. Adjust the drivebelt tension (Chapter 1).

Lower cover

7 Remove the top retaining bolt, which is accessible from in the engine compartment.

8 Raise the front of the vehicle, support it on jackstands and remove the right front wheel and splash panel.

9 Remove the two remaining bolts and lift the cover off the engine.

10 Installation is the reverse of removal.

4 Oil pump body oil seal - replacement

Removal

Refer to illustrations 4.3 and 4.5

1 Remove the timing belt cover (Section 3) and timing belt (Section 5).

2 Referring to the appropriate Sections, remove the crankshaft pulley and sprocket.

3 Pry the oil seal out with a screwdriver **(see illustration)**.

Installation

4 Lubricate the inner diameter of the seal with engine oil and place the seal in position.

5 Tap the seal evenly and fully into the bore using a hammer and suitable size socket **(see illustration)**.

6 Install the crankshaft sprocket and pulley.

7 Replace the timing belt and cover.

5 Timing belt - removal, installation and adjustment

1987 and earlier models

Refer to illustrations 5.2 and 5.3

Removal

1 Remove the timing belt front cover (Section 2).

5.3 Mark the timing belt direction with an arrow if it is going to be reused (1987 and earlier)

2 With the spark plugs removed, use a wrench on the crankshaft pulley bolt to rotate the crankshaft until the timing mark on the crankshaft pulley is aligned with the 0 degree BTDC mark on the indicator scale and the camshaft sprocket A mark lines up with the mark on the front housing **(see illustration)**.

5.7a The crankshaft sprocket marks and the . . .

5.7b . . . camshaft sprocket marks must be aligned as indicated before installing the timing belt (1987 and earlier)

5.8 Apply maximum tension to the spring in the direction shown (arrow) and then tighten the lock bolt snugly before installing the timing belt (1987 and earlier)

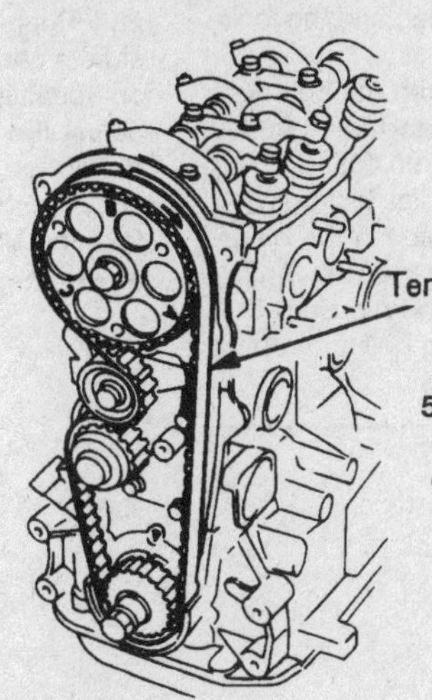

5.9 The timing belt must be installed from the direction of the tension side (1987 and earlier)

3 Remove the six bolts and pull the crankshaft pulley off the timing belt sprocket. Because of insufficient clearance, the pulley cannot be removed from the vehicle, but for this procedure removal won't be necessary. The pulley just has to be moved clear of the sprocket. **Note:** *Mark the timing belt with an arrow indicating direction of rotation before loosening the tension if the belt is to be reused* **(see illustration)**.

4 Loosen the timing belt tensioner lock bolt.

5 Work the belt off the sprockets and remove it from the engine.

6 Inspect the belt for damage, peeling, wear, cracks, hardening, crimping or signs of oil or other moisture. The belt should be replaced with a new one if any of these conditions exist or if the specified mileage has elapsed (Chapter 1).

Installation

Refer to illustrations 5.7a, 5.7b, 5.8 and 5.9

7 Make sure the crankshaft and camshaft sprocket timing marks are aligned **(see illustrations)**.

8 With the spring attached to the tensioner, push on the tensioner to apply maximum pressure and tighten the lock bolt to hold the tensioner in place **(see illustration)**.

9 Work the belt onto the camshaft and crankshaft sprockets from the tension (right) side so that the tension is maintained **(see illustration)**. If the old belt is being reinstalled, make sure the arrow is pointing in the proper direction.

Adjustment

Refer to illustration 5.11

10 Loosen the tensioner lock bolt so that just the spring is applying pressure.

11 Turn the crankshaft twice to the right so that equal tension is applied to both sides of the timing belt and tighten the lock bolt **(see illustration)**.

12 Check the timing marks to make sure they are still properly aligned.

13 Check the deflection of the belt midway between the crankshaft and camshaft sprockets on the tension side to make sure it is within specification. If the tension is not correct, repeat the adjustment operation described in Step 9.

14 Install the timing belt cover.

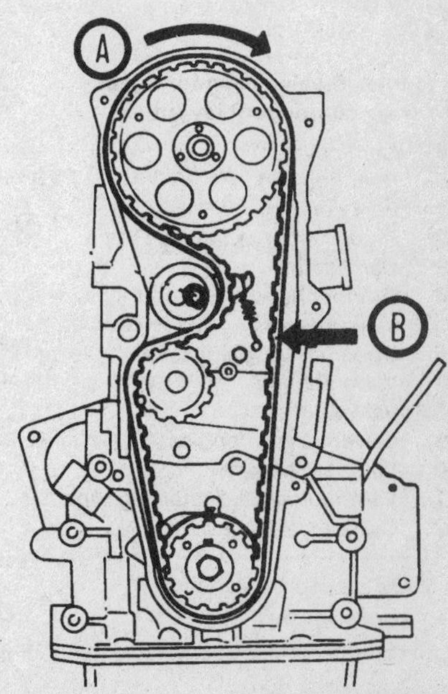

5.11 Rotate the timing belt to the right (A) while checking the tension at point B

1988 and later models

Removal

Refer to illustrations 5.15 and 5.16

15 Remove the timing belt cover **(see illustration)**.

16 Make sure the number 1 arrow on the camshaft pulley is lined up with the timing notch on the housing **(see illustration)**. Rotate the engine if necessary to align the mark and arrow.

17 Loosen the lockbolt, swing the tensioner to the left to release the belt tension, then tighten the lockbolt **(see illustration 3.3b)**.

18 Remove the timing belt.

Installation

19 Make sure the number 1 arrow on the camshaft pulley is lined up with the timing notch and the timing belt pulley mating mark is aligned with the mark on the case.

20 Check the timing belt tensioner to make sure the spring is fully extended and the lockbolt is tight.

21 Install the timing belt, with the belt tight on the water pump pulley and idler pulley (tension) side **(see illustration 5.16)**.

22 Loosen the tensioner pulley lockbolt.

23 Turn the engine over twice in the direction of rotation and check that the pulley marks are aligned as described in Step 9. If they aren't, remove the timing belt and repeat the procedure.

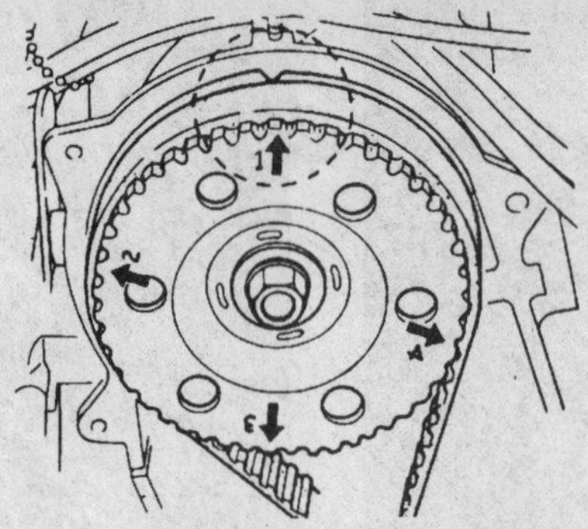

5.15 Line up the number 1 arrow with the timing notch before removing the timing belt (1988 on)

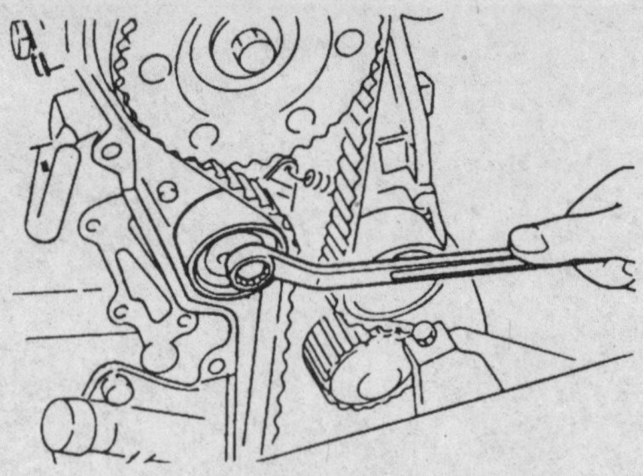

5.16 Loosen the lockbolt and swing the tensioner away from the belt to release the tension (1988 on)

24 Tighten the lockbolt to the specified torque.

25 Push on the timing belt on the tension side to check that the timing belt deflection is as specified. If it is not, loosen the lockbolt, adjust the tensioner to achieve the specified deflection, then tighten the lockbolt to the specified torque.

26 Install the timing belt cover.

6 Camshaft sprocket - removal and installation

Removal

1 Remove the timing belt front cover (Section 3).

2 Remove the timing belt (Section 5).

3 Remove the camshaft cover (Section 2).

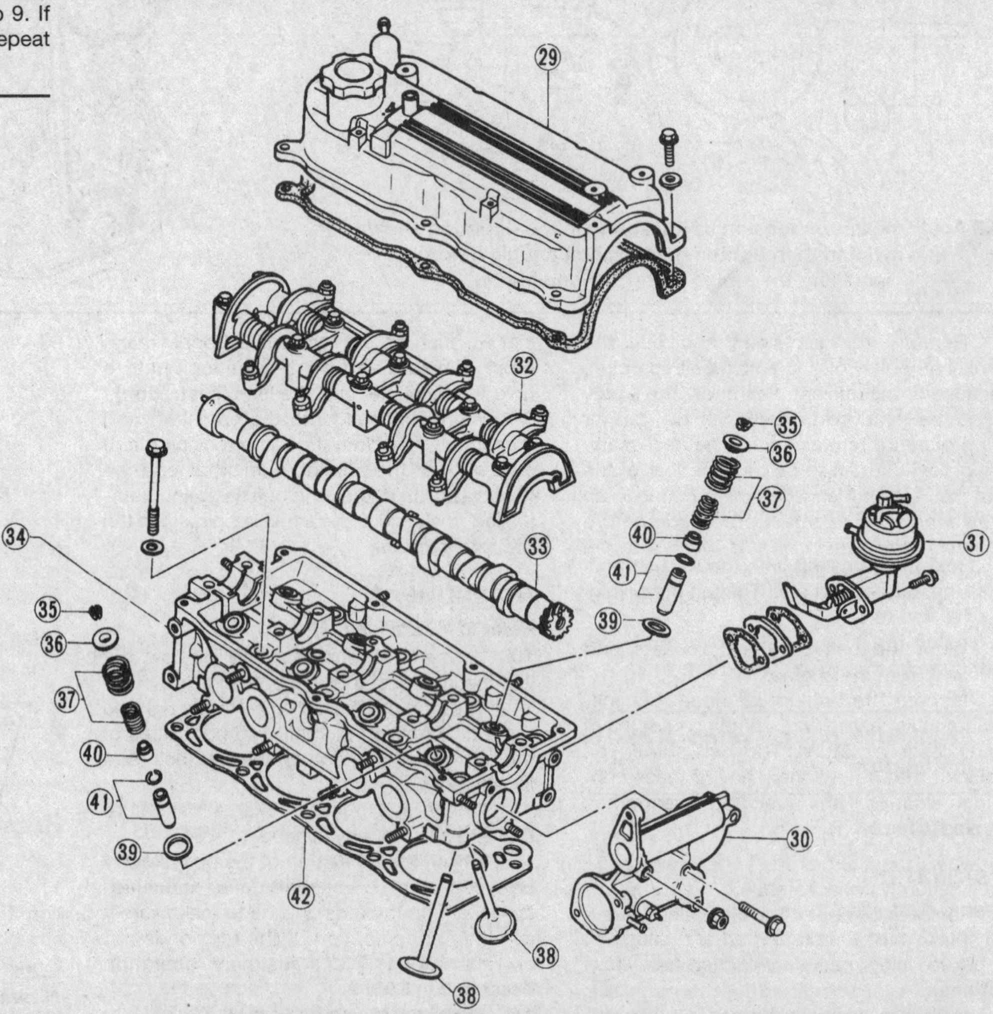

9.1a 8-valve cylinder head component layout

29 Cam cover
30 Rear housing
31 Fuel pump
32 Rocker shaft assembly
33 Camshaft
34 Cylinder head
35 Valve keepers
36 Upper valve spring seats
37 Valve springs
38 Valves
39 Lower valve spring seats
40 Valve stem seals
41 Valve guides and retaining clips
42 Cylinder head gasket

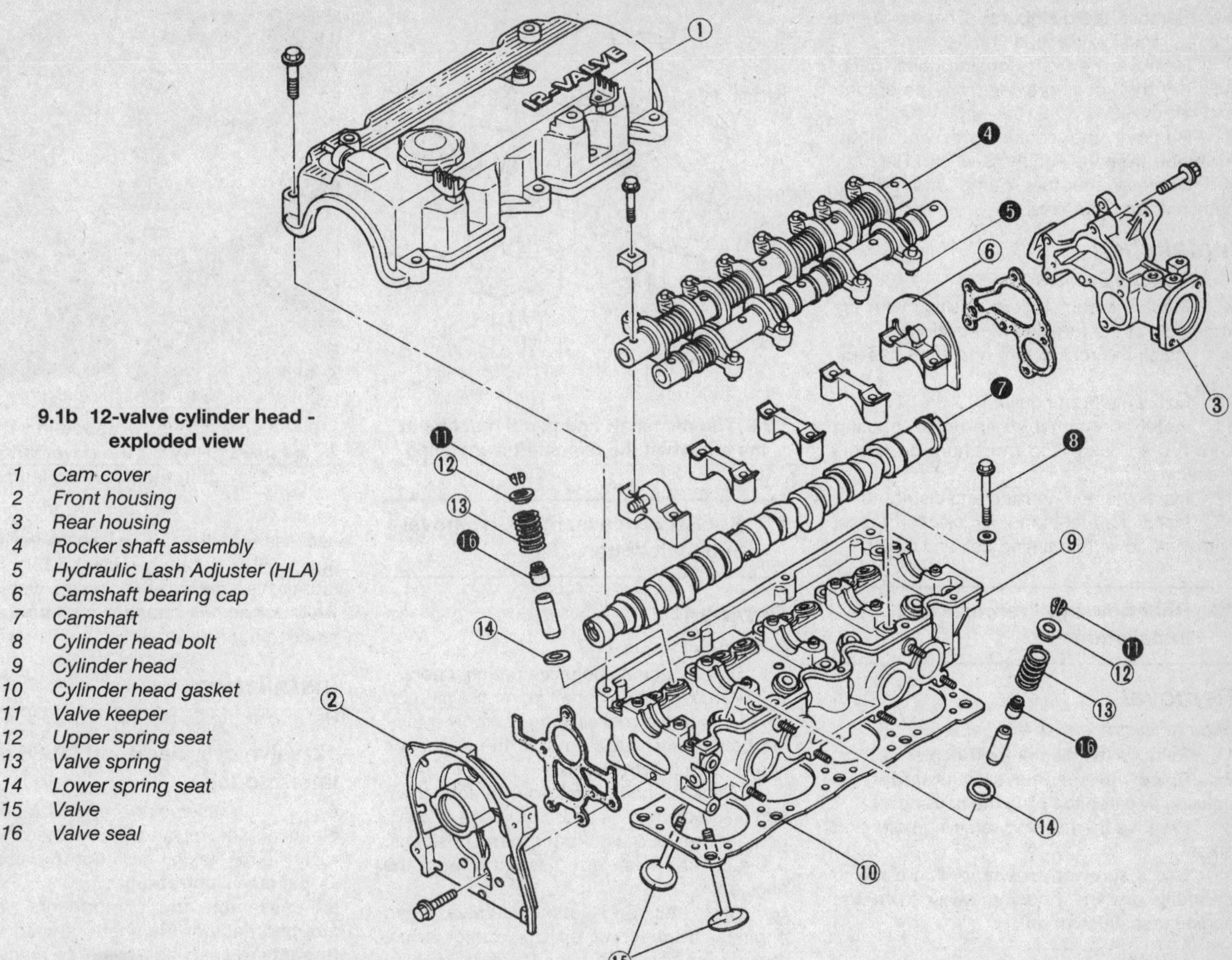

9.1b 12-valve cylinder head - exploded view

1 *Cam cover*
2 *Front housing*
3 *Rear housing*
4 *Rocker shaft assembly*
5 *Hydraulic Lash Adjuster (HLA)*
6 *Camshaft bearing cap*
7 *Camshaft*
8 *Cylinder head bolt*
9 *Cylinder head*
10 *Cylinder head gasket*
11 *Valve keeper*
12 *Upper spring seat*
13 *Valve spring*
14 *Lower spring seat*
15 *Valve*
16 *Valve seal*

4 Hold the sprocket in position so it cannot turn, using an extension and socket on one of the front cover bolts. Remove the sprocket bolt, sprocket and washer.

Installation

5 Place the sprocket in position on the camshaft and align the sprocket and cover marks.

6 Hold the camshaft with the wrench and install the washer and bolt. Tighten the bolt to the specified torque.

7 Install the timing belt, cover and any other components which were removed.

7 Crankshaft pulley - removal and installation

Removal

1 Raise the front of the vehicle and support it securely on jackstands.

2 Remove the right front wheel and fender well splash shield.

3 Remove the pulley retaining bolts.

4 Insert a large screwdriver through the access hole in the bellhousing and into the teeth of the starter ring gear so the crankshaft cannot turn.

5 With an assistant holding the screwdriver so the crankshaft is locked, remove the timing belt sprocket bolt.

6 Lift the crankshaft pulley from the engine.

Installation

7 Place the pulley in position and install the retaining bolts and the timing belt sprocket bolt finger tight.

8 With the crankshaft locked in place, tighten the sprocket bolt and pulley bolts to the specified torque.

9 Install the splash shield and front wheel and lower the vehicle.

8 Timing belt sprocket - removal and installation

Removal

1 Raise the front of the vehicle, support it securely on jackstands and remove the right front wheel and inner fender splash shield.

2 Remove the crankshaft pulley-to-timing belt sprocket bolts (Section 7).

3 Lock the flywheel in place with a screwdriver inserted between the teeth and remove the sprocket bolt and sprocket.

Installation

4 Place the sprocket on the crankshaft and install the crankshaft pulley and sprocket bolts finger tight. Tighten the bolts to the specified torque.

5 Install the splash shield and front wheel and lower the vehicle.

9 Camshaft - removal and installation

Removal

Refer to illustrations 9.1a and 9.1b

1 Remove the front timing belt cover (Section 2), timing belt (Section 5) and camshaft sprocket (Section 6) **(see illustrations)**.

2 Remove camshaft cover (Section 2).

3 Remove the air injection tubes (Chapter 6).

4 Remove the distributor (Chapter 5) and the rear housing (Section 10).
5 Remove the front housing bolts, carefully pry the housing away from the engine and remove it.
6 Remove the rocker arm and shaft assembly from the engine (Section 11).
7 Remove the fuel pump and lift the camshaft from the engine.

Installation

Refer to illustration 9.8

8 Place the camshaft in position with the knock pin at the top **(see illustration)**.
9 Install the rocker arm and shaft assembly.
10 Install the front housing.
11 Install the camshaft sprocket, making sure the sprocket and front housing marks are aligned.
12 Install the rear housing and distributor.
13 Install the fuel pump, air injection tubes, camshaft cover and timing belt and cover.

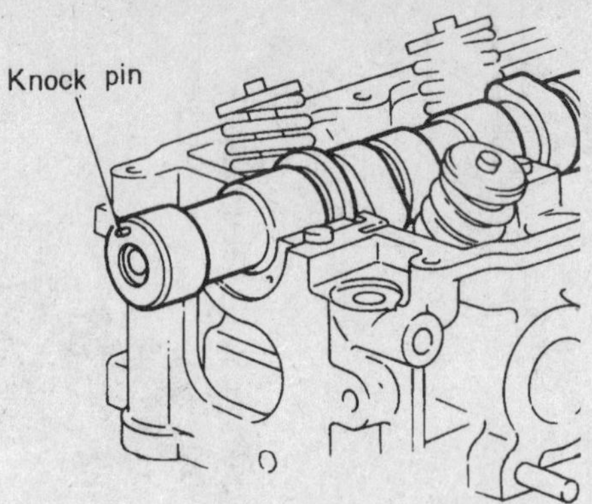

9.8 The camshaft knock pin must be at the top when the camshaft is installed

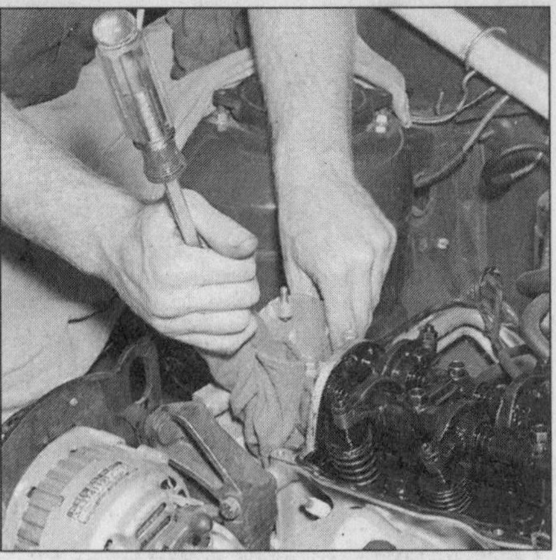

10.4 A screwdriver wrapped in a rag can be used to pry off the cover without damaging the soft aluminum

10 Rear housing - removal and installation

Removal

Refer to illustration 10.4

1 Remove the distributor (Chapter 5).
2 Place newspapers or rags under the housing to catch the oil in the housing.
3 Remove the housing retaining bolts and nuts.
4 Use a screwdriver wrapped in a rag to carefully pry the housing away from the engine **(see illustration)**.

Installation

5 Carefully clean the contact surfaces of the housing and cylinder of old gasket material.
6 Coat the new gasket with sealant and place it in position on the housing.
7 Install the housing on the cylinder head, install the nuts and bolts and tighten them to the specified torque.
8 Install the distributor.

11 Rocker arm assembly - removal and installation

Removal

Refer to illustration 11.3

1 Disconnect the negative battery cable.
2 Remove the camshaft cover (Section 2).
3 Loosen the rocker arm assembly retaining bolts, a little at a time, in the sequence shown **(see illustration)**.
4 Once the bolts are loose, remove them and place them in a numbered piece of cardboard for reinstallation to the same positions.
5 Lift the rocker arm assembly from the engine.
6 On 1988 and later 12-valve head engines, after lifting off the rocker arms, remove the camshaft bearing caps, keeping them in order for installation to the same positions.

HLA units (1988 and later models)

Refer to illustration 11.7

7 Inspect the contact surface of the HLA for wear or damage. Remove the HLA by grasping it (with padded-jaw pliers, if necessary) and pulling it out of the rocker arm **(see illustration)**. Do not remove the HLA unless necessary as the O-ring can be easily damaged. HLA's can be cleaned in solvent (spray-type carburetor cleaner works well), which often will cause a clattering HLA to function normally again.

Installation

Refer to illustrations 11.8, 11.9 and 11.10

12-valve cylinder head (1988 and later models)

8 Fill the reservoirs of the HLA units with clean engine oil and press them into the rocker arms, taking care not to damage the O-ring **(see illustration)**.
9 Assemble the components with the stepped ends of the shafts toward the rear (the intake shaft has twice as many holes) **(see illustration)**.
10 After installing the camshaft, place the camshaft bearing caps in position with the arrows facing toward the front of the engine. The oil passage in the number 3 cap must face toward the rear **(see illustration)**.

All models

Refer to illustrations 11.13, 11.14 and 11.15

11 Carefully clean the contact areas of the

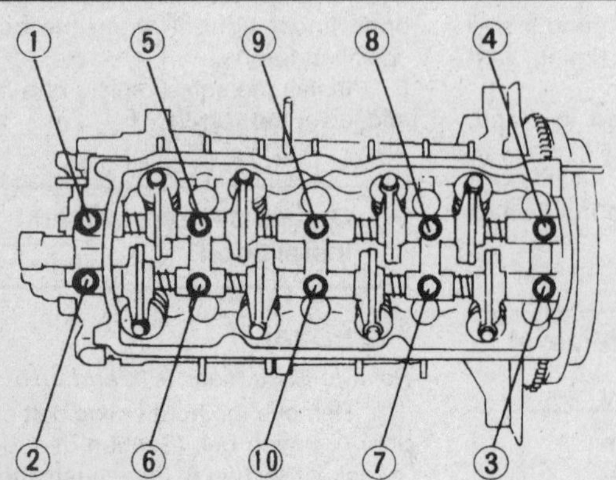

11.3 Rocker arm assembly bolt loosening sequence

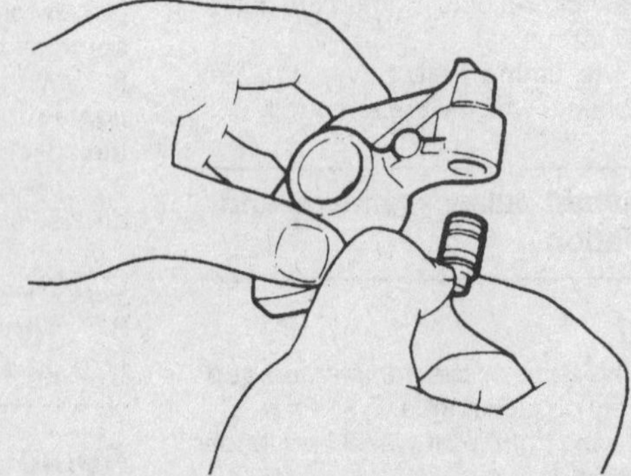

11.7 Pull the HLA unit out of the rocker arm if it is malfunctioning - use padded-jaw pliers if necessary

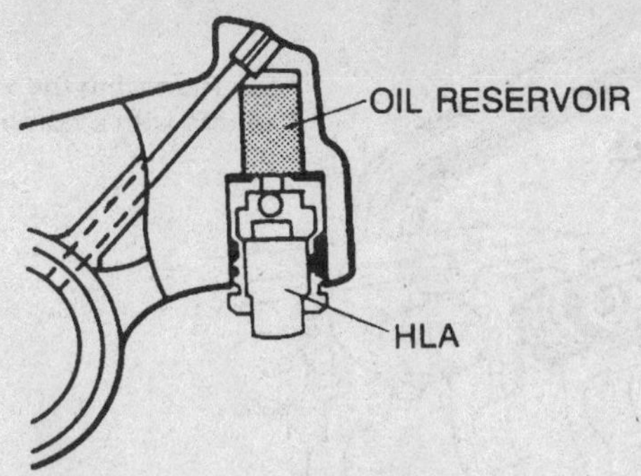

11.8 Fill the reservoir of the new HLA with clean oil

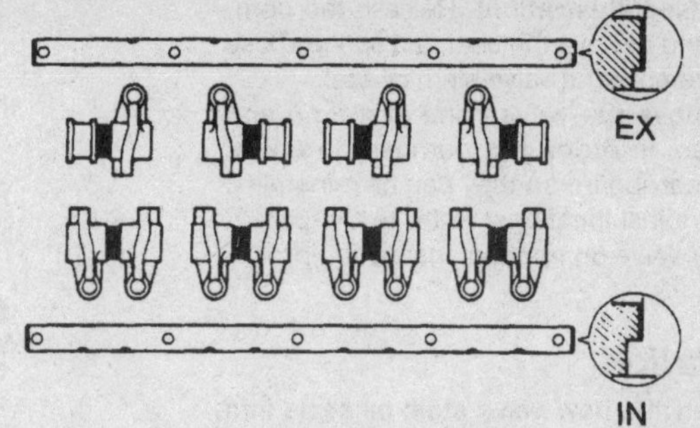

11.9 The proper relationship of the 12-valve rocker gear with the stepped ends toward the rear - the intake shaft has twice as many holes

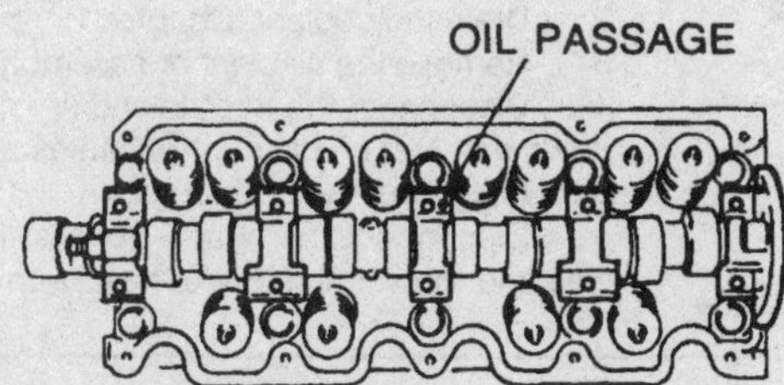

11.10 Make sure the number 3 camshaft bearing is installed in the oil passage as shown

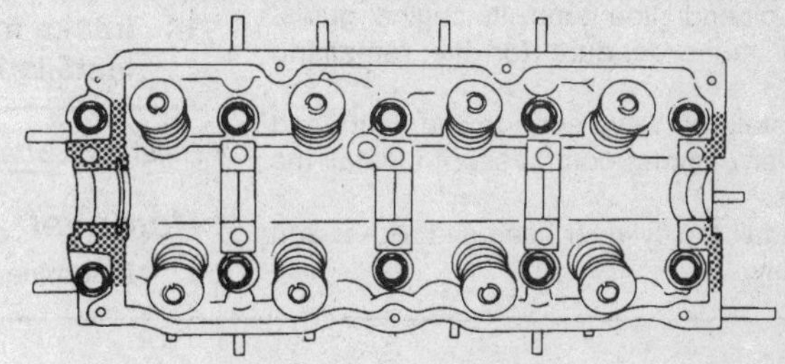

11.13 Apply sealant to the shaded areas before installing the rocker assembly

rocker arm assembly and the cylinder head to remove all traces of sealant.

12 If the assembly has been disassembled, lubricate it liberally with clean engine oil prior to installation.

13 Apply sealant to the cylinder head-to-rocker arm assembly contact areas **(see illustration)**.

14 Lower the rocker arm assembly into place and install the bolts finger tight in their original positions. On 12-valve cylinder heads, make sure the rocker arms or spacers are not caught between the rocker arm and camshaft cap **(see illustration)**.

15 Tighten the bolts, a little at a time, to the specified torque in the sequence **(see illustration)**.

16 Check the valve adjustment, adjusting as necessary (Chapter 1).

17 Install the camshaft cover and connect the battery cable.

12 Front housing oil seal - replacement

1 Remove the timing belt (Section 5).

2 Remove the camshaft sprocket (Section 6).

3 Pry the old oil seal out with a screwdriver, taking care not to damage the sealing surface.

4 Apply a thin coat of engine oil the outer diameter of the new seal.

5 Place the seal squarely in position in the bore.

6 Place the seal in the bore and use a suitable size socket to press it fully and evenly into place.

7 Install the sprocket, timing belt and cover.

13 Valves, springs and valve stem oil seals - removal and installation

Removal

Refer to illustration 13.3

1 Remove the rocker arm assembly (Section 11).

2 Remove the cylinder head (Section 16).

3 Use a compressor to compress the valve springs, one at a time, and remove the valve

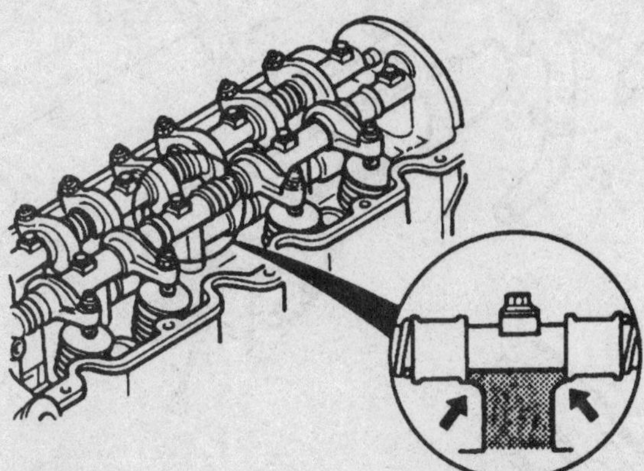

11.14 When installing the rocker arm assembly, check to make sure the rocker arms and spacers don't get caught between the camshaft and the cap

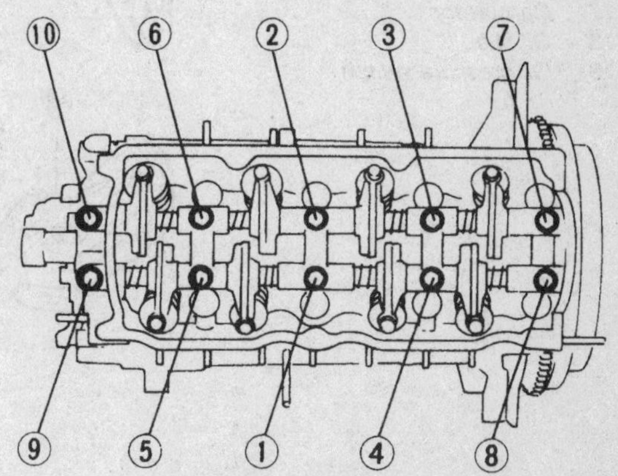

11.15 Rocker arm assembly bolt tightening sequence

keepers **(see illustration)**. Release the compressor and remove the seat and springs. Use pliers to remove the valve stem oil seal.

4 Remove the valves one at a time and keep them in order in a numbered rack or piece of cardboard so they can be reinstalled in their original locations. Refer to Chapter 2, Part B for valve component inspection procedures.

Installation

5 Insert the new valve stem oil seals into the guides and then use a suitable size socket and hammer to tap them fully into place.

6 Coat the first valve stem with clean engine oil and slide it into its original guide. Repeat the procedure for the remaining valves.

7 Install the valve springs and seats and use a valve spring compressor to install the keepers.

8 Install the cylinder head and rocker arm assembly.

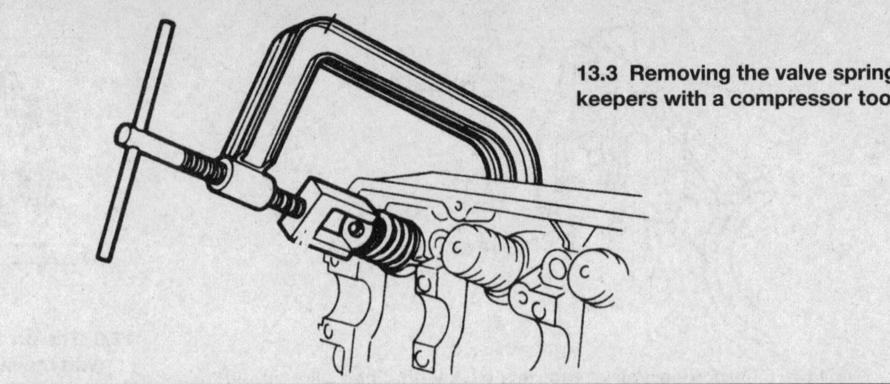

13.3 Removing the valve spring keepers with a compressor tool

14 Intake manifold - removal and installation

Refer to illustration 14.10

Removal

1 Disconnect the negative cable from the battery and remove the air cleaner assembly.

2 Drain the coolant (Chapter 1).

3 Remove the air cleaner assembly.

4 Disconnect the throttle and (if equipped) downshift and cruise control cables and vacuum hose from the carburetor.

5 Disconnect the heater hose at the firewall and the vacuum brake hose from the fit-

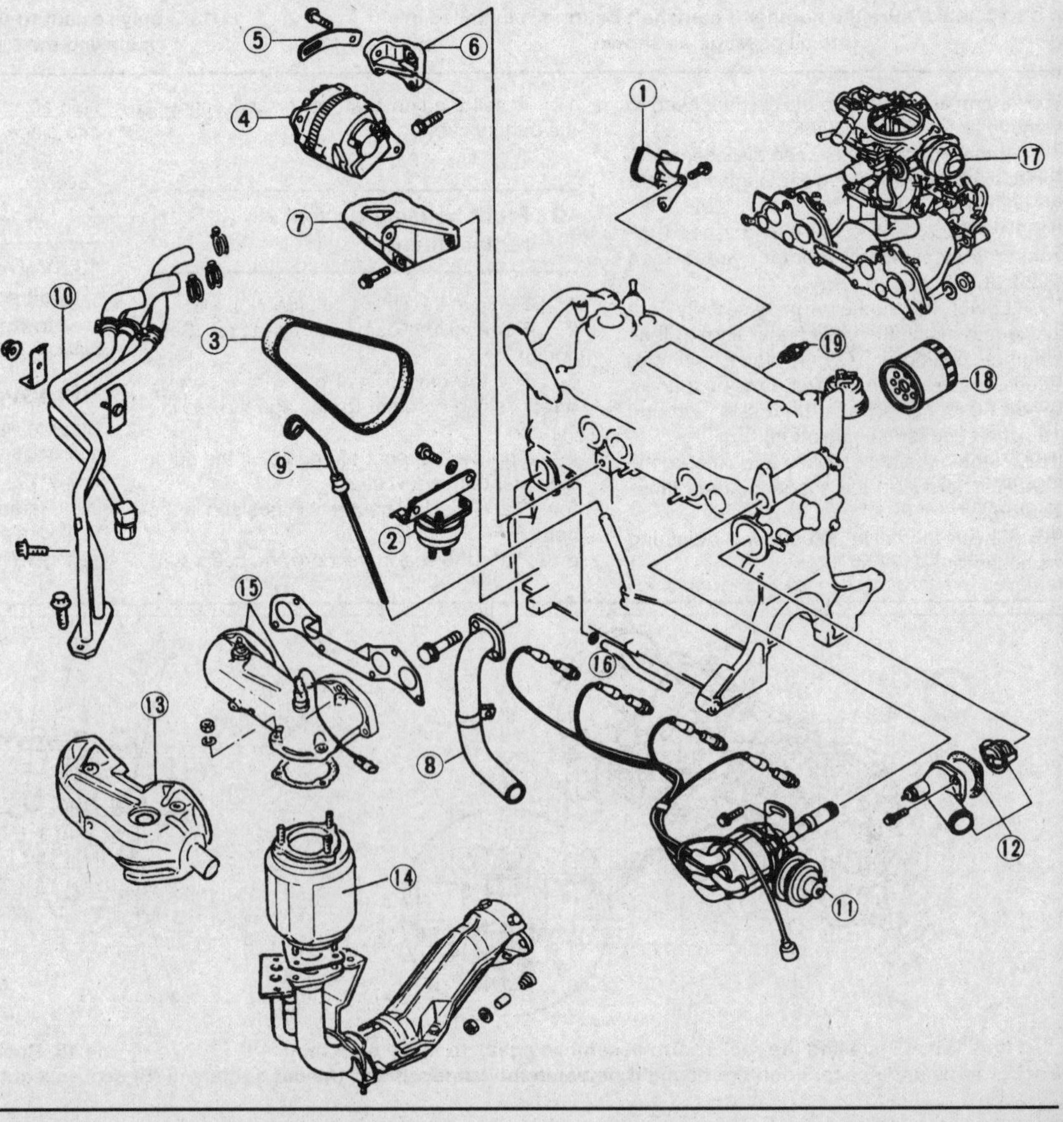

14.10 Engine external component layout

1 *Torque stopper assembly*
2 *Engine mount*
3 *Drivebelt*
4 *Alternator*
5 *Alternator adjusting strap*
6 *Strap bracket*
7 *Alternator bracket*
8 *Lower water inlet pipe assembly and hose*
9 *Oil dipstick assembly*
10 *Air injection pipes*
11 *Spark plugs, wires and distributor*
12 *Thermostat and housing*
13 *Heat shield*
14 *Exhaust pipe*
15 *Exhaust manifold*
16 *Bypass hose assembly*
17 *Carburetor*
18 *Oil filter*
19 *Oil pressure switch*

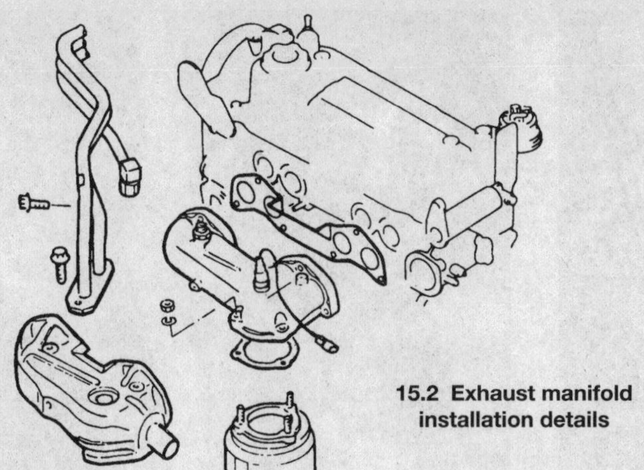

15.2 Exhaust manifold installation details

ting on the vacuum reservoir.

6 Disconnect and plug the fuel line at the fuel pump.

7 Disconnect the charcoal canister hose from the carburetor and the purge hoses from the canister.

8 Disconnect the four electrical connectors adjacent to the carburetor and canister.

9 Mark any remaining hoses and connections which will interfere with manifold removal with numbered pieces of tape and disconnect them.

10 Remove the manifold retaining nuts and bolts, slide the intake manifold off the studs and separate it from the cylinder head **(see illustration)**.

11 Remove the gasket.

Installation

12 Clean all traces of gasket and other foreign material from the manifold and cylinder head mating surfaces, taking care not to gouge the soft aluminum surface.

13 Install a new gasket, place the manifold in position on the studs and install the retaining nuts. Tighten the nuts to the specified torque. Work from the center of the manifold out, in a criss-cross pattern.

14 Install the components which were removed to gain access to the intake manifold.

15 Exhaust manifold - removal and installation

Refer to illustration 15.2

Removal

1 Disconnect the negative cable from the battery.

2 Remove the air injection system pipes **(see illustration)**.

3 Remove the air injection fitting, retaining bolt and oxygen sensor and detach the heat shroud.

4 Apply penetrating oil to the cylinder head and catalytic converter retaining stud threads and allow it to soak for ten minutes.

5 In the engine compartment, remove the nuts retaining exhaust manifold to the cylinder head and to the catalytic converter.

6 Grasp the manifold, separate it from the cylinder head and the catalytic converter and lift it from the engine.

Installation

7 Remove all traces of gasket material from the manifold and cylinder head with a gasket scraper. Take care not to nick or gouge the soft aluminum of the head.

8 Place the manifold in position on the cylinder head, using new gaskets, and install the retaining nuts to hold it in place. Install the nuts and bolts retaining the manifold to the catalytic converter. Tighten the manifold nuts to the specified torque. Work from the center of the manifold out, in a criss-cross pattern.

16 Cylinder head - removal and installation

Refer to illustrations 16.10, 16.11 and 16.14

Note: *The engine must be cold whenever the camshaft/cylinder head bolts are loosened or removed.*

Removal

1 Disconnect the negative cable from the battery and remove the air cleaner assembly and the air injection pipes.

2 Drain the cooling system and disconnect the upper radiator hose.

3 Remove the distributor (Chapter 5) and rear housing (Section 10).

4 Referring to the appropriate Sections, remove the timing belt cover and the belt.

5 Remove the fuel pump (Chapter 4).

6 Remove the intake manifold (Section 14).

7 Remove the alternator. On air conditioned models, remove the compressor through bolt and move the compressor carefully out of the way, taking care not to damage the lines (which are contain high pressure) or the radiator. Remove the alternator/air conditioner bracket-to-cylinder head bolts and loosen the remaining bracket bolts.

8 Remove the camshaft cover (Section 2).

9 Remove the three bolts attaching the exhaust manifold to the catalytic converter and separate the converter from the manifold.

10 Loosen the cylinder head bolts, a few turns at a time, in the sequence shown **(see illustration)**.

11 After they are all loose, remove the cylin-

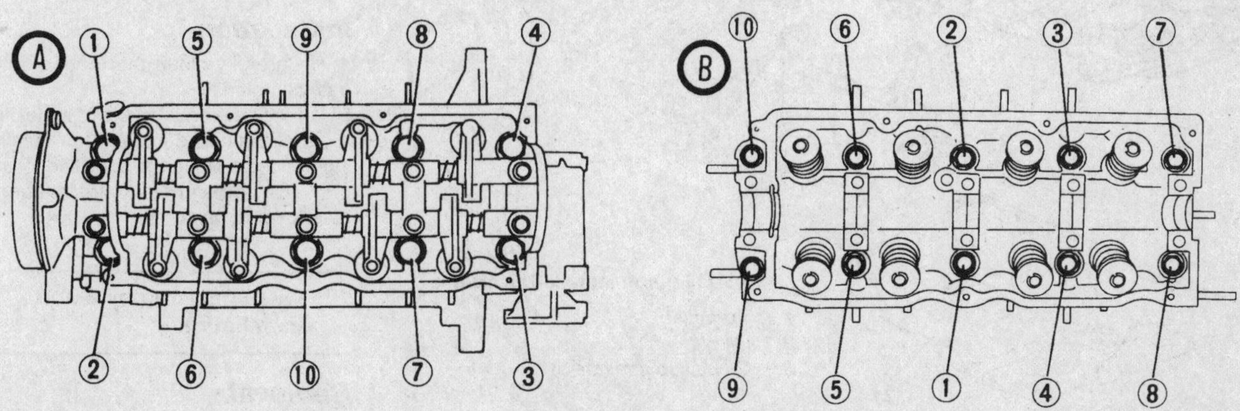

16.10 Cylinder head bolt loosening (A) and tightening (B) sequence

16.11 Use a piece of cardboard to keep the cylinder head bolts in order

16.14 Use a scraper to remove the gasket material

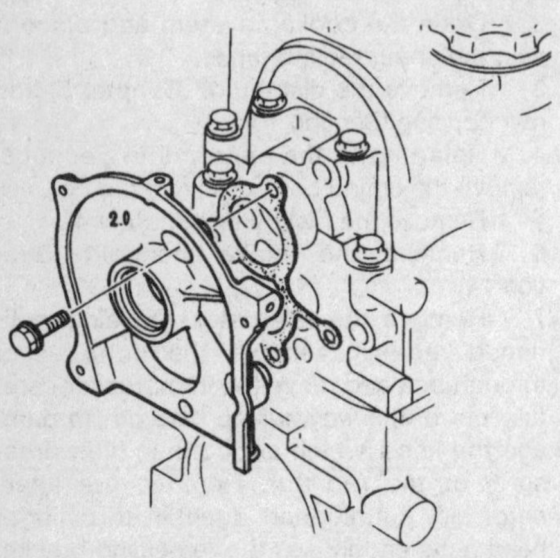

17.3 Front housing installation details

der head bolts and place them in order in a piece of cardboard so they can be reinstalled in their original positions **(see illustration)**.

12 If the cylinder head cannot be lifted off easily, break the gasket seal using a pry bar inserted between the alternator/compressor bracket and the cylinder head.

13 Separate the cylinder head from the engine and remove the gasket.

Installation

14 Remove all traces of gasket material from the engine block and cylinder head **(see illustration)**. Make sure the cylinder head bolt threads and the threaded holes in the block are clean, as this could affect torque readings during installation.

15 Place the new gasket and cylinder head in position, followed by the camshaft and rocker arm assembly.

16 Install the cylinder head bolts and tighten them to the specified torque in the sequence shown in the accompanying illustration.

17 The remainder of the installation procedure is the reverse of removal.

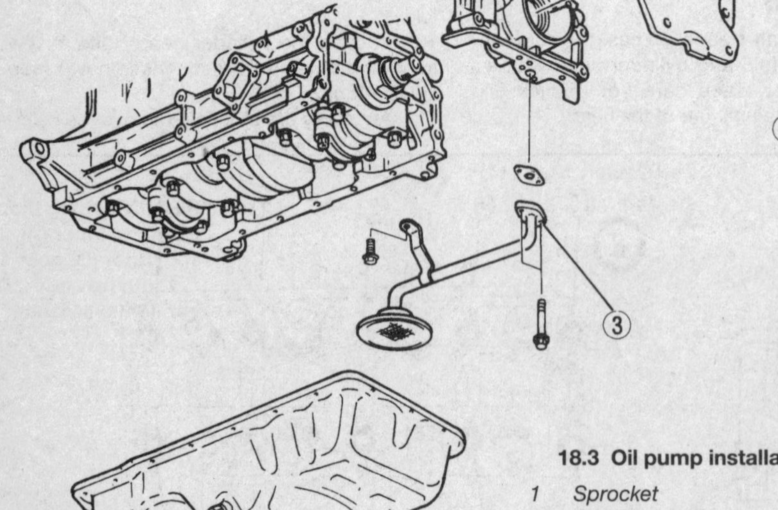

18.3 Oil pump installation details

1 *Sprocket*
2 *Oil pan*
3 *Oil pickup strainer*

17 Front housing cover - removal and installation

Refer to illustration 17.3

Removal

1 Remove the timing cover (Section 2) and timing belt (Section 5).

2 Remove the camshaft sprocket (Section 6).

3 Remove the bolts and carefully separate the cover from the cylinder head, using a screwdriver to break the gasket seal **(see illustration)**.

Installation

4 Carefully clean the mating surfaces of gasket material.

5 Place the housing cover in position using a new gasket and install the retaining bolts. Tighten the bolts to the specified torque.

6 The remainder of installation is the reverse of removal.

18 Oil pump - removal and installation

Removal

Refer to illustration 18.3

1 Remove the timing belt covers, timing

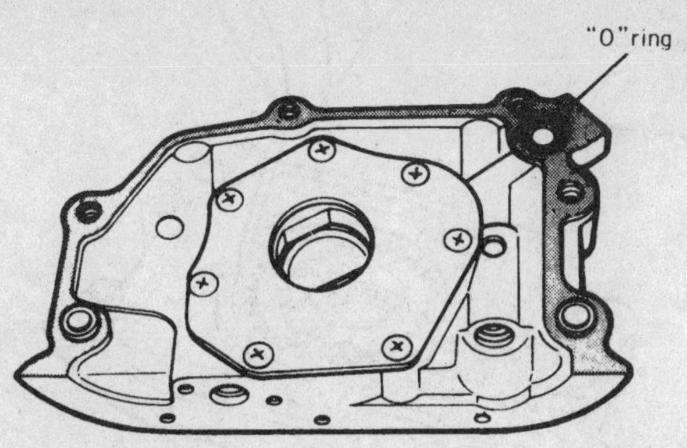

18.7 Apply sealant to the shaded areas of the oil pump housing

19.1 The oil pump cover screw locations (arrows)

belt and crankshaft sprocket.

2 Remove the oil pan.

3 Remove the engine mount plate/front cover bolts **(see illustration)**.

4 Unbolt and remove the pickup tube assembly.

5 Insert a screwdriver at the corner of the cover to break the gasket seal and remove the cover.

6 Clean the oil pump mating surfaces to remove old gasket material.

Installation

Refer to illustration 18.7

7 Coat the O-ring with petroleum jelly and insert it into the pump. Coat the pump housing with sealant as shown **(see illustration)**. Apply clean engine oil to the lip of the oil seal.

8 Place the pump and new gasket in position and install the bolts. Tighten the bolts to the specified torque.

9 Using a new O-ring, install the pickup tube and support assembly. Tighten the bolts to the specified torque.

10 Install the oil pan.

11 Install a new oil filter and replace the oil pressure switch harness.

12 Install the timing belt, covers and the crankshaft sprocket.

19 Oil pump - disassembly, inspection and reassembly

Disassembly

Refer to illustrations 19.1 and 19.2

1 Remove the retaining screws and cover from the rear of the pump **(see illustration)**.

2 Remove the gears from the pump body. It may be necessary to turn the body over to remove the gears by allowing them to fall out **(see illustration)**.

3 Mount the pump body in a soft jawed vise and remove the oil pressure sending unit, plug, pressure regulator valve, plunger and spring.

Inspection

Refer to illustrations 19.6a, 19.6b and 19.6c

4 Wash the oil pump parts in solvent.

5 Inspect the components for wear, cracks or other damage.

6 Check the outer (idler) gear-to-body clearance, inner (drive) gear-to-body clearance,

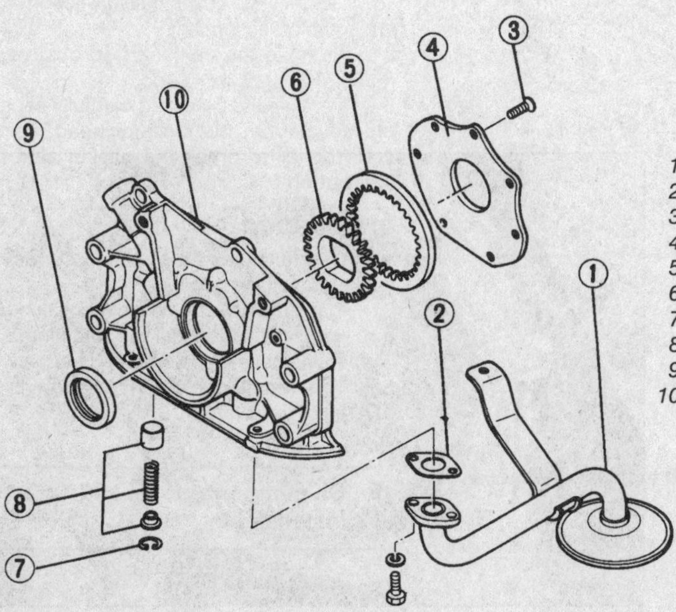

19.2 Oil pump components

1. *Oil strainer*
2. *Gasket*
3. *Bolt*
4. *Pump cover*
5. *Outer gear*
6. *Inner gear*
7. *Snap-ring*
8. *Plunger assembly*
9. *Oil seal*
10. *Pump body*

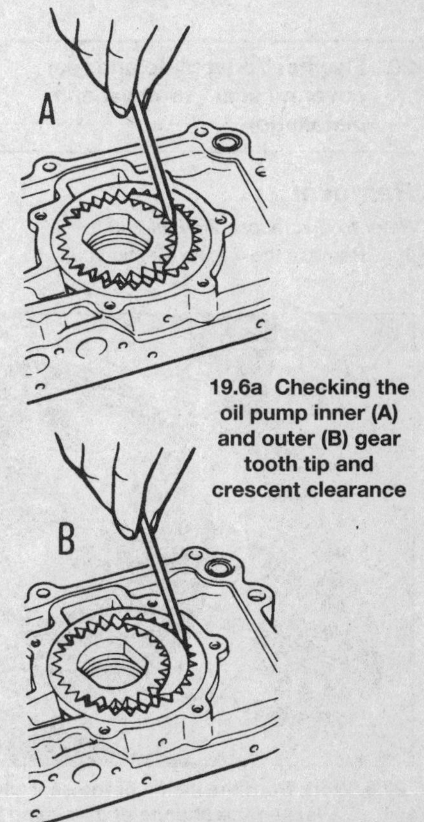

19.6a Checking the oil pump inner (A) and outer (B) gear tooth tip and crescent clearance

2A

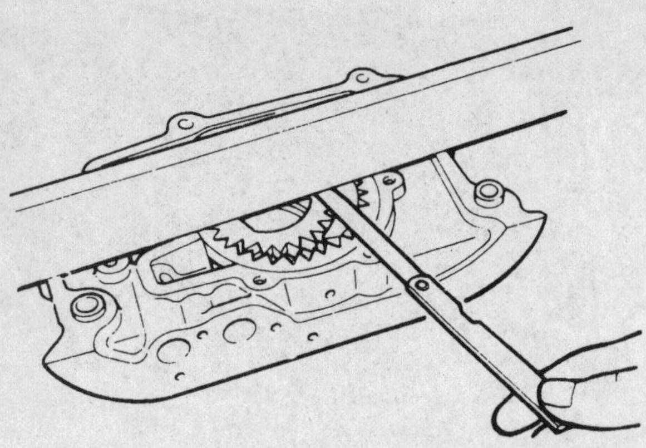
19.6b Measuring the oil pump gear-to-cover clearance

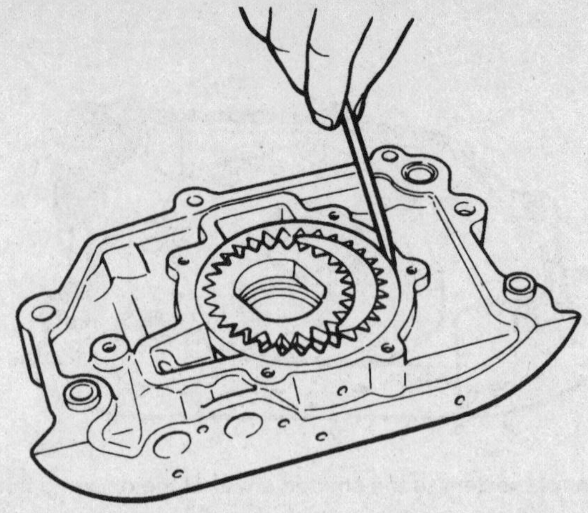
19.6c Checking the oil pump outer gear-to-body clearance

the outer gear-to-pump body clearance and the gear to-cover clearance **(see illustrations)**.

Reassembly

7 Install the valve, plunger and spring assembly.

8 Coat the plug threads with a thread locking compound and tighten to the specified torque.

9 Install the gears, noting that the outer gear is identified by a mark. This mark must face the cover.

10 Install the pump cover and tighten the screws securely.

11 Install the oil pressure sending unit.

20 Flywheel/driveplate and rear cover oil seal - removal and installation

Removal

Refer to illustrations 20.4 and 20.6

1 Remove the engine (Section 22).

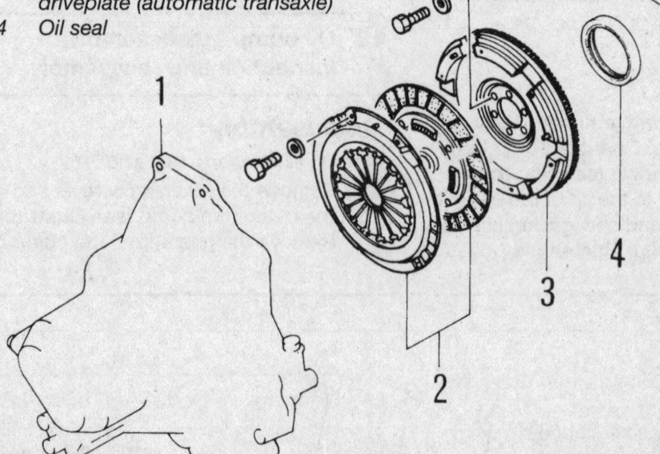

20.4 Details of the rear oil seal installation

1. *Transaxle*
2. *Clutch (manual transaxle)*
3. *Flywheel (manual transaxle) or driveplate (automatic transaxle)*
4. *Oil seal*

20.6 Work from the inside of the seal when prying the seal out to lessen the chance of damaging the bore surface

20.7 Tap lightly around the seal outer circumference with a hammer and punch until the seal is fully seated in the bore

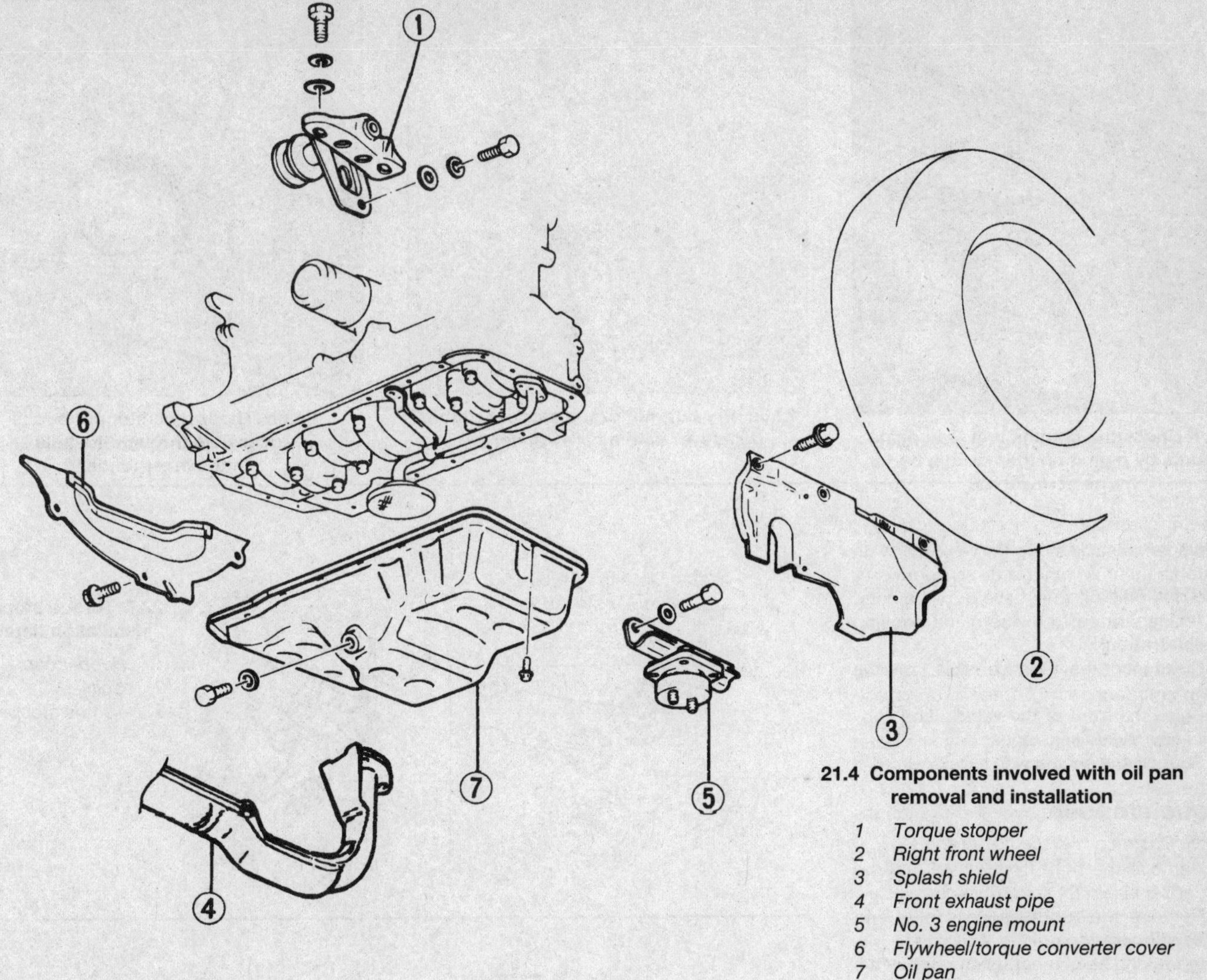

21.4 Components involved with oil pan removal and installation

1 *Torque stopper*
2 *Right front wheel*
3 *Splash shield*
4 *Front exhaust pipe*
5 *No. 3 engine mount*
6 *Flywheel/torque converter cover*
7 *Oil pan*

2 Remove the flywheel/torque converter cover.
3 On automatic transaxle models, remove the torque converter retaining bolts.
4 Remove the bellhousing bolts and separate the transaxle and engine **(see illustration)**.
5 Remove the transaxle driveplate (automatic) or pressure plate, clutch disc and flywheel (manual).
6 Pry the oil seal out using a screwdriver **(see illustration)**.

Installation

Refer to illustration 20.7

7 Insert the new seal squarely into position and tap it into place slowly and carefully, working around the outer circumference until it bottoms in the bore **(see illustration)**.
8 Install the clutch (Chapter 8) and flywheel or driveplate and torque converter assemblies.
9 Connect the engine to the transaxle and install the flywheel/torque converter cover.
10 Install the engine in the vehicle.

21 Oil pan - removal and installation

Removal

Refer to illustration 21.4

1 Disconnect the battery negative cable.
2 Raise the front of the vehicle and support it securely on jackstands.
3 Drain the engine oil.
4 Remove the torque stopper assembly **(refer to illustration)**.
5 Remove the right front wheel and the inner fender panel.
6 Disconnect the front exhaust pipe.
7 Connect a suitable lifting device and raise the engine weight off the number 3 engine mount and unbolt and remove the mount.
8 Remove the flywheel/torque converter driveplate cover.
9 Remove the oil pan bolts.
10 Raise the front of the engine and break the oil pan gasket seal by inserting a screwdriver between the pan and the block.
11 Rotate the front of the oil pan to the left and remove it from the engine.
12 Wash the oil pan thoroughly in solvent.
13 Clean the contact surfaces of the oil pan and engine block.

Installation

14 Apply a 1/4-inch bead of RTV-type sealant to the contact surface of the oil pan.
15 Place the oil pan in position and install the retaining bolts. Tighten the bolts to the specified torque.
16 The remainder of installation is the reverse of removal.
17 After installation fill the engine with the specified amount and grade of oil, start the engine and check for leaks.

22 Engine mounts - replacement with engine in vehicle

Refer to illustration 22.1

1 The engine mounts can be replaced with

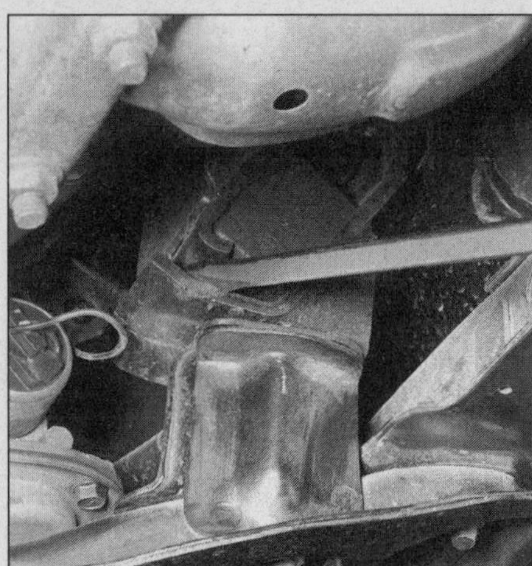

22.1 Check the condition of the engine mounts by prying on them with a bar or large screwdriver

22.6a Pry out the torque stopper rubber cover with a screwdriver

22.6b The torque stopper bolt is accessible through the hole in the inner fender

the engine/transaxle still in the vehicle. Pry on the rubber mounts with a large screwdriver or bar to determine if they have become hard, split, or separated from the metal backing **(see illustration)**.

2 Disconnect the negative cable from the battery.

3 Raise the front of the vehicle and support it securely on jackstands.

4 Support the engine with a jack.

Torque stopper

Refer to illustrations 22.6a, 22.6b and 22.7

5 Remove the right front wheel and the inner fender shield for shield for access.

6 Remove the rubber access plug and bolt **(see illustrations)**.

7 In the engine compartment, remove the bolts and lift the stopper from the engine **(see illustration)**.

Engine mounts

Refer to illustration 22.9

8 From under the vehicle remove the retaining nuts.

9 In the engine compartment, remove the retaining bolts and then lift the mount from the engine **(see illustration)**.

10 Installation is the reverse of removal.

23 Engine - removal and installation

Removal

Refer to illustrations 23.3a, 23.3b, 23.3c, 23.3d, 23.3e, 23.3f, 23.4, 23.7, 23.9, 23.23, 23.26 and 23.30

1 Remove the hood (Chapter 12).

2 Remove the battery and mount and drain the cooling system (Chapter 1).

3 Remove the air cleaner assembly **(see illustrations)**.

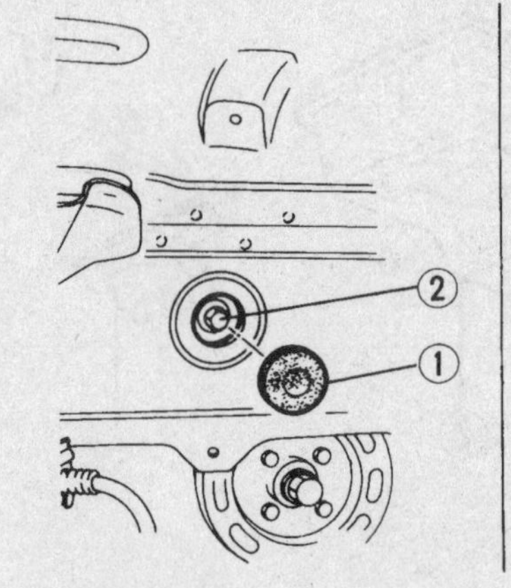

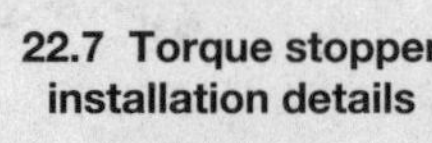

22.7 Torque stopper installation details

1 *Rubber cap*
2 *Bolts*
3 *Torque stopper*

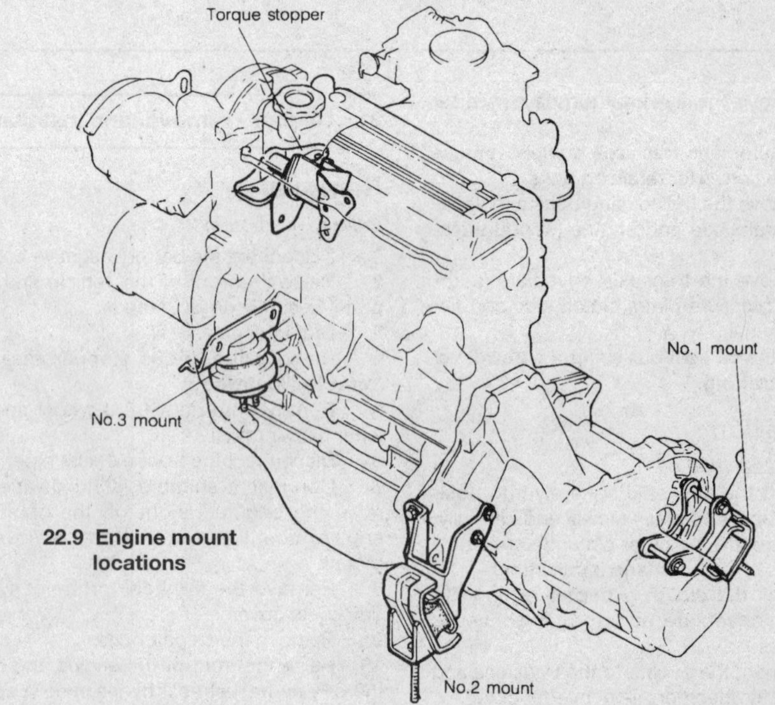

22.9 Engine mount locations

23.3a Removing the air cleaner heat hose

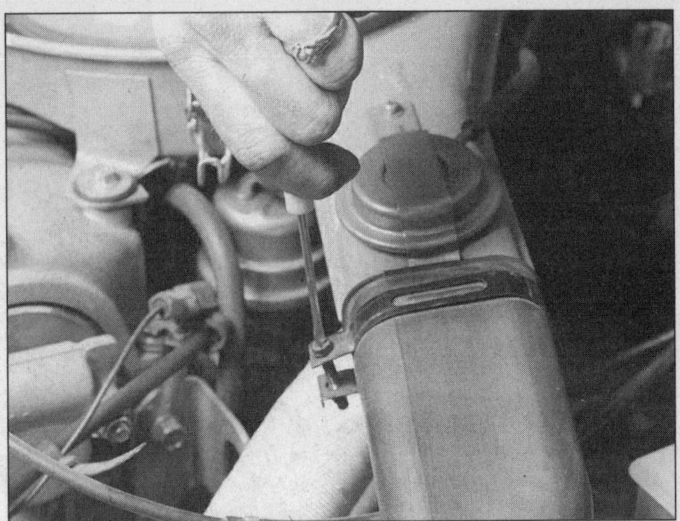
23.3b Removing the air cleaner air pipe

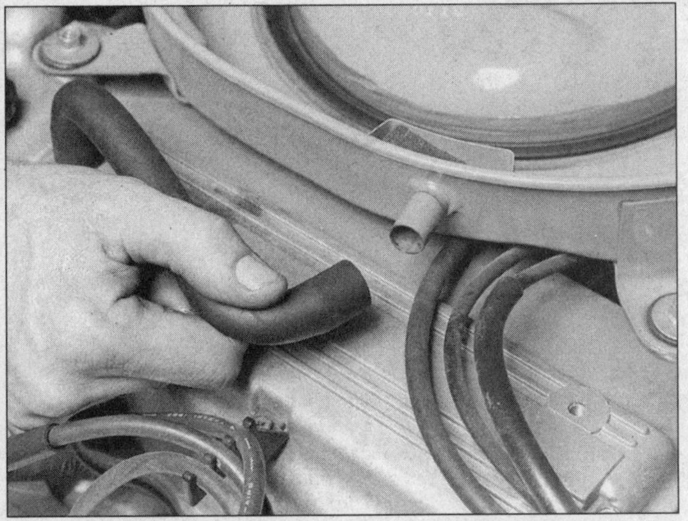
23.3c Removing the PCV hose from the air cleaner

23.3d Disconnecting the air injection hoses from the air cleaner

23.3e Removing the air cleaner-to-camshaft cover bolt

23.3f Removing the carburetor-to-air cleaner bolts

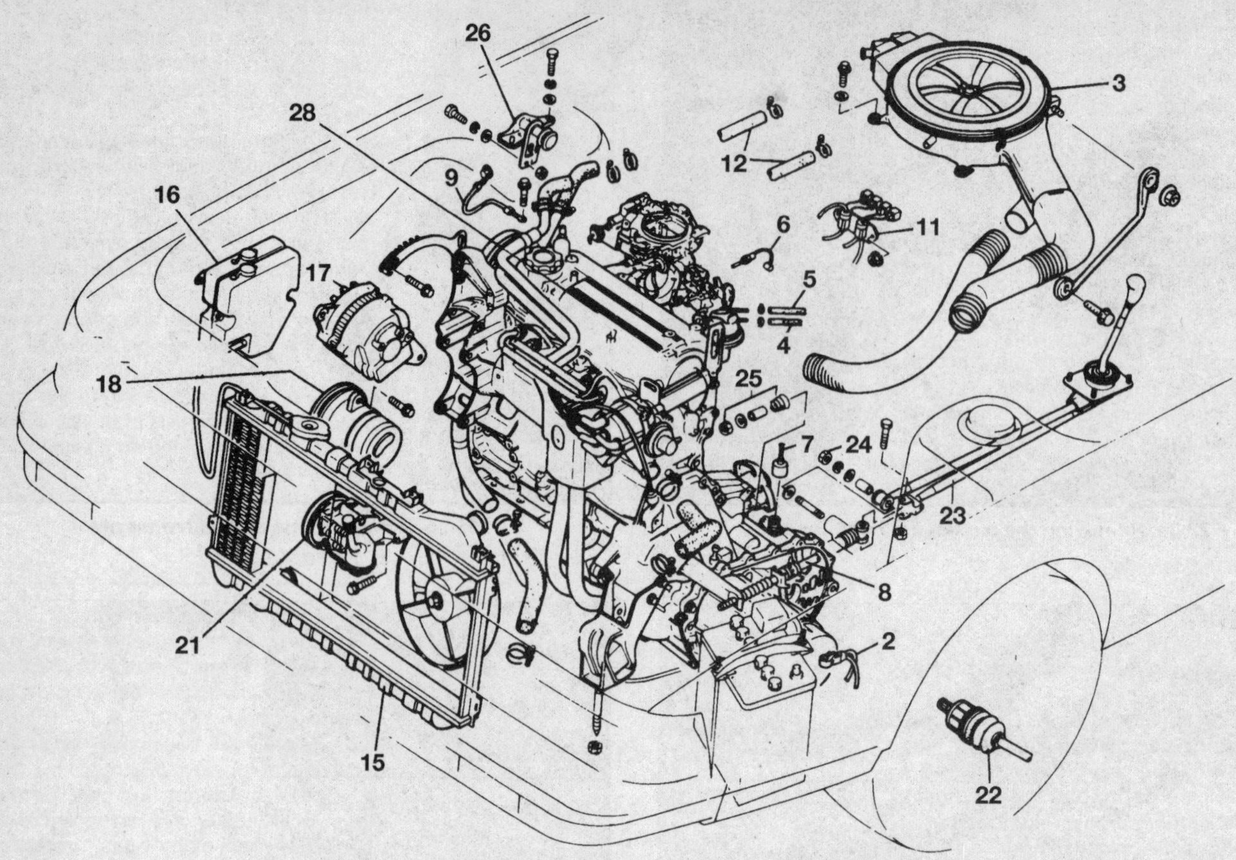

23.4 For engine removal, components listed are removed in the order shown

1 *Hood (not shown)*
2 *Battery negative cable*
3 *Air cleaner assembly*
4 *Fuel hose (carbureted model)*
5 *Fuel return hose (carbureted model)*
6 *Throttle cable*
7 *Speedometer cable*
8 *Clutch*
9 *Engine ground cable*
10 *Power brake vacuum hose (not shown)*
11 *Power steering three-way valve and bracket*
12 *Heater hoses*
13 *Engine-to-transaxle wiring (not shown)*
14 *Evaporative system vacuum hoses (not shown)*
15 *Fan and radiator*
16 *Coolant and windshield washer reservoirs*
17 *Alternator*
18 *Air conditioner compressor*
19 *Front wheels (not shown)*
20 *Splash shields (not shown)*
21 *Power steering pump*
22 *Driveaxles*
23 *Manual transaxle change rod*
24 *Manual transaxle extension bar*
25 *Exhaust system flexible joints, bolts and nuts*
26 *Torque stopper*
27 *Engine and transaxle mounting nuts (not shown)*
28 *Engine and transaxle*

23.7 Remove the shift cable pin with needle nose pliers

23.9 Slide the clamp up the hose so it won't be lost

4 Remove the fuel inlet and return lines at the fuel pump **(see illustrations)**.
5 Disconnect the throttle cable and cruise control cable (if equipped).
6 Disconnect the speedometer cable.
7 Disconnect the clutch (manual) or shift cable (automatic) **(see illustration)**.
8 Disconnect the wiring harness ground connection from the transaxle.
9 Disconnect the power brake vacuum hose **(see illustration)**.
10 Unplug the vacuum switches and remove the bracket.
11 Disconnect the heater hoses.
12 Unplug the duty solenoid and vacuum sensor and unbolt it from the firewall.
13 Unplug the wiring harness connections to the engine.
14 Unplug any remaining electrical connectors.
15 Disconnect the distributor coil wire.
16 Disconnect the evaporative system hoses from the canister.
17 Disconnect the radiator hoses and unplug the fan motor.
18 Remove the radiator (Chapter 3).
19 Remove the radiator coolant and windshield washer reservoirs.
20 Remove the alternator and (if equipped) air conditioning compressor from the bracket. Swing the compressor out of the way, taking care not to damage the hoses (which contain high pressure) and fasten it out of the way with a piece of wire.
21 Raise the front of the vehicle, support it securely on jackstands and remove the front wheels and inner fender splash shields.
22 Remove the power steering pump with the hoses still connected and fasten it out of the way in the engine compartment with a piece of wire.
23 Disconnect the driveaxles from the transaxle by prying them out with a pry bar **(see illustration)**. The joint shaft assembly must remain attached to the engine and inserted into the transaxle during engine removal or the differential will fall into the case, necessitating disassembly of the transaxle (Chapter 7).

23.23 Pry the right axleshaft out of the joint shaft housing (A)

24 Drain the transaxle (Chapter 1).
25 Disconnect the balljoints.
26 Disconnect the exhaust pipe at the muffler **(see illustration)**.
27 Remove the rubber plug and inner fender shield for access and unbolt and remove the torque stopper and drive belt covers.
28 Attach a lifting device to the engine.
29 Disconnect the engine mounts.
30 Raise the engine slowly and carefully with an assistant guiding the engine forward off the muffler studs and moving the wiring harnesses out of the way **(see illustration)**.
31 Raise the engine from the engine compartment and lower it onto suitable working surface. Separate the transaxle from the engine (Section 24). Block the engine in an upright position or mount it on an engine stand.

Installation

32 Reconnect the engine to the transaxle.
33 The front of the vehicle should remain raised to allow access from underneath during installation.
34 Position the engine directly over the engine compartment and lower it carefully and slowly into position.
35 Have an assistant guide the transaxle past the brake master cylinder and then guide the engine mounts and muffler studs into position while another assistant makes sure the power steering pump is moved out of the way as the engine is lowered.
36 The remainder of installation is the reverse of removal, referring to the appropriate Chapters for details of driveaxle insertion and reconnection of the front suspension.

24 Engine and transaxle - separation

1 Remove the starter motor.
2 Remove the joint shaft bracket bolts. The joint shaft must remain inserted into the transaxle or the differential will drop into the transaxle case.
3 Remove the transaxle torque converter cover plate.
4 Lock the starter ring gear teeth with a large screwdriver and remove the torque converter retaining bolts, rotating the crankshaft pulley with a wrench on the pulley bolt to bring each bolt into position.
5 Remove the transaxle-to-engine bolts.
6 Insert a large screwdriver between the engine and transaxle to separate them, working around the bellhousing until the transaxle can be removed. Have an assistant hold the joint shaft in the transaxle as it is moved away from the engine make sure the differential stays in place.

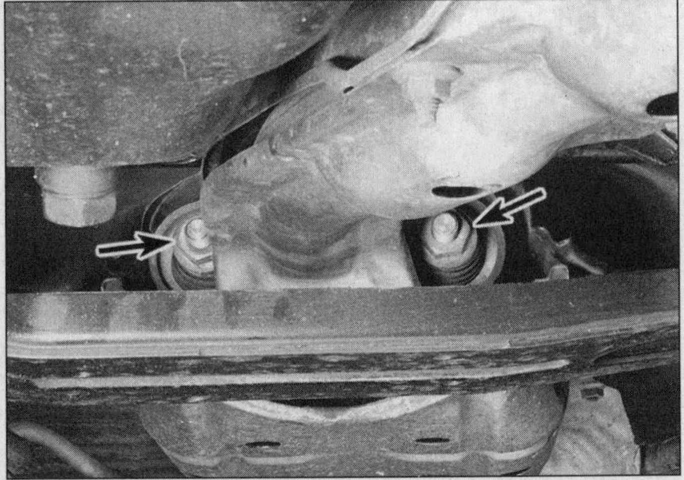

23.26 Exhaust pipe-to-muffler nuts (arrows)

23.30 Move the engine forward and then up to remove it from the engine compartment

Notes

Chapter 2 Part B General engine overhaul procedures

Contents

Specifications

Valves and related components

1987 and earlier

Valve clearance	0.012 in (0.30 mm)
Valve face angle	45°
Valve seat angle	45°
Valve head thickness (margin)	
Intake	0.020 in (0.5 mm)
Exhaust	0.039 in (1.0 mm)
Valve stem diameter	
Intake	
Standard	0.3177 to 0.3185 in (8.07 to 8.09 mm)
Service limit	0.3142 in (7.980 mm)
Exhaust	
Standard	0.3159 to 0.3165 in (8.025 to 8.040 mm)
Service limit	0.3140 in (7.975 mm)
Stem-to-guide clearance (intake and exhaust)	
Standard	0.0010 to 0.0024 in (0.025 to 0.060 mm)
Service limit	0.0079 in (0.020 mm)
Valve seat width	0.047 to 0.063 in (1.2 to 1.6 mm)
Valve seat sinking	
Standard	1.831 in (46.5 mm)
Service limit	1.890 in (48.0 mm)
Valve spring angle limit	0.071 in (1.81 mm)
Valve spring free length	
Inner	
Standard	1.800 in (45.7 mm)
Service limit	1.744 in (44.3 mm)
Outer	
Standard	2.063 in (52.4 mm)
Service limit	1.984 in (50.4 mm)
Rocker arm and shaft	
Rocker arm bore	0.6300 to 0.6310 in (16.000 to 16.027 mm)
Shaft diameter	0.6286 to 0.6293 in (15.966 to 15.984 mm)
Clearance in rocker arm	
Standard	0.0006 to 0.0024 in (0.016 to 0.061 mm)
Service limit	0.004 in (0.010 mm)

Valves and related components (continued)

1988 and later models

Valve clearance	Self adjusting
Valve seat and face angles	45°
Valve head thickness (margin)	
Intake	0.031 in (0.047 mm)
Exhaust	0.051 in (0.067 mm)
Valve stem diameter	
Intake	0.2744 to 0.2750 in (6.070 to 6.985 mm)
Exhaust	0.2742 to 0.2748 in (6.965 to 6.980 mm)
Valve seat width	0.047 to 0.063 in (1.2 to 1.6mm)
Valve seat sinking	
Standard	1.976 in (50.2 mm)
Service limit	2.008 in (51.0 mm)
Valve stem-to-guide clearance	same as 1987 and earlier models
Valve spring angle limit	0.067 in (1.7 mm)
Valve spring free length	
Intake	
Standard	1.949 in (49.5 mm)
Service limit	1.902 in (48.3 mm)
Exhaust	
Standard	1.984 in (50.4 mm)
Service limit	1.937 in (49.2 mm)
Valve guide projection	0.780 to 0.799 in (19.8 to 20.3 mm)
Rocker arm and shaft	
Rocker arm inner diameter	0.748 to 0.749 in (19.000 to 19.033 mm)
Rocker arm shaft inner diameter	0.746 to 0.747 in (18.959 to 18.980 mm)
Clearance in rocker arm	
Standard	0.0008 to 0.0029 in (0.020 to 0.074 mm)
Service limit	0.004 in (0.10 mm)

Crankshaft and connecting rods

Crankshaft end play	
Standard	0.0031 to 0.0071 in (0.08 to 0.18 mm)
Service limit	0.0118 in (0.030 mm)
Connecting rod end play (side clearance)	
Standard	0.004 to 0.010 in (0.110 to 0.262 mm)
Service limit	0.012 in (0.30 mm)
Main bearing journal diameter	
Standard	2.359 to 2.360 in (59.937 to 59.955 mm)
Service limit	0.002 in (0.05 mm)
Grinding limit	0.03 in (0.75 mm)
Main bearing oil clearance	
Standard	0.0012 to 0.0019 in (0.031 to 0.049 mm)
Service limit	0.0031 in (0.08 mm)
Connecting rod bearing journal diameter	
Standard	2.005 to 2.006 in (50.940 to 50.955 mm)
Service limit	0.0020 in (0.05 mm)
Grinding limit	0.03 in (0.75 mm)
Connecting rod wrist pin bore diameter	0.8640 to 0.8646 in (21.943 to 21.961 mm)
Connecting rod bearing oil clearance	
Standard	0.0010 to 0.0026 in (0.027 to 0.067 mm)
Service limit	0.0039 in (0.10 mm)
Crankshaft journal taper/out-of-round limit	0.0020 in (0.05 mm)
Crankshaft runout limit	0.0012 in (0.03 mm)

Engine block

Cylinder bore diameter	
2.0/2.2 liter	3.3859 to 3.3866 in (86.000 to 86.019 mm)
1.6 liter	3.1890 to 3.1897 in (81.000 to 81.019 mm)
Service limit	0.060 in (0.15 mm)
Difference between cylinder bore service limit	0.0007 in (0.019 mm)
Deck warpage limit	0.006 in (0.15 mm)

Pistons and rings

Piston diameter	
2.0/2.2 liter	3.3837 to 3.3845 in (85.944 to 85.964 mm)
1.6 liter	3.1868 to 3.1876 in (80.944 to 80.964 mm)
Piston-to-bore clearance	0.0014 to 0.0030 in (0.036 to 0.075 mm)

Ring groove width	
Top and second	0.059 to 0.060 in (1.52 to 1.54 mm)
Oil	0.1583 to 0.1591 in (4.02 to 4.04 mm)
Piston ring-to-groove clearance	
Top and second	0.0012 to 0.0028 in (0.03 to 0.07 mm)
Service limit	0.006 (0.015 mm)
Piston ring end gap	
Top	0.008 to 0.014 in (0.2 to 0.3 mm)
Second	0.006 to 0.012 in (0.15 to 0.3 mm)
Oil	0.012 to 0.035 in (0.3 to 0.9 mm)
Service limit	0.039 in (1.0 mm)
Piston pin diameter	0.8651 to 0.8654 in (21.974 to 21.980 mm)
Pin-to-piston clearance	Loose - 0 to 0.0009 in (0 to 0.024 mm)
Pin-to-rod clearance	Press fit

Camshaft

Runout	0.0012 in (0.03 mm)
Endplay	0.003 to 0.006 in (0.08 to 0.016 mm)
Service limit	0.008 in (0.20 mm)
Bearing journal diameter	
Front (number 1)	1.257 to 1.258 in (31.940 to 31.965 in
Center (number 2, 3, 4)	1.256 to 1.257 in (31.910 to 31.935 mm)
Rear (number 5)	1.257 to 1.258 in (31.940 to 31.965 mm)
Service limit	0.002 in (0.05 mm)
Bearing oil clearance	
Front (number 1)	0.0014 to 0.0033 in (0.035 to 0.085 mm)
Center (number 2, 3, 4)	0.0026 to 0.0045 in (0.065 to 0.115 mm)
Rear (number 5)	0.0014 to 0.0033 in (0.035 to 0.085 mm)
Service limit	0.0059 in (0.015 mm)
Lobe lift	
Intake	1.5023 in (38.157 mm)
Service limit	1.4944 in (37.957 mm)
Exhaust	1.5024 in (38.160 mm)
Service limit	1.4945 in (37.960 mm)

General

Compression pressure	
Standard	164 psi at 270 rpm
Minimum	115 psi at 270 rpm
Cylinder numbers	1-2-3-4 (front-to-rear)
Firing order	1-3-4-2

Torque specifications

	Ft-lbs	M-kg
Alternator bracket-to-engine bolt	27 to 46	3.7 to 6.3
Alternator adjusting bolt	14 to 25	1.9 to 3.5
Cylinder head bolt		
Engine warm	69 to 80	9.5 to 11.0
Engine cold	59 to 64	8.2 to 8.8
Main bearing cap bolt	61 to 65	8.3 to 8.9
Clutch plate bolt	71 to 96	9.8 to 13.2
Connecting rod nut	37 to 41	5.1 to 5.6
Camshaft pulley bolt	35 to 48	4.8 to 6.6
Camshaft cap bolt	13 to 20	1.8 to 2.8
Camshaft cover bolt	2 to 3	0.28 to 0.41
Crankshaft pulley bolt	8 to 11	1.1 to 1.5
Exhaust manifold bolt	16 to 21	2.2 to 2.9
Engine mount bolts		
Number 1 engine mount-to-transaxle	27 to 38	3.7 to 5.2
Number 1 engine mount-to-body	32 to 40	4.4 to 5.5
Number 2 engine mount-to-transaxle	27 to 38	3.7 to 5.2
Number 2 engine mount-to-body	32 to 40	4.4 to 5.5
Number 3 engine mount-to-body	32 to 40	4.4 to 5.5
Number 3 engine mount-to-engine	41 to 59	5.7 to 8.1
Flywheel bolt	71 to 76	9.8 to 10.5
Intake manifold bolt	14 to 19	1.9 to 2.6
Oil pan bolt	5 to 9	0.7 to 1.2
Timing belt pulley bolt		
1983 through 1984	108 to 116	14.9 to 16.0
1985 on	80 to 87	11.0 to 12.0
Timing belt tensioner lockbolt	27 to 38	3.9 to 5.2

Torque specifications

	Ft-lbs	M-kg
Torque stopper-to-engine bolt	49 to 56	6.8 to 7.7
Torque stopper-to-body bolt	40 to 50	5.5 to 6.9
Oil pressure switch	9 to 13	1.2 to 1.8
Water bypass hose clamp	14 to 25	1.9 to 3.5
Water inlet pipe assembly-to-water pump bolt	14 to 19	1.9 to 2.6
Water inlet pipe bracket-to-engine bolt	28 to 38	3.9 to 5.2

1 General information

Included in this portion of Chapter 2 are the general overhaul procedures for the cylinder head and internal engine components. The information ranges from advice concerning preparation for an overhaul and the purchase of replacement parts to detailed, step-by-step procedures covering removal and installation of internal engine components and the inspection of parts.

The following Sections have been written based on the assumption that the engine has been removed from the vehicle. For information concerning in-vehicle engine repair, as well as removal and installation of the external components necessary for the overhaul, see Part A of this Chapter and Section 2 of this Part.

The specifications included here in Part B are only that necessary for the inspection procedures, which follow. Refer to Part A for additional specifications.

2 Repair operations possible with the engine in the vehicle

Many major repair operations can be accomplished without removing the engine from the vehicle.

It is a very good idea to clean the engine compartment and the exterior of the engine with some type of pressure washer before any work is begun. A clean engine will make the job easier and will prevent the possibility of getting dirt into internal areas of the engine.

Remove the hood (Chapter 11) and cover the fenders to provide as much working room as possible and to prevent damage to the painted surfaces.

If oil or coolant leaks develop, indicating a need for gasket or seal replacement, the repairs can generally be made with the engine in the vehicle. The oil pan gasket, the cylinder head gasket, intake and exhaust manifold gaskets, timing cover gaskets and the front crankshaft oil seal are accessible with the engine in place.

Exterior engine components, such as the water pump, the starter motor, the alternator, the distributor, the fuel pump and the carburetor, as well as the intake and exhaust manifolds, are quite easily removed for repair with the engine in place.

Since the cylinder head can be removed without pulling the engine, valve component servicing can also be accomplished with the engine in the vehicle.

Replacement of, repairs to or inspection of the timing sprockets and belt and the oil pump and front cover seals are all possible with the engine in place.

In extreme cases caused by a lack of necessary equipment, repair or replacement of piston rings, pistons, connecting rods and rod bearings and reconditioning of the cylinder bores is possible with the engine in the vehicle. However, this practice is not recommended because of the cleaning and preparation work that must be done to the components involved.

Detailed removal, inspection, repair and installation procedures for the above mentioned components can be found in the appropriate Part of Chapter 2 or the other Chapters in this manual.

3 Engine overhaul - general information

It is not always easy to determine when, or if, an engine should be completely overhauled, as a number of factors must be considered.

High mileage is not necessarily an indication that an overhaul is needed, while low mileage does not preclude the need for an overhaul. Frequency of servicing is probably the most important consideration. An engine that has had regular and frequent oil and filter changes, as well as other required maintenance, will most likely give many thousands of miles of reliable service. Conversely, a neglected engine may require an overhaul very early in its life.

Excessive oil consumption is an indication that piston rings and/or valve guides are in need of attention. Make sure that oil leaks are not responsible before deciding that the rings and guides are bad. Have a cylinder compression or leakdown test performed by an experienced tune-up mechanic to determine the extent of the work required.

If the engine is making obvious knocking or rumbling noises, the connecting rod and/or main bearings are probably at fault. Check the oil pressure with a gauge installed in place of the oil pressure sending unit and compare it to the Specifications. If it is extremely low, the bearings and/or oil pump are probably worn out.

Loss of power, rough running, excessive valve train noise and high fuel consumption rates may also point to the need for an overhaul, especially if they are all present at the same time. If a complete tune-up does not remedy the situation, major mechanical work is the only solution.

An engine overhaul involves restoring the internal parts to the specifications of a new engine. During an overhaul, the piston rings are replaced and the cylinder walls are reconditioned (rebored and/or honed). If a rebore is done, new pistons are required. The main and connecting rod bearings are replaced with new ones and, if necessary, the crankshaft may be reground to restore the journals. Generally, the valves are serviced as well, since they are usually in less-than-perfect condition at this point. While the engine is being overhauled, other components, such as the carburetor, distributor, starter and alternator, can be rebuilt as well. The end result should be a like new engine that will give many trouble free miles.

Before beginning the engine overhaul, read through the entire procedure to familiarize yourself with the scope and requirements of the job. Overhauling an engine is not difficult, but it is time consuming. Plan on the vehicle being tied up for a minimum of two weeks, especially if parts must be taken to an automotive machine shop for repair or reconditioning. Check on availability of parts and make sure that any necessary special tools and equipment are obtained in advance. Most work can be done with typical hand tools, although a number of precision measuring tools are required for inspecting parts to determine if they must be replaced. Often an automotive machine shop will handle the inspection of parts and offer advice concerning reconditioning and replacement. **Note:** *Always wait until the engine has been completely disassembled and all components, especially the engine block, have been inspected before deciding what service and repair operations must be performed by an automotive machine shop.* Since the block's condition will be the major factor to consider when determining whether to overhaul the original engine or buy a rebuilt one, never purchase parts or have machine work done on other components until the block has been thoroughly inspected. As a general rule, time is the primary cost of an overhaul, so it does not pay to install worn or substandard parts.

As a final note, to ensure maximum life and minimum trouble from a rebuilt engine, everything must be assembled with care in a spotlessly clean environment.

4 Engine rebuilding alternatives

The do-it-yourselfer is faced with a number of options when performing an engine overhaul. The decision to replace the engine block, piston/connecting rod assemblies and crankshaft depends on a number of factors, with the number one consideration being the condition of the block. Other considerations are cost, access to machine shop facilities, parts availability, time required to complete the project and experience.

Some of the rebuilding alternatives include:

Individual parts - If the inspection procedures reveal that the engine block and most engine components are in reusable condition, purchasing individual parts may be the most economical alternative. The block, crankshaft and piston/connecting rod assemblies should all be inspected carefully. Even if the block shows little wear, the cylinder bores should receive a finish hone.

Crankshaft kit - This rebuild package consists of a reground crankshaft and a matched set of pistons and connecting rods. The pistons will already be installed on the connecting rods. Piston rings and the necessary bearings will be included in the kit. These kits are commonly available for standard cylinder bores, as well as for engine blocks that have been bored to a regular oversize.

Short block - A short block consists of an engine block with a crankshaft and piston/connecting rod assemblies already installed. All new bearings are incorporated and all clearances will be correct. The existing camshaft, valve train components, cylinder head and external parts can be bolted to the short block with little or no machine shop work necessary.

Long block - A long block consists of a short block plus an oil pump, oil pan, cylinder head, rocker arm cover, camshaft and valve train components, timing sprockets and belt and timing belt cover. All components are installed with new bearings, seals and gaskets incorporated throughout. The installation of manifolds and external parts is all that is necessary.

Give careful thought to which alternative is best for you and discuss the situation with local automotive machine shops, auto parts dealers or parts store countermen before ordering or purchasing replacement parts.

5 Engine removal - methods and precautions

If it has been decided that an engine must be removed for overhaul or major repair work, certain preliminary steps should be taken.

Locating a suitable work area is extremely important. A shop is, of course, the most desirable place to work. Adequate work space, along with storage space for the vehicle, is very important. If a shop or garage is not available, at the very least a flat, level, clean work surface made of concrete or asphalt is required.

Cleaning the engine compartment and engine prior to removal will help keep tools clean and organized.

An engine hoist or A-frame will also be necessary. Make sure that the equipment is rated in excess of the combined weight of the engine and its accessories. Safety is of primary importance, considering the potential hazards involved in lifting the engine out of the vehicle.

If a novice is removing the engine, a helper should be available. Advice and aid from someone more experienced would also be helpful. There are many instances when one person cannot simultaneously perform all of the operations required when lifting the engine out of the vehicle.

Plan the operation ahead of time. Arrange for or obtain all of the tools and equipment you will need prior to beginning the job. Some of the equipment necessary to perform engine removal and installation safely and with relative ease are (in addition to an engine hoist) a heavy duty floor jack, complete sets of wrenches and sockets as described in the front of this manual, wooden blocks and plenty of rags and cleaning solvent for mopping up the inevitable spills. If the hoist is to be rented, make sure that you arrange for it in advance and perform beforehand all of the operations possible without it. This will save you money and time.

Plan for the vehicle to be out of use for a considerable amount of time. A machine shop will be required to perform some of the work that the do-it-yourselfer cannot accomplish due to a lack of special equipment. These shops often have a busy schedule, so it would be wise to consult them before removing the engine in order to accurately estimate the amount of time required to rebuild or repair components that may need work.

Always use extreme caution when removing and installing the engine. Serious injury can result from careless actions. Plan ahead. Take your time and a job of this nature, although major, can be accomplished successfully.

6 Engine overhaul - disassembly sequence

1 It is much easier to disassemble and work on the engine if it is mounted on a portable engine stand. These stands can often be rented for a reasonable fee from an equipment rental yard. Before the engine is mounted on a stand, the flywheel/driveplate should be removed from the engine (refer to Chapter 8).

2 If a stand is not available, it is possible to disassemble the engine with it blocked up on a sturdy workbench or on the floor. Be extra careful not to tip or drop the engine when working without a stand.

3 If you are going to obtain a rebuilt engine, all external components must come off first in order to be transferred to the replacement engine, just as they will if you are doing a complete engine overhaul yourself. These include:

Alternator and brackets
Emissions control components
Distributor, spark plug wires and spark plugs
Thermostat and housing cover
Water pump
Carburetor
Intake/exhaust manifolds
Oil filter
Fuel pump
Engine mounts
Flywheel/driveplate

Note: *When removing the external components from the engine, pay close attention to details that may be helpful or important during installation. Note the installed position of gaskets, seals, spacers, pins, washers, bolts and other small items.*

4 If you are obtaining a short block, which consists of the engine block, crankshaft, pistons and connecting rods all assembled, then the cylinder head, oil pan and oil pump will have to be removed as well. See Engine rebuilding alternatives for additional information regarding the different possibilities to be considered.

5 If you are planning a complete overhaul, the engine must be disassembled and the internal components removed in the following order:

Timing belt cover
Timing belt
Camshaft cover
Front and rear housings
Cylinder head and camshaft
Oil pan
Oil pump
Piston/connecting rod assemblies
Crankshaft

6 Before beginning the disassembly and overhaul procedures, make sure the following items are available:

Common hand tools
Small cardboard boxes or plastic bags for storing parts
Gasket scraper
Ridge reamer
Vibration damper puller
Micrometers
Telescoping gauges
Dial indicator set
Valve spring compressor
Cylinder surfacing hone
Piston ring groove cleaning tool
Electric drill motor
Tap and die set
Wire brushes
Cleaning solvent

7.2 After removing the valve components, store them together in a plastic bag to keep from mixing them in with the components from other valves

7.3a Use a valve spring compressor to compress the spring and remove the keepers from the valve stem

7.3b If the valve stem won't pull through the guide without binding, the head of the valve is probably mushroomed slightly, which can be corrected by deburring the top of the valve stem with a small file

8.2 Use a gasket scraper to remove all old gasket material. Use a shop towel underneath to keep old gasket material from falling down into the engine

8.5a Use a tap to remove old sealer and rust from all bolt and stud holes

8.5b After tapping out bolt and stud holes, compressed air should be used to blow out the debris left by the cleaning operation

7 Cylinder head - disassembly

Note: *New and rebuilt cylinder heads are commonly available for most engines at dealerships and auto parts stores. Due to the fact that some specialized tools are necessary for the disassembly and inspection procedures, and replacement parts may not be readily available, it may be more practical and economical for the home mechanic to purchase a replacement head rather than taking the time to disassemble, inspect and recondition the original head.*

Refer to illustrations 7.2, 7.3a and 7.3b

1 Cylinder head disassembly involves removal and disassembly of the intake and exhaust valves and their related components. If they are still in place, remove the camshaft and rocker arm assembly from the cylinder head. Label the parts or store them separately so they can be reinstalled in their original locations.

2 Before the valves are removed, arrange to label and store them, along with their related components, so they can be kept separate and reinstalled in the same valve guides they are removed from **(see illustration)**.

3 Compress the valve spring on the first valve with a spring compressor and remove the keepers **(see illustration)**. Carefully release the valve spring compressor and remove the keeper, the retainer, the springs, the valve stem seal and the valve from the head. If the valve binds in the guide (won't pull through), push it back into the head and deburr the area around the keeper groove with a fine file or whetstone **(see illustration)**.

4 Repeat the procedure for the remaining valves. Remember to keep together all the parts for each valve so they can be reinstalled in the same locations.

5 Once the valves have been removed and safely stored, the head should be thoroughly cleaned and inspected. If a complete engine overhaul is being done, finish the engine disassembly procedures before beginning the cylinder head cleaning and inspection process.

8 Cylinder head - cleaning and inspection

1 Thorough cleaning of the cylinder head and related valve train components, followed by a detailed inspection, will enable you to decide how much valve service work must be done during the engine overhaul.

Cleaning

Refer to illustrations 8.2, 8.5a, 8.5b and 8.6

2 Scrape away all traces of old gasket material and sealing compound from the head gasket, intake manifold and exhaust manifold sealing surfaces **(see illustration)**. Be very careful not to gouge the soft aluminum of the cylinder head. Special gasket removal solvents are available at auto parts stores that dissolve the gasket, making removal much easier.

3 Remove any built up scale around the coolant passages.

4 Run a stiff wire brush through the oil holes to remove any deposits that may have

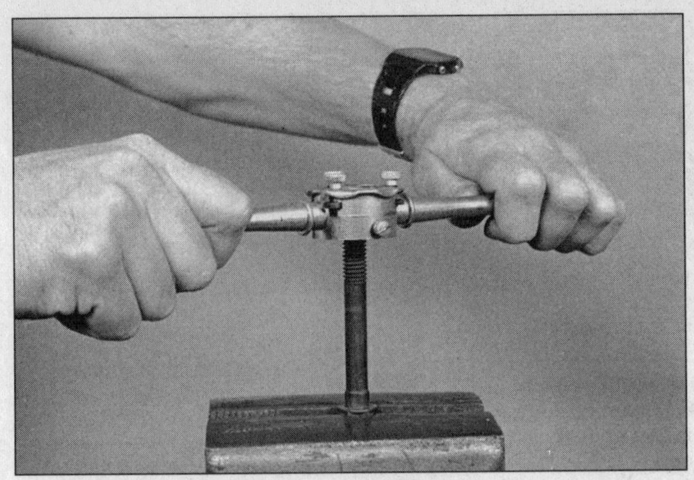

8.6 A die can be use to clean sealant from bolt threads

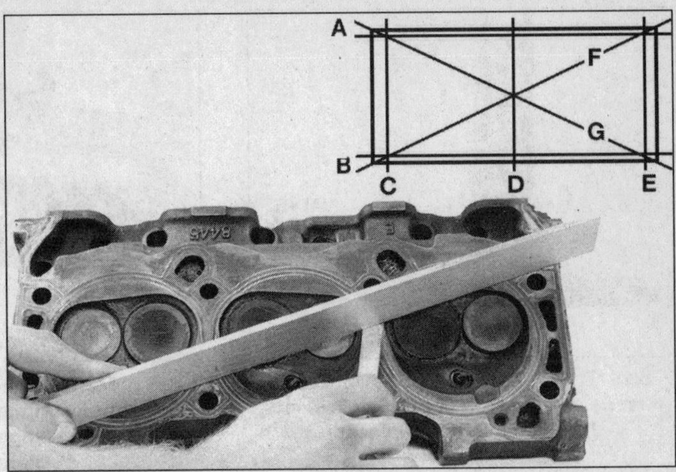

8.12 Check the cylinder head for warpage with a straightedge and feeler gauge on the lines shown

formed in them.

5 Run an appropriate size tap into each of the threaded holes to remove any corrosion and thread sealant that may be present **(see illustration)**. If compressed air is available, use it to clear the holes of debris produced by this operation **(see illustration)**.

6 Clean the exhaust and intake manifold stud threads with an appropriate size die **(see illustration)**. Clean the rocker arm pivot bolt or stud threads with a wire brush.

7 Clean the cylinder head with solvent and dry it thoroughly. Compressed air will speed the drying process and ensure that all holes and recessed areas are clean. **Note:** *Decarbonizing chemicals are available and may prove very useful when cleaning cylinder heads and valve train components. They are very caustic and should be used with caution. Be sure to follow the instructions on the container.*

8 Clean the rocker arms and shafts thoroughly. Compressed air will speed the drying process and can be used to clean out the oil passages.

9 Clean all the valve springs, keepers and retainers with solvent and dry them thoroughly. Do the components from one valve at a time to avoid mixing up the parts.

10 Scrape off any heavy deposits that may have formed on the valves, then use a motorized wire brush to remove deposits from the valve heads and stems. Again, make sure the valves do not get mixed up.

Inspection

Cylinder head

Refer to illustrations 8.12, 8.14a and 8.14b

11 Inspect the head very carefully for cracks, evidence of coolant leakage or other damage. If cracks are found, a new cylinder head should be obtained.

12 Using a straightedge and feeler gauge, check the head gasket mating surface for warpage. If the warpage exceeds 0.006-inch over the length of the head, it can be resurfaced at an automotive machine shop **(see illustrations)**.

13 Examine the valve seats in each of the combustion chambers. If they are pitted, cracked or burned, the head will require valve service that is beyond the scope of the home mechanic.

14 Check the valve stem to valve guide clearance. Use a dial indicator to measure the lateral movement of each valve stem with the valve in the guide and approximately 1/16-inch off the seat **(see illustrations)**. If, after this check, there is still some doubt as to the condition of the valve guides, the exact clearance and condition of the guides can be checked by an automotive machine shop, usually for a very small fee.

Rocker arm components

Refer to illustration 8.16

15 Check the rocker arm faces where they contact the camshaft and valve stems for pits, wear and rough spots. Check the rocker shaft contact areas as well.

16 Inspect the rocker shaft sliding surfaces for scuffing and excessive wear. Measure the rocker shaft and rocker arm contact surfaces to determine if the clearance is within specifications **(see illustration)**.

17 Any damaged or excessively worn parts must be replaced with new ones.

2B

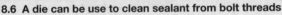

8.14a Mount a dial indicator on the head with the stem against the valve just above the valve guide, lift the valve slightly off the seat, then rock it back and forth to check for valve stem-to-guide clearance

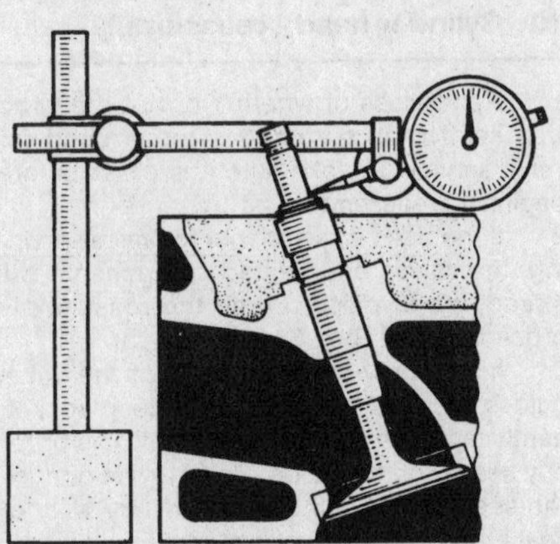

8.14b A dial indicator can be used to determine stem-to-guide clearance

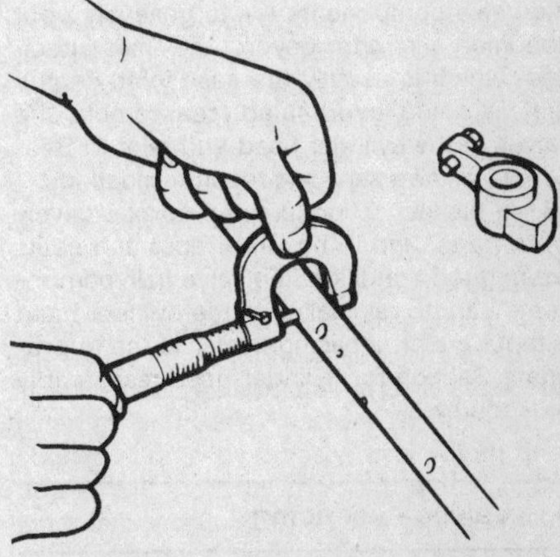

8.16 Measure the rocker arm shaft and rocker arm bore to determine clearance

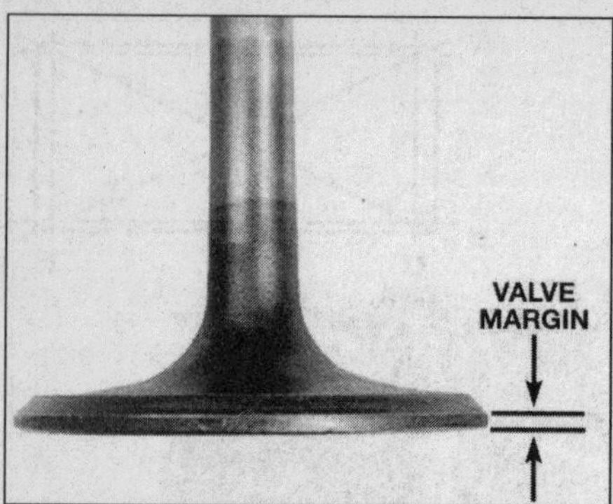

8.19 The margin width on each valve must be as specified (if no margin exists, the valve must be replaced)

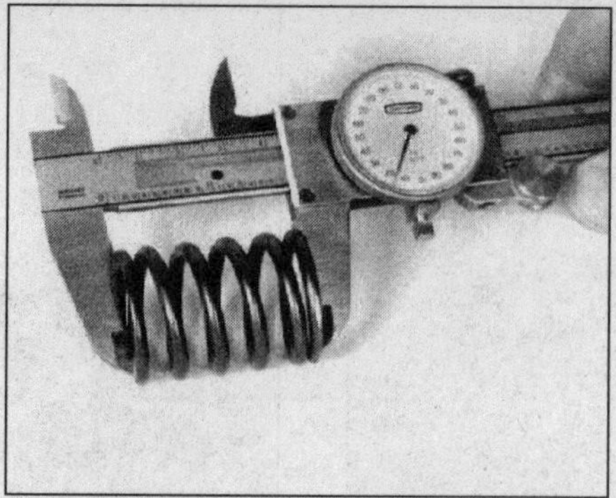
8.20a Measure the free length of each valve spring with a dial caliper. Springs that have sagged in use should be replaced

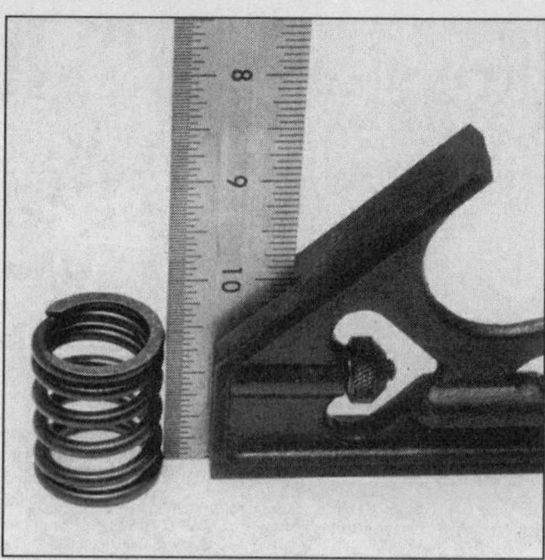
8.20b Check each valve spring for squareness and replace any which have sagged off center

Valves

Refer to illustration 8.19

18 Carefully inspect each valve face for cracks, pits and burned spots. Check the valve stem and neck for cracks. Rotate the valve and check for any obvious indication that it is bent. Check the end of the stem for pits and excessive wear. The presence of any of these conditions indicates the need for valve service by an automotive machine shop.

19 Measure the width of the valve margin on each valve and compare it to Specifications **(see illustration)**. Any valve with a margin narrower than specified will have to be replaced with a new one.

Valve components

Refer to illustrations 8.20a and 8.20b

20 Check each valve spring for wear (on the ends) and pits. Measure the free length and compare it to the Specifications **(see illustration)**. Any springs that are shorter than specified have sagged and should not be reused. Stand the spring on a flat surface and check it for squareness **(see illustration)**.

21 Check the spring retainers and keepers for obvious wear and cracks. Any questionable parts should be replaced with new ones, as extensive damage will occur in the event of failure during engine operation.

22 If the inspection process indicates that the valve components are in generally poor condition and worn beyond the limits specified, which is usually the case in an engine that is being overhauled, reassemble the valves in the cylinder head and refer to Section 9 for valve servicing recommendations.

23 If the inspection turns up no excessively worn parts, and if the valve faces and seats are in good condition, the valve train components can be reinstalled in the cylinder head without major servicing. Refer to the appropriate Section for cylinder head reassembly procedures.

9 Valves - servicing

1 Because of the complex nature of the job and the special tools and equipment needed, servicing of the valves, the valve seats and the valve guides, commonly known as a valve job, is best left to a professional.

2 The home mechanic can remove and disassemble the head, do the initial cleaning and inspection, then reassemble and deliver the head to a dealer service department or an automotive machine shop for the actual valve servicing.

3 The dealer service department, or automotive machine shop, will remove the valves and springs, recondition or replace the valves and valve seats, recondition the valve guides, check and replace the valve springs, spring retainers and keepers (as necessary), replace the valve seals with new ones, reassemble the valve components and make sure the installed spring height is correct. The cylinder head gasket surface will also be resurfaced if it is warped.

4 After the valve job has been performed by a professional, the head will be in like new condition. When the head is returned, be sure to clean it again before installation on the engine to remove any metal particles and abrasive grit that may still be present from the valve service or head resurfacing operations. Use compressed air, if available, to blow out all the oil holes and passages.

10 Cylinder head - reassembly

1 Regardless of whether or not the head was sent to an automotive repair shop for valve servicing, make sure it is clean before beginning reassembly.

2 If the head was sent out for valve servicing, the valves and related components will already be in place. Begin the reassembly procedure with Step 6.

3 Install new seals on each of the valve guides. Using a hammer and a deep socket, gently tap each seal into place until it is properly seated on the guide. Do not twist or cock the seals during installation or they will not seal properly on the valve stems.

4 Install the valves, taking care not to damage the new valve stem oil seals, drop the valve spring shim(s) around the valve guide boss and set the valve spring, cap and retainer in place.

11.1 A ridge reamer must be used to remove the wear ridge at the top of each cylinder before the pistons can be removed

5 Compress the spring with a valve compressor tool and install the keepers. Release the compressor, making sure the keepers are seated properly in the valve stem upper groove. If necessary, grease can be used to hold the keepers in place until the compressor is released.

6 Install the camshaft (Chapter 2, Part A).

7 Lubricate the rocker arm and shaft assembly with clean engine oil. Install the assembly and tighten the bolts to the specified torque (Chapter 2, Part A).

11 Piston/connecting rod assembly - removal

Refer to illustrations 11.1, 11.2, 11.4, 11.5a, 11.5b, 11.6 and 11.7

1 Using a ridge reamer, completely remove the ridge at the top of each cylinder. Follow the manufacturer's instructions provided with the ridge reaming tool **(see illus-**

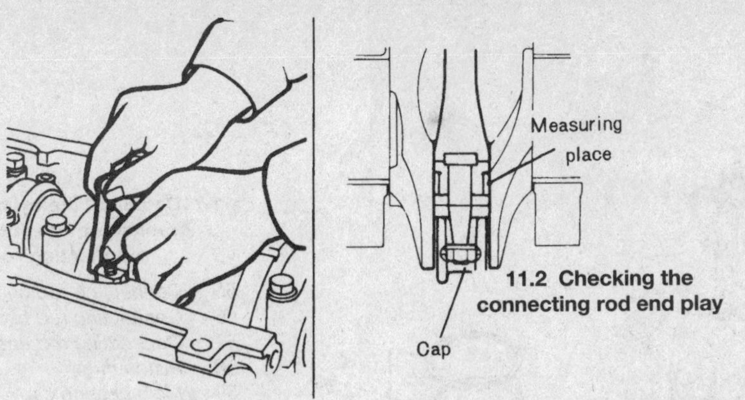

11.2 Checking the connecting rod end play

tration). Failure to remove the ridge before attempting to remove the piston/connecting rod assemblies will result in piston breakage.

2 Before the connecting rods are removed, check the end play. Mount a dial indicator with its stem in line with the crankshaft and touching the side of the number one connecting rod cap **(see illustration)**.

3 Push the connecting rod backward, as far as possible, and zero the dial indicator. Next, push the connecting rod all the way to the front and check the reading on the dial indicator. The distance that it moves is the end play. If the end play exceeds the service limit, a new connecting rod will be required. Repeat the procedure for the remaining connecting rods.

4 An alternative method is to slip feeler gauges between the connecting rod and the crankshaft throw until the play is removed **(see illustration)**. The end play is equal to the thickness of the feeler gauge.

5 Check the connecting rods and connecting rod caps for identification marks. If they are not plainly marked, identify each rod and cap, using a small punch to make the appropriate number of indentations to indicate the cylinders they are associated with **(see illustrations)**.

6 Loosen each of the connecting rod cap nuts 1/2-turn. Remove the number one connecting rod cap and bearing insert. Do not drop the bearing insert out of the cap. Slip a short length of plastic or rubber hose over each connecting rod cap bolt to protect the crankshaft journal and cylinder wall when the piston is removed **(see illustration)** and push the connecting rod/piston assembly out through the top of the engine. Use a wooden tool to push on the upper bearing insert in the connecting rod. If resistance is felt, double-check to make sure that all of the ridge was removed from the cylinder.

11.4 A feeler gauge slipped between the side of the rod and the machined face of the crankshaft measures the rod side clearance

11.5a Use a centerpunch to identify the rods before removing them from the block

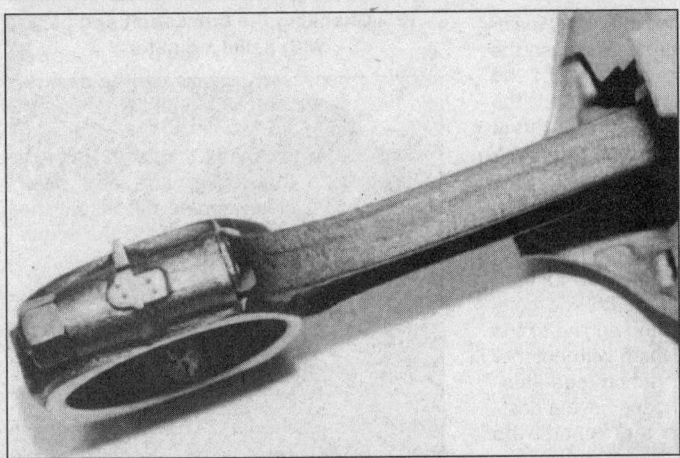
11.5b The centerpunch marks should indicate the number of the cylinder the rod came out of, and the marks should be made on both the cap and rod to prevent mix-ups and to make sure the cap goes on the right way

11.6 To keep the crankshaft and cylinder walls from being scratched by the rod bolt threads, slip sections of fuel line hose over the bolts before attempting to remove the rods

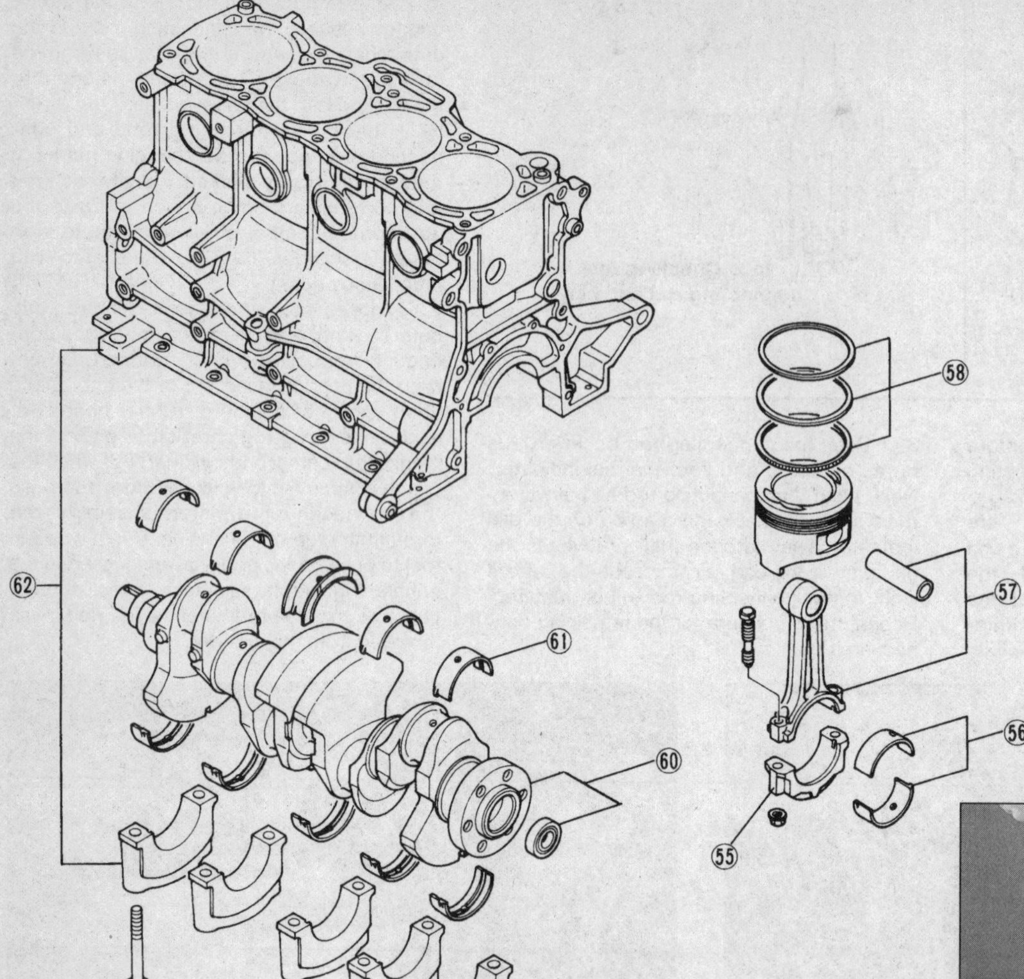

11.7 Details of the cylinder block, crankshaft, bearings and connecting rod

55 *Connecting rod cap*
56 *Connecting rod bearings*
57 *Connecting rod and wrist pin*
58 *Piston rings*
59 *Main bearing cap*
60 *Crankshaft and pilot bearing*
61 *Main bearing*
62 *Cylinder block*

7 Repeat the procedure for the remaining cylinders **(see illustration)**. After removal, reassemble the connecting rod caps and bearing inserts in their respective connecting rods and install the cap nuts finger tight. Leaving the old bearing inserts in place until reassembly will help prevent the connecting rod bearing surfaces from being accidentally nicked or gouged.

12 Crankshaft - removal

Refer to illustrations 12.2, 12.3, 12.4a, 12.4b and 12.6

1 Before the crankshaft is removed, check the end play. Mount a dial indicator with the stem in line with the crankshaft and just touching one of the crank throws **(see illustration)**.

2 Push the crankshaft all the way to the rear and zero the dial indicator. Next, pry the crankshaft to the front as far as possible and check the reading on the dial indicator. The distance that it moves is the end play. If it is greater than specified, check the crankshaft thrust surfaces for wear. If no wear is apparent, new main bearings should correct the endplay.

3 If a dial indicator is not available, feeler gauges can be used. Gently pry or push the crankshaft all the way to the front of the engine. Slip feeler gauges between the crankshaft and the front face of the thrust (center) main bearing to determine the clearance **(see illustration)**.

4 Loosen each of the main bearing cap bolts 1/4-turn at a time, until they can be removed by hand. Check the main bearing caps to see if they are marked as to their locations. They are usually numbered consecutively from the front of the engine to the rear. If they are not, mark them with number stamping dies or a center punch **(see illustration)**. The main bearing caps have a cast-in arrow, which points to the front of the engine **(see illustration)**.

5 Gently tap the caps with a soft-face hammer, then separate them from the engine block. If necessary, use the main bearing cap bolts as levers to remove the caps. Try not to

12.2 Checking the crankshaft end play with a dial indicator

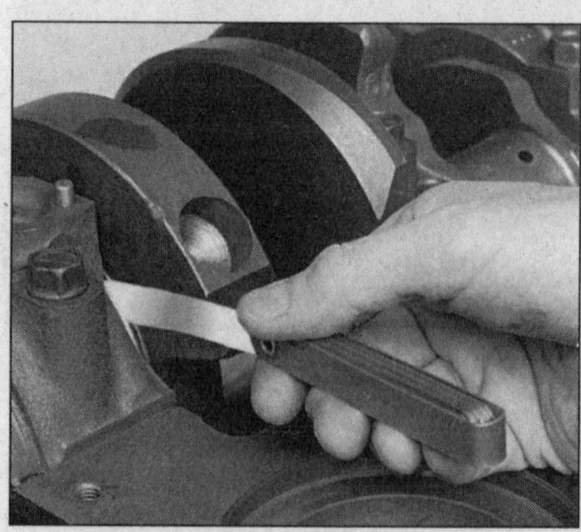

12.3 Crankshaft end play is measured by inserting a feeler gauge between the machined face of the crankshaft and the thrust bearing

drop the bearing insert if it comes out with the cap.

6 Carefully lift the crankshaft out of the engine. It is a good idea to have an assistant available, since the crankshaft is quite heavy. With the bearing inserts in place in the engine block and in the main bearing caps, return the caps to their respective locations on the engine block and tighten the bolts finger tight. On manual transaxle models, remove the pilot bearing from the end of the crankshaft, using a slide hammer (available a tool rental stores) **(see illustration)**.

12.4a Most main bearing caps are factory numbered and have a cast-in arrow indicating the front of the engine

12.4b If the main caps are not identified by numbers and arrows to indicate position and direction of installation, mark them with a centerpunch

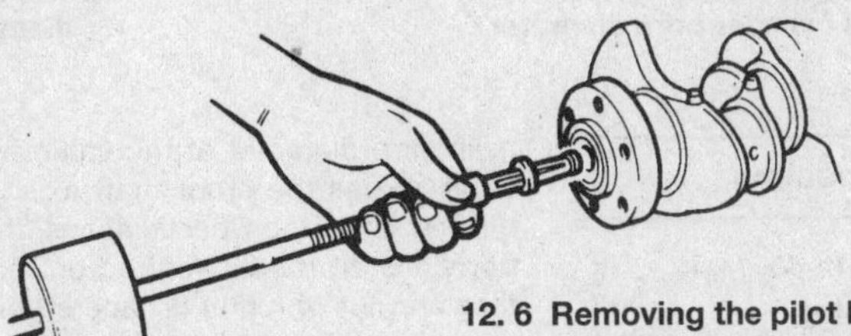

12. 6 Removing the pilot bearing from the crankshaft (manual transaxle models)

13 Engine block - cleaning

Refer to illustrations 13. 1a, 13.1b and 13.10

1 Remove the soft plugs from the engine block. To do this, knock the plugs into the block, using a hammer and punch, then grasp them with large pliers and pull them back through the holes **(see illustrations)**.

2 Using a gasket scraper, remove all traces of gasket material from the engine block. Be very careful not to nick or gouge the gasket sealing surfaces.

3 Remove the main bearing caps and separate the bearing inserts from the caps and the engine block. Tag the bearings according to which cylinder they removed from and whether they were in the cap or the block and set them aside.

4 Using a Allen wrench of the appropriate size, remove any threaded oil gallery plugs from the block.

5 If the engine is extremely dirty it should be taken to an automotive machine shop to be steam cleaned or hot tanked.

6 After the block is returned, clean all oil holes and oil galleries one more time. Brushes for cleaning oil holes and galleries are available at most auto parts stores. Flush the passages with warm water until the water runs clear, dry the block thoroughly and wipe all machined surfaces with a light, rust preventative oil. If you have access to compressed air, use it to speed the drying process and to blow out all the oil holes and galleries.

7 If the block is not extremely dirty or sludged up, you can do an adequate cleaning job with warm soapy water and a stiff brush. Take plenty of time and do a thorough job. Regardless of the cleaning method used, be very sure to thoroughly clean all oil holes and galleries, dry the block completely and coat all machined surfaces with light oil.

8 The threaded holes in the block must be clean to ensure accurate torque readings during reassembly. Run the proper size tap into each of the holes to remove any rust, corrosion, thread sealant or sludge and to restore any damaged threads. If possible, use compressed air to clear the holes of debris produced by this operation. Thoroughly clean the threads on the head bolts and the main bearing cap bolts as well.

9 Reinstall the main bearing caps and tighten the bolts finger tight.

10 After coating the sealing surfaces of the new soft plugs with a good quality gasket sealer, install them in the engine block. Make sure they are driven in straight and seated properly or leakage could result. Special tools are available for this purpose, but equally good results can be obtained using a large socket, with an outside diameter that will just slip into the soft plug, and a hammer **(see illustration)**.

11 If the engine is not going to be reassembled right away, cover it with a large plastic trash bag to keep it clean.

13.1a Use a large punch to drive the soft plug into the block

13.1b After the soft plug has been driven into the block it can be grabbed with pliers and pulled out at an angle

13.10 Coat the new soft plug with silicone sealant, then use a large socket to drive it into the block, being careful to keep it straight

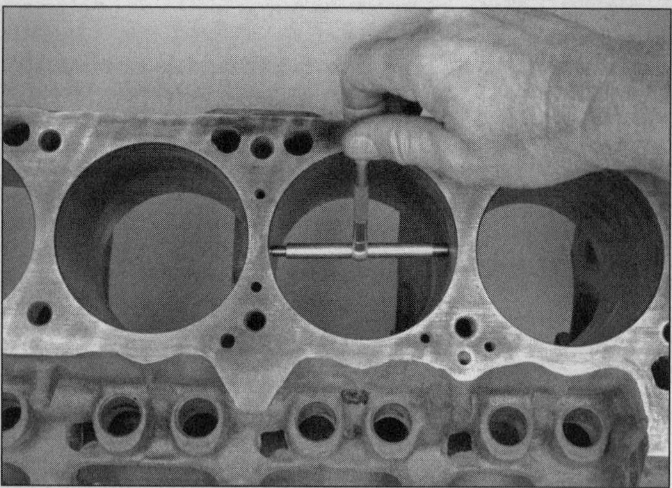

14.4a A telescoping gauge (snap gauge) is used to measure cylinder bore diameter

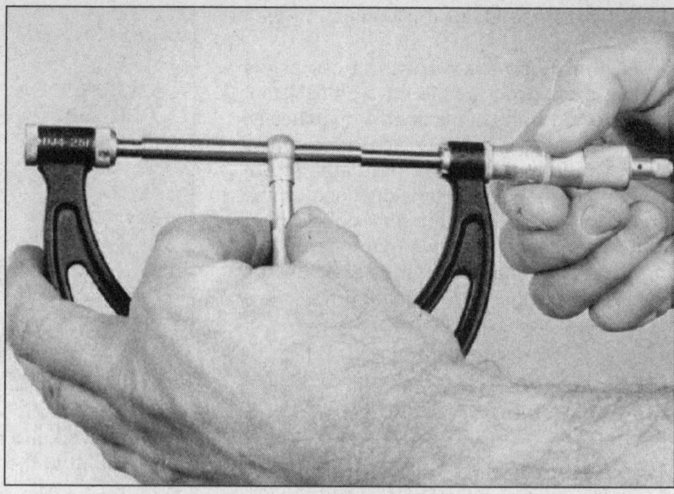

14.4b After extending the telescoping gauge to the cylinder diameter, it is removed and measured with a micrometer to determine bore size, taper and out-of-round

14 Engine block - inspection

Refer to illustrations 14.4a, 14.4b, 14.4c, 14.7a and 14.7b

1 Thoroughly clean the engine block as described in Section 13 and double-check to make sure that the ridge at the top of each cylinder has been completely removed.

2 Visually check the block for cracks, rust and corrosion. Look for stripped threads in the threaded holes. It is also a good idea to have the block checked for hidden cracks by an automotive machine shop that has the special equipment to do this type of work. If defects are found, have the block repaired, if possible, or replaced.

3 Check the cylinder bores for scuffing and scoring.

4 Measure each cylinder's diameter at the top (just under the ridge), center and bottom of the cylinder bore, parallel to the crankshaft axis **(see illustrations)**. Next, measure each cylinder's diameter at the same three locations across the crankshaft axis. Compare the results to the Specifications. If the cylinder walls are badly scuffed or scored, or if they are out of round or tapered beyond the limits given in the Specifications, have the engine block rebored and honed at an automotive machine shop. If a rebore is done, oversize pistons and rings will be required.

5 If the cylinders are in reasonably good condition and not worn to the outside of the limits, and if the piston-to-cylinder clearances can be maintained properly, then they do not have to be rebored. Honing is all that is necessary.

6 Before honing the cylinders, install the main bearing caps (without the bearings) and tighten the bolts to the specified torque.

7 To perform the honing operation you will need the proper size flexible hone (with fine stones), plenty of light oil or honing oil, some rags and an electric drill motor. Mount the hone in the drill motor, compress the stones and slip the hone into the first cylinder **(see illustration)**. Lubricate the cylinder thoroughly, turn on the drill and move the hone up and down in the cylinder at a pace which will produce a fine crosshatch pattern on the cylinder walls with the crosshatch lines intersecting at approximately a 60-degree angle **(see illustration)**. Be sure to use plenty of lubricant. Do not withdraw the hone from the cylinder while it is running. Instead, shut off the drill and continue moving the hone up and down in the cylinder until it comes to a complete stop, then compress the stones and withdraw the hone. Wipe the oil out of the cylinder and repeat the procedure on the remaining cylinders. If you do not have the tools or do not desire to perform the honing operation, most automotive machine shops will do it for a reasonable fee.

8 After the honing job is complete, chamfer the top edges of the cylinder bores with a small file so the rings will not catch when the pistons are installed.

9 The entire engine block must be thoroughly washed again with warm, soapy water

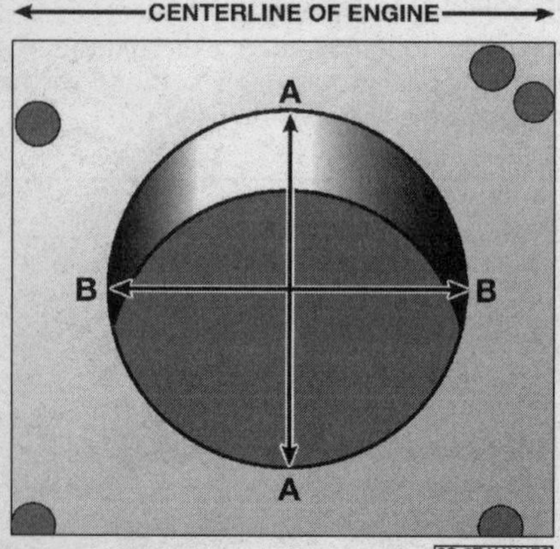

14.4c Measure the diameter of each cylinder just under the wear ridge (X and Y) and at the center and bottom

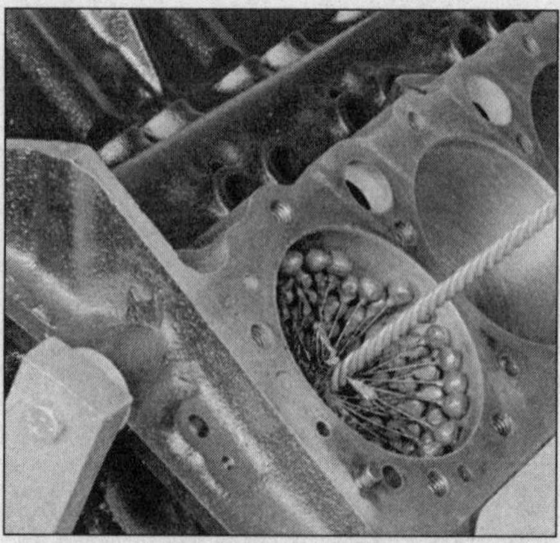

14.7a Cylinders should always be honed before installing new rings to give the bore the proper surface for proper ring seating

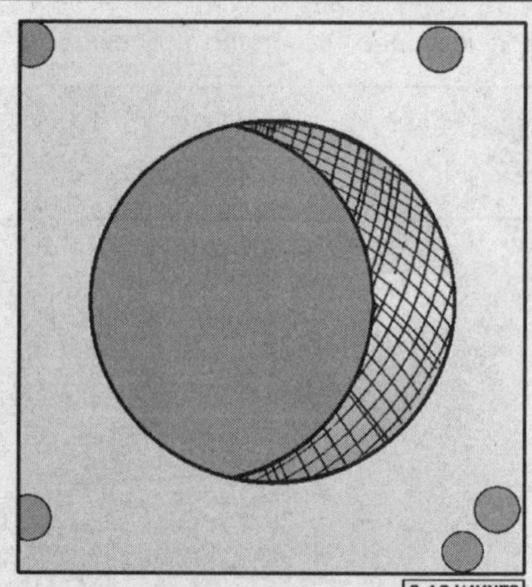

14.7b The cylinder hone should leave a cross-hatch pattern with the lines intersecting at approximately a 60-degree angle

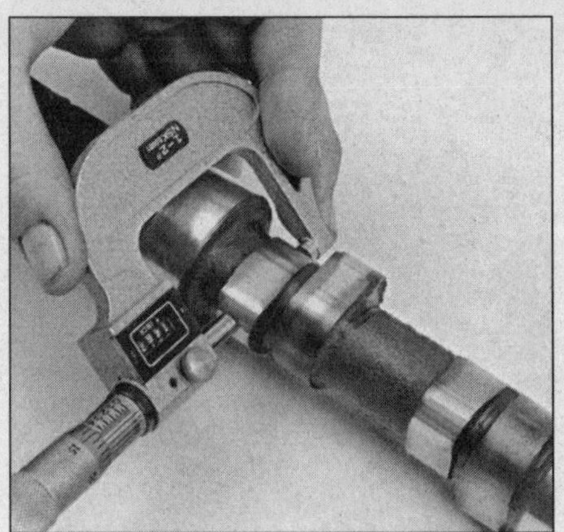
15.2 Measuring the camshaft lobes

to remove all traces of the abrasive grit produced during the honing operation. Be sure to run a brush through all oil holes and galleries and flush them with running water. After rinsing, dry the block and apply a coat of light rust preventative oil to all machined surfaces. Wrap the block in a plastic trash bag to keep it clean and set it aside until reassembly.

15 Camshaft - inspection

Refer to illustrations 15.2, 15.4a, 15.4b, 15.5 and 15.6

1 Once the camshaft has been removed from the engine, cleaned with solvent and dried, inspect the bearing journals for uneven wear, pitting or evidence of seizure. If the journals are damaged, the bearing areas of the cylinder head and camshaft caps are probably damaged as well. If the damage is severe, the camshaft, caps and the cylinder head will have to be replaced.

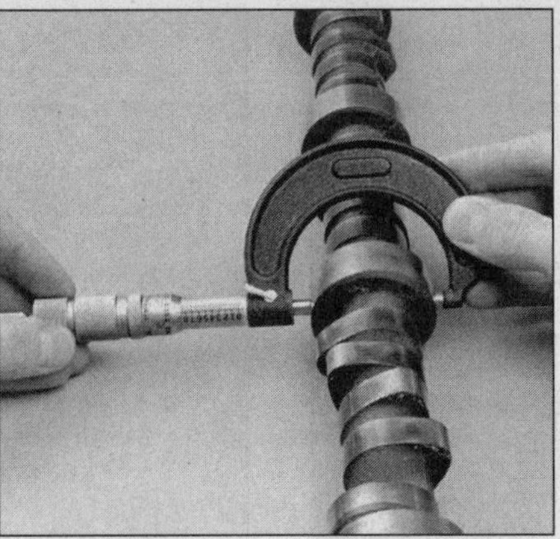
15.4a Measure the camshaft bearing journal diameter and subtract that figure from the bearing inside diameter to obtain the camshaft oil clearance

2 Measure the camshaft lobes with a micrometer and compare the measurements to Specifications to determine if they are worn **(see illustration)**.

3 Check the camshaft lobes for heat discoloration, score marks, chipped areas, pitting or uneven wear. If the lobes are in good condition and if the lobe lift measurements are as specified, the camshaft can be reused.

4 Measure the bearing journals with a micrometer to determine if they are excessively worn or out of round **(see illustration)**. If they are more than 0.020-inch out of round, the camshaft should be replaced with a new one. Measure the journals and the front oil seal surface and compare these measurements to Specifications to determine if wear is excessive **(see illustration)**.

5 With the camshaft mounted in V-blocks, check runout as shown **(see illustration)**.

6 Place the camshaft in the cylinder head and check the end play with a dial indicator by pushing the camshaft fully rearward and then forward **(see illustration)**.

7 The camshaft oil clearance is checked during final assembly of the engine with the cylinder head bolted in place (Chapter 2, Part A). With the camshaft, caps and journals and completely clean and free of oil, lay a strip of Plastigage material across each journal parallel to the camshaft axis, install the caps and tighten the bolts to the specified torque. Remove the caps and measure the crushed Plastigage with the scale printed on the package to determine the oil clearance. If the clearance is out of specification, the cylinder head and camshaft caps must be replaced with new ones.

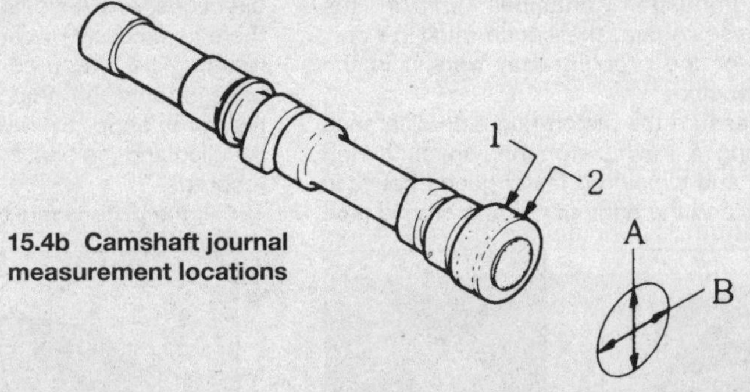

15.4b Camshaft journal measurement locations

16 Piston/connecting rod assembly - inspection

2B

Refer to illustrations 16.4a, 16.4b, 16.5, 16.10 and 16.11

1 Before the inspection process can be carried out, the piston/connecting rod assemblies must be cleaned and the original piston rings removed from the pistons. **Note:** *Always use new piston rings when the engine is reassembled.*

2 Using a piston ring installation tool, carefully remove the rings from the pistons. Do not nick or gouge the pistons in the process.

3 Scrape all traces of carbon from the top (or crown) of the piston. A hand-held wire brush or a piece of fine emery cloth can be used once the majority of the deposits have been scraped away. Do not, under any circumstances, use a wire brush mounted in a drill motor to remove deposits from the pistons. The piston material is soft and will be eroded away by the wire brush.

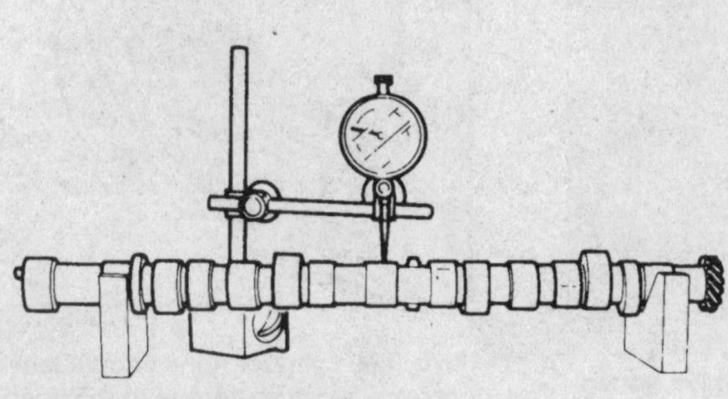
15.5 Checking camshaft runout with a dial indicator

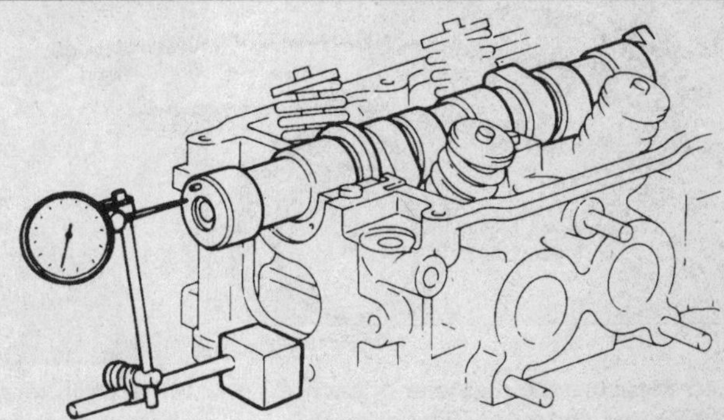
15.6 Checking the camshaft end play with a dial indicator

16.4a Use a piece of broken ring to carefully remove carbon deposits from the ring grooves. Use caution not to remove any of the piston material

16.4b If available, a ring groove cleaning tool can be used to remove carbon from the ring grooves

4 Use a piston ring groove cleaning tool to remove any carbon deposits from the ring grooves. If a tool is not available, a piece broken off the old ring will do the job. Be very careful to remove only the carbon deposits. Do not remove any metal and do not nick or scratch the sides of the ring grooves **(see illustrations)**.

5 Once the deposits have been removed, clean the piston/rod assemblies with solvent and dry them thoroughly. Make sure that the oil return holes in the back sides of the ring grooves are clear **(see illustration)**.

6 If the pistons are not damaged or worn excessively, and if the engine block is not rebored, new pistons will not be necessary. Normal piston wear appears as even vertical wear on the piston thrust surfaces and slight looseness of the top ring in its groove. New piston rings should always be used when an engine is rebuilt.

7 Carefully inspect each piston for cracks around the skirt, at the pin bosses and at the ring lands.

8 Look for scoring and scuffing on the thrust faces of the skirt, holes in the piston crown and burned areas at the edge of the crown. If the skirt is scored or scuffed, the engine may have been suffering from overheating and/or abnormal combustion, which caused excessively high operating temperatures. The cooling and lubrication systems should be checked thoroughly. A hole in the piston crown is an indication that abnormal combustion (preignition) was occurring. Burned areas at the edge of the piston crown are usually evidence of spark knock (detonation). If any of the above problems exist, the causes must be corrected or the damage will occur again.

9 Corrosion of the piston, evidenced by pitting, indicates that coolant is leaking into the combustion chamber and/or the crankcase. Again, the cause must be corrected or the problem may persist in the rebuilt engine.

10 Measure the piston ring side clearance by laying a new piston ring in each ring groove and slipping a feeler gauge between the ring and the edge of the ring groove **(see illustration)**. Check the clearance at three or four locations around each groove. Be sure to use the correct ring for each groove; they are different. If the side clearance is greater than specified, new pistons will have to be used.

11 Check the piston-to-bore clearance by measuring the bore (see Section 14) and the piston diameter. Make sure that the pistons and bores are correctly matched. Measure the piston across the skirt **(see illustration)**. Subtract the piston diameter from the bore diameter to obtain the clearance. If it is greater than specified, the block will have to be rebored and new pistons and rings installed. Check the piston-to-rod clearance by twisting the piston and rod in opposite directions. Any noticeable play indicates that there is excessive wear, which must be corrected. The piston/connecting rod assemblies should be taken to an automotive machine shop to have new piston pins installed and the pistons and connecting rods rebored.

12 If the pistons must be removed from the

16.5 Make sure the oil return holes in the back of the oil ring groove are open

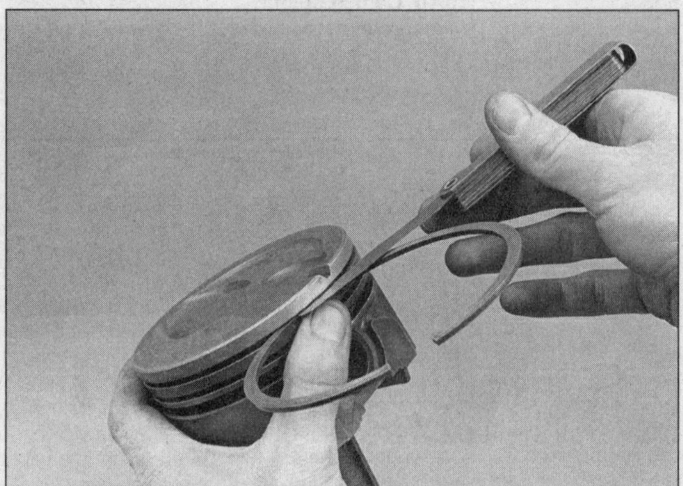

16.10 To check ring side clearance, insert the ring in the groove then use a feeler gauge to check the remaining gap

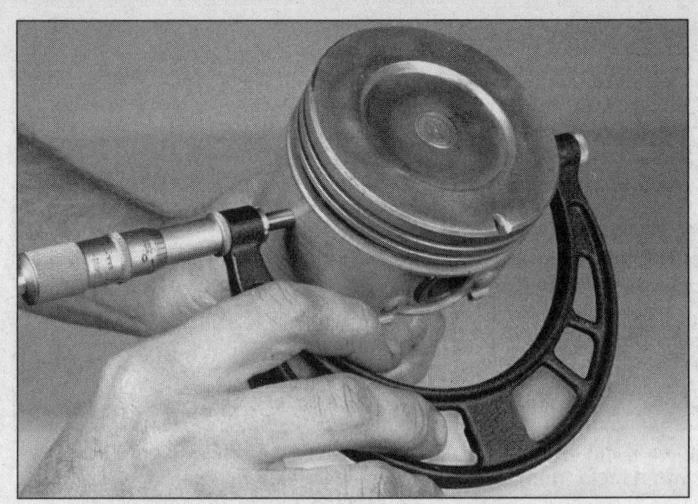
16.11 Measure the piston diameter at the thrust faces, 90 degrees to the piston pin hole

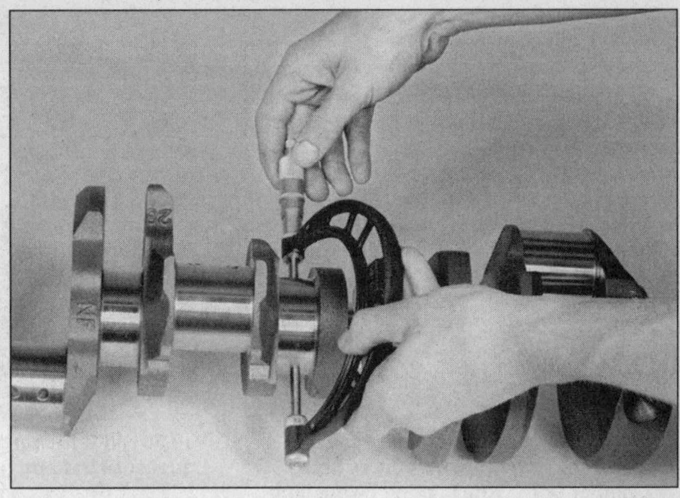
17.2a Measure the diameter of each crankshaft journal at several places to detect taper and out-of-round conditions

connecting rods, such as when new pistons must be installed, or if the piston pins have too much play in them, they should be taken to an automotive machine shop. While they are there have the connecting rods checked for bend and twist, as automotive machine shops have special equipment for this purpose. Unless new pistons or connecting rods must be installed, do not disassemble the pistons from the connecting rods.

13 Check the connecting rods for cracks and other damage. Temporarily remove the rod caps, lift out the old bearing inserts, wipe the rod and cap bearing surfaces clean and inspect them for nicks, gouges or scratches. After checking the rods, replace the old bearings, slip the caps into place and tighten the nuts finger tight.

17 Crankshaft - inspection

Refer to illustrations 17.2a and 17.2b

1 Clean the crankshaft with solvent and dry it thoroughly. Be sure to clean the oil holes with a stiff brush and flush them with solvent. Check the main and connecting rod bearing journals for uneven wear, scoring, pitting or cracks. Check the remainder of the crankshaft for cracks and damage.

2 Using a micrometer, measure the diameter of the main and connecting rod journals and compare the results to the Specifications. By measuring the diameter at a number of points around the journal's circumference, you will be able to determine whether or not the journal is out of round. Take the measurement at each end of the journal, near the crank counterweights, to determine whether the journal is tapered **(see illustrations)**.

3 If the crankshaft journals are damaged, tapered, out of round or worn beyond the limits given in the Specifications, have the crankshaft reground by a reputable automotive machine shop. Be sure to use the correct size bearing inserts if the crankshaft is reconditioned to maintain proper oil clearance.

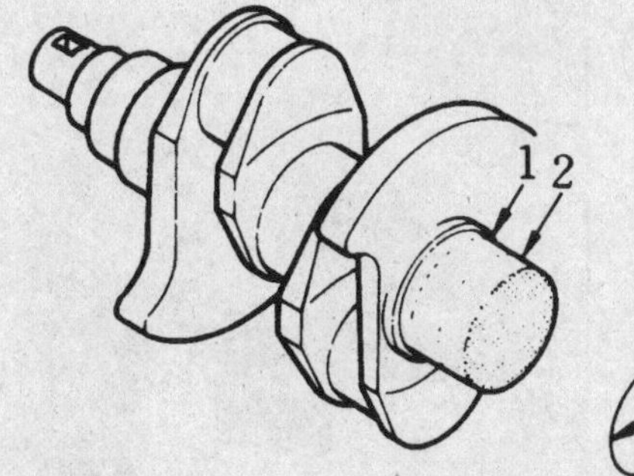

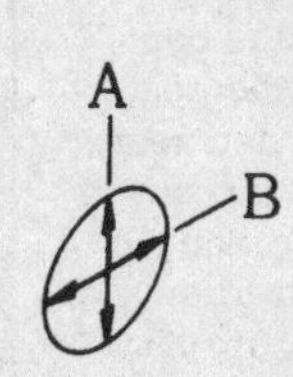

17.2b Measure the crankshaft at the two points (1 and 2) and the four locations (A and B) on each journal

4 Refer to Section 18 and examine the main and rod bearing inserts for unusual wear patterns.

18 Main and connecting rod bearings - inspection

1 Even though the main and connecting rod bearings should be replaced with new ones during the engine overhaul, the old bearings should be retained for close examination, as they may reveal valuable information about the condition of the engine.

2 Bearing failure occurs because of lack of lubrication, the presence of dirt or other foreign particles, overloading the engine and corrosion. Regardless of the cause of bearing failure, it must be corrected before the engine is reassembled to prevent it from happening again.

3 When examining the bearings, remove them from the engine block, the main bearing caps, the connecting rods and the rod caps and lay them out on a clean surface in the same general position as their location in the engine. This will enable you to match any bearing problems with the corresponding crankshaft journal.

4 Dirt and other foreign particles get into the engine in a variety of ways. If may be left in the engine during assembly, or it may pass through filters or breathers. It may get into the oil, and from there into the bearings. Metal chips from machining operations and normal engine wear are often present. Abrasives are sometimes left in engine components after reconditioning, especially when parts are not thoroughly cleaned using the proper cleaning methods. Whatever the source, these foreign objects often end up embedded in the soft bearing material and are easily recognized. Large particles will not embed in the bearing and will score or gouge the bearing and shaft. The best prevention for this cause of bearing failure is to clean all parts thoroughly and keep everything spotlessly clean during engine assembly. Frequent and regular engine oil and filter changes are also recommended to prevent premature bearing wear.

5 Lack of lubrication (or lubrication breakdown) has a number of interrelated causes. Excessive heat (which thins the oil), overloading (which squeezes the oil from the bearing face) and oil leakage or throw off (from excessive bearing clearances, worn oil pump or high engine speeds) all contribute to lubrication breakdown. Blocked oil passages, which usually are the result of misaligned oil holes in a bearing shell, will also oil starve a bearing and destroy it. When lack of lubrication is the cause of bearing failure, the bearing material is wiped or extruded from the steel backing of the bearing. Temperatures may increase to the point where the steel backing turns blue from overheating which can also affect the rod cap and rod bolts.

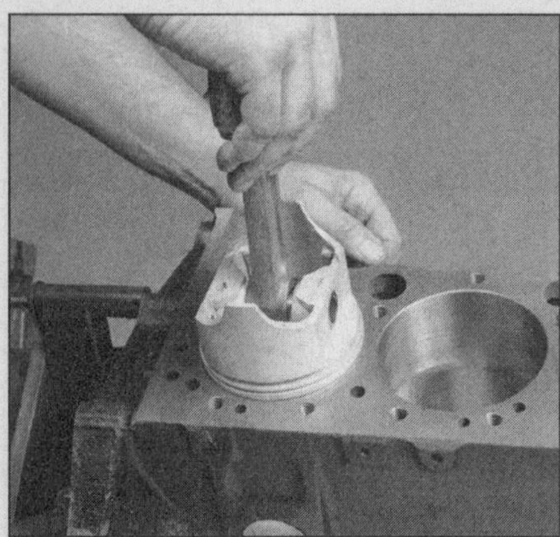
19.3a Before checking piston ring end gap the ring must be square in the cylinder bore. This is done by pushing the ring down into the cylinder with the top of a piston

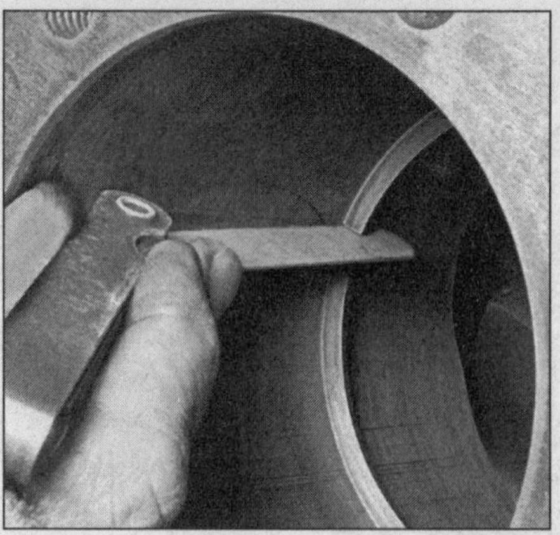
19.3b With the ring square in the cylinder, measure the end gap with a feeler gauge

19.5 To increase ring end gap, mount a file in a vise and file the ring, from the outside in only, until the proper gap is obtained

19.9a Install the oil control ring expander in the lower piston groove, making sure the ends interlock properly

19.9b Roll the oil control ring side rails into place above and below the oil control ring expander. Do not use a ring expander tool to install oil ring side rails

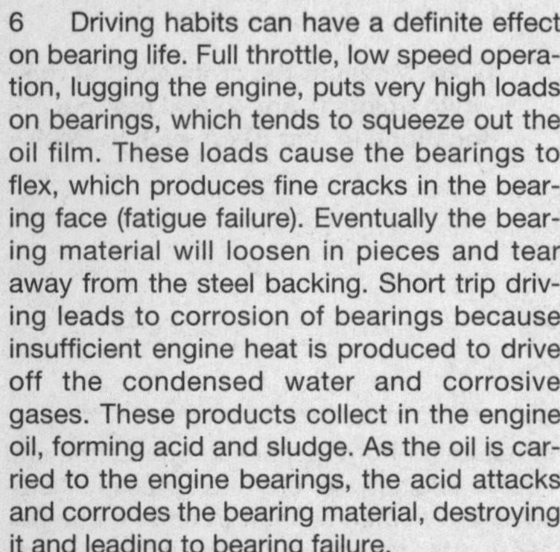

6 Driving habits can have a definite effect on bearing life. Full throttle, low speed operation, lugging the engine, puts very high loads on bearings, which tends to squeeze out the oil film. These loads cause the bearings to flex, which produces fine cracks in the bearing face (fatigue failure). Eventually the bearing material will loosen in pieces and tear away from the steel backing. Short trip driving leads to corrosion of bearings because insufficient engine heat is produced to drive off the condensed water and corrosive gases. These products collect in the engine oil, forming acid and sludge. As the oil is carried to the engine bearings, the acid attacks and corrodes the bearing material, destroying it and leading to bearing failure.

7 Incorrect bearing installation during engine assembly will lead to bearing failure as well. Tight fitting bearings leave insufficient bearing oil clearance and will result in oil starvation. Dirt or foreign particles trapped behind a bearing insert result in high spots on the bearing which lead to failure.

19 Piston rings - installation

Refer to illustrations 19.3a, 19.3b, 19.5, 19.9a, 19.9b, 19.10, 19.11, 19.12 and 19.13

1 Before installing the new piston rings, the ring end gaps must be checked. It is assumed that the piston ring side clearance in the piston has been checked and verified correct (Section 16).

2 Lay out the piston/connecting rod assemblies and the new ring sets so the ring sets will be matched with the same piston and cylinder during the end gap measurement and engine assembly.

3 Insert the top (number one) ring into the first cylinder and square it up with the cylinder walls by pushing it in with the top of the piston **(see illustration)**. The ring should be near the bottom of the cylinder at the lower limit of ring travel. To measure the end gap, slip a feeler gauge between the ends of the ring **(see illustration)**. Compare the measurement to the Specifications.

4 If the gap is larger or smaller than specified, double-check to make sure that you have the correct rings before proceeding.

5 If the gap is too small, it must be enlarged or the ring ends may come in contact with each other during engine operation, which can cause serious damage to the engine. The end gap can be increased by filing the ring ends very carefully with a fine file. Mount the file in a vise equipped with soft jaws, slip the ring over the file with the ends contacting the file face and slowly move the ring to remove material from the ends **(see illustration)**. When performing this operation, file only from the outside in.

6 Excess end gap is not critical unless it is greater than 0.040-inch (1 mm). Again, double-check to make sure you have the correct rings for your engine.

7 Repeat the procedure for each ring that will be installed in the first cylinder and for each ring in the remaining cylinders. Remember to keep rings, pistons and cylinders matched up.

8 Once the ring end gaps have been checked/corrected, the rings can be installed on the pistons.

9 The oil control ring (lowest one on the piston) is installed first. It is composed of three separate components. Slip the spacer/expander into the groove **(see illustration)**, then install the lower side rail. Do not use a piston ring installation tool on the oil ring side rails, as they may be damaged. Instead, place one end of the side rail into the groove between the spacer/expander and the ring land, hold it firmly in place and slide a finger around the piston while pushing the rail into the groove **(see illustration)**. Next, install the upper side rail in the same manner.

10 After the three oil ring components have been installed, check to make sure that both the upper and lower side rails can be turned smoothly in the ring groove. Refer to the accompanying illustration for proper positioning of the oil ring gaps **(see illustration)**.

11 The number two (middle) ring is installed next. It is stamped with an R mark which should face toward the top of the piston **(see illustration)**. **Note:** *Always follow the instructions printed on the ring package or box - different manufacturers may require different*

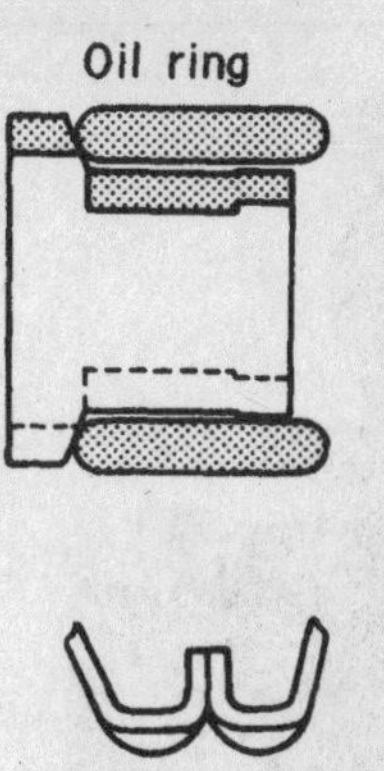

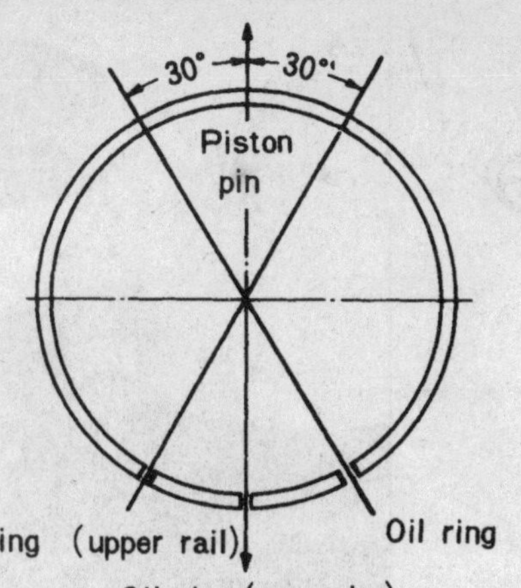

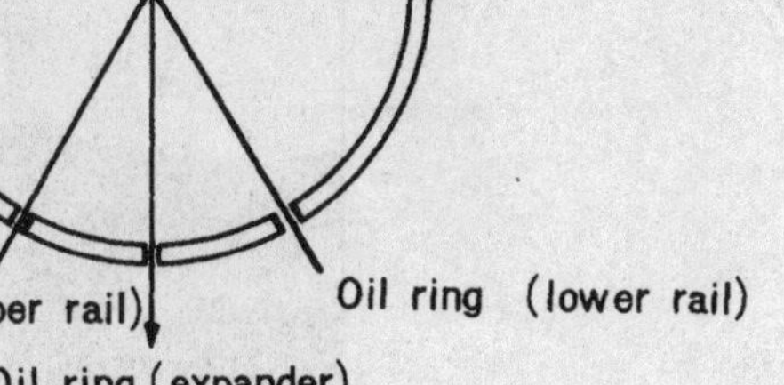

19.10 Oil ring installation and gap positioning

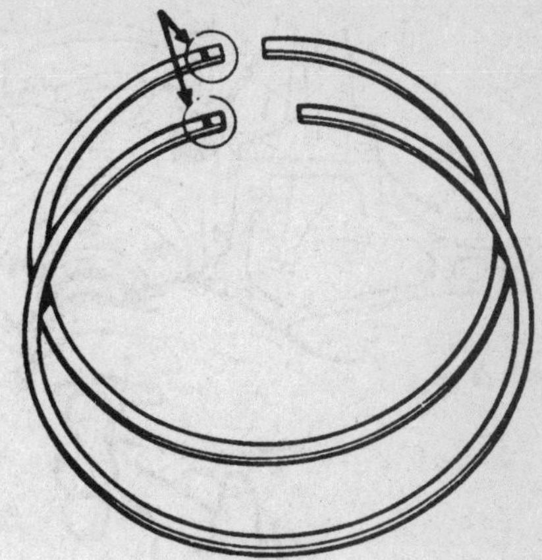

19.11 The piston ring markings must face up

approaches. Do not mix up the top and middle rings, as they have different cross sections.

12 Use a piston ring installation tool and make sure that the identification mark is facing the top of the piston, then slip the ring into the middle groove on the piston **(see illustration)**. Do not expand the ring any more than is necessary to slide it over the piston.

13 Install the number one (top) ring in the same manner. Make sure the identifying mark is facing up. Be careful not to confuse the number one and number two rings. Make sure the ring gaps are properly positioned **(see illustration)**.

20 Crankshaft - installation and main bearing oil clearance check

Refer to illustration 20.19

1 Crankshaft installation is the first step in engine reassembly. It is assumed at this point that the engine block and crankshaft have been cleaned, inspected and repaired or reconditioned.

2 Position the engine with the bottom facing up.

3 Remove the main bearing cap bolts and lift out the caps. Lay them out in the proper order to ensure that they are installed correctly.

4 If they are still in place, remove the old bearing inserts from the block and the main bearing caps. Wipe the main bearing surfaces of the block and caps with a clean, lint free cloth. They must be kept spotlessly clean.

5 Clean the back sides of the new main bearing inserts and lay one bearing half in each main bearing saddle in the block. Lay the other bearing half from each bearing set in the corresponding main bearing cap. Make sure the tab on the bearing insert fits into the recess in the block or cap. Also, the oil holes in the block must line up with the oil holes in the bearing insert. Do not hammer the bearing into place and do not nick or gouge the bearing faces. No lubrication should be used at this time.

6 The flanged thrust bearing must be installed in the number three (3) cap and saddle.

7 Clean the faces of the bearings in the block and the crankshaft main bearing journals with a clean, lint free cloth. Check or clean the oil holes in the crankshaft, as any dirt here can go only one way - straight through the new bearings.

8 Once you are certain that the crankshaft is clean, carefully lay it in position (an assistant would be very helpful here) in the main bearings.

9 Before the crankshaft can be permanently installed, the main bearing oil clearance must be checked.

10 Trim several pieces of the appropriate size of Plastigage, so they are slightly shorter than the width of the main bearings, and place one piece on each crankshaft main bearing journal, parallel with the journal axis.

11 Clean the faces of the bearings in the caps and install the caps in their respective positions (do not mix them up) with the arrows pointing toward the front of the engine. Do not disturb the Plastigage.

19.12 Use a ring expander to install the compression rings. Be sure the mark (usually one or two dots) are facing up, and that the number one and two rings aren't mixed up

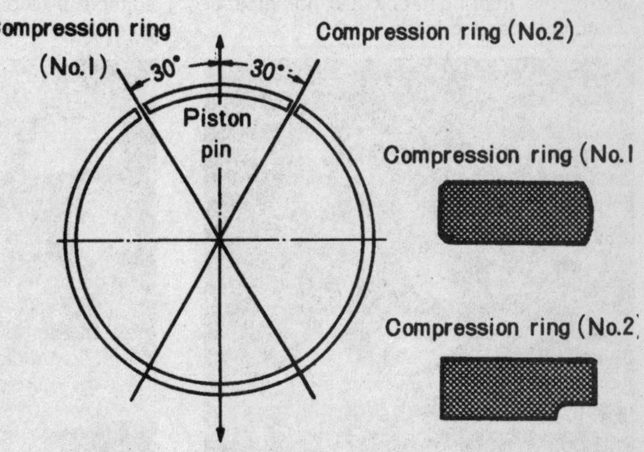

19.13 Compression piston ring installation and gap positioning

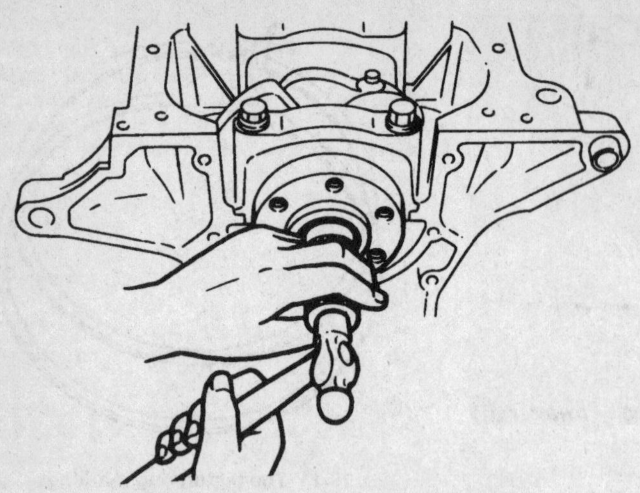

20.19 Installing the pilot bearing into the crankshaft (manual transaxle models)

21.6 When installing the pistons and rings, leave a portion of the piston skirt extended below the ring compressor to center the piston in the cylinder

12 Starting with the center main and working out toward the ends, tighten the main bearing cap bolts, in three steps, to the specified torque. Do not rotate the crankshaft at any time during this operation.

13 Remove the bolts and carefully lift off the main bearing caps. Keep them in order. Do not disturb the Plastigage or rotate the crankshaft. If any of the main bearing caps are difficult to remove, tap them gently from side-to-side with a soft-face hammer to loosen them.

14 Compare the width of the crushed Plastigage on each journal to the scale printed on the Plastigage container to obtain the main bearing oil clearance. Check the Specifications to make sure it is correct.

15 If the clearance is not correct, double-check to make sure you have the right size bearing inserts. Also, make sure that no dirt or oil was between the bearing inserts and the main bearing caps or the block when the clearance was measured.

16 Carefully scrape all traces of the Plastigage material off the main bearing journals and/or the bearing faces. Do not nick or scratch the bearing faces.

17 Carefully lift the crankshaft out of the engine. Clean the bearing faces in the block, then apply a thin, uniform layer of clean, high quality moly-base grease or engine assembly lube to each of the bearing surfaces. Be sure to coat the thrust flange faces as well as the journal face of the thrust bearing.

18 Make sure the crankshaft journals are clean, then lay the crankshaft back in place in the block. Clean the faces of the bearings in the caps, then apply a thin, uniform layer of clean, moly-base grease to each of the bearing faces. Install the caps in their respective positions with the arrows pointing toward the front of the engine. Install the bolts and tighten them to the specified torque, starting with the center main and working out toward the ends. Work up to the final torque in three steps.

19 On manual transaxle models, install a new pilot bearing in the end of the crankshaft. Lubricate the crankshaft cavity and the outer circumference of the bearing with clean engine oil and place the bearing in position. Tap it fully and evenly into the cavity using a suitable size piece of pipe and a hammer **(see illustration)**. Lubricate the inside of the bearing with grease.

20 Rotate the crankshaft a number of times by hand to check for any obvious binding.

21 The final step is to check the crankshaft end play with a feeler gauge or a dial indicator as described in Section 12.

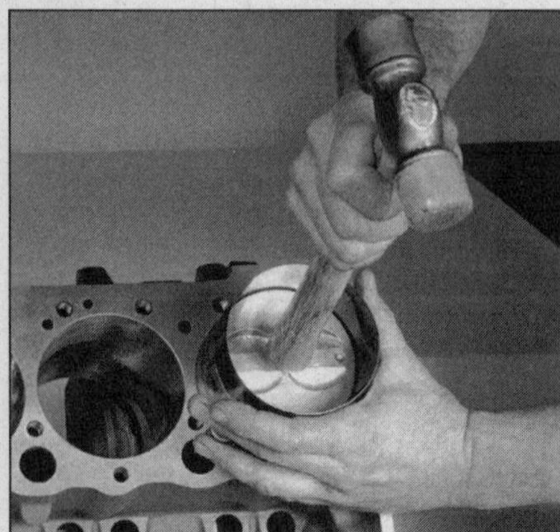

21.9 Gently drive the piston into the cylinder bore with the end of a wooden hammer handle

21.11 Lay a piece of the proper size Plastigage across the rod journal before installing the rod cap

21 Piston/connecting rod assembly - installation and bearing oil clearance check

Refer to illustrations 21.6, 21.9, 21.11, 21.13, 21.14, 21.16a and 21.16b

1 Before installing the piston/connecting rod assemblies the cylinder walls must be perfectly clean, the top edge of each cylinder must be chamfered, and the crankshaft must be in place.

2 Remove the connecting rod cap from the end of the number one connecting rod. Remove the old bearing inserts and wipe the bearing surfaces of the connecting rod and cap with a clean, lint free cloth. They must be kept spotlessly clean.

3 Clean the back side of the new upper bearing half, then lay it in place in the connecting rod. Make sure that the tab on the bearing fits into the recess in the rod. Do not hammer the bearing insert into place and be very careful not to nick or gouge the bearing face. Do not lubricate the bearing at this time.

4 Clean the back side of the other bearing insert and install it in the rod cap. Again, make sure the tab on the bearing fits into the recess in the cap, and do not apply any lubricant. It is critically important that the mating surfaces of the bearing and connecting rod are perfectly clean and oil free when they are assembled.

5 Position the piston ring gaps **(see illustrations 19.10, 19.11 and 19.13)**, then slip a section of plastic or rubber hose over the connecting rod cap bolts.

6 Lubricate the piston and rings with clean engine oil and attach a piston ring compres-

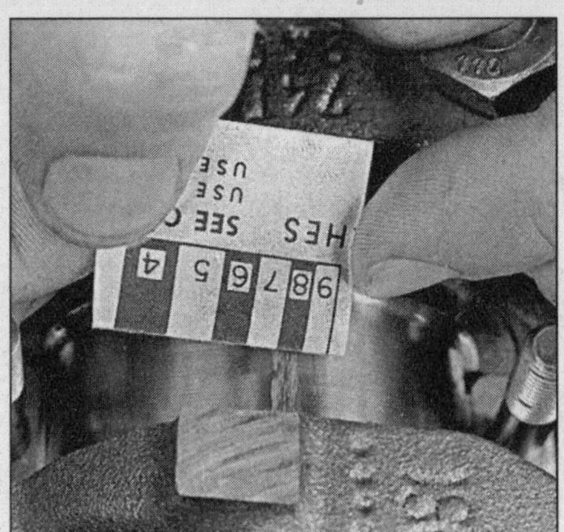
21.13 After removing the rod cap, compare the width of the crushed Plastigage to the scale on the package to determine the oil clearance

21.14 Use rubber boots to protect the cylinder walls and crankshaft journal from the rod bolts, and pull the rod up snugly against the rod journal

sor to the piston. Leave the skirt protruding about 1/4-inch to guide the piston into the cylinder **(see illustration)**. The rings must be compressed as far as possible.

7 Rotate the crankshaft until the number one connecting rod journal is as far from the number one cylinder as possible (bottom dead center), and apply a coat of engine oil to the cylinder walls.

8 With the notch on top of the piston facing to the front of the engine, gently place the piston/connecting rod assembly into the number one cylinder bore and rest the bottom edge of the ring compressor on the engine block. Tap the top edge of the ring compressor to make sure it is contacting the block around its entire circumference.

9 Carefully tap on the top of the piston with the end of a wooden hammer handle **(see illustration)** while guiding the end of the connecting rod into place on the crankshaft journal. The piston rings may try to pop out of the ring compressor just before entering the cylinder bore, so keep some downward pressure on the ring compressor. Work slowly, and if any resistance is felt as the piston enters the cylinder, stop immediately. Find out what is hanging up and fix it before proceeding. Do not, for any reason, force the piston into the cylinder, as you will break a ring and/or the piston.

10 Once the piston/connecting rod assembly is installed, the connecting rod bearing oil clearance must be checked before the rod cap is permanently bolted in place.

11 Cut a piece of the appropriate size Plastigage slightly shorter than the width of the connecting rod bearing and lay it in place on the number one connecting rod journal, parallel with the journal axis **(see illustration)**. It must not cross the oil hole in the journal.

12 Clean the connecting rod cap bearing face, remove the protective hoses from the connecting rod bolts and install the rod cap. Make sure the mating mark on the cap is on the same side as the mark on the connecting rod. Install the nuts and tighten them to the specified torque, working up to it in three steps. Do not rotate the crankshaft at any time during this operation.

13 Remove the rod cap, being very careful not to disturb the Plastigage. Compare the width of the crushed Plastigage to the scale printed on the Plastigage container to obtain the oil clearance **(see illustration)**. Compare it to the Specifications to make sure the clearance is correct. If the clearance is not correct, double-check to make sure that you have the correct size bearing inserts. Also, recheck the crankshaft connecting rod journal diameter and make sure that no dirt or oil was between the bearing inserts and the connecting rod or cap when the clearance was measured.

14 Carefully scrape all traces of the Plastigage material off the rod journal and/or bearing face. Be very careful not to scratch the bearing- use your fingernail or a piece of hardwood. Make sure the bearing faces are perfectly clean, then apply a uniform layer of clean, high quality moly-base grease or engine assembly lube to both of them. You will have to push the piston into the cylinder to expose the face of the bearing insert in the connecting rod. Be sure to slip the protective hoses over the rod bolts first **(see illustration)**.

15 Slide the connecting rod back into place on the journal, remove the protective hoses from the rod cap bolts, install the rod cap and tighten the nuts to the specified torque. Again, work up to the torque in three steps.

16 Repeat the entire procedure for the remaining piston/connecting rod assemblies. Keep the back sides of the bearing inserts and the inside of the connecting rod and cap perfectly clean when assembling them. Make sure you have the correct piston for the cylinder and that the notch on the piston faces to the front of the engine when the piston is installed **(see illustrations)**. Remember, use plenty of oil to lubricate the piston before installing the ring compressor. Also, when installing the rod caps for the final time, be sure to lubricate the bearing faces adequately.

17 After all the piston/connecting rod assemblies have been properly installed, rotate the crankshaft a number of times by hand to check for any obvious binding.

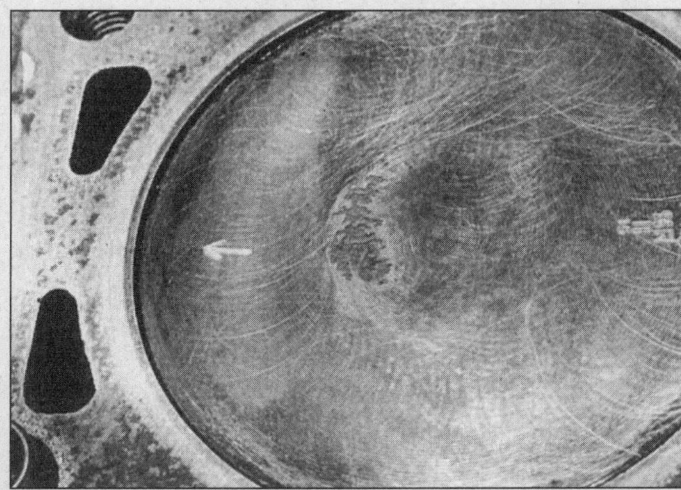
21.16a An arrow at one edge of the piston should point to the front of the engine after installation

21.16b Some pistons use a notch to indicate which side of the piston should face the front of the engine

18 As a final step, the connecting rod end play must be checked. Refer to Section 11 for this procedure. Compare the measured end play to the Specifications to make sure it is correct.

22 Rear oil seal and cover - installation

Refer to illustration 22.4

1 Lubricate the outer circumference of the oil seal lightly with assembly lube or clean engine oil and place the seal in position in the rear cover bore. Press the seal fully and evenly into the bore using a suitable size socket.
2 Apply gasket sealant to the gasket and rear cover contact surfaces.
3 Apply a light coat of clean engine oil to the seal lip, place the rear cover and gasket in position and install the retaining bolts. Tighten the bolts to the specified torque.
4 Carefully cut away the portion of the gasket that extends from the rear cover into the oil pan contact area as shown in the **(see illustration)**.

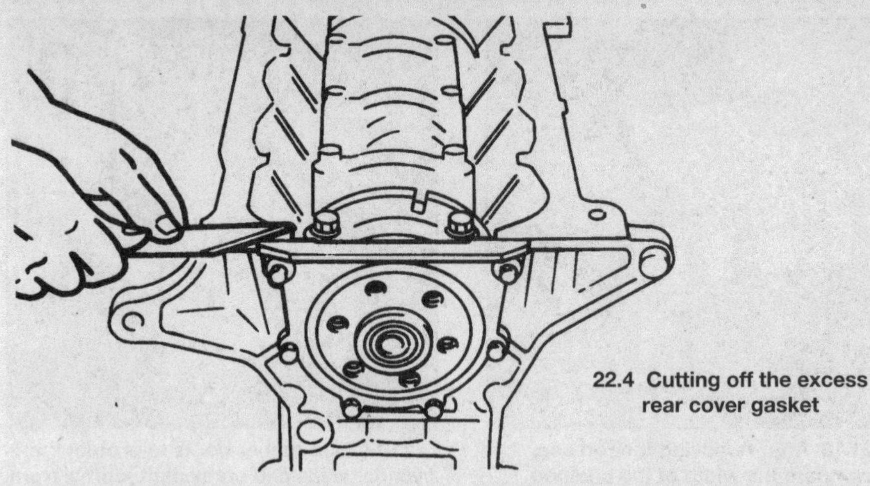

22.4 Cutting off the excess rear cover gasket

23 Engine overhaul - reassembly sequence

1 Before beginning engine reassembly, make sure you have all the necessary new parts, gaskets and seals as well as the following items on hand:

Common hand tools
A 1/2-inch drive torque wrench
Piston ring installation tool
Piston ring compressor
Short lengths of rubber or plastic hose to fit over connecting rod bolts
Plastigage
Feeler gauges
A fine-tooth file
New engine oil
Engine assembly lube or moly-base grease
RTV-type gasket sealant
Anaerobic-type gasket sealant
Thread locking compound

2 In order to save time and avoid problems, engine reassembly must be done in the following order.

Crankshaft and main bearings
Crankshaft pilot bearing (manual transaxle models)
Piston rings
Piston/connecting rod assemblies
Rear oil seal and cover
Engine end plate
Oil pump and oil strainer
Oil pan
Flywheel/driveplate
Front engine mount bracket
Water pump
Cylinder head, camshaft and rocker arm assembly
Front housing and oil seal
Timing belt sprockets and tensioner
Timing belt and cover
Fuel pump
Rear housing
Camshaft cover
Oil pressure switch
Oil filter
Thermostat and housing cover
Distributor, spark plug wires and spark plugs
Water hose and pipe assemblies
Intake and exhaust manifolds
Alternator and brackets
Emissions control components

24 Initial start-up and break-in after overhaul

1 Once the engine has been properly installed in the vehicle, double check the engine oil and coolant levels.
2 With the spark plugs out of the engine and the coil high tension lead grounded to the engine block, crank the engine until oil pressure registers on the gauge (if so equipped) or until the oil light goes off.
3 Install the spark plugs, hook up the plug wires and the coil high tension lead.
4 Make sure the carburetor choke plate is closed, then start the engine. It may take a few moments for the gasoline to reach the carburetor, but the engine should start without a great deal of effort.
5 As soon as the engine starts it should be set at a fast idle to ensure proper oil circulation and allowed to warm up to normal operating temperature. While the engine is warming up, make a thorough check for oil and coolant leaks.
6 Shut the engine off and recheck the engine oil and coolant levels. Restart the engine and check the ignition timing and the engine idle speed (refer to Chapter 1). Make any necessary adjustments.
7 Drive the vehicle to an area with minimum traffic, accelerate at full throttle from 30 to 50 mph, then allow the vehicle to slow to 30 mph with the throttle closed. Repeat the procedure 10 or 12 times. This will load the piston rings and cause them to seat properly against the cylinder walls. Check again for oil and coolant leaks.
8 Drive the vehicle gently for the first 500 miles (no sustained high speeds) and keep a constant check on the oil level. It is not unusual for an engine to use oil during the break-in period.
9 At approximately 500 to 600 miles, change the oil and filter, retorque the cylinder head bolts and recheck the valve clearances (if applicable).
10 For the next few hundred miles, drive the vehicle normally. Do not either pamper it or abuse it.
11 After 2000 miles, change the oil and filter again and consider the engine fully broken in.

Chapter 3
Cooling, heating and air conditioning systems

Contents

Specifications

Radiator cap pressure cap rating	15 psi
Coolant capacity	7.4 qts
Thermostat rating	193°F (89.5°C)
Water temperature switch	
On at	194°F (90°C)
Off at	206°F (97°C)
Cooling fan motor current	8 to 11 amperes

Torque specifications

	Ft-lbs	M-kg
Fan thermo switch	22 to 29	3.0 to 4.0
Temperature gauge unit	5 to 7	0.5 to 1.0
Thermostat housing bolt	13 to 22	1.9 to 3.1
Water pump-to-block bolt	14 to 19	1.9 to 2.6

1 General information

The cooling system consists of a radiator, an engine driven water pump and thermostat controlled coolant flow.

The fan is driven by an electric motor that is mounted in the radiator shroud and is activated by a temperature switch. **Warning:** *The fan can start even when the engine is Off as long as the ignition switch is On.* The battery negative cable should be disconnected whenever you are working in the vicinity of the fan.

The water pump is mounted on the front of the engine and is driven by the timing belt.

The heater utilizes the heat produced by the engine, which is absorbed by the coolant to warm the vehicle interior. The coolant passes through a heater core similar to a small radiator in the passenger compartment. The coolant flow through the core and air which is directed through the heater core and duct system to heat the vehicle interior are controlled by the driver or passenger.

Air conditioning is available as an option on these vehicles. The air conditioning system is located in the engine compartment and the crankshaft pulley by way of a drivebelt drives the compressor.

2 Antifreeze - general information

Warning: *Do not allow antifreeze to come in contact with your skin or painted surfaces of the vehicle. Flush contacted areas immediately with plenty of water. Antifreeze can be fatal to children and pets. They like it because it is sweet. Just a few licks can cause death. Wipe up garage floor and drip pan coolant spills immediately. Keep antifreeze containers covered and repair leaks in your cooling system immediately.*

The cooling system should be filled with a water/ethylene glycol based antifreeze solution, which will prevent freezing down to at least -20°F at all times. It also provides protection against corrosion and increases the coolant boiling point.

The cooling system should be drained, flushed and refilled at least every other year (see Chapter 1). The use of antifreeze solutions for periods of longer than two years is likely to cause damage and encourage the formation of rust and scale in the system.

Before adding antifreeze to the system, check all hose connections and retorque the cylinder head bolts. Antifreeze tends to search out and leak through very minute openings.

The exact mixture of antifreeze-to-water that you should use depends on the relative weather conditions. The mixture should contain at least 50 percent antifreeze, but should never contain more than 70 percent antifreeze.

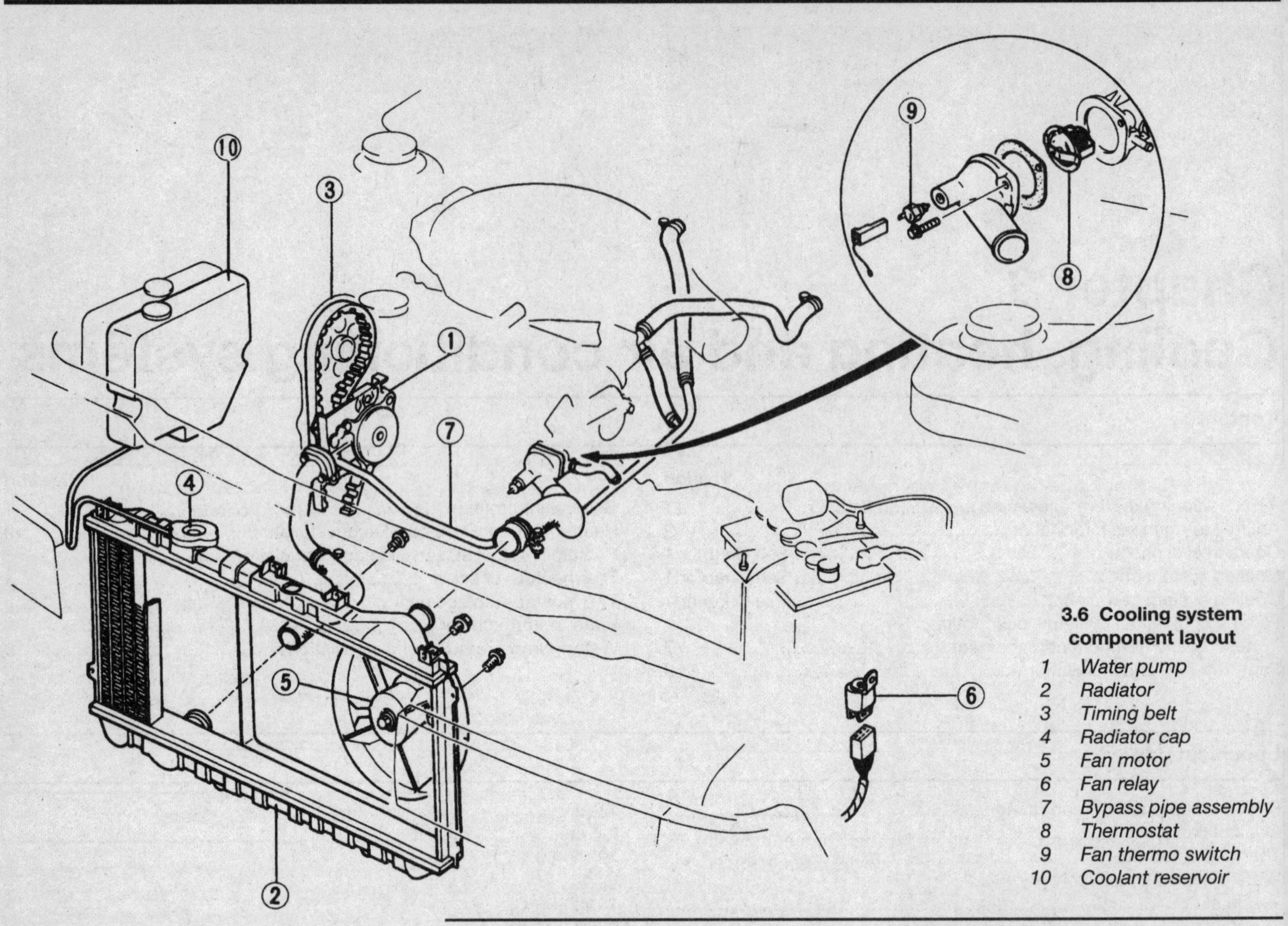

3.6 Cooling system component layout

1. *Water pump*
2. *Radiator*
3. *Timing belt*
4. *Radiator cap*
5. *Fan motor*
6. *Fan relay*
7. *Bypass pipe assembly*
8. *Thermostat*
9. *Fan thermo switch*
10. *Coolant reservoir*

3 Thermostat - replacement

Refer to illustrations 3.6, 3.7a, 3.7b, 3.8 and 3.12

Warning: *The engine must be completely cool before beginning this procedure. Also, when working in the vicinity of the electric fan, disconnect the negative battery cable from the battery to prevent the fan from coming on accidentally.*

1 Refer to the Warning in Section 2.

2 Disconnect the cable from the negative battery terminal (if not done previously).

3 Remove the distributor (Chapter 5) to provide access to the thermostat housing.

4 Drain the cooling system until the level is below the thermostat by loosening the radiator cap and opening the petcock at the bottom of the radiator. Close the petcock when enough coolant has drained.

5 Remove the upper radiator hose from the water outlet housing.

6 Unplug the fan thermo switch connector **(see illustration)**.

7 Remove the two housing nuts and separate the housing from the engine. It may be

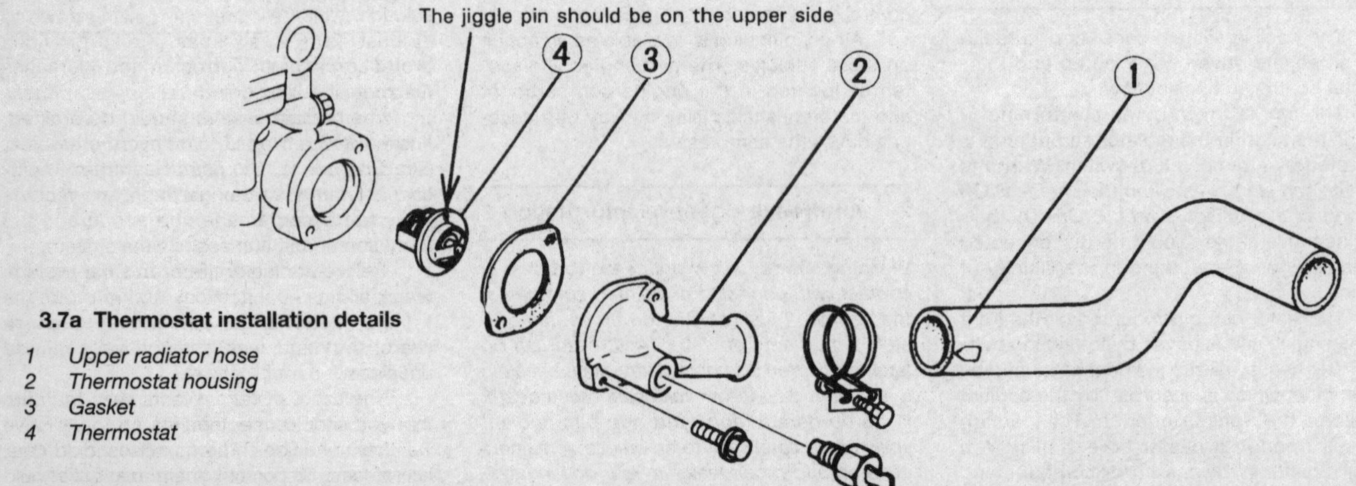
The jiggle pin should be on the upper side

3.7a Thermostat installation details

1. *Upper radiator hose*
2. *Thermostat housing*
3. *Gasket*
4. *Thermostat*

3.7b Break free the thermostat housing gasket with a rubber mallet

3.8 Note the direction of installation when removing the thermostat

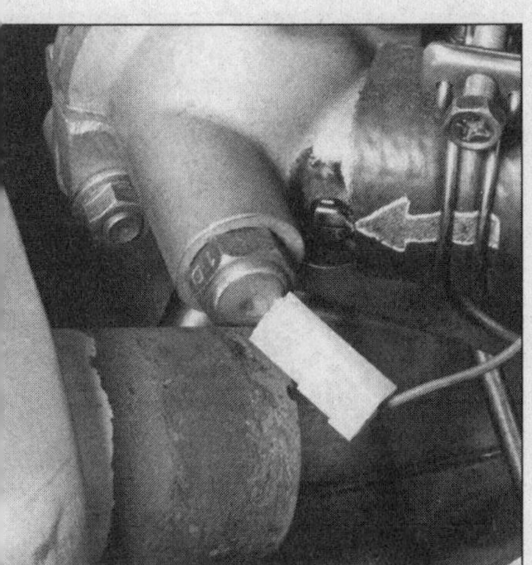

3.12 Make sure the arrow on the radiator hose aligns with the tab on the housing

necessary to use a rubber mallet to break the housing gasket seal **(see illustrations)**.

8 Remove the thermostat from the thermostat housing **(see illustration)**.

9 Before installing the thermostat, clean the gasket sealing surfaces on the water outlet and thermostat housing.

10 Apply a thin coat of sealant to both sides of the new gasket.

11 Place the thermostat in the housing, install the gasket with the printed side facing the thermostat and install the water outlet. Tighten the water outlet bolts to the specified torque.

12 Connect the upper radiator hose and tighten the hose clamp securely. Make sure the arrow on the hose aligns with the tab on the housing **(see illustration)**.

13 Plug in the thermo switch connector.

14 Install the distributor.

15 Fill the cooling system with the proper antifreeze/water mixture (refer to Chapter 1).

16 Reconnect the battery cable and start the engine.

17 Run the engine with the radiator cap removed until the upper radiator hose is hot (thermostat open).

18 With the engine idling, add coolant to the radiator until the level reaches the bottom of the filler neck.

19 Install the radiator cap.

4 Thermostat - check

1 The best way to check the operation of the thermostat is with it removed from the engine. In most cases, if the thermostat is suspect, it is more economical to simply buy and install a replacement thermostat, as they are not very costly.

2 To check, first remove the thermostat as described in Section 3.

3 Inspect the thermostat for excessive corrosion and damage. Replace it with a new one if either of these conditions is noted.

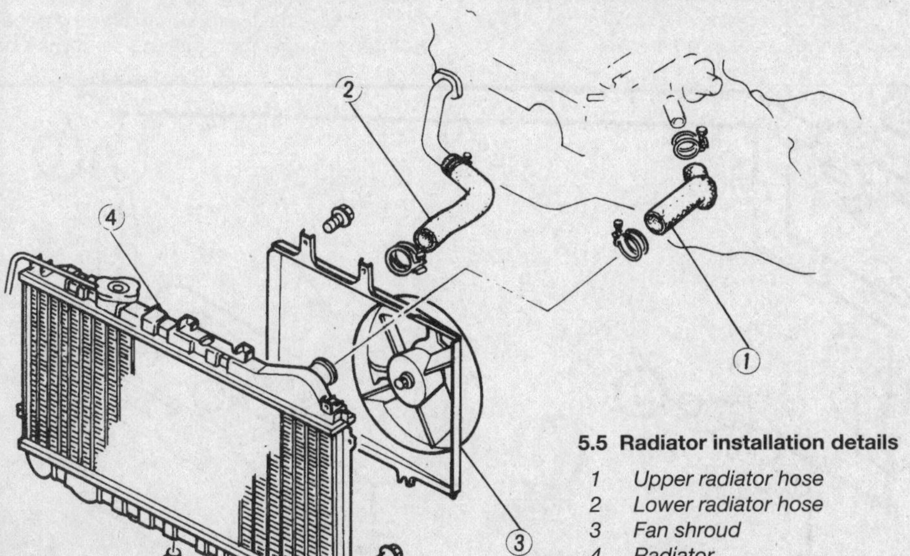

5.5 Radiator installation details

1 *Upper radiator hose*
2 *Lower radiator hose*
3 *Fan shroud*
4 *Radiator*

5 Radiator - removal, servicing and installation

Refer to illustrations 5.5, 5.6a, 5.6b and 5.12

Warning: *The engine must be completely cool before beginning this procedure. Also, when working in the vicinity of the electric fan, disconnect the negative battery cable from the battery to prevent the fan from coming on accidentally.*

1 Refer to the Warning in Section 2.

2 Drain the radiator (refer to Chapter 1, if necessary).

3 For access, remove the air cleaner intake and disconnect the ignition coil wire and move it out of the way.

4 Unplug the fan motor and radiator thermo switch connectors.

5 Remove the radiator hoses from the radiator and disconnect the coolant recovery hose **(see illustration)**.

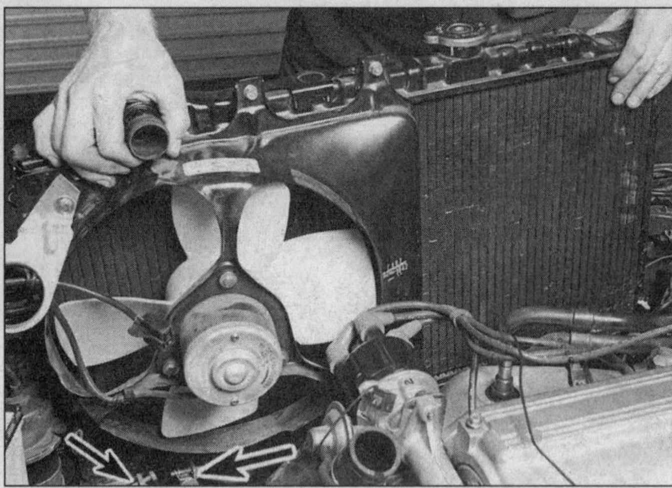

5.6a Lift the radiator for access to the automatic transaxle hose connections (arrows)

5.6b Hold the hoses out of the way and lift the radiator straight up to avoid damage to the fins

6 Remove the radiator attaching bolts and clamps and lift out the radiator. On automatic transaxle models, raise the radiator sufficiently for access to the cooler lines and disconnect and plug them. Remove the radiator from the engine compartment **(see illustrations)**.

7 Carefully examine the radiator for evidence of leaks and damage. It is recommended that any necessary repairs be performed by a radiator repair shop.

8 With the radiator removed, brush accumulations of insects and leaves from the fins and examine and replace, if necessary, any hoses or clamps which have deteriorated.

9 The radiator can be flushed as described in Chapter 1.

10 Replace the radiator cap with a new one of the same rating, or if the cap is comparatively new, have it tested by a service station.

11 If you are installing a new radiator, transfer the fittings from the old unit.

12 Installation is the reverse of removal, making sure the radiator seats securely in the mounts **(see illustration)**.

13 After installing the radiator, refill it with the proper coolant mixture (refer to Chapter 1), then start the engine and check for leaks.

6 Fan - removal and installation

Warning: *The engine must be completely cool before beginning this procedure. Also, when working in the vicinity of the electric fan, disconnect the negative battery cable from the battery to prevent the fan from coming on accidentally.*

1 To provide access, remove the distributor (Chapter 5) and the air cleaner assembly intake tube.

2 Unplug the fan connector.

3 Drain the coolant until the level is below the upper radiator hose by removing the

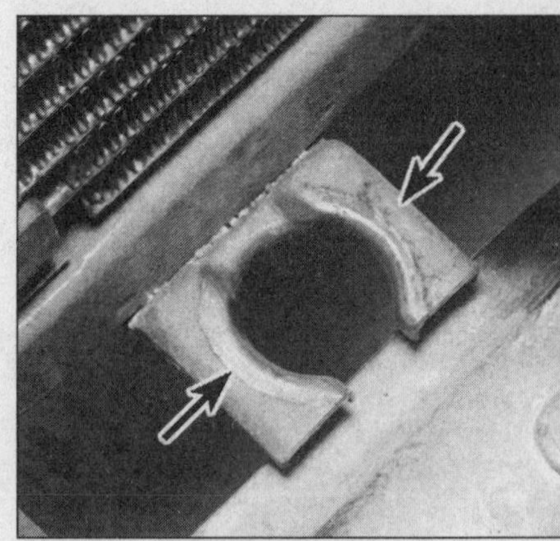

5.12 Check the radiator frame mount contact areas (arrows) for rust and damage

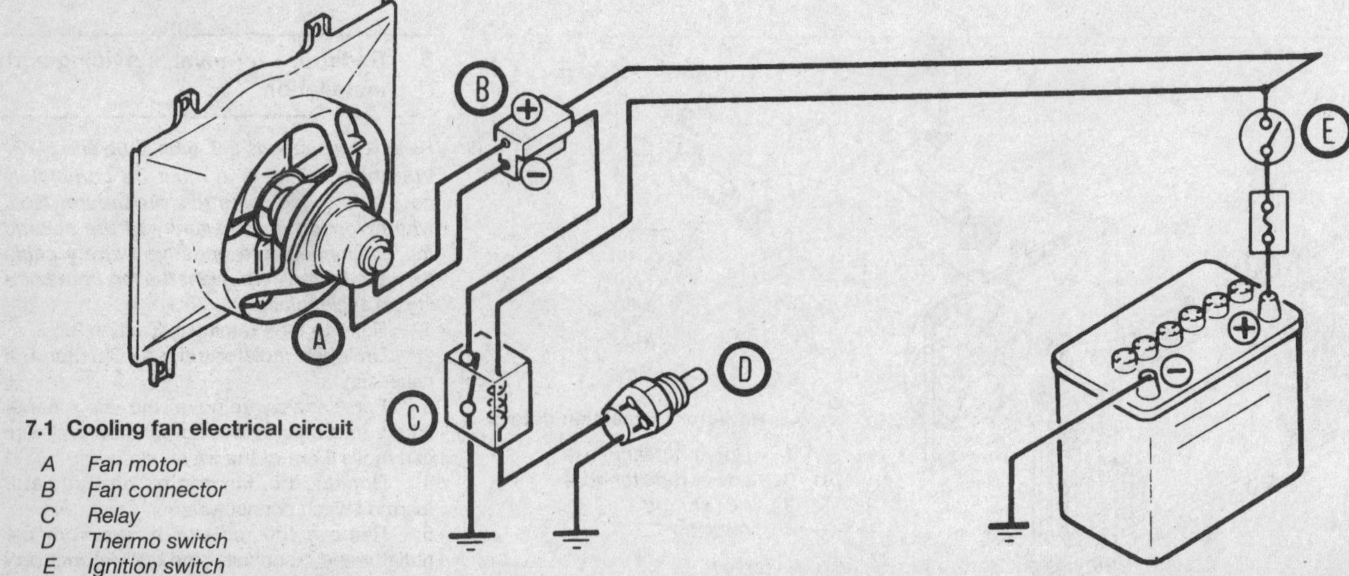

7.1 Cooling fan electrical circuit

A Fan motor
B Fan connector
C Relay
D Thermo switch
E Ignition switch

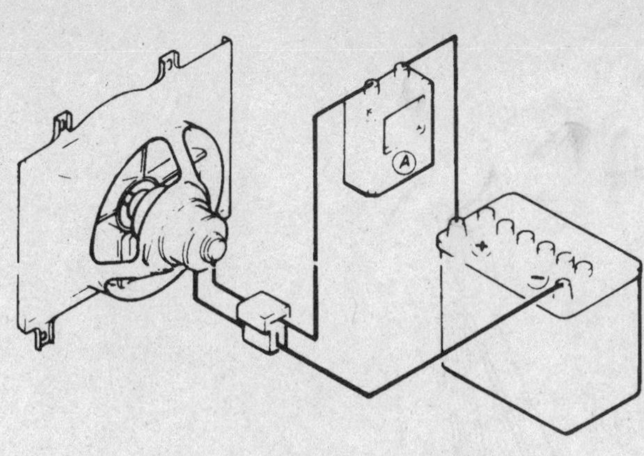

7.4 Cooling fan motor test

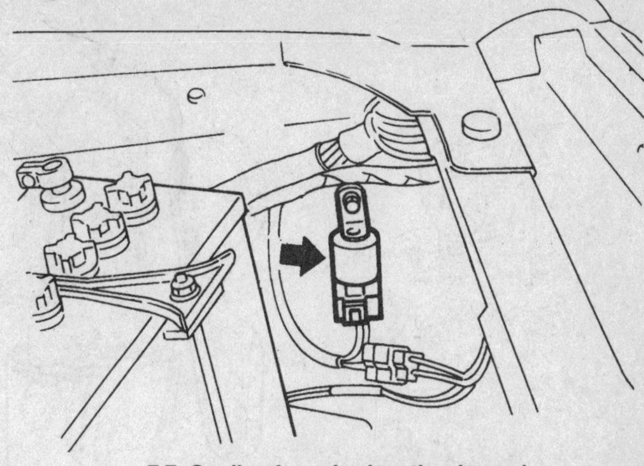
7.7 Cooling fan relay location (arrow)

drain plug at the bottom of the radiator.

4 Remove the upper radiator hose.

5 Remove the retaining bolts and lift the fan motor and cowling assembly from the radiator.

6 Installation is the reverse of removal.

7 Fill the radiator to the proper level, connect the negative battery cable and check for proper operation as the engine warms to operating temperature.

7 Electric cooling fan system - description, testing and component placement

Description

Refer to illustration 7.1

1 The electric cooling fan system consists of a fan motor and blade assembly mounted in a cowling which bolts to the radiator, a fan relay located on the left inner fender panel and a thermo switch threaded into the thermostat housing **(see illustration)**.

2 When the coolant in the thermostat housing reaches operating temperature for the fan (206.6°F) the thermo switch opens, sending electrical current through the relay and turning the fan motor on. When the temperature is below 194°F the switch is closed and the fan motor is off.

Testing and replacement

Fan motor

Refer to illustration 7.4

3 Trace the wire from the motor to the connector and separate the connector using a screwdriver.

4 Test the motor using an ammeter and battery, to make sure the fan motor operates at the specified current **(see illustration)**.

5 If the fan motor does not operate at the specified current, replace it with a new one (Section 6).

Fan relay

Refer to illustration 7.7

6 Unplug the water thermo switch connector and check to see if the fan turns when the ignition switch is turned On, indicating that the relay is operating properly.

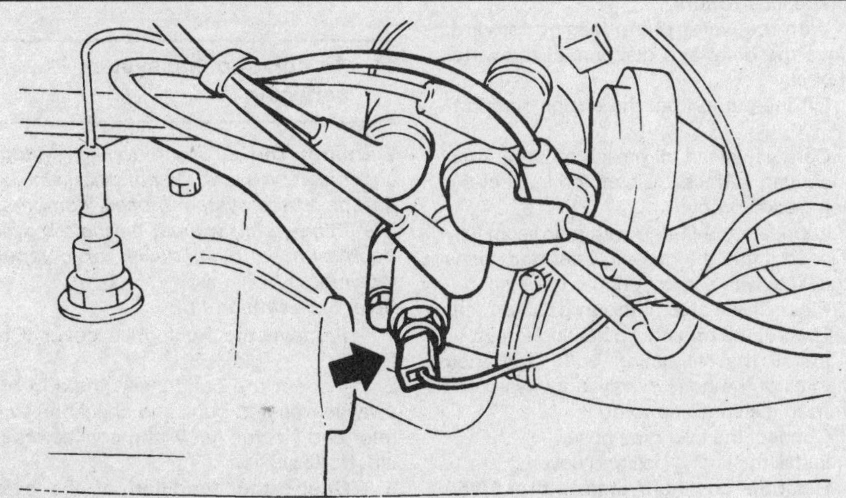
7.8 Cooling fan thermo switch location (arrow)

7 If the fan does not turn, check for a loose connection or faulty fuse. If the fuse and connections are good, replace the relay with a new one. The relay is replaced by unplugging the connector and removing the retaining screws **(see illustration)**.

Thermo switch

Refer to illustration 7.8

Note: *Do not disconnect the thermo switch with the ignition switch On or the fan will go on automatically.*

8 Disconnect the connector and remove the thermo switch **(see illustration)**.

9 Place the thermo switch in a container of hot water and check that there is continuity, indicating that the switch is operating properly.

10 When reinstalling the switch, make sure that the O-ring is installed or leaks will result.

8 Water pump - check

1 A failure of the water pump can cause overheating and serious engine damage (the pump will not circulate coolant through the engine).

2 There are three ways to check the operation of the water pump while it is still installed on the engine. If the pump is defective, it should be replaced with a new or rebuilt unit.

3 With the engine at normal operating temperature, squeeze the upper radiator hose. If the water pump is working properly, a pressure surge will be felt as the hose is released.

4 Water pumps are equipped with weep or vent holes. If a pump seal failure occurs, small amounts of coolant will leak from the weep holes. It will be necessary to remove the timing belt lower cover and use a flashlight from under the vehicle to see evidence of leakage from this point on the pump body.

5 If the water pump shaft bearings fail, there may be a squealing sound emitted from the front of the engine while it is running. Shaft wear can be felt if the water pump pulley is forced up and down.

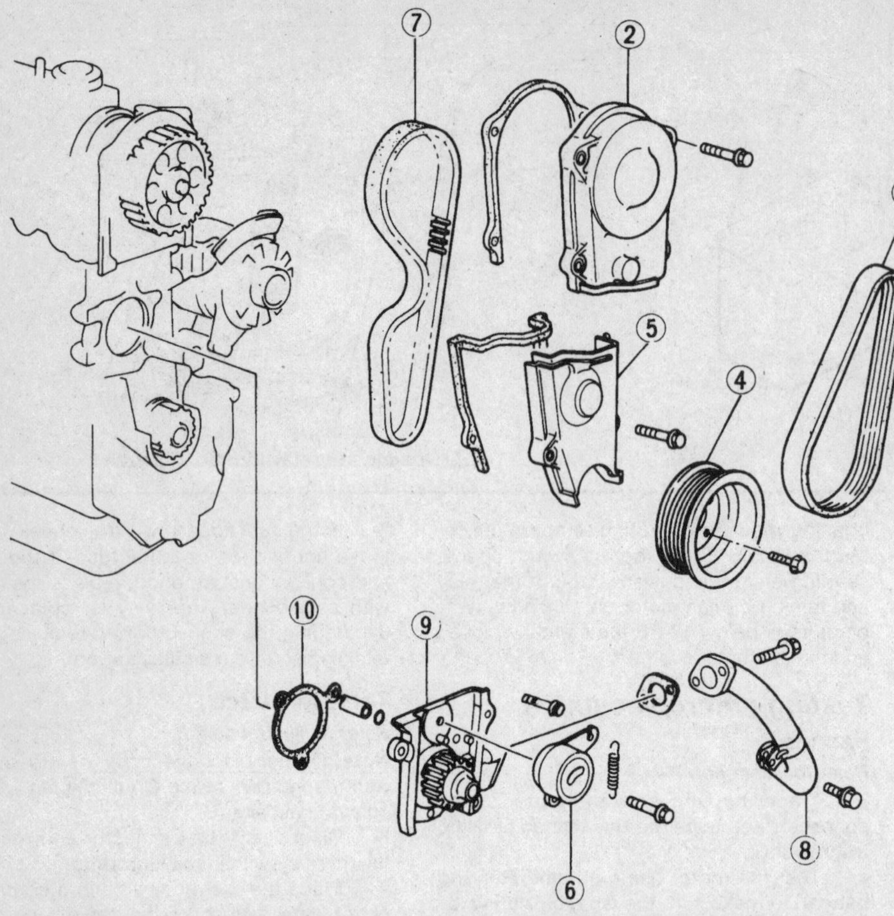

9.5 Water pump installation details

1 Drivebelt
2 Upper timing belt cover
4 Crankshaft pulley
5 Lower timing belt cover
6 Idler
7 Timing belt
8 Hose
9 Water pump
10 Gasket

9 Water pump - removal and installation

Refer to illustrations 9.5 and 9.6

Warning: *The engine must be completely cool before beginning this procedure. Also, when working in the vicinity of the electric fan, disconnect the negative battery cable from the battery to prevent the fan from coming on accidentally.*

1 Refer to the Caution in Section 2.

2 Drain the cooling system (refer to Chapter 1, if necessary).

9.6 Pry the water pump out from the engine with a large screwdriver

3 Remove the timing belt covers and the belt (Chapter 2).

4 Disconnect the water pump inlet pipe hose.

5 Remove the water pump bolts **(see illustration)**.

6 Use a large screwdriver or a suitable pry bar to pry on the water pump while using a rocking motion to disengage the pump O-ring **(see illustration)**.

7 With the water pump leaning forward, remove the bolts and disconnect the water inlet pipe.

8 Lift the pump from the engine compartment.

9 Carefully clean all gasket material from all mounting surfaces. Clean and inspect the O-ring gasket groove.

10 Lubricate the O-ring with petroleum jelly and insert it into the groove. Coat both sides the gaskets with sealant prior to installation.

11 Place the water pump in position and install two of the retaining bolts finger tight.

12 Install the remaining bolts and then tighten all of the bolts evenly in a criss-cross pattern to the specified torque.

13 Connect the inlet pipe hose.

14 Install the timing belt and covers.

15 Refill the cooling system with a 50/50 solution of water and the specified coolant (Chapter 1).

10 Heater fan motor - removal and installation

Refer to illustration 10.2

1 Disconnect the battery negative cable.

2 Unplug the electrical connectors, remove the retaining screws and lift the motor from the housing **(see illustration)**.

3 Installation is the reverse of removal.

11 Air conditioning system - servicing

Warning: *The air conditioning system is under high pressure. Do not disassemble any portion of the system (hoses, compressor, line fittings, etc.) without having the system depressurized by a dealer or competent repair facility.*

Refer to illustration 11.2

1 Remove the front grille cover (Chapter 11).

2 Inspect the condenser fins and brush away leaves and bugs and check the evaporator and electric fan wiring connectors **(see illustration)**.

3 Check the condition of the system hoses. If there is any sign of deterioration or hardening, have them replaced by a dealer or

10.2 The heater fan motor retaining screws and electrical connector locations (arrows)

11.2 The air conditioner fan (A), condenser (B) and evaporator (C)

air conditioning repair facility.

4 At the recommended intervals, check and adjust the compressor drivebelt as described in Chapter 1.

5 Because of the special tools, equipment and skills required to service air conditioning systems, and the differences between the various systems that may be installed on vehicles, major air conditioning servicing procedures cannot be covered in this manual.

Notes

Chapter 4
Fuel and exhaust systems

Contents

Specifications

Carburetor specifications

Air horn dry float adjustment
Air horn inverted, clearance H
US models .... 0.53 in (13.5 mm)
UK models .... 0.394 in (10 mm)
Air horn upright, clearance L .... 1.929 in (49 mm)
Choke diaphragm clearance G (vacuum applied) .... 0.077 to 0.87 in (1.95 to 2.20 mm)
Fast idle cam clearance G .... 0.028 to 0.043 in (0.70 to 1.10 mm)
Choke valve clearance R .... 0.031 to 0.39 in (0.080 to 0.082 mm)
Choke unloader clearance R .... 0.128 to 0.144 in (3.25 to 3.65 mm)
Secondary throttle valve clearance .... 0.244 to 0.283 in (6.2 to 7.2 mm)

Fuel injection system specifications

Fuel pressure
1986
Pump activated (engine NOT running) .... 44 to 49 PSI
At idle .... 35 to 41 PSI
1987 and later
Pump activated (engine NOT running) .... 35 to 41 PSI
At idle .... 27 to 33 PSI

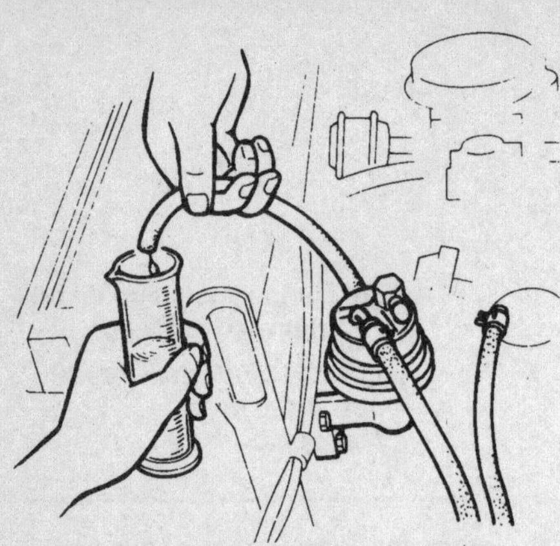

2.8 Testing the fuel pump (carbureted models)

1 General information

Carbureted models

The fuel system consists of a rear mounted fuel tank, a mechanically operated fuel pump and carburetor and an air cleaner assembly.

Fuel injected models

The exhaust system includes a catalytic converter, muffler, related emissions equipment and associated pipes and hardware.

The exhaust system on all models includes a muffler, catalytic converter and associated pipes and hardware.

2 Fuel pump/fuel pressure - check

Warning: *Gasoline is extremely flammable, so take extra precautions when you work on any part of the fuel system. Don't smoke or allow open flames or bare light bulbs near the work area, and don't work in a garage where a natural gas-type appliance (such as a water heater or a clothes dryer) with a pilot light is present. Since gasoline is carcinogenic, wear latex gloves when there's a possibility of being exposed to fuel, and, if you spill any fuel on your skin, rinse it off immediately with soap and water. Mop up any spills immediately and do not store fuel-soaked rags where they could ignite. The fuel system is under constant pressure, so, if any fuel lines are to be disconnected, the fuel pressure in the system must be relieved first. When you perform any kind of work on the fuel system, wear safety glasses and have a Class B type fire extinguisher on hand.*

Carbureted models

Refer to illustration 2.8

1 The fuel pump bolts to the cylinder head on the back (firewall side) of the engine.

2 A fuel pump is sealed and no repairs are possible. However, it can be inspected and tested on the vehicle as follows.

3 Make sure that there is fuel in the fuel tank.

4 With the engine running, check for leaks at all gasoline line connections between the fuel tank and the carburetor. Tighten any loose connections.

5 Inspect all hoses for flat spots and kinks which would restrict the fuel flow. Air leaks or restrictions on the suction side of the fuel pump will greatly affect pump output.

6 Check for leaks at the fuel pump diaphragm flange.

7 Disconnect the ignition coil wire at the distributor, carefully ground the wire to the engine to prevent sparks, then disconnect the fuel inlet line from the carburetor and place it in a container.

8 Crank the engine a few revolutions and make sure that well defined spurts of fuel are ejected from the open end of the line **(see illustration)**. If not, the fuel line is clogged or the fuel pump is defective.

9 Disconnect the fuel line at both ends and blow through it with compressed air. If the fuel line is not clogged, replace the fuel pump with a new one.

Fuel injected models

Refer to illustrations 2.11, 2.14 and 2.16

10 Relieve the fuel system pressure (see Section 11). Reconnect the fuel pump wire harness connector, or the circuit opening relay wire.

11 Disconnect the hose from the fuel filter to the distribution pipe and install a fuel pressure gauge with a T-fitting **(see illustration)**.

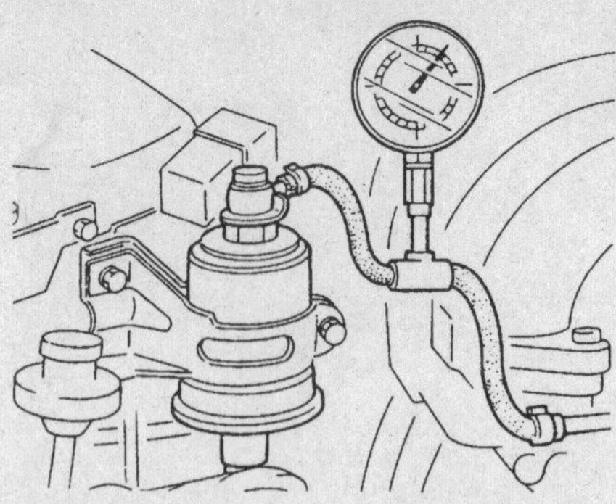

2.11 To check the fuel pressure on fuel injected models, install a gauge between the fuel filter and the distribution pipe with a T-fitting and a short section of hose

12 Start the engine and let it idle. The pressure should be as noted in the Specifications.

13 If there is no pressure (even though the pump is running), the in-line fuel filter is probably clogged. Replace it and check the pressure again. If there is still zero pressure, the fuel feed line may be clogged. If the fuel feed line is clear, check the fuel pump inlet filter.

14 If the fuel pressure is low, the in-line fuel filter may be partially clogged. Replace it and check the pressure again. If it's still low, check for a loose fuel line fitting or a punctured fuel line. Also check the pressure regulator, fuel distribution pipe and injectors for leaks (refer to Section 13). If nothing is leaking, block the fuel return line (the hose connected to the fuel pressure regulator) and bridge the fuel pump test connector terminals on the firewall with a jumper wire **(see illustration)**. Note the indicated pressure. If the pressure is now above the upper limit, the fuel pressure regulator is faulty. If the pressure is still low, replace the fuel pump.

15 If the fuel pressure is high, disconnect the fuel return line flexible hose and attach a 5/16-inch ID rubber hose to the pressure regulator side of the return line. Insert the other end in an approved gasoline container. Note the fuel pressure while bridging the test connector terminals. If pressure is still above the upper limit, replace the regulator. If the fuel pressure is now as specified, the return line is restricted. Locate and remove the restriction.

16 To check fuel pump resistance, remove the rear seat and unplug the pump wire harness connector. Measure the resistance between terminals A and B with an ohmmeter. The reading should be approximately 0.3-ohms **(see illustration)**. If it isn't, replace the pump.

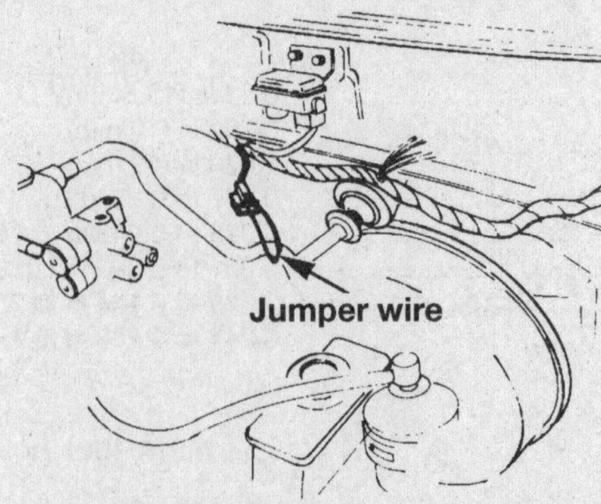

2.14 The fuel pump can be activated by bridging the fuel pump test connector terminals with a jumper wire

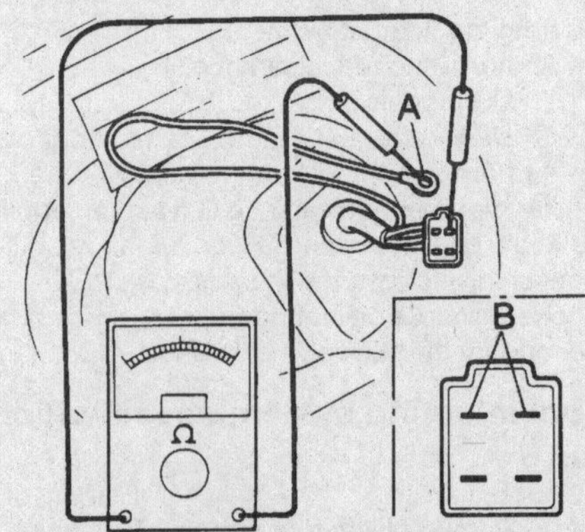

2.16 Check the fuel pump resistance with an ohmmeter - measure between the two B terminals and the ground wire A

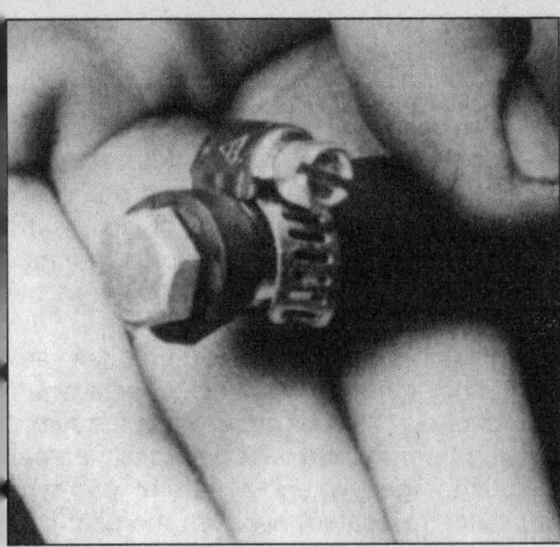

3.2 A bolt can be used to plug the fuel hose

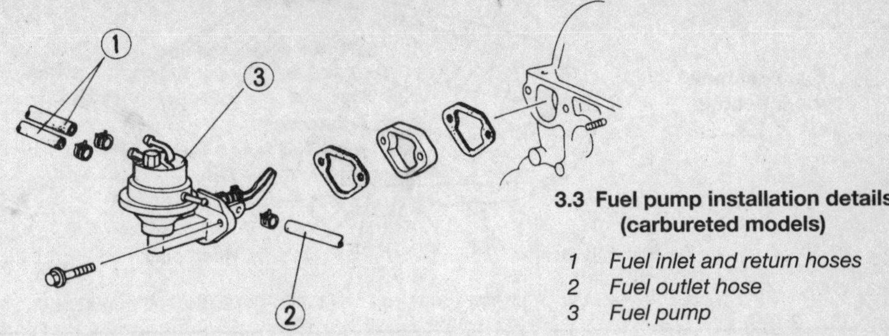

3.3 Fuel pump installation details (carbureted models)

1 *Fuel inlet and return hoses*
2 *Fuel outlet hose*
3 *Fuel pump*

3 Fuel pump - removal and installation

Warning: *Gasoline is extremely flammable, so take extra precautions when you work on any part of the fuel system. Don't smoke or allow open flames or bare light bulbs near the work area, and don't work in a garage where a natural gas-type appliance (such as a water heater or a clothes dryer) with a pilot light is present. Since gasoline is carcinogenic, wear latex gloves when there's a possibility of being exposed to fuel, and, if you spill any fuel on your skin, rinse it off immediately with soap and water. Mop up any spills immediately and do not store fuel-soaked rags where they could ignite. The fuel system is under constant pressure, so, if any fuel lines are to be disconnected, the fuel pressure in the system must be relieved first. When you perform any kind of work on the fuel system, wear safety glasses and have a Class B type fire extinguisher on hand.*

Carbureted models

Refer to illustrations 3.2 and 3.3

1 Disconnect the cable from the negative battery terminal.

2 Use pliers to release the clips and then remove and plug the fuel inlet and outlet hoses **(see illustration)**.

3 Remove the fuel pump mounting bolts, the pump and the gasket **(see illustration)**.

4 Install the pump using a new gasket.

5 Connect the fuel lines, start the engine and check for leaks.

Fuel injected models

Refer to illustrations 3.8, 3.9 and 3.11

6 Relieve the fuel system pressure (Section 12), then disconnect the cable from the negative battery terminal.

7 Remove the service hole cover and push the rubber grommet and harness connector through the opening.

8 Mark the fuel main and return hoses with pieces of tape. Loosen the hose clamps and disconnect the hoses **(see illustration)**.

9 Remove the pump bracket screws and lift the fuel pump and bracket out of the fuel tank **(see illustration)**.

10 Disconnect the electrical leads from the pump terminals.

11 Loosen the pump clamp screw, slide the hose clamps toward the center of the hose, then swing the bottom of the pump out of the bracket. Pull the pump assembly and hose from the bracket **(see illustration)**.

12 Remove the rubber cushion and in-tank filter from the lower end of the fuel pump by prying the retaining clip off.

13 Installation is the reverse of removal. Be sure to use a new gasket between the fuel tank and the pump bracket.

4 Fuel line - repair and replacement

Warning: *Gasoline is extremely flammable, so take extra precautions when you work on any part of the fuel system. Don't smoke or allow open flames or bare light bulbs near the work area, and don't work in a garage where a natural gas-type appliance (such as a water heater or a clothes dryer) with a pilot light is present. Since gasoline is carcinogenic, wear latex gloves when there's a possibility of being exposed to fuel, and, if you spill any fuel on your skin, rinse it off immediately with soap and water. Mop up any spills immediately and do not store fuel-soaked rags where they could ignite. The fuel system is under constant pressure, so, if any fuel lines are to be disconnected, the fuel pressure in the system must be relieved first. When you perform any kind of work on the fuel system, wear safety glasses and have a Class B type fire extinguisher on hand.*

1 If a section of metal fuel line must be replaced, only seamless steel tubing should be used, since copper or aluminum does not have enough durability to withstand normal operating vibrations.

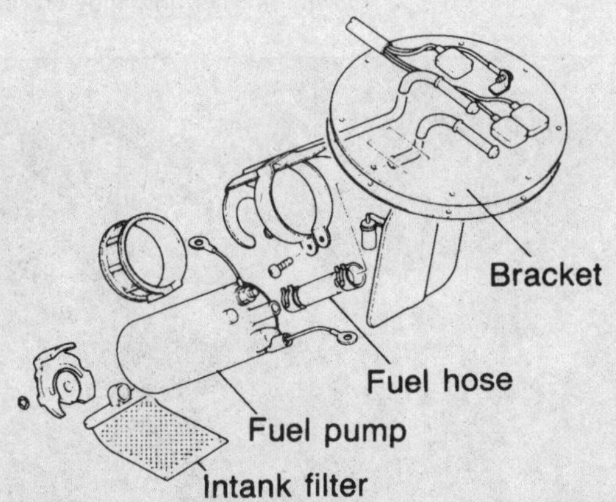

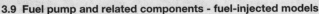

3.9 Fuel pump and related components - fuel-injected models

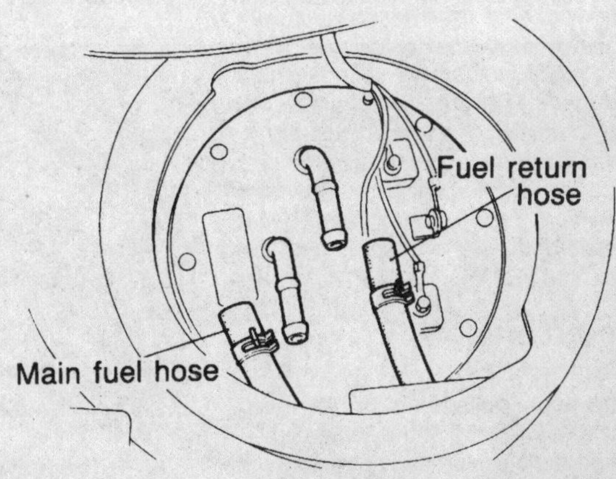

3.11 Fuel injected model electric fuel pump installation details

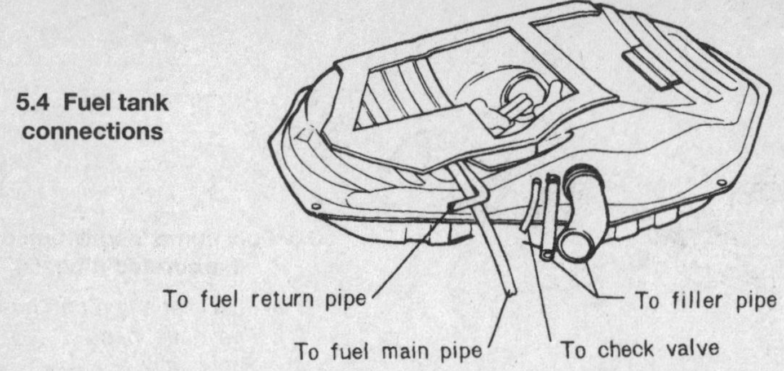

5.4 Fuel tank connections

2 If only one section of a metal fuel line is damaged, it can be cut out and replaced with a piece of rubber hose. Be sure to use only reinforced fuel resistant hose, identified by the word "Fluroelastomer" on the hose. The inside diameter of the hose should match the outside diameter of the metal line. The rubber hose should be cut four inches longer than the section it's replacing, so there are two inches of overlap between the rubber and metal line at either end of the section. Hose clamps should be used to secure both ends of the repaired section.

3 If a section of metal line longer than six inches is being removed, use a combination of metal tubing and rubber hose so the hose lengths will be no longer than 10 inches.

4 Never use rubber hose within four inches of any part of the exhaust system or within 10 inches of the catalytic converter.

5 Fuel tank - removal and installation

Refer to illustration 5.4

Warning: *Gasoline is extremely flammable, so take extra precautions when you work on any part of the fuel system. Don't smoke or allow open flames or bare light bulbs near the work area, and don't work in a garage where a natural gas-type appliance (such as a water heater or a clothes dryer) with a pilot light is present. Since gasoline is carcinogenic, wear latex gloves when there's a possibility of being exposed to fuel, and, if you spill any fuel on your skin, rinse it off immediately with soap and water. Mop up any spills immediately and do not store fuel-soaked rags where they could ignite. The fuel system is under constant pressure, so, if any fuel lines are to be disconnected, the fuel pressure in the system must be relieved first. When you perform any kind of work on the fuel system, wear safety glasses and have a Class B type fire extinguisher on hand.*

1 Raise the rear of the vehicle and support it on jackstands.

2 Remove the cable from the negative battery terminal.

3 Drain all fuel from the tank into a clean container.

4 Mark and disconnect the fuel lines and the filler pipe at the fuel tank **(see illustration)**.

5 While the tank is supported by an assistant or a floor jack, remove the five retaining bolts.

6 Carefully lower the tank, unplug the gauge unit connector and remove the tank from the vehicle.

7 **Warning:** *Never perform any repair work involving heat or flame on the tank until it has been purged of gas and vapors. All repair work should be performed by a professional* (see the following Section).

8 Before reinstalling the tank make sure that all traces of dirt and corrosion are cleaned from it. A coat of rust preventative paint is recommended. If the tank is rusted internally, however, it should be replaced with a new one.

9 Installation is the reverse of the removal procedure.

6 Fuel tank - repair

1 Any repairs to the fuel tank or filler neck should be carried out by a professional who has experience in this critical and potentially dangerous work. Even after cleaning and flushing of the fuel system, explosive fumes can remain and ignite during repair of the tank.

2 If the fuel tank is removed from the vehicle, it should not be placed in an area where sparks or open flames could ignite the fumes coming from the tank. Be especially careful inside garages where a natural gas-type appliance is located, because the pilot light could cause an explosion.

7 Carburetor - removal and installation

Refer to illustrations 7.3a, 7.3b, 7.9 and 7.10

Warning: *Gasoline is extremely flammable, so take extra precautions when you work on any part of the fuel system. Don't smoke or allow open flames or bare light bulbs near the work area, and don't work in a garage where a natural gas-type appliance (such as a water heater or a clothes dryer) with a pilot light is present. Since gasoline is carcinogenic, wear latex gloves when there's a possibility of being exposed to fuel, and, if you spill any fuel on your skin, rinse it off immediately with soap and water. Mop up any spills immediately and do not store fuel-soaked rags where they could ignite. The fuel system is under constant pressure, so, if any fuel lines are to be disconnected, the fuel pressure in the system must be relieved first. When you perform any kind of work on the fuel system, wear safety glasses and have a Class B type fire extinguisher on hand.*

1 Remove the cable from the negative battery terminal.

2 Remove the air cleaner assembly.

3 Disconnect the throttle linkage and (if equipped) cruise control cables **(see illustrations)**.

4 Disconnect the fuel lines, making very careful note of how they are attached. Tags

7.3a Remove the throttle linkage clip with a screwdriver and ...

7.3b ... use two wrenches to loosen the retaining nuts

7.9 Insert a screwdriver blade under the carburetor spacer to break the gasket seal

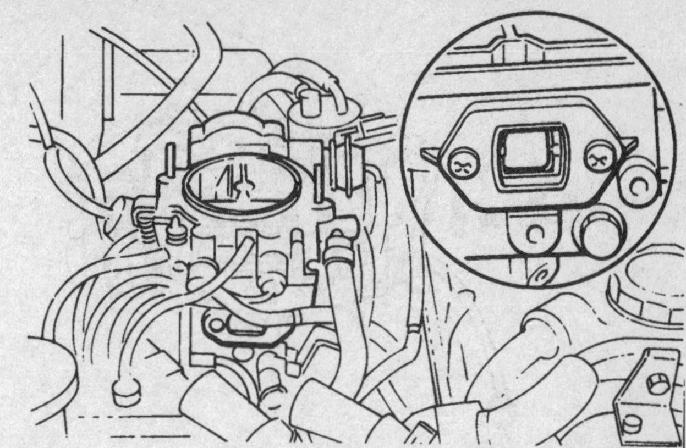
7.10 The carburetor fuel level can be checked at the sight glass

or coded pieces of tape will help.

5 Unplug the electrical harness.

6 Disconnect the evaporative system canister hoses.

7 Disconnect the vacuum lines from the carburetor, noting their locations.

8 Remove the mounting nuts, lift the carburetor sufficiently to allow disconnection of the choke heater wire and remove the carburetor from the manifold.

9 Remove the spacer from the manifold, using a screwdriver to break the seal **(see illustration)**.

10 Installation is the reverse of the removal procedure, but the following points should be noted:

a) *By filling the carburetor bowl with fuel, the initial start-up will be easier and less drain on the battery.*
b) *New gaskets should be used on both sides of the spacer.*
c) *After installation, start the engine, check for leaks and make sure fuel level is even with the mark on the carburetor sight glass* **(see illustration)**. *If it is not, adjust the float level as described in Section 8.*
d) *Idle speed and mixture settings should be checked and, if necessary, adjusted.*

8 Carburetor - overhaul and adjustment

Note: *Carburetor overhaul is an involved procedure that requires some experience. The home mechanic without much experience should have the overhaul done by a dealer service department or repair shop. Because of running production changes, some details of the unit overhauled here may not exactly match those of your carburetor, although the home mechanic with previous experience should be able to detect the differences and modify the procedure.*

Disassembly

Air horn and automatic choke

Refer to illustrations 8.1a, 8.1b, 8.2 and 8.3

1 Mount the carburetor on a punch or suitable tool placed in a vise as a work stand and disconnect the vacuum tube, accelerator pump rod and lever and spring **(see illustrations)**.

8.1a It will be much easier to work on the carburetor if it is mounted on a punch held securely in a vise

2 Separate the air vent solenoid valve electrical lead from the connector and disconnect the choke rod **(see illustration)**.

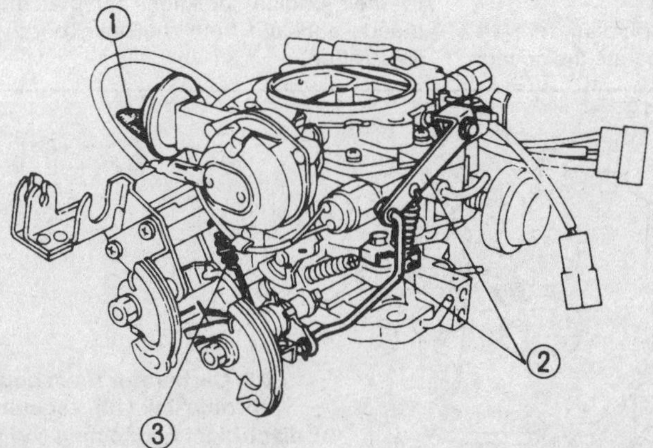

8.1b Carburetor air horn and choke assembly

1 *Vacuum tube*
2 *Accelerator pump*
3 *Spring*

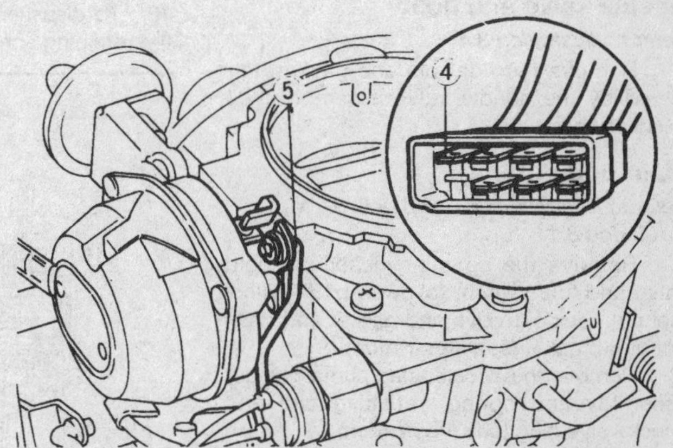

8.2 Air horn and choke air vent solenoid lead (4) and choke rod (5)

4

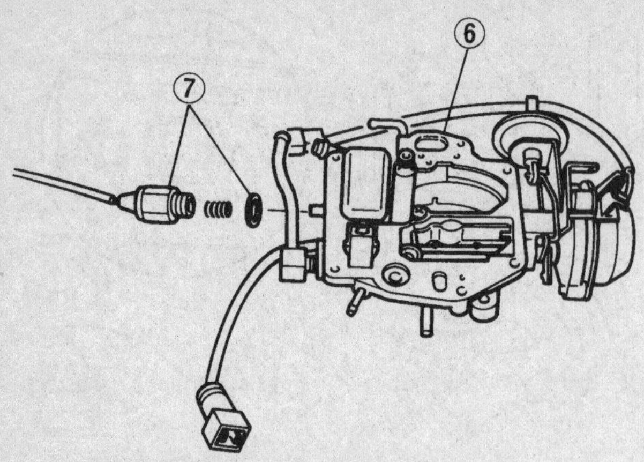

8.3 Air horn and automatic choke assembly (6) and air vent solenoid and gasket (7)

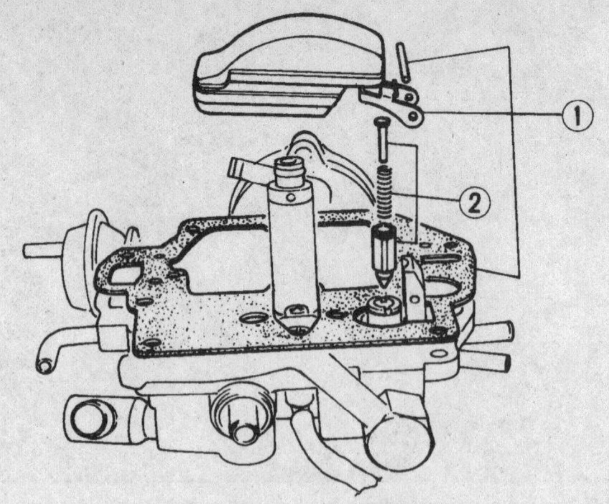

8.4 Needle valve and float assembly

1 Float, pin and gasket
2 Needle valve assembly

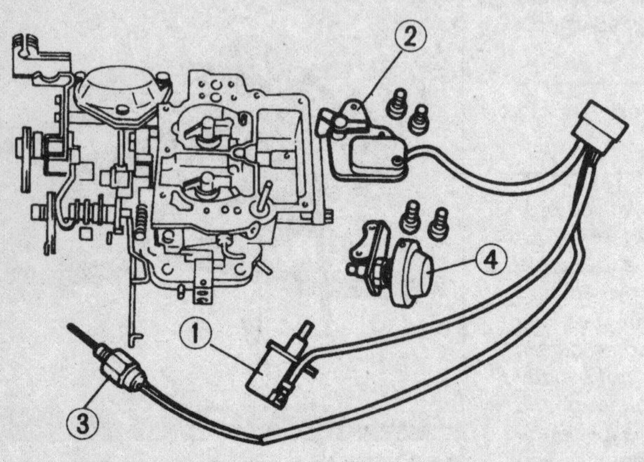

8.5 Carburetor main body solenoid switch component details

1 Coasting richer solenoid valve
2 Idle switch
3 Slow fuel cut solenoid
4 Dashpot and bracket

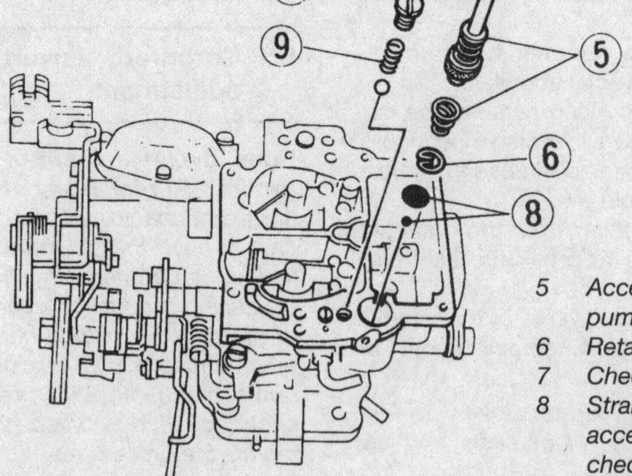

5 Accelerating pump/plunger assembly
6 Retaining clip
7 Check valve plug
8 Strainer and accelerating pump inlet check ball
9 Accelerating pump outlet ball and spring

8.6 Carburetor main body accelerating pump components

3 Remove the air horn and choke assembly and air vent solenoid and gasket from the main body **(see illustration)**.

Needle valve and float

Refer to illustration 8.4

4 Remove the float pin and gasket, followed by the needle valve assembly **(see illustration)**.

Main body

Refer to illustrations 8.5, 8.6, 8.8, 8.10a, 8.10b and 8.11

5 Remove the coasting richer solenoid valve and idle switch, followed by the slow fuel cut solenoid valve and gasket and dash pot and bracket **(see illustration)**.

6 Remove the accelerating pump plunger assembly and spring, retaining clip and check valve plug **(see illustration)**.

7 Turn the main body over and remove the strainer and accelerating pump inlet check ball and pump outlet check ball and spring.

8 Disconnect the throttle link and diaphragm connecting rod **(see illustration)**.

9 Separate the throttle body (one of the bolts is located inside) and the diaphragm assembly screws and gasket.

10 To disassemble the diaphragm, remove the retaining screws and separate the covers and remove the spring and diaphragm and throttle lever hanger **(see illustrations)**.

11 Noting the sizes for ease of installation to their original position, remove the air bleeds and jets from the main body **(see illustration)**.

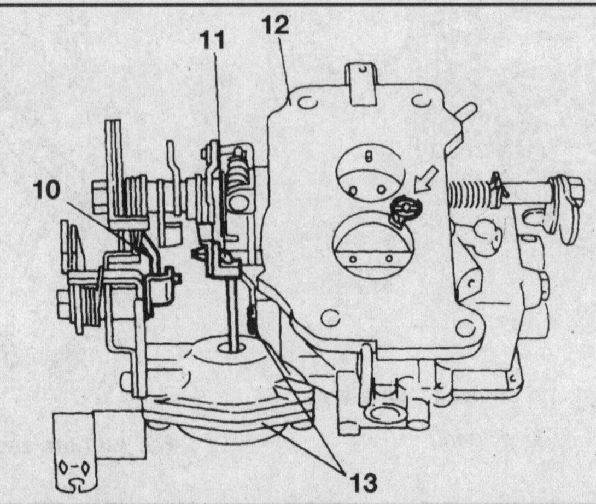

8.8 Carburetor main body throttle link (10), vacuum diaphragm connecting rod (11), throttle body (12) and diaphragm assembly (13)

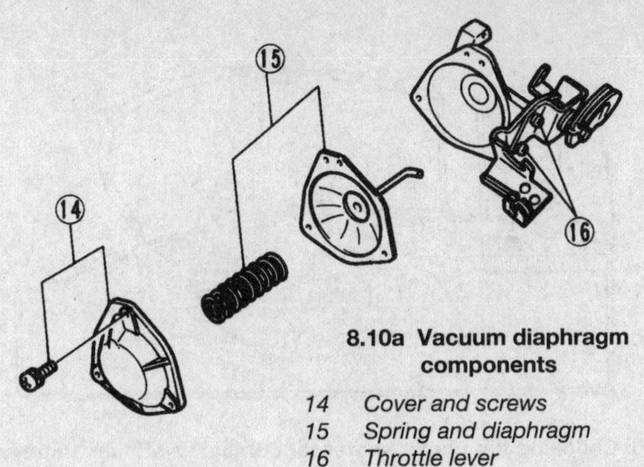

8.10a Vacuum diaphragm components

14 Cover and screws
15 Spring and diaphragm
16 Throttle lever

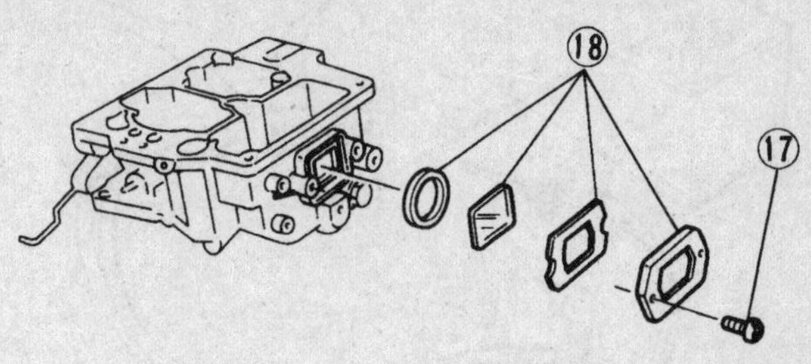

8.10b Carburetor main body fuel bowl sight glass assembly

17 Screws
18 Cover, gasket, glass and rubber gasket

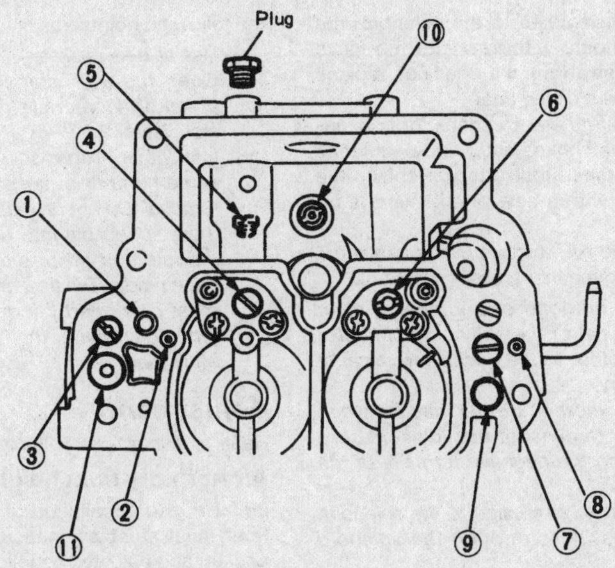

8.11 Carburetor main body air bleeds and jets

1 Step jet #80
2 Secondary step air bleed (No. 1) #80
3 Richer air bleed (N0. 2) #80
4 Secondary main air bleed #50
5 Secondary main jet #150
6 Primary main air bleed
7 Slow jet #46 and plug
8 Primary slow air bleed (No. 1) #80
9 Primary slow air bleed (No. 2) #150
10 Primary main jet #94
11 Richer air bleed (No. 1) (#200 for automatic transaxle, #250 for manual) and richer jet #42

4

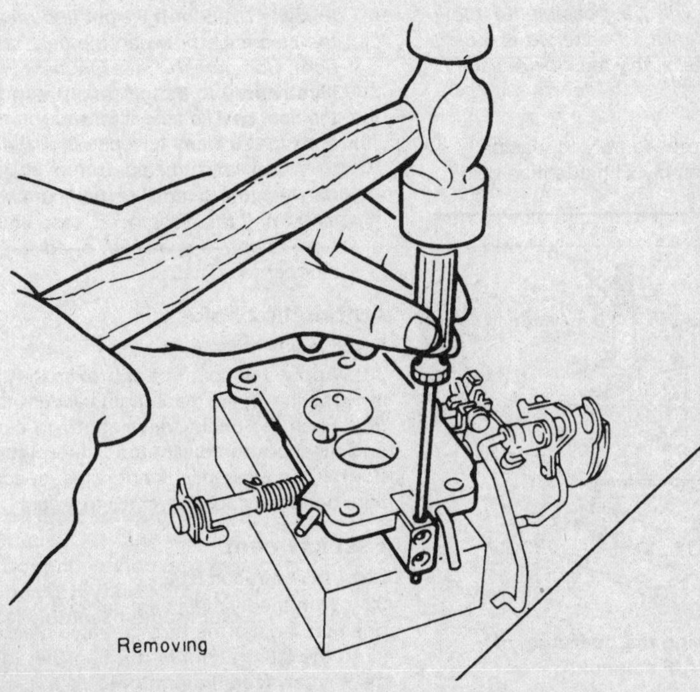

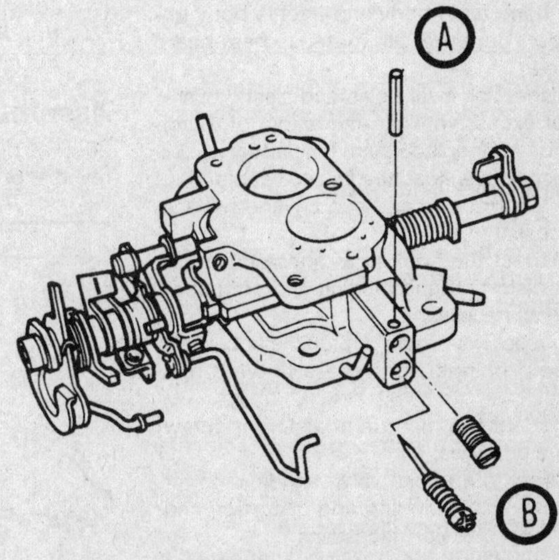

8.12 Remove the carburetor throttle body mixture adjustment screw by driving out the spring pin

A Spring pin
B Mixture adjustment screw

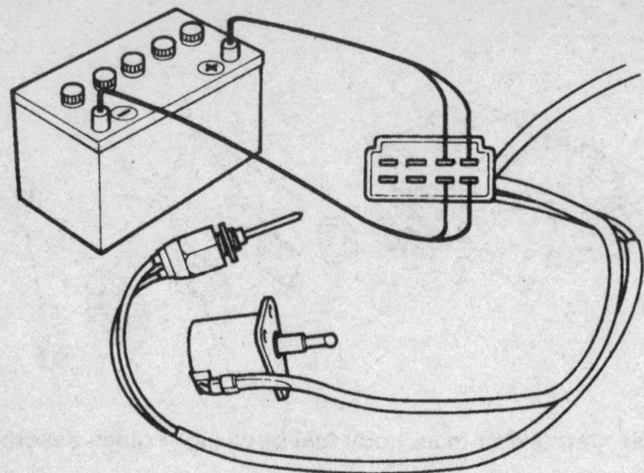

8.25 Checking solenoid operation)

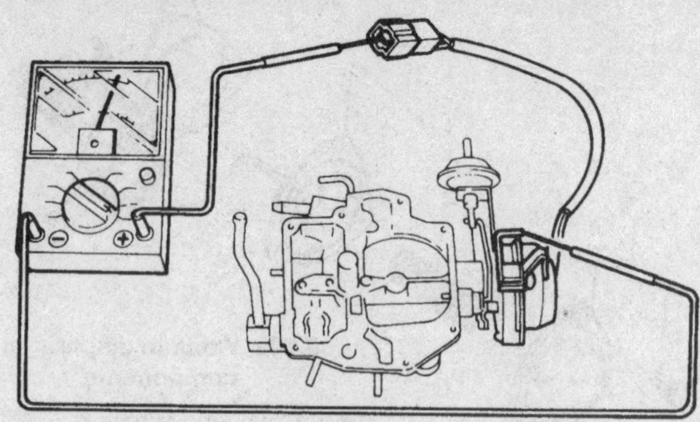

8.26 Checking the choke heater for continuity with an ohmmeter

Throttle body

Refer to illustration 8.12,

12 Carefully drive out the spring pin and remove the mixture adjustment screw, recording the number of turns so that it can be reinstalled in the same position **(see illustration)**.

Cleaning and inspection

Refer to illustration 8.25, 8.26 and 8. 27

13 Wash all components in clean solvent and blow them dry with compressed air. A can of compressed air can be used if an air compressor is not available. Do not use a piece of wire for cleaning the jets and passages.

14 The A/F mixture control solenoid, automatic choke, diaphragm and other electrical, rubber and plastic parts should not be immersed in carburetor cleaner because they will harden, swell or distort.

15 Make sure all fuel passages, jets and other metering components are free of burrs and dirt.

16 Inspect the upper and lower surfaces of the air horn, main body and throttle body for damage. Be sure all material has been removed.

17 Inspect all lever holes and plastic bushings for excessive wear and an out of round condition and replace them if necessary.

18 Inspect the float needle and seat for dirt, deep wear grooves and scoring and replace it if necessary.

19 Inspect the float, float arms and hinge pin for distortion and binding and correct or replace as necessary.

20 Inspect the rubber cup on the accelerating pump plunger for excessive wear and cracks.

21 Inspect the mixture adjustment screw for burrs or ridges.

22 Check the choke valve and linkage for excessive wear, binding and distortion and correct or replace as necessary.

23 Inspect the choke vacuum diaphragm for leaks and replace if necessary.

24 Check the choke valve for freedom of movement.

25 Check the solenoid operation by connecting the solenoid to the positive battery terminal with the body grounded. With the battery current applied to the solenoid, the valve stem should withdraw into the valve body **(see illustration)**. If it does not, replace the solenoid with a new one.

26 Use an ohmmeter to check for continuity between the choke heater and coupler as shown in the **(see illustration)**. Replace the choke heater with a new one if there is no continuity.

27 Check the A/F mixture control solenoid in the following manner **(see illustration)**.

a) Connect one end of a jumper wire to one terminal of the solenoid connector and the other to the positive terminal of the battery.

b) Connect another jumper wire between the other terminal of the solenoid connector and the negative terminal of the battery.

c) When current is applied to the solenoid, air will not pass through the solenoid valve.

d) When current is not applied to the solenoid, it will be possible to blow through the valve. If solenoid is faulty, the air horn assembly must be replaced.

Assembly

28 Carburetor reassembly is basically a reversal of disassembly with attention paid to the following points:

a) Use all new gaskets.

b) Coat the A/F solenoid O-ring with assembly lube or clean gasoline prior to installation.

c) Install the mixture adjustment screw the same number of turns recorded during removal. Do not drive the mixture adjustment spring pin into position until after the idle and mixture adjustments have been made. The final mixture adjustment must be done by a dealer or qualified technician with the required testing equipment.

"O" ring

8.27 Checking the operation of the A/F solenoid

Adjustment

Refer to illustrations 8.29a and 8.29b

Air horn dry float height

29 Prior to installation of the air horn, the float level must be measured (without the gasket) and adjusted as follows.

a) With the air horn inverted, allow the float to lower by its own weight and measure the clearance between the float and air horn. Compare the measurement H ***(see illustration)*** *to Specifications and bend the float seal lip as necessary.*

b) Turn the air horn upright, allow the float to lower and measure the distance between the bottom of the float and the air horn. If the clearance L ***(see illustration)*** *is not as specified, bend the float stopper to adjust.*

Automatic choke

Refer to illustration 8.31

30 Apply a vacuum of approximately 15.7 in-Hg to the choke diaphragm vacuum tube.

31 Push the choke valve lightly to close it and measure the clearance R **(see illustration)**. If the clearance is not within specification, bend the choke lever (D) to adjust.

Fast idle cam

Refer to illustration 8.32

32 With the fast idle cam set to the second position, adjust the throttle valve clearance (G in the illustration) by turning the adjustment screw **(see illustration)**.

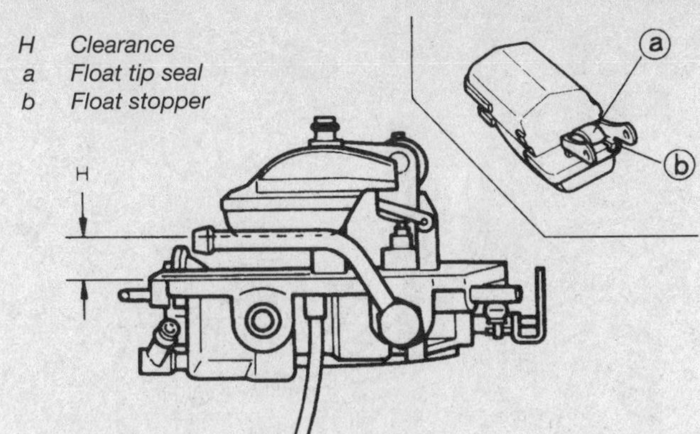

H Clearance
a Float tip seal
b Float stopper

8.29a Carburetor dry float measurement and adjustment procedure (with body inverted)

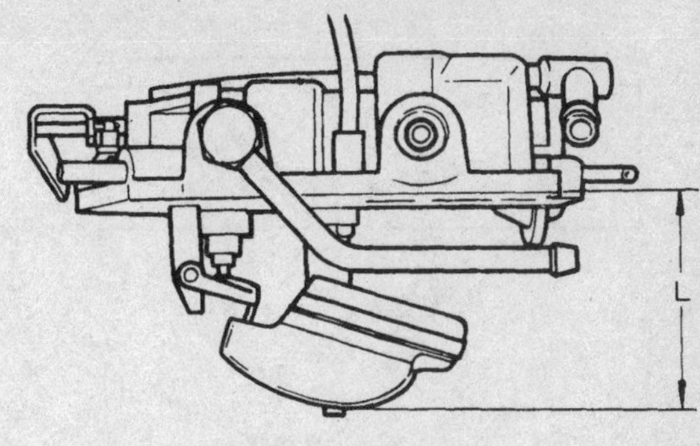

8.29b Carburetor dry float measurement and adjustment procedure (with air horn upright)

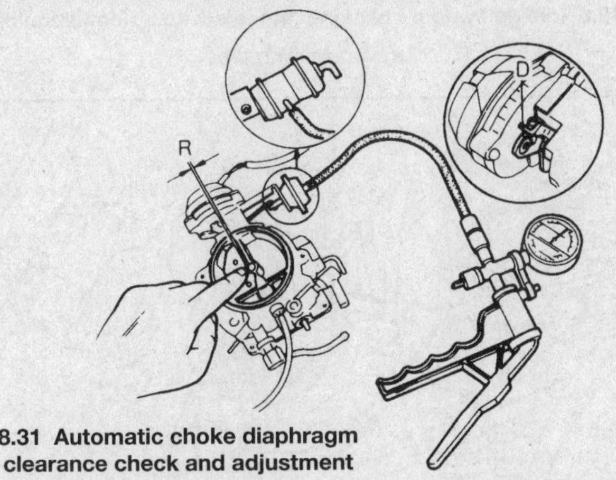

8.31 Automatic choke diaphragm clearance check and adjustment

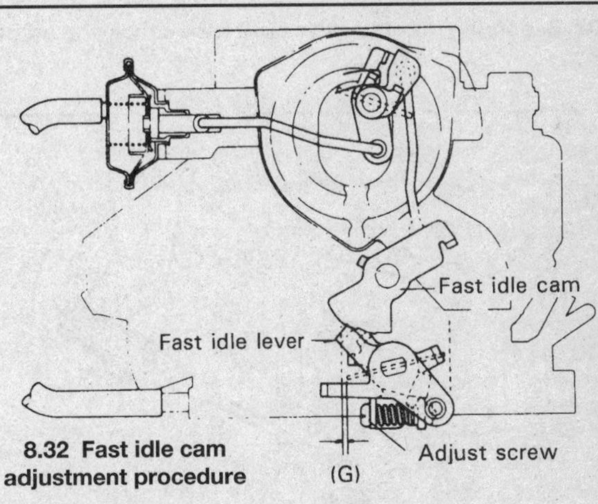

8.32 Fast idle cam adjustment procedure

G Clearance

Choke plate clearance

Refer to illustration 8.33

33 Set the fast idle cam to the second position and check the choke plate clearance R **(see illustration)**.

34 Bend the starting arm (B in the illustration) if necessary to bring the clearance within specification. To make a larger adjustment, bend the choke rod itself.

Choke unloader

Refer to illustration 8.35

35 Open the primary throttle valve fully and measure the clearance R **(see illustration)**.

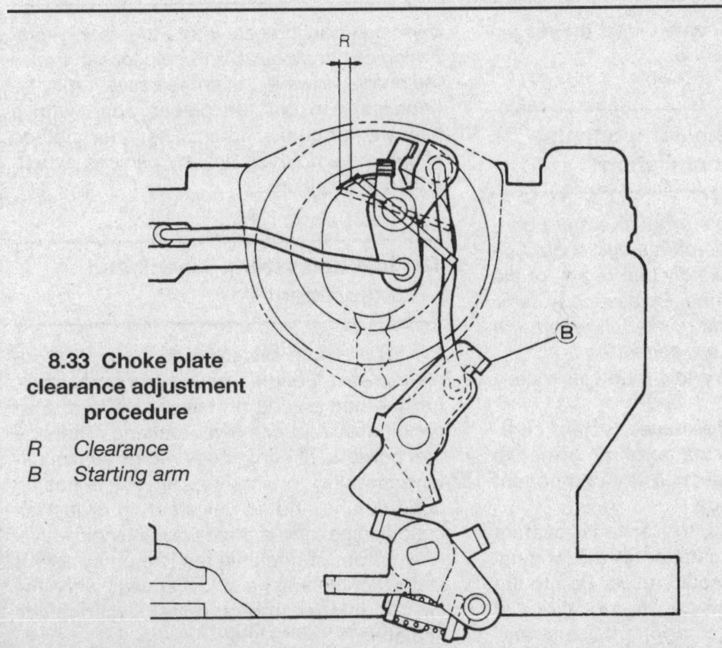

8.33 Choke plate clearance adjustment procedure

R Clearance
B Starting arm

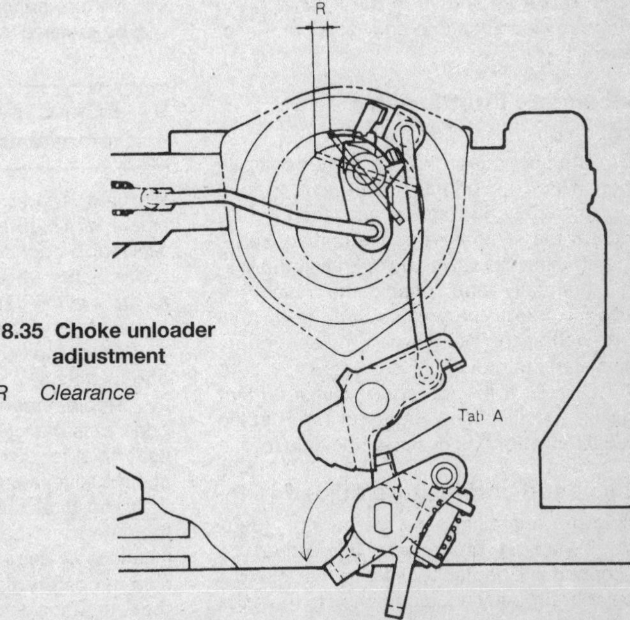

8.35 Choke unloader adjustment

R Clearance

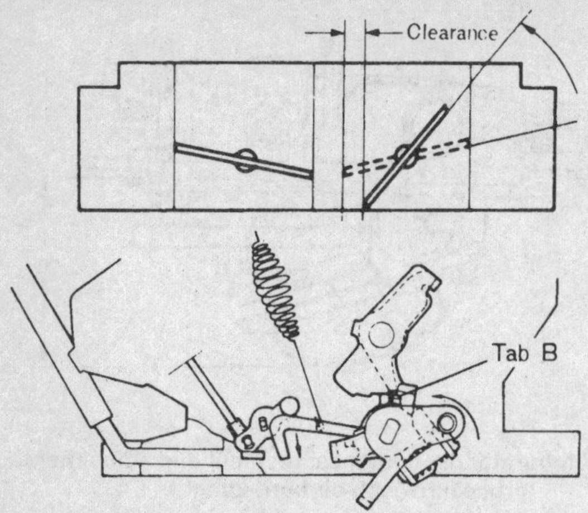

8.37 Secondary throttle valve clearance check and adjustment

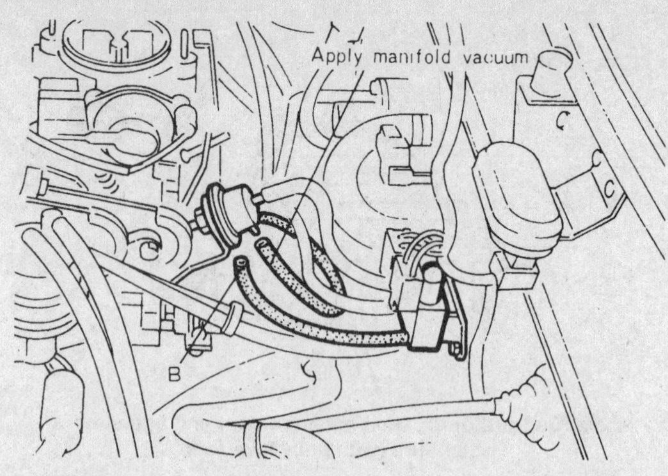

10.6 Idle up system checking (models with air conditioning)

B Vacuum sensing tube

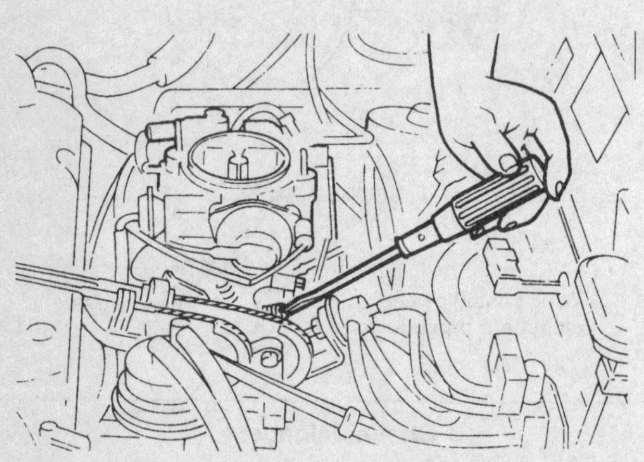

10.7 Idle up system servo diaphragm adjustment (power steering equipped models)

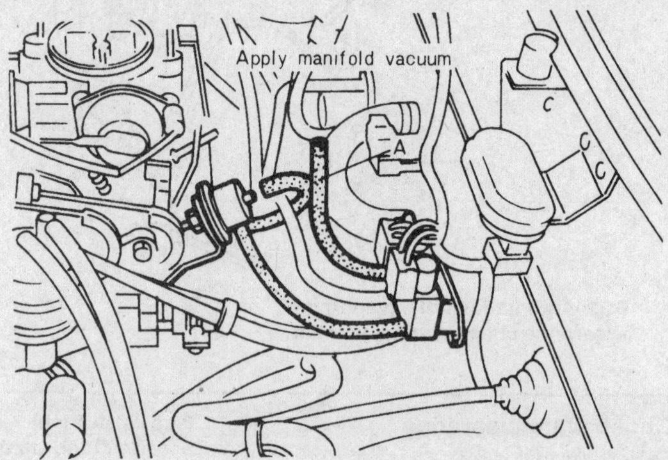

10.8a Power steering equipped model idle up system servo diaphragm check

Bend Tab A as shown in the illustration to bring the clearance into specification, if necessary.

Secondary throttle valve

Refer to illustration 8.37

36 The secondary throttle valve begins to open when the primary valve has opened approximately 53 degrees and then is fully open at the same time as the primary valve. Open the throttle valves by operating the linkage manually and check the clearance between the primary valve and the throttle bore wall at the point when the secondary valve starts to move.

37 Check the clearance measurement against specifications and bend Tab B in the **(see illustration)** as necessary to adjust.

Idle speed and mixture adjustment

38 After installing the carburetor (Section 7), adjust the engine idle speed as described in Chapter 1. Drive the vehicle to a dealer or properly equipped shop to have the idle mixture adjusted, after which the roll pin can be pressed into place.

9 Exhaust system components - removal and installation

Warning: *The vehicle's exhaust system generates very high temperatures and should be allowed to cool completely before any of the components are touched. Be especially careful around the catalytic converter, where the highest temperatures are generated.*

1 Raise the vehicle and support it securely on jackstands.

2 Replacement of exhaust system components is basically a matter of removing the heat shields, disconnecting the component and installing a new one.

3 The heat shields and exhaust system hangers must be reinstalled in the original locations or damage could result. Due to the high temperatures and exposed locations of the exhaust system components, rust and corrosion can "freeze" parts together. Penetrating oils are available to help loosen frozen fasteners. However, in some cases it may be necessary to cut the pieces apart with a hacksaw or cutting torch. The latter method should be employed only by persons experienced in this work.

10 Idle up system - check and adjustment

1 The idle up system used on some models increases engine speed to compensate for the load placed on the engine by the air conditioner and/or power steering. The system consists of servo diaphragms (which differ according to whether the vehicle has air conditioning and power steering or just air conditioning) and a three way solenoid valve. A symptom of a fault in the idle up system is stalling of the engine at low speeds when the air conditioner and/or power steering are actuated.

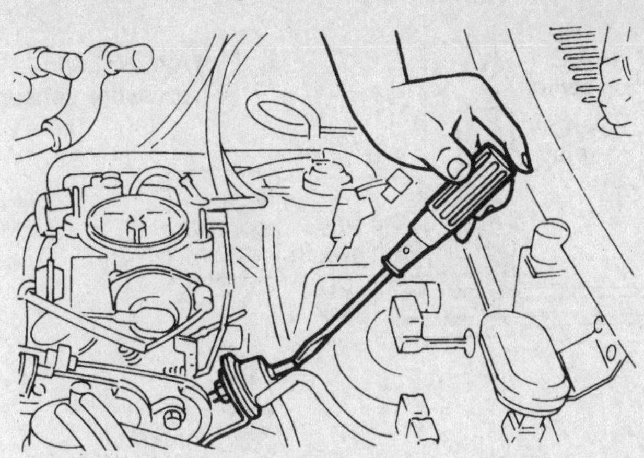
10.8b Idle up servo adjustment (air conditioned models)

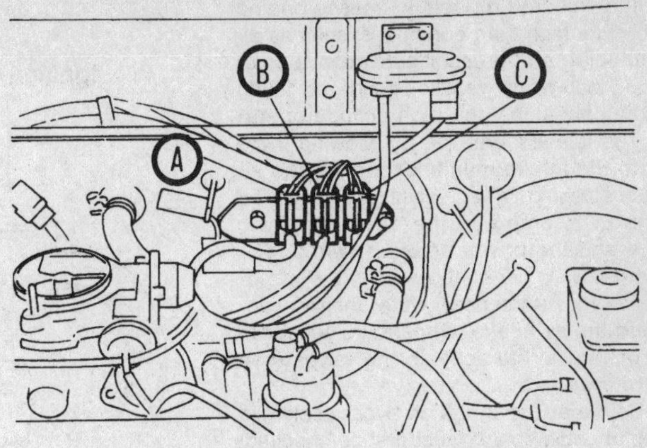

10.9 Three-way solenoid valve locations

A Power steering
B No. 2 ACV
C Air conditioner

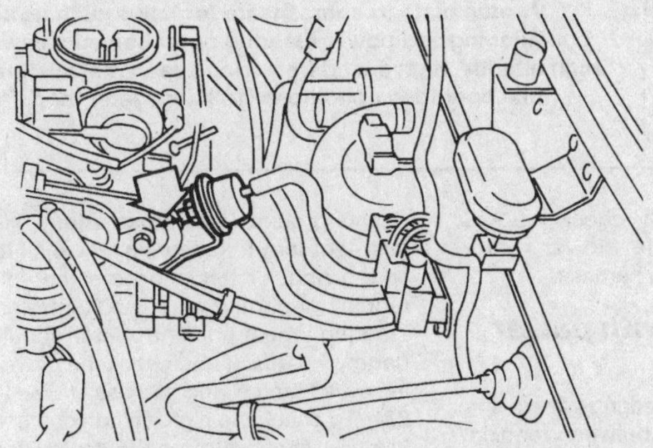
10.13 The servo diaphragm stem (arrow) should move if the 3-way solenoid valve is operating properly

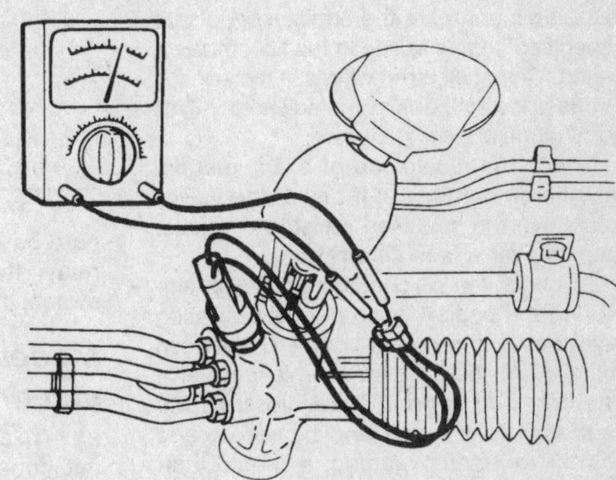
10.15 Power steering switch continuity check

Carbureted models

Servo diaphragm

2 Remove the air cleaner assembly.

3 Turn off all accessories and disconnect the electric cooling fan.

4 Disconnect and plug the hoses of the idle compensator, reed valves and thermo sensor.

5 Warm the engine to normal operating temperature and connect a tachometer.

Models equipped with air conditioning

Refer to illustrations 10.6 and 10.7

6 Disconnect the vacuum sensing tube (B) **(see illustration).**

7 Apply manifold vacuum to the servo diaphragm and check that the engine idle increases to between 1300 to 1400 rpm. If the increase is not as specified, turn the adjustment screw to adjust **(see illustration).**

Models equipped with power steering

Refer to illustrations 10.8a, 10.8b and 10.9

8 Perform Steps 2 through 4. On models also equipped with air conditioning, check and adjust the servo diaphragm **(see illustrations).**

9 Disconnect the vacuum sensing tube A and apply manifold vacuum to the servo diaphragm **(see illustration).**

10 The engine speed should increase to between 900 to 1000 rpm on manual transaxle models and 1150 to 1250 rpm on automatic transaxle models. If the rpm increase is not within specification, disconnect the vacuum tube and rotate the adjusting screw on the diaphragm to adjust.

11 Reconnect the vacuum tube and recheck the engine speed.

Three way solenoid valve

Refer to illustration 10.13

12 The three way solenoid valve is connected between intake manifold and servo diaphragm. On air conditioned models the three way solenoid valve restricts the vacuum flow in accordance with the signal sent through the control unit from the air conditioning switch. The three way solenoid valve on power steering equipped models restricts the vacuum flow according to the signal from the power steering switch.

13 With the engine idling, turn on the air conditioning and check that the servo diaphragm raises, indicating the three way solenoid is operating properly **(see illustration).**

14 Turn the air conditioning off and turn the steering wheel full lock to the right or left and check that the servo diaphragm raises, indicating that the three way solenoid and power steering switch are operating properly.

Power steering switch

Refer to illustration 10.15

15 Unplug the power steering switch connector and check for continuity **(see illustration).** With the engine idling turn the steering wheel full lock to the right or left to make sure there is continuity.

Fuel injected models

Models equipped with air conditioning

Refer to illustrations 10.16, 10.19, 10.20, 10.21, 10.22 and 10.23

16 The idle-up system used on 1986 and

later fuel injected models increases engine RPM under high-load conditions, such as air conditioning compressor activation, power steering load at low vehicle speeds, or during hot idle conditions and high altitude operation. The idle is increased by allowing more air into the intake manifold through the air bypass solenoid valves, which are controlled by the EGI computer, the air conditioning switch and the power steering switch. The computer also uses inputs from the atmospheric pressure sensor, water thermo sensor and the air intake temperature sensor to determine when to activate the valves **(see illustration)**.

17 Before adjusting the air bypass solenoid valves, the idle speed must first be checked, and adjusted if necessary. Refer to Chapter 1.

18 Connect a tachometer to the engine. With the connector to the air bypass solenoid valve disconnected, apply 12-volts to each BAT terminal and ground each GRD terminal, in pairs, then compare the engine speed with the specified engine speed in the accompanying chart. Check all three valves. If the speeds aren't as specified, adjust the solenoid valves by turning the adjusting screws.

19 Check the resistance of each solenoid valve with an ohmmeter. If any of the valves aren't within the specified resistance values, replace the valve **(see illustration)**.

20 To check the air conditioner idle-up signal, bring the engine up to normal operating temperature and attach a voltmeter between terminal A (of the air bypass solenoid valve connector) and ground **(see illustration)**. Turn the air conditioner and blower on and check the voltmeter reading. It should indicate battery voltage. If not, check the A/C relay, the A/C switch, the blower motor switch, the fuses and wiring harness.

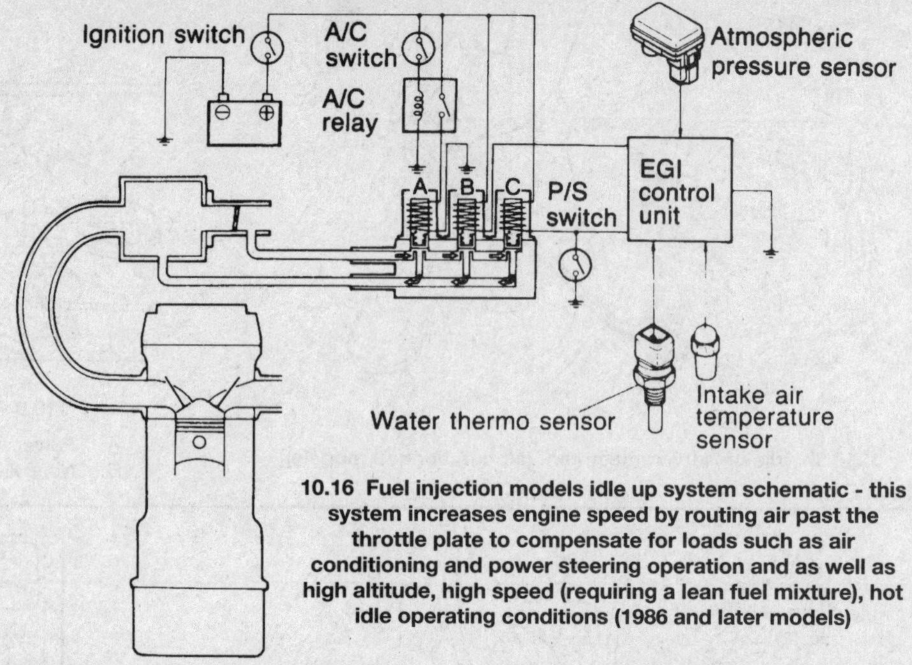

10.16 Fuel injection models idle up system schematic - this system increases engine speed by routing air past the throttle plate to compensate for loads such as air conditioning and power steering operation and as well as high altitude, high speed (requiring a lean fuel mixture), hot idle operating conditions (1986 and later models)

Models equipped with power steering

21 To check the power steering idle-up signal, connect the voltmeter between terminal D and ground **(see illustration)**. Have an assistant turn the steering wheel all the way to the right or left and note the voltmeter reading. It should read 0-volts. Release the steering wheel and the meter should read battery voltage. If not, check the power steering switch and wiring harness.

22 To check the high altitude compensation idle-up signal, warm up the engine and run it

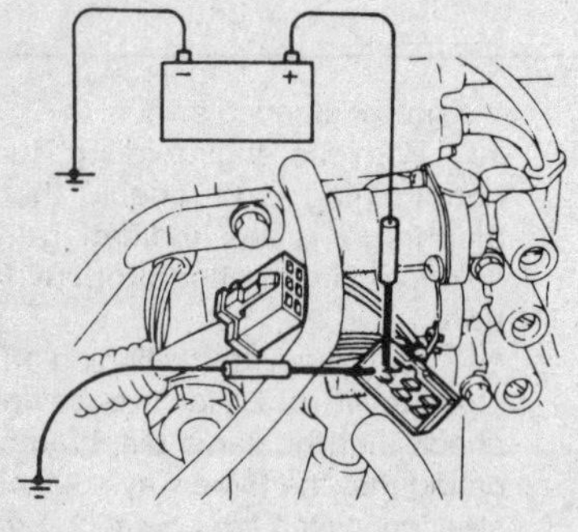

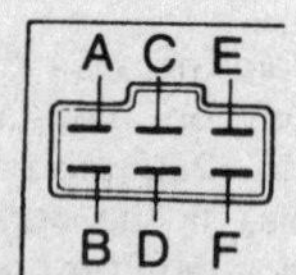

Valve	BAT	GRD	Engine speed
A (for A/C)	A	B	1250 ~ 1350 rpm
B (for high Altitude and hot idle compensations)	C	D	900 ~ 1000 rpm (MTX)
C (for P/S and high altitude compensation)	E	F	1000 ~ 1100 rpm (ATX)

10.19 Activate each air bypass solenoid and not if the engine speed is as specified in the chart - if not, adjust by turning the screw on the respective air bypass solenoid (ATX=automatic transaxle; MTX=manual transaxle

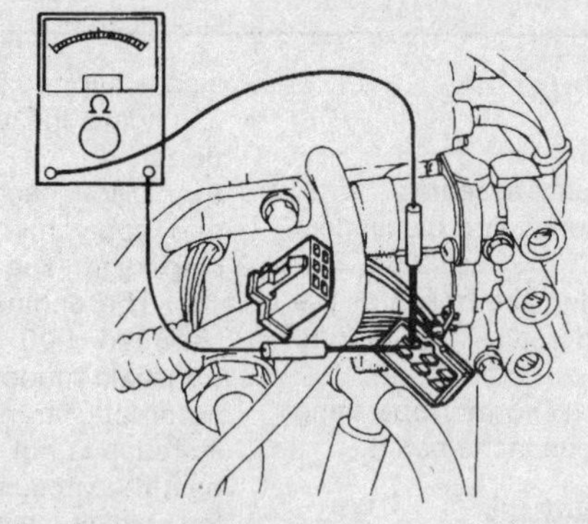

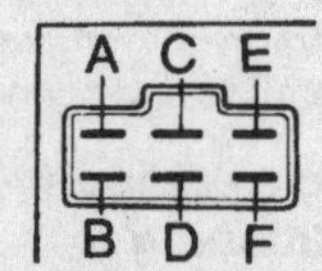

Terminals	Resistance
A ↔ B	17 ~ 23 Ω
C ↔ D	27 ~ 38 Ω
E ↔ F	27 ~ 38 Ω

10.20 Checking the resistance of the air bypass solenoid valves (if the readings obtained aren't as specified, replace the valve

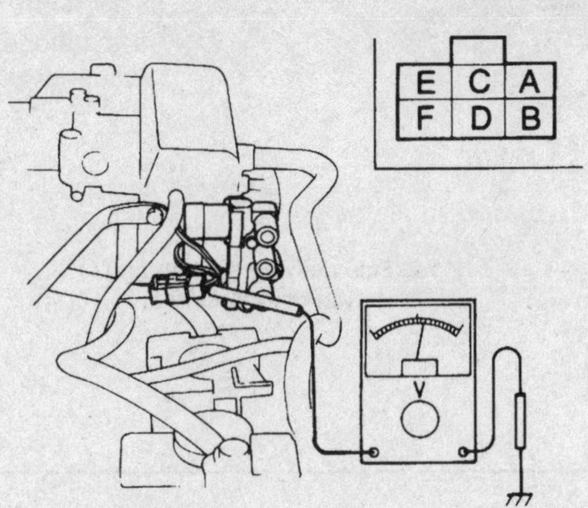

10.21 **Check the air conditioning and power steering idle up signals at the air bypass solenoid valve electrical connector**

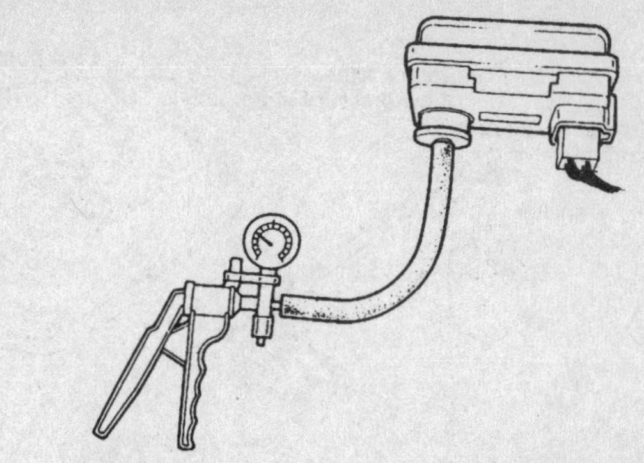

Terminal	Vacuum Amount
D	155 mmHg (6.10 inHg)
F	85 mmHg (3.35 inHg)

10.22 **Connect a vacuum pump to the atmospheric pressure sensor and attach a voltmeter to the terminals of the air bypass solenoid valve indicated in the chart - with vacuum applied, the voltmeter should read 0-volts**

at idle. Connect a vacuum pump to the port on the atmospheric pressure sensor and attach a voltmeter to the terminals shown in the chart **(see illustration)**. With vacuum applied, the voltmeter should read 0-volts. With the vacuum released, the meter should indicate battery voltage. If not, check the atmospheric pressure sensor and wiring harness.

23 To check the hot idle compensation idle-up signal, warm up the engine and run it at idle. Connect a voltmeter between the intake air temperature sensor terminal THA (located in the air flow meter electrical connector) and ground **(see illustration)**. Using a heat lamp, heat up the intake air temperature sensor to more than 131-degrees F. The voltmeter should read 0-volts. If not, check the intake air temperature sensor.

11 Fuel injection system - general information

Later model engines are equipped with an Electronic Fuel Injection (EFI) system. The EFI system is composed of three basic subsystems: a fuel system, an air intake system and an electronic control system. The following checks apply to 1986 and 1987 models and most later models. Refer to the following Sections for fuel injection system check and replacement procedure. Fuel injection system checking on some later models may require the use of a special tester tool and this should be left to a dealer.

Fuel delivery system

Refer to illustration 11.2

An electric pump located inside the tank supplies fuel under constant pressure to the fuel distribution pipe, which distributes it to all four injectors. From the distribution pipe, fuel is injected into the intake ports, just above the intake valves, by the four fuel injectors. The amount of fuel supplied by the injectors is precisely controlled by an electronic control module called the EGI control unit. A pressure regulator controls system pressure in relation to intake manifold vacuum. The fuel filter, mounted between the distribution pipe and fuel pump, protects the components of the system **(see illustration)**.

Air Intake system

Refer to illustrations 11.3a and 11.3b

The air intake system consists of an air filter housing, an air flow meter and a throttle body. An auxiliary air valve and air bypass solenoid valve control the idle speed under different operating conditions **(see illustrations)**. The air flow meter is an information gathering device for the EGI control unit. A potentiometer measures intake air flow and a temperature sensor measures intake air temperature. This information helps the EGI determine the amount (duration) of fuel to be injected by the injectors. The throttle plate inside the throttle body is controlled by the driver. As the throttle plate opens, the amount of air that can pass through the system increases, so the potentiometer opens further and the EGI signals the injectors to increase the amount of fuel delivered to the intake ports.

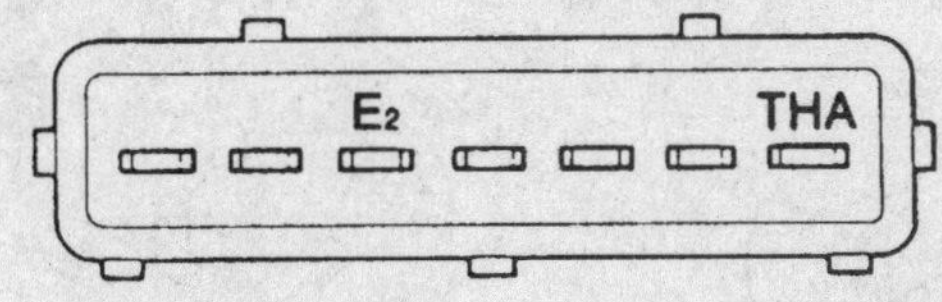

Intake Air Temperature	Resistance
−20°C (−4°F)	13.6 ~ 18.4 kΩ
20°C (68°F)	2.205 ~ 2.695 kΩ
60°C (140°F)	0.493 ~ 0.667 kΩ

10.23 **Unplug the air flow meter electrical connector, then check the resistance of the air intake temperature sensor across the terminals shown, at the temperatures indicated in the chart**

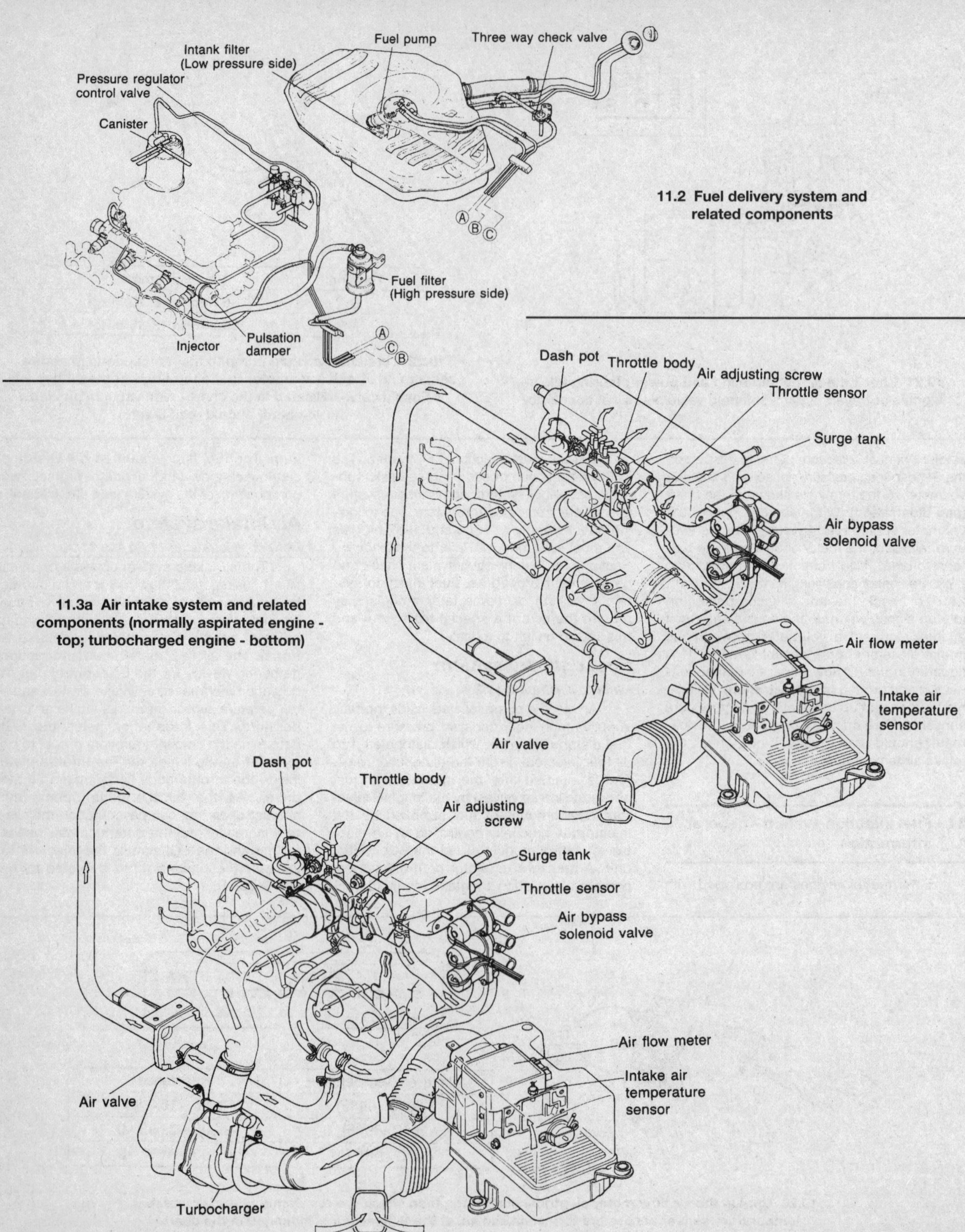

11.2 Fuel delivery system and related components

11.3a Air intake system and related components (normally aspirated engine - top; turbocharged engine - bottom)

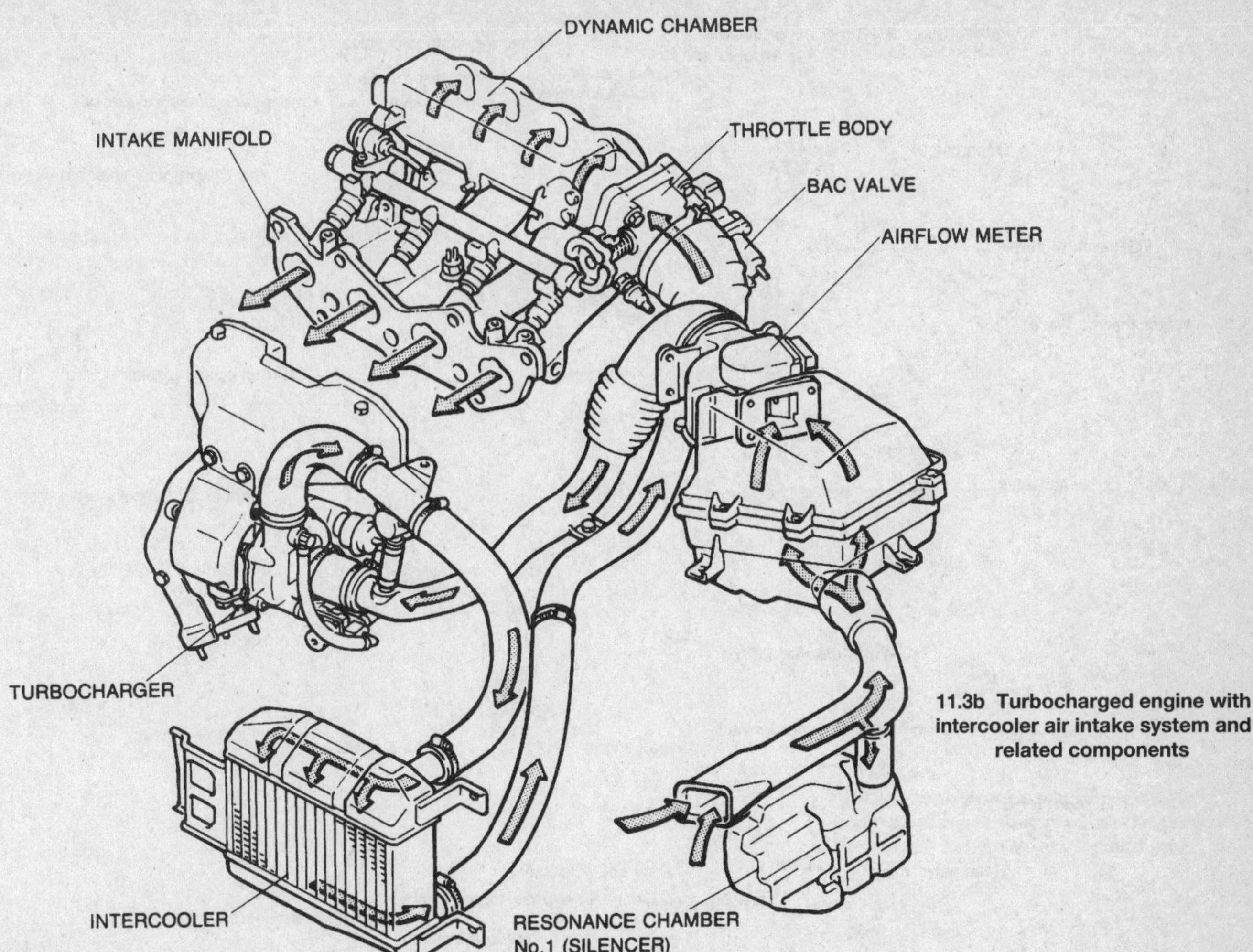

11.3b Turbocharged engine with intercooler air intake system and related components

Electronic control system

Refer to illustration 11.4

The electronic control system controls the EFI and other systems through an electronic control module, which employs a microcomputer called the EGI control unit. The EGI receives signals from a number of information sensors that monitor such variables as intake air volume, intake air temperature, coolant temperature, engine rpm, acceleration/deceleration and exhaust oxygen content. These signals help the EGI determine the injection duration necessary for the optimum fuel/air ratio. Some of the sensors and the corresponding EGI-controlled solenoids are not contained within EFI components, but are scattered throughout the engine compartment **(see illustration on next page)**.

General diagnosis

Warning: *Gasoline is extremely flammable, so take extra precautions when you work on any part of the fuel system. Don't smoke or allow open flames or bare light bulbs near the work area, and don't work in a garage where a natural gas-type appliance (such as a water heater or a clothes dryer) with a pilot light is present. Since gasoline is carcinogenic, wear latex gloves when there's a possibility of being exposed to fuel, and, if you spill any fuel on your skin, rinse it off immediately with soap and water. Mop up any spills immediately and do not store fuel-soaked rags where they could ignite. The fuel system is under constant pressure, so, if any fuel lines are to be disconnected, the fuel pressure in the system must be relieved first. When you perform any kind of work on the fuel system, wear safety glasses and have a Class B type fire extinguisher on hand.*

The EFI system is not usually the direct cause of engine problems. Trouble is usually caused by a bad contact in the wiring connectors or contaminated fuel, which could clog the injectors. Always make sure that all connections are secure by tapping or wiggling the connectors to see if the signal changes. Make sure that the connector terminals are not bent and that the connectors are pushed completely together and locked.

Before troubleshooting the EFI system, always check the condition of the ignition system. Make sure the battery, all fuses, fusible links and ground connections, the ignition coil, the coil high tension wire, the distributor, the plug wires and the spark plugs are all in good condition, properly connected and functioning correctly. Also check the ignition timing and the idle speed.

Check the general engine condition, such as compression pressure and valve clearances. Refer to Chapter 1 for the compression check and valve adjustment procedures.

Check the fuel delivery system for fuel leaks. Make sure the fuel pump is operating properly and the filter is not clogged.

Check the air intake system for vacuum leaks. Removal of components such as the engine oil dipstick, oil filler cap, PCV hose, etc. can cause the engine to run poorly. Check for a restricted air filter element.

Although this system requires a special tester for complete diagnosis, some checks of the individual components may be performed using regular shop test equipment.

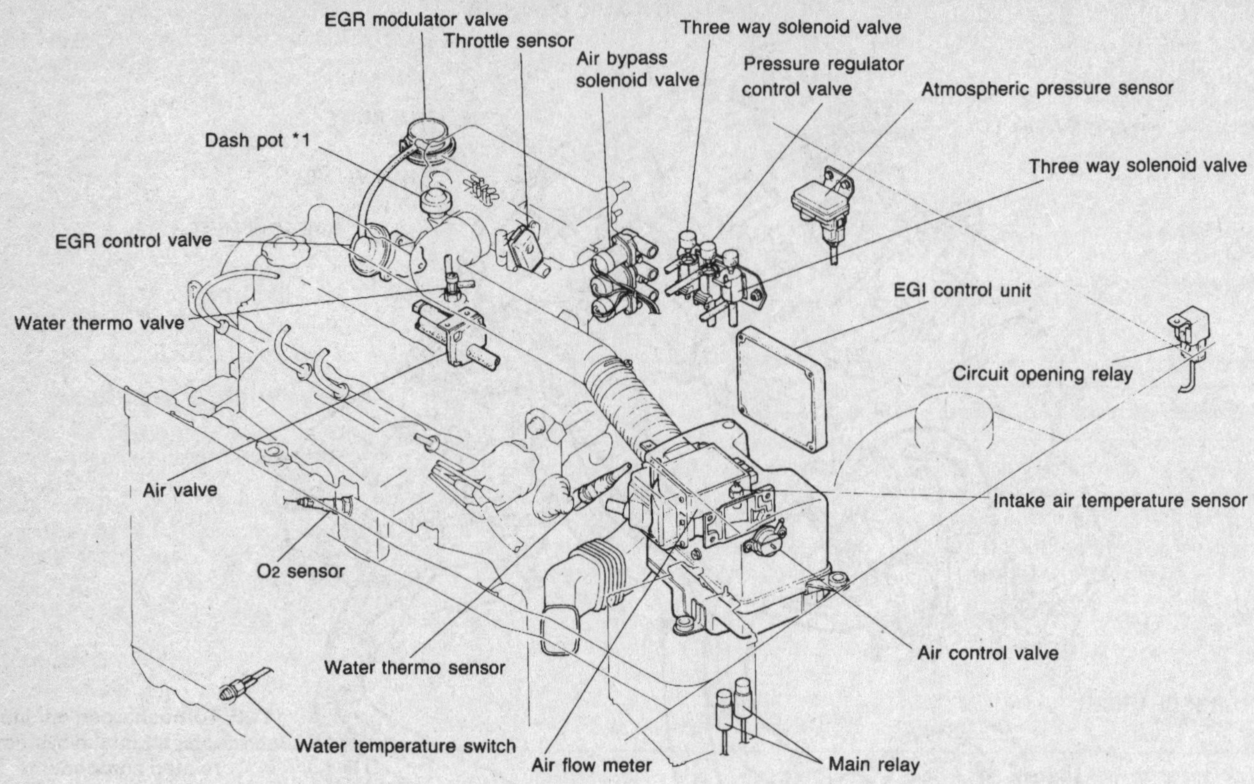

*1...Except for EC-AT

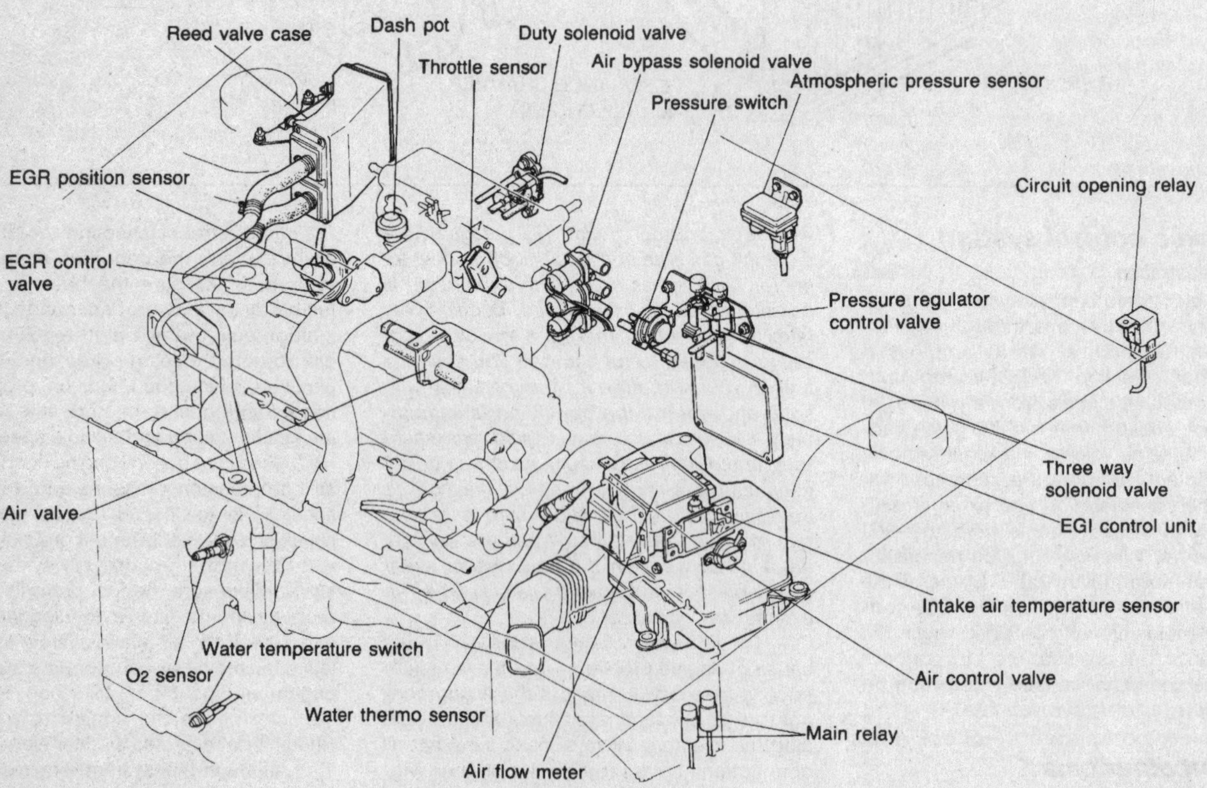

11.4 Electronic control system and related components (normally aspirated engine - top; turbocharged engine - bottom

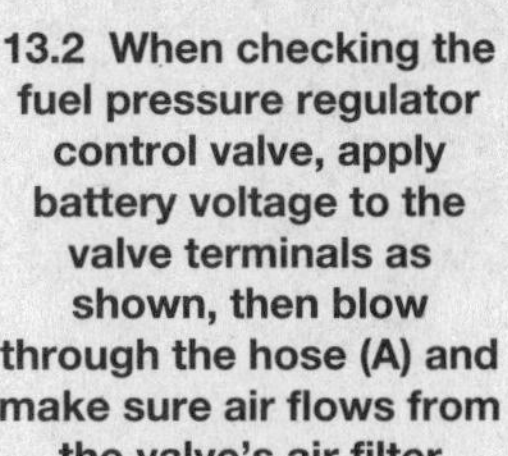

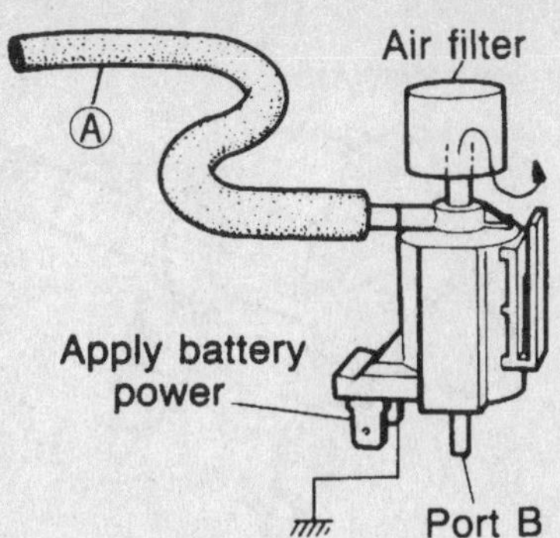

13.2 When checking the fuel pressure regulator control valve, apply battery voltage to the valve terminals as shown, then blow through the hose (A) and make sure air flows from the valve's air filter

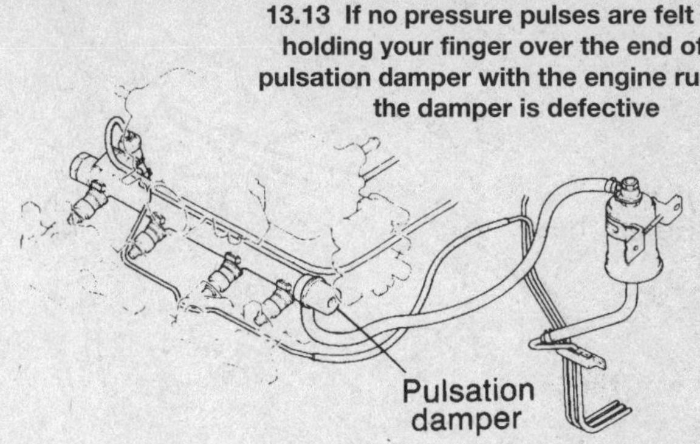

13.13 If no pressure pulses are felt when holding your finger over the end of the pulsation damper with the engine running, the damper is defective

12 Fuel pressure relief procedure

Warning: *Gasoline is extremely flammable, so take extra precautions when you work on any part of the fuel system. Don't smoke or allow open flames or bare light bulbs near the work area, and don't work in a garage where a natural gas-type appliance (such as a water heater or a clothes dryer) with a pilot light is present. Since gasoline is carcinogenic, wear latex gloves when there's a possibility of being exposed to fuel, and, if you spill any fuel on your skin, rinse it off immediately with soap and water. Mop up any spills immediately and do not store fuel-soaked rags where they could ignite. The fuel system is under constant pressure, so, if any fuel lines are to be disconnected, the fuel pressure in the system must be relieved first. When you perform any kind of work on the fuel system, wear safety glasses and have a Class B type fire extinguisher on hand.*

Note: *After the fuel pressure has been relieved. it's a good idea to lay a shop towel over any fuel connection to be disassembled, to absorb the residual fuel that may leak out when servicing the fuel system.*

1 On 1986 and 1987 models, remove the rear seat cushions to gain access to the fuel pump wire harness connector. On 1988 and later models, open the hood and locate the circuit opening relay in the engine compartment adjacent to the clutch pedal.

2 On 1986 and 1987 models, start the engine and unplug the connector or on 1988 and later models, disconnect the wire from the circuit opening relay. The engine will die within a few seconds.

3 Even though the fuel pressure should now be safely relieved, it's always a good idea to disconnect the negative battery cable from the battery and place a shop rag over any fuel fitting before loosening it.

13 Fuel injection system fuel delivery components - check and replacement

Warning: *Gasoline is extremely flammable, so take extra precautions when you work on any part of the fuel system. Don't smoke or allow open flames or bare light bulbs near the work area, and don't work in a garage where a natural gas-type appliance (such as a water heater or a clothes dryer) with a pilot light is present. Since gasoline is carcinogenic, wear latex gloves when there's a possibility of being exposed to fuel, and, if you spill any fuel on your skin, rinse it off immediately with soap and water. Mop up any spills immediately and do not store fuel-soaked rags where they could ignite. The fuel system is under constant pressure, so, if any fuel lines are to be disconnected, the fuel pressure in the system must be relieved first. When you perform any kind of work on the fuel system, wear safety glasses and have a Class B type fire extinguisher on hand.*

Note: *After the fuel pressure has been relieved. it's a good idea to lay a shop towel over any fuel connection to be disassembled, to absorb the residual fuel that may leak out when servicing the fuel system.*

Warning: *Gasoline is extremely flammable, so extra precautions must be taken when working on any part of the fuel system. DO NOT smoke or allow open flames or bare light bulbs near the work area. Also, don't work in a garage if a natural gas appliance (such as a water heater or clothes dryer) is present.*

Fuel pressure regulator control valve

Refer to illustration 13.2

1 The fuel pressure regulator control valve is located on the firewall, between the two three way solenoid valves. It's an EGI controlled electrovalve, which in turn controls the fuel pressure regulator through vacuum modulation.

2 To check the valve, connect a vacuum hose to the upper port **(see illustration)**. Blow through the hose and make sure air comes out of the lower port. Using two jumper wires, ground one terminal of the valve and apply battery voltage to the other. Blow into the hose and see if air now flows out of the valve's air filter. If the valve fails either test, replace it.

3 To remove the valve, mark and disconnect the two vacuum hoses and wires. Lift the end of the plastic retaining tab and slide the valve off of the mounting bracket. Installation is the reverse of removal.

Fuel pressure regulator

4 For fuel pressure regulator diagnosis, see the fuel pressure check procedure above.

5 Relieve the fuel system pressure, then disconnect the negative battery cable.

6 Loosen the return hose clamp and remove the hose from the pressure regulator. It's a good idea to place rags under the hose to catch spilled fuel.

7 Remove the vacuum sensing hose from the regulator.

8 Remove the two regulator mounting bolts and detach the regulator from the distribution pipe.

9 Place the pressure regulator, with a new seal, in position on the distribution pipe and install the bolts. Tighten them snugly.

10 Connect the fuel return and vacuum sensing hoses.

11 Connect the battery cable and turn the ignition to the On position. Energize the fuel pump by bridging the fuel pump test connector terminals to pressurize the system, then check for leaks.

Pulsation damper

Refer to illustration 13.13

12 The pulsation damper acts as a shock absorber in the distribution pipe, reducing the pulsating effect of the fuel that results from the injectors opening and closing.

13 To check the damper, place a finger over the hole in the end of the damper and feel for pressure pulses with the engine running **(see illustration)**. If nothing is felt, replace the damper.

14 To replace the damper, first relieve the fuel system pressure (Section 12) then disconnect the cable from the negative terminal of the battery.

15 Disconnect the fuel feed line and unscrew the damper from the distribution pipe.

16 Installation is the reverse of the removal procedure.

Distribution pipe

17 Relieve the fuel system pressure (Section 12) then disconnect the negative battery cable.

18 Disconnect the fuel return hose from the pressure regulator and the feed line from the

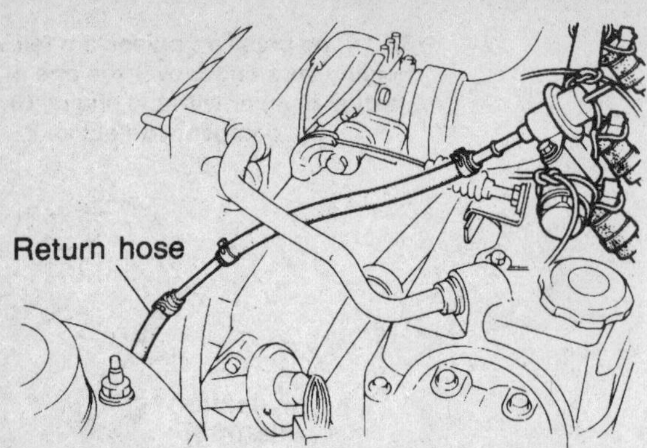

13.24 Connect a length of hose with a short section of tubing between the fuel pressure regulator and the return hose when repositioning the distribution pipe for the injector leakage check

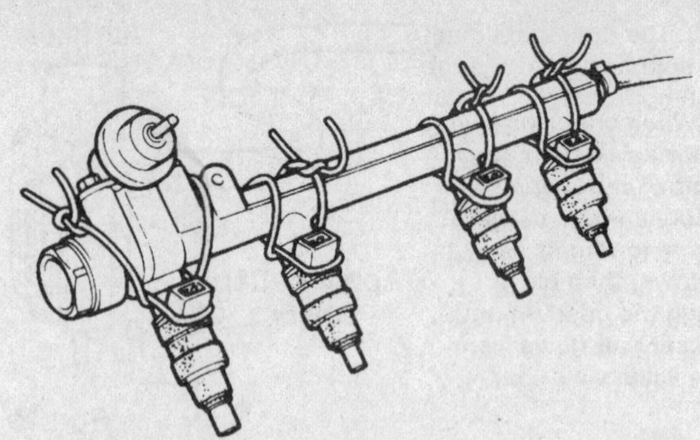

13.25 Wire the injectors to the distribution pipe to prevent them from popping out during the injector leakage check

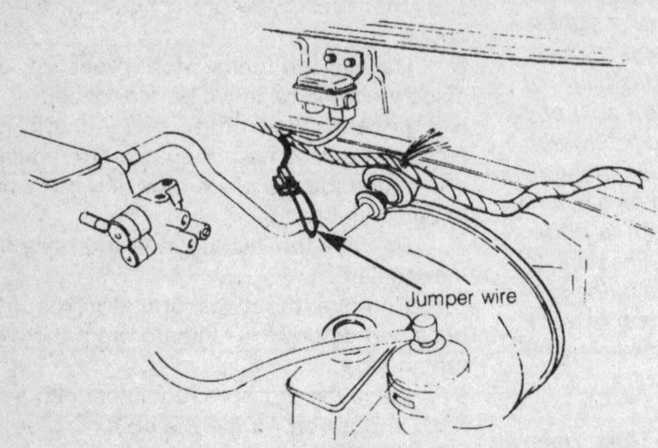

13.26 The fuel pump can be activated by bridging the fuel pump test connector terminals with a jumper wire

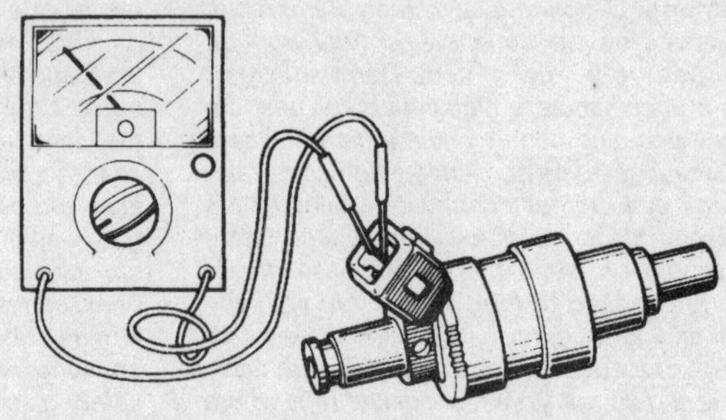

13.27 Check the injector solenoid resistance with an ohmmeter (it's not necessary to remove the injector from the distribution pipe to perform this check

pulsation damper.

19 Unplug the injector electrical connectors.

20 Remove the two mounting bolts and carefully pull the distribution pipe and injectors from the manifold. Guide the assembly out from under the throttle body and surge tank.

21 Installation is the reverse of the removal procedure. Be sure to inspect the injector-to-intake manifold rubber insulators and replace them if they are cracked, hardened or deformed.

Fuel injectors

Refer to illustrations 13.24, 13.25, 13.26, 13.27 and 13.30

22 To check injector operation, place the tip of a screwdriver or stethoscope against each injector body and listen for a clicking noise while the engine is running. If no sound is heard, check the injector resistance.

23 Remove the distribution pipe as outlined in Steps 17 through 20.

24 To check for injector fuel leakage, connect the hose from the fuel filter to the inlet fitting on the distribution pipe. Using a piece of extra fuel hose and a coupler, connect the return hose to the fuel pressure regulator **(see illustration)**.

25 Wire the injectors to the distribution pipe so they won't pop off when fuel pressure builds up **(see illustration)**.

26 Place some rags under the injectors. Turn the ignition to the On position and energize the fuel pump by jumping the fuel pump test connector terminals **(see illustration)**. Look for drops or seeping fuel at the injectors. Replace any injectors that leak. **Note:** *A very slight amount of leakage after five minutes is acceptable.*

27 To check injector resistance, connect an ohmmeter across the injector terminals. The reading should be 12-to-16 ohms **(see illustration)**. If it isn't, replace the injector.

28 To replace a fuel injector, disconnect the extra hose that was connected to perform the leak test. Wrap a rag around the hose when removing it to control the fuel spray, as the pressure relief procedure can't be followed with the distribution pipe removed.

29 Pull the injector out of the distribution pipe using a twisting motion. Inspect the rubber insulator, grommet and O-ring. It's a good idea to routinely replace them to eliminate the possibility of fuel leaks.

30 Install the new O-ring, grommet and insulator. Apply a light coat of engine oil to the O-ring and insulator to ease installation and reduce the possibility of tearing them **(see illustration)**.

31 Insert the injector into the fuel distribution pipe. Be sure to push it in straight, otherwise the O-ring may be damaged. The electrical connector must face up.

32 Install the fuel distribution pipe and injectors and tighten the bolts securely. Connect the fuel feed, return and vacuum sens-

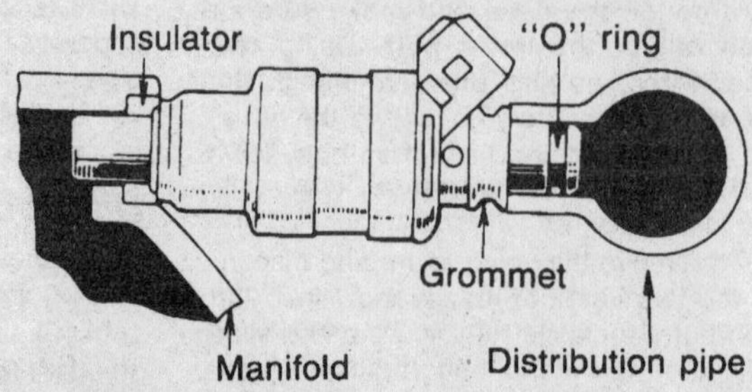

13.30 Fuel injector mounting details (it's a good idea to replace all of the rubber insulators, and O-rings whenever any of the injectors are removed)

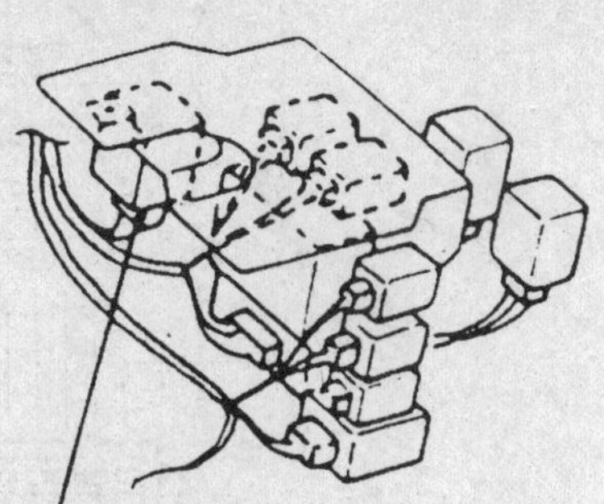

13.33 The circuit opening relay supplies power to the fuel pump from the time the engine is cranked until the ignition switch is turned off - if the fuel pump doesn't run when the engine is cranked, but does run when the power is supplied directly to it, the circuit opening relay should be checked

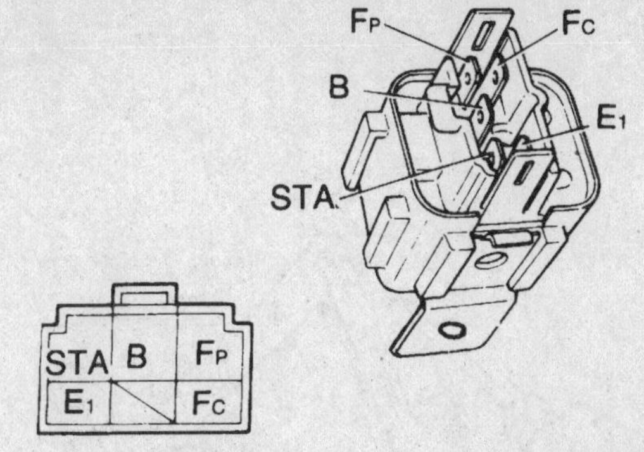

Between terminals	Resistance (Ω)
STA ↔ E1	15~30
B ↔ Fc	80~150
B ↔ Fp	∞

13.35 Check the circuit opening relay resistance between the indicated terminals - if the values aren't correct, replace the relay

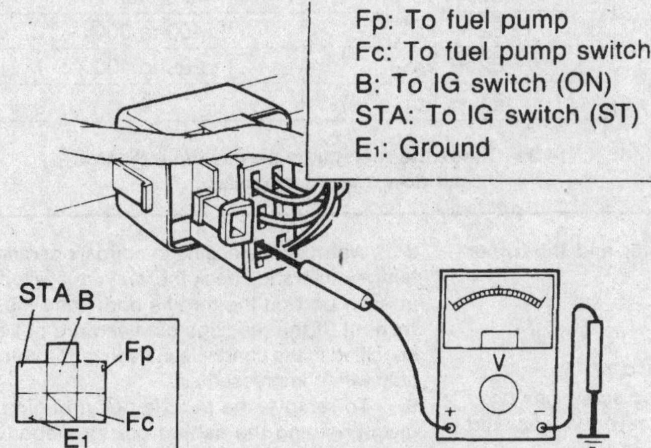

Terminal / Condition	Fp	F c	B	STA	E1
IG SW: ON	0V	12V	12V	0V	0V
Measuring plate: opened	12V	0V	12V	0V	0V
IG SW: ST	12V	0V	12V	12V	0V

13.34 Check the circuit opening relay terminal voltages and compare your readings with the chart

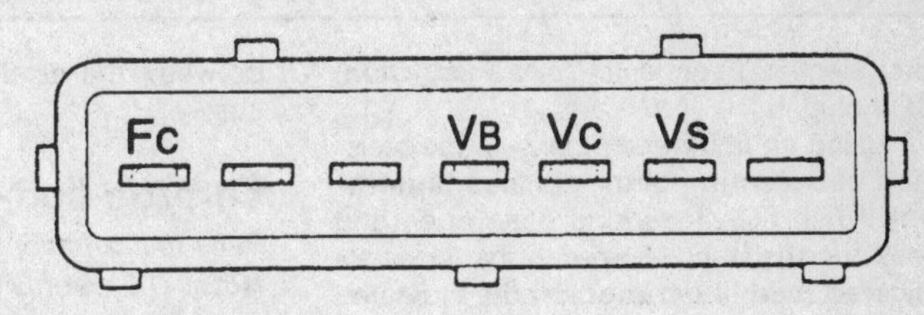

Terminal	Voltage
Vs	0.7~2.7 V
Vc	6~10 V
VB	Approx. 12 V
Fc(fuel pump switch)	Approx. 12 V

14.1 Without unplugging the air flow meter electrical connector, peel back the rubber boot and check the terminal voltages as shown

ing hoses. Pressurize the fuel system by bridging the fuel pump test connector terminals and check for leaks.

Circuit opening relay

Refer to illustrations 13.33, 13.34 and 13.35

33 A circuit opening relay, located under the dash on the relay panel, supplies power to the fuel pump when the starter is operated **(see illustration)**. It continues to feed the pump until the key is turned off, at which time the relay resets itself (no power is directed to the pump when the ignition key is turned to the On position - the engine must be turned over first).

34 To check the relay and related wiring harnesses, block open the measuring plate inside the air flow meter and measure the voltage at each terminal on the relay connector with the relay still connected **(see illustration)**. If the B-terminal voltage is incorrect, check the fuses and the wiring harness from the ignition switch. If the STA-terminal voltage is incorrect, also check the wiring harness from the ignition switch. If the E1-terminal voltage is incorrect, check the ground harness. If incorrect at the Fc-terminal, check the air flow meter or the circuit opening relay resistance. If the Fp-terminal voltage is incorrect, check the circuit opening relay resistance also.

35 Check the resistance between the terminals of the relay **(see illustration)**. If the resistance values are not within the specified limits, replace the relay.

36 To replace the relay, unplug the electrical connector and remove the mounting screw. Installation is the reverse of the removal procedure.

14 Fuel injection air intake system components - check and replacement

Air flow meter

Refer to illustrations 14.1, 14.2, 14.3a, 14.3b and 14.5

1 Remove the two screws and peel back the rubber boot on the air flow meter electrical connector. Turn the ignition switch to the On position and measure the voltage between each terminal and ground. Compare your readings to the accompanying chart **(see illustration)**. If the voltages are not as specified, check the main fuse, the main relay in the air flow meter and the wiring harness.

2 Release the spring clip on the air flow

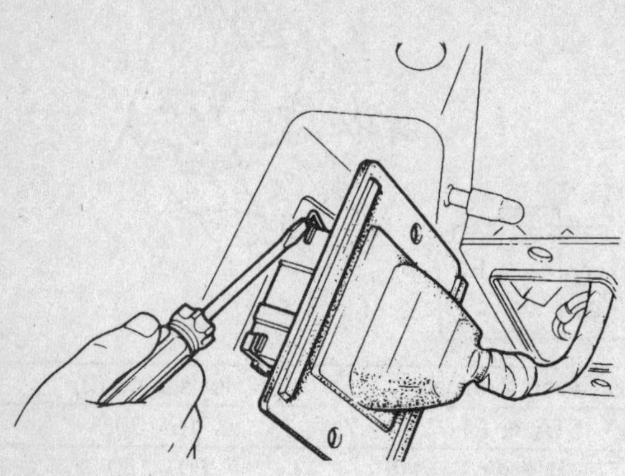

14.2 To unplug the air flow meter electrical connector, release the spring clip with a small screwdriver

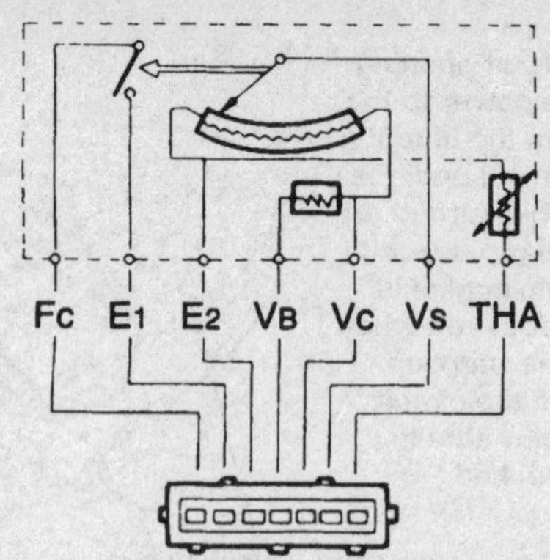

Terminal	Resistance (Ω)
E2 ↔ Vs	More than 20
E2 ↔ Vc	100 to 300
E2 ↔ VB	200 to 400
E1 ↔ Fc	∞

14.3a Check the resistance across the indicated air flow meter terminals . . .

meter electrical connector **(see illustration)** and unplug it.

3 Using an ohmmeter, measure the resistance between the terminals **(see illustration)**. Push the measuring plate open and check the resistance between the terminals indicated **(see illustration)**. If the indicated measurements are not as specified in the accompanying charts, replace the air flow meter.

4 To replace the air flow meter, loosen the air intake hose clamp and slide the hose off the air cleaner upper case. Unplug the electrical connector. Remove the vacuum hose from the air control valve.

5 Separate the air cleaner upper case from the air cleaner base and detach the air flow meter from the upper case **(see illustration)**.

6 Installation is the reverse of the removal procedure. Be sure to replace the rubber seal between the air flow meter and the upper case.

Throttle body

Refer to illustrations 14.8 and 14.15

Note: *The throttle adjusting screw has been factory preset and should never be tampered with.*

7 Check the throttle linkage for smooth operation. If it binds, the problem may be a buildup of sludge behind the throttle plate caused by the PCV hose that directs crankcase vapors into the surge tank/intake manifold. Removing the duct to the throttle body, opening the throttle plate and carefully wiping out the sludge with a shop rag can clean out this buildup. However, do not remove the thin material coating the throttle valve and the inside of the bore.

8 Warm up the engine to normal operating temperature and check the vacuum available at each port on the throttle body **(see illustration)**. If the readings obtained are not as specified in the chart, clean each port, preferably with compressed air.

9 To remove the throttle body, begin by disconnecting the cable from the negative terminal of the battery.

10 Remove the duct between the air flow meter and the throttle body.

11 Disconnect the throttle return spring.

12 Remove the accelerator cable from the throttle lever.

13 Label and disconnect the vacuum hoses on the top of the throttle body **(see illustration 14.8)**.

14 Unplug the throttle position sensor electrical connector.

15 Drain approximately two quarts of

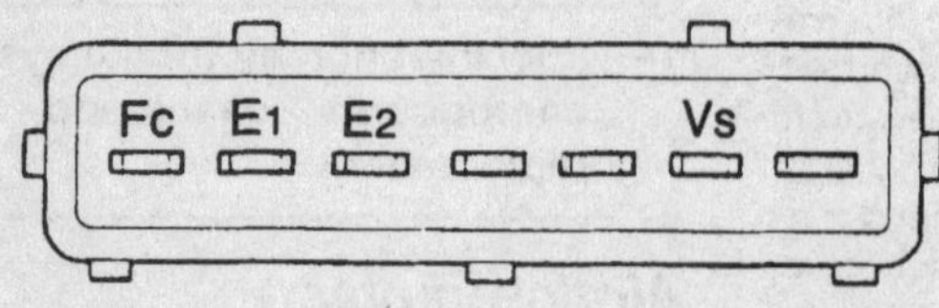

Terminals	Resistance (Ω)
E2 ↔ Vs	Less than 400
E1 ↔ Fc	0 (continuity)

14.3b . . . then push the air flow meter measuring plate open and measure the resistance across the terminals shown here

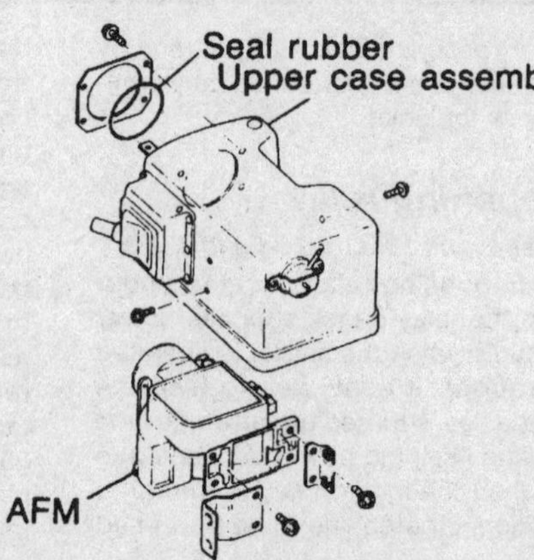

14.5 A typical air flow meter is retained in the upper air cleaner case with brackets and screws (be sure to replace the seal rubber when installing the air flow meter)

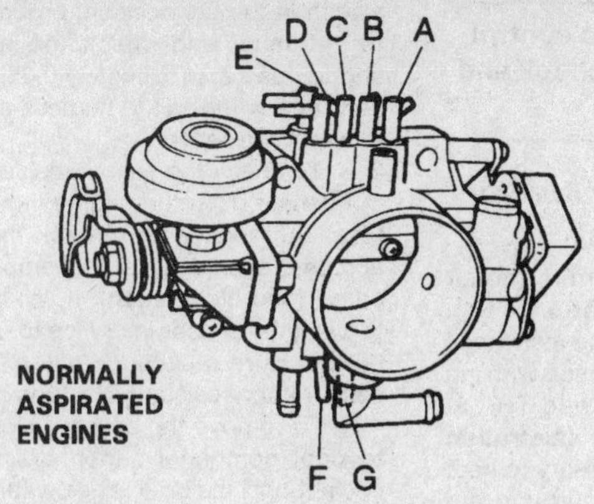

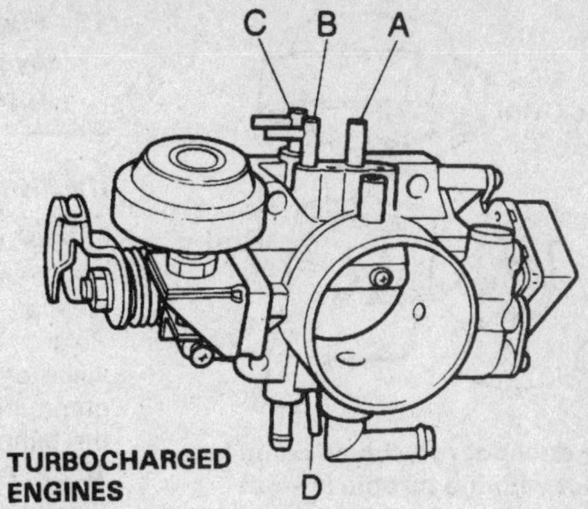

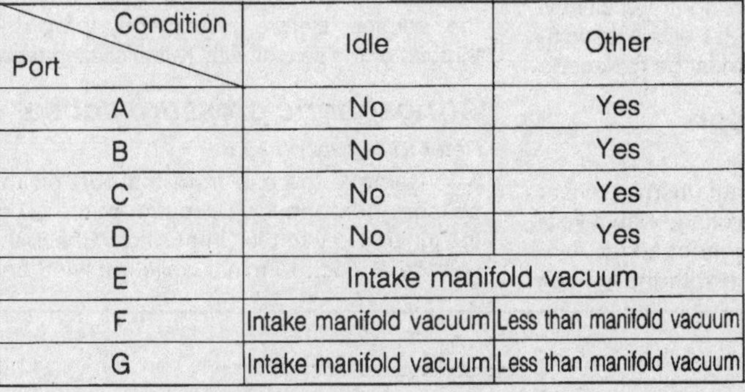

Port \ Condition	Idle	Other
A	No	Yes
B	No	Yes
C	No	Yes
D	No	Yes
E	Intake manifold vacuum	
F	Intake manifold vacuum	Less than manifold vacuum
G	Intake manifold vacuum	Less than manifold vacuum

Port \ Condition	Idle	Other
A	No	Yes
B	No	Yes
C	Intake manifold vacuum	
D	Intake manifold vacuum	Less than manifold vacuum

14.8 Check the vacuum available at the ports on the throttle body under the conditions indicated in the chart

coolant from the radiator (see Chapter 1). Disconnect the water hoses and the air bypass hose from the throttle body **(see illustration)**.

16 Remove the four throttle body mounting nuts and detach the throttle body.

17 Remove the old gasket material from the surge tank and the throttle body with a razor blade. Failure to do so will result in an air leak when the throttle body is reinstalled.

18 Wash all residue and sludge buildup from the throttle body with fresh solvent or carburetor cleaner. Pay particular attention to the throttle plate area. **Caution:** *Do not immerse the throttle position sensor in solvent or cleaning fluid of any kind. The plastic housing and the electronic circuitry inside may be damaged.*

19 Blow out the vacuum passages with compressed air, if available.

20 Installation is the reverse of removal.

Air valve

Refer to illustration 14.21

21 Start the engine and run it at idle. While the engine is still cold, pinch the air bypass hose with a pair of pliers **(see illustration)**. The idle speed should be reduced slightly. If it isn't reduced, check the air valve and hose for leaks.

22 Allow the engine to warm up to normal operating temperature. Pinch the hose again and the speed drop should be within 100-to-200 RPM. If the idle speed drops more than 200 RPM, check the voltage at the air valve.

23 To check the terminal voltage, disconnect the electrical connector and check for battery voltage with a voltmeter. If the voltage is low (or nonexistent), check the circuit opening relay and the wiring harness.

24 Check the resistance of the air valve with an ohmmeter. The reading should be 30-to-45 ohms. If it isn't within this range, replace the air valve.

25 The valve operation can be checked by removing one of the hoses from the air valve, attaching a length of hose to the valve and blowing into the valve with the ignition turned On. Air should pass through the valve when the valve temperature is 68-degrees F or less. No air should pass through the valve when the temperature is above 68-degrees F.

26 To replace the valve, loosen the hose clamps and slide the hoses off the valve. Unplug the electrical connector, remove the mounting bolts and detach the valve. Installation is the reverse of the removal procedure.

14.15 Typical throttle body mounting details

Dashpot (1986 and 1987 models)

Refer to illustration 14.28

27 To check the dashpot, push in on the rod with your finger. The rod should resist the pressure and go in slowly. The rod should come out rapidly when released.

28 Connect a tachometer to the engine and increase the engine speed to 2500 RPM. Slowly decrease the engine speed and watch

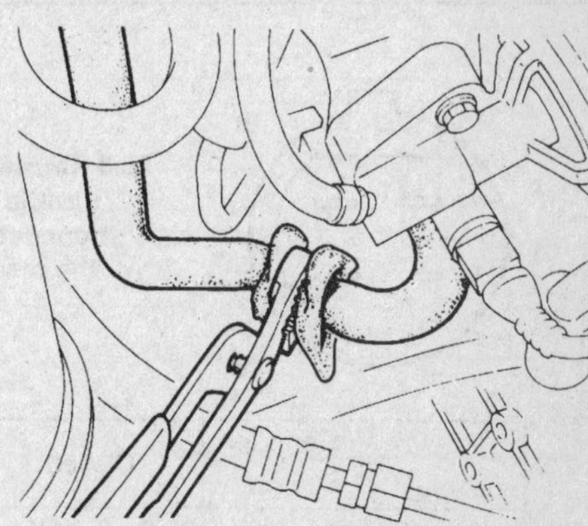

14.21 When checking the air valve operation, wrap a rag around the bypass hose and pinch it closed with a pair of pliers (1986 and 1987 models)

4

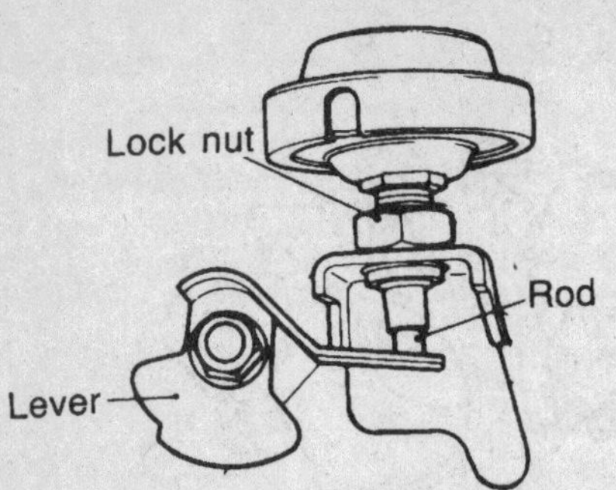

14.28 The dashpot rod should come into contact with the throttle lever at approximately 2000 rpm during deceleration

for the dashpot rod to come into contact with the throttle lever **(see illustration)**. It should contact the lever at approximately 1900-to-2000 RPM. If not, loosen the locknut and turn the dashpot to adjust it. To replace the dashpot, loosen the locknut and unscrew the unit from the bracket.

15 Fuel injection electronic control system components - check and replacement

Intake air temperature sensor (1986 and 1987 models)

1 Remove the upper cover from the air cleaner assembly **(see illustration 11.4)**. Refer to Section 10 and check the resistance value of the air flow meter sensor with an ohmmeter across terminals E2 and THA at the temperatures indicated **(see illustration 10.23)**. A heat lamp will be necessary to heat the sensor and dry ice packed around the sensor will be useful in cooling it sufficiently. If the resistance values aren't within specifications, the air flow meter must be replaced.

Water thermo sensor

Refer to illustration 15.3

2 Begin checking the water thermo sensor by measuring the terminal voltage with a voltmeter. Peel back the rubber boot on the sensor electrical connector and with the ignition switch in the On position, probe the connector terminal and check the meter, which should read approximately 0.05-volt. If incorrect, check the wiring harness and the resistance of the sensor.

3 To check the sensor resistance, remove the sensor from the engine (refer to Step 4). Heat the sensor and check the resistance across the terminals at the temperatures indicated **(see illustration)**. It will be necessary to pack the sensor in dry ice to check the low temperature resistance value. Replace the sensor if the resistance isn't as specified.

4 To remove the sensor, allow the engine to cool completely, then drain the engine coolant until the level is below the sensor. Disconnect the electrical connector and unscrew the sensor. Before installation, wrap the threads of the sensor with Teflon sealing tape.

Atmospheric pressure sensor

Refer to illustration 15.5

5 Remove the cap from the port on the sensor and connect a vacuum pump. Turn the ignition key to the On position. Check the voltage at each terminal while applying and

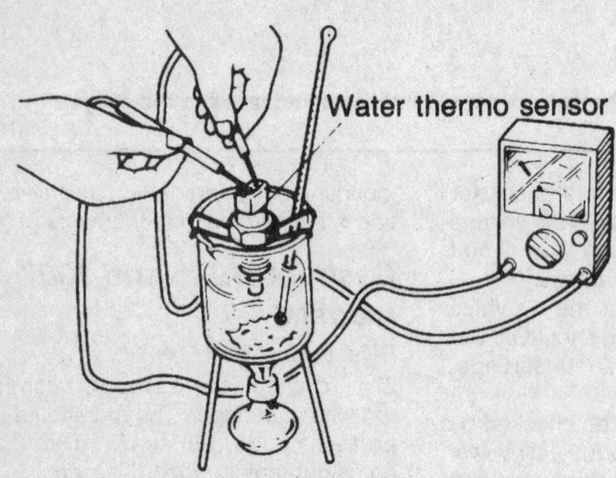

15.3 Check the resistance of the water thermo sensor at the temperatures indicated (if the resistance readings are incorrect, replace the sensor)

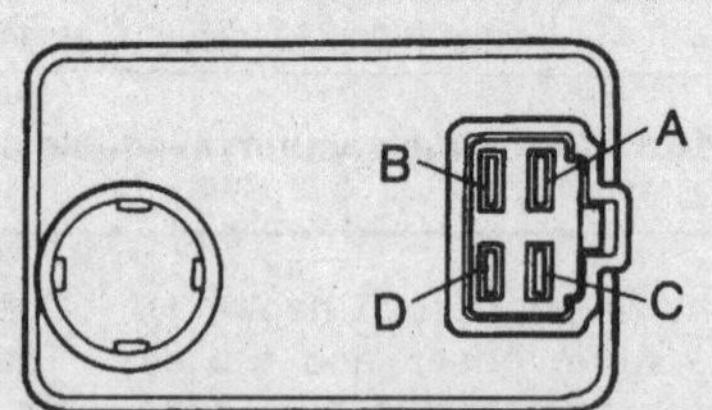

Terminal (Color)	Voltage
A (YG)	Approx. 12V
B (Lg)	1.4 ~ 4.9V
C (LgR)	Below 1.5V
D (LgW)	4.5 ~ 5.5V

15.5 Check the terminal voltages at the atmospheric pressure sensor while applying and releasing vacuum to the sensor with a vacuum pump

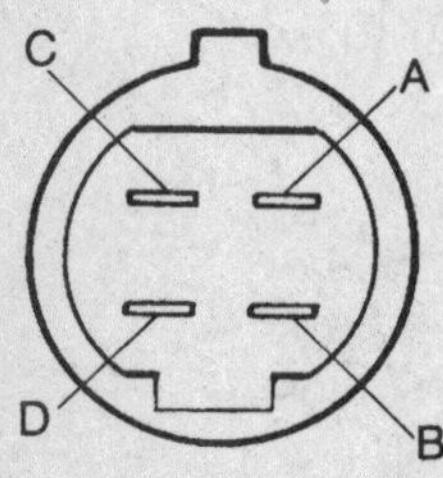

Terminal \ Condition	Closed	Fully opened
A (V_T)	0.4 ~ 0.6V	Approx. 4.0V
B (GND)	Below 1.5 V	
C (V_S)	4.5 ~ 5.5 V	
D (IDL)	Below 1.5 V	Approx. 12 V

15.8 Check the voltages at the throttle position sensor connector and compare the results to the chart

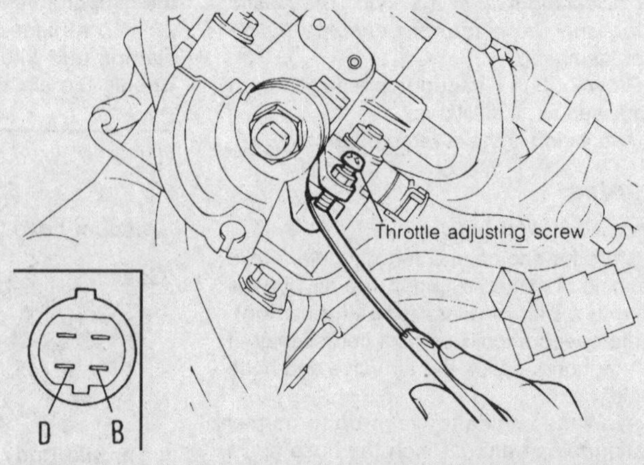

15.9 Insert a feeler gauge between the throttle adjusting screw and the throttle lever while checking for continuity between terminals D and B

releasing vacuum to the sensor **(see illustration)**. If the voltage reading at terminals A, C or D is incorrect, check the wiring harness. If the voltage at these terminals is correct but the B terminal voltage is incorrect, replace the atmospheric pressure sensor.

6 To replace the sensor, disconnect the electrical connector and remove the two mounting bolts. Installation is the reverse of the removal procedure.

Water temperature sensor

7 Allow the engine to cool completely. Drain the engine coolant until the level is below the sensor. Disconnect the electrical connector and remove the sensor from the radiator. Measure the sensor resistance with an ohmmeter. There should be continuity at temperatures of 59 to 66 degrees F and above. If not, install a new sensor.

Throttle position sensor

Refer to illustrations 15.8, 15.9 and 15.10

8 Peel back the rubber boot from the sensor connector and turn the ignition switch to the On position. Measure the voltage between each terminal and ground, recording the voltmeter readings. Repeat the voltage checks, this time with the throttle plate wide open **(see illustration)**. If only the D terminal voltage is incorrect, check the throttle position sensor setting. If the other terminal voltages are incorrect, check the resistance at the throttle position sensor terminals (Step 10).

9 To check the throttle position sensor setting on 1986 and 1987 models, insert a 0.016-inch thick feeler gauge between the lever and throttle adjusting screw **(see illustration)**. With an ohmmeter, check for continuity between terminals B and D. Replace the feeler gauge with a 0.022-inch gauge. There should now be no continuity. If this is not the case, adjust the sensor by rotating it either way until the desired setting is obtained.

10 To check the resistance of the throttle position sensor, unplug the wire harness connector and attach the ohmmeter leads between the sensor terminals **(see illustration)**. If the readings are incorrect, replace the throttle position sensor.

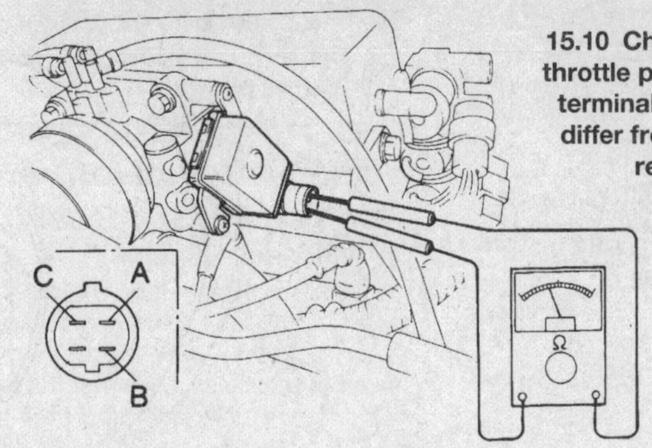

15.10 Check the resistance of the throttle position sensor across the terminals shown (if the readings differ from the specified values, replace the sensor)

Terminal \ Condition	Closed	Fully opened
A ↔ B	Approx. 500 Ω	Approx. 4.5 kΩ
B ↔ C	4~6 kΩ	

11 To replace the throttle position sensor, unplug the electrical connector and remove the two screws. To install the sensor, align the blade on the throttle shaft with the slot in the sensor, rotate the sensor into position and install the two screws. Adjust the sensor as described in Step 9.

Intake manifold pressure switch (earlier turbocharged engines only)

Refer to illustration 15.12

12 Disconnect the pressure hose from the switch. Apply approximately 10 PSI air pressure to the valve. **Caution:** *Do not exceed 14 PSI, or the valve will be damaged. Check the terminal voltage of the switch at the brown/white wire of the switch connector* **(see illustration)**. The voltage reading should be below 1.5-volt with the air pressure applied and approximately 12-volts without pressure. If incorrect readings are obtained, check the wiring harness and the switch resistance.

13 To check the switch resistance, unplug the electrical connector and attach ohmmeter leads to the switch terminals. Apply compressed air as in Step 12 and read the meter. There should be continuity. Check the switch without the pressure applied. There should be no continuity under this condition. If the resistance values are incorrect, replace the switch.

Power steering switch

Refer to illustration 15.14

14 To check the power steering switch operation, start the engine and allow it to idle. Unplug the electrical connector at the switch and hook up an ohmmeter across the switch terminals **(see illustration)**. Have an assistant turn the steering wheel to full right or left lock. The meter should show continuity. Conversely, there should be no continuity when the steering wheel is released. If the switch fails either test, replace it.

15 When installing a new switch, allow the engine to cool completely, then with the

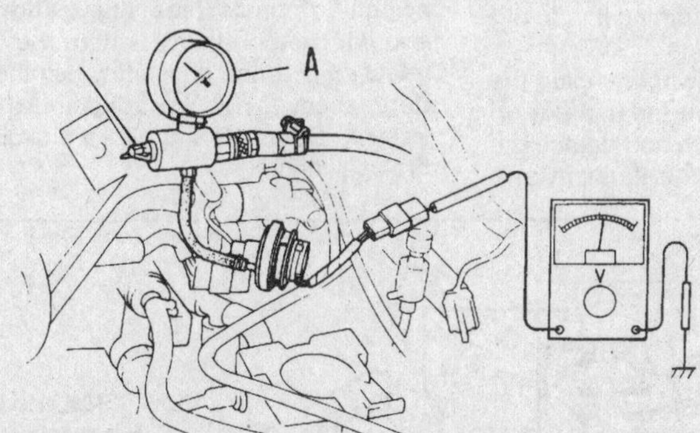

15.12 Check the intake manifold pressure switch terminal voltage with approximately 10 psi of air pressure applied to the switch through the pressure hose

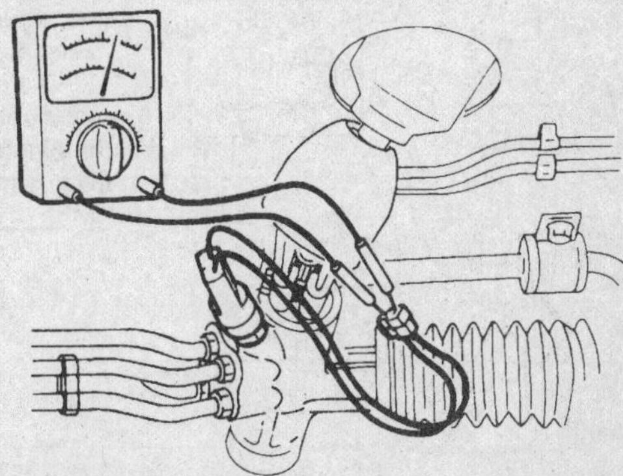

15.14 When checking the resistance of the power steering switch with the steering wheel at full-lock, there should be continuity - there should be no continuity when the steering wheel is in any other position

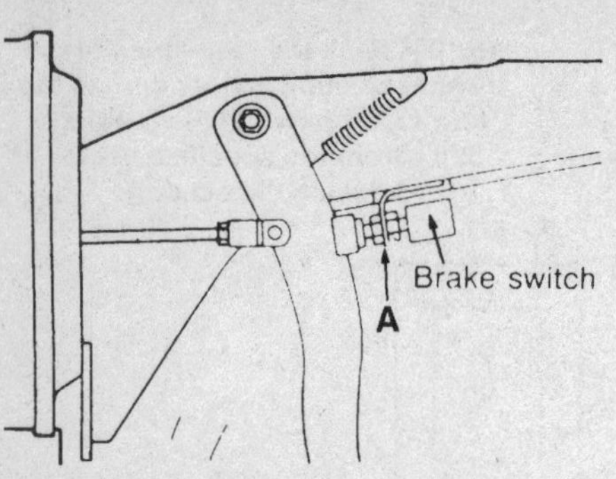

15.17 To adjust the brake switch, loosen the jam nut (A) and turn the switch in or out as required

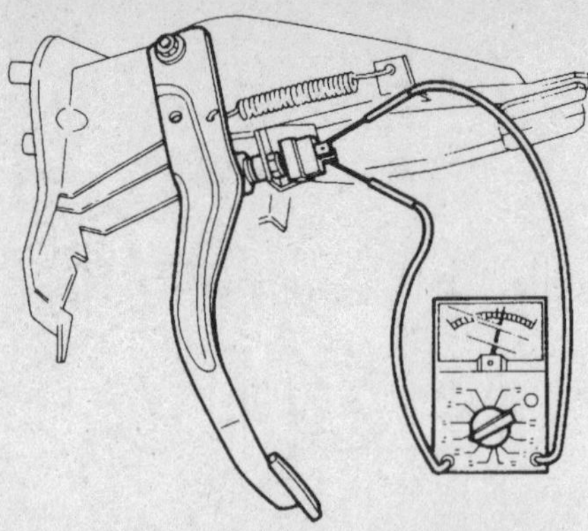

15.18 When checking the clutch switch, there should be continuity when the pedal is released (out) but no continuity when the pedal is depressed

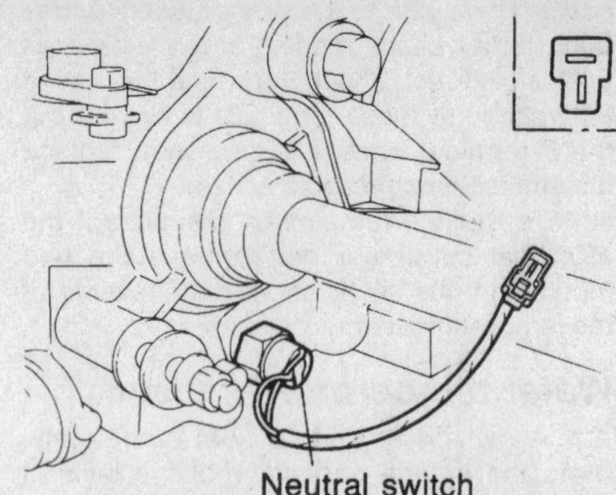

15.19 When the manual transaxle is placed in Neutral, there should be no continuity through the Neutral switch (continuity should exist in all gears)

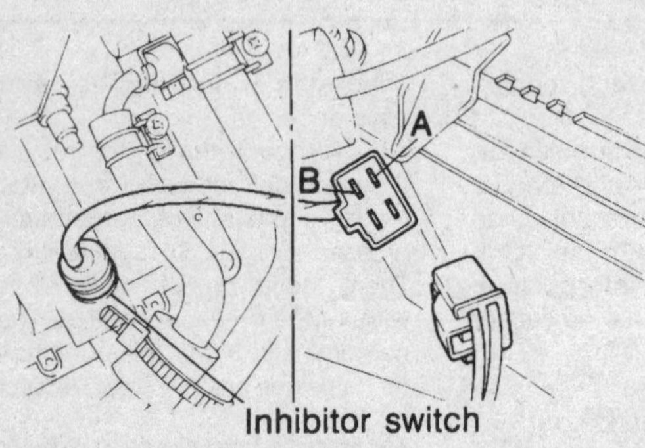

15.20 Check for continuity between terminals A and B of the inhibitor switch with the gear selector in Park or Neutral - there should be no continuity with the gear selector in any other range

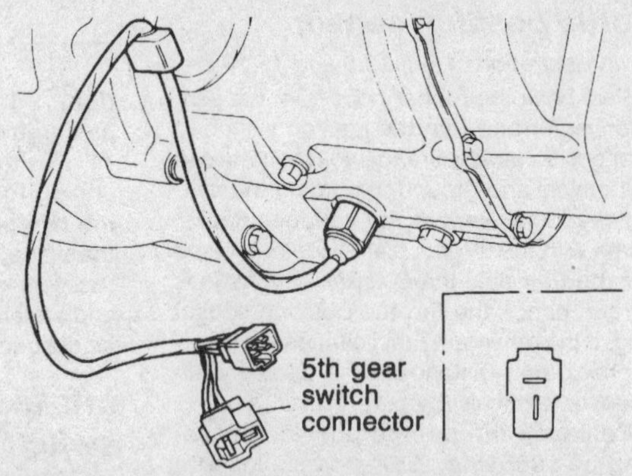

15.21 When the transaxle is in 5th gear, there should be no continuity through the 5th gear switch - in any other position there should be continuity

engine off, turn the steering wheel back-and-forth to bleed off any residual pressure in the steering gear unit. Unplug the electrical connector and unscrew the switch. Wrap the new switch with Teflon tape and start it into the steering gear by hand, then tighten it securely with a wrench. Plug in the electrical connector and check the fluid level.

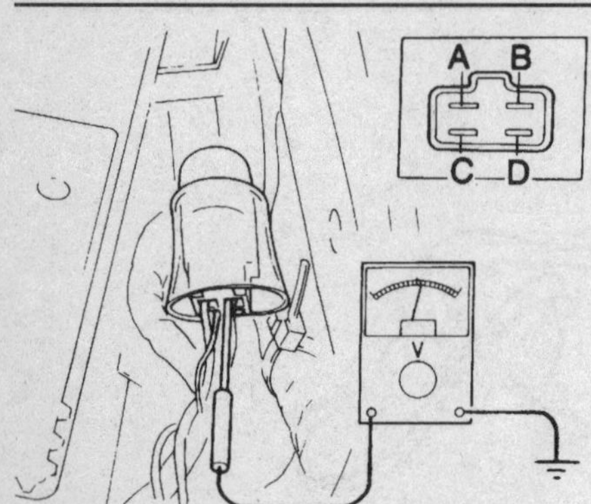

15.23 Check the voltage at each terminal of the main relay (all should indicate 12-volts except terminal B, which should read 0-volts)

Brake switch

Refer to illustration 15.17

16 Unplug the electrical connector to the brake switch under the dash. Connect an ohmmeter across the two terminals and measure the resistance of the switch with the pedal depressed. There should be continuity. There should be no continuity when the brake pedal is released. If the switch fails either test, attempt to adjust it by turning it in or out as necessary.

17 To replace the brake switch, unplug the electrical connector, remove the jam nut on the plunger side of the switch and detach the switch from the bracket **(see illustration)**. Installation is the reverse of removal. Use the test described in Step 17 to adjust the switch, moving the switch fore-and-aft as necessary.

Clutch switch

Refer to illustration 15.18

18 Detach the electrical connector from the switch and hook up an ohmmeter across the switch terminals **(see illustration)**. There should be continuity when the pedal is released and no continuity when the pedal is depressed. If not, try adjusting the switch (refer to Steps 16 and 17 - it's similar to the brake switch).

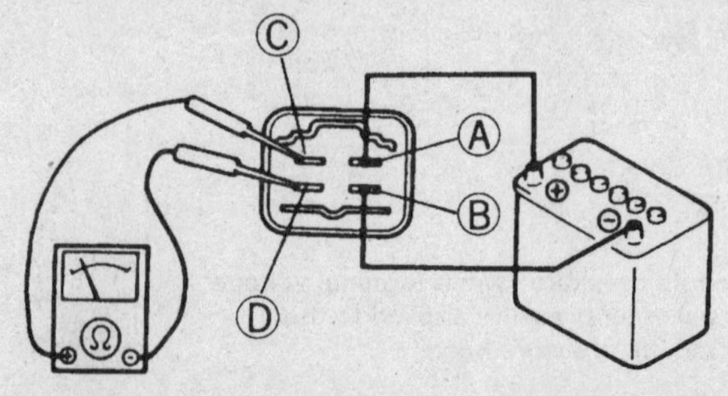

15.26 1988 and later main relay checking details

Neutral switch (manual transaxle equipped vehicles)

Refer to illustration 15.19

19 Unplug the connector from the Neutral switch, which is mounted on the transaxle **(see illustration)**. Connect an ohmmeter across the terminals of the switch and read the meter. There should be no continuity when the transaxle is in Neutral. When the shifter is moved to any other position, the ohmmeter should indicate continuity. If the readings are not correct, replace the switch. Wrap the threads on the new switch with Teflon tape to prevent leaks.

Inhibitor switch (automatic transaxle equipped vehicles)

Refer to illustration 15.20

20 Locate the inhibitor switch, which is mounted on the transaxle, and follow the harness until the connector is found. Unplug the connector and attach an ohmmeter to terminals A and B on the switch side of the connector **(see illustration)**. The ohmmeter should indicate continuity when the transaxle is in Neutral or Park. In any other gear there should be no continuity. If the switch fails either test it must be replaced.

5th gear switch (manual transaxle equipped vehicles)

Refer to illustration 15.21

21 Locate the switch on the transaxle housing and unplug the connector **(see illustration)**. Connect an ohmmeter across the two terminals and read the resistance value in fifth gear. It should be infinite ohms (no continuity). Check the resistance values in all of the other gears, including Neutral. The ohmmeter reading should be 0-ohms, indicating continuity. If the readings are incorrect, replace the switch.

22 To replace the switch, raise the vehicle and support it securely on jackstands. Position a drain pan under the transaxle and remove the switch from the transaxle case. Wrap the threads on the new switch with Teflon tape, start the switch by hand then tighten it snugly with a wrench. Fill the transaxle with the specified type and amount of lubricant (refer to Chapter 1).

Main relay

1986 and 1987 models

Refer to illustration 15.23

23 Using a voltmeter, check each terminal of the main relay **(see illustration)**. The meter should indicate approximately 12-volts at terminals A, C and D, with terminal B showing 0-volts. If the readings are incorrect, proceed to the next Step and measure the relay resistance.

24 Remove the relay from the vehicle and measure the resistance between terminals A and B with an ohmmeter. The meter should indicate approximately 70-ohms. Next, using two jumper wires, apply battery voltage to terminal A and ground terminal B while checking for continuity between terminals C and D. If the relay fails either test, replace it.

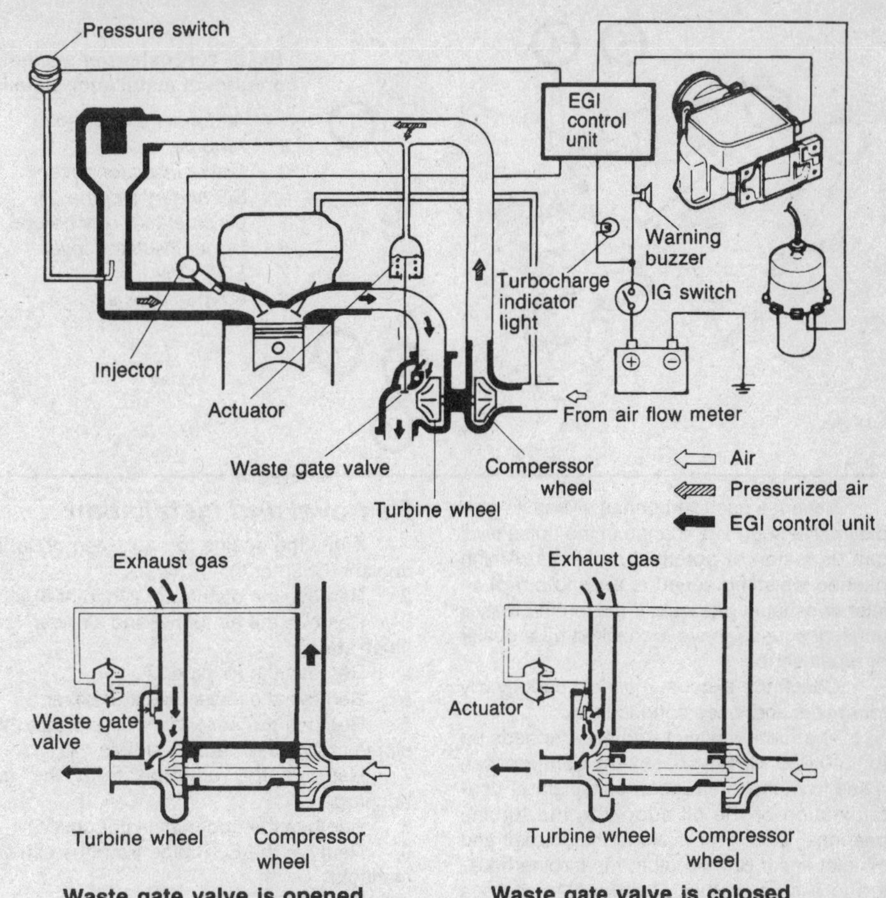

16.1a Turbocharger and related component details

1988 and later models

Refer to illustration 15.26

25 Make sure there is a clicking sound from the main relay when the ignition switch is turned on and off.

26 Check the relay as described in step 24 and check that there is continuity at the C and D terminals with power applied and none with no power applied **(see illustration)**.

EGI control unit

27 Due to the specialized test equipment and expertise required to check the control unit, diagnosis and replacement should be left to a dealer service department or a repair shop.

16 Turbocharger - description and checking

General information

Refer to illustrations 16.1a and 16.1b

The turbocharger increases power by using an exhaust gas driven turbine to pressurize the fuel/air mixture before it enters the combustion chambers, effectively forcing more fuel/air mixture into each cylinder than a normally aspirated engine. The amount of boost (intake manifold pressure) is controlled by the wastegate and actuator (operated by a spring loaded actuator assembly, regulated by manifold pressure), which controls the maximum boost level by allowing some of the exhaust gas to bypass the turbine **(see illustration)**. Later turbocharged models use an intercooler, a radiator-like cooler in the intake system which cools the air before it enters the turbocharger **(see illustration)**.

Check

While a comparatively simple design, the turbocharger is a precision device that can be severely damaged by an interrupted oil or coolant supply or loose or damaged ducts. Due to the special techniques and equipment required, diagnosis of suspected problems should be left to a dealer service department or repair shop. The home mechanic can, however, check the connections and linkages for damage and proper installation, as well as remove and install the turbocharger and save the labor expense of replacing the turbo unit.

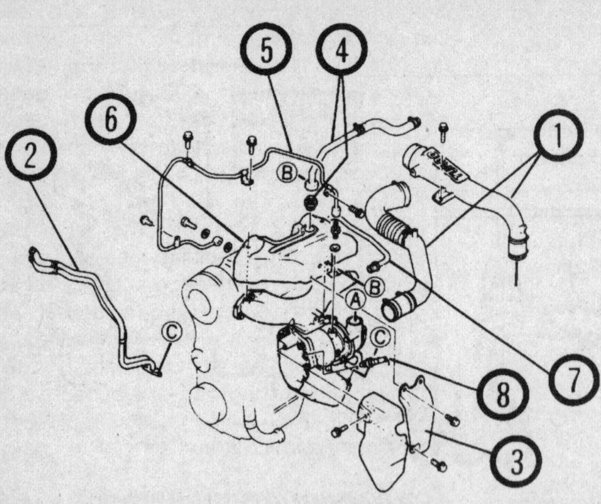

16.1b Turbocharger system component installation details

1. *Air funnel and air hose*
2. *Air pipe*
3. *Lower insulator cover*
4. *Secondary air pipe*
5. *Oil pipe (to turbocharger)*
6. *Upper insulator cover*
7. *EGR pipe*
8. *Oxygen sensor*

Because each turbocharger has its own distinctive sound, a change in the noise level can be a sign of potential problems. A high pitched whistling sound is a symptom of an inlet or exhaust gas leak. If the turbine makes unusual sounds, have it checked by a dealer or repair shop.

Check the exhaust manifold periodically for cracks and loose connections.

The turbine wheel rotates at speeds up to 140,000 RPM, so severe damage can result from the interruption of coolant or contamination of the oil supply to the turbine bearings. Check for leaks in the coolant and oil inlet lines. Burned oil in the turbine housing is a sign of this. **Caution:** *Any time a major engine bearing such as a main, connecting rod or camshaft bearing is replaced, the turbocharger should be flushed with clean engine oil.*

Removal and installation

1 Allow the engine to cool, then drain the coolant (Chapter 1).

2 Remove the distributor (Chapter 5).

3 Remove the air funnel and air hose **(see illustration)**.

4 Remove the air pipe.

5 Remove the lower insulator cover.

6 Remove the secondary air pipe and the nipple from the exhaust manifold.

7 Remove the oil pipe from the turbocharger.

8 Remove the upper insulator cover.

9 Remove the EGR pipe from the exhaust manifold.

10 Remove the water hoses.

11 Remove the oxygen sensor from the exhaust manifold.

12 Remove the front pipe from the catalytic converter.

13 Remove the turbocharger bracket bolts.

14 Remove the exhaust manifold bolts and detach the turbocharger, exhaust manifold and front catalytic converter as an assembly.

15 Remove the nuts securing the catalytic converter and exhaust manifold to the turbocharger.

16 The turbine rotor can now be inspected for freedom of movement and excessive play. If any axial or radial movement is felt, the turbocharger must be replaced.

17 Before installing the turbocharger, add 25 cubic centimeters of engine oil to the turbocharger through the oil passage to pre-oil the bearing.

18 Attach the exhaust manifold and the catalytic converter to the turbocharger. Be sure to use new gaskets. Tighten the nuts to the specified torque.

19 The remainder of installation is the reverse of the removal procedure.

20 Before starting the engine, detach the connector from the negative terminal of the ignition coil. Crank the engine for 20-seconds to ensure that oil pressure is built up throughout the lubrication system. Reconnect the coil wire and start the engine, allowing it to idle for at least 30-seconds before increasing the engine speed.

17 Turbocharger knock control system - description and checking

General description

Refer to illustration 17.1

The knock control system consists of the knock sensor, knock control unit and EGI

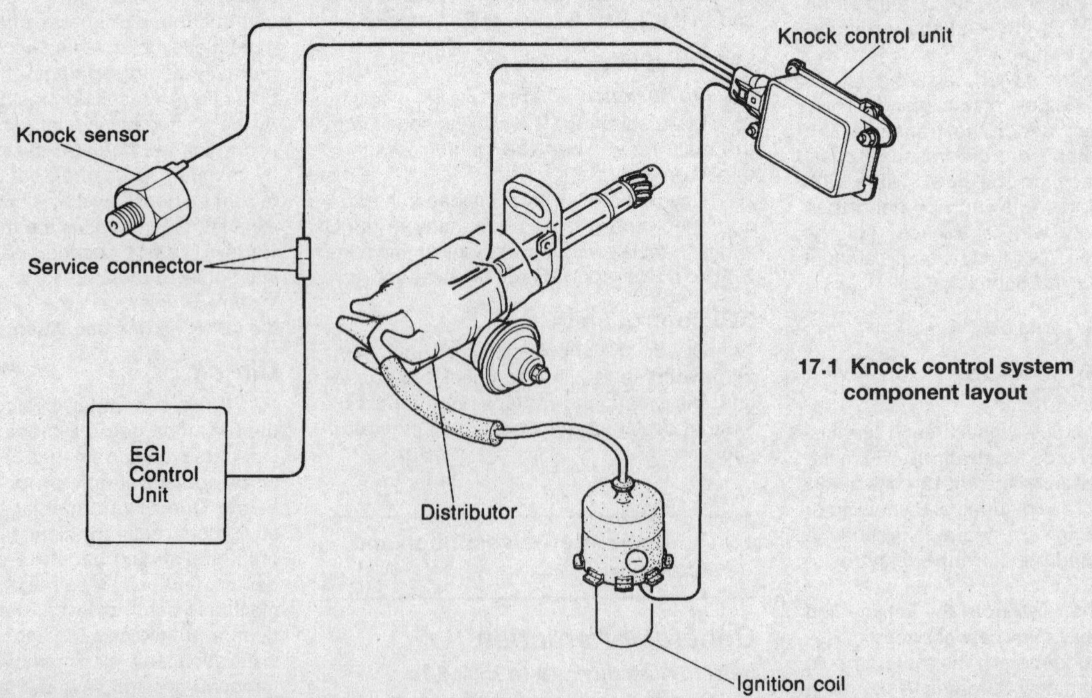

17.1 Knock control system component layout

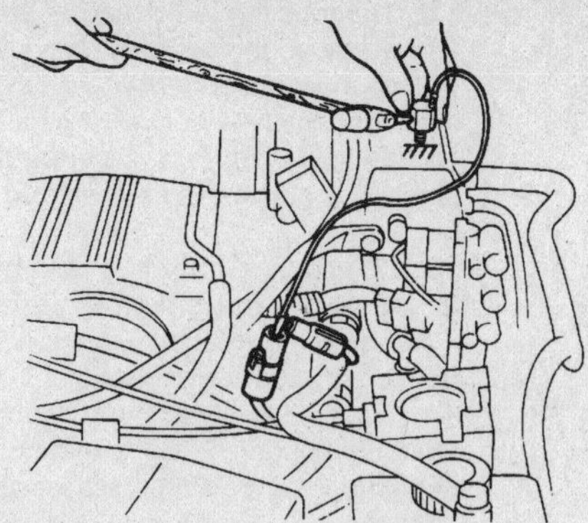

17.2 To confirm a defective knock control sensor, connect a known good sensor to the wiring connector, ground the sensor and tap it with a hammer - if the timing now retards, the original sensor is defective

control unit **(see illustration)**. The knock sensor, mounted on the back side of the engine block, senses abnormal vibrations from preignition and detonation and sends a signal to the knock control unit. The knock control unit differentiates a true knocking signal from other vibrations. If it is a knock signal, the knock control unit will retard the timing, depending on the magnitude of the vibration, up to 6-degrees. The EGI control unit sends a signal to the knock control unit, which inhibits spark retardation at engine speeds below 1650 and above 4500 RPM, or when the intake manifold pressure is lower than atmospheric pressure.

Checking

Refer to illustration 17.2

Note: *This following procedure is possible on 1986 and 1987 models only; later models require the use of a special tester tool and the job should be left to a dealer.*

1 Using a voltmeter, carefully probe terminal 1U on the EGI control unit. The indicated voltage should be 0-volts at idle. If it isn't, check the wire from the EGI control unit to the knock control unit (terminal G).

2 Check the ignition timing at idle, then disconnect the service connector from the EGI control unit **(see illustration)**. Tap the surge tank lightly with a hammer and see if the ignition timing retards. If it doesn't, go on to Step 3. If it does, reconnect the service connector and tap the surge tank again. Make sure the timing does not retard, indicating a properly functioning knock control system. If it does retard, the knock control unit is defective.

3 If the timing doesn't retard when performing the first test, unplug the service connector, connect a known good knock sensor to the connector and ground the sensor. Tap the sensor and make sure the timing retards. If it does, the original sensor is bad. If it doesn't, check the wiring from the sensor to the control unit. If the wiring is okay, replace the knock control unit.

Component replacement

4 To remove the knock control sensor, unplug the wire harness and unscrew the sensor from the block. Installation is the reverse of the removal procedure.

5 To remove the knock control unit, first disconnect the cable from the negative battery terminal. Unplug the wire harness from the unit and remove the two mounting nuts. Installation is the reverse of the removal procedure.

Notes

Chapter 5 Engine electrical systems

Contents

Specifications

Alternator

No load adjustment voltage test

Ammeter reading	5 amps
Voltmeter reading (adjustment voltage)	15 volts

Ignition coil

Secondary coil resistance	10 to 30 ohms
Primary terminal-to-case resistance	Over 10,000 ohms

Torque specifications

Torque specifications	Ft-lbs	M-kg
Alternator through-bolt	27 to 46	3.8 to 6.4
Starter motor bolt	27 to 46	3.8 to 6.4

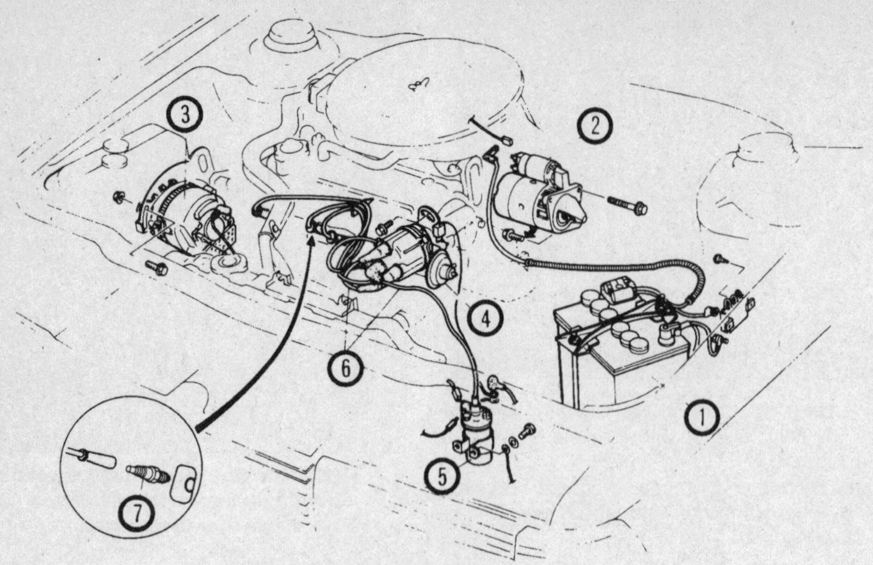

1.1 Engine electrical system components

1 *Battery*
2 *Starter motor*
3 *Alternator*
4 *Distributor*
5 *Ignition coil*
6 *Spark plug wires*
7 *Spark plug*

1 Ignition system - general information and precautions

Refer to illustration 1.1

The ignition system is composed of the battery, distributor, coil, ignition switch, spark plugs and the primary (low tension) and secondary (high tension) wiring circuits **(see illustration)**.

This system works in conjunction with the control unit and uses a magnetic pickup assembly located inside the distributor, which contains a rotor, reluctor, a pick up coil, centrifugal advance mechanism, vacuum control unit and breaker switch.

All ignition timing changes in this distributor are accomplished by the interaction of the data from various engine sensors and the control unit which computes the desired spark timing and signals the distributor to change the timing accordingly. **Warning:** *Because of the very high voltage generated by this system, extreme care should be taken whenever an operation involving ignition components is performed. This not only includes the distributor, coil and spark plug wires, but related items that are connected to the systems as well, such as the plug connections, tachometer, and testing equipment. Consequently, before any work is performed, the ignition should be turned off and the negative battery cable disconnected.*

2 Battery - removal and installation

Refer to illustration 2.4

1 The battery is located at the front of the engine compartment. It is held in place by a hold-down brace across the top of the case.

2 Hydrogen gas is produced by the battery, so keep open flames and lighted cigarettes away from it at all times.

3 Always keep the battery in an upright position. Spilled electrolyte should be rinsed off immediately with large quantities of water. Always wear eye protection when working around the battery.

4 Always disconnect the negative (-) battery cable first, followed by the positive (+) cable **(see illustration)**.

5 After the cables are disconnected from the battery, remove the nuts and the hold-down brace.

6 Carefully lift the battery out of the engine compartment.

7 Installation is the reverse of removal. The cable brace nuts should be tight, but do not overtighten them as damage to the battery case can occur. The battery posts and cable ends should be cleaned prior to connection (Chapter 1).

3 Battery - emergency jump starting

Refer to the booster battery (jump) starting procedure at the front of this manual.

4 Battery cables - check and replacement

1 Periodically inspect the entire length of each battery cable for damage, cracked or burned insulation and corrosion. Poor battery cable connections can cause starting problems and decreased engine performance.

2 Check the cable-to-terminal connections at the ends of the cables for cracks,

2.4 Hold the negative cable steady when loosening the nut as the battery post can be easily damaged

loose wire strands and corrosion. The presence of white, fluffy deposits under the insulation at the cable terminal connection is a sign the cable is corroded and should be replaced. Check the terminals for distortion missing mounting bolts or nuts and corrosion.

3 If only the positive cable is to be replaced, be sure to disconnect the negative cable from the battery first.

4 Disconnect and remove the cable from the vehicle. Make sure the replacement cable is the same length and diameter.

5 Clean the threads of the starter or ground connection with a wire brush to remove rust and corrosion. Apply a light coat of petroleum jelly to the threads to ease installation and prevent future corrosion. Inspect the connections frequently to make sure they are clean and tight.

6 Attach the cable to the starter or ground connection and tighten the mounting nut securely.

7 Before connecting the new cables to the battery, make sure they reach the terminals without having to be stretched.

8 Connect the positive cable first, followed by the negative cable. Tighten the nuts and apply a thin coat of petroleum jelly to the terminal and cable connection.

5 Ignition system - check

Warning: *Because of the very high voltage generated by the ignition system, extreme care should be taken whenever an operation is performed involving ignition components. This not only includes the distributor, coil and spark plug wires, but related items that are connected to the system as well, such as the plug connections, tachometer and any test equipment. Consequently, before any work is performed, the ignition should be turned off or the battery ground cable disconnected.*

Refer to illustration 5.1

1 If the engine turns over but will not start remove the spark plug wire from a spark plug

5.1 To use a calibrated ignition tester (available at most auto parts stores), remove an ignition wire from a cylinder, connect the spark plug boot to the tester and clip the tester to a good ground - if there is enough voltage to fire the plug, sparks will be clearly visible between the electrode tip and the tester body as the engine is cranked

and, use a calibrated ignition tester to check for spark **(see illustration)**.

2 If there is no spark, check another wire in the same manner. A few sparks, then no spark, should be considered as no spark.

3 If there is good spark, check the spark plugs (refer to Chapter 1) and/or the fuel system (refer to Chapter 4).

4 If there is a weak spark or no spark, unplug the coil lead from the distributor, hold it about 1/4-inch from a good ground and check for spark as described above.

5 If there is no spark, have the system checked by a dealer or repair shop.

6 If there is a spark, check the distributor cap and/or rotor (refer to Chapter 1).

7 Further checks of the ignition system must be done by a dealer or repair shop.

6 Distributor - removal and installation

Removal

Refer to illustrations 6.4 and 6.5

1 Disconnect the battery negative cable.

2 Disconnect the coil positive terminal wire.

3 Remove the two retaining screws and lift off the distributor cap.

4 Use a wrench on the crankshaft pulley bolt to rotate the engine until the distributor rotor is vertical **(see illustration)**.

5 Mark the distributor flange to engine rear housing relationship for reference **(see illustration)**.

6 Disconnect the vacuum advance hoses, remove retaining bolt and lift the distributor from the engine.

Installation if the crankshaft was not turned after distributor removal

7 Lubricate the O-ring with clean engine oil.

8 Insert the distributor into the engine rear housing with the rotor in the vertical position, align the marks made during removal and install the retaining bolt.

9 Connect the vacuum hoses and the coil wire.

Installation if the crankshaft was turned after distributor removal

10 Remove the number one spark plug and place your finger over the spark plug hole while turning the crankshaft with a wrench on the pulley bolt at the front of the engine. When you feel compression, continue turning the crankshaft slowly until the timing mark on the crankshaft pulley is aligned with the T on the engine timing indicator.

11 Complete the installation by referring to Steps 7 through 9.

6.4 The distributor rotor must be pointing straight up as shown before the distributor is removed

7 Distributor rotor - replacement

1 Disconnect the negative battery cable.

2 Remove the distributor cap.

3 Remove the retaining screws and lift off the distributor rotor.

4 Installation is the reverse of removal.

8 Distributor - dismantling and reassembly

Disassembly

Refer to illustrations 8.5, 8.6, 8.7, 8.8a and 8.8b

1 Remove the distributor (Section 6).

2 Remove the mounting tab plate from the distributor housing.

3 Mount the distributor in a vise, using a cloth to protect the surface.

4 Remove the two screws and lift off the rotor.

5 Noting their positions for ease of reassembly, remove the two advance springs **(see illustration)**.

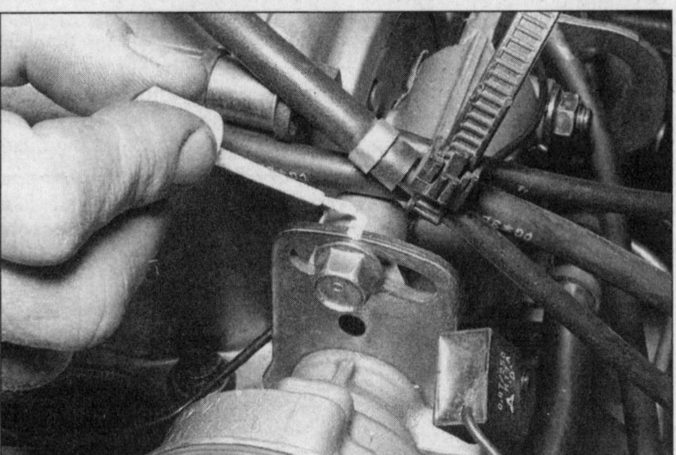

6.5 Marking the distributor-to-engine housing relationship

8.5 Disconnect the advance mechanism springs (arrows)

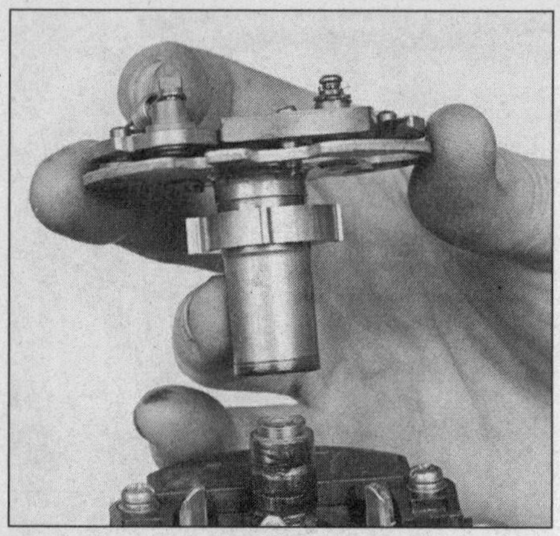

8.6 Removing the distributor advance mechanism

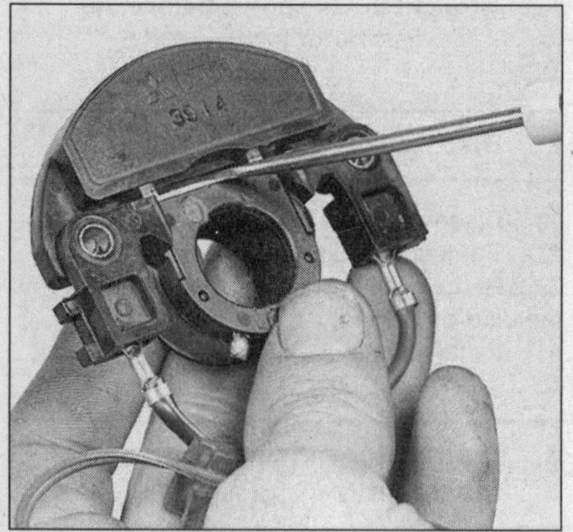

8.8a Pry the module carefully away from the pickup coil with a small screwdriver

6 Remove the retaining bolt and lift the advance mechanism from the shaft **(see illustration)**.

7 Remove the two screws and lift the pick up coil **(see illustration)**.

8 Use a small screwdriver to disengage the module from the pick up coil **(see illustrations)**.

9 Remove the two screws and extract the vacuum diaphragm assembly from the housing.

8.11b Rotate the mechanism while engaging the arm (arrow)

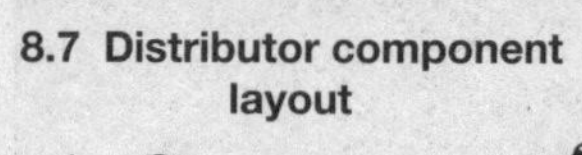

8.7 Distributor component layout

1 *Cap*
2 *Rotor*
3 *Advance mechanism*
4 *Pickup coil*
5 *Vacuum control unit*
6 *Breaker assembly*
7 *Driven gear*
8 *Shaft*

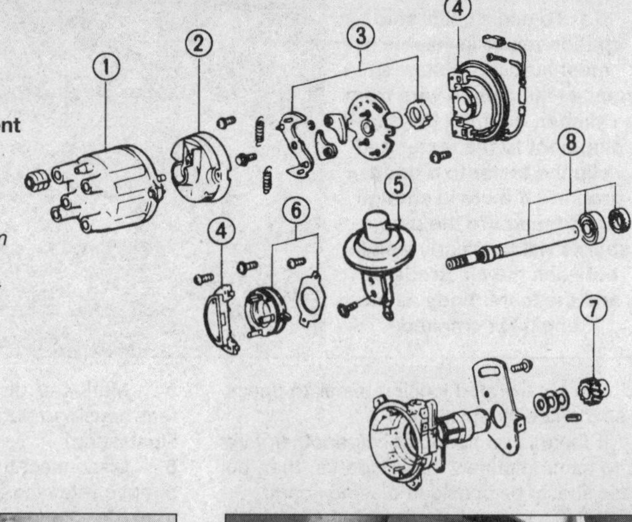

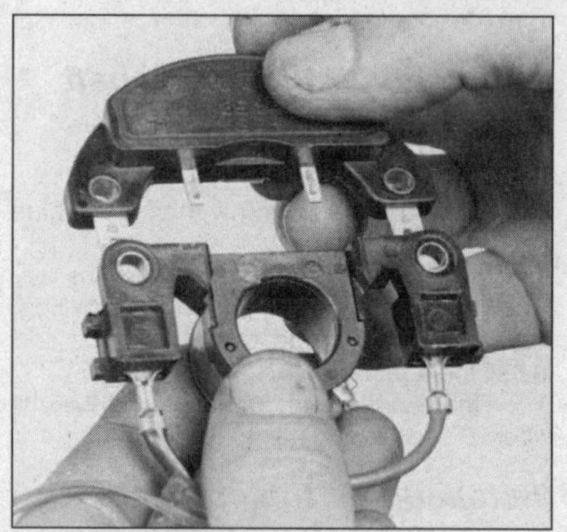

8.8b Lift the module away from the pickup coil

Reassembly

Refer to illustrations 8.11a and 8.11b

10 Lubricate the distributor shaft with lithium grease.

11 Insert the arm of the vacuum control unit into the distributor housing and latch it onto the mechanism in the housing base, turning the mechanism to lock the assembly in place **(see illustrations)**.

12 Install the pickup coil, making sure it locks onto the mounting tabs before tightening the screws.

13 Install the advance mechanism and reconnect the springs.

14 Install the rotor and distributor cap.

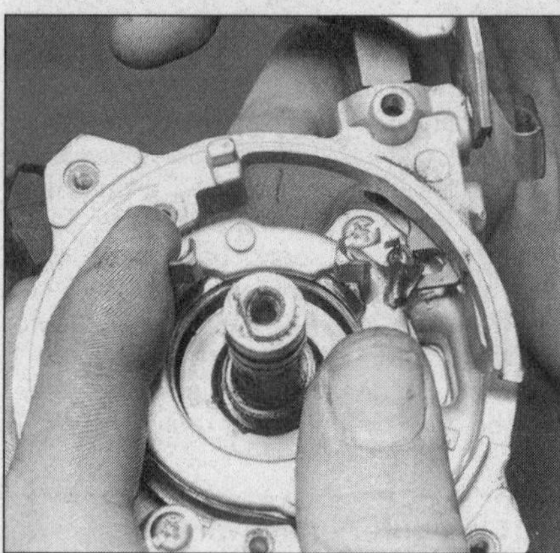

8.11a Connect the vacuum advance arm

9 Ignition coil - testing

Refer to illustrations 9.2, 9.4 and 9.5

1 Remove the boot and disconnect the coil wires.

2 Connect an ohmmeter as shown in the to check the primary circuit **(see illustration)**.

3 If the coil primary circuit is operating properly there will be no continuity.

4 Measure the resistance of the coil secondary resistance with an ohmmeter and compare the reading to those in the Specifications section **(see illustration)**.

5 Measure the insulation resistance between the primary terminal and the case

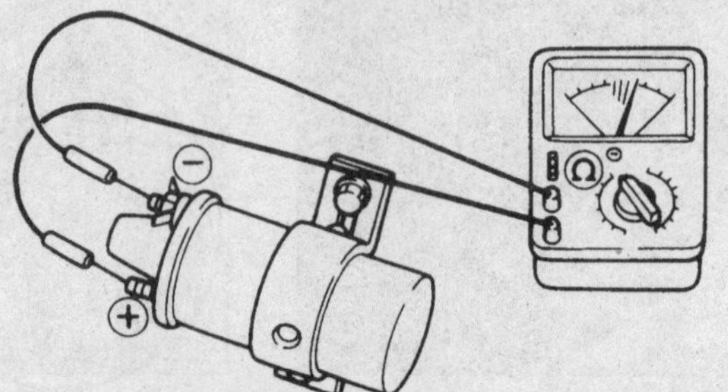

9.2 Testing the ignition coil primary circuit

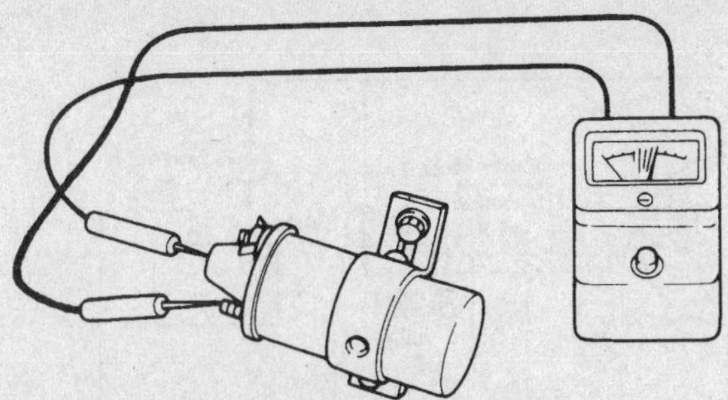

9.4 Testing the secondary coil resistance

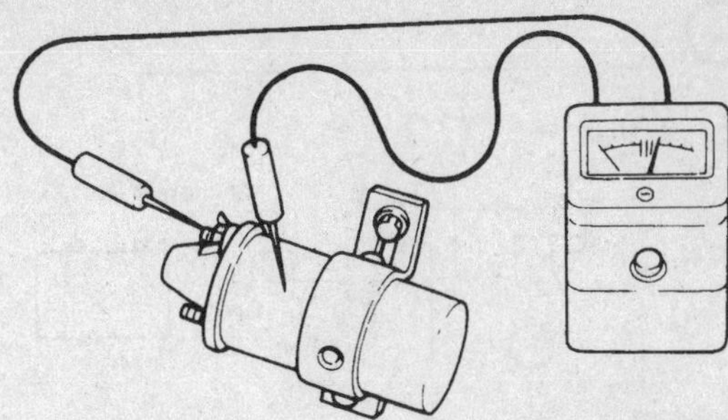

9.5 Testing the ignition coil insulation resistance

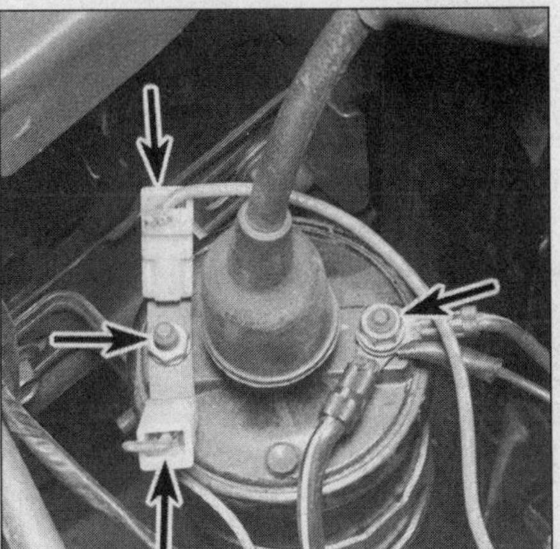

10.2 Ignition coil wire connections (arrows)

with a multimeter **(see illustration)**.

6 Replace the ignition coil with a new one if it fails any of the tests.

10 Ignition coil - removal and installation

Removal

Refer to illustrations 10.2 and 10.3

1 Disconnect the battery negative cable.

2 Pull the rubber boot off and, noting their positions, disconnect the coil wires **(see illustration)**.

3 Remove the retaining bolts and bracket and lift the coil from the radiator brace **(see illustration)**.

Installation

4 Place the coil in position, install the bracket and bolts. Tighten the bolts securely.

5 Connect the coil wires and install the boot securely on the top of the coil.

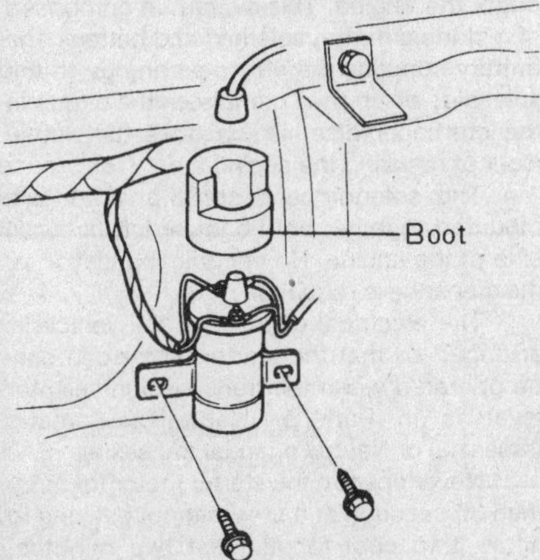

10.3 Ignition coil installation details

11 Charging system - general information and precautions

The charging system is made up of the alternator, voltage regulator and battery. These components work together to supply electrical power for the engine ignition, lights, radio, etc.

The alternator is turned by a drivebelt at the front of the engine. When the engine is operating, voltage is generated by the internal components of the alternator to be sent to the battery for storage.

The purpose of the voltage regulator is to limit the alternator voltage to a preset value. This prevents power surges, circuit overloads, etc., during peak voltage output. On all models with which this manual is concerned, the voltage regulator is contained within the alternator housing.

The charging system does not ordinarily require periodic maintenance. The drivebelts, electrical wiring and connections should, however, be inspected at the intervals suggested in Chapter 1.

Take extreme care when making circuit connections to a vehicle equipped with an alternator and note the following. When making connections to the alternator from a battery, always match correct polarity. Before using arc welding equipment to repair any part of the vehicle, disconnect the wires from the alternator and the battery terminal. Never start the engine with a battery charger connected. Always disconnect both battery leads before using a battery charger.

12 Charging system - check

Refer to illustrations 12.2, 12.3 and 12.7

1 If a malfunction occurs in the charging circuit, do not immediately assume that the alternator is causing the problem. First check the following items:

a) The battery cables where they connect to the battery (make sure the connections are clean and tight).

b) The battery electrolyte specific gravity (if it is low, charge the battery).

c) Check the external alternator wiring and connections (they must be in good condition).

d) Check the drivebelt condition and tension (see Chapter 1).

e) Check the alternator mount bolts for tightness.

f) Run the engine and check the alternator for abnormal noise.

2 Using a voltmeter, check the battery voltage with the engine off at the B terminal as shown in the **(see illustration)**. It should be approximately 12 volts. **Caution:** *When checking the alternator, do not ground the L terminal while the engine is running or start the engine with the L and R terminals disconnected.*

5

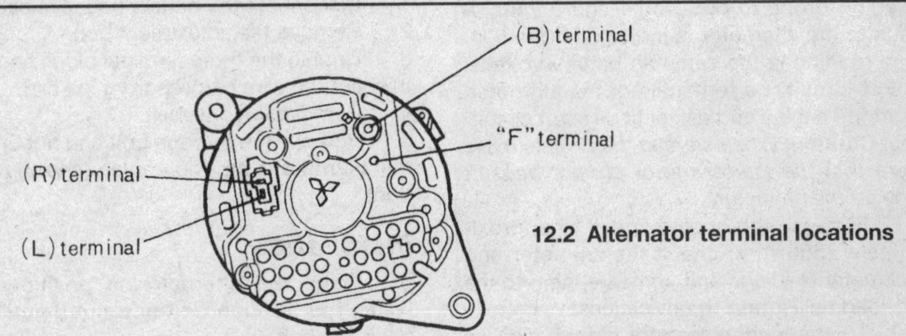

12.2 Alternator terminal locations

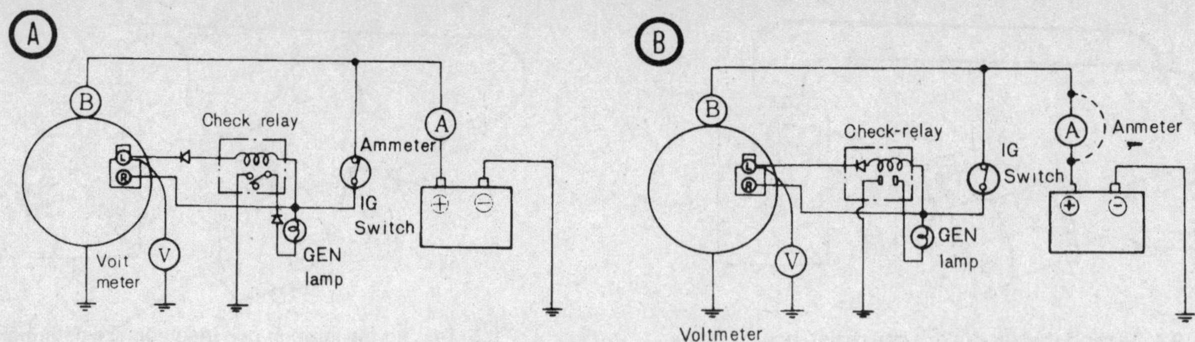

12.3 Alternator check connections

A System check
B No load adjustment check

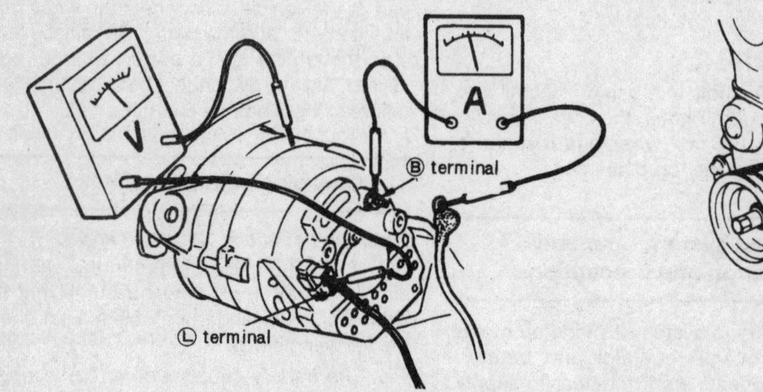

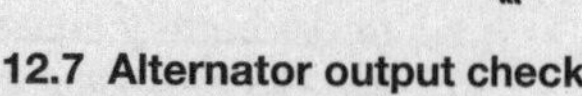

12.7 Alternator output check

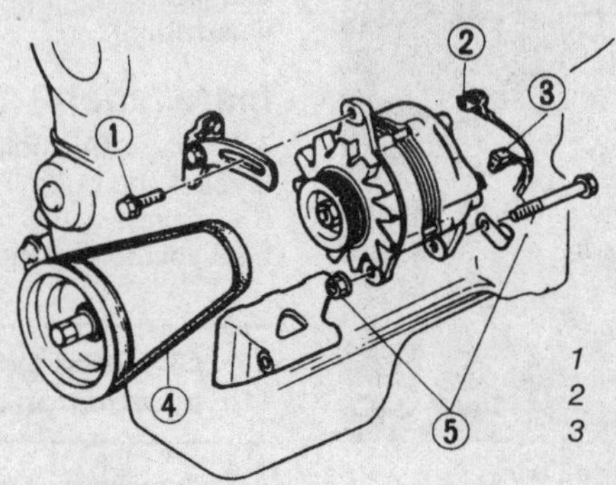

1 *Adjustment bolt*
2 *B terminal connection*
3 *L and R terminal connections*
4 *Drivebelt*
5 *Through bolt and nut*

13.5 Alternator installation details

3 To check the charging system, make the connections shown in the **(see illustration)**. With the engine off, check the voltage between the alternator L terminal and ground. If the reading is not 0 volts, the alternator is faulty. Turn the ignition On and check the voltage. If the reading is 0 volts, there is a fault in the alternator or wiring. If the voltage is close to battery voltage (12 volts), short circuit between the F terminal and alternator rear bracket and check the voltage. There is a fault in the IC regulator if the voltage drops.

4 To check the no-load adjustment voltage, make sure the battery is fully charged and connect an ammeter and voltmeter as shown in the illustration. The voltmeter reading should be 0 volts.

5 Turn the ignition On and make sure the reading drops to between 1 and 3 volts. A fault in the alternator is indicated if the voltage reading is the same as battery voltage. Short circuit the terminals of the ammeter, start the engine and discontinue short circuiting. **Caution:** *When starting the engine, make sure that the starter motor current doesn't flow to the ammeter.*

6 Increase the engine speed to approximately 2500 rpm, check the ammeter and voltmeter readings and compare them to the no-load adjustment specifications.

7 To check the alternator output, disconnect the negative battery cable and connect an ammeter and voltmeter as shown in the **(see illustration)**.

8 Connect the negative battery cable, start the engine and apply a load by turning on the headlights. Increase the engine speed gradually and check the current output. The system is operating properly if the voltage is no higher than battery voltage and there is output current.

13 Alternator - removal and installation

Removal

Refer to illustration 13.5

1 Disconnect the battery negative cable.
2 Remove the adjustment bolt.
3 Unplug the three terminal plugs and disconnect the wire harness from the clip.
4 Remove the drivebelt.
5 Remove the through bolt and nut and lift the alternator from the engine **(see illustration)**.

Installation

6 Place the alternator in position and install the through bolt and nut. Install the adjusting bolt.
7 Install the drivebelt and adjust the tension (Chapter 1).
8 Plug in the alternator connectors.
9 Connect the battery negative cable.

14 Starting system - general information

The function of the starting system is to crank the engine. This system is composed of a starting motor, solenoid and battery. The battery supplies the electrical energy to the solenoid, which then completes the circuit to the starting motor, which does the actual work of cranking the engine.

The solenoid and starting motor are mounted together on the lower left (firewall) side of the engine. No periodic lubrication or maintenance is required.

The electrical circuitry of the vehicle is arranged so that the starter motor can only be operated when the transmission selector lever is in Park or Neutral (automatic transaxle) or Neutral (manual transaxle).

Never operate the starter motor for more than 30 seconds at a time without pausing to allow it to cool for at least two minutes. Excessive cranking can cause overheating, which can seriously damage the starter.

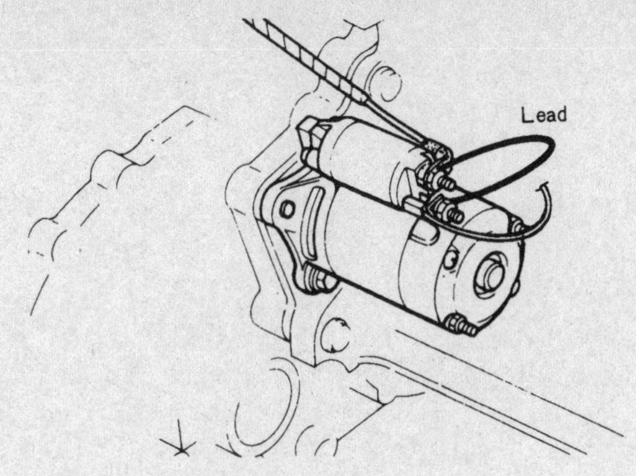

15.5 Starter solenoid check

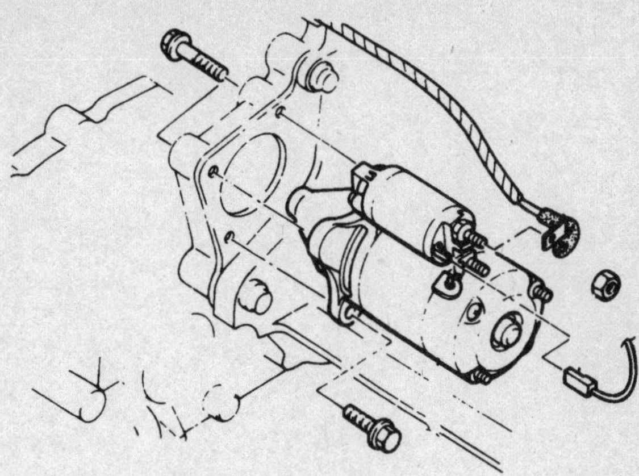

16.3 Starter motor installation details

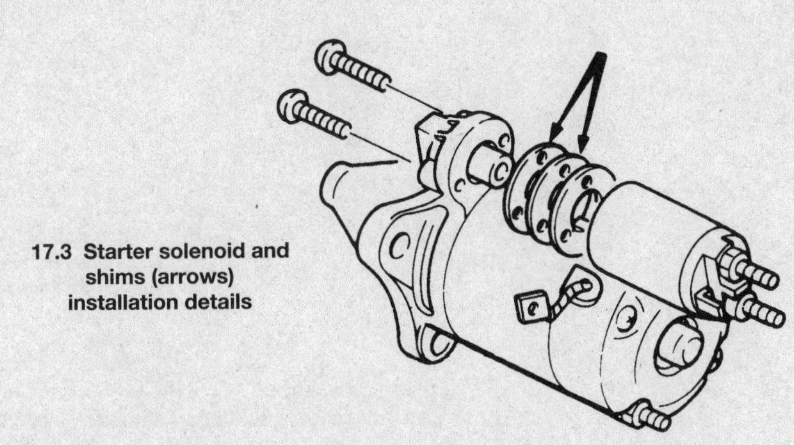

17.3 Starter solenoid and shims (arrows) installation details

15 Starter motor - testing in vehicle

Refer to illustration 15.5

1 If the starter motor does not turn at all when the switch is operated, make sure that the shift lever is in Neutral or Park (automatic transaxle) or Neutral (manual transaxle).

2 Make sure that the battery is charged and that all cables, both at the battery and starter solenoid terminals, are secure.

3 If, when the switch is actuated, the starter motor does not operate at all but the solenoid clicks, and the battery is fully charged, then the problem is in the main solenoid contacts or the starter motor itself.

4 If the solenoid plunger cannot be heard when the switch is actuated, the solenoid itself is defective or the solenoid circuit is open.

5 To check the solenoid, connect a jumper lead between the battery (B) and the M terminal on the solenoid **(see illustration)**. If the starter motor now operates, the solenoid is OK and the problem is in the ignition switch, neutral start switch or in the wiring.

6 If the starter motor still does not operate, remove the starter/solenoid assembly for disassembly, testing and repair by your dealer or a properly equipped shop.

16 Starter motor - removal and installation

Refer to illustration 16.3

1 Disconnect the negative battery cable.

2 Raise the front of the vehicle and support it securely on jackstands.

3 From under the vehicle, disconnect the solenoid wires and battery cable from the starter motor **(see illustration)**.

4 Remove the retaining bolts and lower the starter motor from the engine.

5 Installation is the reverse of the removal procedure.

17 Starter solenoid - removal and installation

Removal

Refer to illustration 17.3

1 After removing the starter motor (Section 16), disconnect the motor strap.

2 Remove the two screws which secure the solenoid housing to the starter end frame.

3 Twist the solenoid to disengage it and remove it from the starter body, taking care not to lose any of the shims **(see illustration)**.

Installation

4 Place the solenoid with shims in place and rotate it into position in the starter end frame.

5 Install the two solenoid screws and connect the motor strap.

Notes

Chapter 6
Emissions control systems

Contents

Specifications

Control unit terminals, connections and voltage readings

Terminal	Connection to	Voltage with ignition On
A (input)	Ignition coil (-) terminal	Approximately 12 volts
B (input)	Ignition power supply	Approximately 12 volts
C (input)	Air conditioner relay	Below 1.5 volts (12 volts with blower on)
E, I (output)	System check terminal	E: approximately 12 volts; after 0.4 seconds: below 1.5 volts
F (output)	A/F solenoid valve	Approximately 12 volts
H (output)	Coasting richer solenoid valve	Approximately 12 volts
D (output)	Slow fuel cut solenoid valve	Below 1.5 volts
J (output)	Air conditioner solenoid	Approximately 12 volts
K, L (output)	Duty solenoid valve	Approximately 12 volts
M (output)	Solenoid valve for Air Control Valve	Approximately 12 volts
N, R (ground)	Engine ground	0 volts
a (input)	Oxygen sensor	Below 1.5 volts
b (output)	Oxygen sensor	Below 1.5 volts
c (output)	Water thermo sensor	Approximately 3.4 volts at 140°F (60°C), approximately 1.1 volts at 175°F (80°C)
d (ground)	Water thermo sensor ground	Below 1.5 volts
e (output)	Vacuum sensor	Approximately 4 volts
f (ground)	Vacuum sensor ground	Below 1.5 volts
g (power)	Vacuum sensor	Approximately 1.5 volts
h (ground)	EGR position sensor	Below 1.5 volts
j (output)	EGR position sensor	Below 1.5 volts
l (power)	EGR position sensor	Approximately 5 volts
k (input)	Vacuum switch	Approximately 12 volts
m (input)	Clutch switch, neutral switch	Below 1.5 volts
n (input)	Ignition switch START terminal	Below 1.5 volts (10 volts at START)
o (input)	Idle switch	Approximately 12 volts
p (ground)	Idle switch and vacuum ground switch	Below 1.5 volts
q (input)	Water thermo switch	Below 1.5 volts above 61°F (17°C)

EGR system water thermo sensor resistance

Water temperature	Resistance
-4°F (-20°C)	Approximately 1.62 ohms
68°F (20°C)	Approximately 2.45 ohms
176°F (80°C)	Approximately 0.032 ohms

6

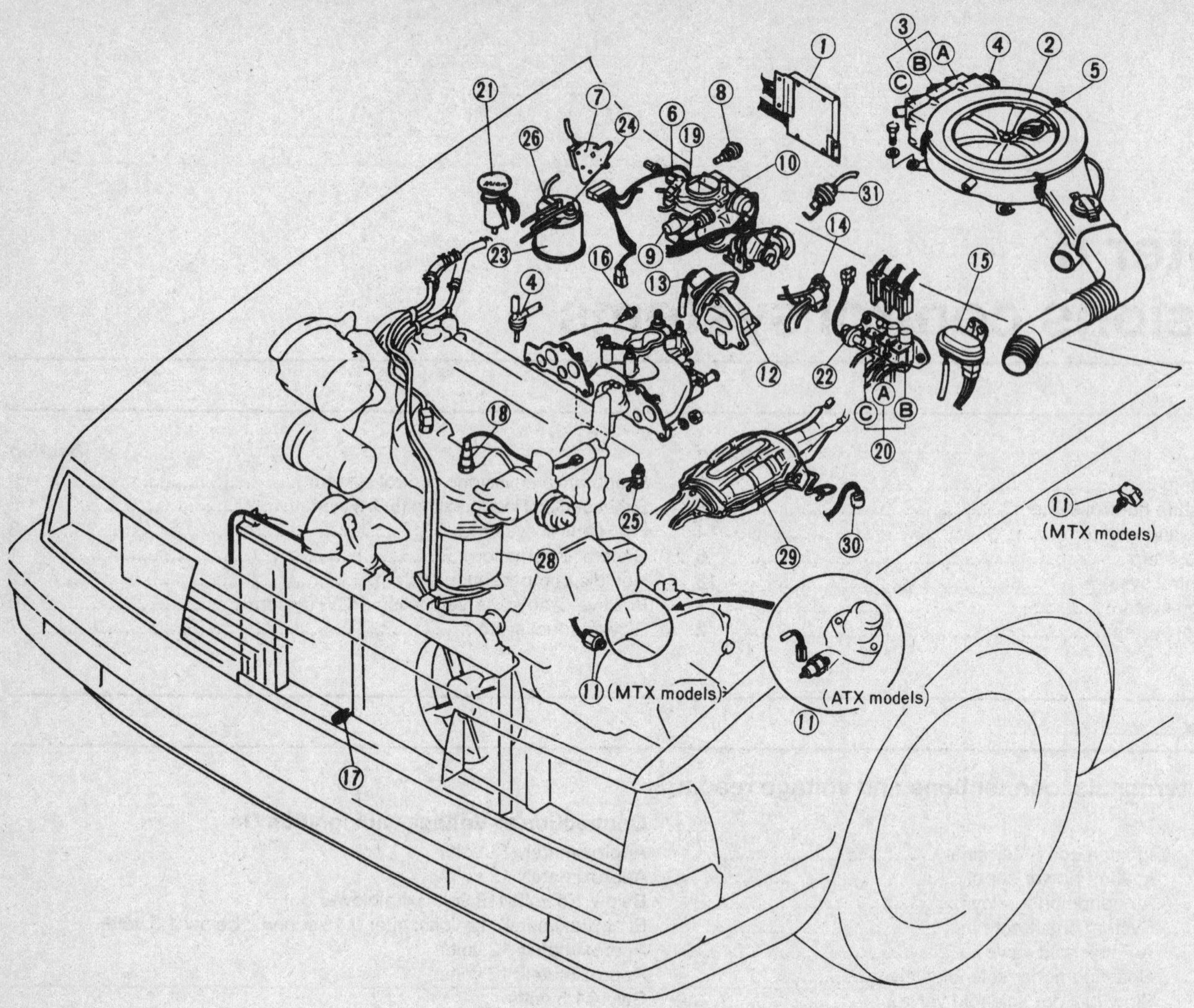

1.1 Typical emissions system component layout

1 Control unit
2 Air cleaner assembly
3 Reed valve
4 No. 1 air control valve
5 Idle compensator valve
6 Air vent solenoid valve
7 Idle switch
8 Dashpot
9 Coasting richer solenoid
10 Slow cut fuel solenoid valve
11 Clutch switch and neutral switch
12 EGR valve
13 EGR position sensor
14 Duty solenoid valve
15 Vacuum sensor
16 Water thermo sensor
17 Water thermo switch
18 Oxygen sensor
19 A/F solenoid valve
20 Three-way solenoid valve
21 Altitude compensator
22 Vacuum switch
23 Evaporative emissions system canister
24 Purge control valve No. 1
25 Water thermo valve
26 Purge control valve
27 Check valve
28 Front catalytic converter
29 Rear catalytic converter
30 Power steering switch
31 Servo diaphragm

1 General information

Refer to illustration 1.1

To prevent pollution of the atmosphere from burned and evaporating gases, a number of emissions control systems are incorporated on the vehicles covered by this manual **(see illustration)**. The combination of systems used depends on the year in which the vehicle was manufactured, the locality to which it was originally delivered and the engine type. The major systems incorporated on the vehicles with which this manual is concerned include the:

Fuel control system
Electronic ignition system
Air injection system
Coasting richer system
Slow cut system
Deceleration control system
Evaporative emissions control system
Hot idle compensation system
Air inlet temperature control system
Exhaust Gas Recirculation (EGR)
Evaporative emissions control
Positive Crankcase Ventilation (PCV)
Altitude compensation system

All of these systems are linked, directly or indirectly, to the control unit.

The Sections in this Chapter include general descriptions, checking procedures (where possible) and component replacement procedures (where applicable) for each of the systems listed above.

Before assuming that an emissions control system is malfunctioning, check the fuel

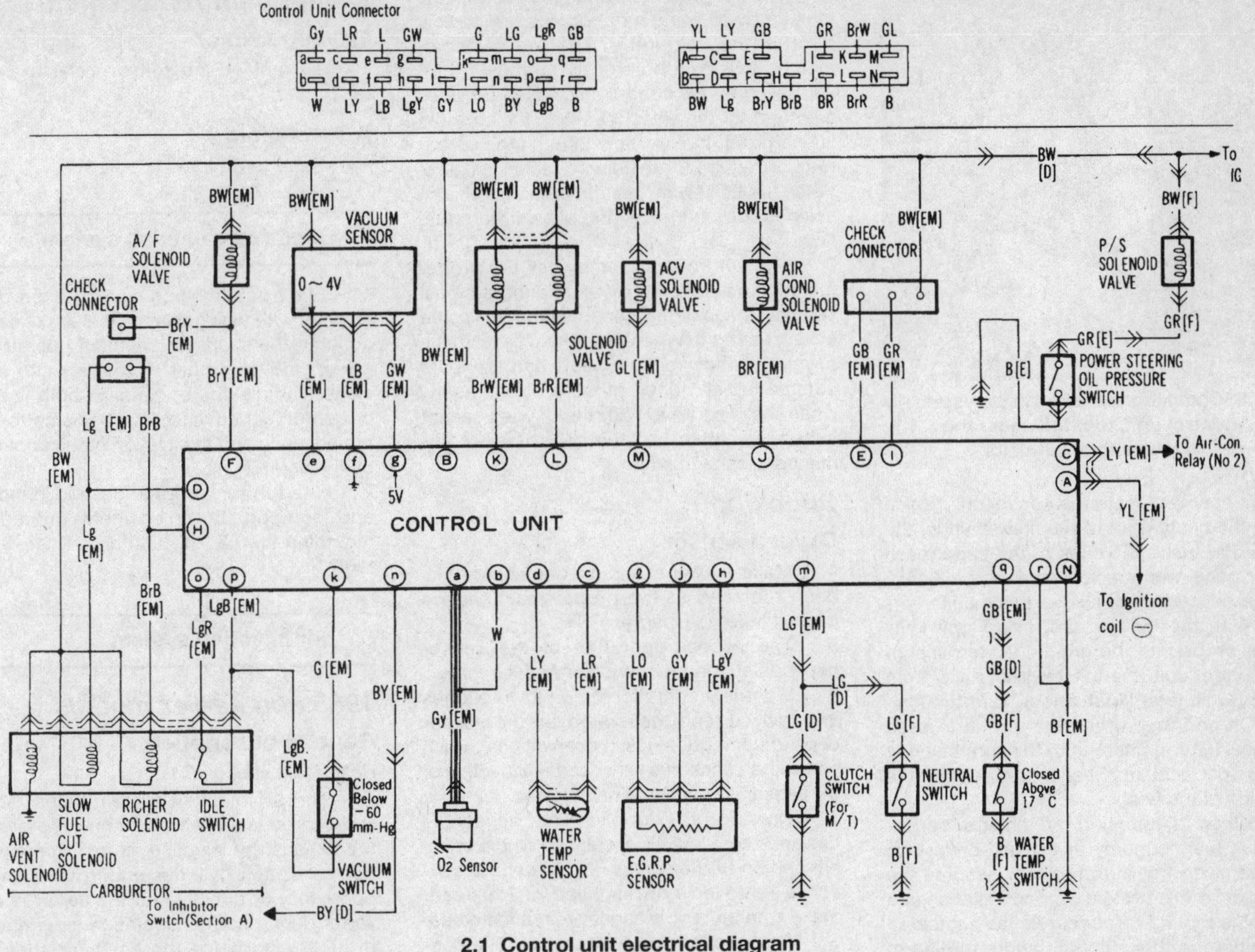

2.1 Control unit electrical diagram

and ignition systems carefully. In some cases special tools and equipment, as well as specialized training, are required to accurately diagnose the causes of a rough running or difficult to start engine. If checking and servicing become too difficult, or if a procedure is beyond the scope of the home mechanic, consult your dealer service department. This does not necessarily mean, however, that the emissions control systems are particularly difficult to maintain and repair. You can quickly and easily perform many checks and do most (if not all) of the regular maintenance at home with common tune-up and hand tools. **Note:** *The most frequent cause of emissions system problems is simply a loose or broken vacuum hose or wiring connection. Therefore, always check the hose and wiring connections first.*

Pay close attention to any special precautions outlined in this Chapter. It should be noted that the illustrations of the various systems might not exactly match the system installed on your particular vehicle due to changes made by the manufacturer during production or from year to year.

A Vehicle Emissions Control Information label is located in the engine compartment of all vehicles with which this manual is concerned. This label contains important emissions specifications and setting procedures, as well as a vacuum hose schematic with emissions components identified. When servicing the engine or emissions systems, the VECI label in your particular vehicle should always be checked for up-to-date information.

2 Emissions control system

General description

Refer to illustration 2.1

1 The emissions control system used on these models links the related emissions systems with one another so they work together. It consists of sensors that send information to the control unit and various engine components that respond to commands from the control unit **(see illustration)**.

2 Here's a specific example of how one portion of this system operates. An oxygen sensor, mounted in the exhaust manifold and protruding into the exhaust gas stream, constantly monitors the oxygen content of the exhaust gas as it travels through the exhaust pipe. If the percentage of oxygen in the exhaust gas is incorrect, an electrical signal is sent to the control unit. The control unit takes this information, processes it and then sends a command to the carburetor Air/Fuel (A/F) solenoid, telling it to change the air/fuel mixture. To be effective, all this happens in a fraction of a second, and it goes on continuously while the engine is running. The end result is an air/fuel ratio that is constantly kept at a predetermined proportion, regardless of driving conditions.

Testing

Refer to illustration 2.6

3 One might think that a system which uses exotic electrical sensors and is controlled by an on-board computer would be difficult to diagnose. This is not necessarily the case.

4 The emissions control system control unit can be checked with a voltmeter to determine in just what area of the emissions system a fault is located. You or a dealer mechanic can easily troubleshoot this system.

5 To check the control unit to isolate the area in the emissions control system in which

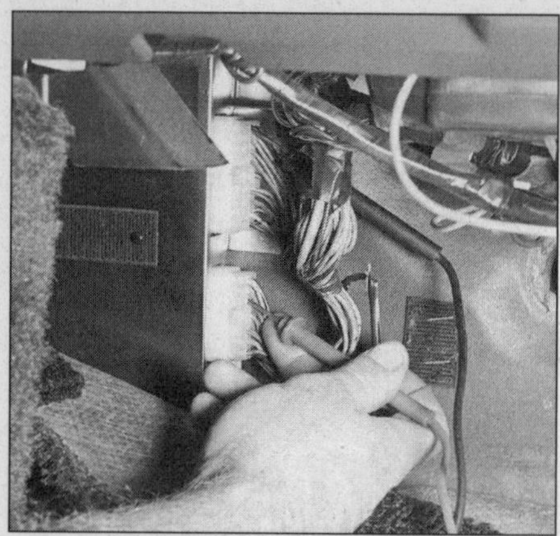

2.6 Checking the emissions system control unit, located under the dash, with a voltmeter

a fault may lie, locate the control unit, which is on the center part of the firewall under the dash. Pry loose the clips of the under dash cover panel with a screwdriver and roll back the carpeting to gain access to the unit.

6 With the ignition Off, insert one voltmeter probe into the ground (N) terminal of the control unit (the top terminal away from the firewall) **(see illustration)**. Turn the ignition On and touch the other probe to each terminal in turn, referring to the and the chart in the Specifications Section to determine the location of the fault.

7 When diagnosing an engine performance, fuel economy or exhaust emissions problem, do not automatically assume the fault lies in this system. Perform all standard troubleshooting procedures, as indicated elsewhere in this manual, before turning to the control unit. Since this is an electronic system, you should have a basic knowledge of automotive electronics before attempting any diagnosis. Damage to the control unit could occur if care is not exercised.

Control unit voltage check

8 Refer to the list of control unit terminals, the component or system to which they are connected and their voltage readings in the Specifications Section. Checking the control unit will isolate the location of a fault so that further checks and repairs can be made. If the problem persists after repairs or replacements have been made, the vehicle must be diagnosed by a professional mechanic who can use specialized diagnostic tools and advanced troubleshooting methods to check the system.

3 Fuel Control System

General description

1 The function of this system is to control the flow of fuel through the carburetor idle and main metering circuits. The major components of the system are the Air/Fuel (A/F) solenoid and the oxygen sensor.

2 The A/F solenoid changes the air/fuel mixture by allowing more or less fuel to flow through the carburetor. The A/F solenoid, located in the carburetor air horn, is in turn controlled by the control unit, which provides a ground for the solenoid. When the solenoid is energized, the fuel flow through the carburetor is reduced, providing a leaner mixture. When the ECM removes the ground path, the solenoid de-energizes and allows more fuel flow.

3 The control unit determines the proper fuel mixture required by monitoring a signal sent by the oxygen sensor, located in the exhaust stream. When the mixture is lean, the oxygen sensor voltage is low and the ECM commands a richer mixture. Conversely, when the mixture is rich, the oxygen sensor voltage is higher and the control unit commands a leaner mixture.

Checking

Oxygen sensor

4 Make sure that the oxygen sensor has been replaced at the proper maintenance interval (refer to Chapter 1).

5 The proper operation of the sensor depends on the four conditions which follow:

6 Electrical conditions: The low voltages and low currents generated by the sensor depend upon good, clean connections, which should be checked whenever a malfunction of the sensor is suspected or indicated.

7 Outside air supply: The sensor is designed to allow air circulation to the internal portion of the sensor. Whenever the sensor is removed and installed or replaced, make sure the air passages are not restricted.

8 Proper operating temperature: The control unit will not react to the sensor signal until the sensor reaches approximately 600°F (315°C). This factor must be taken into consideration when evaluating the performance of the sensor.

9 Unleaded fuel: The use of unleaded fuel is essential for proper operation of the sensor. Make sure the fuel you are using is of this type.

10 In addition to observing the above conditions, special care must be taken whenever the sensor is handled, as directed in Chapter 1. Violation of any of these cautionary procedures may lead to sensor failure. **Caution:** *Do not attempt to measure the voltage output of the oxygen sensor, because the current drain from a conventional voltmeter would be enough to permanently damage the sensor. For the same reason, never hook up test leads, jumpers or other electrical connections.*

Mixture control solenoid

11 Check the wiring connectors and wires leading to the mixture control solenoid for looseness, fraying and other damage. Repair or replace any damaged wiring as necessary.

12 Check the mixture control solenoid for apparent physical damage. Replace the mixture control solenoid with a new one if damage is found.

Component replacement

Oxygen sensor

13 To replace the sensor, refer to Chapter 1.

A/F solenoid

14 Refer to Chapter 4.

4 Electronic ignition system

1 Electronic ignition system used on all engines with which this manual is concerned controls the spark for optimum operation of the engine for proper driveability and emissions. The distributor contains both vacuum or centrifugal advance mechanisms to control advance and the ignition coil is controlled by the control unit.

2 For further information and checking and component replacement procedures regarding the EST distributor, refer to Chapter 5.

5 Air injection system

1985 and earlier models

General description

Refer to illustration 5.1

1 The air injection system helps reduce hydrocarbons and carbon monoxide levels in the exhaust by injecting air into the exhaust ports of each cylinder during cold engine operation, or directly into the catalytic converter during normal operation **(see illustration)**. It also helps the catalytic converter reach proper operating temperature quickly during warm-up.

2 The air injection system uses exhaust pressure pulses to draw air into the exhaust system and utilizes fresh air that is filtered by the air cleaner.

3 Components utilized in the system include the reed valves located in the air cleaner assembly, the Air Control Valves (ACV), the solenoid valves and external tubes and hoses.

Checking

4 Exhaust gas blowing back through the air cleaner assembly is a symptom of a fault in the air injection system. Begin any inspection by carefully checking all hoses, vacuum lines and wires. Be sure they are in good condition and that all connections are tight and clean.

5 A simple, functional test of this system can be performed with the engine running.

6 Remove the top of the air cleaner assembly and the filter element.

Reed valve

Refer to illustration 5.7

7 With the engine idling at normal operating temperature, place a piece of paper over the reed valve inlet port. With the engine idling there should be a steady stream of air

Vehicles for states other than california

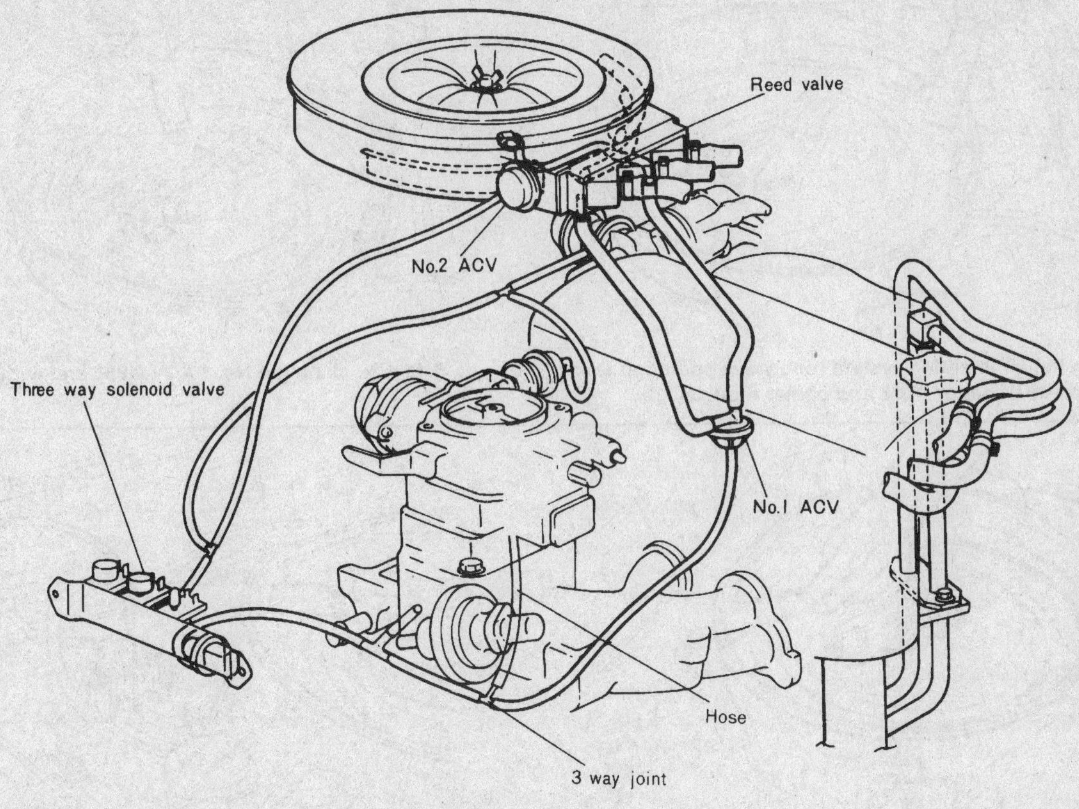

Vehicles for california and canada

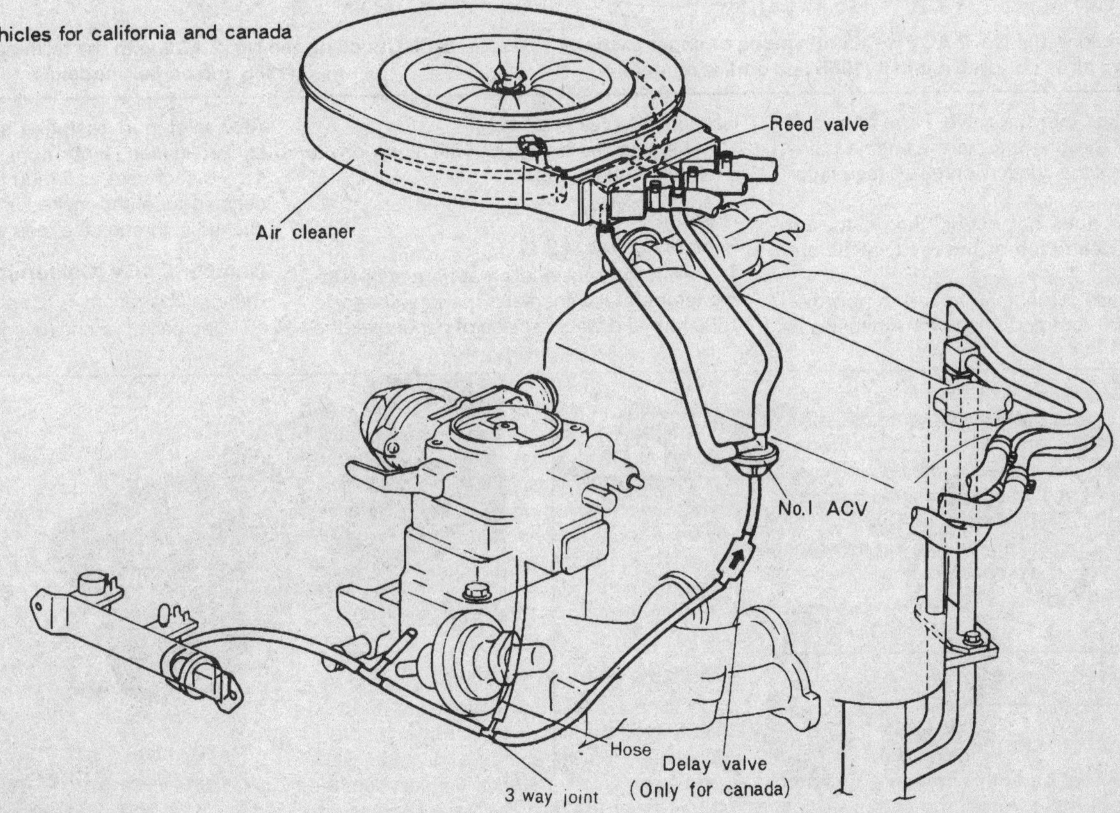

5.1 Air injection system component layout (1985 and earlier models)

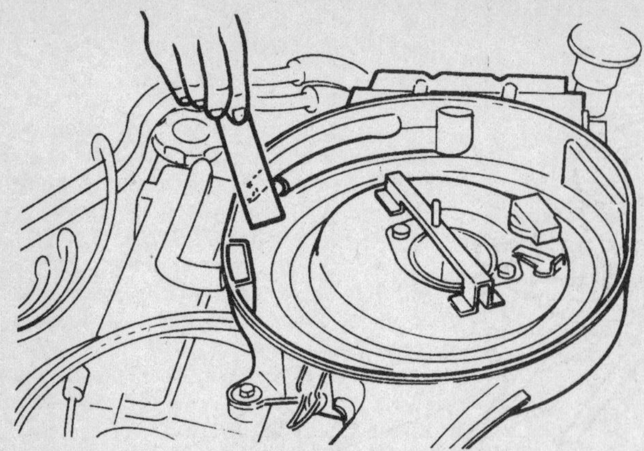

5.7 Checking the air injection system reed valve operation with a piece of paper (1985 and earlier models)

5.11 Checking the No. 1 ACV (1985 and earlier models)

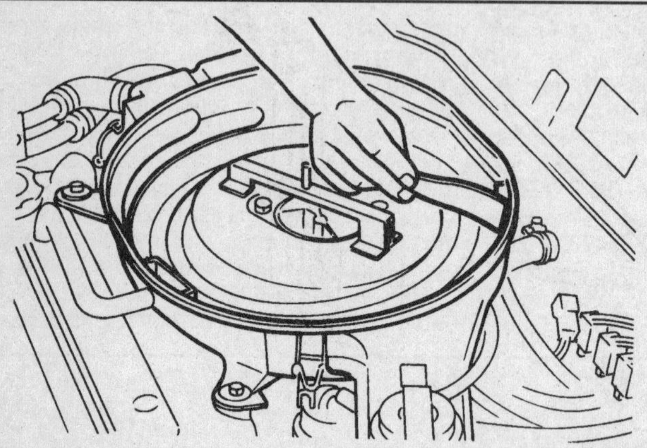

5.13 Checking the No. 2 ACV with a thin piece of paper to make sure air is not drawn into it (1985 and earlier models)

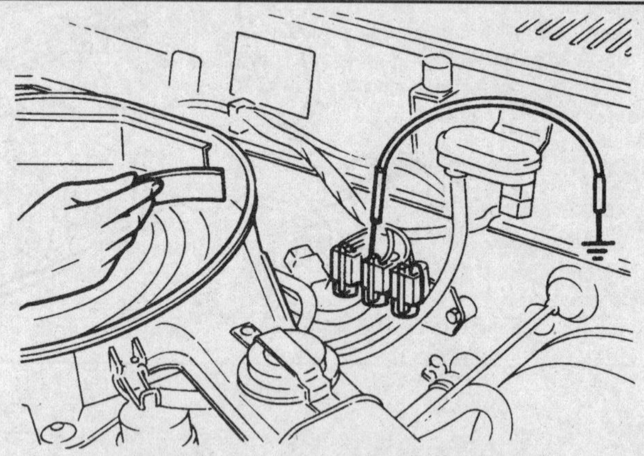

5.14 Checking the No. 2 ACV with the terminal grounded (1985 and earlier models)

being sucked into the valve. Have an assistant apply throttle, and as the engine gains speed, see if the suction increases **(see illustration)**.

8 If this does not occur, the hoses are leaking or restricted or the reed valves are faulty.

9 Increase the engine speed to approximately 1500 rpm and check for exhaust gas leakage at the air inlet fitting.

10 Replace the reed valve with a new one if it fails either test.

Number 1 ACV

Refer to illustration 5.11

11 With the engine idling at normal operating temperature, increase the idle speed to 1500 rpm and place a piece of paper over the ACV inlet port to make sure air is being sucked in **(see illustration)**.

12 Disconnect and plug the ACV vacuum sensing tube and make sure air is not being sucked in through the reed valve.

Number 2 ACV (California models)

Refer to illustrations 5.13 and 5.14

13 Increase the engine speed to 1500 rpm

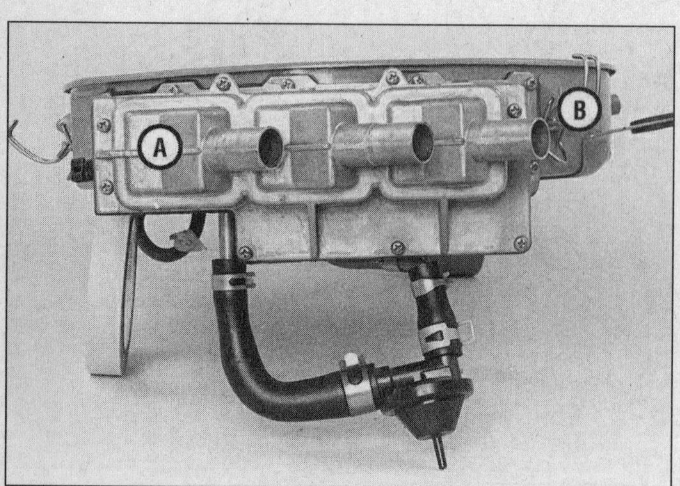

5.16a The reed valve assembly (A) is attached to the air cleaner housing (B) by screws

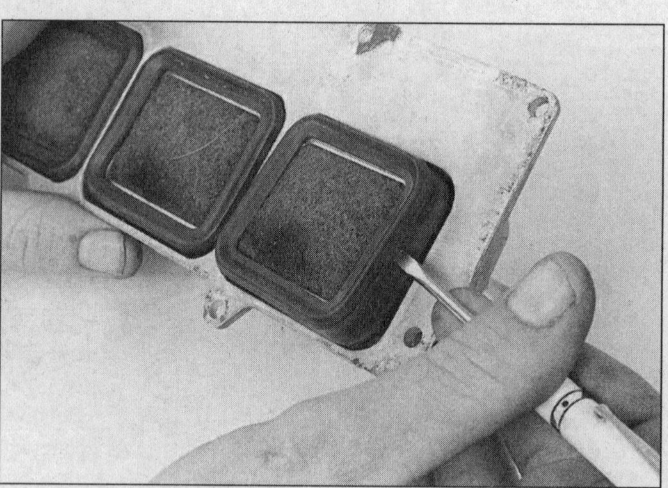

5.16b Use a small screwdriver to pry the reed valve loose

and place a piece of paper over the ACV inlet port to make sure air is not being sucked in **(see illustration)**.

14 Ground the three way solenoid GL terminal with a jumper wire as shown in the **(see illustration)** and check to make sure that air is now sucked into the inlet port.

Component replacement

15 Remove the air cleaner and disconnect the negative cable from the battery.

Reed valve

Refer to illustrations 5.16a, 5.16b and 5.16c

16 Remove the reed valve housing cover retaining screws and lift the valves and filters from the housing **(see illustrations)**.

ACV

17 Mark the hose connections for installation to the same positions. On the Number 1 ACV, remove the retaining clips and disengage the ACV from the hose. On the Number 2 ACV, remove the screws and lift the ACV from the reed valve housing.

1986 and later models

General description

Refer to illustration 5.18

18 The air injection system includes the air control valve and the reed valve, both of which are mounted in the air cleaner housing.

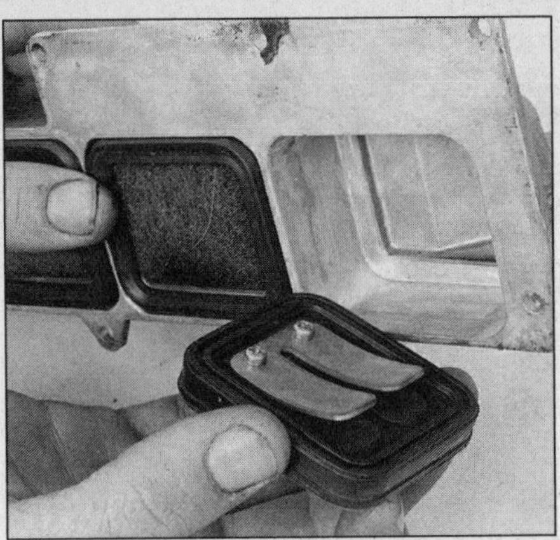

5.16c Removing the reed valve from the housing

Turbocharged engines have remotely mounted reed valves, located on the right shock tower, in addition to the reed valve in the air cleaner housing **(see illustration)**.

19 When intake manifold vacuum increases to a certain level, the air control valve opens and fresh air is drawn into the exhaust manifold by the exhaust pressure pulses. This burns off any leftover fuel and reduces hydrocarbon (HC) emissions. The two remotely mounted reed valves on the turbocharged engine operate whenever the exhaust pulses are sufficient to pull air through the valves (usually from 2500 RPM and up).

Checking

20 To check the air injection system, lift up the air cleaner upper case and run the engine at idle. Feel for air being sucked into the air passage. A strip of paper held near the opening will help determine this.

21 Increase the engine speed to 2500 RPM and make sure that no air is drawn into the passage. Check to see that no exhaust gas is coming from the passage.

22 If the system doesn't work as described, check the air control valve and the reed valve as described below.

23 To check the air control valve, remove it from the housing (Step 26) and connect a vacuum pump. Apply vacuum gradually and check for stem movement at 7-to-11 inches of mercury. If the valve fails the test or leaks, replace it.

24 To check the reed valve, warm up the engine and run it at idle. Attach a vacuum pump to the air control valve and apply a vacuum of 19.5-inches of mercury. Lift up the air cleaner housing and check for air flow into the passage. Increase the engine speed to 2500 RPM and make sure that no exhaust gas is coming from the passage. If it fails either test, replace the reed valve.

25 To check the remotely mounted reed

Air control valve
Reed valve A
Reed valve
Air control unit
Reed valve

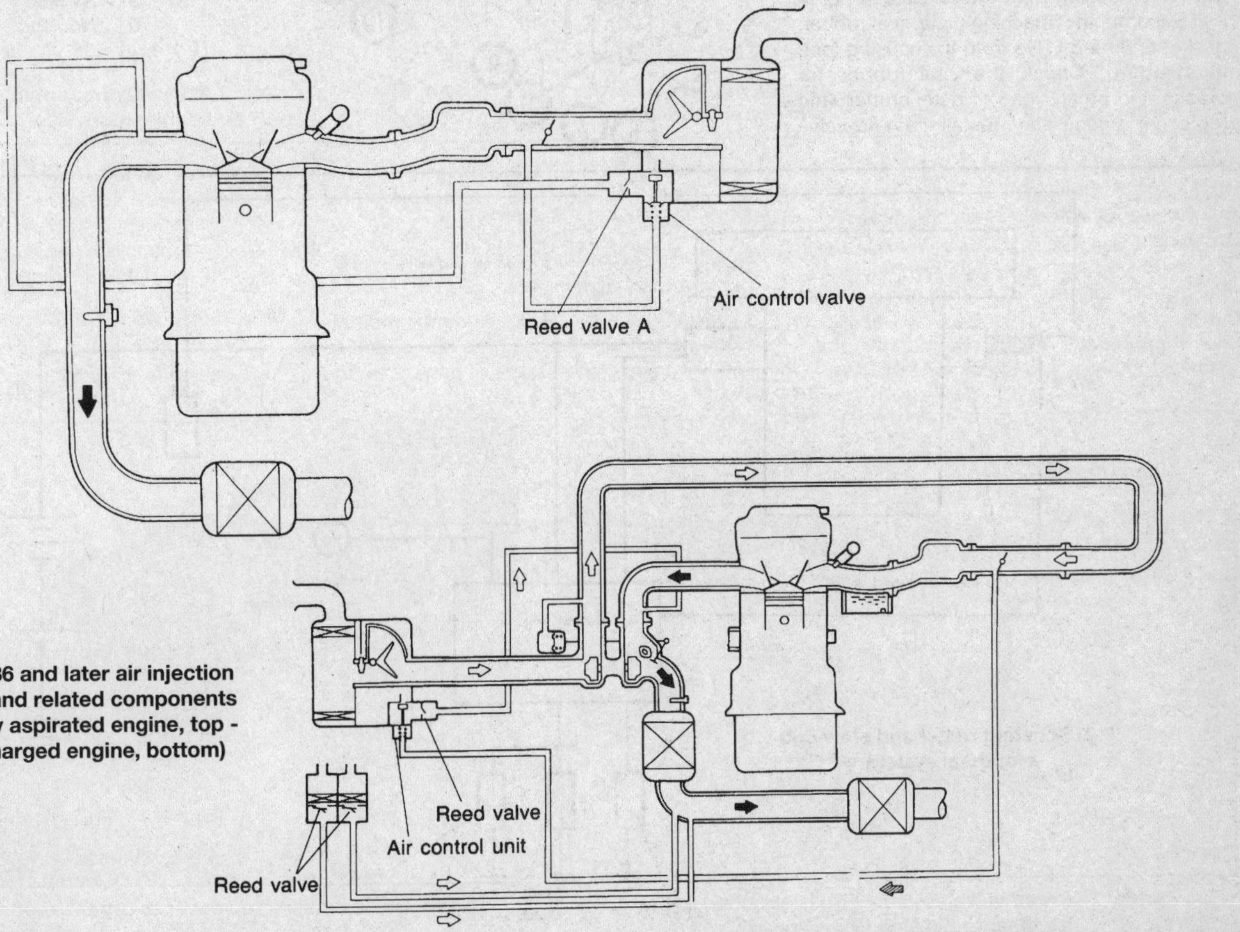

5.18 1986 and later air injection system and related components (normally aspirated engine, top - turbocharged engine, bottom)

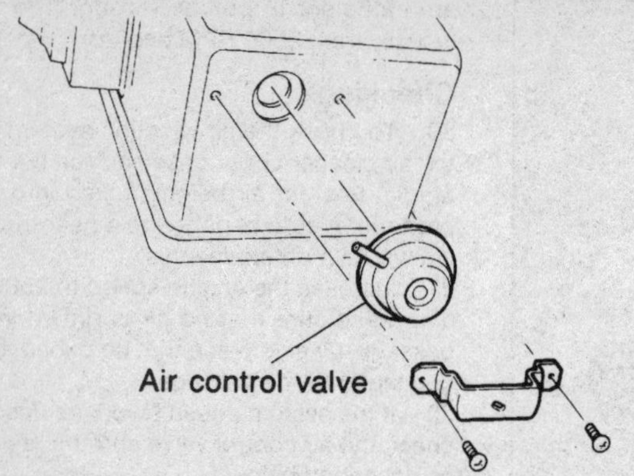

5.26a 1986 and later air control valve mounting details

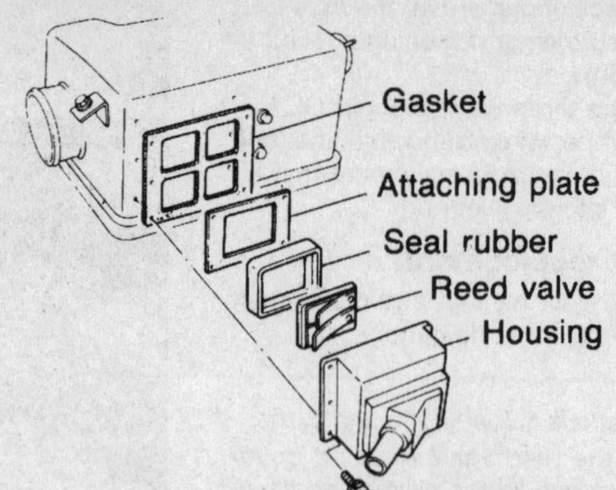

5.26b Reed valve mounting details (1986 and 1987 models)

valves (turbocharged engines only), run the engine at 2500 RPM and check for air being sucked into the passages. Verify that no exhaust gas is coming from the valves. If either valve fails either of the tests, replace it.

Component replacement

Refer to illustrations 5.26a, 5.26b and 5.27

26 To remove the air control valve, remove the two valve mounting screws and detach the valve from the air cleaner housing **(see illustrations)**. To install the valve, reverse the removal procedure.

27 To remove the reed valve, first remove the valve housing from the air cleaner housing. Separate the attaching plate, seal rubber, gasket and reed valve from the housing **(see illustration)**. Check the seal rubber for cracks and other signs of deterioration and replace it if necessary. Install the reed valve

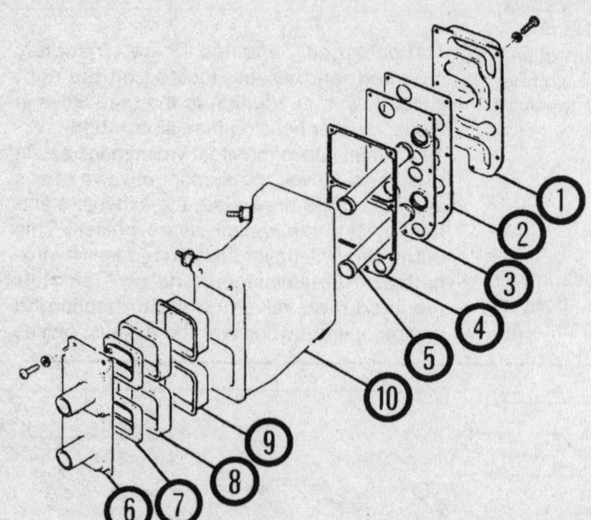

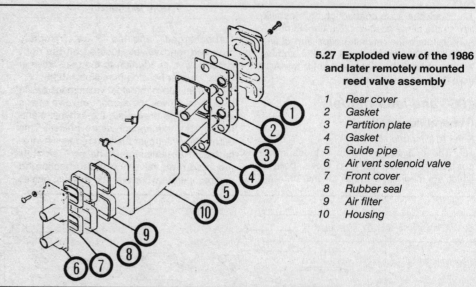

5.27 Exploded view of the 1986 and later remotely mounted reed valve assembly

1 *Rear cover*
2 *Gasket*
3 *Partition plate*
4 *Gasket*
5 *Guide pipe*
6 *Air vent solenoid valve*
7 *Front cover*
8 *Rubber seal*
9 *Air filter*
10 *Housing*

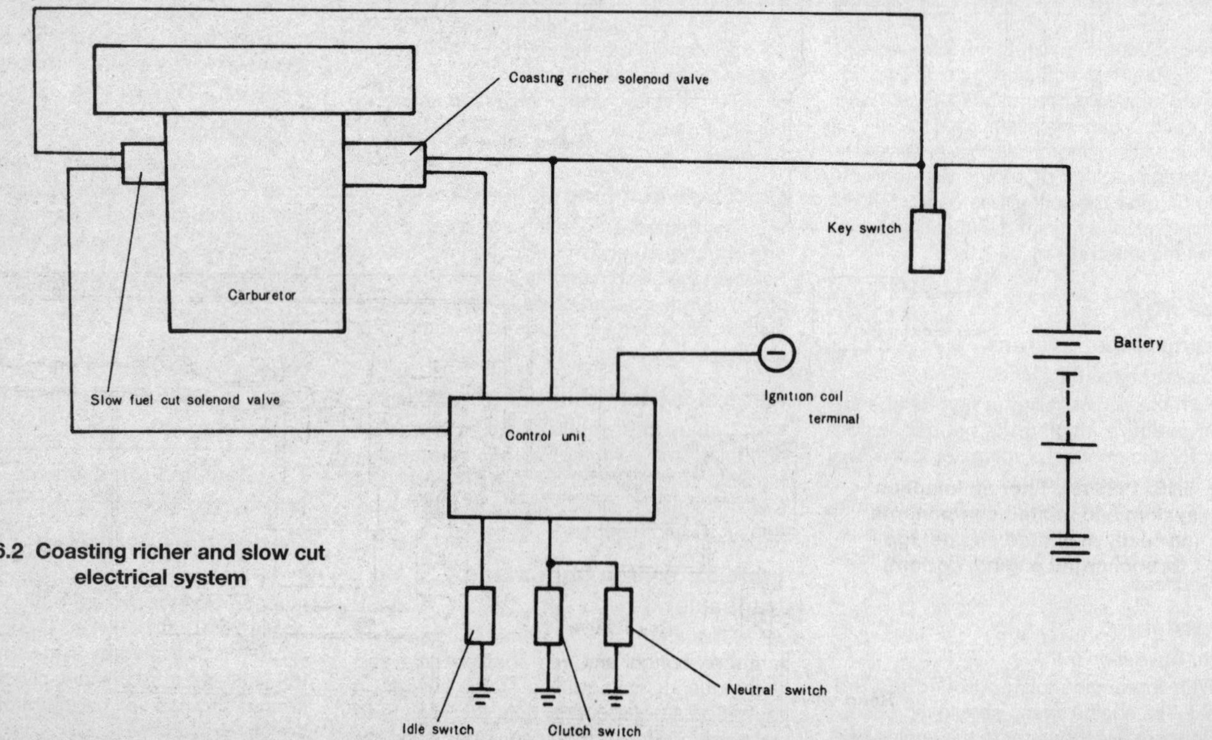

6.2 Coasting richer and slow cut electrical system

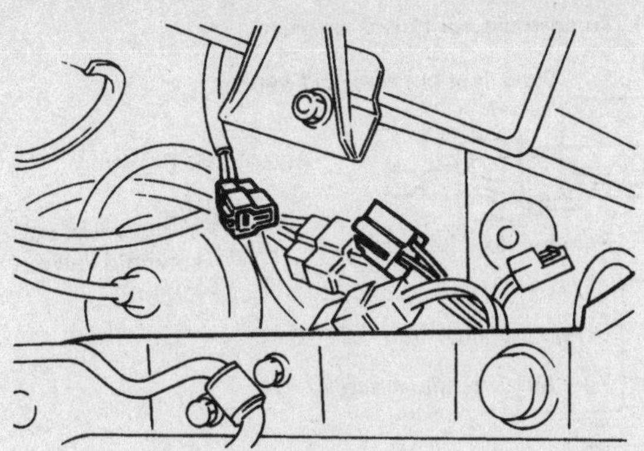

6.3 Unplug the neutral switch to test the coasting richer and the slow cut systems

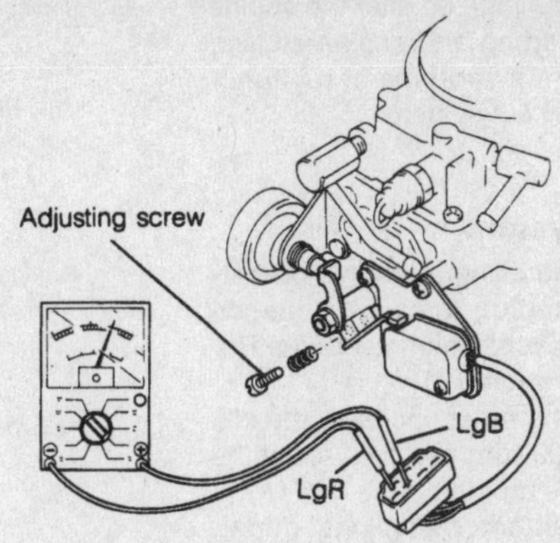

6.6 Coasting richer and slow fuel cut idle switch test

by reversing the removal sequence. Be sure to use a new gasket.

28 To remove the remotely mounted reed valves (turbocharged engines only), remove the reed valve housing from the right shock tower and place the unit on a clean work surface. Remove the four screws on each end of the housing and separate the components of the reed valve assembly as shown in **(see illustration 5.27)**. During reassembly, use new gaskets and replace the seal rubber if necessary.

Richer air bleeds
Secondary main air bleed
Coasting richer solenoid valve
Richer jet
Secondary throttle valve
To secondary main jet

6.15 Coasting richer solenoid system details

6 Coasting richer system

General description

Refer to illustration 6.2

1 The coasting richer system opens the fuel passage to the secondary stage of the carburetor during deceleration between 1400 and 2000 rpm. It is actuated by signals from the control unit sent from the idle, clutch and neutral or inhibitor switches.

2 Rough idling and/or stalling, excessively high idle speed, lack of engine braking and running on after the engine has been shut off are symptoms of a fault in the coasting richer system **(see illustration)**.

Checking

Coasting richer system

Refer to illustration 6.3

3 With the engine idling at normal operating temperature, unplug the neutral switch connector and connect a voltmeter to the Brb terminal **(see illustration)**.

4 Connect a tachometer, increase the idle speed and check the voltmeter readings, comparing them to the chart in the Specifications Section.

Idle switch

Refer to illustration 6.6

5 With the engine idling, ground the Brb terminal. The engine speed should increase.

6 Connect a tachometer to the engine and then connect a voltmeter to the idle switch connectors as shown in the **(see illustration)**.

7 With the engine idling, increase the engine speed to above 2000 rpm, allow it to decelerate then check the voltmeter reading. At idle the reading should be approximately 12 volts and above 1200 to 1300 rpm it should be less than 1.5 volts.

8 Turn the idle switch adjusting screw to bring the readings to within specifications, if necessary.

Clutch switch (manual transaxle)

9 Disconnect the clutch switch, connect an ohmmeter and check for continuity between the switch terminals.

10 When the clutch pedal is depressed the switch should be closed and when it is released it should be open.

Neutral switch (manual transaxle)

11 Unplug the neutral switch connector and insert the voltmeter probes into the terminals. With the transaxle in Neutral the switch should be closed and in all other positions it should be open.

Inhibitor switch (automatic transaxle)

12 Checking the automatic transaxle inhibitor switch requires special tools and techniques. Consequently, if you suspect a fault in this component, take the vehicle to your dealer or a properly equipped shop for checking and replacement. Refer to Chapter 7 for more information on the inhibitor switch.

Component replacement

Neutral and clutch switch

13 The neutral and/or clutch switches are replaced by unplugging the connector and unscrewing the switch from the transaxle housing.

Idle switch

14 Disconnect the vacuum tube and electrical connector, remove the retaining screws and lift the idle switch from the carburetor. Installation is the reverse of removal.

Coasting richer solenoid

Refer to illustration 6.15

15 Refer to Chapter 5 for coasting richer solenoid valve (part of the carburetor main body) replacement **(see illustration)**.

7 Slow fuel cut system

General description

1 The slow fuel cut system closes the primary carburetor system during deceleration above 2000 rpm or when the ignition switch is off. It is activated by signals from the control unit sent from the idle, clutch and neutral (manual transaxle) or inhibitor (automatic transaxle) switches.

2 Rough idling, running on after the engine is shut off, hard starting and engine stalling during warm up are symptoms of malfunctions in the slow fuel cut system.

Checking

Slow cut fuel system

3 With the engine idling at normal operating temperature, unplug the neutral switch connector and connect a voltmeter to the Brb terminal **(see illustration 6.6)**.
4 Connect a tachometer, increase the idle speed to above 3000 rpm and then allow the engine to decelerate rapidly.
5 Check the voltmeter readings during deceleration. Above 2000 rpm the reading should be 12 volts and below 2000 rpm the reading should be less than 1.5 volts.

Idle, clutch and neutral or inhibitor switches

6 Refer to Section 6 for testing and replacement procedures.

Slow fuel cut solenoid valve

Refer to illustration 7.7

7 With the engine idling, unplug the slow cut solenoid connector. If the engine stops, the solenoid valve is operating properly **(see illustration)**.

Idle switch

8 With a tachometer connected and the engine running at idle at normal operating temperature, connect a voltmeter to the idle switch connector terminals.
9 Increase the engine speed to over 2000 rpm and then allow it to decelerate slowly.

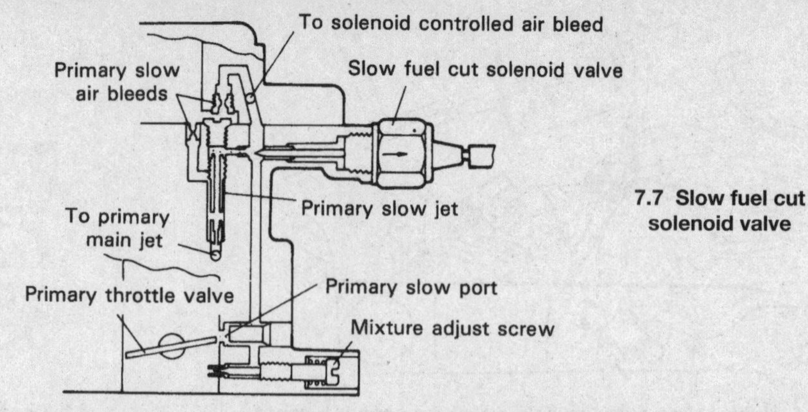

7.7 Slow fuel cut solenoid valve

The voltmeter reading should be approximately 12 volts at idle and below 1.5 volts above 1200 to 1300 rpm.

Component replacement

Slow fuel cut solenoid valve

10 After unplugging the connector, the solenoid valve can be removed from the carburetor by unscrewing it.

8 Exhaust Gas Recirculation (EGR) system

1985 and earlier models

General description

Refer to illustration 8.1

1 The EGR system meters exhaust gases into the engine induction system through passages cast into the intake manifold. From there the exhaust gases pass into the fuel/air mixture for the purpose of lowering combustion temperatures, thereby reducing the amount of oxides of nitrogen (NOX) formed **(see illustration)**.
2 The amount of exhaust gas admitted is regulated by a control unit vacuum duty solenoid valve controlled EGR valve in response to engine operating conditions. The EGR valve position sensor in turn sends a signal to the control unit. Models with automatic transaxle also have a vacuum delay valve.
3 Common engine problems associated with the EGR system are rough idling or stalling at idle, rough engine performance during light throttle application and stalling during deceleration.

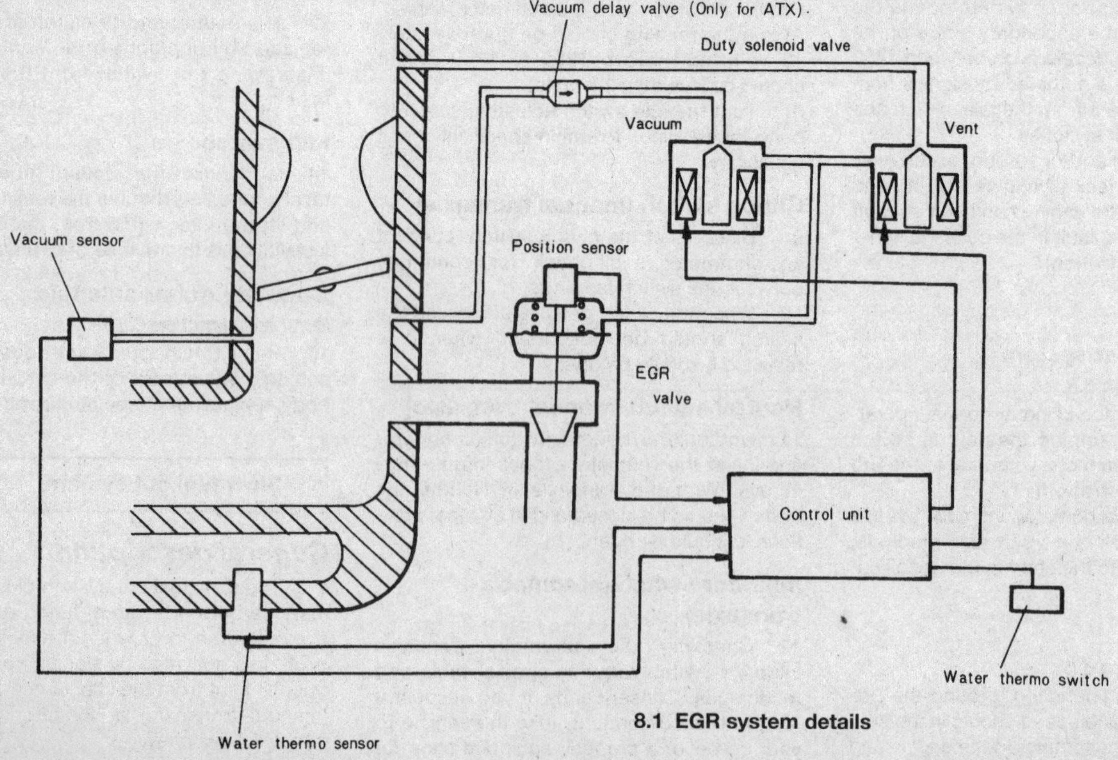

8.1 EGR system details

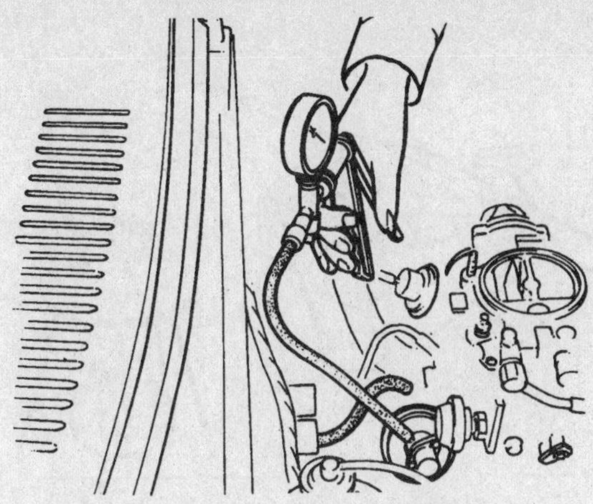
8.6 Applying vacuum to the EGR valve

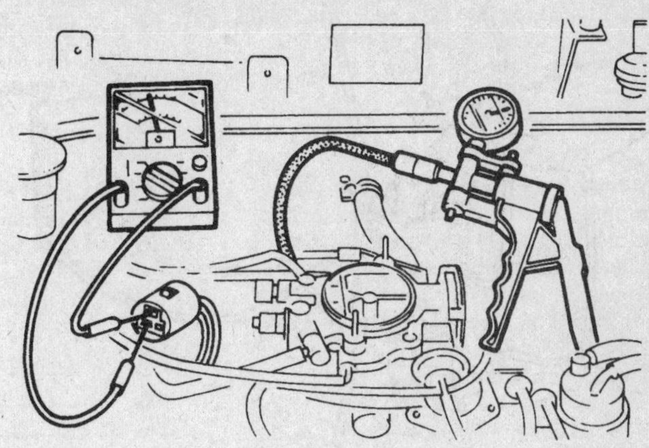
8.7 Testing the position sensor

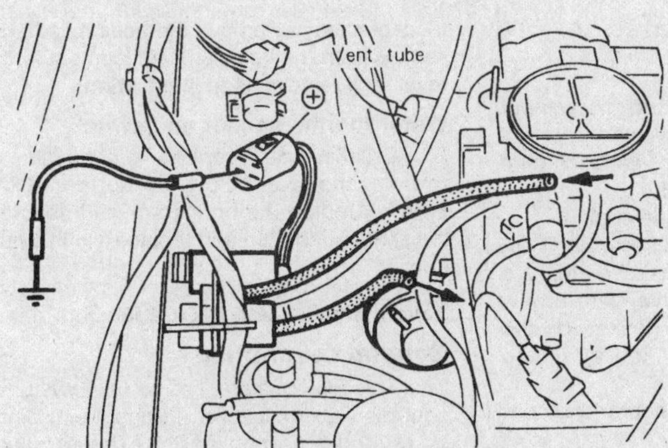

8.9 Testing the duty solenoid valve

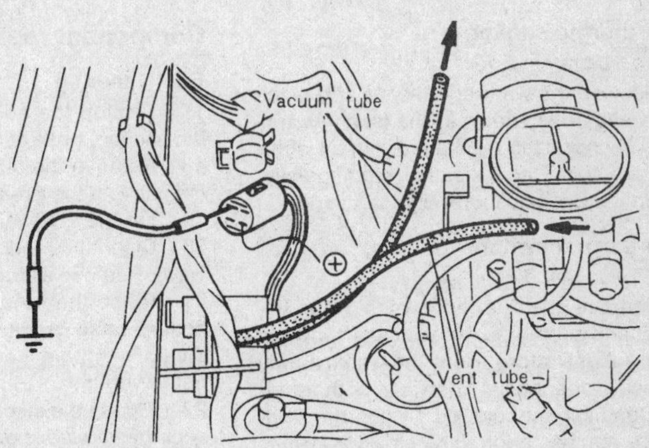

8.10 Testing the duty solenoid vacuum valve

6

Checking

EGR valve

Refer to illustration 8.6

4 Refer to Chapter 1 for EGR valve checking procedures.

5 If the EGR valve appears to be in proper operating condition, carefully check all hoses connected to the valve for breaks, leaks or kinks. Replace or repair the valve/hoses as necessary.

6 With the engine at normal operating temperature, remove the air cleaner assembly and plug the hoses of the idle compensator, thermo sensor and reed valves. Disconnect and plug the vacuum hose from the EGR valve and connect a vacuum pump **(see illustration)**. When vacuum is applied with the engine idling, the engine should stumble or die, indicating the vacuum diaphragm is operating properly. Replace the EGR valve with a new one if the test does not affect the idle.

Position sensor

Refer to illustration 8.7

7 Unplug the position sensor connector and connect an ohmmeter as shown in the **(see illustration)**. If the meter shows resistance, the position sensor is operating properly.

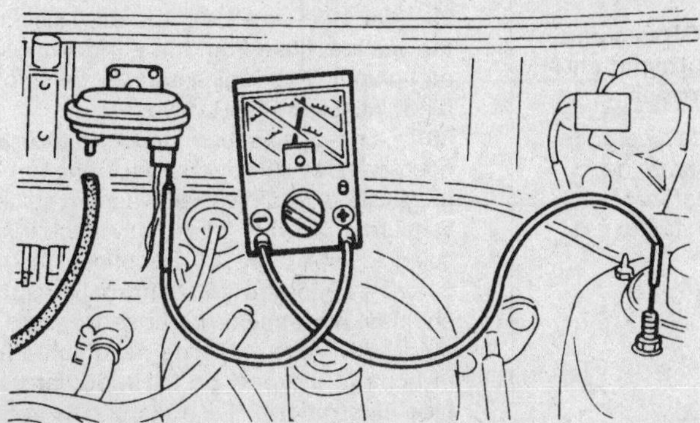
8.12 Testing the EGR system vacuum sensor

Duty solenoid valve

Refer to illustrations 8.9 and 8.10

8 Disconnect the EGR valve vacuum sensing tube and blow through it to make sure air passes through the valve.

9 Unplug the connector, apply battery power to the terminal as shown in the **(see illustration)** and blow through the hose again to make sure that air does not pass.

10 To check the duty solenoid vacuum valve, disconnect the vacuum sensing tube located between the valve and the intake manifold and blow through the valve to make sure no air passes. With battery power applied to the connector terminal as shown in the **(see illustration)** air should now pass.

11 Replace the duty solenoid valve with a new one if it fails either test.

Vacuum sensor

Refer to illustration 8.12

12 With the engine idling, connect a voltmeter to the vacuum sensor L terminal as shown in the **(see illustration)** and make sure the reading is one volt. When the vacuum tube is disconnected from the vacuum sensor the reading should be approximately four volts.

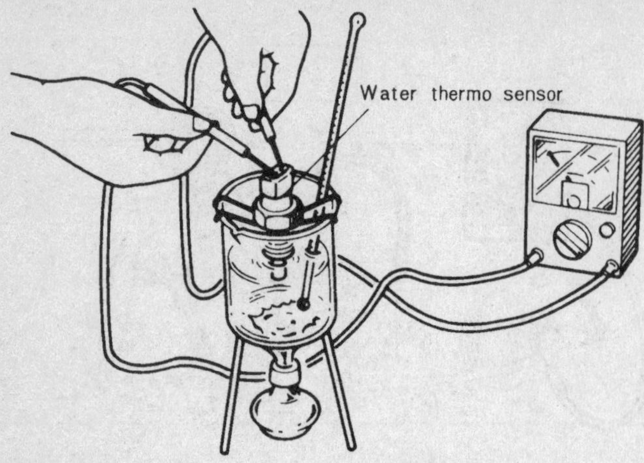

8.13 Checking the EGR water thermo sensor

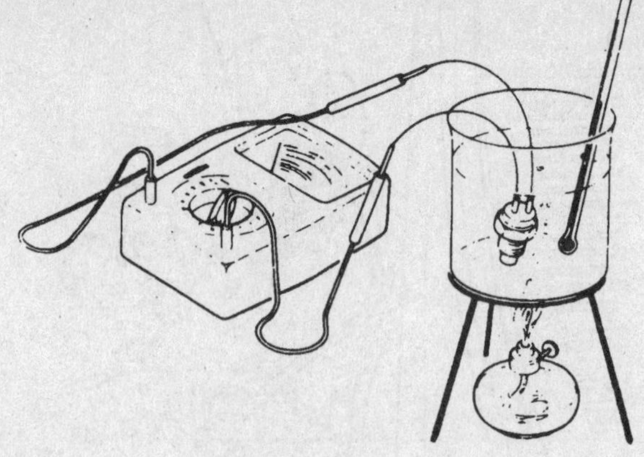

8.14 Checking the water thermo switch

Water thermo sensor

Refer to illustration 8.13

13 Remove the water thermo sensor, place it in hot water as shown in the **(see illustration)** and check the resistance with an ohmmeter. Compare the resistance readings with those in the Specifications section.

Water thermo switch

Refer to illustration 8.14

14 Remove the thermo switch from the radiator and submerge it in water as shown in the **(see illustration)**. Heat the water slowly and check for continuity between both terminals. Continuity should exist when the temperature reaches approximately 65°F (19°C). The switch should be replaced with a new one if it is not within specification.

Vacuum delay valve (automatic transaxle models)

15 Remove the vacuum delay valve and connect a 3.28 foot (1.0 m) piece of tubing between the valve and a vacuum pump and hold your thumb over the end of the tube.

16 Apply approximately 20 in Hg (500 mm Hg) vacuum with the pump and check that the time required for the vacuum to drop to 3.9 in Hg (100 mm Hg) is approximately two seconds. If it is not, replace the vacuum delay valve.

Component replacement

EGR valve

17 Unplug the connector and disconnect the vacuum hose at the EGR valve.

18 Remove the nuts or bolts which secure the valve to the intake manifold.

19 Lift the EGR valve from the engine.

20 Clean the mounting surfaces of the EGR valve. Remove all traces of gasket material.

21 Place the new EGR valve, with a new lithium-base grease coated gasket, on the intake manifold and tighten the attaching nuts or bolts.

22 Plug in the electrical connector and connect the vacuum signal hose.

Position sensor

23 Disconnect the vacuum hose and the linkage, remove the nut and lift the sensor from the bracket. Replacement is the reverse of removal.

Duty solenoid valve

24 Disconnect the vacuum hose, unplug the connector, remove the retaining nuts and lift the valve from the firewall. Replacement is the reverse of removal.

Vacuum sensor

Refer to illustration 8.25

25 Disconnect the vacuum hose and electrical connector, remove the bolts and lift the sensor from the vehicle. Replacement is the reverse of removal **(see illustration)**.

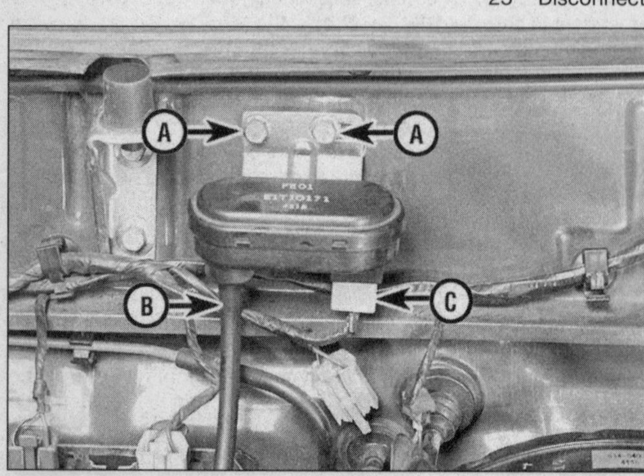

8.25 EGR vacuum sensor attachments (arrows)

A Retaining bolts
B Vacuum hose
C Electrical connector

Water thermo sensor and switch

26 Drain sufficient coolant from the radiator to bring the level below the bottom of the switch. Unplug the connector and unscrew the sensor or switch and replace it with a new one.

1986 and later models

General description

27 This EGR system, like all EGR systems, controls NOx (oxides of nitrogen) emissions by routing a portion of the exhaust gases back into the intake manifold. Operation of the system depends on vacuum level, exhaust pressure, engine coolant and radiator temperature and on turbocharged vehicles, engine load and speed. The checking and service procedures differ from the previous system described in Chapter 6.

Checking

Refer to illustrations 8.31, 8.32, 8.34, 8.37, 8.39, 8.42, 8.43a and 8.43b

28 Check all of the vacuum hoses for deterioration, kinks, leaks, proper connection and routing. On 1988 through 1991 models, reach under the EGR valve and push up on the diaphragm, making sure it moves easily. Start the engine and make sure the EGR diaphragm moves up when engine speed is increased.

29 On 1986 and 1987 models, disconnect the vacuum hose from the EGR control valve and plug it. The engine should run smoothly. If not, check the EGR valve.

30 Connect a vacuum gauge to the disconnected hose (turbocharged engine). The gauge should indicate zero vacuum at idle and vacuum at 2500 RPM. If not, check the duty solenoid valve (Step 42). Reconnect the hose.

31 On 1986 and 1987 normally aspirated engines, disconnect the hose from the EGR modulator valve and plug it. Attach a length of hose to the port on the modulator valve **(see illustration)**. Raise the engine speed to

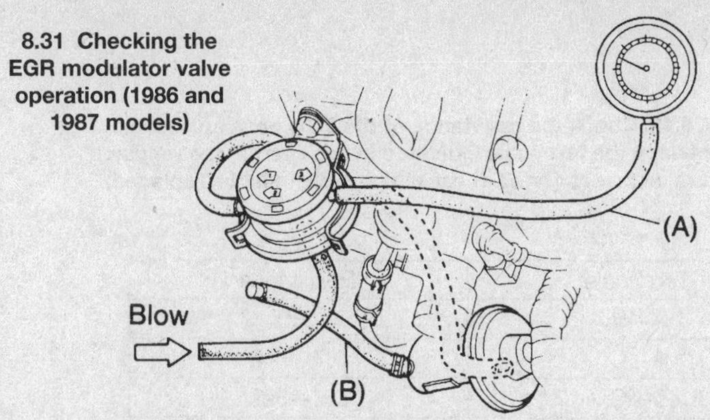

8.31 Checking the EGR modulator valve operation (1986 and 1987 models)

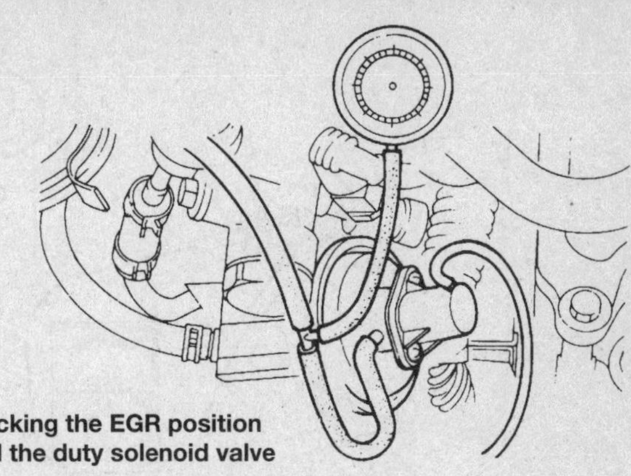
8.32 Checking the EGR position sensor and the duty solenoid valve

2500 RPM, blow into the hose and check to see that the vacuum reading increases. If it doesn't, check the modulator valve (Step 37). Reconnect the hoses.

32 On turbocharged engines, connect a vacuum gauge between the duty solenoid valve and the EGR control valve **(see illustration)**. Raise the engine speed and note the vacuum reading. Now, disconnect the hose from the EGR control valve and plug it. The vacuum reading should be greater than the previous reading. If it isn't, check the EGR position sensor (Step 38) and the duty solenoid valve (Step 42).

33 With the vacuum hose still plugged, disconnect the water temperature switch connector located on the radiator tank. Increase the engine speed to 2500 RPM and make sure no vacuum registers on the gauge. If vacuum is present, check the duty solenoid valve (Step 42).

34 On 1986 and 1987 normally aspirated engines, disconnect the vacuum hose from the EGR modulator valve and connect a vacuum gauge to it at 2500 RPM and verify that the vacuum reading is greater than 5.6-inches of mercury **(see illustration)**. If it's less, check the three way solenoid valve (Step 46). Now disconnect the water temperature switch located on the radiator side tank and make sure no vacuum registers on the gauge. If it does, check the three way solenoid valve.

35 To check the EGR control valve (normally aspirated and turbocharged engines), run the engine until normal operating temperature is reached, then disconnect the hose from the EGR control valve and plug it. The engine should run smoothly. If it doesn't, remove the EGR control valve and clean the exhaust gas passage and the valve pintle.

36 Connect a vacuum pump to the control valve and apply a vacuum of at least 3-inches of mercury. The engine should run extremely rough or even stall. If it doesn't, replace the EGR valve. Further checks of the valve can be found in Chapter 1.

37 To check the EGR modulator valve (normally aspirated engines only), remove it from the engine. Connect a vacuum pump to the number three port, plug the number one port and blow into the exhaust gas port while operating the vacuum pump **(see illustration)**. Verify that vacuum is retained in the modulator. Now stop blowing into the exhaust gas port. The vacuum should not hold. If it does, replace the modulator valve.

38 To check the EGR position sensor (turbocharged engines only), peel back the rubber boot on the sensor electrical connector but don't unplug the connector.

39 Detach the vacuum hose from the EGR control valve and connect a vacuum pump to the valve. Turn the ignition switch to the On position and, referring to the chart check the voltage at each terminal under the conditions shown in the table **(see illustration)**.

6

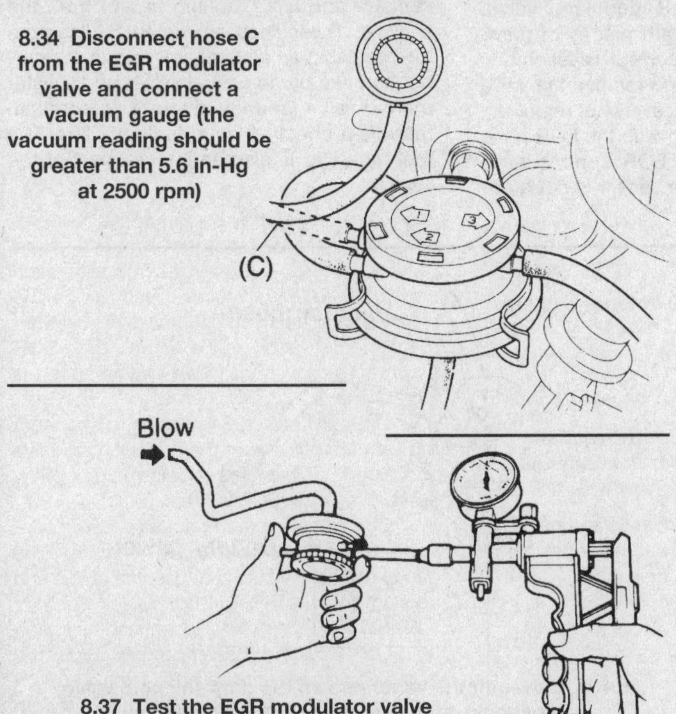

8.34 Disconnect hose C from the EGR modulator valve and connect a vacuum gauge (the vacuum reading should be greater than 5.6 in-Hg at 2500 rpm)

8.37 Test the EGR modulator valve with a vacuum pump

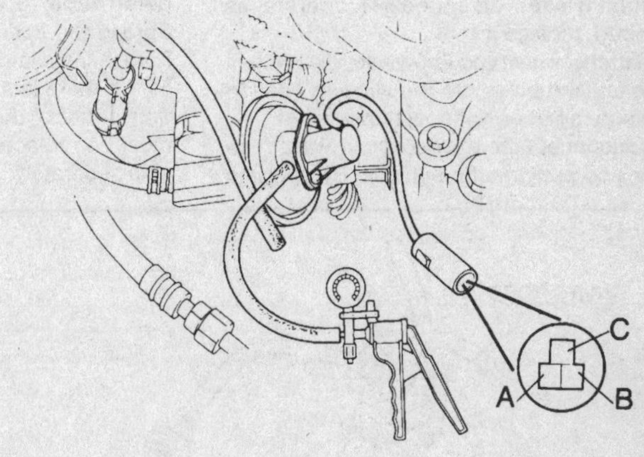

Terminal / Vacuum to the valve	No vacuum	150 mmHg (5.9 inHg)
C	Approx. 0.7V	Approx. 4.7V
B	Below 1.5V	
A	4.5 ~ 5.5V	

8.39 Check the EGR position sensor terminal voltage under the conditions shown

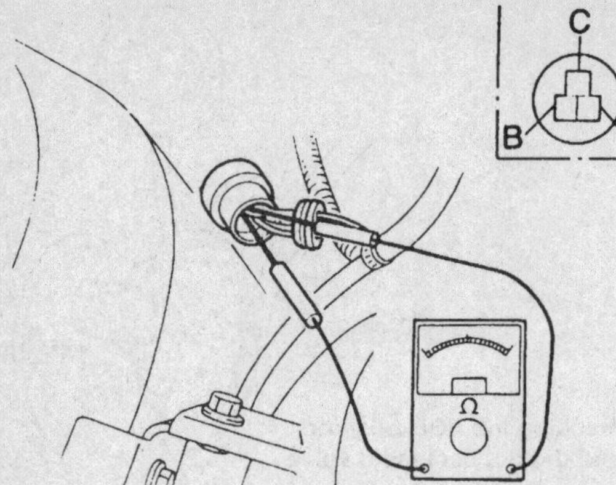

8.42 Check the resistance of the EGR position sensor between the terminals indicated in the chart (if the readings are incorrect, the EGR valve assembly must be replaced)

Terminals	Resistance
A—B	5kΩ
A—C	0.7 ~ 5kΩ
B—C	0.7 ~ 5kΩ

40 If the voltage is incorrect at the A or B terminal, check the wiring harness and have a dealer service department check the EGI control unit. If incorrect at the C terminal, check the resistance of the sensor, then check the wiring harness and have a dealer service department check the EGI control unit.

41 Unplug the wire connector and check the resistance of the sensor between the terminals indicated **(see illustration 8.39)**. If any of the resistance values are not as specified, replace the EGR valve assembly (the position sensor is not available separately).

42 The duty solenoid valve (turbocharged engines only) is composed of two valves: a vent valve and a vacuum valve. To check the vent valve, disconnect the hoses and blow through the vent hose to verify that air passes through **(see illustration)**.

43 Unplug the electrical connector and apply battery voltage to the terminals as shown **(see illustrations)**. Blow into the vent hose again and verify that air doesn't flow through. If the valve doesn't operate as described, replace it.

44 To check the vacuum valve, disconnect the hoses and blow into the vacuum hose to make sure air does not flow through.

45 Disconnect the duty solenoid valve connector and activate the solenoid by applying battery voltage to the two terminals **(see illustration 8.43a)**. Once again blow into the vacuum hose. Air should now pass through the valve. If it doesn't, replace the valve.

46 To check the three way solenoid valve, refer to Section 9 (it's similar to the three way solenoid valve for the Evaporative Emissions Control system).

47 The water temperature switch check and replacement procedure is described in Chapter 4.

48 Check the water thermo sensor (see Chapter 4).

Component replacement

49 To remove the EGR control valve, first allow the engine to cool completely. Mark and disconnect the vacuum hoses, remove the three bolts and detach the valve. Scrape all gasket material from the mating surfaces. To install the valve, reverse the removal procedure.

50 To remove the EGR modulator valve, mark all of the hoses with pieces of numbered tape to ensure correct reassembly. Spread the spring clip and remove the valve from it. Installation is the reverse of removal.

51 If there is a problem with the EGR position sensor, the entire EGR control valve must be replaced, as the sensor is not available separately.

52 To replace the duty solenoid valve, mark the hoses with pieces of numbered tape to ensure correct reassembly and disconnect them. Unscrew the mounting nuts and remove the duty solenoid valve from the firewall. Installation is the reverse of removal.

9 Evaporative emissions control system

1985 and earlier models

General description

Refer to illustration 9.2

1 This system is designed to trap and store fuel that evaporates from the carburetor and fuel tank which would normally enter the atmosphere and contribute to hydrocarbon (HC) emissions.

2 The system consists of a charcoal filled canister and lines running to and from the canister. These lines include a vent line from the fuel tank, an air vent solenoid in the carburetor, two purge control valves and a water thermo valve **(see illustration)**. In addition, there is a check valve in fuel tank line. The fuel tank cap is also an integral part of the system.

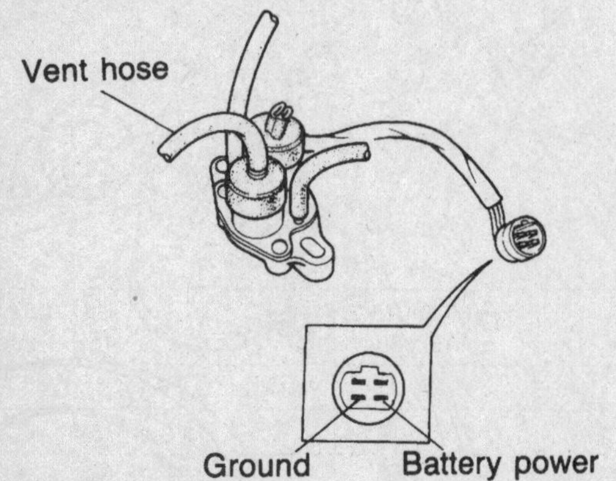

8.43a Blow into the vent hose on the duty solenoid valve - air should flow through when the valve is off, but NOT when the valve is activated

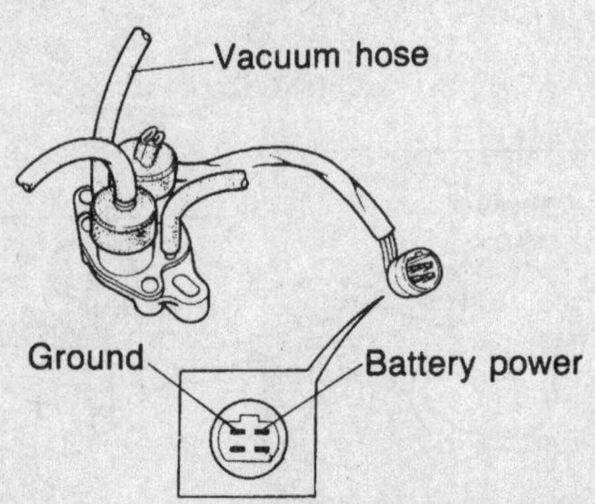

8.43b Blow into the vent hose on the duty solenoid valve - air should NOT pass through (air should flow through when the valve is activated)

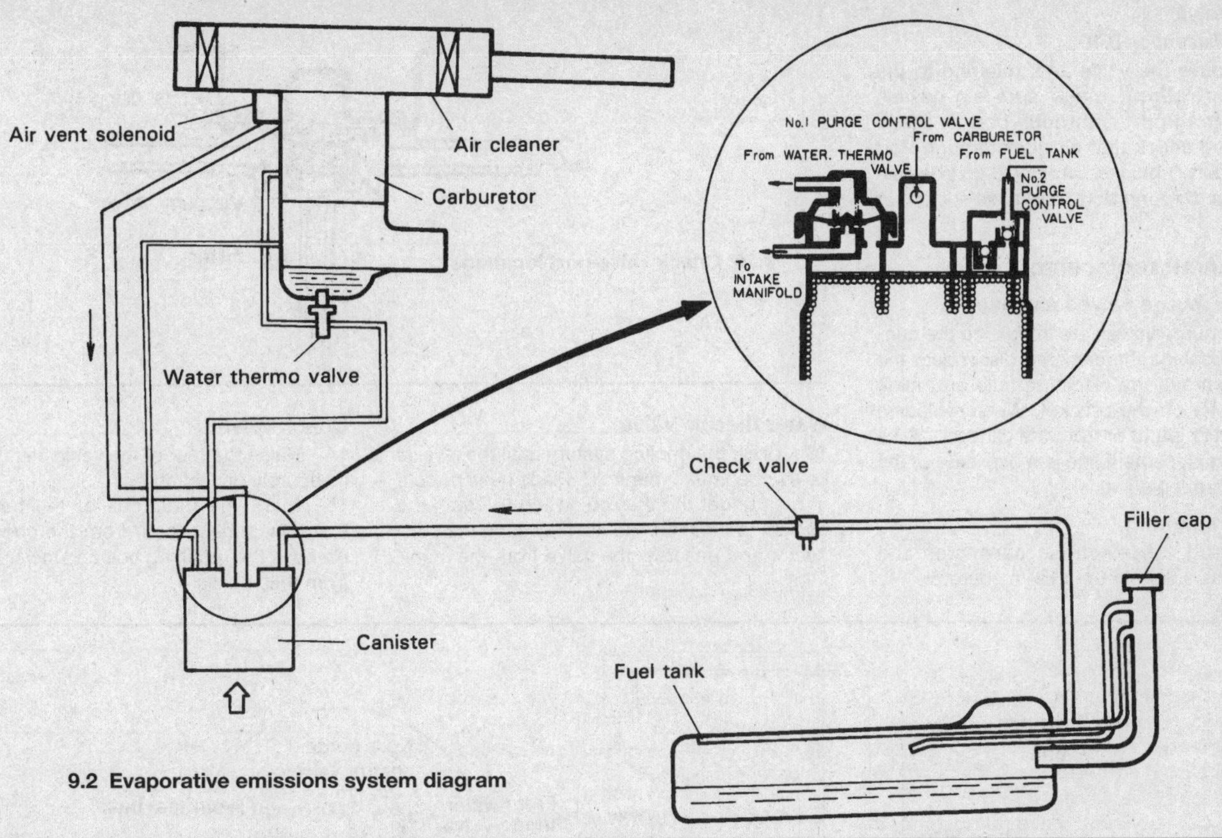

9.2 Evaporative emissions system diagram

Checking

Canister and lines

3 Check all lines in and out of the canister for kinks, leaks and breaks along their entire lengths. Repair or replace as necessary.

4 Check the gasket in the gas cap for signs of drying, cracking or breaks. Replace the gas cap with a new one if defects are found.

Air vent solenoid valve

5 Remove the air cleaner assembly, press the air vent solenoid valve and turn the ignition switch On and then Off. There should be a clicking noise, indicating the solenoid is working properly. If there is not, replace the solenoid valve with a new one.

No. 1 purge control valve

Refer to illustration 9.7

6 With the air cleaner removed, disconnect and plug the idle compensator, thermo sensor, reed valves, and the air vent hose.

7 With the engine idling at normal operating temperature, place your hand under the canister and slowly increase engine speed. Air should be sucked into the canister as the engine speed increases, indicating that the No. 1 purge control valve and thermo sensor are operating properly **(see illustration)**.

No. 2 purge control valve

Refer to illustration 9.8

8 Disconnect the vacuum sensing tube A and make sure that it is possible to both blow and suck air through the valve **(see illustration)**.

Water thermo valve

9 Remove the thermo valve, place it in a container of water and slowly heat the water. If it is possible to blow through the valve when the temperature is above 129°F (54°C), the valve is operating properly.

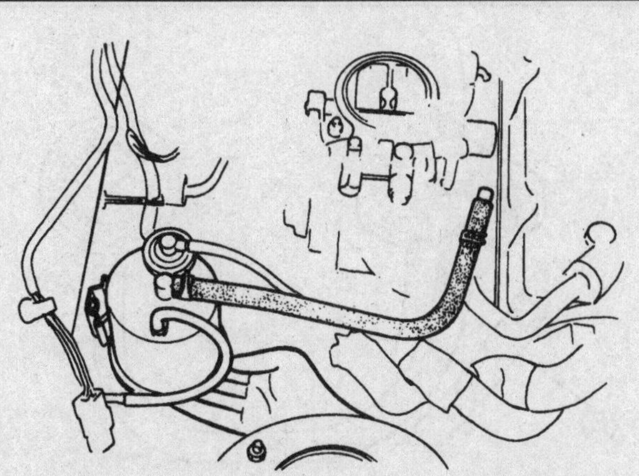

9.7 Checking the No. 1 purge valve operation

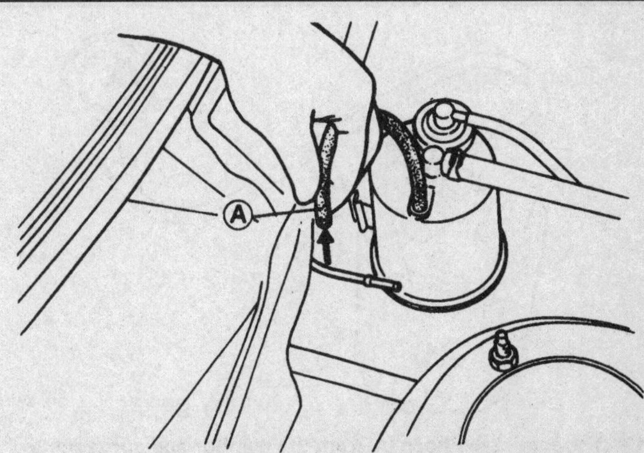

9.8 Checking the evaporative system No. 2 purge valve at the vacuum tube (A)

Check valve

Refer to illustration 9.10

10 Remove the valve and, referring to the **(see illustration)**, make sure air passes through from port A through port B. Block port B and check that air goes through Port C. With port B blocked, it should be possible to suck air through port A and feel suction at port C.

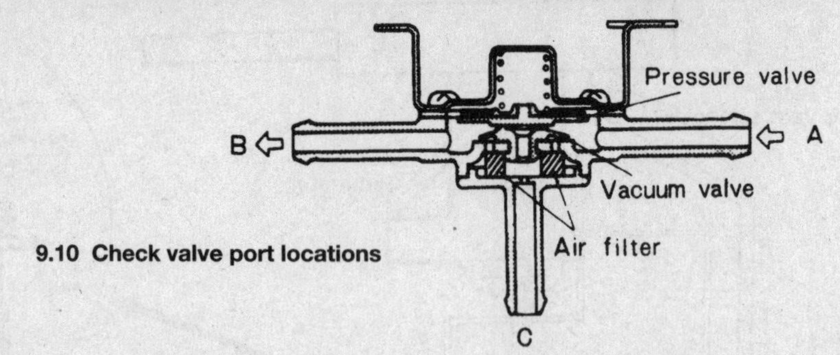

9.10 Check valve port locations

Component replacement

Canister, purge valves and lines

11 The purge valves are integral to the canister. To replace the canister, disconnect the hoses, remove the retaining nuts and slide the canister off the bracket. When replacing any line running to or from the canister, make sure the replacement line is a duplicate of the one you are replacing.

Air vent solenoid

12 Unplug the electrical connector and remove the solenoid from the carburetor.

Water thermo valve

13 Drain the cooling system until the level is below the intake manifold. Place newspapers or rags under the thermo switch to catch the coolant in the manifold itself. Unplug the connector and unscrew the valve from the manifold.

Check valve

14 Raise the rear of the vehicle and support it securely on jackstands.

15 Mark the locations of the hoses and then disconnect them from the check valve. Remove the retaining bolt and lower the valve from the vehicle.

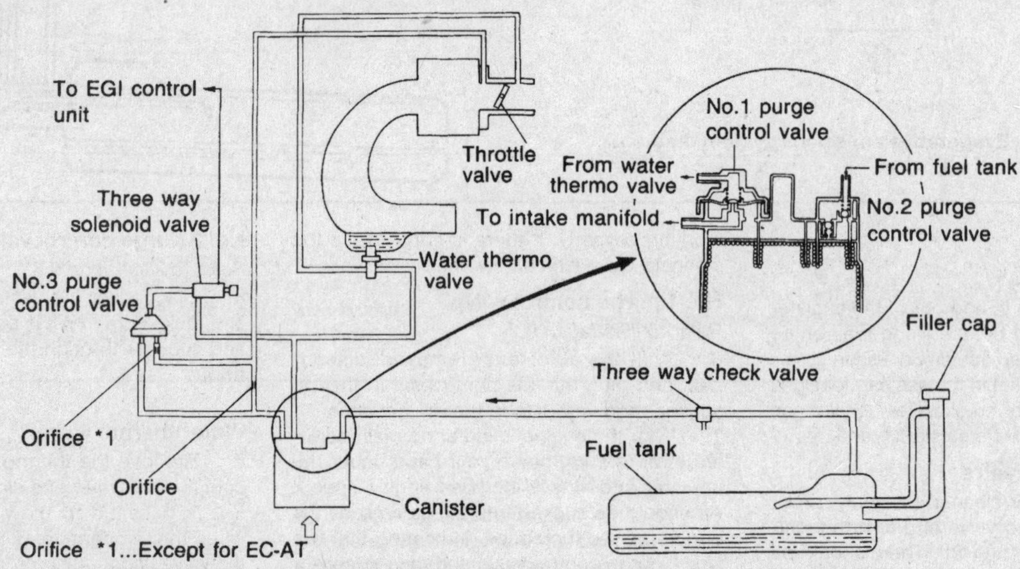

9.16 1986 and later model Evaporative Emissions system Control (EEC) system layout

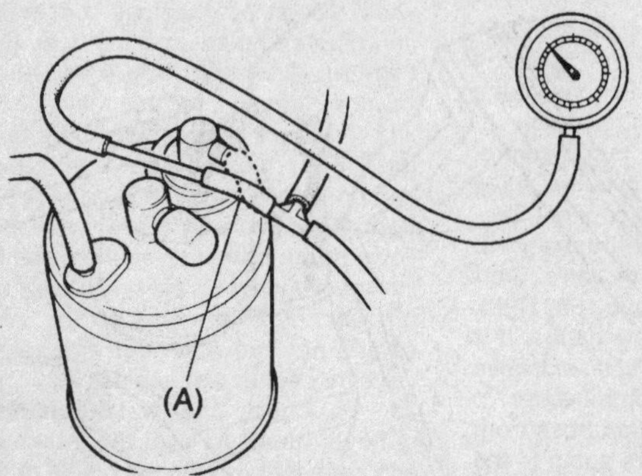

9.17 Disconnect the hose (A) from the number one purge control valve and connect a vacuum gauge to the hose to check the operation of the water thermo valve

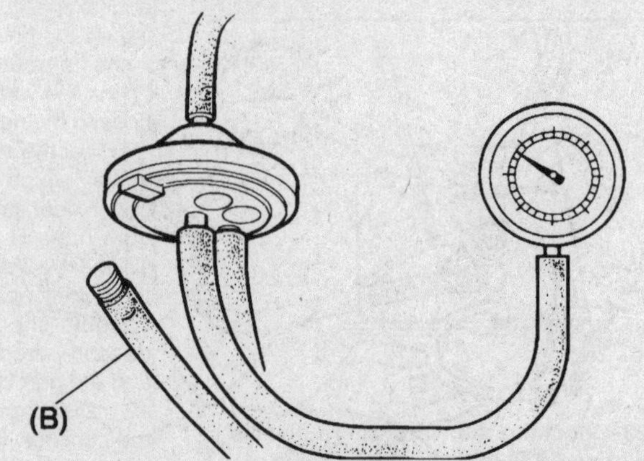

9.18 Disconnect the hose (B) and plug it, then install vacuum gauge and check for vacuum at 1500 rpm

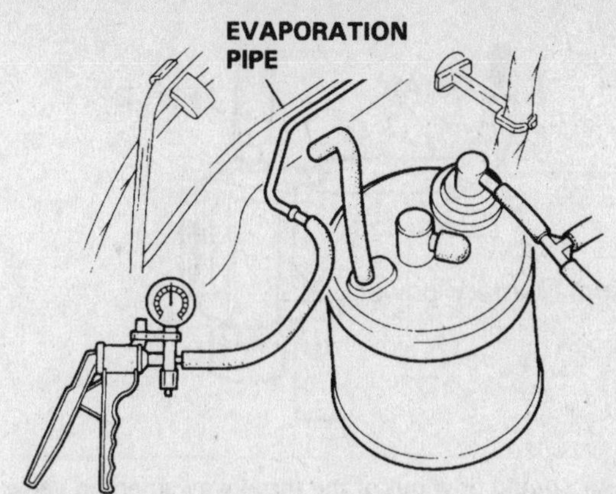

9.19 Disconnect the evaporation hose from the pipe and connect a vacuum pump, then try to apply vacuum - if the vacuum can be maintained, there is an obstruction in the evaporation pipe of the three-way check valve

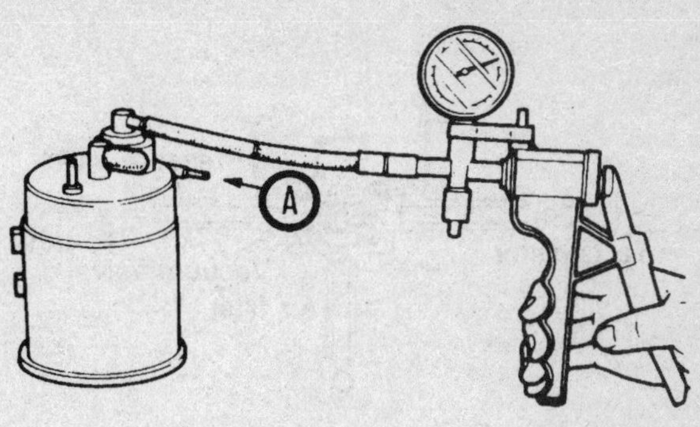

9.20 Connect a vacuum pump to the number one purge control valve and blow into Port A - with the vacuum applied, air should flow through

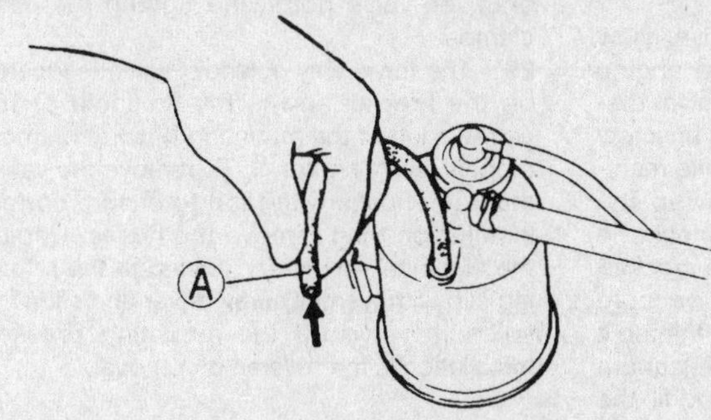

9.21 If the air doesn't flow through the number two purge control valve when you blow into hose A, replace the canister

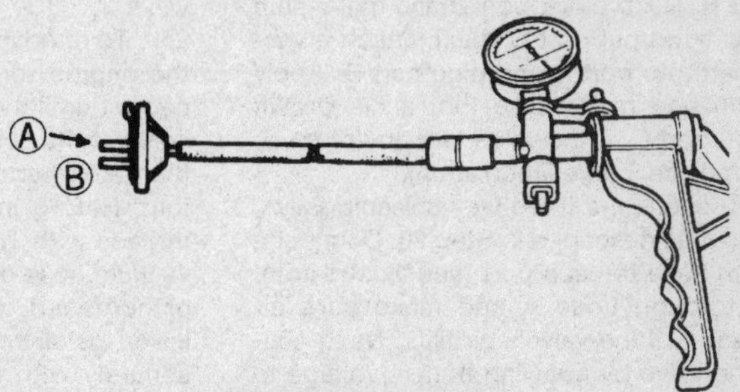

9.22 Connect a vacuum pump to the port on the number three purge control valve, then blow into port A (air should NOT flow through the valve when the vacuum is below 2.6 in-Hg, but should when the vacuum is greater

1986 and later models

General description

Refer to illustration 9.16

16 This system stores fuel vapors in the charcoal canister when the engine is not running. When the engine is started, the vapors are sucked into the surge tank and burned during engine operation **(see illustration)**.

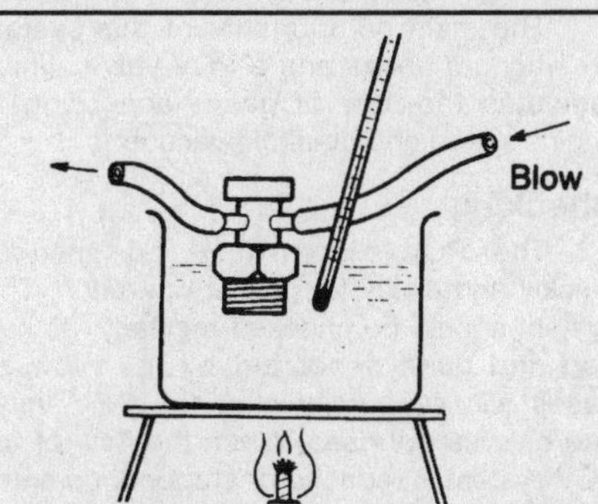

9.23 Checking the water thermo valve (air should flow through the valve at temperatures of 130-degrees F and higher - be careful not to burn yourself while performing this test!)

Checking

Refer to illustrations 9.17, 9.18, 9.19, 9.20, 9.21, 9.22, 9.23, 9.24 and 9.25

17 To check the system operation, warm up the engine and run it at idle. Disconnect the hose from the number one purge control valve and attach a vacuum gauge to the disconnected hose **(see illustration)**. Increase the engine speed to 2500 RPM and note the reading on the gauge. It should be more than 5.9-inches of mercury. If the reading is incorrect, check the water thermo valve. Reconnect the hose to the number 1 purge control valve.

18 Locate the number three purge control valve, which is mounted above the valve cover near the distributor. Disconnect vacuum hose B and plug it **(see illustration)**. Connect a vacuum gauge to the valve. Start the engine and run it at more than 1500 RPM. Vacuum should register on the gauge. If it doesn't, check the three way solenoid valve and the number three purge control valve.

19 Disconnect the evaporation hose from the canister. Connect a vacuum pump to the evaporation hose and attempt to apply vacuum, which should be impossible unless the evaporation pipe or three way check valve is clogged **(see illustration)**.

20 To check the number one purge control valve, blow into port A **(see illustration)**. Air should not flow through the valve. Connect a vacuum pump to the number one purge control valve and apply a vacuum of 5-inches of mercury. Air should now flow through the valve when you blow into port A. If not, replace the canister.

21 To check the number two purge control valve, disconnect the hose from the evaporation pipe and blow into the hose **(see illustration)**. Air should flow freely through the valve. if it doesn't, replace the canister.

22 To check the number three purge control valve, remove the valve from the vehicle and connect a vacuum pump **(see illustration)**. Blow into port A and make sure no air flows through the valve when less than 2.6-inches of vacuum is present. Apply a vacuum of 3-inches of mercury to the switch. Air should now flow through the valve. If the valve fails either test, replace it.

23 To check the water thermo valve, remove the valve from the intake manifold and connect hoses to each side of the valve. Immerse the switch in 130-degree F water and blow into the hose **(see illustration)**. Air should pass through freely. If it doesn't, replace the valve.

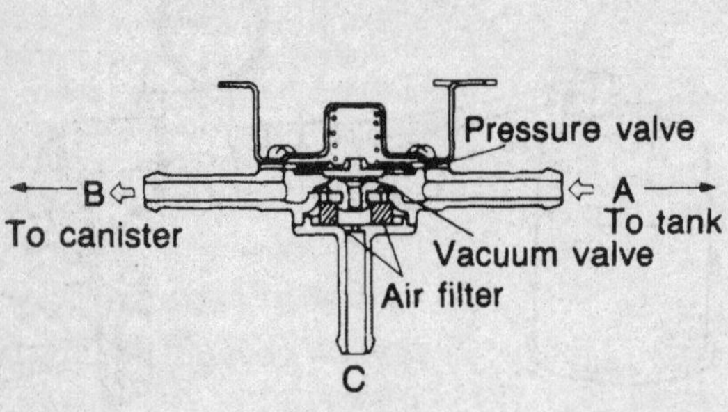

9.24 Use this diagram along with the procedure described in the text to test the three way check valve

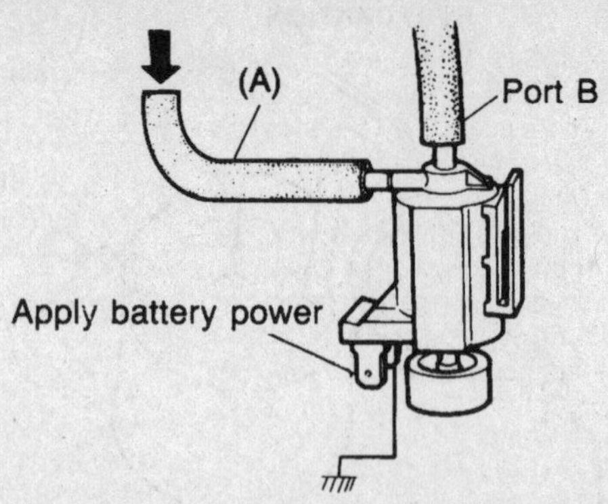

9.25 Air should flow out of the three way solenoid valve at port B when the solenoid is activated

24 To check the three way check valve, remove the valve from the vehicle (Step 28). Blow into port A and make sure air flows out of port B. Next, block port B and make sure air now flows out port C. Next, attach a vacuum pump to port A and plug port B. Apply vacuum and make sure that air is drawn through port C. If the valve fails any of these tests, replace it **(see illustration)**.

25 To check the three way solenoid valve, remove it as described in Step 29. Connect a vacuum hose to each port **(see illustration)**. Blow through hose A and make sure air comes out of the valve's air filter. Next, activate the valve by applying battery voltage to the terminals. Air should now come out of port B. If the valve fails the tests, replace it.

Component replacement

26 Two of the purge control valves are integral with the evaporative emissions control canister and are not replaceable separately. Refer to Chapter 6 for the canister removal procedure. To replace the number three purge control valve, disconnect the hoses one at a time and attach them to the new valve.

27 To remove the water thermo valve, allow the engine to cool, then drain the engine coolant until the level is below the valve. Disconnect the two vacuum hoses and unscrew the water thermo valve from the intake manifold. Before installing the valve, wrap the threads with Teflon sealing tape. Check the vacuum hose ends to see if they are cracked or hardened, which may result in vacuum leaks. Install the valve by hand, then tighten it securely with a wrench. Push the vacuum hoses onto the ports on the valve and fill the cooling system with coolant (see Chapter 1).

28 The three way check valve is located at the rear of the vehicle near the fuel tank. Mark the three hoses on the valve with pieces of tape to ensure correct installation, then loosen the hose clamps and disconnect the hoses from the valve. Remove the mounting screws and the valve. If the hoses are cracked or hardened, replace them. Installation is the reverse of removal. Push the hoses onto the valve ports and tighten the hose clamps.

29 The three way solenoid valve is located on the firewall and is the solenoid at the extreme left of the mounting bracket on most models (see Chapter 4). To remove the valve, mark the hoses with tape to ensure correct installation then remove the hoses. Unplug the electrical connector. Dislodge the retaining clip with a small screwdriver and slide the solenoid valve off the mounting bracket. Installation is the reverse of removal.

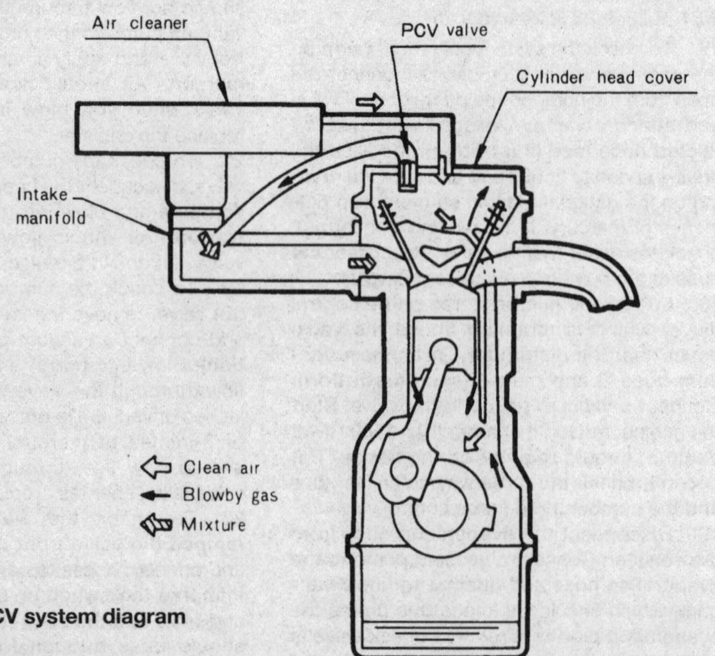

10.1 PCV system diagram

10 Positive Crankcase Ventilation (PCV) system

1985 and earlier models

General description

Refer to illustration 10.1

1 The positive crankcase ventilation system reduces hydrocarbon emissions by circulating fresh air through the crankcase to pick up blow by gases, which are then rerouted through the carburetor to be burned in the engine **(see illustration)**.

2 The main components of this system are vacuum hoses and a PCV valve, which regulates the flow of gases according to engine speed and manifold vacuum.

Checking

3 The PCV system can be checked quickly and easily for proper operation. This system should be checked regularly, as carbon and gunk deposited by the blow by gases will eventually clog the PCV valve and/or system hoses. When the flow of the PCV system is reduced or stopped, common symptoms are rough idling or reduced engine speed at idle.

4 To check for proper vacuum in the system, remove the top plate of the air cleaner and locate the small PCV filter on the inside of the air cleaner housing.

5 Disconnect the hose leading to this filter.

6 With the engine idling, place your thumb over the end of the hose. You should feel a slight vacuum. The suction may be heard as your thumb is released. This will indicate that air is being drawn all the way through the system. If a vacuum is felt, the system is functioning properly. Check that the filter inside the air cleaner housing is not clogged or dirty. If in doubt, replace the filter with a new one, an inexpensive safeguard (refer to Chapter 1).

7 If there is very little vacuum or none at all at the end of the hose, the system is clogged and must be inspected further.

8 Shut off the engine and locate the PCV valve. Carefully pull it from its rubber grommet. Shake it and listen for a clicking sound. That is the rattle of the check ball. If the valve does not click freely, replace it with a new one.

9 Start the engine and run it at idle speed with the PCV valve removed. Place your thumb over the end of the valve and feel for suction. This should be a relatively strong vacuum which will be felt immediately.

10 If little or no vacuum is felt at the PCV valve, turn off the engine and disconnect the vacuum hose from the other end of the valve. Run the engine at idle speed and check for vacuum at the end of the hose just disconnected. No vacuum at this point indicates that the vacuum hose or inlet fitting at the engine is plugged. If it is the hose which is blocked, replace it with a new one or remove it from the engine and blow it out sufficiently with compressed air. A clogged passage at the carburetor or manifold requires that the component be removed and thoroughly cleaned to remove carbon build up. A strong vacuum felt going into the PCV valve, but little or no vacuum coming out of the valve, indicates a failure of the PCV valve requiring replacement with a new one.

11 When purchasing a new PCV valve, make sure it is the correct one for your engine. An incorrect PCV valve may pull too little or too much vacuum, possibly leading to engine damage.

Component replacement

12 The replacement procedures for both the PCV valve and filter are covered in Chapter

1986 and later models

General description

13 The PCV system installed on the fuel injected engine is almost identical to the system described above the exception of the valve checking procedure.

Checking

14 Warm up the engine to normal operating temperature and allow it to idle. Pull the PCV valve from the cylinder head cover and place your finger over the valve. If the idle speed drops, the valve is functioning properly.

Component replacement

15 Refer to Chapter 1 for the PCV valve replacement procedure.

11 Air inlet temperature control system

General description

1 The air inlet temperature control system is provided to improve engine efficiency and reduce hydrocarbon emissions during the initial warm-up period by maintaining a controlled air temperature at the carburetor. This temperature control of the incoming air allows leaner carburetor and choke calibrations.

2 The system uses a damper assembly, located in the snorkel of the air cleaner housing, to control the ratio of cold and warm air directed into the carburetor. This damper is controlled by a vacuum diaphragm, which is, in turn, modulated by a thermo sensor in the air cleaner.

3 It is during the first few miles of driving (depending on outside temperature) that this system has its greatest effect on engine performance and emissions output. When the engine is cold, the damper flap blocks off the air cleaner inlet snorkel, allowing only warm air from around the exhaust manifold to enter the carburetor. Gradually, as the engine warms up, the flap opens the snorkel passage, increasing the amount of cold air allowed in. Once the engine reaches normal operating temperature, the flap opens completely, allowing only cold, fresh air to enter.

4 Because of this cold-engine-only function, it is important to periodically check this system to prevent poor engine performance when cold or overheating of the fuel mixture once the engine has reached operating temperatures. If the air cleaner valve sticks in the no heat position, the engine will run poorly, stall and waste gas until it has warmed up on its own. A valve sticking in the heat position causes the engine to run as if it is out of tune due to the constant flow of hot air to the carburetor.

Checking

5 Refer to Chapter 1 for maintenance and checking procedures for this system. If problems were encountered in the system's performance while performing the routine maintenance checks, refer to the procedures that follow.

6 If the damper door did not close off snorkel air when the cold engine was first started, disconnect the vacuum hose at the snorkel vacuum diaphragm and place your thumb over the hose end, checking for vacuum. If there is vacuum going to the diaphragm, check that the damper door and link are not frozen or binding within the air cleaner snorkel. If a vacuum pump is available, disconnect the vacuum hose and apply vacuum to the motor to make sure the damper door actuates. Replace the vacuum diaphragm if the application of vacuum does not open the door and the hose routing is correct but the damper door moves freely.

7 If there was no vacuum going to the diaphragm in the above test, check the hoses for cracks, crimps and proper connection. If the hoses are clear and in good condition, replace the thermo sensor inside the air cleaner housing.

Component replacement

Air cleaner vacuum diaphragm

8 Disconnect the vacuum hose from the diaphragm.

9 Remove the retaining screw, unhook the linkage and rotate the diaphragm up and out of the air cleaner housing.

10 To install, insert the diaphragm in the housing, rotate it into position, connect the linkage and install the retaining screw.

11 Connect the vacuum hose.

Air cleaner thermo sensor

Refer to illustration 11.14

12 Mark their locations and disconnect the vacuum hoses at the sensor.

13 Carefully note the position of the sensor as it must be installed in exactly the same position.

14 Lift the sensor from the air cleaner **(see illustration)**.

15 Install the new sensor in the same position as the old one and connect the vacuum hoses.

12 Hot idle compensation system

General description

Refer to illustration 12.1

1 The hot idle compensation system aids idling and starting by venting air directly from the air cleaner into the intake manifold when the engine is hot **(see illustration)**.

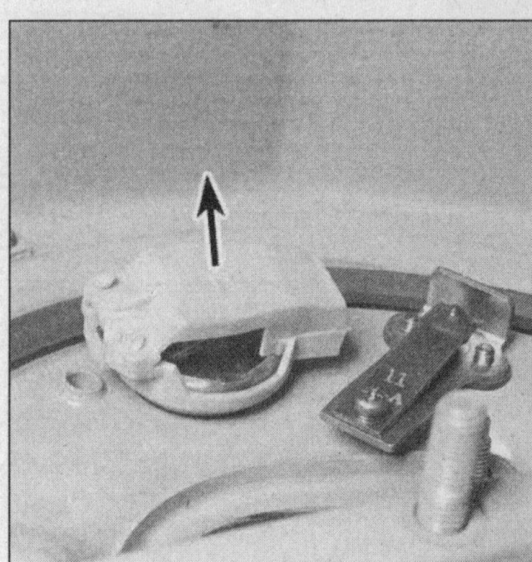

11.14 The air inlet thermo sensor can be lifted straight up (arrow) after disconnecting the vacuum hoses under the air cleaner assembly

6

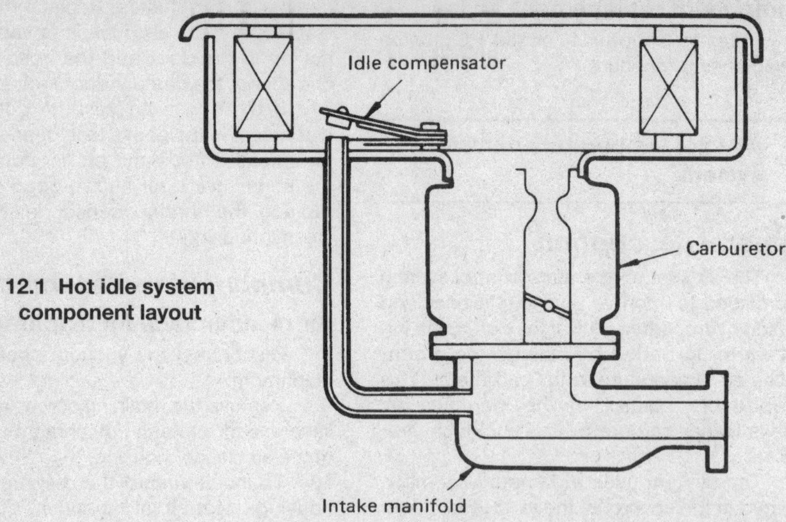

12.1 Hot idle system component layout

2 Symptoms of a fault in the hot idle compensation system are hard starting when the engine is cold, rough idling or an unusually high idle speed.

Component checking

3 With the engine cold, remove the air cleaner top plate and make sure the idle compensator is closed.
4 Install the top plate, start the engine and run it until normal operating temperature is reached. The air temperature in the air cleaner housing should be 156° F (69°C). Remove the top plate and check that the idle compensator is open.
5 If the idle compensator fails either check, replace it with a new one.

Component replacement

6 Marking all hoses for ease of installation to their original positions and remove the air cleaner housing. Remove the attaching screws and lift the idle compensator from the housing.
7 Installation is the reverse of removal.

13 Deceleration control system

General description

Refer to illustration 13.2

1 The deceleration control system gradually closes the throttle during sudden deceleration so that excessive unburned fuel is not dumped into the exhaust, causing increased emissions.
2 The components of this system an anti-afterburn valve used only on automatic transaxle models with air conditioning and a dashpot on the carburetor which operates the throttle **(see illustration)**.
3 A symptom of a fault in this system is immediate closing of the throttle on deceleration.

Component checking

Anti-afterburn valve

4 With the engine idling, block off the intake port of the anti-afterburn valve and check that air is not sucked in.
5 Turn the air conditioning switch On and check that air is now sucked into the valve intake port for approximately two seconds. Replace the valve with a new one if it fails either test.

Dashpot

Refer to illustration 13.7

6 Pull the throttle lever sharply away from the dashpot and check that the dashpot rod immediately extends fully. Release the throttle lever and make sure that it slowly returns to the idle position after contacting the dashpot rod.
7 To adjust the dashpot, run the engine at idle at normal operating temperature and connect a tachometer. Slowly increase the engine speed and check that the dashpot rod separates from the lever at approximately 2000 rpm. Loosen the locknut and turn the dashpot to adjust **(see illustration)**.
8 If adjustment does not bring the dashpot into specification, replace it with a new one.

Component replacement

Anti-afterburn valve

9 Unplug the connector, remove the vacuum hose and unsnap the valve from the bracket.

Dashpot

10 Loosen the locknut and unscrew the dashpot from the bracket.

14 Altitude compensation system

General description

Refer to illustration 14.1

1 Some non-California vehicles are equipped with an altitude compensation system **(see illustration)**. This system features a compensator that opens above 3609 feet to allow more air into the carburetor. In addition, a vacuum switch sends a signal to the control unit when the manifold vacuum drops so the

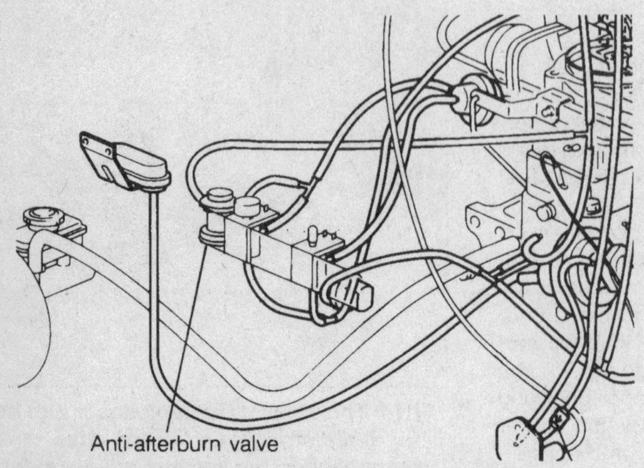

13.2 Anti-afterburn valve location

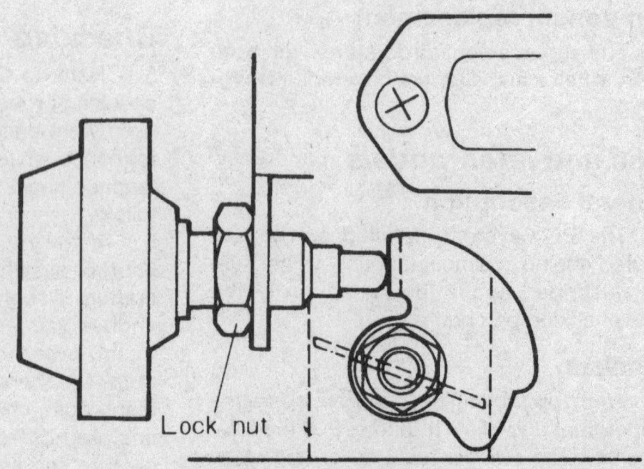

13.7 Dashpot adjustment

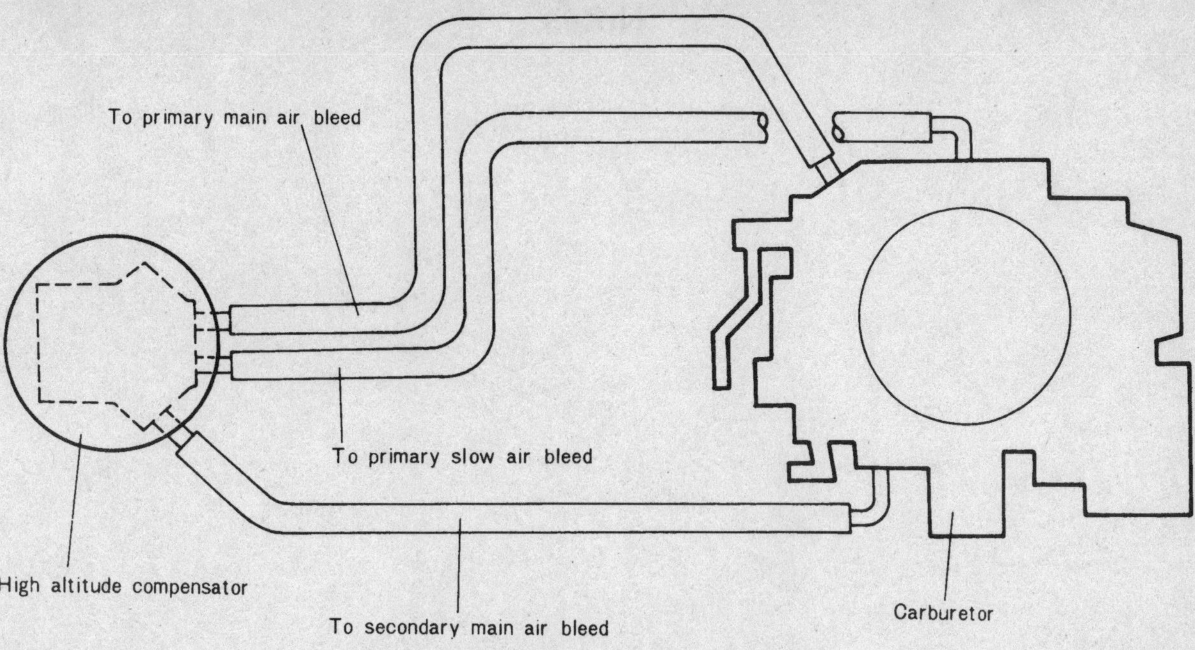

14.1 Altitude compensation system diagram

A/F solenoid valve supplies additional fuel.

2 Symptoms of a fault in the altitude compensation system are rough idle or stalling and an excessively high idle speed.

Checking

Refer to illustration 14.3

3 Disconnect the air hose from the carburetor and blow into it **(see illustration)**.

4 Above 3609 feet air can be blown through the hose and below this altitude air will not pass if the compensator is working properly.

5 Further testing of the altitude compensation system requires special equipment and techniques and should be left to your dealer.

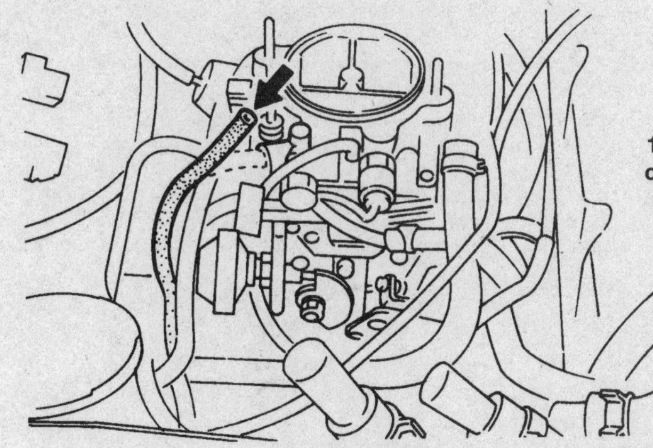

14.3 The altitude compensator can be tested by disconnecting the hose and blowing into the end (arrow)

Notes

Chapter 7 Part A Manual transaxle

Contents

Specifications

Reverse lever-to-idler clearance	
Standard	0.004 to 0.013 in (0.1 to 0.32 mm)
Service limit	0.020 in (0.5 mm)
Shift fork-to-clutch sleeve clearance	
Standard	0.008 to 0.018 in (0.2 to 0.46 mm)
Service limit	0.020 in (0.5 mm)
Gear synchronizer ring-to-gear clearance	
Standard	0.059 in (1.5 mm)
Service limit	0.021 in (0.53 mm)
Thrust clearances	
First gear	
Standard	0.002 to 0.021 in (0.05 to 0.53 mm)
Service limit	0.024 in (0.6 mm)
Second gear	
Standard	0.02 to 0.039 in (0.5 to 1.0 mm)
Service limit	0.039 in (1.0 mm)
Third gear	
Standard	0.02 to 0.017 in (0.5 to 0.43 mm)
Service limit	0.020 in (0.5 mm)
Fourth gear	
Standard	0.01 to 0.014 in (0.25 to 0.355 mm)
Service limit	0.020 in (0.5 mm)
Primary shaft gear bearing preload	0.4 to 1.7 in-lbs
Differential side bearing preload	0.69 to 1.56 in-lbs
Side gear and pinion gear backlash	0.004 in (0.1 mm)

Torque specifications

	Ft-lbs	M-kg
Rear crossmember		
Front nuts and bolts	32 to 40	4.4 to 5.5
Rear bolt	90 to 85	9.5 to 11.8
Lower balljoint bolt	32 to 40	4.4 to 5.5
Transaxle		
Case bolts	27 to 39	3.7 to 5.5
Gate lock bolt	8.7 to 11.6	1.2 to 1.6
Gear shaft locknut	94 to 152	13 to 21
Guide bolt	6 to 10	0.9 to 1.4
Rear cover bolt	6 to 8	0.9 to 1.1
Transaxle-to-engine bolts	65 to 87	9.1 to 11.9
Transaxle mount-to-engine bolts	40	5.5
Transaxle mount-to-transaxle bolts and nuts	27 to 38	3.8 to 5.4
Transaxle mount-to-body nuts	32 to 40	4.4 to 5.5

1 General information

All manual transmission models are equipped with either a 4-speed or 5-speed transaxle that incorporates the transmission and differential into one unit. Power from the engine passes through the transaxle gears and then to the differential gears, which drive the axleshafts.

All forward gears are synchromesh and the floor mounted gear shift lever operates the transaxle internal shift mechanism by way of a shift control rod.

2 Transaxle mounts - check and replacement

Checking

1 Watch the mount as an assistant pulls up and pushes down on the transaxle. If the rubber separates from the plate or the case moves up but not down, indicating the mount is bottomed out, replace the mount with a new one.

Replacement

2 Disconnect the battery negative cable.
3 Support the transaxle with a jack.
4 Remove the transaxle mount-to-engine bolts.

7A

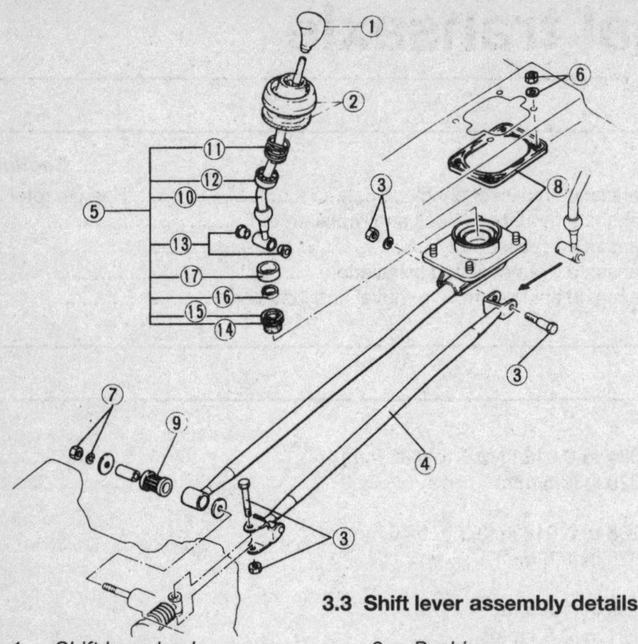

3.3 Shift lever assembly details

1	*Shift lever knob*	9	*Bushing*
2	*Boot*	10	*Shift lever*
3	*Bolts and nuts*	11	*Spring*
4	*Change control rod*	12	*Upper ball seat*
5	*Change lever components*	13	*Bushings*
6	*Bracket nuts*	14	*Boot*
7	*Nut and washer*	15	*Plate*
8	*Extension bar and bracket assembly*	16	*Holder*
		17	*Lower ball seat*

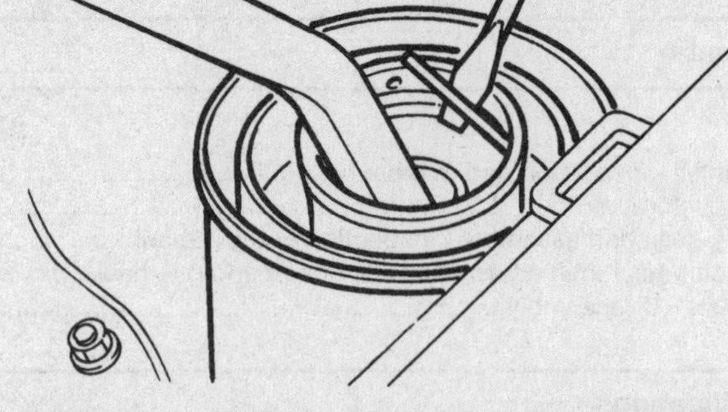

3.4 Release the shift lever spring clip with a screwdriver

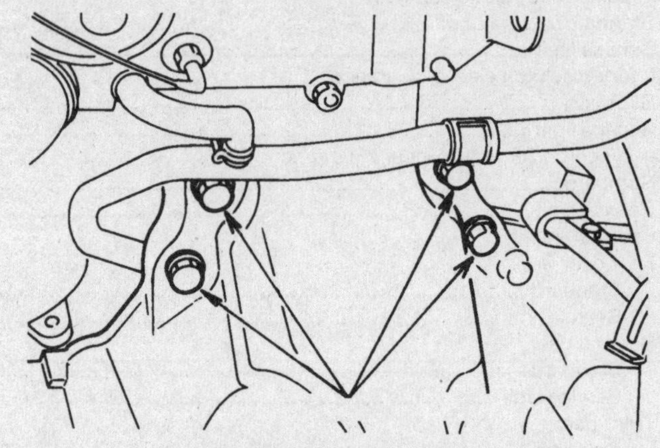

4.7 Upper transaxle bolt locations (arrows)

5 Remove the mount-to-body nuts and remove the mount.
6 Place the new mount in position and install the mount-to-transaxle bolts. Tighten the bolts to the specified torque.
7 Install the mount-to-body nuts and tighten them to the specified torque.
8 Remove the jack and connect the battery negative cable.

3 Transaxle shift lever assembly - removal and installation

Refer to illustrations 3.3 and 3.4

1 Inside the vehicle passenger compartment, remove the shift lever knob, shift boot and the front and rear consoles (Chapter 11).
2 Raise the front of the vehicle and support it securely on jackstands.
3 Remove the retaining nuts and bolts and lower the change rod from the vehicle **(see illustration)**.
4 Remove the shift lever spring clip with a screwdriver and lift the lever assembly from the vehicle **(see illustration)**.
5 Remove the extension bar retaining nuts and bolts and remove the bar, bracket and gasket assembly.
6 Installation is the reverse of removal.

4 Transaxle - removal and installation

Removal

Refer to illustrations 4.7, 4.15 and 4.16

1 Disconnect the battery negative cable.
2 Disconnect speedometer cable.
3 Remove the mounting bolts from the clutch cable bracket and disconnect the clutch cable from the release lever. If equipped with hydraulic system, remove the clutch release cylinder (see Chapter 13).
4 Remove the ground cable retaining bolt and the wire harness clip.
5 Remove the starter motor (Chapter 5).
6 There are two principal ways of supporting the weight of the engine during the removal of the crossmember and transaxle. A special support fixture can be obtained which rests on the suspension strut towers, or an engine hoist can be used. If the engine support fixture is being used, install it at this time. If the engine hoist is being used to support the engine, the hood must be removed to gain sufficient clearance (Chapter 11).
7 Remove the four top transaxle-to-engine mounting bolts **(see illustration)**.
8 Raise the front of the vehicle, support it securely on jackstands and drain the transaxle oil (Chapter 1).
9 Remove the front wheels and splash panels and disconnect the stabilizer bar control link.
10 Remove the lower balljoint and steering knuckle coupling bolt and separate the lower suspension arm from the knuckle (Chapter 10).
11 Remove the left driveaxle (Chapter 8).
12 Remove the right driveaxle and joint shaft (Chapter 8).
13 Separate the change control rod from the change rod and remove the extension bar from the transaxle.
14 Remove the transaxle under cover.
15 Unbolt and remove the crossmember and lower suspension arm assembly **(see illustration)**.
16 Support the transaxle with a jack and fasten the transaxle to the jack **(see illustration)**.
17 Remove the two remaining bolts, separate the transaxle from the engine and lower the transaxle from the vehicle.

Installation

18 Apply a thin coat of moly grease to the transaxle input shaft splines.
19 Raise the transaxle into position and install the bolts. Tighten the bolts to the proper torque.
20 Install the extension bar onto the transaxle and the change rod to the change control rod.
21 Install the crossmember and lower arm assembly.
22 Install the transaxle under cover.

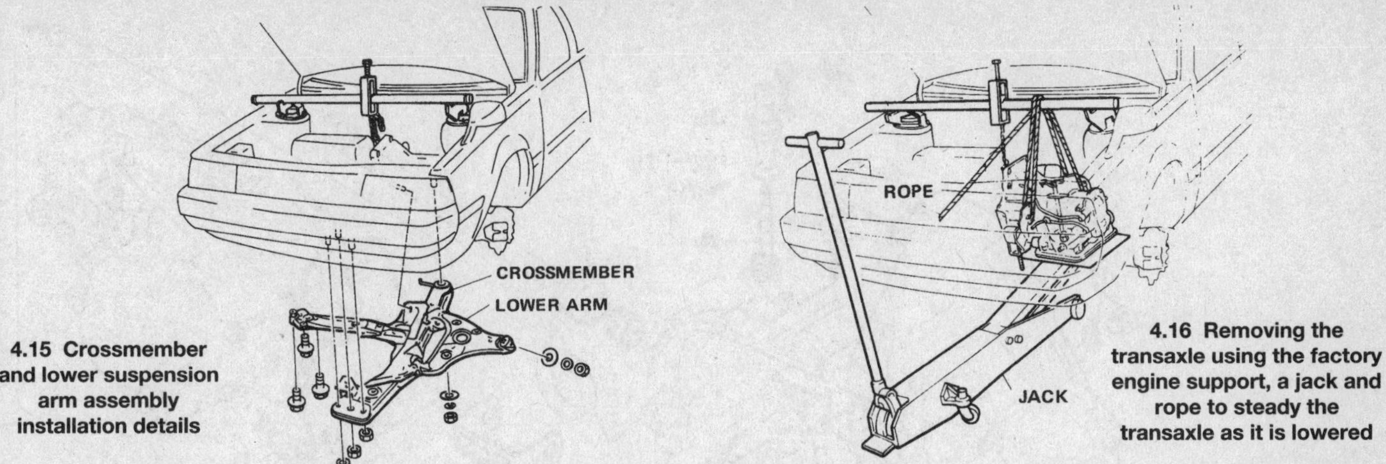

4.15 Crossmember and lower suspension arm assembly installation details

4.16 Removing the transaxle using the factory engine support, a jack and rope to steady the transaxle as it is lowered

23 Install the right driveaxle (Chapter 8).
24 Install the left driveaxle (Chapter 8).
25 Connect the lower balljoint to the knuckle and install the nuts and bolts, tightening them to the specified torque.
26 Connect the stabilizer bar link.
27 Install the splash shields and the front wheels.
28 Install the starter motor.
29 Remove the jack from the transaxle and lower the vehicle.
30 Install the four transaxle–to–engine retaining bolts. Tighten the bolts to the specified torque.
31 Install the wiring harness clips and the ground cable bolt and connect the clutch cable.
32 Fill the transaxle with the specified oil (Chapter 1).
33 Connect the clutch cable to the release lever. Install and tighten the bracket mounting bolts. If equipped with hydraulically actuated clutch, install the clutch release cylinder and bleed the system (see Chapter 13).
34 Connect the speedometer cable.
35 Connect the battery negative cable.

5 Transaxle - disassembly

Refer to illustrations 5.1a, 5.1b, 5.3a, 5.3b, 5.4, 5.6, 5.7, 5.10a, 5.10b, 5.11, 5.13, 5.14, 5.15, 5.16a, 5.16b, 5.18a, 5.18b, 5.19, 5.20, 5.22, 5.23, 5.25, 5.27, 5.33 and 5.35

1 Unbolt and remove the rear cover (5-

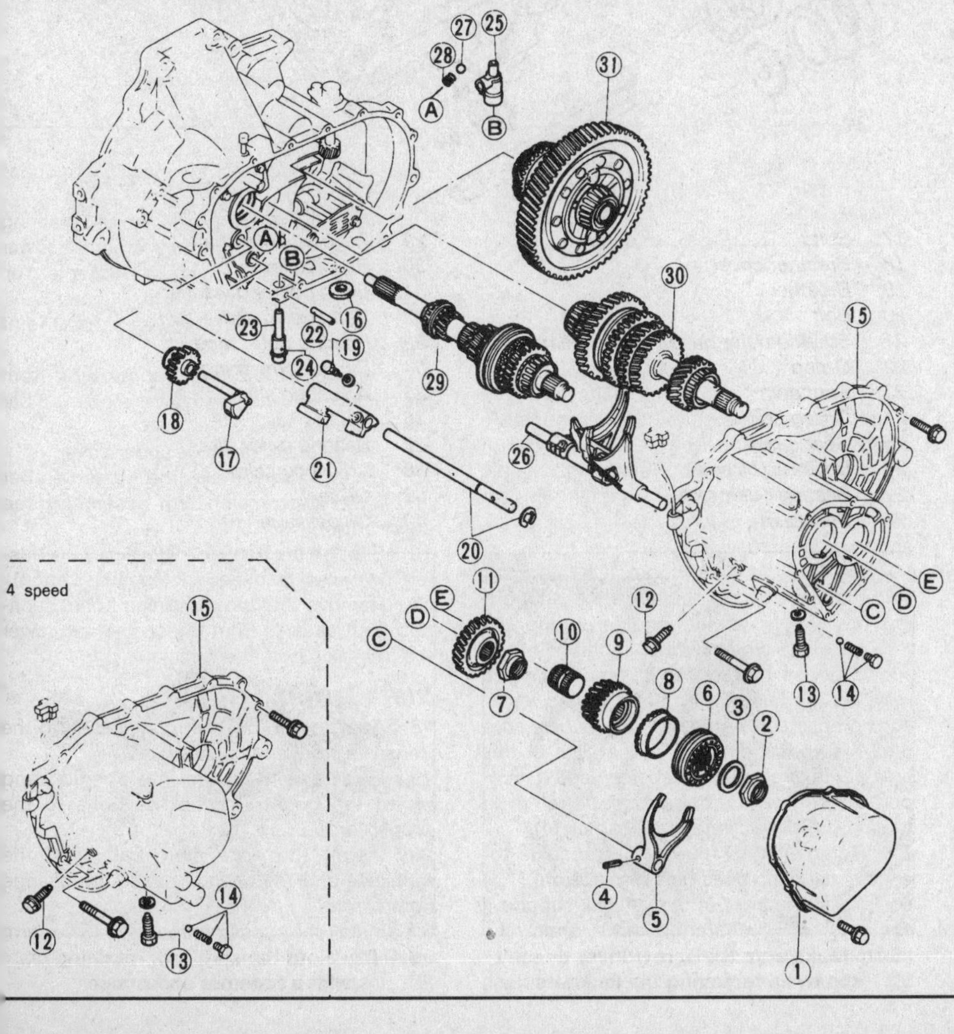

4 speed

5.1a Transaxle component layout

1 *Rear cover (5-speed)*
2 *Locknut (5-speed)*
3 *Stop plate (5-speed)*
4 *Springpin (5-speed)*
5 *Shift fork (5-speed)*
6 *Clutch hub assembly (5-speed)*
7 *Locknut (5-speed)*
8 *Synchronizer ring (5-speed)*
9 *5th gear (5-speed)*
10 *Gear sleeve (5-speed)*
11 *Primary gear (5-speed)*
12 *Lock bolt*
13 *Guide bolt*
14 *Lock bolt and ball and spring*
15 *Transaxle case assembly*
16 *Magnet*
17 *Reverse idle shaft*
18 *Reverse idle gear*
19 *Lock bolt*
20 *Shift rod (5th and reverse) and clip*
21 *Gate*
22 *Springpin*
23 *Crank lever shaft*
24 *O-ring*
25 *Crank lever assembly*
26 *Shift fork and shift rod assembly*
27 *Steel ball*
28 *Spring*
29 *Primary shaft gear assembly*
30 *Secondary shaft gear assembly*
31 *Ring gear and differential assembly*

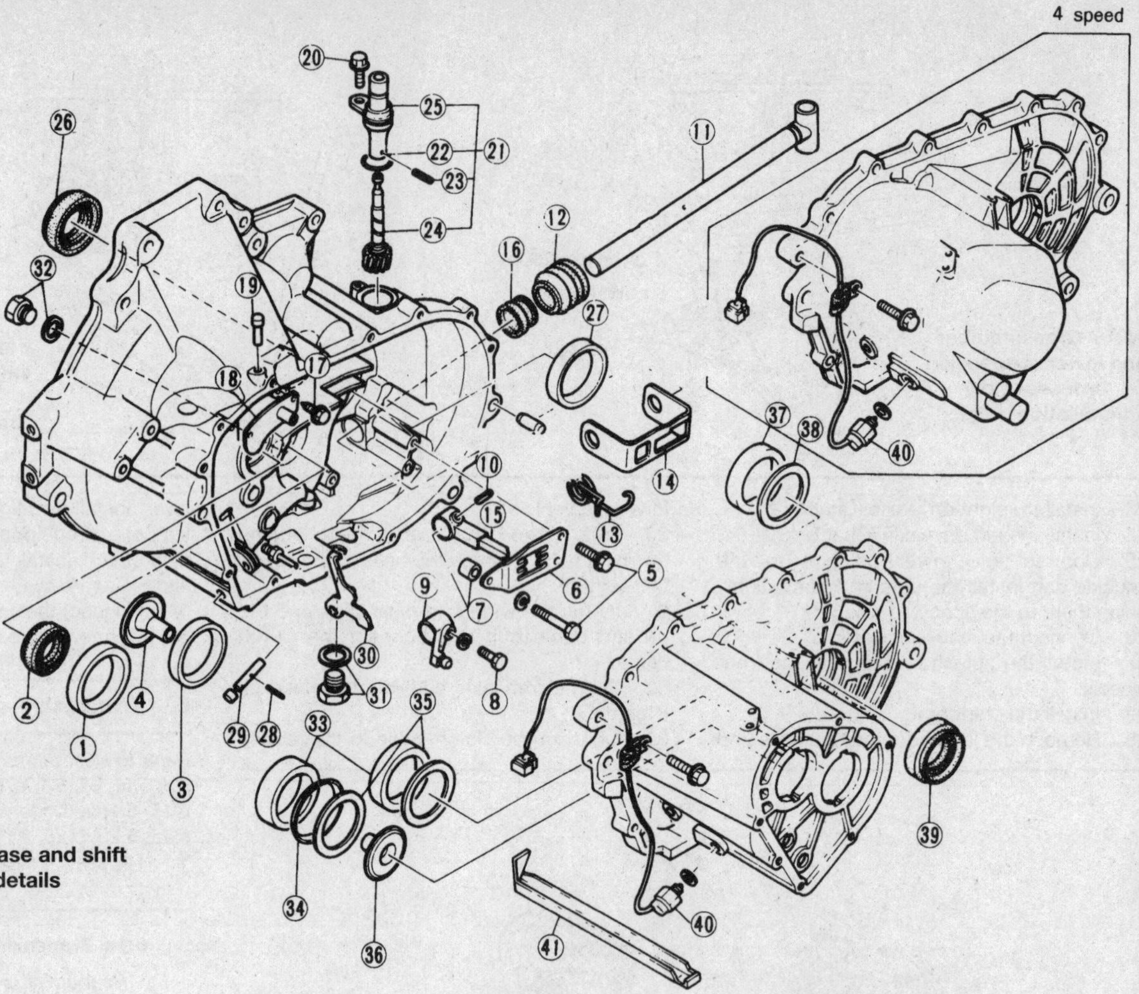

4 speed

5.1b Transaxle case and shift assembly details

1 Bearing outer race
2 Oil seal
3 Bearing outer race
4 Funnel
5 Bolts
6 Guide plate
7 Pipe
8 Bolt
9 Change arm
10 Springpin
11 Change rod
12 Boot
13 Spring (5-speed)
14 Reverse gate (5-speed)
15 Selector
16 Oil seal
17 Bolts
18 Breather cover
19 Breather
20 Bolt
21 Speedometer driven gear assembly
22 O-ring
23 Springpin
24 Driven gear
25 Gear case
26 Driveaxle oil seal
27 Bearing outer race
28 Springpin
29 Reverse lever shaft
30 Reverse lever
31 Drain bolt and washer
32 Bolt and washer
33 Bearing outer race
34 Diaphragm spring
35 Adjusting shim
36 Funnel
37 Bearing outer race
38 Adjusting shim
39 Oil seal
40 Oil passage

5.3a Insert a screwdriver into the gear teeth to lock the shaft

5.3b Make sure the screwdriver doesn't slip while removing the locknuts

5.4 Drive out the shift fork retaining pin with a hammer and punch

5.6 Remove the lock bolt

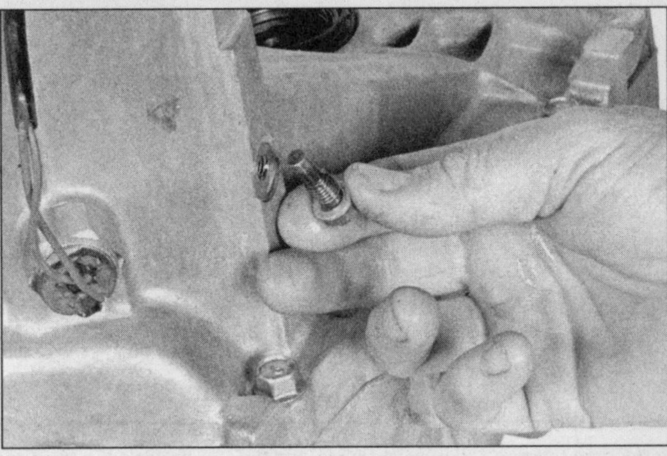

5.7 Remove the guide bolt from the case

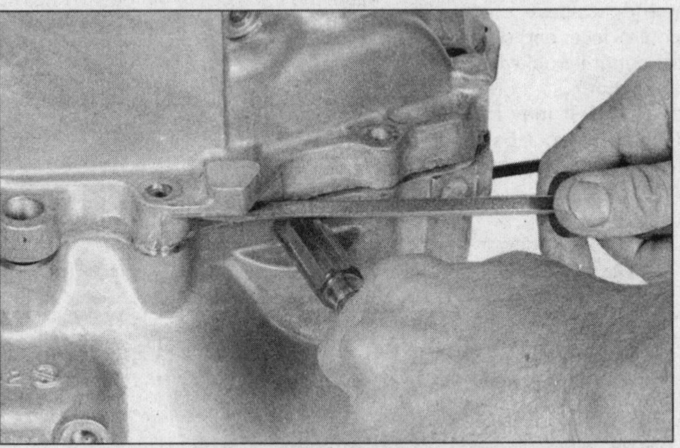

5.10a Use two screwdrivers to carefully separate the transaxle case halves

5.10b Carefully lift the case half off the shafts

speed) **(see illustrations)**.

2 Use a punch to drive the locknut collar back from the groove on each of the locknuts (5-speed).

3 Carefully lock the gear teeth with a screwdriver or similar tool and remove the locknuts **(see illustrations)**.

4 Remove the 5th gear shift fork retaining pin and the shift fork **(see illustration)**.

5 Remove the 5th gear stop plate, clutch hub, synchro ring, gear sleeve and gear.

6 Remove the lock bolt from the transaxle case **(see illustration)**.

7 Remove the guide bolt from the case **(see illustration)**.

8 Unscrew the backup light connector from the case.

9 Mark the location of the wiring clamp for ease of reassembly and remove the transaxle bolts.

10 Carefully separate the halves of the case **(see illustrations)**.

11 Remove the 5th gear oil passage **(see illustration)**.

12 Remove the magnet from the case.

13 Remove the idler shaft and gear **(see illustration)**.

14 Remove the lock bolt from the 5th gear and the reverse lock plate **(see illustration)**.

15 On 4-speed models, remove the shift

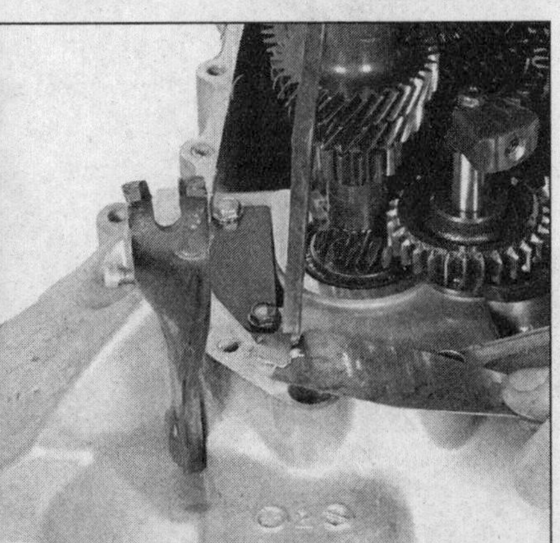

5.11 Use a scraper to remove the 5th-gear oil passage which is held in place with gasket sealant

5.13 Lift out the reverse idle shaft and remove the gear

5.14 Remove the 5th-gear and reverse lock plate bolt

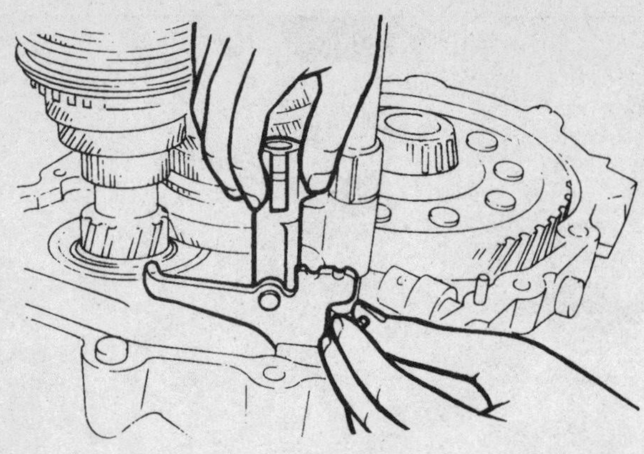
5.15 The 4-speed gearshift and lever are removed as a unit

5.16a Use a screwdriver to lift out the 5th gear and reverse rod

gate and reverse lever as a unit, with the shifter in Neutral **(see illustration)**.
16 Remove the 5th gear and reverse rod **(see illustrations)**.
17 Remove the 5th and reverse gear shift gate.
18 Drive out the crank lever retaining pin and remove the pin (5-speed) **(see illustrations)**.
19 Remove the crank lever assembly while moving the shift rod to assist in it's release (5-speed) **(see illustration)**.
20 Making sure the interlock sleeve end surface is flush with the control lever end surface, turn the change rod counterclockwise as far as it will go **(see illustration)**.
21 Pull up on the change rod. It may be necessary to pry upward on the interlock ball.
22 Drive out the retaining pin from the change rod **(see illustration)**.
23 Place the transaxle in 4th gear by pulling upward on the upper shift fork **(see illustration)**.
24 Pull the shift rod carefully out of the housing. When the rod is clear of the housing, the steel ball will fall from the reverse lever shaft.
25 Lift the secondary gear shaft and shift fork assembly from the transaxle case **(see**

5.16b Remove the 5th gear and reverse lock plate

5.18a Use a punch to drive out the crank lever retaining pin

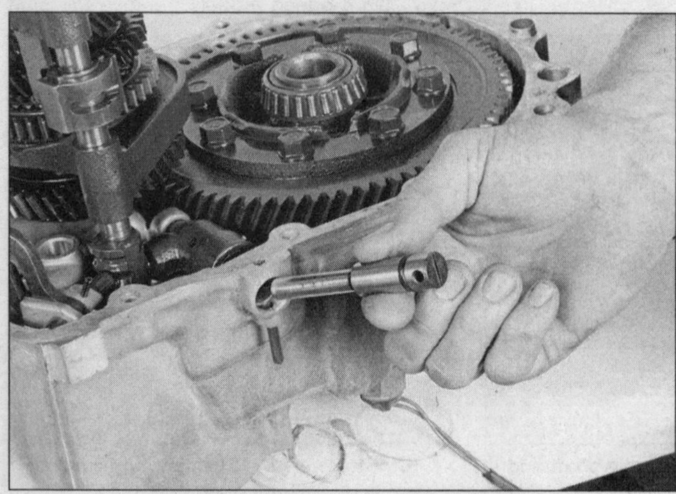
5.18b Remove the crank lever shaft

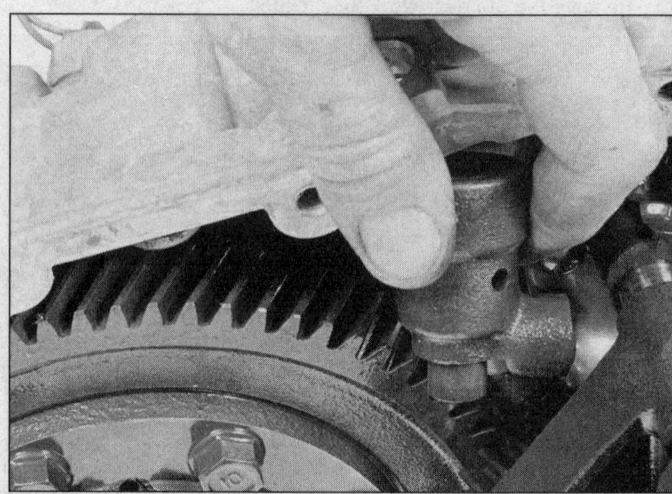
5.19 Lift out the crank lever while moving the shifter

5.20 Rotate the control rod counterclockwise

5.22 Use a punch to drive the retaining pin from the control end of the rod

illustration).
26 Remove the primary gear assembly.
27 Remove the differential assembly **(see illustration)**.
28 Remove the Neutral switch.
29 Remove the input shaft oil seals and bearing races.
30 Remove the funnel from the transaxle case.
31 Unbolt and remove the shifter guide plate and arm.
32 Drive out the shift arm retaining pin, making sure the selector lever is centered.
33 Remove the change shaft boot from the transaxle housing and withdraw the shaft **(see illustration)**.
34 Remove the reverse gate spring bushing and selector.

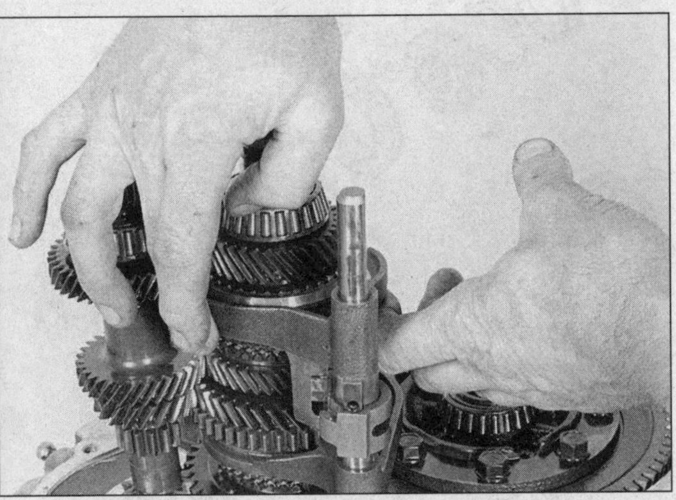
5.23 Shift into 4th gear by pulling the shift fork upward

5.25 Remove the secondary gearshaft assembly by lifting it carefully upward

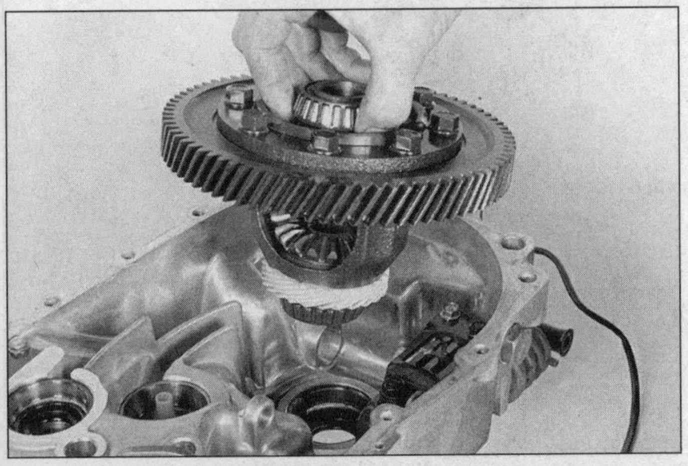
5.27 Lift the differential assembly from the transaxle case

5.33 Withdraw the boot and change shaft

35 Carefully drive out the bearing races **(see illustration)**.
36 Remove the change rod seal from the case.
37 Remove the driveaxle seals from the case by tapping them out with a hammer and punch, working around the circumference.
38 Remove the differential bearing race.
39 Remove the breather baffle.
40 Remove the control lever spring.
41 Lift the shift fork away from the secondary gear shaft with the control lever lug aligned with the shifter fork notch and remove the shaft assembly.
42 Remove the primary shaft assembly.

6 Secondary gear shaft assembly - inspection and overhaul

Refer to illustrations 6.1, 6.2, 6.17 and 6.21

1 Remove the secondary gear shaft from the transaxle (Section 5) **(see illustration)**.
2 Place the shaft in a vise, using two blocks of wood to protect it from damage. Check the gear thrust clearances with a feeler gauge and check them against Specifications **(see illustration)**.
3 Use a puller to remove the roller bearing from the end of the shaft and lift off 4th gear.

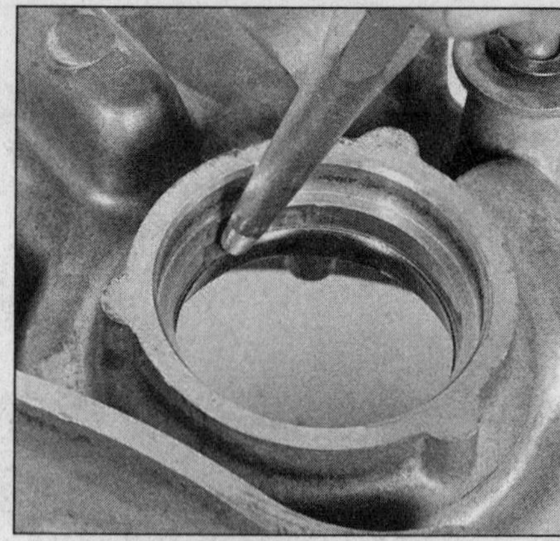

5.35 Drive the bearing race out by tapping evenly around the circumference with a punch and hammer

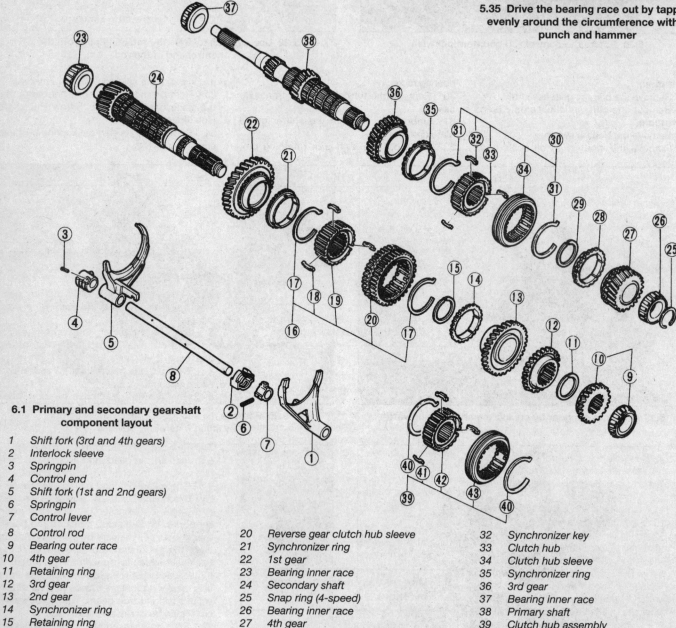

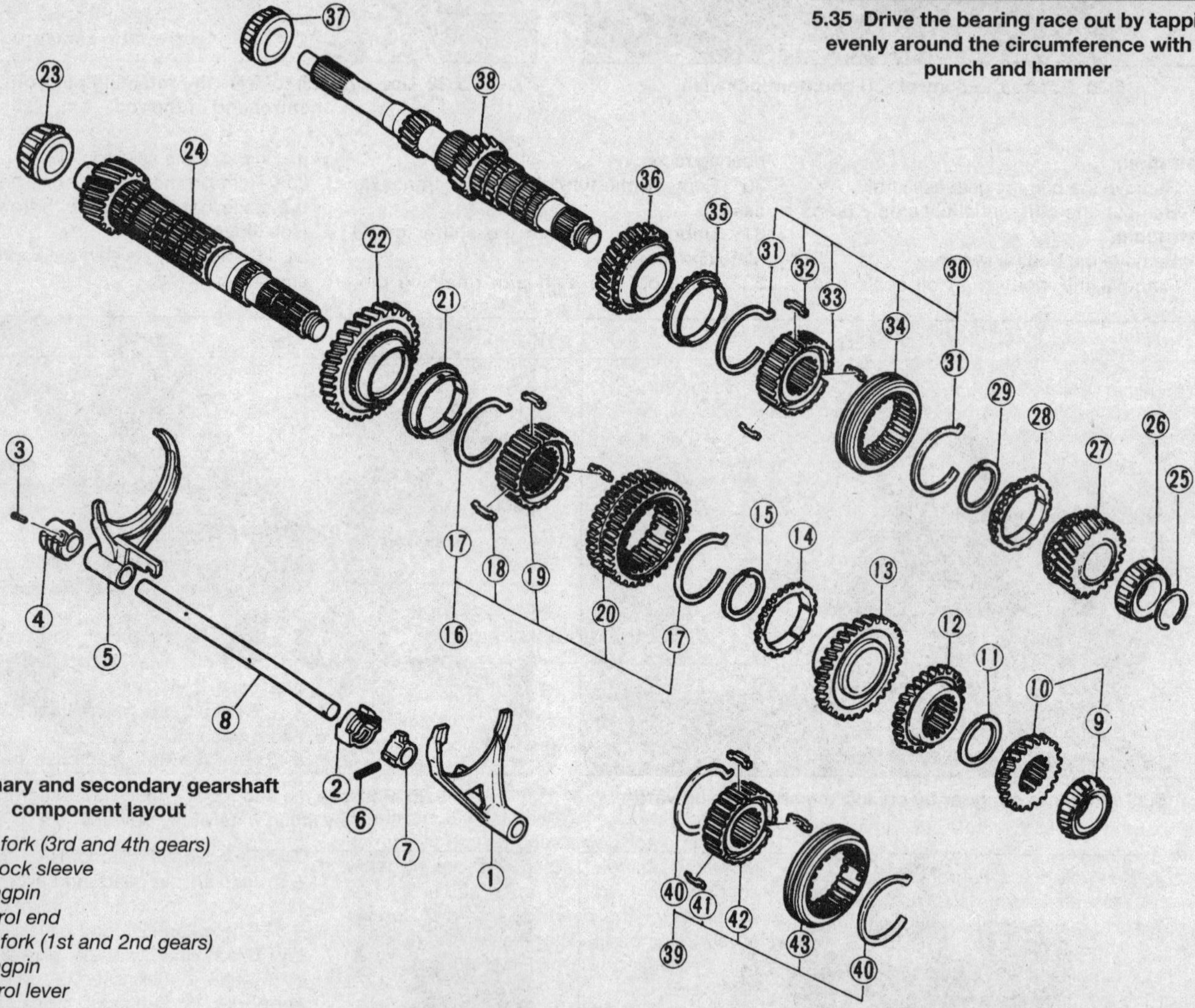

6.1 Primary and secondary gearshaft component layout

1 *Shift fork (3rd and 4th gears)*
2 *Interlock sleeve*
3 *Springpin*
4 *Control end*
5 *Shift fork (1st and 2nd gears)*
6 *Springpin*
7 *Control lever*
8 *Control rod*
9 *Bearing outer race*
10 *4th gear*
11 *Retaining ring*
12 *3rd gear*
13 *2nd gear*
14 *Synchronizer ring*
15 *Retaining ring*
16 *Clutch hub assembly*
17 *Synchronizer spring*
18 *Synchronizer key*
19 *Clutch hub*
20 *Reverse gear clutch hub sleeve*
21 *Synchronizer ring*
22 *1st gear*
23 *Bearing inner race*
24 *Secondary shaft*
25 *Snap ring (4-speed)*
26 *Bearing inner race*
27 *4th gear*
28 *Synchronizer ring*
29 *Retaining ring*
30 *3rd and 4th gear clutch hub assembly*
31 *Synchronizer spring*
32 *Synchronizer key*
33 *Clutch hub*
34 *Clutch hub sleeve*
35 *Synchronizer ring*
36 *3rd gear*
37 *Bearing inner race*
38 *Primary shaft*
39 *Clutch hub assembly*
40 *Synchronizer spring*
41 *Synchronizer key*
42 *Clutch hub*
43 *Clutch hub sleeve*

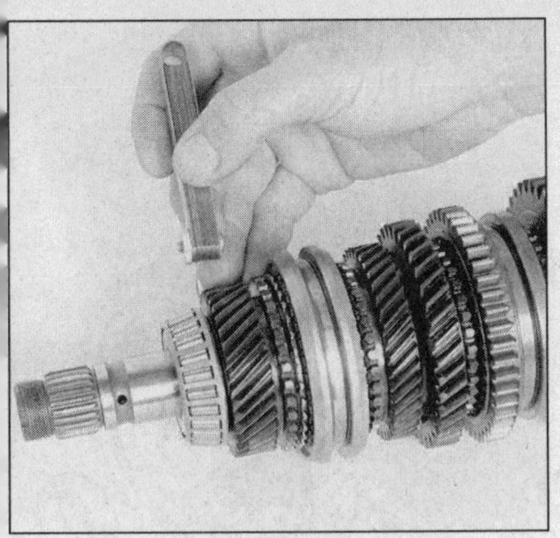

6.2 Check gear thrust clearances with a feeler gauge

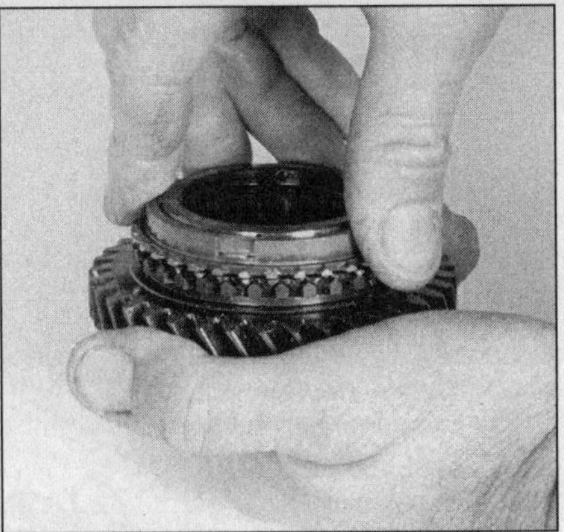

6.17 Check the synchro ring for free movement

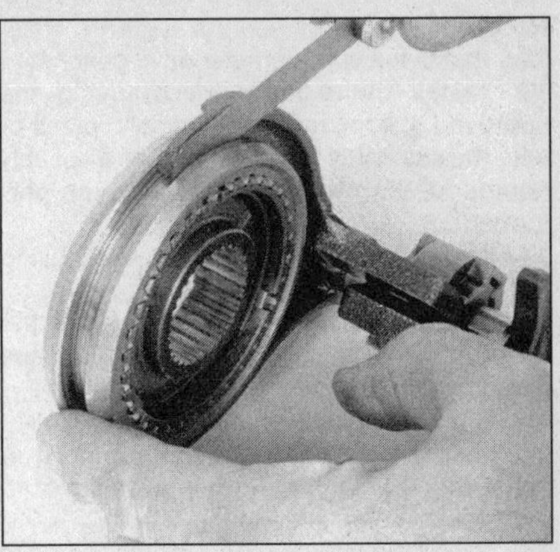

6.21 Check the clutch hub and shifter clearance

4 Remove the synchronizer ring.
5 Remove the 3rd and 4th gear clutch hub assembly retaining rings.
6 Carefully pry the 3rd and 4th gear clutch hub assembly off the shaft.
7 Remove the 3rd gear synchronizer ring.
8 Remove the 3rd gear assembly.
9 Remove the thrust washer retaining ring, followed by the thrust washers.
10 Remove 2nd gear.
11 Remove the synchronizer ring.
12 Remove the 1st gear retaining ring.
13 Special tools are required to press off the 1st gear and the 1st and 2nd gear synchronizer assembly. This operation will have to be performed by your dealer or a properly equipped shop.
14 Remove the bearing with a puller.
15 Inspect the gears for worn or damaged synchro cones, hub sleeve wear, worn or damaged teeth or worn surfaces.
16 Check the secondary shaft for worn or damaged sliding and contact surfaces, splines or teeth as well as for clogged oil passages.
17 Check the synchro rings by pressing them into position and then rotating them to make sure they slide smoothly. Measure the clearance with a feeler gauge and compare them to Specifications **(see illustration)**.
18 Inspect the clutch hub assembly and shifter for grooves, galling and wear.
19 Disassemble the synchronizer hub and inspect the splines and surfaces for wear and the springs to make sure they are not bent or weak.
20 Reassemble the hub with the raised portion of the key facing the outer edge of the hub. When installing the spring, make sure it is in the center indentation of the keys.
21 Check the clutch hub-to-shifter clearance with a feeler gauge **(see illustration)**.
22 Replace any worn or damaged components with new ones.
23 Install the bearing on the gear end of the shaft.
24 Invert the shaft and install 1st and 2nd gear clutch hubs assembly with the shift fork groove downward.
25 Install the 1st and 2nd gear assembly snap rings.
26 Install the synchro ring into the hub, aligning the groove with the keys in the hub.
27 Install 2nd gear.
28 Install the synchro ring into the hub, aligning the groove with the keys in the hub.
29 Install the thrust washer retaining rings.
30 Install 3rd gear and the 3rd gear synchro ring.
31 Install the 3rd/4th gear synchro with the grooved surfaces downward and the keys aligned. Installation may require the use of a press.
32 Install the 3rd/4th gear retaining ring.
33 Install the 4th gear synchro ring, followed by 4th gear.
34 Take the shaft to a dealer or properly equipped shop to have the bearing pressed onto the shaft.

7 Primary gear shaft assembly - inspection and overhaul

Refer to illustration 7.2

1 Remove the assembly and place it securely in a vise using wood blocks to protect the shaft surface.
2 Use a puller to remove the bearings from both ends of the shaft **(see illustration)**.
3 Inspect the shaft and gears for worn or damaged splines, sliding surfaces or damaged teeth.
4 Inspect the bearings for wear, looseness, galling or pitting of the bearing rollers.
5 Replace any worn components with new ones.
6 Press the bearings onto the shaft and reinstall the assembly.

8 Differential - inspection and overhaul

Refer to illustration 8.2

1 Remove the differential from the transaxle (Section 5) and place it securely in a vise, using wood blocks to protect the surface.

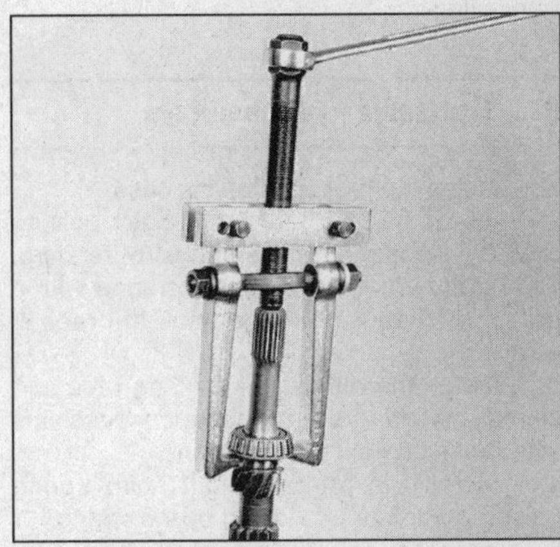

7.2 Remove the primary shaft bearing with a puller tool

2 Remove the bolts and lift the ring gear from the gear case **(see illustration on next page)**.
3 Remove the pinion shaft spring pin by driving it out from the opposite side of the gear case.
4 Remove the pinion shaft, gears and thrust washers.
5 Remove the gear case bearing inner race using a press and bearing removal tool.
6 Remove the remaining bearing with a puller.
7 Remove the speedometer drive gear.
8 Inspect the gears and sliding and contact surfaces for wear, cracks and galling.
9 Check the side and pinion gear assembly. This is done with the driveaxles inserted in the differential assembly. With the axles supported on B-blocks, measure the backlash of both pinion gears by manually moving them the full distance of free travel. If the backlash exceeds specification, obtain a thrust washer of the proper thickness from your dealer and install it between the differential case and side gears. The thrust washers should be of similar thickness.
10 Prior to reassembly, wash each part thoroughly in solvent.
11 During reassembly, apply clean transmission oil to all sliding surfaces and replace with new ones any spring pins which were

removed.
12 Install the speedometer drive gear.
13 Install the side bearings, using the approved special tool and hydraulic press or take the assembly to your dealer or a suitably equipped shop to have this operation performed.
14 Install the pinion and side gears, using the appropriate thrust washers.
15 Install the pinion shaft, making sure the spring pin hole is aligned with the hole in the gear case.
16 Install the pinion shaft lock.
17 Install the spring pin by tapping it in place with a hammer and drift, working from the speedometer gear side.
18 Install the ring gear and tighten the bolts to the specified torque.
19 Install the differential assembly in the transaxle.

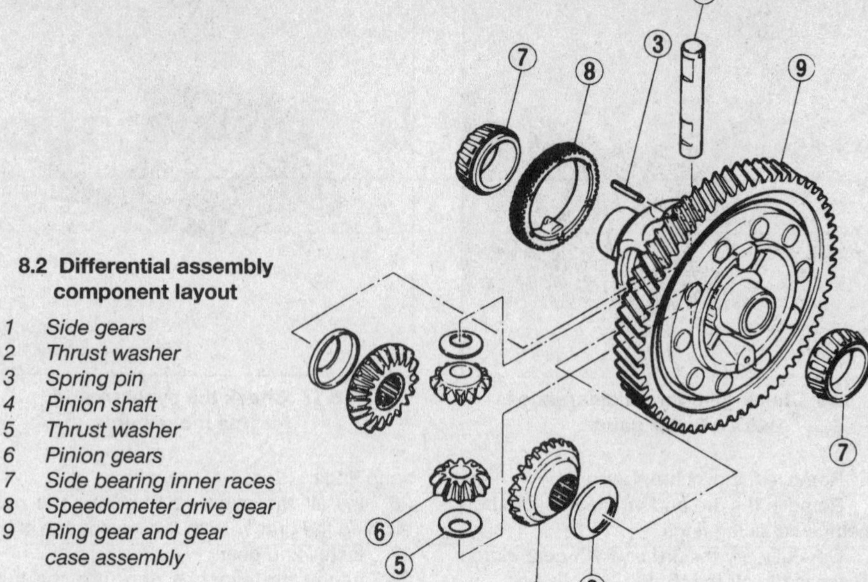

8.2 Differential assembly component layout

1 *Side gears*
2 *Thrust washer*
3 *Spring pin*
4 *Pinion shaft*
5 *Thrust washer*
6 *Pinion gears*
7 *Side bearing inner races*
8 *Speedometer drive gear*
9 *Ring gear and gear case assembly*

9 Transaxle - reassembly

1 Install the drain plug in the case.
2 Install the secondary shaft outer bearing race by placing it in position with its shim. Tap lightly around the circumference with a drift punch and a hammer until the race is seated.
3 Install the differential bearing race and shims, matching the numbers on the shims with those on the removed items.
4 Install the primary shaft shim spring (raised portion up), followed by the spring.
5 Install the reverse lever shaft and spring.
6 Install the oil deflector.
7 Install the shift rod oil seal.
8 Insert the shift rod and install the shifter, making sure the spring pin is in the proper position.
9 Place the selector rod tip through the right hole of the reverse gate and lower the assembly into position so that the shift rod can be inserted.
10 Place the reverse gate spring in position and insert the reverse shift rod through the spring on the end of the gate.
11 Position the shift arm onto the end of the shift rod.
12 Secure the selector to the shift rod with the spring pin.
13 Secure the selector guide plate with the three bolts. The bolts are dissimilar and the one without a washer is installed at the upper right corner. The reverse gate spring must be installed around the rear bolt spacer.
14 Install the lock bolt and washer onto the shift arm.
15 Install the gear lube funnel, followed by the secondary shaft bearing race.
16 Install the primary shaft seal with the open end upward.
17 Install the primary shaft bearing into the case and tap it into place.
18 Place the magnet in the slot in the transaxle case.
19 Install the differential in the case.
20 Lubricate the inner lip of the differential seal with clean transaxle oil and install it in the case.
21 Install the spring in the reverse lever shaft.
22 Position the shift fork assembly on the secondary shaft gear assembly. Use care when installing and make sure the gears are properly meshed with the differential and primary shaft. The shift fork assembly must be inserted into the proper boss in the transaxle case.
23 Carefully pull the shift fork assembly slightly upward and outward of its boss by tilting the secondary gear shaft assembly. Slide the control up as far as it will go and rotate it 90° from the Neutral position. Place the ball in the end of the reverse lever shaft and rotate the rod into the Neutral position. Carefully reinsert the rod into its transaxle case boss.
24 Install the spring pin into the shift fork assembly rod control end and tap it into place.
25 Install the crank lever assembly which connects the shift arm to the shift fork assembly rod control end.
26 Install a new O-ring on the crank lever shaft. Lubricate the crank lever with clean transaxle oil and install it. Secure the lever with the spring retaining pin.
27 Place the reverse gate in place and slide the 5th gear and reverse rod into position with the dimple on the rod facing out. The hole in the shift rod must be aligned with the reverse gate.
28 Install the reverse idler gear and shaft. Place the gear in position, insert the shaft with the shaft hole lined up with the rib in the transaxle case.
29 On 5-speed models, use RTV-type sealant to install the oil passage on the transaxle case.
30 Install the transaxle case onto the differential case, carefully placing it so the primary and secondary gear shafts seat in their bosses. It may be necessary to align the magnet with the slot in the upper case half.
31 Install the transaxle case retaining bolts and tighten them to the specified torque in a criss-cross pattern.
32 Install the primary shift rod lock bolt and seal washer. It may be necessary to lift up on the secondary shift shaft to properly align the lock bolt. Tighten the bolt securely (5-speed).
33 Install the reverse idler shaft lock bolt (5-speed).
34 Install the primary gear and locknut, with the nut finger tight (5-speed).
35 Lubricate the primary shaft gear sleeve with clean transaxle fluid and slide it into place (5-speed).
36 Lubricate and install the 5th gear.
37 Install the 5th speed synchronizer ring.
38 Install the clutch hub assembly and shift fork, aligning the keys with the slots in the synchronizer ring securing the fork with the roll pin (5-speed).
39 Install the synchronizer stopper plate (5-speed).
40 Install the secondary shaft lock nut finger tight (5-speed).
41 Tighten both locknuts and use a punch and hammer to peen the nut collars into the shaft grooves to keep them from turning (5-speed).
42 Apply sealant to the transaxle 5th speed cover and install the cover and bolts, tightening to the specified torque.
43 Install the axleshaft seals.
44 Install the backup light switch in the case.
45 Lightly lubricate the O-ring with clean transaxle oil, install it on the speedometer gear assembly. Install the speedometer gear assembly.
46 Install the transaxle (Section 4).

Chapter 7 Part B Automatic transaxle

Contents

Specifications

Torque specifications

	Ft-lbs	M-kg
Crossmember		
All 10 mm bolts	32 to 40	4.4 to 5.5
12 mm bolt	69 to 85	9.5 to 11.8
Torque converter bolt	25 to 36	3.5 to 5.0
Transaxle-to-engine bolt	66 to 86	9.1 to 11.9

1 General information

Refer to illustration 1.1

Due to the complexity of the clutches and the hydraulic control system, and because of the special tools and expertise required to perform an automatic transaxle overhaul, this should not be undertaken by the home mechanic **(see illustration)**. Therefore, the procedures in this Chapter are limited to general diagnosis, routine maintenance and adjustment, transaxle removal and installation and replacement of the input and output shaft seals.

If the transaxle requires major repair work, it should be left to a dealer service department or a transmission repair shop. You can, however, remove and install the transaxle yourself and save the expense, even if the repair work is done by a transmission specialist.

Adjustments that the home mechanic can perform include those involving the kickdown switch and solenoid, the inhibitor (neutral start) switch, vacuum diaphragm and the shift linkage. **Caution:** *Never tow a disabled vehicle at speeds greater than 30 mph or distances over 50 miles unless the front wheels are off the ground. Failure to observe this precaution may result in severe transmission damage caused by lack of lubrication.*

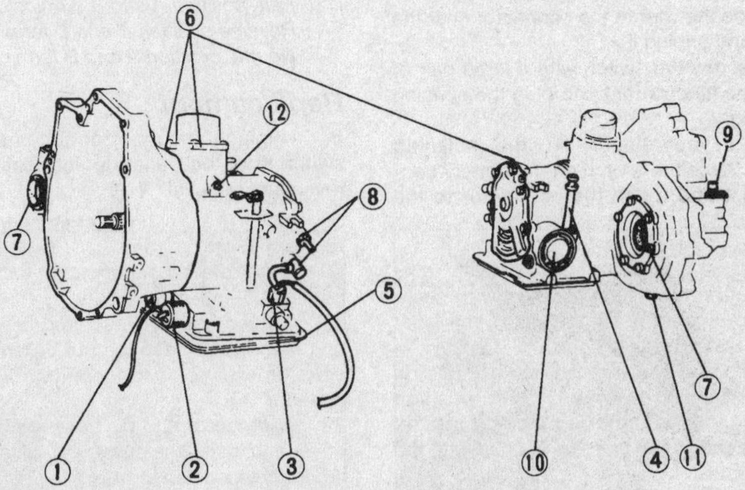

1.1 Automatic transaxle details

1 Vacuum diaphragm
2 Kickdown solenoid
3 Inhibitor switch
4 Oil level tube
5 Oil pan
6 Case
7 Oil seal
8 Oil pipe
9 Speedometer gear
10 Servo retainer
11 Drain plug
12 Fluid pressure detection plug

7B

2 Diagnosis - general

Automatic transmission malfunctions may be caused by four general conditions: poor engine performance, improper adjustments, hydraulic malfunctions and mechanical malfunctions. Diagnosis of these problems should always begin with a check of the easily repaired items: fluid level and condition, shift linkage adjustment and throttle linkage adjustment. Next, perform a road test to determine if the problem has been corrected or if more diagnosis is necessary. If the problem persists after the preliminary tests and corrections are completed, additional diagnosis should be done by a dealer service department or a transmission repair shop.

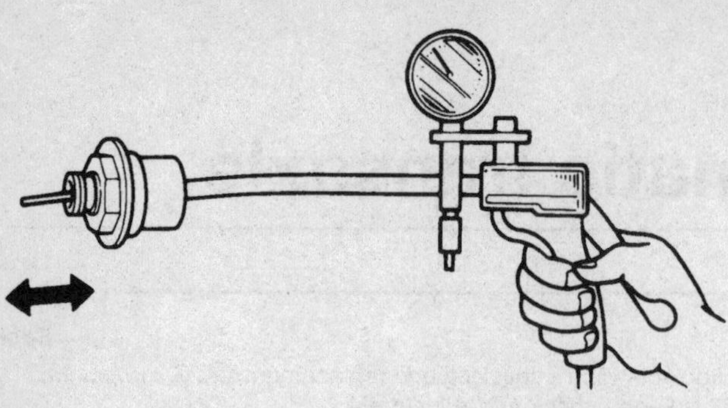

3.4 Checking the vacuum diaphragm

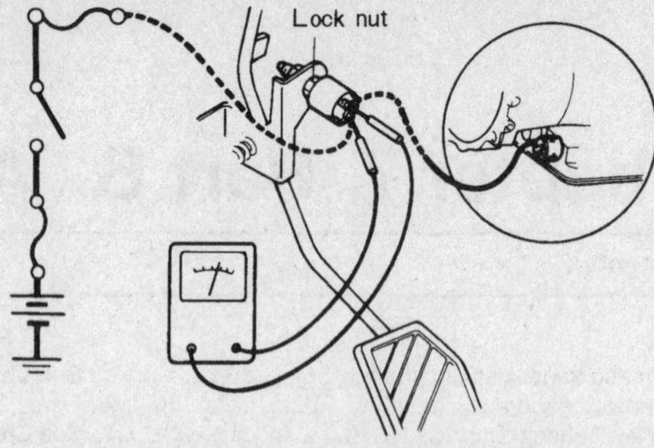

4.2 Checking the kickdown switch for continuity

3 Vacuum diaphragm - testing and replacement

Refer to illustration 3.4

1 Symptoms of a fault in the vacuum diaphragm include vibration during shifts and incomplete shifts.

2 Drain approximately one quart of fluid from the transaxle so the level will be below the vacuum diaphragm (Chapter 1).

3 Disconnect the vacuum hose and remove the vacuum diaphragm from the transaxle.

4 Connect a vacuum pump to the diaphragm and check that the rod moves when vacuum is applied **(see illustration)**. If the rod does not move or moves less than one inch, replace the diaphragm with a new one.

5 After installation, check the fluid level and add as necessary (Chapter 1).

4 Kickdown switch - checking and adjustment

1 If the transaxle will not shift down when the throttle pedal is fully depressed and the kickdown solenoid is operating properly (Section 5), the kickdown switch could be faulty or out of adjustment.

Checking

Refer to illustration 4.2

2 With the throttle pedal completely depressed, use an ohmmeter to make sure there is continuity between the terminals as shown **(see illustration)**.

Adjustment

3 Loosen the locknut and turn the kickdown switch until the ohmmeter indicates continuity when the throttle pedal is depressed seven-eighths of full travel. Tighten the locknut.

5 Kickdown solenoid - checking

Refer to illustrations 5.4 and 5.5

1 A fault in the kickdown solenoid is indicated if the transaxle will not shift down when the throttle is depressed or if the downshift is hesitant or rough.

2 Raise the front of the vehicle and support it securely on jackstands.

3 Trace the wire to the connector near the battery and unplug it.

4 Unscrew the switch with a large pair of pliers **(see illustration)** and plug the opening with a rag.

5 Hold your finger on the solenoid plunger. Place the switch on the battery negative post and touch the connector to the positive post to make sure the plunger retracts **(see illustration)**.

6 Replace the solenoid switch with a new one if there is any doubt about its condition.

6 Inhibitor switch - checking and replacement

Checking

Refer to illustrations 6.3a and 6.3b

1 Check the inhibitor switch for proper operation by making sure that the engine starts only with the shifter in the Park and Neutral positions.

2 Trace the wire from the switch to the connector and unplug the connector.

3 Check the switch connector terminals for continuity in Park, Reverse and Neutral with an ohmmeter **(see illustrations)**.

4 With the ignition on and the shifter in the noted positions, there should be continuity between **(see illustration 6.3b)**:

Park position A and B terminals
Reverse position C and D terminals
Neutral position A and B terminals

Replacement

5 Unplug the connector and unscrew the switch from the transaxle. Installation is the reverse of removal.

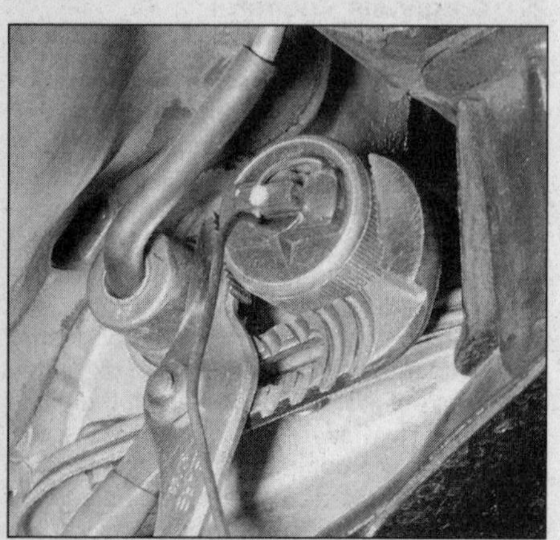

5.4 Use large pliers to unscrew the kickdown solenoid from the transaxle case

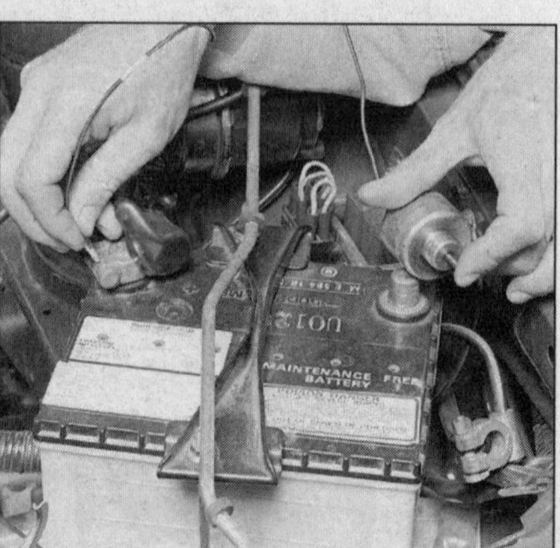

5.5 Testing the kickdown solenoid

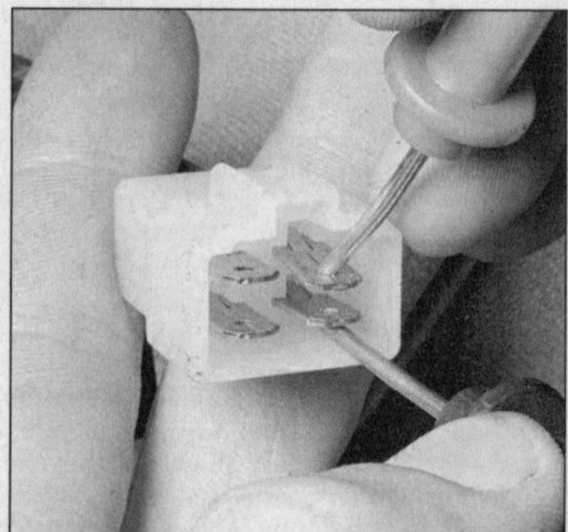

6.3a Checking the inhibitor switch

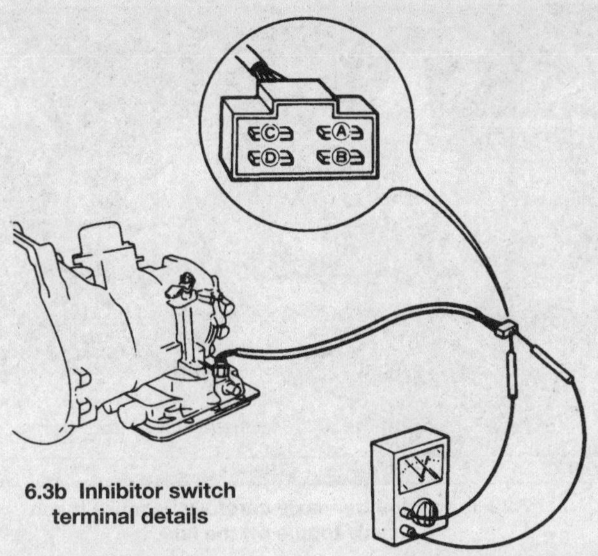

6.3b Inhibitor switch terminal details

7.3 Use needle nose pliers to remove the shift cable retaining clip

7.8 The engine must be supported during transaxle removal

7.11 Transaxle bolt locations (arrows)

7 Transaxle - removal and installation

Removal

Refer to illustrations 7.3, 7.8, 7.11, 7.16, 7.17 and 7.22

1 Disconnect the battery negative cable.
2 Disconnect the speedometer cable.
3 Disconnect the shift control cable from the transaxle **(see illustration)**.
4 Disconnect the battery negative cable and ground wires from the transaxle.
5 Disconnect the inhibitor switch and kickdown solenoid.
6 Remove the starter motor (Chapter 5).
7 There are two principal ways of supporting the weight of the engine during the removal of the transaxle. A special support fixture can be obtained which rests on the suspension strut mount towers or an engine hoist can be used. If the engine support fixture is being used, install it at this time. If the engine hoist is being used to support the engine, the hood must be removed to gain sufficient clearance (see Chapter 11).
8 Connect the support to the engine and raise the vehicle to provide sufficient clearance for lowering the transaxle and support it securely on jackstands **(see illustration)**.
9 Disconnect the oil cooler lines at the transaxle.
10 Disconnect and tag any remaining vacuum or electrical connectors that are attached to the transaxle or will interfere with the removal of the transaxle.
11 Remove the upper transaxle-to-engine bolts **(see illustration)**.
12 Remove the front wheels and splash shields.
13 Disconnect the stabilizer bar, remove the lower balljoint-to-steering knuckle bolts and nuts and separate the balljoint from the knuckle (Chapter 10).
14 Remove the right driveaxle and disconnect the left driveaxle from the transaxle (Chapter 8). Use a piece of wire to fasten the left driveaxle out of the way.
15 Remove the joint shaft and bracket assembly (Chapter 8).
16 Remove the torque converter access plate and separating plate **(see illustration)**.
17 With an assistant rotating the engine

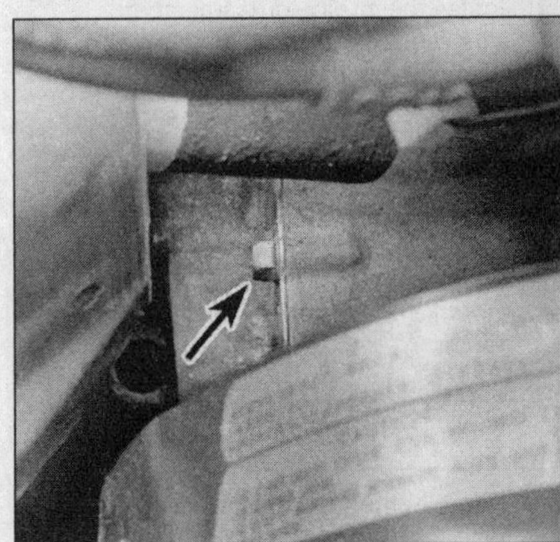

7.16 Torque converter access cover bolt location (arrow)

7.17 Lock the flywheel gear teeth with a screwdriver when removing the torque converter bolts

7.22 Lower the transaxle carefully because it can easily topple off the jack

with a wrench on the crankshaft pulley bolt to bring them into position, remove the torque converter bolts **(see illustration)**.

18 Remove all but two of the crossmember assembly bolts.

19 Place a jack under the crossmember, remove the bolts and lower the crossmember assembly.

20 Support the transaxle with the jack.

21 Making sure the engine weight is supported by the lift, remove the two lower transaxle-to-engine bolts.

22 Slide the transaxle away from the engine and carefully lower the jack until it is clear of the vehicle **(see illustration)**.

Installation

23 Raise the transaxle into position while an assistant guides it, making sure the torque converter is not dislodged.

24 Install the transaxle-to-engine mounting bolts, tightening to the specified torque.

25 Install the engine crossmember.

26 The rest of the installation procedure is the reverse of the removal procedure with the following notes:

a) *Make sure all nuts and bolts are torqued to the proper value.*
b) *The suspension alignment should be checked by a dealer or suitably equipped shop.*
c) *Check the transaxle fluid level* (Chapter 1).

8 Transaxle seals - replacement

1 Remove the transaxle (Section 7).

Input shaft seal

Refer to illustrations 8.2 and 8.3

2 Pry the old seal out using a small screwdriver or punch **(see illustration)**.

3 Coat the inner circumference of the seal with clean engine oil and tap it into the bore until it is flush with the housing **(see illustration)**.

8.2 Use a punch or similar tool to pry the input shaft seal out of its bore

8.3 The head of the punch and hammer can be used to seat the new seal fully into the bore

Axleshaft seals

Refer to illustrations 8.4 and 8.5

4 Pry the old seal out with a screwdriver **(see illustration)**.

5 Lubricate the inner circumference of the new seal with clean engine oil or white lithium base grease. Place the lip of the new seal into a piece of pipe or a large socket of 1-3/4 inch diameter and tap it evenly into the bore **(see illustration)**.

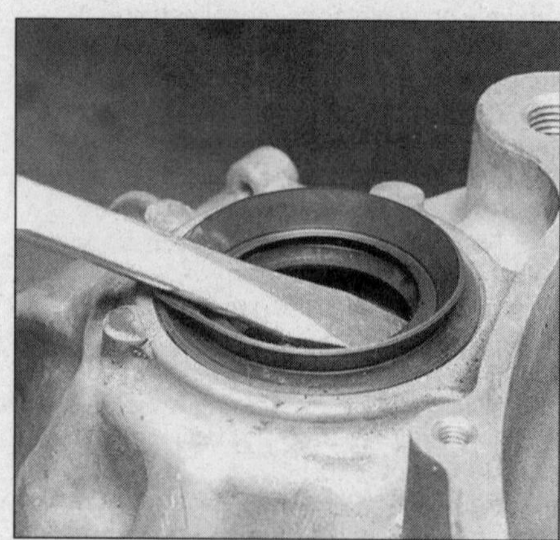

8.4 Pry out the old axleshaft seal with a screwdriver

8.5 Use a socket and rubber mallet to tap the new axleshaft seal fully into the transaxle case bore

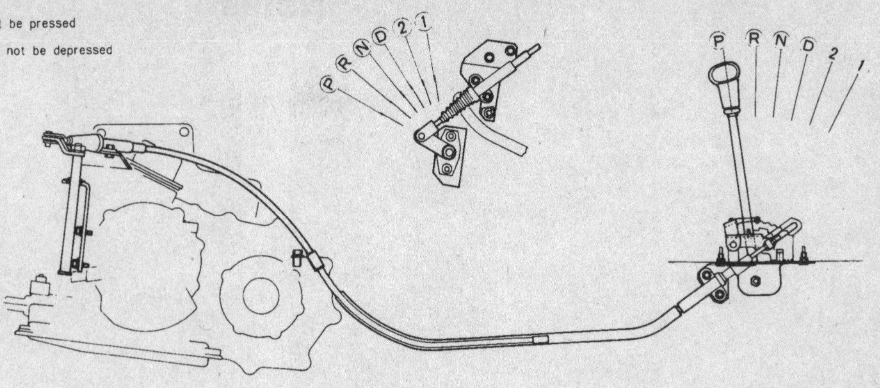

9.1 Shift linkage detent positions

9 Shift linkage - check and adjustment

Refer to illustrations 9.1 and 9.3

1 Move the shifter through each position, making sure the movement into each detent is positive and corresponds to the shifter plate **(see illustration)**. Slight resistance should be felt entering each detent.

2 The shifter should move between Drive and Neutral without the need to depress the button on the shifter handle. The button must be depressed when moving from Drive to Reverse.

3 If the button is loose or if the shifter can be moved from Drive to Reverse without pressing the button, adjust the shifter knob **(see illustration)**. Loosen the locknut, twist the shifter knob until proper operation of the linkage is attained and tighten the locknut.

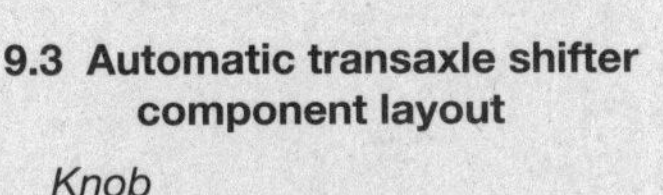

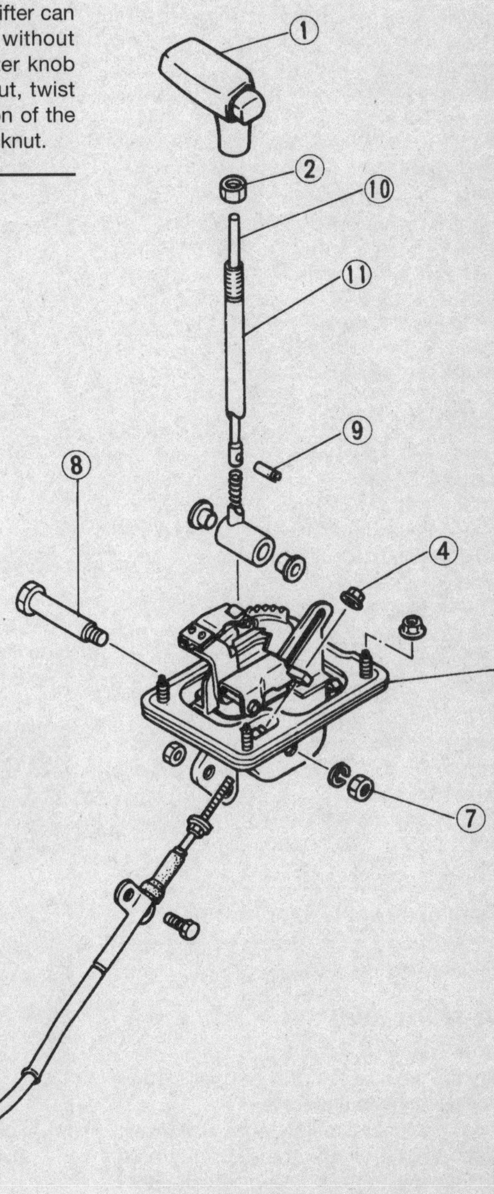

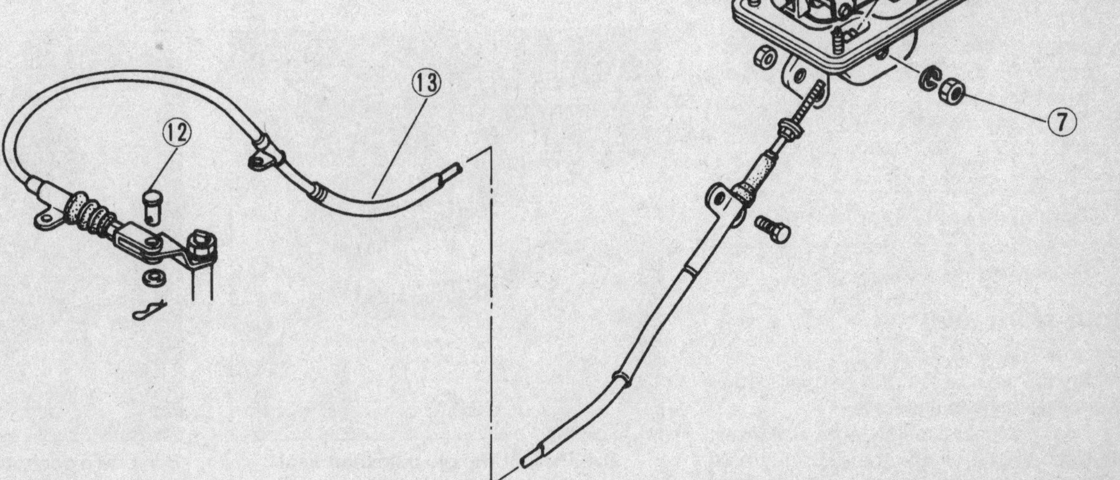

9.3 Automatic transaxle shifter component layout

1 *Knob*
2 *Knob locknut*
4 *Cable locknut*
6 *Shifter lever bracket*
7 *Nut and washer*
8 *Lever mounting bolt*
9 *Guide pin*
10 *Push rod*
11 *Shifter lever*
12 *Cable-to-transaxle pin*
13 *Shifter cable*

Notes

Chapter 8
Clutch and driveaxles

Contents

Specifications

Clutch pilot bearing-to-crankshaft end surface clearance (Dimension A in illustration 8.16c)	0.087 to 0.110 in
Hydraulic clutch minimum disengagement height	2.7 in (68 mm)

Torque specifications

Torque specifications	Ft-lbs	M-kg (unless otherwise indicated
Clutch release lever and fork bolt	20	2.7
Clutch pressure plate-to-flywheel bolt	13 to 20	1.8 to 2.7
Flywheel bolt		
1983 through 1984 models	71 to 76	9.8 to 10.5
1985 models	108 to 116	14.5 to 16.0
1986 and later models	71 to 75	96 to 103 Nm
Clutch cover-to-flywheel	13 to 20.3	18 to 26 Nm
Clutch master cylinder mounting bolts	14 to 19	19 to 26 Nm
Clutch release cylinder mounting bolts	14 to 19	19 to 26 Nm
Stabilizer bar nut	9 to 13	1.2 to 1.8
Steering knuckle-to-shock absorber bolt	69 to 86	9.5 to 11.9
Steering knuckle-to-balljoint	32 to 40	4.4 to 5.5
Wheel nut	65 to 87	9.0 to 12.0

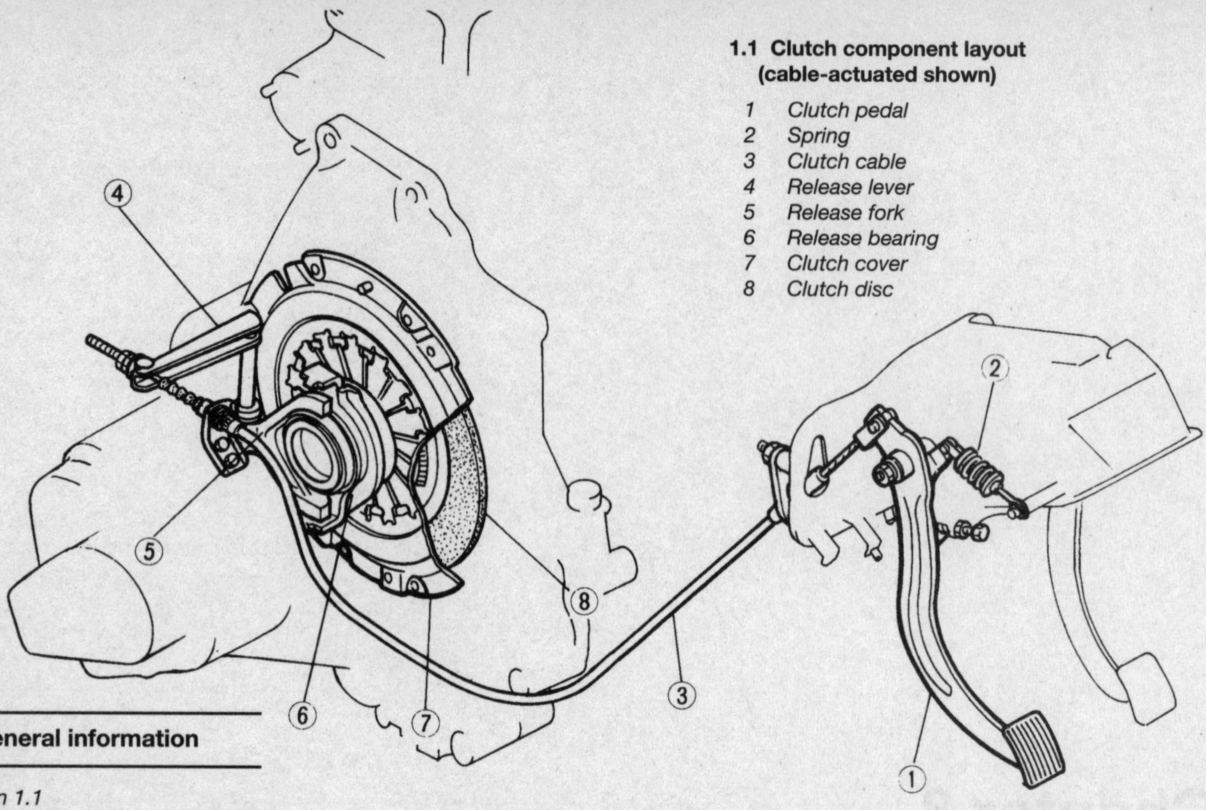

1.1 Clutch component layout (cable-actuated shown)

1 *Clutch pedal*
2 *Spring*
3 *Clutch cable*
4 *Release lever*
5 *Release fork*
6 *Release bearing*
7 *Clutch cover*
8 *Clutch disc*

1 Clutch - general information

Refer to illustration 1.1

Manual transaxle equipped vehicles use a single dry plate, diaphragm spring-type clutch. Operation is through a foot pedal, cable or hydraulic actuation, release lever and fork assembly and a release bearing **(see illustration)**.

Models through 1985 used a clutch system actuated by a cable. Beginning in 1986, a hydraulic actuation system, using a master cylinder and slave cylinder, became available.

2 Clutch operation - checking

Cable-operated clutch

1 Before performing any operations on the clutch, several checks can be made to determine if there is actually a fault in the clutch itself.

2 With the engine running and the brake applied, hold the clutch pedal approximately 1/2-inch from the floor and shift back and forth several times. If the shifts are smooth, the clutch is releasing properly. If it is not the clutch is not releasing fully and the linkage should be checked.

3 Inspect the clutch pedal bushings for wear or binding.

4 Refer to Chapter 1 for further information on clutch and clutch pedal adjustment.

Hydraulic clutch

5 1986 and later models are equipped with a clutch release system operated by hydraulic pressure. The hydraulic release system consists of the clutch pedal, master cylinder and fluid reservoir, the hydraulic line, slave cylinder that actuates the clutch release lever, and the clutch release bearing. Refer to Chapter 1 for information on adjustments involved with the hydraulic clutch system.

6 Other than replacing components that have obvious damage, some preliminary checks should be performed to diagnose a clutch system failure. The first check should be of the fluid level in the clutch master cylinder. If the fluid level is low, add fluid as necessary and inspect the hydraulic clutch system for leaks. To check for complete clutch release, check the release cylinder push-rod travel. With the clutch pedal depressed completely, the release cylinder push-rod should extend substantially.

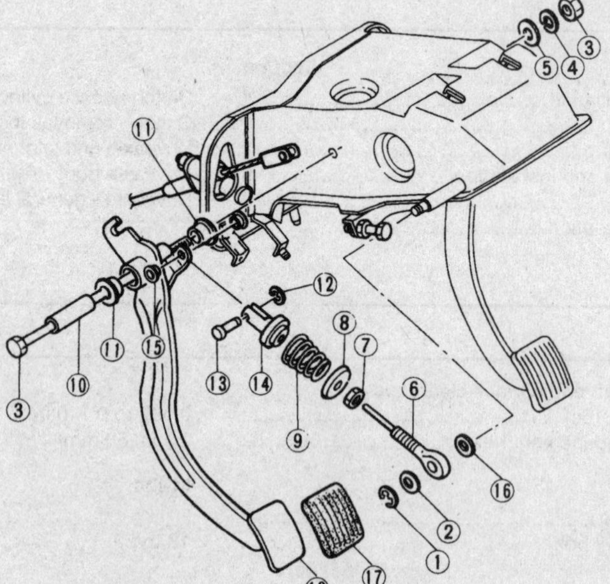

3.2 Clutch pedal installation details (cable-actuated shown)

1 *Clip*
2 *Though bolt and washer*
3 *Bolt and nut*
4 *Spring washer*
5 *Plain washer*
6 *Rod*
7 *Nut*
8 *Assist seat*
9 *Assist spring*
10 *Spacer*
11 *Bushings*
12 *Clip*
13 *Pin*
14 *Spring seat*
15 *Bushings*
16 *Plain washer*
17 *Pad*
18 *Clutch pedal*

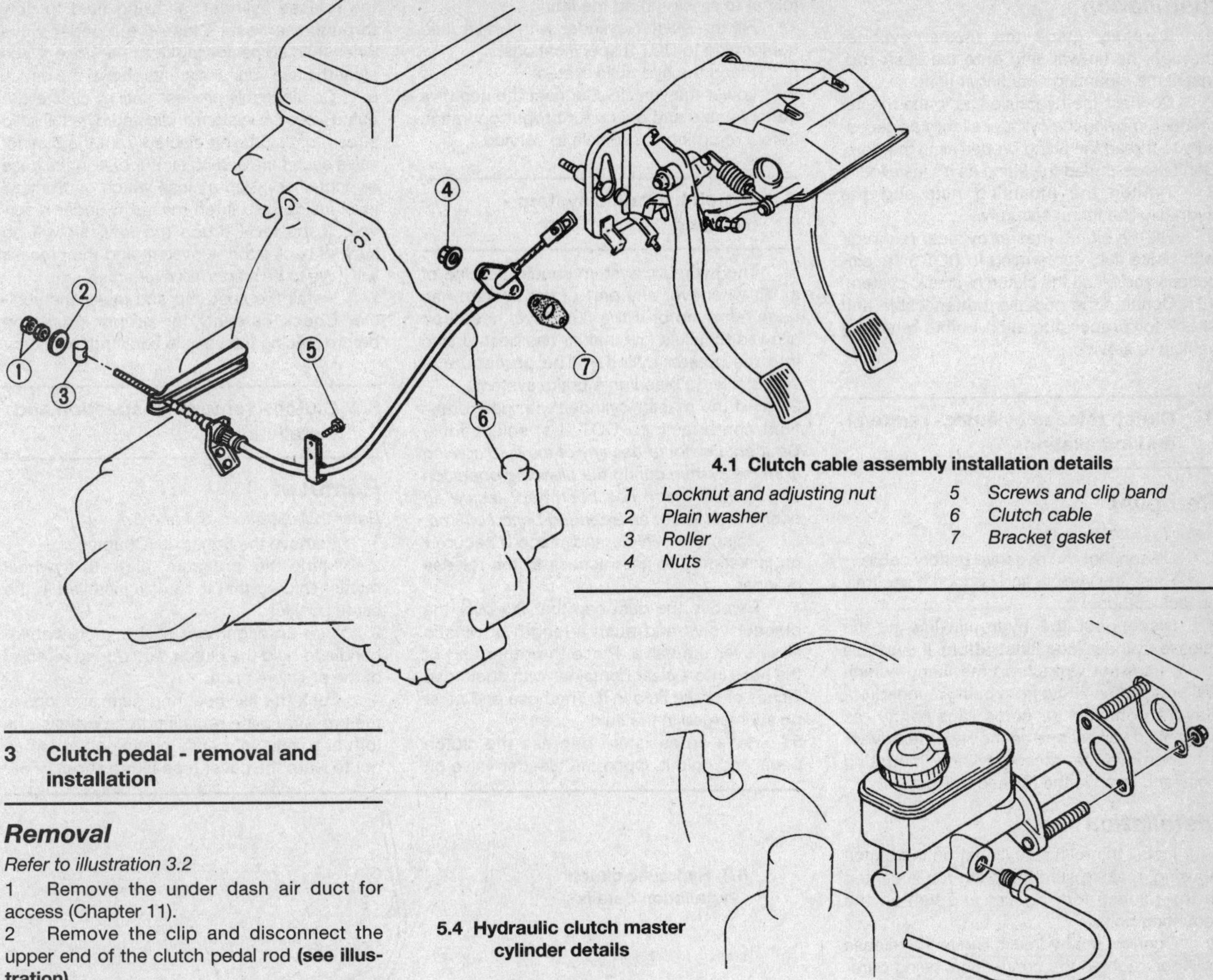

4.1 Clutch cable assembly installation details

1. Locknut and adjusting nut
2. Plain washer
3. Roller
4. Nuts
5. Screws and clip band
6. Clutch cable
7. Bracket gasket

5.4 Hydraulic clutch master cylinder details

3 Clutch pedal - removal and installation

Removal

Refer to illustration 3.2

1 Remove the under dash air duct for access (Chapter 11).

2 Remove the clip and disconnect the upper end of the clutch pedal rod **(see illustration)**.

3 Remove the pedal through bolt and nut, disengage the clutch cable or hydraulic master cylinder rod and remove the pedal and rod assembly from the vehicle.

Installation

4 Prior to installation, lubricate the pedal bushing and cable hook liberally with lithium base grease.

5 Place the pedal in position, install the through bolt and nut and connect the clutch cable or master cylinder rod.

6 Connect the pedal rod.

7 Refer to Chapter 1 and check the clutch pedal height and free play, adjusting as necessary.

8 Install the air duct.

4 Clutch cable - removal and installation

Removal

Refer to illustration 4.1

1 In the engine compartment, remove the locknut, adjusting nut and washer from the end of the cable and disengage it from the release lever **(see illustration)**.

2 Pull the cable from the bracket on the transaxle.

3 Remove the clip band and bracket retaining the cable.

4 Inside the passenger compartment remove the under dash air duct for clearance.

5 Disengage the cable from the pedal and remove it from the vehicle.

Installation

6 Prior to installation, lubricate the contact surfaces of the roller and the release lever.

7 Insert the cable through the firewall and connect it to the clutch pedal.

8 Insert the cable in the release arm and install the bracket and clip band.

9 Install the washer, adjusting nut and locknut.

10 Adjust the pedal free play (Chapter 1).

11 Install the air duct.

5 Clutch master cylinder - removal and installation

Removal

Refer to illustration 5.4

1 Disconnect the negative battery cable.

2 On some models, it may be necessary to remove the ABS relay box.

3 Disconnect the hydraulic line at the clutch master cylinder. If available, use a flare-nut wrench on the fitting, which will prevent the fitting from being rounded off. Have rags or a container handy as some fluid will be lost as the line is removed. **Caution:** *Don't allow brake fluid to come into contact with the paint, as it will damage the finish.*

4 Remove the nuts which secure the master cylinder to the engine firewall **(see illustration)**. You will find one nut on the firewall and the other nut under the dash on the brake pedal bracket.

5 Carefully guide the master cylinder off the push-rod and through the firewall.

Installation

6 Carefully guide the master cylinder through the firewall and onto the push-rod. Install the mounting nuts finger tight.

7 Connect the hydraulic line to the master cylinder, moving the cylinder slightly as necessary to thread the fitting properly into the bore. Don't cross-thread the fitting as it's installed.

8 Tighten the mounting nuts and the hydraulic line fitting securely.

9 Fill the clutch master cylinder reservoir with brake fluid conforming to DOT 3 specifications and bleed the clutch hydraulic system.

10 Connect the negative battery cable and check for proper operation before returning vehicle to service.

6 Clutch release cylinder - removal and installation

Removal

Refer to illustration 6.3

1 Disconnect the negative battery cable.

2 Raise the vehicle and support it securely on jack stands.

3 Disconnect the hydraulic line at the release cylinder **(see illustration)**. If available use a flare-nut wrench on the fitting, which will prevent the fitting from being rounded off. Have a container or some rags handy, as some fluid will escape as the line is removed.

4 Remove the release cylinder mounting bolts and remove the release cylinder.

Installation

5 Install the release cylinder on the clutch housing, making sure the push-rod is seated in the release fork pocket and tighten the mounting bolts.

6 Connect the hydraulic line to the release cylinder. Tighten the connection, being careful not to cross-thread the fitting.

7 Fill the master cylinder with brake fluid conforming to DOT 3 specifications.

8 Bleed the hydraulic system.

9 Lower the vehicle. Connect the negative battery cable and check for proper operation before returning the vehicle to service.

7 Clutch hydraulic system - bleeding

1 The hydraulic system should be bled of all air whenever any part of the system has been removed or if the fluid level has been allowed to fall so low that air has been drawn into the master cylinder. The procedure is very similar to bleeding a brake system.

2 Fill the master cylinder with new brake fluid conforming to DOT 3 specifications. **Caution:** *Do not re-use any of the fluid coming from the system during the bleeding operation or use fluid which has been kept inside an open container for an extended period of time.*

3 Raise the vehicle and place it securely on jackstands to gain access to the release cylinder.

4 Remove the dust cap that fits over the bleeder valve and push a length of plastic hose over the valve. Place the other end of the hose into a clear container with about two inches of brake fluid in it. The hose end must be submerged in the fluid.

5 Have an assistant depress the clutch pedal and hold it. Open the bleeder valve on the release cylinder, allowing fluid to flow through the hose. Close the bleeder valve when fluid stops flowing from the hose. Once closed, have your assistant release the pedal.

6 Continue this process until all air is evacuated from the system, indicated by a full solid stream of fluid being ejected from the bleeder valve each time and no air bubbles in the hose or container. Keep a close watch on the fluid level inside the clutch master cylinder reservoir; if the level drops too low, air will be sucked back into the system and the process will have to be started all over again.

7 Install the dust cap and lower the vehicle. Check carefully for proper operation before placing the vehicle back into service.

8 Clutch - removal, inspection and installation

Removal

Refer to illustrations 8.4 and 8.7

1 Remove the transaxle (Chapter 7).

2 Mark the pressure plate-to-flywheel relationship so that it can be installed in the same position.

3 Use an alignment tool or screwdriver handle to hold the clutch disc during removal of the pressure plate.

4 Lock the flywheel ring gear and loosen the pressure plate retaining bolts evenly, one turn at a time, in a criss-cross pattern so as not to warp the cover **(see illustration)**.

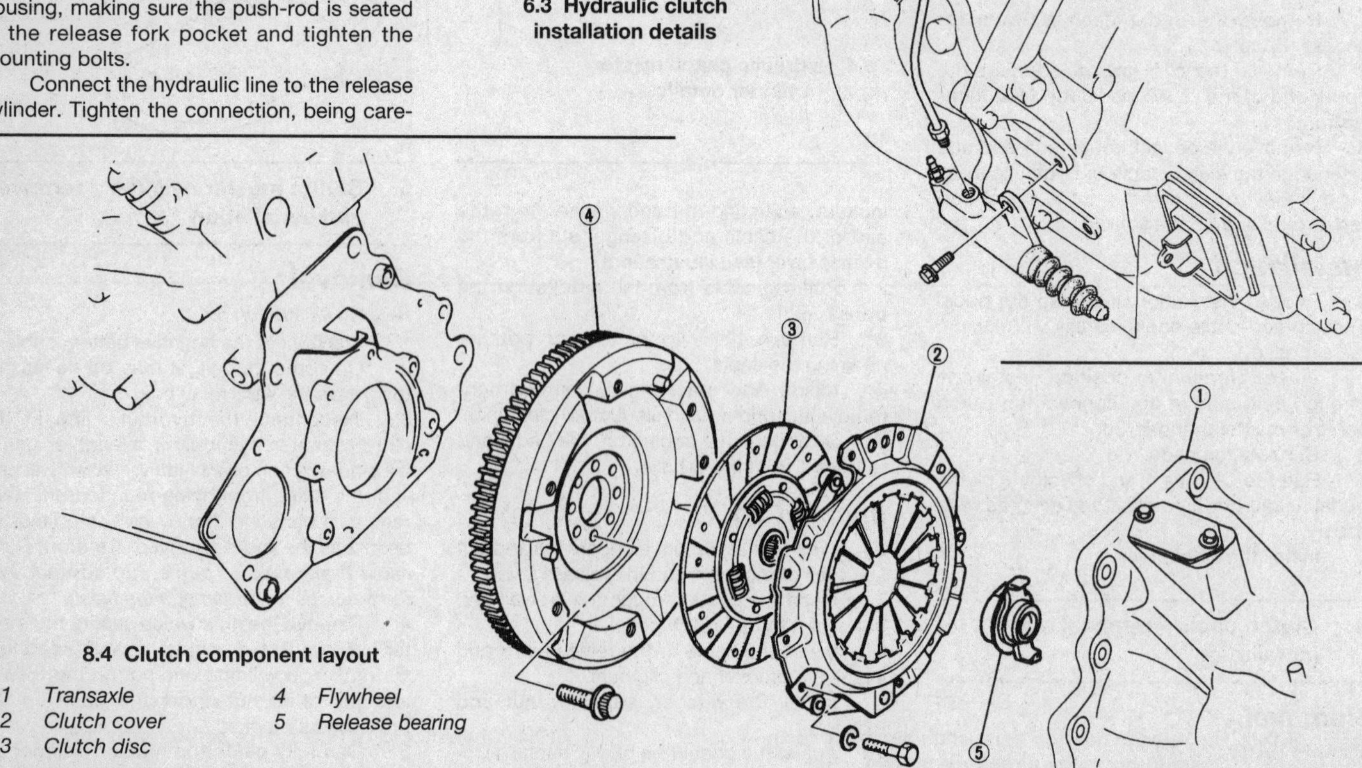

6.3 Hydraulic clutch installation details

8.4 Clutch component layout

1 Transaxle
2 Clutch cover
3 Clutch disc
4 Flywheel
5 Release bearing

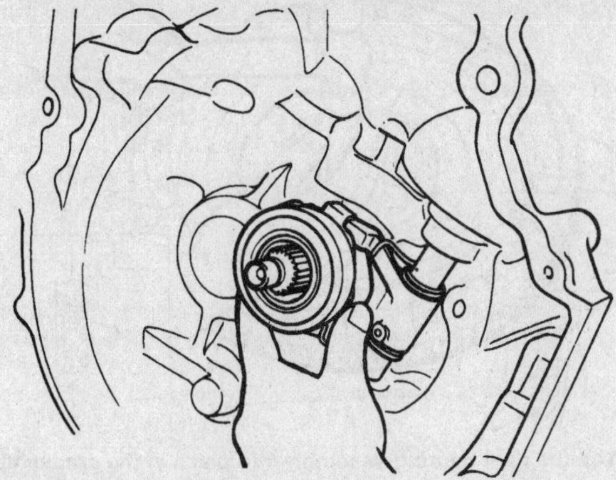
8.7 Removing the clutch release bearing

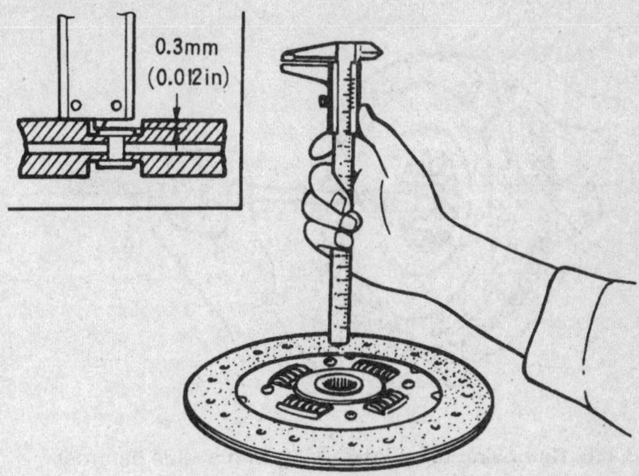

8.12 Measuring the clutch lining

5 Remove the pressure plate and clutch disc.
6 Handle the disc carefully, taking care not to touch the lining surface, and set it aside.
7 Disconnect the return spring from the release fork hook, twist the release lever and remove the release bearing **(see illustration)**.
8 Remove the release fork bolt and lift the fork and lever away as a unit.

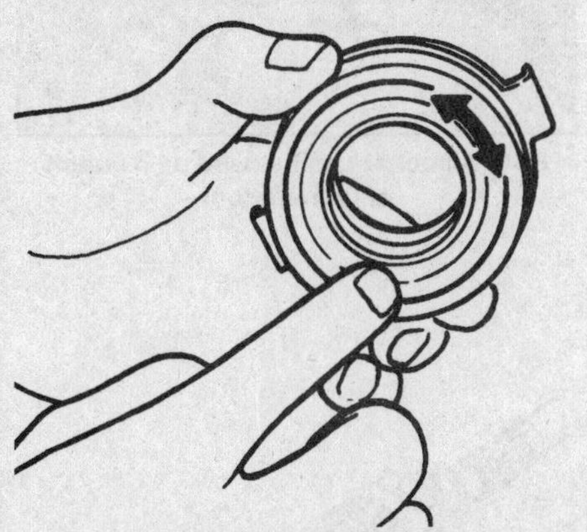
8.14a Check the release bearing to make sure that it rotates smoothly

Inspection

Refer to illustrations 8.12, 8.14a, 8.14b, 8.16a. 8.16b and 8.16c

9 Clean the dust out of the clutch housing using a vacuum cleaner or clean cloth. Do not use compressed air as the dust can endanger your health if inhaled.
10 Inspect the pressure plate for damage and wear of the diaphragm spring, scratches, scoring or color changes (indicating overheating) of the friction surface and damage or distortion of the cover. Although minor imperfections of the friction surface can be removed with fine sandpaper, the pressure plate should be replaced with a new unit if there is any doubt as to its condition.
11 Inspect the surface of the flywheel for signs of uneven contact, indicating improper mounting or damaged clutch springs. Check the surface for burned areas, grooves, cracks or other signs of wear. It may be necessary to remove a badly grooved flywheel and have it machined to restore the surface. Light glazing of the flywheel surface can be removed with fine sandpaper.
12 Inspect the clutch lining for contamination by oil, grease or any other substance and replace the disc with a new one if any is present. Check for wear by measuring the distance from the rivet head to the material surface and checking this measurement against those in the Specifications Section **(see illustration)**.
13 Inspect the disc for distortion, wear, loose rivets, weak springs and damaged splines. Slide the disc onto the input shaft temporarily to make sure the fit is snug and the splines are not burred or worn. Replace the disc with a new one if there is any question as to its condition.
14 Check the release bearing for wear and distortion and make sure that it turns and slides easily on the input shaft **(see illustrations)**. Unless the vehicle has very low miles, it is a good idea to replace the bearing with a new one whenever the clutch is removed.
15 Inspect the clutch housing mounting surface, release lever and return spring for wear, cracking, distortion, damage and fatigue, replacing as necessary.
16 Check the pilot bearing in the crankshaft to make sure it turns easily and smoothly by applying force with your finger and rotating it **(see illustration)**. Replace the bearing if necessary by removing it with a slide hammer

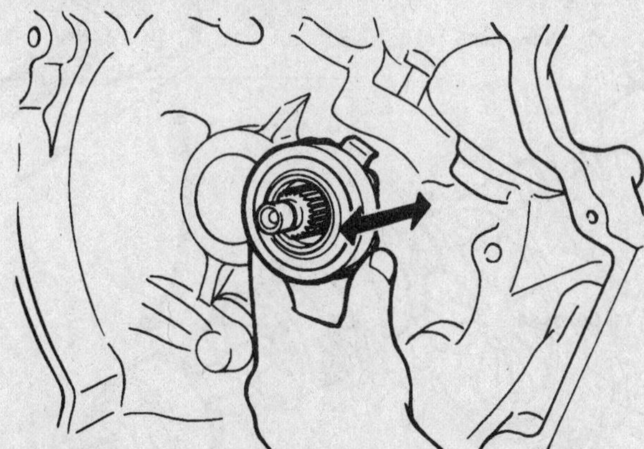
8.14b The release bearing must slide back and forth smoothly in the directions shown

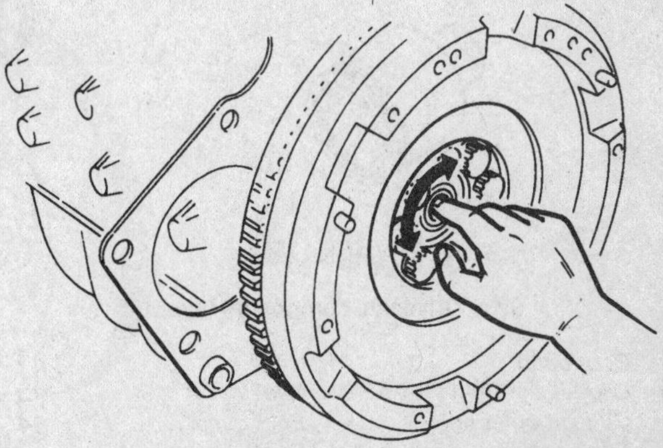
8.16a Check the pilot bearing for smooth rotation

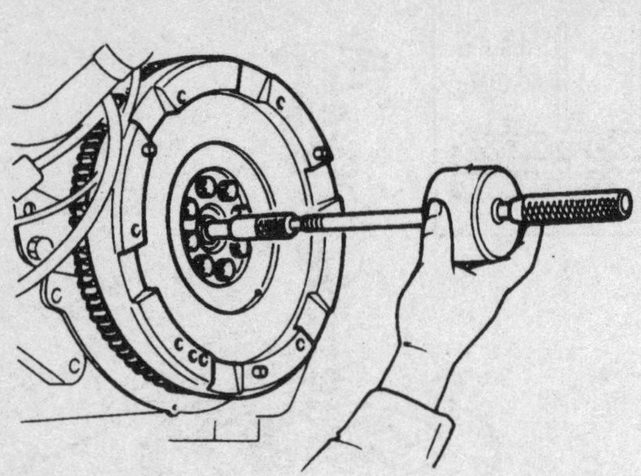
8.16b Removing the pilot bearing with a slide hammer

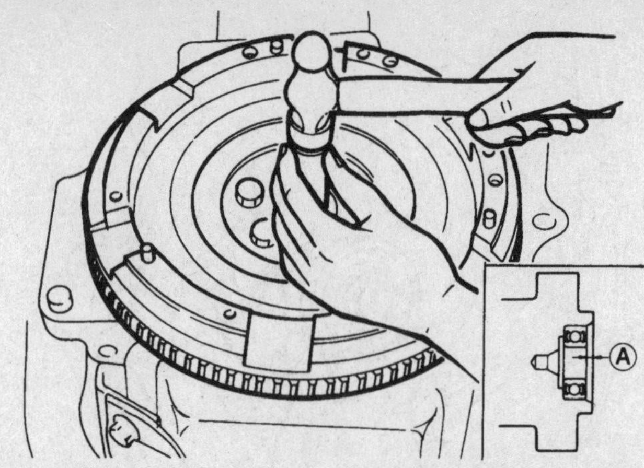

8.16c Tap the pilot bearing assembly into place in the crankshaft

and tapping a new one into the crankshaft bore using a socket or piece of pipe and a hammer **(see illustrations)**.

Installation

Refer to illustration 8.18

17 Prior to installation, lubricate the clutch release bearing, input shaft and clutch disc splines lightly with moly-base grease.

18 With the disc held in place by an alignment tool or socket **(see illustration)**, place the pressure plate in position and align it with any marks made prior to removal.

19 Install the bolts and tighten them in a criss-cross pattern, one or two turns at a time, until they are tightened to the specified torque.

20 Install the release lever, fork, spring and bearing.

21 Remove the alignment tool and install the transaxle.

9 Driveaxle - general information

Refer to illustrations 9.1a, 9.1b and 9.1c

Power is transmitted from the transaxle to the front wheels by driveaxles, which consist of splined solid axles with constant velocity (CV) joints at each end **(see illustrations)**. The driveaxles are of equal length with a joint shaft located between the transaxle and the right driveaxle. The CV joints are protected by rubber boots that are retained by straps to keep the joints from being contaminated by water and dirt.

8.18 A socket can be used as a clutch alignment tool

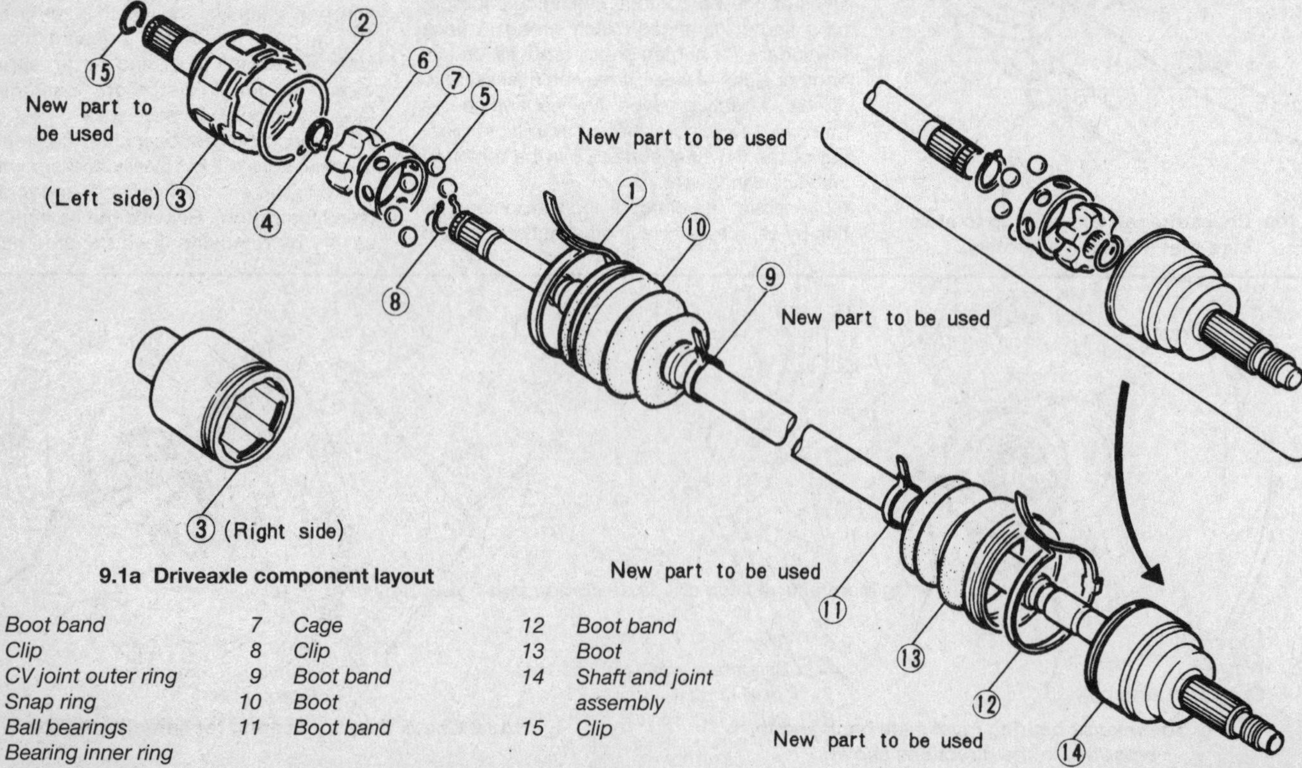

9.1a Driveaxle component layout

1 Boot band
2 Clip
3 CV joint outer ring
4 Snap ring
5 Ball bearings
6 Bearing inner ring
7 Cage
8 Clip
9 Boot band
10 Boot
11 Boot band
12 Boot band
13 Boot
14 Shaft and joint assembly
15 Clip

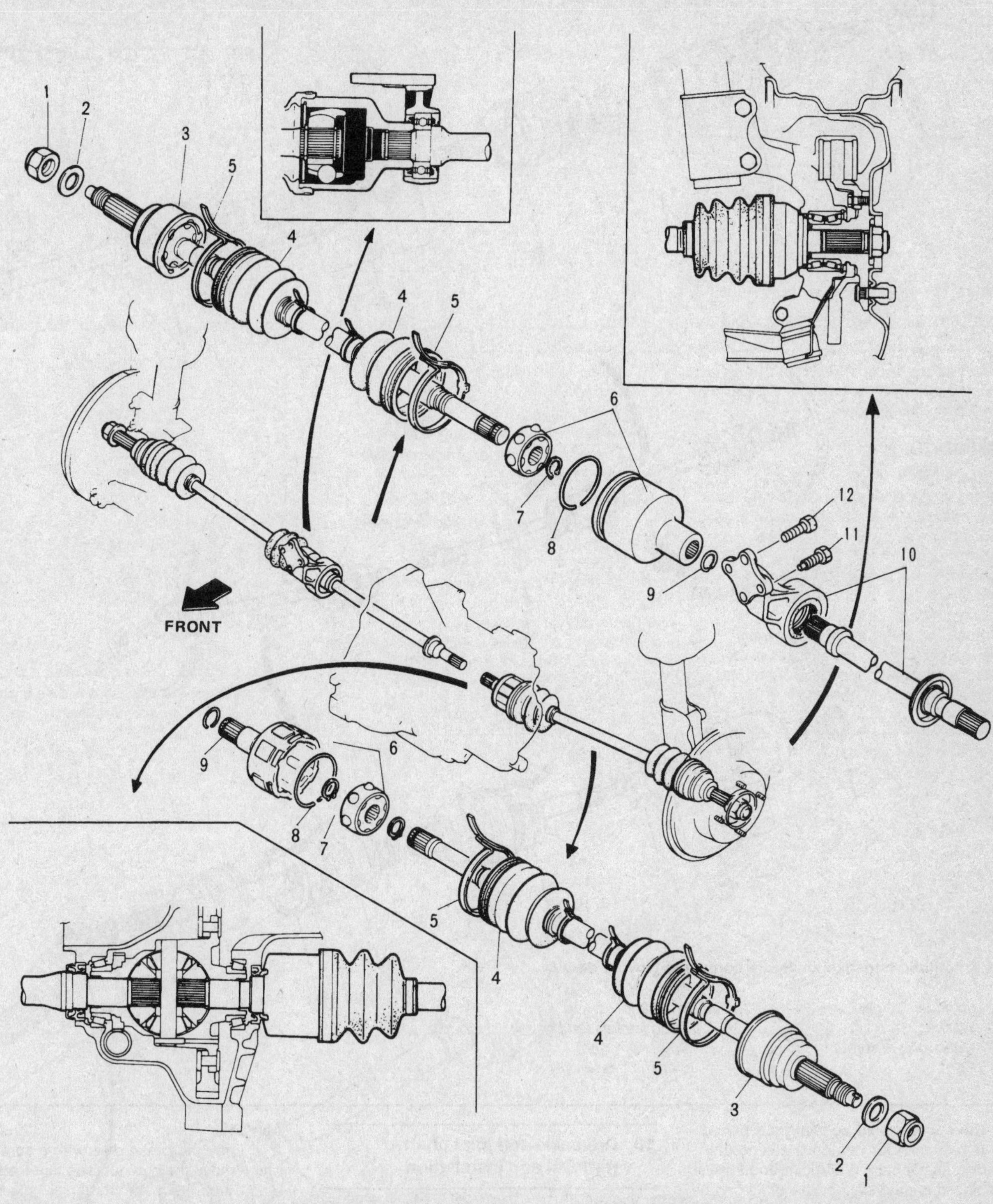

9.1b Manual transaxle driveaxle component layout details

1 Locknut
2 Washer
3 Outer joint assembly
4 Boot
5 Boot band
6 Differential side joint assembly
7 Snap ring
8 Clip
9 Clip
10 Joint shaft assembly
11 Reamer bolt
12 Joint shaft bracket mounting bolt

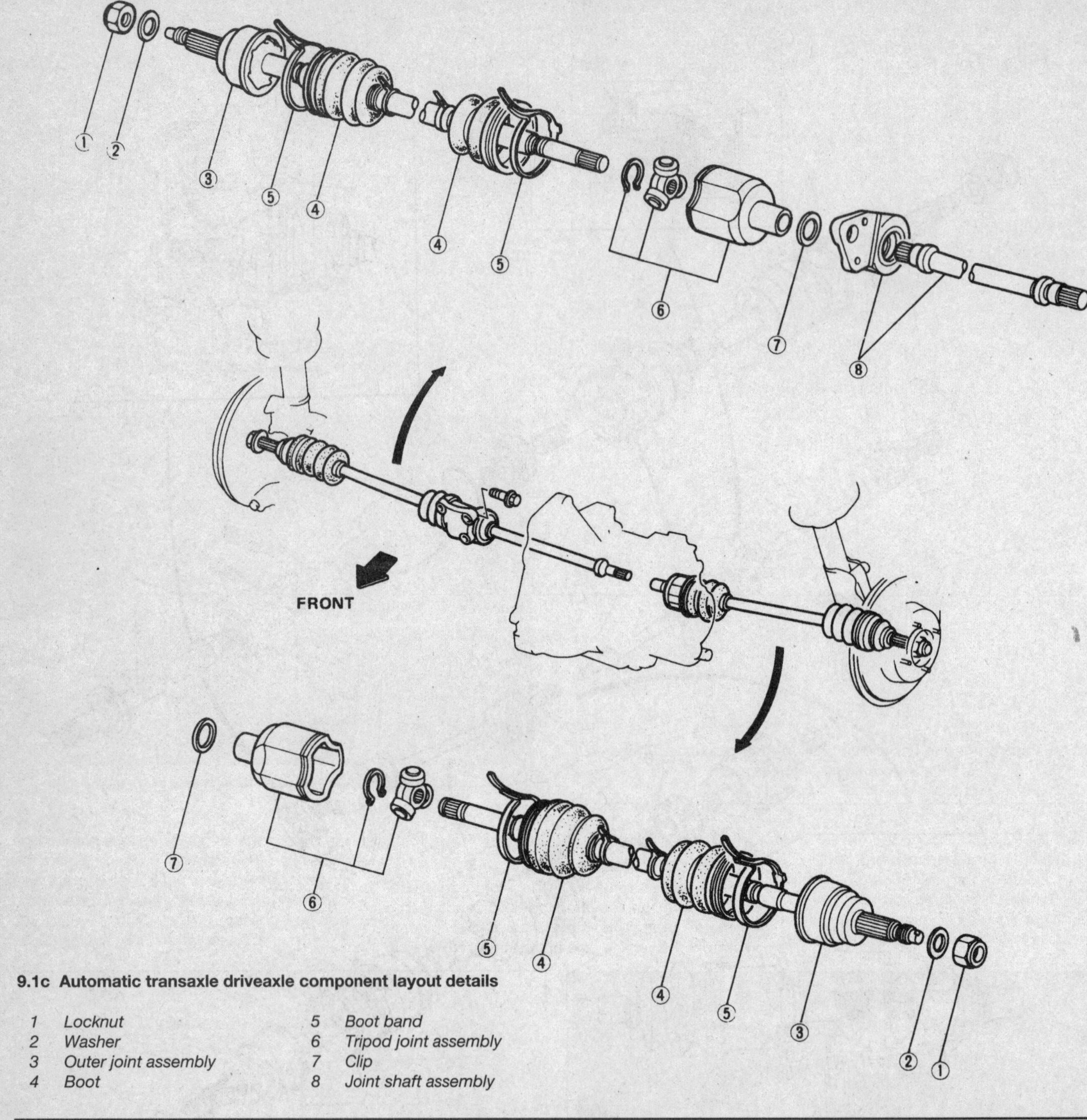

9.1c Automatic transaxle driveaxle component layout details

1 *Locknut*
2 *Washer*
3 *Outer joint assembly*
4 *Boot*
5 *Boot band*
6 *Tripod joint assembly*
7 *Clip*
8 *Joint shaft assembly*

The boots should be inspected periodically (Chapter 1) for damage, leaking lubricant or cuts. Damaged CV joint boots must be replaced immediately or the joints can be damaged. Boot replacement involves removing the driveaxles (Section 10).

The most common symptom of worn or damaged CV joints besides lubricant leaks are a clicking noise in turns, a clunk when accelerating from a coasting condition or vibration at highway speeds.

10 Driveaxle and joint shaft - removal and installation

Removal

Driveaxle

Refer to illustrations 10.2, 10.4a, 10.4b, 10.5 and 10.6

1 Raise the front of the vehicle, support it securely on jackstands, remove the front wheels and splash shields and drain the transaxle.

2 Lock the brake disc with a screwdriver and remove the hub nut **(see illustration)**.

3 Disconnect the stabilizer link, remove the balljoint and steering knuckle nuts and bolts and disconnect the strut from the balljoint (Chapter 10).

4 Carefully pry the inner end of the axle from the transaxle or joint shaft **(see illustration)**. On automatic transaxle models it may be necessary to insert a chisel between the driveaxle and housing, tapping the end of the

10.2 A screwdriver inserted into the rotor through the caliper will hold the hub stationary when loosening and tightening the hub locknut

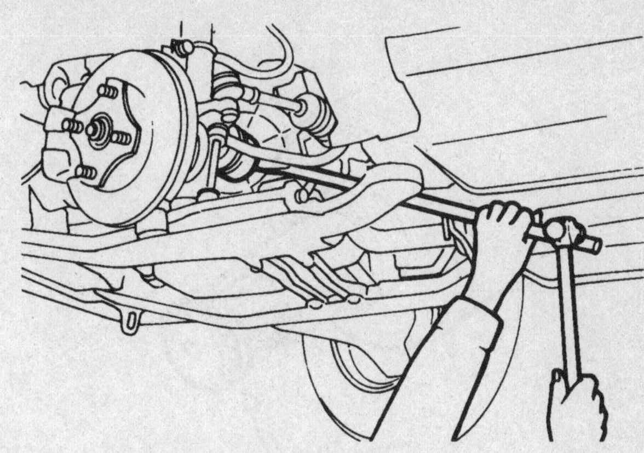

10.4a Disconnect the left driveaxle from the manual transaxle by tapping it out

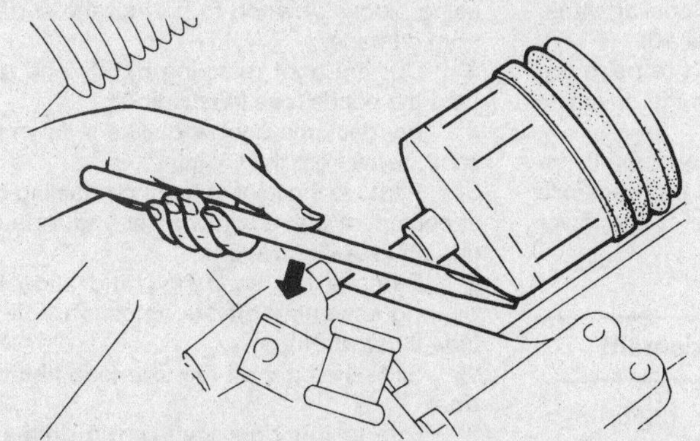

10.4b Disengage the left driveaxle from the transaxle differential on automatic transaxle models

10.5 Use a puller to disengage the driveaxle from the hub

chisel lightly to disengage the driveaxle from the differential **(see illustration)**.

5 Disengage the driveaxle from the hub by using a puller **(see illustration)**.

6 Support the CV joints and remove the driveaxle from the vehicle **(see illustration)**.

Joint shaft

Refer to illustrations 10.7 and 10.8

7 After removing the right driveaxle, remove the retaining bolts, disengage the joint shaft from the transaxle and lower it from the vehicle **(see illustration)**. **Note:** *Plug the hole in the transaxle case whenever the driveaxle is removed. When both the driveaxle and the joint shaft are removed, take care not to move the transaxle differential side gear splines.*

8 Prior to installation, install new clips

10.6 Support the CV joints and carefully withdraw the driveaxle past the hub assembly

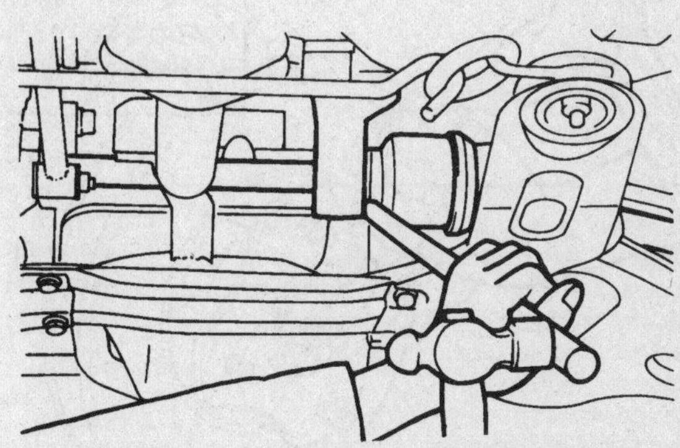

10.7 Use a lever and hammer as shown to disengage the right driveaxle and joint shaft from the transaxle

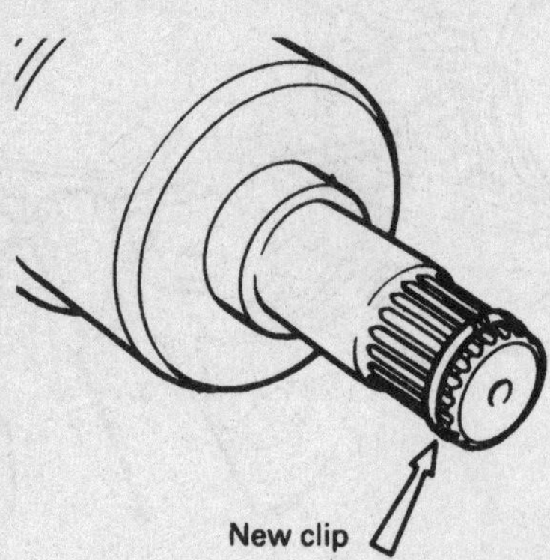

10.8 The clip must be replaced with a new one whenever the driveaxles or joint shaft are removed

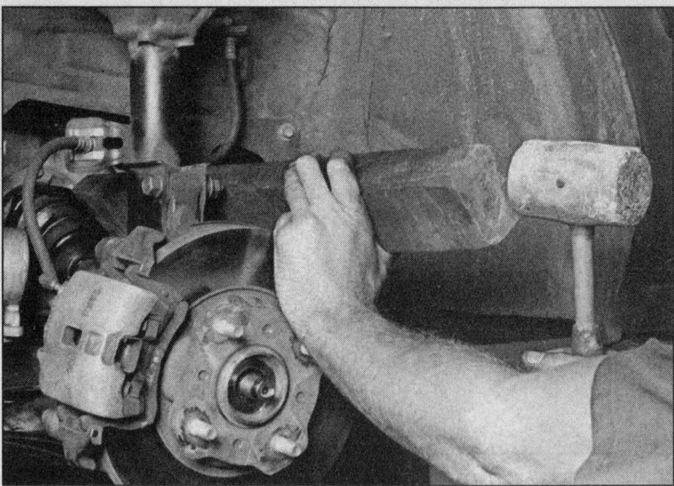

10.11 Use a hammer and a piece of wood to seat the driveaxle in the transaxle

(available at your dealer) in the driveaxle and joint shaft grooves and lubricate the splines with transaxle lubricant **(see illustration)**.

Installation

Joint shaft

9 Insert the joint shaft into the transaxle, install the retaining bolts and tighten them to the specified torque.

Driveaxle

Refer to illustrations 10.11 and 10.15

10 Raise the driveaxle into position while supporting the CV joints and insert the splined ends into the hub and transaxle.

11 Seat the driveaxle into the differential by gently tapping it with a piece of wood and a hammer **(see illustration)**.

12 Place the steering knuckle in position and install the bolts (Chapter 10).

13 Install the hub nuts.

14 Lock the disc so that it cannot turn, using a screwdriver or punch inserted through the caliper into a disc cooling vane, and tighten the hub nut (Chapter 10).

15 Use a hammer and punch to peen the locknut collar into the groove in the driveaxle **(see illustration)**.

16 Connect the stabilizer bar, install the splash shields and wheels, fill the transaxle with the specified fluid (Chapter 1) and lower the vehicle.

11 Driveaxle boot - replacement

Refer to illustrations 11.3, 11.5a, 11.5b, 11.6, 11.7, 11.11, 11.12a, 11.12b, 11.16a and 11.16b

Note: *Prior to beginning work, obtain the proper boot kit from your dealer. The boot kit contains special moly-base lubricant required for use on Constant Velocity (CV) joints, and no other type should be used.*

1 Remove the driveaxle (Section 10).

2 Place the driveaxle assembly in a vise, using blocks of wood to protect the surface from damage.

3 Cut the boot retaining bands and discard the bands **(see illustration)**.

4 Pry back the boot and slide it down the shaft, away from the CV joint.

5 Remove the joint outer ring retaining clip (if equipped) with a screwdriver and slide the ring off **(see illustrations)**.

6 Remove the snap ring and slide the bearing assembly off the axleshaft splines **(see illustration)**.

7 Slide the boot off the axle **(see illustration)**.

8 Due to the work involved in driveaxle removal and installation, it is a good idea to replace both boots even if only one boot is damaged, unless the vehicle has covered very few miles.

9 Clean the bearing assembly and shaft splines carefully and inspect for wear, damage, and contamination by dirt and water. Replace any damaged components with new

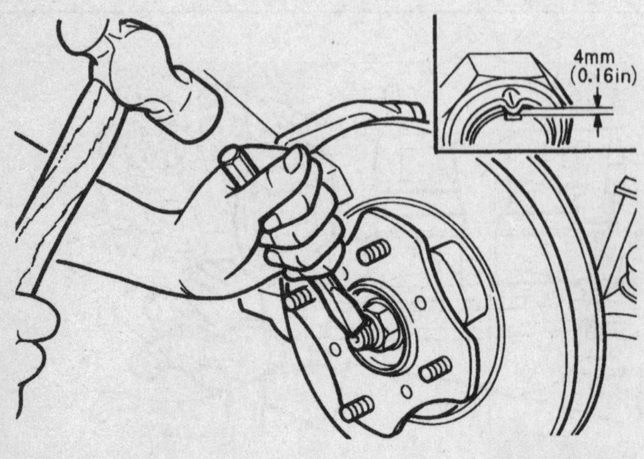

10.15 Peen the locknut collar into the driveaxle groove with a hammer and punch or dull chisel

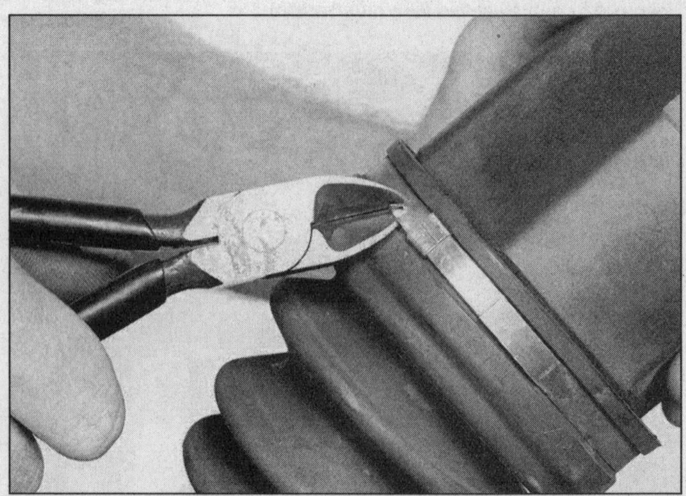

11.3 Cut the driveaxle boot retaining band with a pair of wire cutters

11.5a Remove the CV joint outer ring retaining clip with a screwdriver

11.5b Remove the outer ring

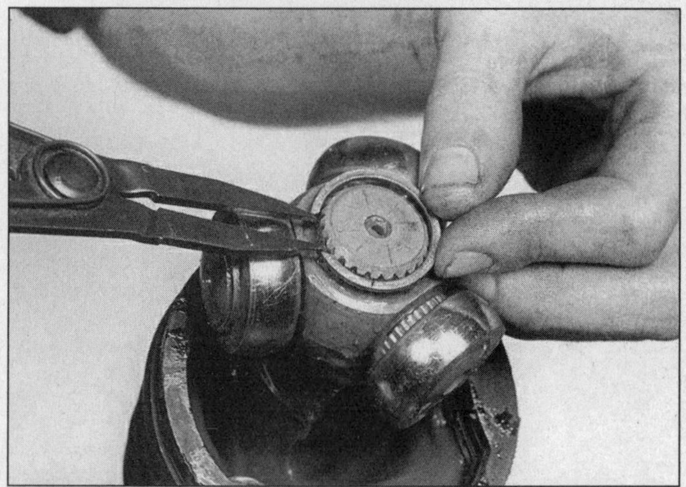

11.6 Remove the bearing snap-ring (tripod-type bearing)

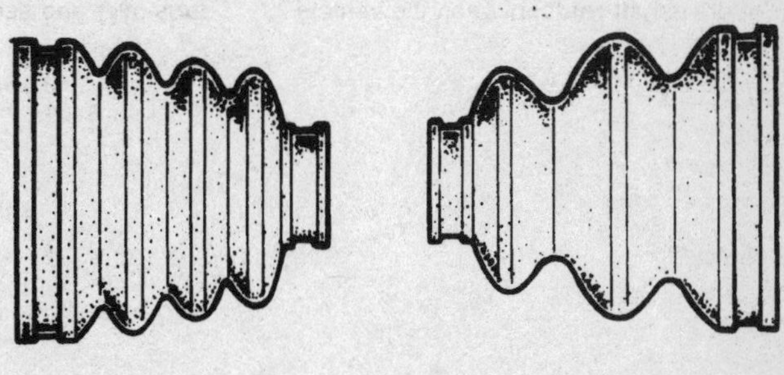

11.7 The wheel side (left) and differential side driveaxle boots are different and should not be interchanged

ones.

10 Wrap tape around the shaft splines to avoid damaging the sealing surface of the new boot during installation. Lightly lubricate the inner diameter of the new boot and slide it onto the driveaxle. Note: Different boots are used on the wheel and differential sides, which should not be mixed up.

11 Remove the tape, apply a light coat of grease to the splines and install the bearing assembly and snap ring with the tapered edge facing the shaft **(see illustration)**.

12 Pack the bearing cavity with the special moly base grease **(see illustrations)**.

13 Install the outer ring.

11.11 The chamfer (arrow) must face toward the axle

11.12a Carefully pack grease into the cavity

11.12b Cover the bearing cavity

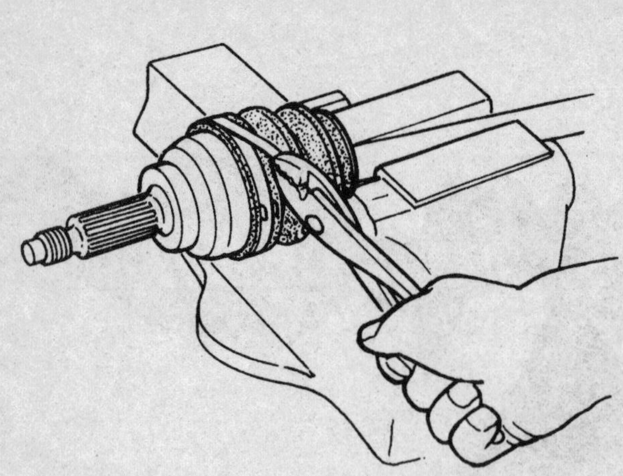

11.16a Bend the boot band locking clip flat and lock it securely with a punch

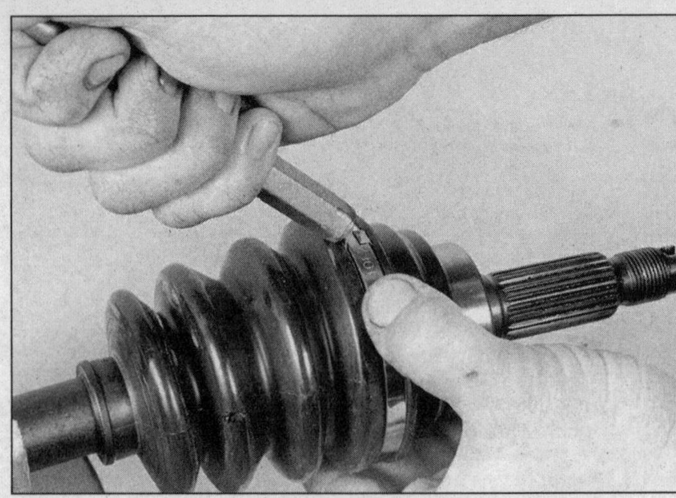

11.16b Use pliers to pull the boot band tight

14 Seat the boot in the grooves.

15 Install the boot retaining bands so that the tightening tab folds in the opposite direction of driveshaft rotation when the vehicle is moving forward.

16 Pull the band tight with a pair of pliers and lock it tightly in place by bending the tabs over and securing them with a blunt tool such as a large punch **(see illustrations)**.

17 Install the driveaxle.

Chapter 9 Brakes

Contents

Specifications

Disc brakes

Front pad thickness	
Standard	0.39 in (10 mm)
Service limit	0.006 in (0.15 mm)
Rear brake pad minimum thickness	0.04 in (1 mm)
Caliper bore	2.160 in (54 mm)
Front rotor	
Thickness	
Standard	0.055 in (14 mm)
Service limit	0.49 in (12.5 mm)
Runout (maximum)	0.0039 in (0.1 mm)
Rear rotor	
Thickness	
Standard	0.39 in (10 mm)
Service limit	0.31 in (8 mm)
Runout limit	0.04 in (1 mm

Rear drum brakes

Lining thickness	
Standard	0.19 in (5.0 mm)
Service limit	0.04 in (1.0 mm)
Drum diameter	
Standard	7.87 in (200 mm)
Service limit	7.91 in (201 mm)
Wheel cylinder	
Bore	0.748 in (1.95 mm)
Piston-to-bore clearance	
Standard	0.02 to 0.005 in (0.040 to 0.125 mm)
Service limit	0.006 in (0.15 mm)

Master cylinder

Bore diameter	7/8-in (22.22 mm)
Piston-to-bore clearance	0.002 to 0.005 in (0.05 to 0.127 mm)
Wear limit	0.006 in (0.15 mm)

Torque specifications

	Ft-lbs	M-kg (unless otherwise indicated)
Brake pedal-to-bracket	14.5 to 25.3	2 to 3.5
Front disc brake caliper mounting bolts		
Upper	12 to 18	1.6 to 3.5
Lower	14.5 to 21.7	2 to 3
Rear disc brake caliper mounting bolts		
1987	46 to 61	63 to 82 Nm
1988 and later	16 to 24	12 to 17 Nm
Steering knuckle bolts	36 to 55	5 to 7.6

9

Torque specifications (continued)

	Ft-lbs	M-kg (unless otherwise indicated)
Flexible brake hose-to-caliper		
Front	16 to 19	2.2 to 2.6
Rear	17 to 25	2.3 to 3.5
Wheel cylinder retaining bolt	7 to 11	1 to 1.5
Rear spindle-to-backing plate bolts	50	6.9
Brake pipe flare nut	9.4 to 16	1.3 to 2.2
Wheel lug nuts	65 to 87	9 to 12

1 General information

Refer to illustration 1.1

All vehicles covered by this manual are equipped with hydraulically operated front and rear brake systems **(see illustration)**. 1986 and earlier front brake systems are disc type while the rear brakes are disc or drum type.

Some 1987 and later models use disc brakes on the rear wheels. The rear disc brake pad, caliper and disc checking procedures are basically the same as for the front disc brake. 1988 and later models have sealed rear wheel bearings which do not require adjustment (see Chapter 10). Because of the special tools required, overhaul of the rear caliper must be left to a dealer.

All brakes are self adjusting. The front disc brakes automatically compensate for pad wear while the rear drum brakes incorporate an adjustment mechanism which is activated as the brakes are applied until the thickness of the brake lining decreases to less than 0.078 in (2 mm).

The hydraulic system consists of two separate front and rear circuits. The master cylinder has separate reservoirs for the two circuits and in the event of a leak or failure in one hydraulic circuit, the other circuit will remain operative. A dual proportioning valve modulates the hydraulic pressure between the front and rear braking systems to prevent wheel lockup. A visual warning of low fluid level is given by a warning light activated by a switch in the master cylinder reservoir.

The parking brake mechanically operates the rear brakes only. It is activated by a pull handle in the center console between the front seats.

The power brake booster, located in the engine compartment on the firewall, uses engine manifold vacuum and atmospheric pressure to provide assistance to the hydraulically operated brakes.

After completing any operation involving the disassembly of any part of the brake system, always test drive the vehicle to check for proper braking performance before resuming normal driving. Test the brakes while driving on a clean, dry, flat surface. Conditions other than these can lead to inaccurate test results. Test the brakes at various speeds with both light and heavy pedal pressure. The vehicle should stop evenly without pulling to one side or the other. Avoid locking the brakes because this slides the tires and diminishes braking efficiency and control.

Tires, vehicle load and front end alignment are factors which also affect braking performance.

ABS system

Refer to illustration 1.10

The ABS system was introduced in 1988 and is designed to maintain vehicle control under severe braking conditions. The system performs this function by monitoring the rotational speed of each wheel and then controlling the brake line pressure to prevent wheel lock-up. An amber indicator lamp on the dash will flash if there is a malfunction in the system.

The ABS system consists of the hydraulic unit, relay box, control unit and wheel speed sensors **(see illustration)**. The control unit, located in the passenger compartment is essentially the "brain" for the ABS system. It accepts and processes information received from the wheel speed sensors and produces control commands for the relay box and hydraulic unit. Due to the complicated nature of this system, diagnosis and repair must be done by a dealer. Take care whenever working in the area of the wheels, suspension or brakes to avoid damaging the wheel speed sensors.

2 Disc brake pads - replacement

Note: *Disc brake pads should be replaced on both wheels at the same time. Work on one brake at a time, using the other, assembled brake, for reference if necessary.*

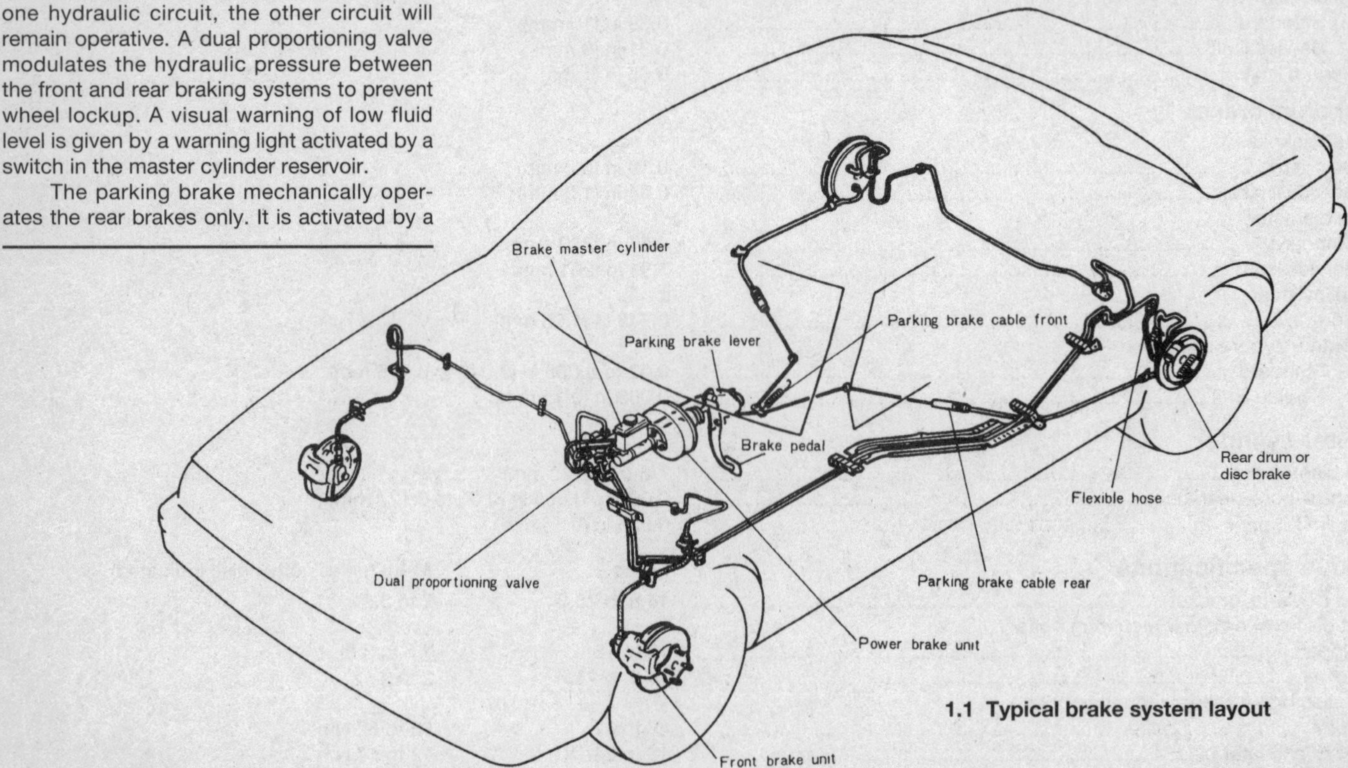

1.1 Typical brake system layout

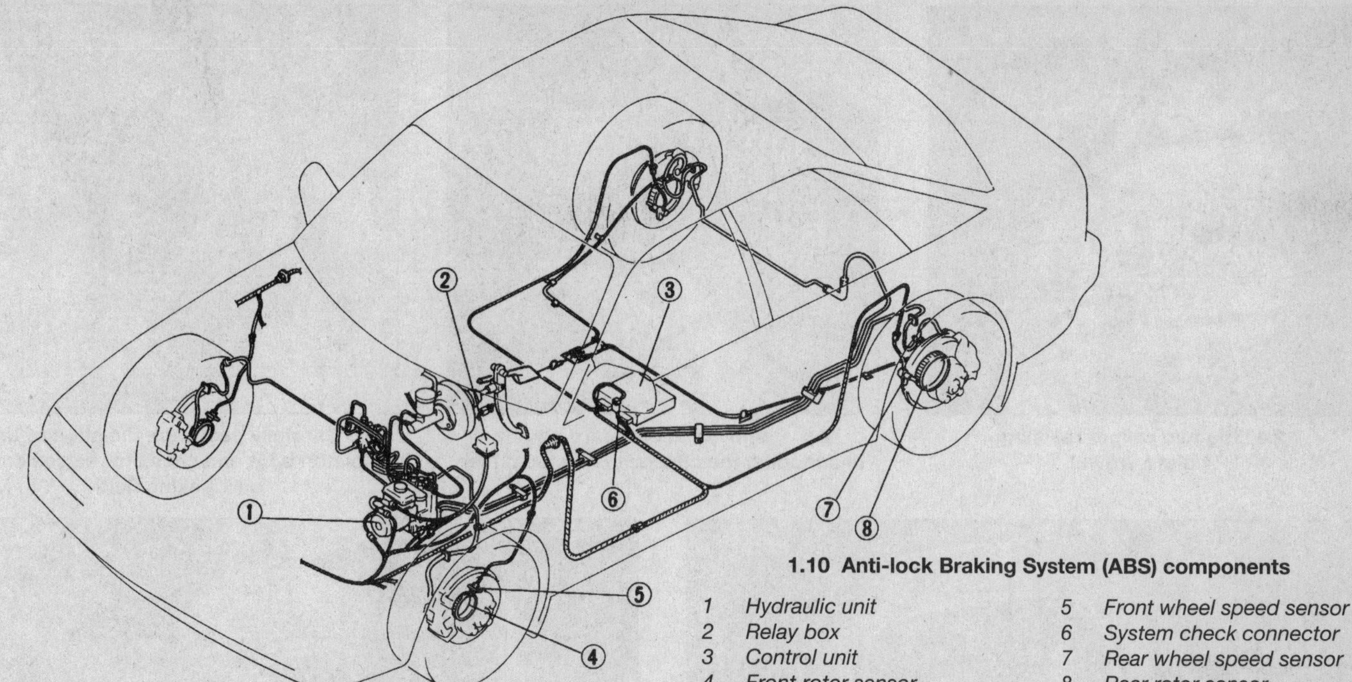

1.10 Anti-lock Braking System (ABS) components

1. *Hydraulic unit*
2. *Relay box*
3. *Control unit*
4. *Front rotor sensor*
5. *Front wheel speed sensor*
6. *System check connector*
7. *Rear wheel speed sensor*
8. *Rear rotor sensor*

Front disc brake pad replacement

Refer to illustrations 2.3, 2.4, 2.6, 2.8, 2.9 and 2.10

1 Whenever you are working on the brake system, be aware that asbestos dust is present and be careful not to inhale any of it as this could be harmful to your health.

2 Remove the cover from the brake fluid reservoir and siphon off about two ounces of the fluid into a container and discard it.

3 Loosen the front wheel bolts, raise the front of the vehicle, support it securely on jackstands and remove the front wheels **(see illustration)**.

4 Remove the two caliper bolts **(see illustration)**.

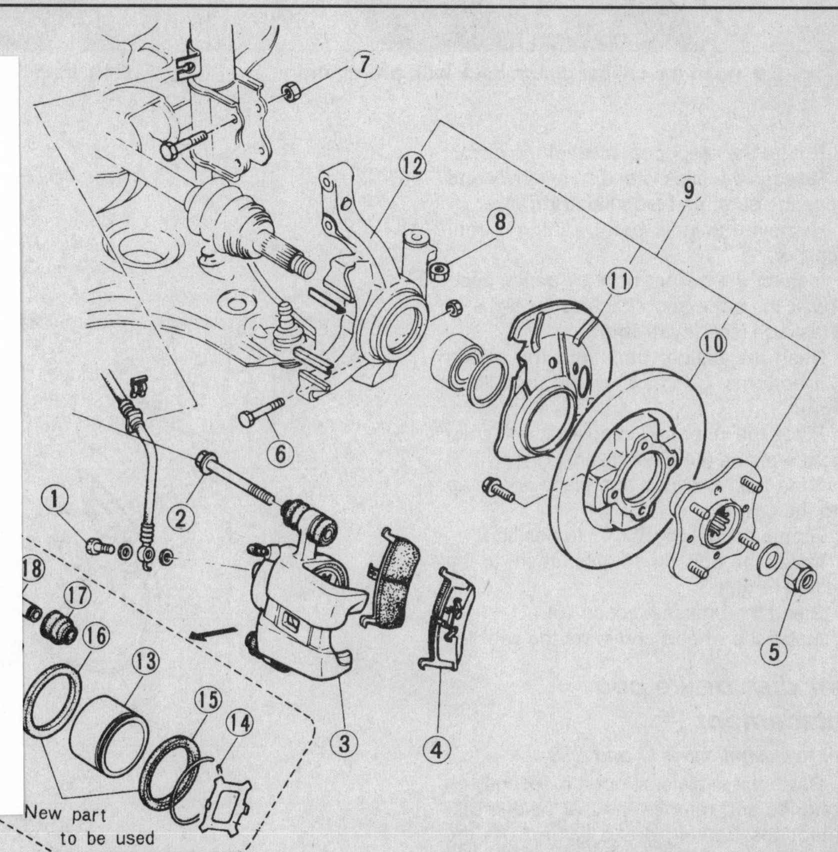

2.4 The two caliper retaining bolts (arrows)

2.6 Remove the outboard pad by unsnapping the clips with a screwdriver

2.8 Carefully peel back the edge of the piston boot and check for corrosion and leaking fluid

2.9 Push the caliper piston back with a C-clamp

2.10 Install the inner pad by snapping the clip into the piston

5 Rotate the caliper up, clear of the disc.

6 Release the clips with a screwdriver and remove the outer pad **(see illustration)**.

7 Remove the inner pad by lifting it from the caliper.

8 Inspect the caliper boot by gently peeling back the edge and checking for signs of fluid leakage **(see illustration)**.

9 Push the caliper back into the piston until it bottoms, using a C-clamp **(see illustration)**.

10 Place the inner pad in position and snap it into the piston **(see illustration)**.

11 Slide the outer pad into place and snap it into the caliper.

12 Rotate the caliper back into position.

13 Install the bolts and tighten them to the specified torque.

14 Bleed the brakes (Section 15).

15 Install the wheels and lower the vehicle.

Rear disc brake pad replacement

Refer to illustrations 2.17 and 2.18

16 Raise the vehicle, support it securely on jackstands and remove the rear wheel. Disconnect the parking brake cable from the bracket and caliper lever.

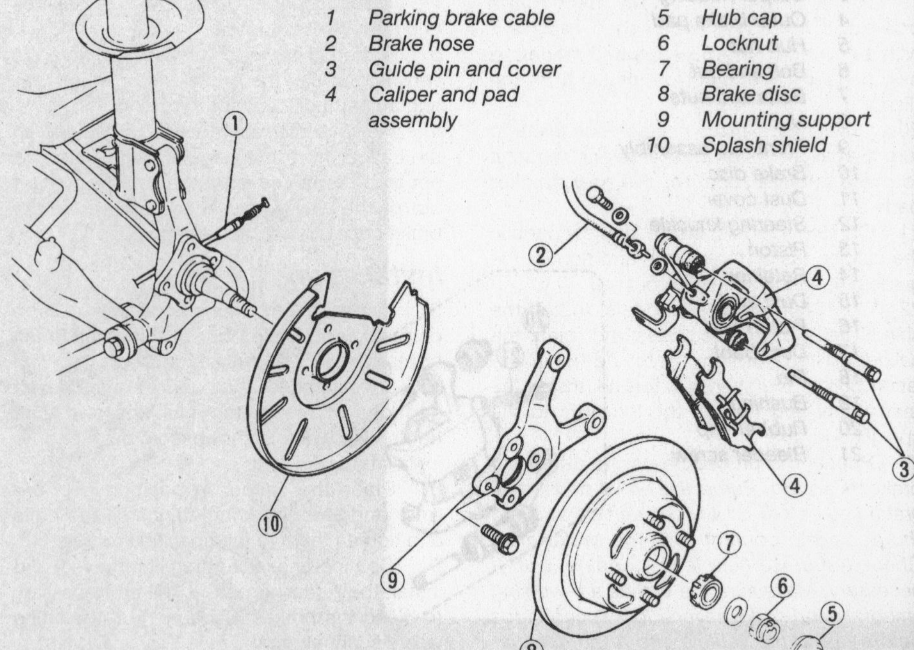

2.17 1987 rear disc brake assembly - exploded view

1 *Parking brake cable*
2 *Brake hose*
3 *Guide pin and cover*
4 *Caliper and pad assembly*
5 *Hub cap*
6 *Locknut*
7 *Bearing*
8 *Brake disc*
9 *Mounting support*
10 *Splash shield*

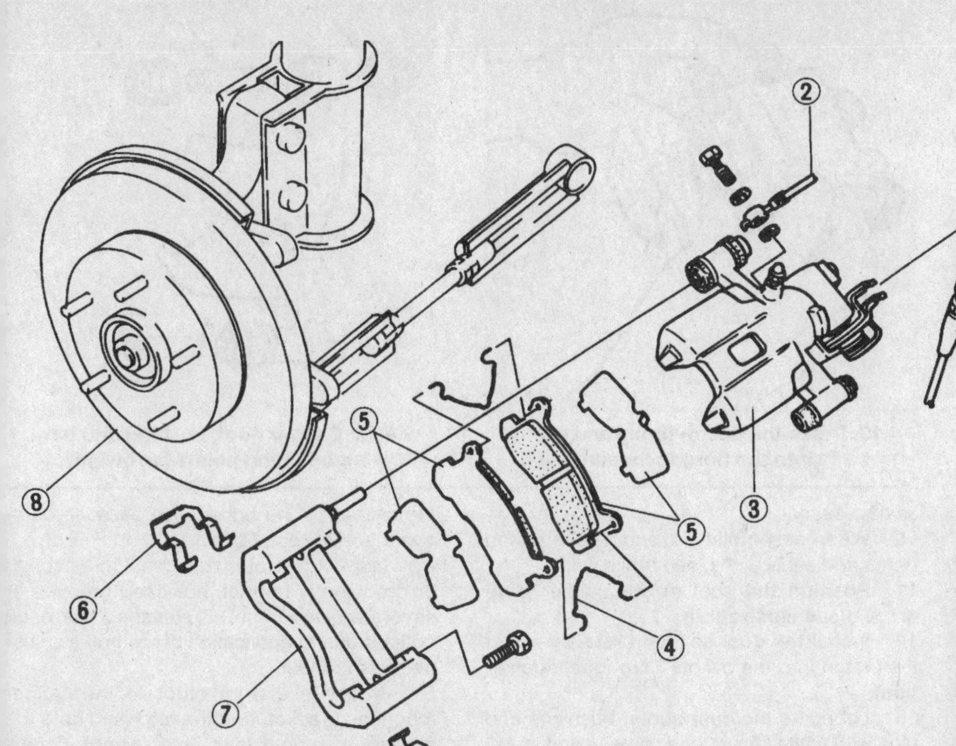

2.18 1988 and later rear disc brake assembly - exploded view

1. *Parking brake cable*
2. *Brake hose*
3. *Caliper*
4. *V-spring*
5. *Pad and shim*
6. *Guide plate*
7. *Mounting support*
8. *Brake disc*

17 On 1987 models, remove the guide pins and detach the caliper **(see illustration)**. Pry the pads out of the caliper with a screwdriver.

18 On 1988 and later models, remove the upper installation bolt and pivot the caliper down for access to the pads **(see illustration)**. Remove the V-springs, brake pads, shims and guide plates.

19 Refer to Chapter 9 and inspect the brake disc. If the disc is damaged, replace it with a new one. On ABS equipped models, a new sensor wheel must be installed on the disc.

20 On all models, use needle nose pliers to turn the caliper piston clockwise and retract it to make enough room for the new, thicker pads.

21 On 1987 models, install the new pads in the caliper. Install the caliper and tighten the guide pins to the specified torque.

22 On 1988 and later models, install the shims, pads and guide plates and rotate the caliper up into position, tightening the installation bolt to the specified torque. Install the rear wheel and tighten the lug nuts to the specified torque.

23 Repeat the procedure on the other rear brake. **Warning:** *Pump the brake pedal several times before driving the vehicle to bring the pads into contact with the brake disc. Check the brake fluid level, topping it off if necessary. Make sure the brakes are working smoothly and make several low speed stops before taking the vehicle into a traffic situation.*

3 Disc brake caliper - removal and installation

Removal

1 Remove the cover from the brake fluid reservoir and siphon off two-thirds of the fluid into a container and discard it.

2 Loosen the wheel nuts, raise the front of the vehicle, support it securely on jackstands and remove the wheels.

3 If the caliper is to be removed from the vehicle, remove the brake line hose inlet fitting bolt and disconnect the fitting.

4 Remove the two mounting bolts and lift the caliper from the vehicle. If the caliper is not to be removed from the vehicle, hang it out of the way with a piece of wire so the brake hose will not be damaged.

Installation

5 Inspect the mounting bolts for excessive corrosion and the rubber bushings and dust boots for tears and damage, replacing with new ones if necessary. Lubricate the contact surfaces of the bolts, bushings and dust boots with white lithium base grease prior to installation.

6 Place the caliper in position over the rotor and steering knuckle, install the bolts and tighten them to the specified torque.

7 Connect the inlet fitting (if removed) and install the retaining bolt. It will be necessary to bleed the brakes (Section 15) if the fitting was disconnected.

8 Install the wheels and lower the vehicle.

4.1 Use a block of wood to protect the caliper when using hydraulic pressure to force the piston out. Be sure to keep your fingers out of the way

4 Disc brake caliper - overhaul

Note: *Purchase a brake caliper overhaul kit for your particular vehicle before beginning this procedure.*

Refer to illustrations 4.1, 4.11, 4.12 and 4.14

1 Remove the caliper (Section 3) and brake pads (Section 2). There are two methods of removing the caliper piston. Step 4 details the procedure for removal with the caliper off the vehicle. With the brake line still connected and the pads removed, the piston can be pushed out, using hydraulic pressure. Protect the caliper with a piece of wood or folded rags and take care to not place your fingers between the piston and the caliper. Have an assistant very slowly apply the brakes to push the piston out and be prepared for a rush of brake fluid as the piston is ejected **(see illustration)**.

2 Clean the exterior of the brake caliper with brake fluid (never use gasoline, kerosene or cleaning solvents), then place the caliper on a clean workbench.

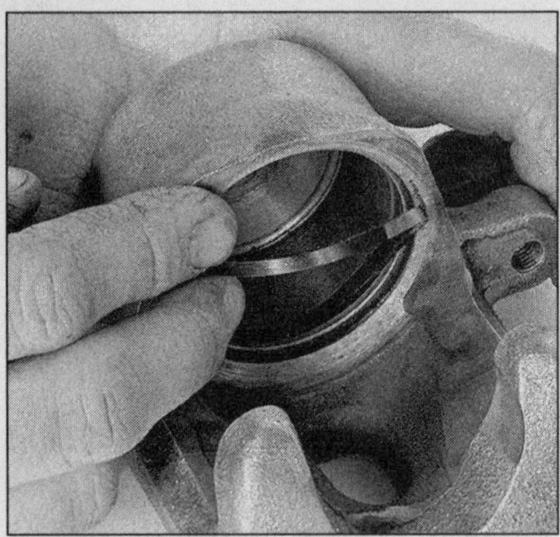
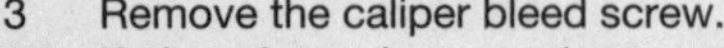

4.11 Insert the piston seal into the groove of the caliper

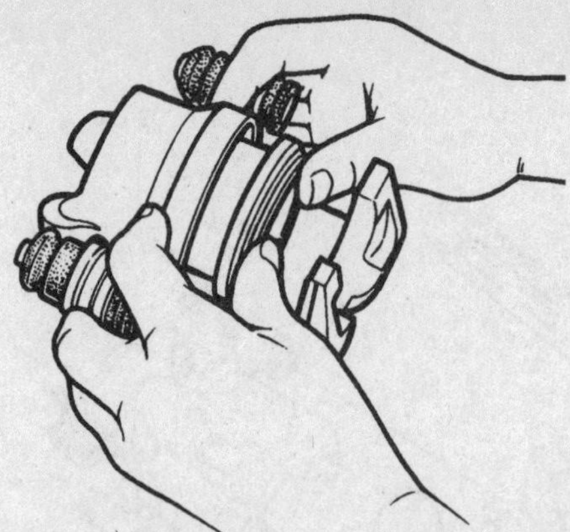

4.12 Press the piston firmly and evenly into the bore to install

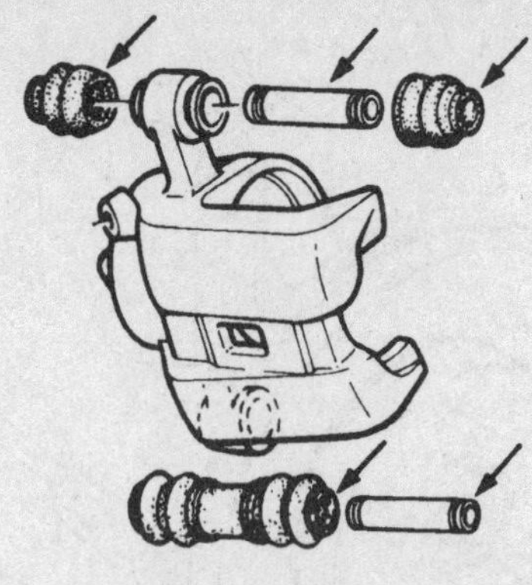

4.14 Caliper boot, bushing and pin lubrication points (arrows)

3 Remove the caliper bleed screw.

4 If the piston has not been removed, place a wooden block or shop rag in the caliper as a cushion, then use compressed air to remove the piston from the caliper. Use only enough air pressure to ease the piston out of the bore. If the piston is blown out, even with the cushion in place, it may be damaged. **Warning:** *Never place your fingers in front of the piston in an attempt to catch or protect it when applying compressed air. Serious injury could occur.*

5 Remove the retainer and dust seal from the piston caliper bore.

6 Using a wood or plastic tool, remove the piston seal from the groove in the caliper bore. Metal tools may cause bore damage.

7 Remove the dust boots, pins and bushings from the caliper ears.

8 Clean the remaining parts with brake fluid. Allow them to drain and then shake them vigorously to remove as much fluid as possible.

9 Carefully examine the piston and caliper bore for nicks, burrs, corrosion and loss of plating. If surface defects are present, parts must be replaced although the caliper bore can be lightly polished with crocus cloth to remove light corrosion and stains. Inspect the mounting bolts, pins and bushings for corrosion and damage, replacing with new parts as necessary.

10 When assembling, lubricate the piston bores and seals with clean brake fluid.

11 Position the seal in the caliper bore groove **(see illustration)**.

12 Install the dust seal and retainer insert the piston into the caliper bore **(see illustration)**.

13 Lubricate the dust boots, bushings and pins with white lithium base grease and install the caliper.

14 Lubricate the brake pad shim with a light coat of white lithium base grease and install the brake pads **(see illustration)**.

15 Install the caliper and bleed the brakes (Section 15).

5 Disc brake rotor - inspection, removal and installation

Refer to illustrations 5.5 and 5.6

1 Raise the vehicle and place it securely on jackstands.

2 Remove the wheel and tire.

3 Remove the brake caliper assembly (refer to Section 3). **Note:** *It is not necessary to disconnect the brake hose. After removing the caliper mounting bolts, hang the caliper out of the way on a piece of wire. Never hang the caliper by the brake hose because damage to the hose will occur.*

4 Inspect the rotor surfaces. Light scoring or grooving is normal, but deep grooves or severe erosion is not. If pulsating has been noticed during application of the brakes, suspect disc runout.

5 Attach a dial indicator to the caliper mounting bracket, turn the rotor and note the amount of runout **(see illustration)**. Check both inboard and outboard surfaces. If the runout is more than the maximum allowable, the rotor must be removed from the vehicle and taken to an automotive machine shop for resurfacing.

6 Using a micrometer, measure the thickness of the rotor **(see illustration)**. If it is less than the minimum specified, replace the rotor with a new one. Also measure the disc thickness at several points to determine variations in the surface. Any variation over 0.0005-inch may cause pedal pulsations during brake application. If this condition exists and the disc thickness is not below the minimum, the rotor can be removed and taken to an automotive machine shop for resurfacing.

7 Special tools and techniques are required to remove the disc from the hub. Consequently, the hub should be removed (Chapter 10) and the assembly taken to your dealer or a properly equipped shop to have the disc turned or replaced.

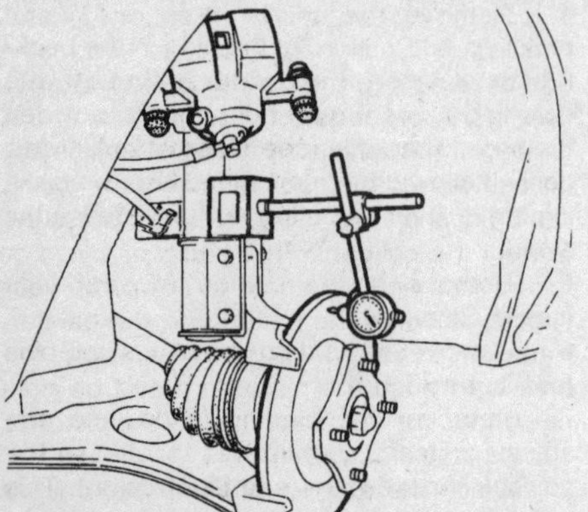

5.5 Checking the brake disc runout

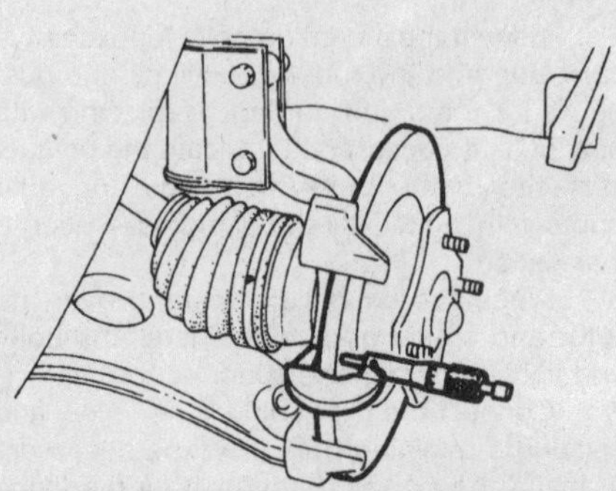

5.6 Measuring the brake disc thickness

6 Drum brake shoes - replacement

Refer to illustrations 6.4a, 6.4b, 6.5, 6.6a, 6.6b, 6.7, 6.9, 6.10, 6.14, 6.17 and 6.18

1 Whenever working on the brake system, be aware that asbestos dust is present. It has been proven to be harmful to your health, so be careful not to inhale it.

2 Raise the vehicle and support it securely on jackstands.

3 Remove the wheel. **Note:** *All four rear shoes should be replaced at the same time, but to avoid mixing up parts, work on only one brake assembly at a time.*

4 Remove the drum/hub assembly (Chapter 1) **(see illustration)**. If the drum cannot be

New part to be used
New part to be used

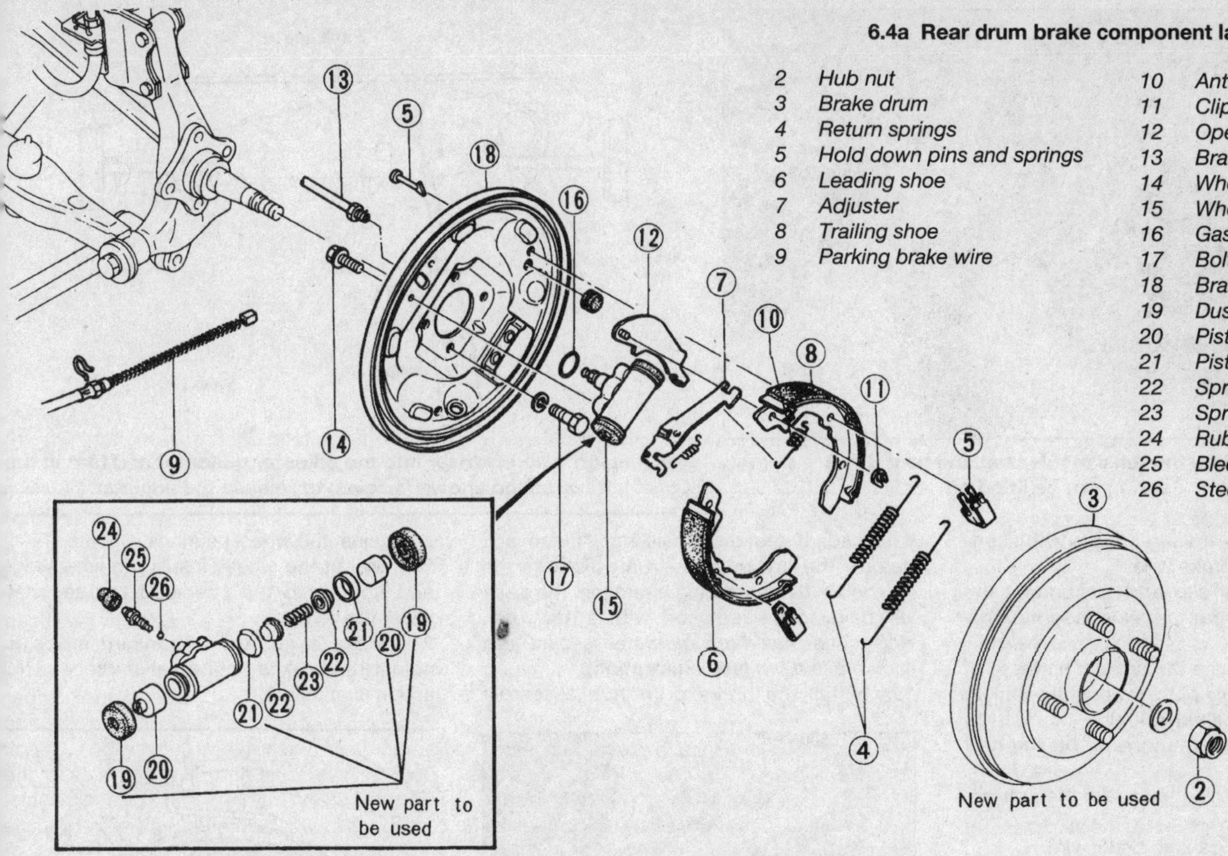

6.4a Rear drum brake component layout

2 *Hub nut*
3 *Brake drum*
4 *Return springs*
5 *Hold down pins and springs*
6 *Leading shoe*
7 *Adjuster*
8 *Trailing shoe*
9 *Parking brake wire*
10 *Anti-rattle spring*
11 *Clip*
12 *Operating lever*
13 *Brake line*
14 *Wheel cylinder bolt*
15 *Wheel cylinder*
16 *Gasket*
17 *Bolts*
18 *Brake backing plate*
19 *Dust boots*
20 *Pistons*
21 *Piston cups*
22 *Spring cups*
23 *Spring*
24 *Rubber cap*
25 *Bleeder screw*
26 *Steel ball*

Shoe hold spring
Operating lever
Back plate
Driver

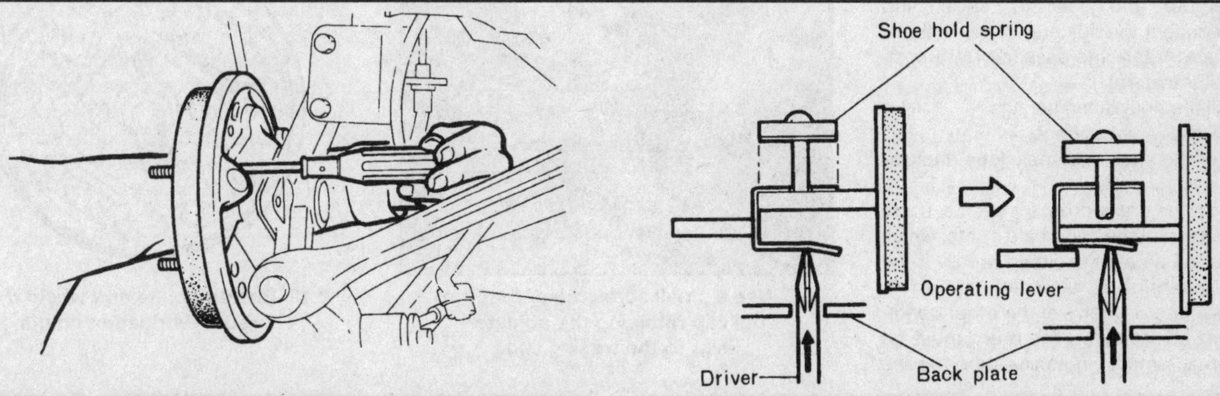

6.4b Release the shoe hold down springs by inserting a screwdriver through the backing plate

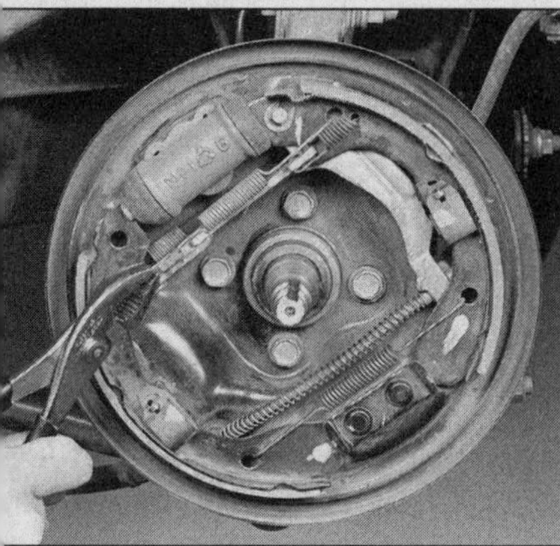

6.5 Use pliers to remove the return springs

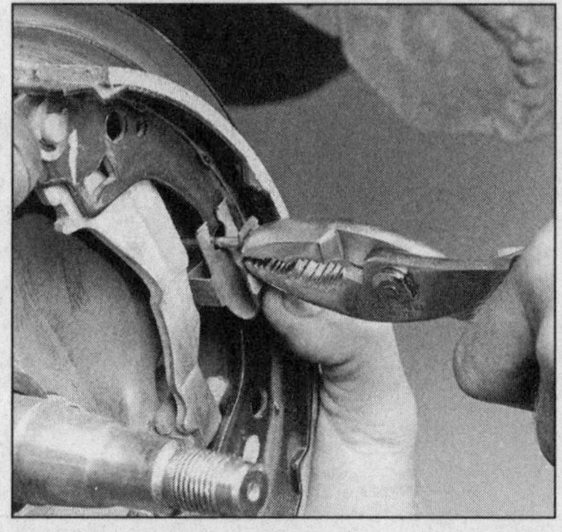

6.6a Compress the hold down spring and rotate the pin to release it from the spring

removed easily, remove the plug in the backing plate, insert a screwdriver through the hole and press on the hold spring to widen the shoe clearance **(see illustration).** If this doesn't allow drum removal, loosen the parking brake lever adjusting nut to increase the stroke.

5 Remove the brake shoe return springs **(see illustration).**

6 Remove the hold down springs and pins **(see illustrations).**

7 Remove the leading shoe and the adjuster. Use a screwdriver to release the adjuster if necessary **(see illustration).** This will release the tension on the hold-down spring and ease the removal of the leading shoe.

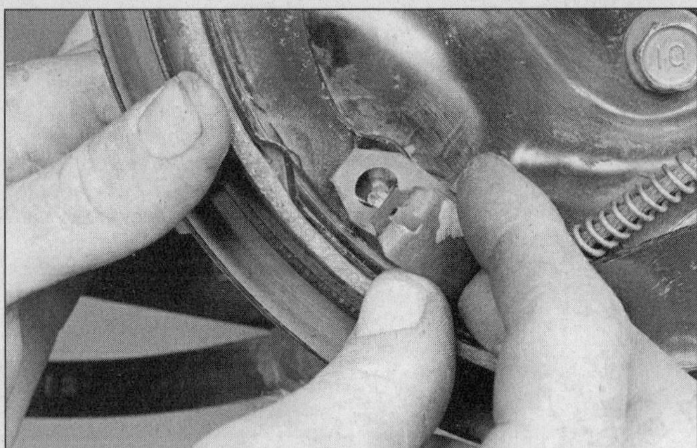

6.6b With the tension released, the hold down spring can be lifted off

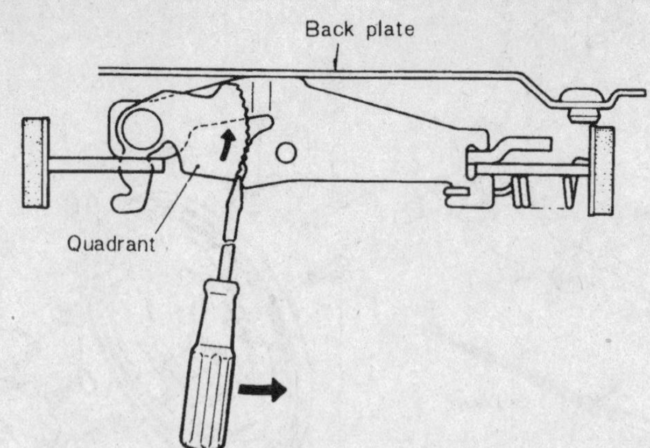

6.7 Insert a screwdriver into the adjuster quadrant and turn in the direction shown (arrows) to release the adjuster

8 Remove the trailing shoe and disconnect the parking brake wire.

9 Remove the clip and disconnect the operating lever from the shoe **(see illustration)**.

10 Lightly lubricate the contact surfaces of the brake backing plate with white lithium base grease **(see illustration)**.

11 Install the operating lever on the new trailing shoe.

12 Install the trailing shoe with the anti-rattle spring in place.

13 Connect the parking brake wire.

14 Assemble the leading shoe and adjuster, connect the adjuster to the anti-rattle spring and rotate the assembly into position **(see illustration)**.

15 Install the hold down springs.

16 Install the return springs.

17 Center the shoe assembly **(see illustration)**.

18 Inspect the brake drum for cracks, score marks, deep scratches and hard spots, which will appear as small discolored areas. If the hard spots cannot be removed with a fine emery cloth and/or if any of the other conditions listed above exist, the drum must be taken to an automotive machine shop to have it turned. If the drum will not "clean up" before the maximum drum diameter is reached in the machining operation, the drum will have to be replaced with a new one. **Note:** *The maximum diameter is cast into each brake drum* **(see illustration)**.

19 Install the brake drum/hub assembly and adjust the wheel bearings (Chapter 1).

20 Mount the wheel, install the wheel lugs and tighten to the specified torque, then lower the vehicle.

21 Make a number of forward stops to adjust the brakes until a satisfactory pedal action is obtained.

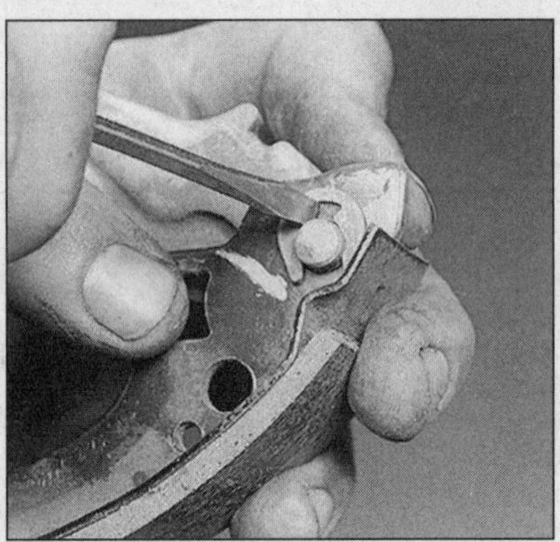

6.9 Use a small screwdriver to remove the clip retaining the adjuster lever to the trailing shoe

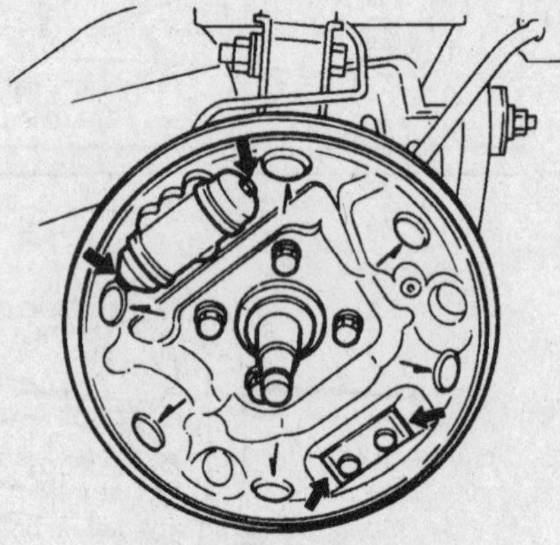

6.10 Backing plate and wheel cylinder boot lubrication points

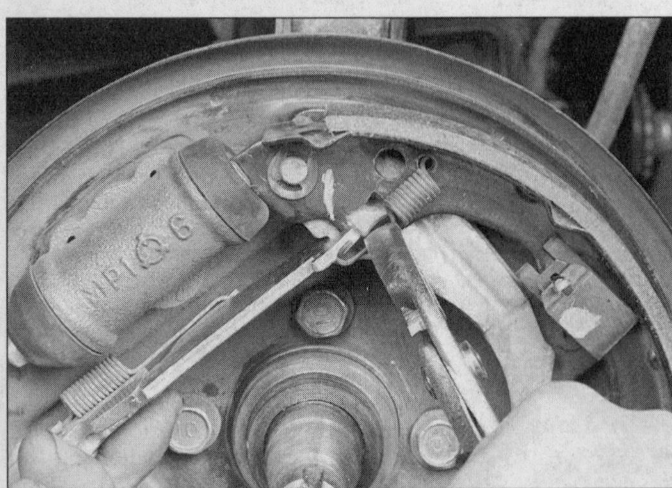

6.14 Connect the anti-rattle spring to the adjuster using pliers

6.17 With all of the components installed, rock the brake assembly back and forth to ensure that all parts are seated

6.18 The maximum diameter allowed is marked inside the brake drum

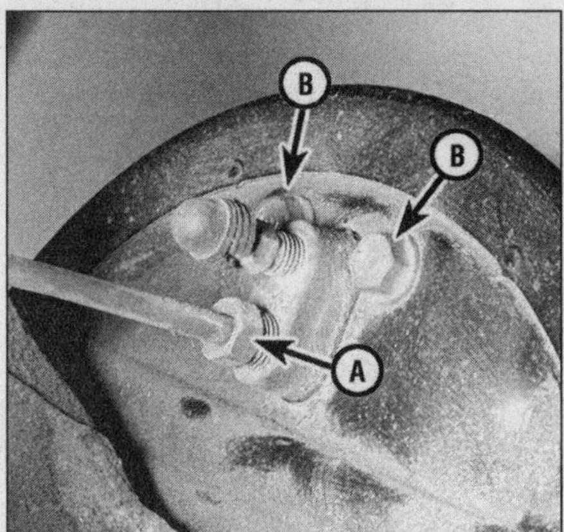

7.4 Wheel cylinder inlet tube (A) and retaining bolts (B)

7 Drum brake wheel cylinder - removal, overhaul and installation

Removal

Refer to illustration 7.4

1 Raise the rear of the vehicle and support it securely on jackstands.

2 Remove the brake shoe assembly (Section 6).

3 Carefully clean all dirt and foreign material from around the wheel cylinder.

4 Disconnect and plug the fluid inlet tube and remove the wheel cylinder retaining bolts **(see illustration)**.

5 Remove the wheel cylinder from the brake backing plate and place it on a clean workbench.

Overhaul

6 Obtain a wheel cylinder rebuild kit from your dealer or an automotive parts store.

7 Remove the bleeder screw and steel ball. It may be necessary to tap the wheel cylinder body on a block of wood to dislodge the ball.

8 Remove the dust boots and pistons from the cylinder bore and then separate the boots from the piston assembly.

9 Push from one end of the piston to remove the rubber cups and piston assembly from the cylinder body.

10 Clean the wheel cylinder with brake fluid, denatured alcohol or brake system cleaner. Do not, under any circumstances, use petroleum based solvents to clean brake parts.

11 Use compressed air to remove excess fluid from the wheel cylinder and to blow out the passages.

12 Check the cylinder bore for corrosion and scoring. Crocus cloth may be used to remove light corrosion and stains, but the cylinder must be replaced with a new one if the defects cannot be removed easily, or if the bore is scored.

13 Lubricate the new seals and the cylinder bore with clean brake fluid.

14 Assemble the piston components and insert the assembly into the piston, making sure the boots are properly seated.

15 Install the steel ball and bleeder screw.

Installation

16 Place the wheel cylinder in position and screw the fluid inlet nut into the cylinder finger tight, making sure it is not cross threaded.

17 Install the retaining bolts and tighten them securely.

18 Tighten the inlet nut securely and install brake shoe assembly.

19 Bleed the brakes (Section 15) and lower the vehicle.

8 Master cylinder - removal, overhaul and installation

Refer to illustrations 8.3, 8.4, 8.5 and 8.17

1 A master cylinder overhaul kit should be purchased before beginning this procedure. The kit will include all the replacement parts necessary for the overhaul procedure. The rubber replacement parts, particularly the seals, are the key to fluid control within the master cylinder. As such, it's very important that they be installed securely and facing in the proper direction. Be careful during the rebuild procedure that no grease or mineral-based solvents come in contact with the rubber parts.

2 Completely cover the front fender and cowling area of the vehicle, as brake fluid can ruin painted surfaces if it is spilled.

3 Disconnect the brake line connections. Rags or newspapers should be placed under the master cylinder to soak up the fluid that will drain out. Unplug the fluid level sensor connector, remove the two master cylinder mounting nuts and lift the master cylinder from the vehicle **(see illustration)**.

4 Drain any remaining fluid from the reservoir. Remove the reservoir by grasping the master cylinder firmly and rocking the reservoir from side to side **(see illustration)**.

5 Place the master cylinder in the vertical position (with the front end down), depress

8.3 Master cylinder retaining nuts (A), fluid pipe connections (B) and level sensor connector (C)

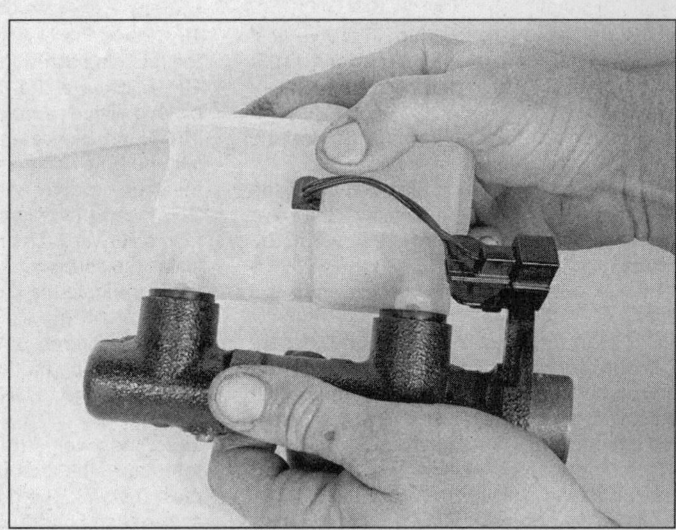

8.4 Grasp the master cylinder firmly and rock the reservoir from side to side to remove it

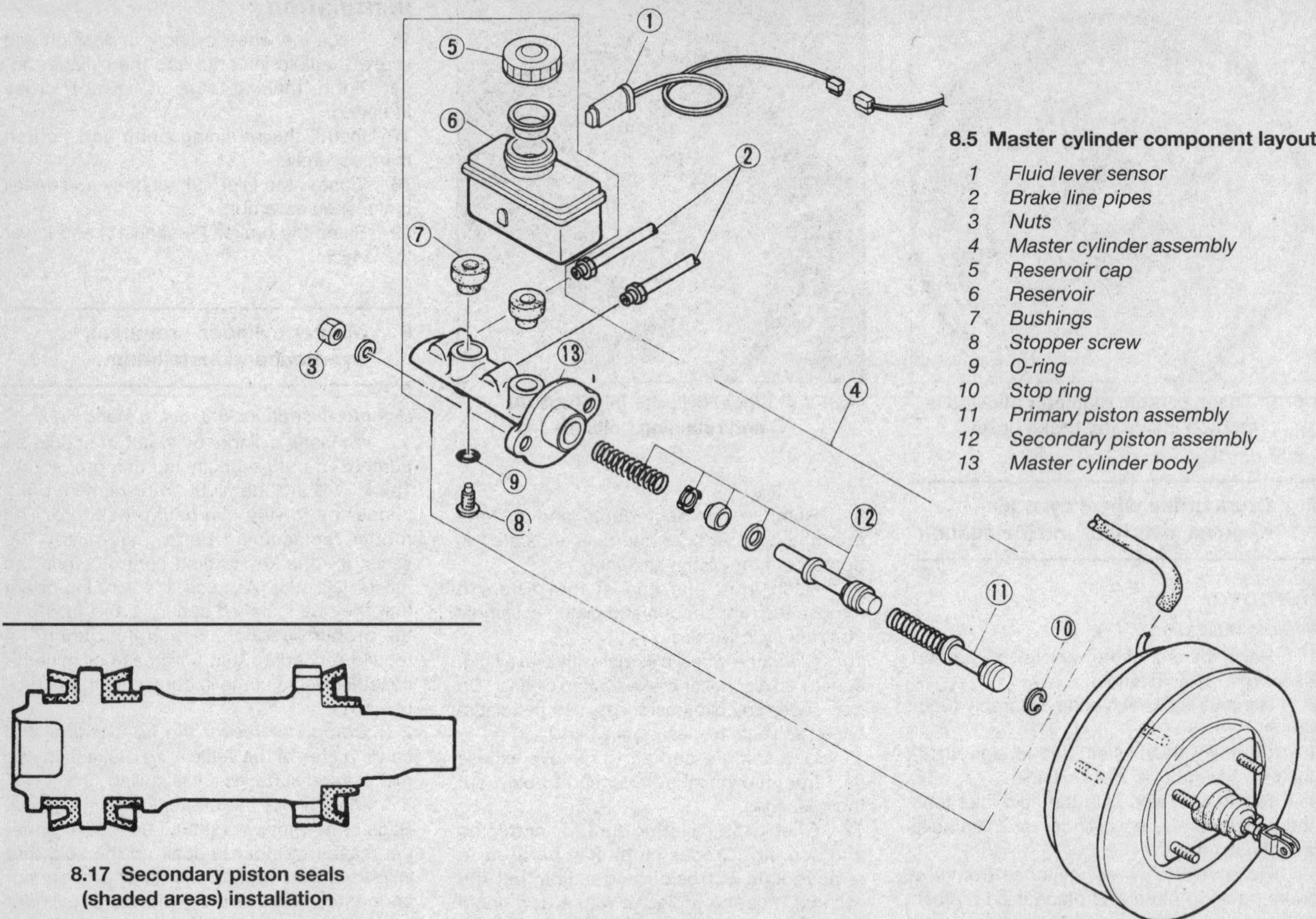

8.5 Master cylinder component layout

1 *Fluid lever sensor*
2 *Brake line pipes*
3 *Nuts*
4 *Master cylinder assembly*
5 *Reservoir cap*
6 *Reservoir*
7 *Bushings*
8 *Stopper screw*
9 *O-ring*
10 *Stop ring*
11 *Primary piston assembly*
12 *Secondary piston assembly*
13 *Master cylinder body*

8.17 Secondary piston seals (shaded areas) installation

the primary piston and remove the snap ring **(see illustration)**.

6 Remove the primary piston and discard it. The overhaul kit will have a replacement unit.

7 Use a wooden dowel to depress the secondary piston. Remove the O-ring and retaining screw.

8 With the master cylinder in the vertical position with the rear end downward, tap it on a block of wood to remove the secondary piston.

9 Remove the spring from the front of the secondary piston.

10 From the secondary piston, remove the rear spreader and cylinder cup seal, the valve shims and the two seals from the rear of the piston.

11 Remove the reservoir bushings, cap and float.

12 Clean the master cylinder and inspect the bore for corrosion and damage. If any corrosion or damage is found, replace the master cylinder body with a new one unless the imperfections are very minor.

13 Inspect the reservoir for cracks and worn bushings, replacing with new components as necessary.

14 Lubricate all components prior to assembly with clean brake fluid.

15 Install the valve shim on the front of the secondary piston. Place the seal (open end forward) on the piston.

16 Install the center seal onto the secondary piston with the open end forward.

17 Install the rear secondary piston seal with the open end toward the rear **(see illustration)**.

18 Place the O-ring on the secondary piston retaining screw.

19 Lubricate the primary and secondary pistons with clean brake fluid.

20 Push the secondary piston assembly into the bore using a wooden dowel. Depress the spring slightly and insert the set screw.

21 Insert the primary piston with the spring facing forward. Depress it slightly and then install the snap ring.

22 Lubricate the reservoir bushings, lay the reservoir on a hard surface and press the master cylinder body onto the reservoir, using a rocking motion.

23 Install the reservoir level float and baffle assembly.

24 Whenever the master cylinder is removed, the complete hydraulic system must be bled. The time required to bleed the system can be reduced if the master cylinder is filled with fluid and primed or "bench bled" before the master cylinder is installed on the vehicle. Fill the reservoir with brake fluid and slowly push the piston all the way in using the wood dowel or a Phillips screwdriver. Before releasing the piston block the brake line ports to keep air from being drawn back into the master cylinder, then release the piston. Repeat the procedure until only brake fluid (no air) is expelled from the brake line ports. Be careful not to let the reservoir run dry during the bleeding process.

25 Place the master cylinder in position over the power brake reservoir studs and install the brake line flare nuts finger tight, making sure not to cross thread them.

26 Install the master cylinder retaining nuts, tightening them securely.

27 Tighten the brake line flare nuts securely and plug in the level sensor connector.

28 Bleed the brakes at the wheel bleed valves (refer to Section 15).

9 Hydraulic brake hoses and lines - inspection and replacement

1 About every six months, with the vehicle raised and placed securely on jackstands, the flexible hoses which connect the steel brake lines with the front and rear brake assemblies should be inspected for cracks,

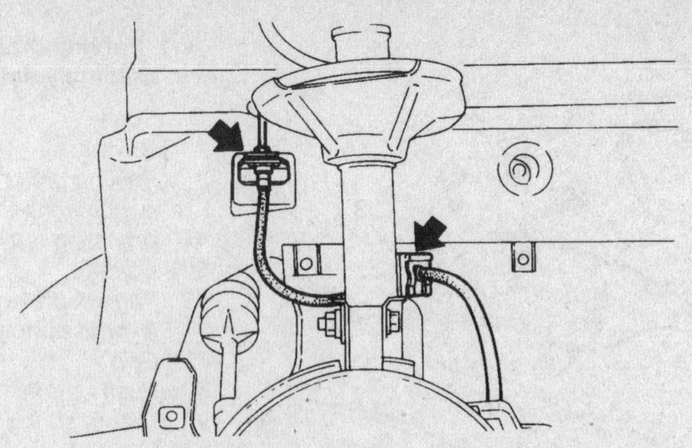

9.2 Front disc brake hose clip locations

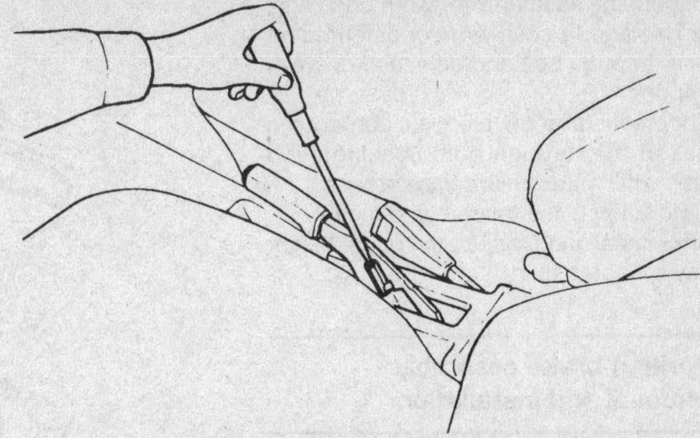

10.3 Adjusting the parking brake stroke

chafing of the outer cover, leaks, blisters and other damage. These are important and vulnerable parts of the brake system and inspection should be complete. A light and mirror will prove helpful for a thorough check. If a hose exhibits any of the above conditions, replace it as follows:

Front brake hose

Refer to illustration 9.2

2 When disconnecting a flexible hose and a brake line pipe, use a back-up wrench and loosen the flare nut, then remove the clip **(see illustration)**. When connecting, install the clip, then tighten the flare nut.

3 When installing make sure all bolt threads are clean.

4 When the brake hose installation is complete, there should be no kinks in the hose. Also, make sure the hose does not contact any part of the suspension. Check this by turning the wheels to the extreme left and right positions. If the hose makes contact, remove the hose and correct the installation as necessary.

Rear brake hose

5 Using a back-up wrench, disconnect the hose at both ends, being careful not to bend the bracket or steel lines.

6 Remove any clips with pliers and separate the female fittings from the brackets.

7 Unbolt the hose retaining clip and remove the hose.

8 Without twisting the hose, install the female ends of the hose in the frame brackets.

9 Install the clips retaining the female end to the bracket.

10 Using a back-up wrench, attach the steel line fittings to the female fittings. Again, be careful not to bend the bracket or steel line.

11 Check that the hose installation did not loosen the frame bracket. Retorque the bracket if necessary.

12 Fill the master cylinder reservoir and bleed the system (refer to Section 13).

Steel brake lines

13 When it becomes necessary to replace steel lines, use only double wall steel tubing. Never substitute copper tubing because copper is subject to fatigue cracking and corrosion. The outside diameter of the tubing is used for sizing.

14 Auto parts stores and brake supply houses carry various lengths of prefabricated brake line.

15 If prefabricated lengths are not available, obtain the recommended steel tubing and fittings to match the line to be replaced. Determine the correct length by measuring the old brake line, and cut the new tubing to length, leaving about 1/2-inch extra for flaring the ends.

16 Install the fittings onto the cut tubing and flare the ends using an ISO flaring tool.

17 Using a tubing bender, bend the tubing to match the shape of the old brake line.

18 Tube flaring and bending can usually be performed by a local auto parts store if the proper equipment is not available.

19 When installing the brake line, leave at least 3/4-inch clearance between the line and any moving parts.

10 Parking brake - checking and adjustment

Checking

1 Pull up on the parking brake handle and make sure that sure that full engagement takes place between 7 and 9 clicks.

Adjustment

Refer to illustration 10.3

2 Start the engine, pump the brake pedal two or three times and shut the engine off.

3 Remove the parking brake cover and use a screwdriver to turn the adjusting nut until the lever stroke is within specification **(see illustration)**. The parking brake warning light on the dash should illuminate after the lever is pulled one notch.

11 Brake pedal assembly - removal and installation

Refer to illustration 11.2

1 Remove the under dash air duct for access.

2 Remove the split pin and withdraw the clevis pin **(see illustration)**.

3 Remove the through bolt, nut and washers.

4 Disconnect the return spring and lift the pedal from the vehicle.

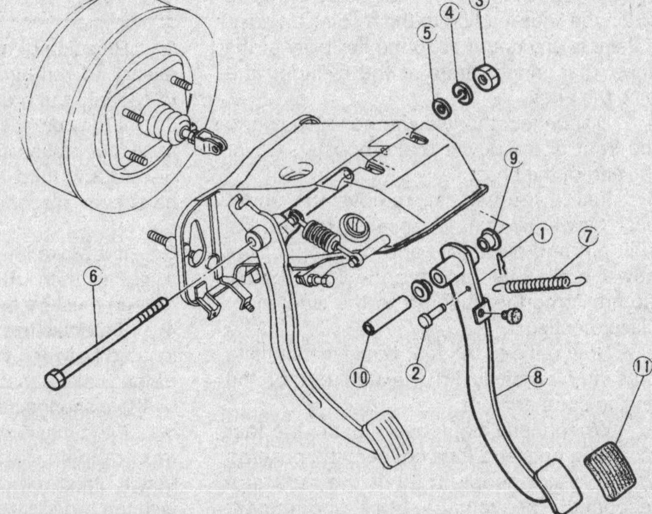

11.2 Brake pedal assembly installation details

1 Split pin
2 Clevis pin
3 Nut
4 Spring washer
5 Plain washer
6 Bolt
7 Return spring
8 Pedal
9 Bushings
10 Shaft
11 Pad
12 Rubber stopper

5 Inspect the assembly for worn bushings, bent or damaged pedal, worn or deteriorated pad, bent through bolt and damaged or weak return spring.

6 Prior to installation, lubricate contact the surfaces of the through bolt, bushings and clevis pin with white lithium base grease.

7 Installation is the reverse of removal.

8 After installation, adjust the pedal height and play (Chapter 1).

12 Parking brake assembly - removal and installation

Refer to illustration 12.1

1 Remove the parking brake cover **(see illustration)**.

2 Disconnect the switch.

3 Remove the adjustment screw.

4 Remove the retaining bolts, disconnect the parking brake cable and lift the handle assembly from the vehicle.

5 Inspect the sector and ratchet pawl for damaged teeth and check the return spring to make sure it is not weak or damaged, replacing as necessary with new components.

6 Lubricate the sector and ratchet teeth lightly with white lithium-based grease prior to installation.

7 Installation is the reverse of removal.

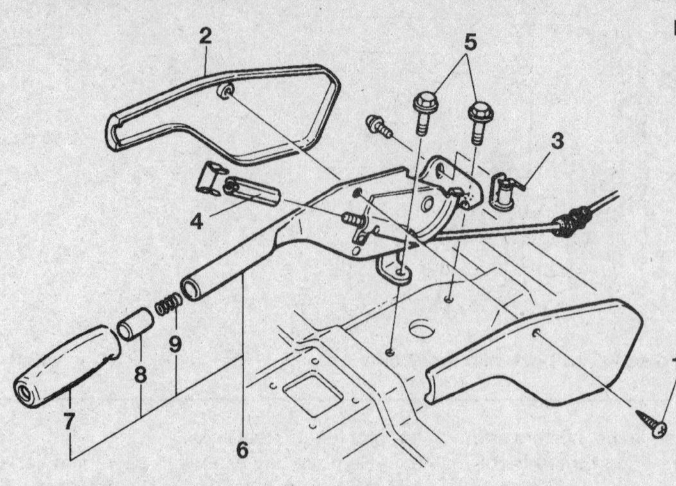

12.1 Parking brake lever assembly details

1 *Screw*
2 *Covers*
3 *Parking brake switch connector*
4 *Adjusting nut*
5 *Bolts*
6 *Parking brake lever assembly*
7 *Grip*
8 *Push button*
9 *Return spring*

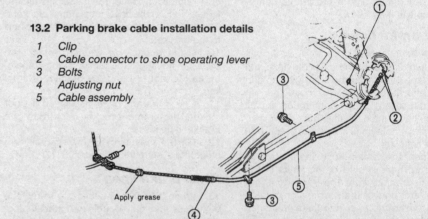

13 Parking brake cable - removal and installation

Refer to illustration 13.2

1 Raise the rear of the vehicle and support it securely on jackstands.

2 Remove the cable clip **(see illustration)**.

3 Remove the trailing brake shoe assembly (Section 6) and disconnect the cable from the shoe operating lever.

4 Remove the retaining bolts and the adjusting nut and remove the cable assembly from the vehicle.

5 Installation is the reverse of removal. Prior to installation, apply white lithium base grease to the cable grommet. After installation, turn the adjusting nut until the equalizer is at a 90-degree angle to the front brake cable.

13.2 Parking brake cable installation details

1 *Clip*
2 *Cable connector to shoe operating lever*
3 *Bolts*
4 *Adjusting nut*
5 *Cable assembly*

Apply grease

14 Power brake booster - inspection, removal and installation

Refer to illustration 14.3

1 The power brake unit requires no special maintenance apart from periodic inspection of the hoses and inspection of the air filter beneath the boot at the pedal pushrod end.

2 Dismantling of the power brake unit requires special tools. If a problem develops, it is recommended that a new or factory exchange unit be installed rather than trying to overhaul the original booster.

3 Remove the mounting nuts which hold the master cylinder to the power brake unit **(see illustration)**. Unplug the brake fluid level sensor connector and position the master cylinder out of the way, being careful not to strain the lines leading to the master cylinder. If there is any doubt as to the flexibility of the lines, disconnect them at the cylinder and plug the ends.

4 Disconnect the vacuum hose leading to the front of the power brake booster. Cover the end of the hose.

5 Inside the vehicle, remove the under dash blower air duct for access. Remove the split pin and clevis pin and disconnect the power brake pushrod from the brake pedal. Do not force the pushrod to the side when disconnecting it.

6 Now remove the four booster mounting nuts and carefully lift the unit out of the engine compartment.

7 When installing, loosely install the four mounting nuts and then connect the pushrod to the brake pedal. Tighten the nuts and reconnect the vacuum hose and master cylinder. If the hydraulic brake lines were disconnected, the entire brake system should be bled to eliminate any air which has entered the system (refer to Section 15).

15 Hydraulic system - bleeding

1 Bleeding of the hydraulic system is necessary to remove air whenever it is introduced into the brake system.

2 It may be necessary to bleed the system at all four brakes if air has entered the system due to low fluid level, or if the brake lines have been disconnected at the master cylinder.

3 If a brake line was disconnected only at a wheel, then only that wheel cylinder (or caliper) must be bled.

4 If a brake line is disconnected at a fitting located between the master cylinder and any of the brakes, that part of the system served by the disconnected line must be bled.

5 If the master cylinder has been removed from the vehicle, refer to Section 8 for the bench bleeding procedure before proceeding with the procedure which follows.

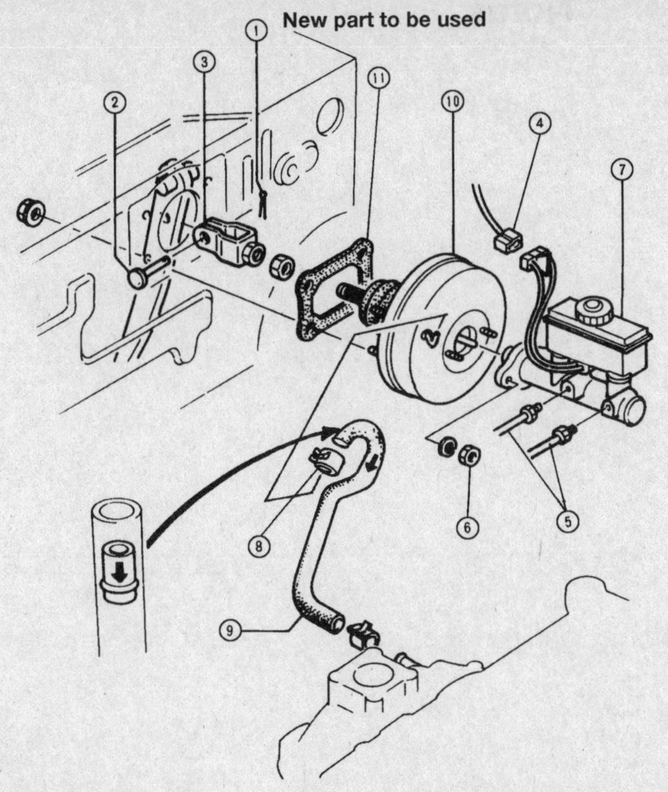

14.3 Power brake booster installation details

1 Split pin
2 Clevis pin
3 Fork and nut
4 Fluid level sensor connector
5 Brake line pipes
6 Nuts
7 Master cylinder assembly
8 Hose clamps
9 Vacuum hose
10 Booster unit
11 Gasket

6 If the master cylinder is installed on the vehicle but is known to have, or is suspected of having air in the bore, the master cylinder must be bled before any wheel cylinder (or caliper) is bled. Follow Steps 7 through 16 to bleed the master cylinder while it is installed on the vehicle.

7 Remove the vacuum reserve from the brake power booster by applying the brake several times with the engine off.

8 Remove the master cylinder reservoir cover and fill the reservoirs with brake fluid, then keep checking the fluid level often during the bleeding operation, adding fluid as necessary to keep the reservoirs full. Reinstall the cover.

9 Disconnect the forward brake line connection at the master cylinder.

10 Allow brake fluid to fill the master cylinder bore until it begins to flow from the forward line connector port. Have a container and shop rags handy to catch and clean up spilled fluid.

11 Reconnect the forward brake line to the master cylinder.

12 Have an assistant depress the brake pedal very slowly (one time only) and hold it down.

13 Loosen the forward brake line at the master cylinder to purge the air from the bore, retighten the connection, then have the brake pedal released slowly.

14 Wait 15 seconds (important).

15 Repeat the sequence, including the 15 second wait, until all air is removed from the bore.

16 After the forward port has been completely purged of air, bleed the rear port in the same manner.

17 To bleed the individual wheel cylinders or calipers, first refer to Steps 7 and 8.

18 Have an assistant on hand, as well as a supply of new brake fluid, an empty clear plastic container, a length of 3/16-inch plastic, rubber or vinyl tubing to fit over the bleeder valve and a wrench to open and close the bleeder valve. The vehicle may have to be raised and placed on jackstands for clearance.

19 Beginning at the right rear wheel, loosen the bleeder valve slightly, then tighten it to a point where it is snug but can still be loosened quickly and easily.

20 Place one end of the tubing over the bleeder valve and submerge the other end in brake fluid in the container.

21 Have the assistant pump the brakes a few times to get pressure in the system, then hold the pedal firmly depressed.

22 While the pedal is held depressed, open the bleeder valve just enough to allow a flow of fluid to leave the valve. Watch for air bubbles to exit the submerged end of the tube. When the fluid flow slows after a couple of seconds, close the valve again and have your assistant release the pedal.

23 Repeat Steps 21 and 22 until no more air is seen leaving the tube, then tighten the bleeder valve and proceed to the left rear wheel, the right front wheel and the left front wheel, in that order, and perform the same procedure. Be sure to check the fluid in the master cylinder reservoir frequently.

24 Never use old brake fluid because it attracts moisture which will deteriorate the brake system components.

25 Fill the master cylinder with fluid at the end of the operation.

26 If any difficulty is experienced in bleeding the hydraulic system, or if an assistant is not available, a pressure bleeding kit is a worthwhile investment. If connected in accordance with the instructions, each bleeder valve can be opened in turn to allow the fluid to be pressure ejected until it is clear of air bubbles without the need to replenish the master cylinder reservoir during the process.

Notes

Chapter 10
Suspension and steering

Contents

Specifications

Torque specifications	Ft-lbs	M-kg (unless otherwise indicated)
Front suspension		
Driveaxle locknut	116 to 174	16 to 24
Upper strut damper nuts	25 to 34	3.0 to 6.4
Lower strut damper nuts and bolts	69 to 86	9.5 to 11.9
Balljoint-to-steering knuckle bolt and nut	32 to 40	4.4 to 5.5
Lower suspension arm through-bolts and nuts	69 to 86	9.5 to 11.9
Stabilizer bar bracket bolts	32 to 40	4.4 to 5.5
Rear suspension		
Upper strut damper nuts	16 to 20	2.2 to 2.7
Lower strut damper bolts and nuts	69 to 86	9.5 to 11.9
Lateral link through-bolt	46 to 55	6.1 to 7.5
Lateral link-to-crossmember	69 to 86	9.5 to 11.9
Lateral link-to-rear hub spindle	69 to 86	9.5 to 11.9
Trailing link-to-body	43 to 54	6.0 to 7.5
Trailing link-to-rear hub spindle	40 to 50	5.5 to 6.9
Trailing link-to-stabilizer bar	23 to 34	3.2 to 4.7
Steering		
Tie rod end nut	22 to 33	3.0 to 4.5
Intermediate shaft nut	13 to 20	1.8 to 2.7
Rack and pinion body-to-chassis	23 to 34	3.2 to 4.7

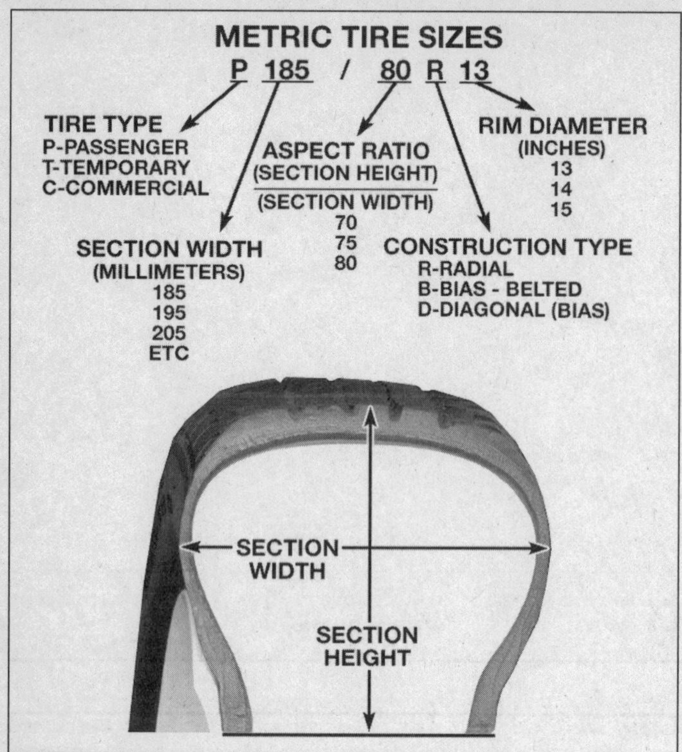

1.1 Metric size code

3.1 Caster, camber and toe-in angles

1 Wheels and tires - general information

Refer to illustration 1.1

All models covered by this manual are equipped with metric-sized radial tires **(see illustration)**. Use of other size or type of tires may affect the ride and handling of the vehicle. Don't mix different types of tires, such as radials and bias belted, on the same vehicle as handling may be seriously affected. It's recommended that tires are replaced in pairs on the same axle, but if only one tire is being replaced, be sure it's the same size, structure and tread design as the other.

Because tire pressure has a substantial effect on handling and wear, the pressure on all tires should be checked at least once a month or before any extended trips (see Chapter 1).

Wheels must be replaced if they are bent, dented, leak air, have elongated bolt holes, are heavily rusted, out of vertical symmetry or if the lug nuts won't stay tight. Wheel repairs that use welding or peening are not recommended.

Tire and wheel balance is important to the overall handling, braking and performance of the vehicle. Unbalanced wheels can adversely affect handling and ride characteristics as well as tire life. Whenever a tire is installed on a wheel, the tire and wheel should be balanced by a shop with the proper equipment.

2 Wheel and tire - removal and installation

1 With the car on a level surface, the parking brake on and the car in gear (manual transaxles should be in Reverse, automatic transaxles should be in Park) remove the wheel cover (if equipped) and loosen, but do not remove, the wheel lug nuts.

2 Using a jack positioned in the proper location on the car, raise the car just enough so that the tire clears the ground.

3 Remove the lug nuts.

4 Remove the wheel and tire.

5 If a flat tire is being replaced, ensure that there is adequate ground clearance for the new inflated tire, then mount the wheel and tire on the wheel studs.

6 Apply a light coat of spray lubricant or light oil to the wheel stud threads and install the lug nuts snugly with the cone shaped end facing the wheel.

7 Lower the car until the tire contacts the ground and the wheel studs are centered in their wheel holes.

8 Tighten the lug nuts evenly and in a cross pattern, and torque to specs.

9 Lower the car completely and remove the jack.

10 Replace the wheel cover.

3 Wheel alignment - general information

Refer to illustration 3.1

A wheel alignment refers to the adjustments made to the wheels so they are in proper angular relationship to the suspension and the ground. Wheels that are out of proper alignment not only affect steering control, but also increase tire wear **(see illustration)**.

Getting the proper wheel alignment is a very exacting process, one in which complicated and expensive machines are necessary to perform the job properly. Because of this, you should have a technician with the proper equipment perform these tasks. We will, however, use this space to give you a basic idea of what is involved with wheel alignment so you can better understand the process and deal intelligently with the shop that does the work.

Toe-in is the turning in of the front wheels (and rear wheels on later models). The purpose of a toe specification is to ensure parallel rolling of the wheels. In a vehicle with zero toe-in, the distance between the front edges of the wheels will be the same as the distance between the rear edges of the wheels. The actual amount of toe-in is normally only a fraction of an inch. Toe-in adjustment is controlled by the tie-rod end position on the tie-rod. Incorrect toe-in will cause the tires to wear improperly by making them scrub against the road surface.

Camber is the tilting of the wheels from the vertical when viewed from the front of the vehicle. When the wheels tilt out at the top, the camber is said to be positive (+). When the wheels tilt in at the top the camber is negative (-). The amount of tilt is measured in degrees from the vertical and this measurement is called the camber angle. This angle affects the amount of tire tread which contacts the road

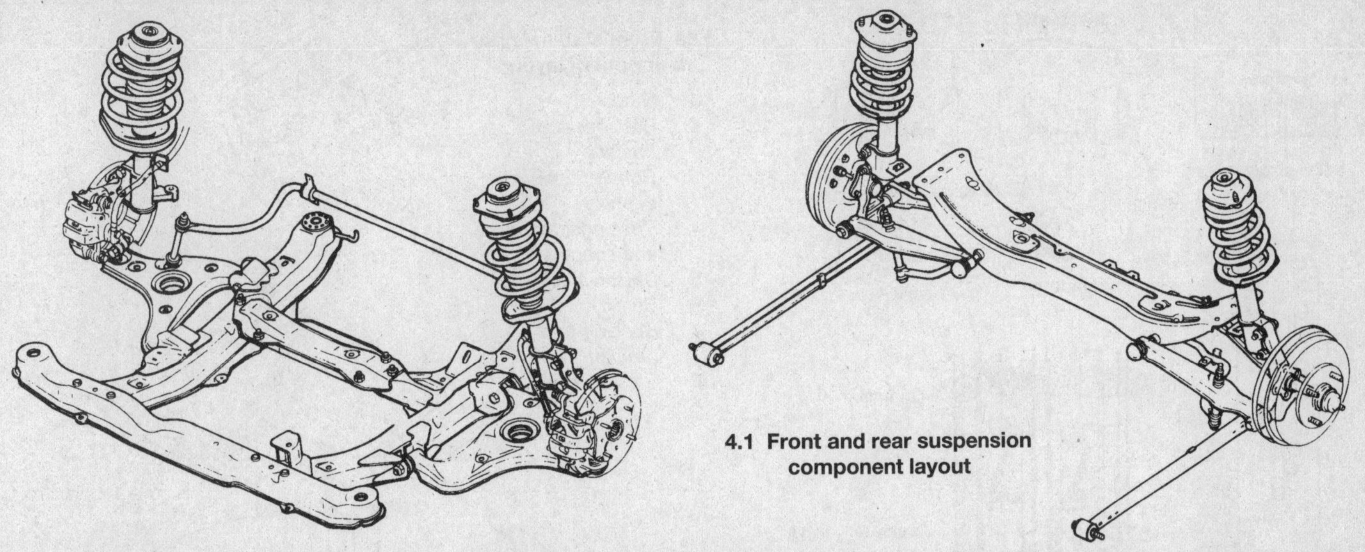
4.1 Front and rear suspension component layout

and compensates for changes in the suspension geometry when the vehicle is cornering or traveling over an undulating surface.

Caster is the tilting of the top of the front steering axis from the vertical. A tilt toward the rear is positive caster and a tilt toward the front is negative caster.

4 Suspension system - general information

Refer to illustrations 4.1, 4.2 and 4.3

These models are equipped with independent front and rear strut-type suspension. This design uses a combination spring and shock absorber assembly mounted directly to the knuckle **(see illustration)**. A lower control arm that pivots on the chassis is also attached to the knuckle. At the rear, trailing links are used to locate the knuckle. In addition, stabilizer bars are used at the front and rear on some models.

Some later models are equipped with a 4-Wheel Steering (4WS) system. This system connects the front steering gear to a solenoid operated steering gear at the rear wheels by way of a steering angle shaft and allows the rear wheels to be steered under certain conditions **(see illustration)**. All checks and adjustments to the 4WS system should be left to your dealer.

Some models are also equipped with a three way damping system which adjusts the damping of the shock absorbers, either manually or automatically. This is accomplished by actuators mounted at the top of the struts that rotate the control rod approximately 60° to vary damping action **(see illustration)**. These models use gas shock absorbers, while non-adjustable models use conventional sealed hydraulic units.

Never attempt to heat or straighten any suspension part, as this can weaken the metal or in other ways damage the part.

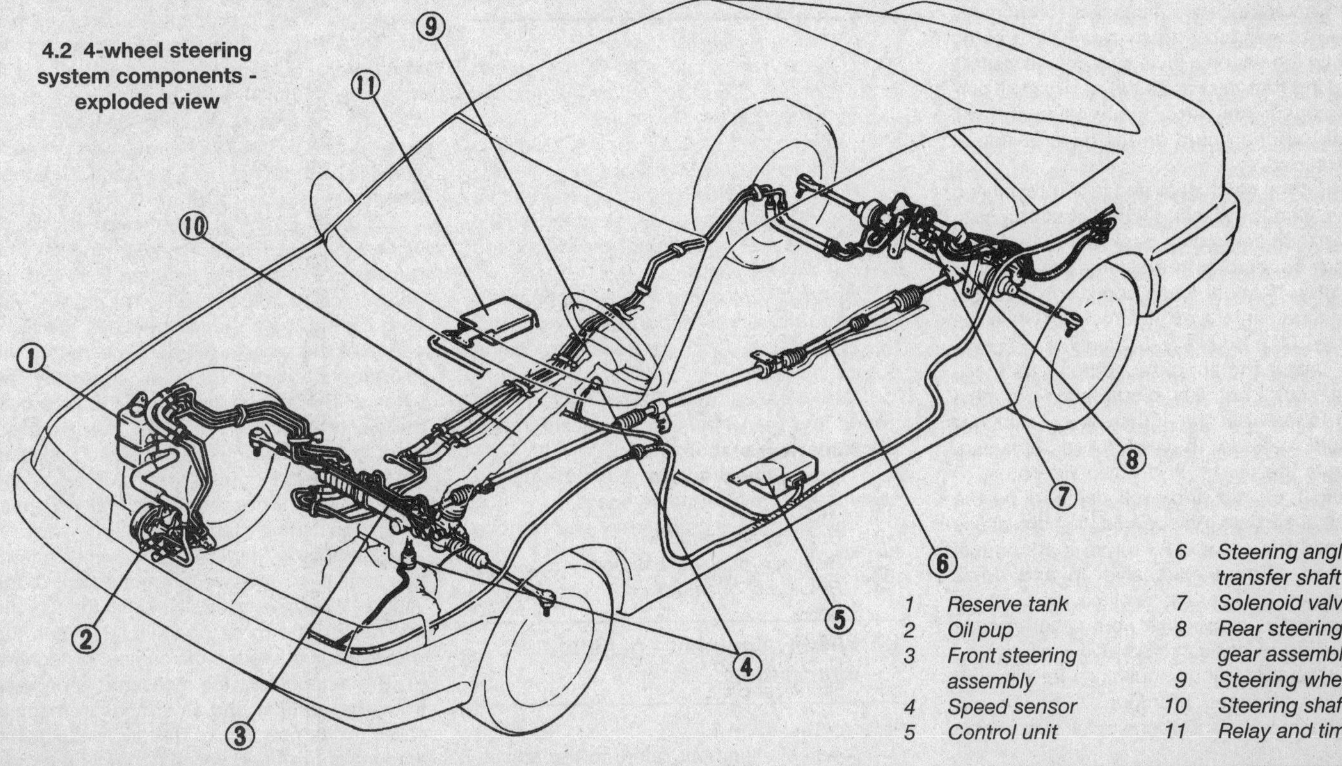

4.2 4-wheel steering system components - exploded view

1 Reserve tank
2 Oil pup
3 Front steering assembly
4 Speed sensor
5 Control unit
6 Steering angle transfer shaft
7 Solenoid valve
8 Rear steering gear assembly
9 Steering wheel
10 Steering shaft
11 Relay and timer

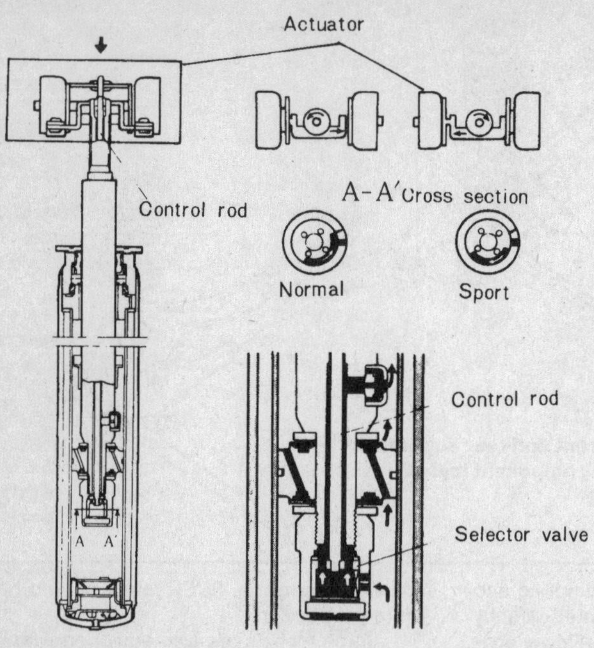

4.3 The optional three way damping system operates the strut control rod to change the damping action

6.3a Front stabilizer bar component layout

1. *Nuts*
2. *Retainer and bushing*
3. *Bolt, retainer and bushing*
4. *Bushings, retainers and spacers*
5. *Splash shields*
6. *Bolts*
7. *Bushing and bracket*
8. *Stabilizer bar*

5 Suspension system - inspection

1 Suspension components should normally last a long time, except in cases where damage has occurred due to an accident. The suspension parts, however, should be checked from time to time for signs of wear which will result in a loss of precision handling and riding comfort.

2 Check that the suspension components have not sagged due to wear. Do this by parking the car on a level surface and visually checking that the car sits level. This will normally occur only after many miles and will usually appear more on the driver's side of the vehicle.

3 Put the car in gear and take off the hand brake. Grip the steering wheel at the top with both hands and rock it back and forth. Listen for any squeaks or metallic noises. Feel for free play. If any of these conditions is found, have an assistant do the rocking while the source of the trouble is located.

4 Check the shock absorbers, as these are the parts of the suspension system most likely to wear out first. If there is any evidence of fluid leakage, they will need replacing. Bounce the car up and down vigorously. It should feel stiff and well damped by the shock absorbers. As soon as the bouncing is stopped the car should return to its normal position without excessive up and down movement. Do not replace the shock absorbers as single units, but rather in pairs unless failure has occurred at low mileage.

5 Check all rubber bushings for signs of deterioration and cracking. If necessary, replace the rubber portions of the suspension arm.

6 Stabilizer bar - removal and installation

Refer to illustrations 6.3a, 6.3b, 6.8, 6.9 and 6.11

1 Raise the vehicle and support it securely on jackstands.

2 On the front stabilizer bar, remove the front wheels and splash shields.

3 Remove the stabilizer bar-to-suspension arm bolts **(see illustrations)**.

4 Remove the bushing and bracket bolts.

5 Remove the rear stabilizer bar from the vehicle.

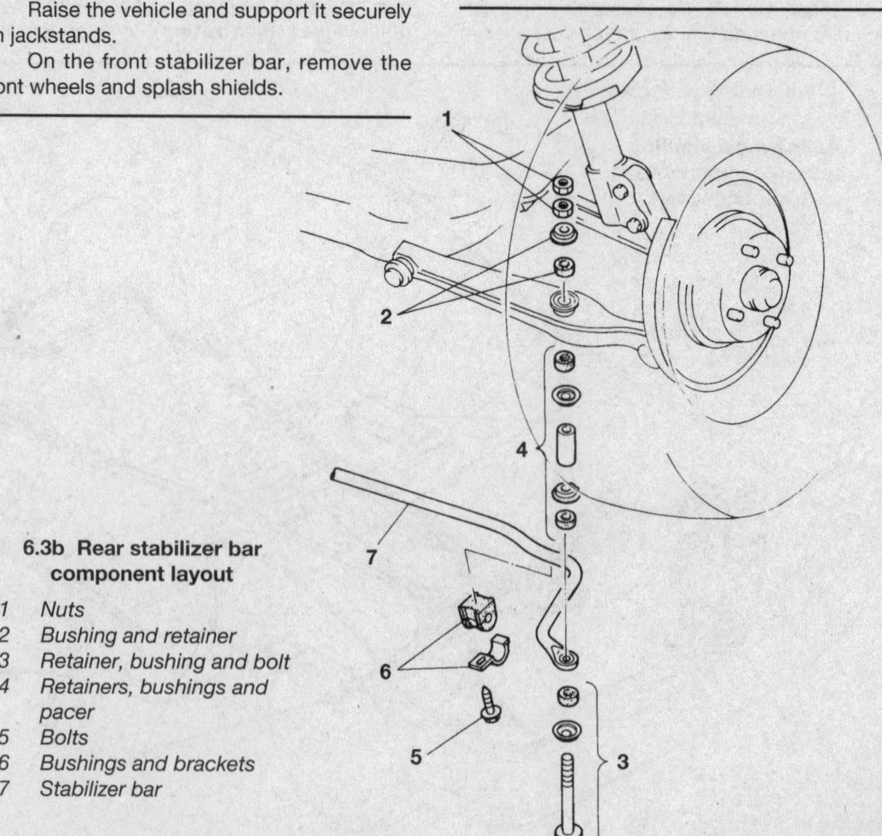

6.3b Rear stabilizer bar component layout

1. *Nuts*
2. *Bushing and retainer*
3. *Retainer, bushing and bolt*
4. *Retainers, bushings and pacer*
5. *Bolts*
6. *Bushings and brackets*
7. *Stabilizer bar*

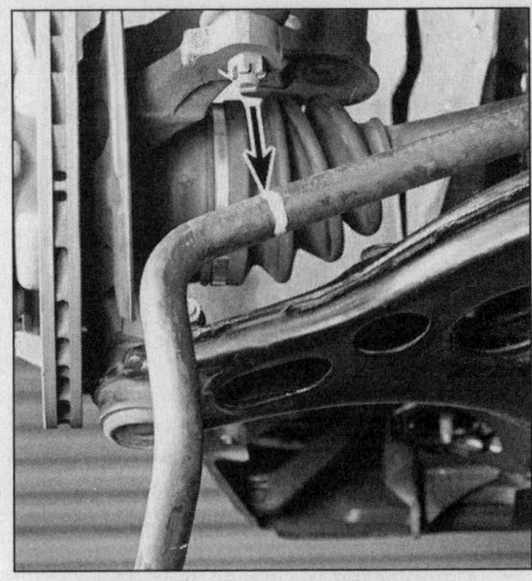
6.8 **Front stabilizer bar bushing alignment mark (arrow)**

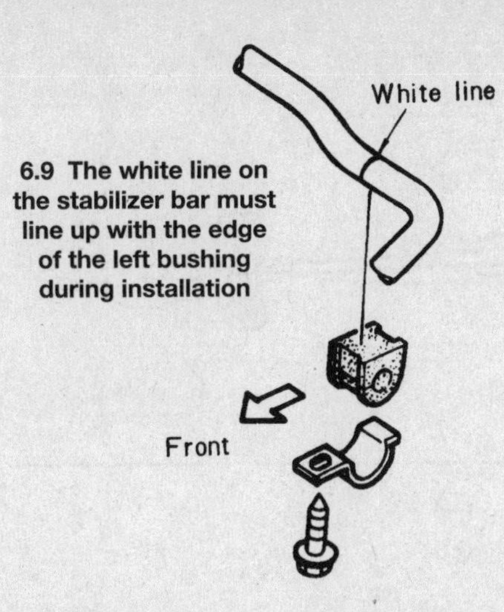

6.9 The white line on the stabilizer bar must line up with the edge of the left bushing during installation

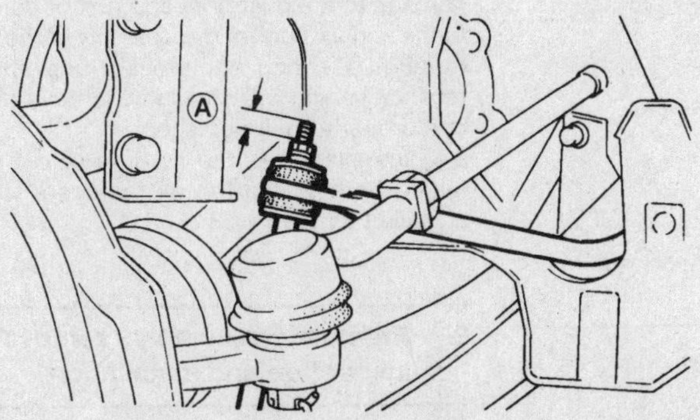

6.11 After tightening, the stabilizer bar link bolt must have one inch of thread exposed

6 On the front stabilizer bar, remove the rack and pinion assembly retaining bolts, pry the assembly up and then remove the bar by carefully working it past the rack and pinion and out through the left wheel well.

7 Inspect the bushings to be sure they are not hardened, cracked or excessively worn, and replace if necessary.

8 Place the stabilizer bar in position. Make sure the bar is inserted with the bushing alignment mark on the left side of the vehicle **(see illustration)**.

9 Install the front stabilizer bar left side bushing with the edge aligned with the mark and the notch facing the rear of the vehicle **(see illustration)**.

10 After installing the bushing bracket bolts, tighten them to the specified torque.

11 Install the end bolts and nuts and tighten them securely with one inch of thread exposed after tightening **(see illustration)**.

7 Front lower control arm - removal and installation

Refer to illustrations 7.4 and 7.8

1 Raise the front of the car and support it on jackstands.

2 If only one lower control arm is being removed, disconnect only that end of the stabilizer bar. If both lower control arms are being removed, remove the stabilizer bar completely. Refer to Section 6.

3 Remove the wheel(s) and splash shield(s).

4 Remove the control arm bushing bolts that secure the control arm to the engine cradle **(see illustration)**.

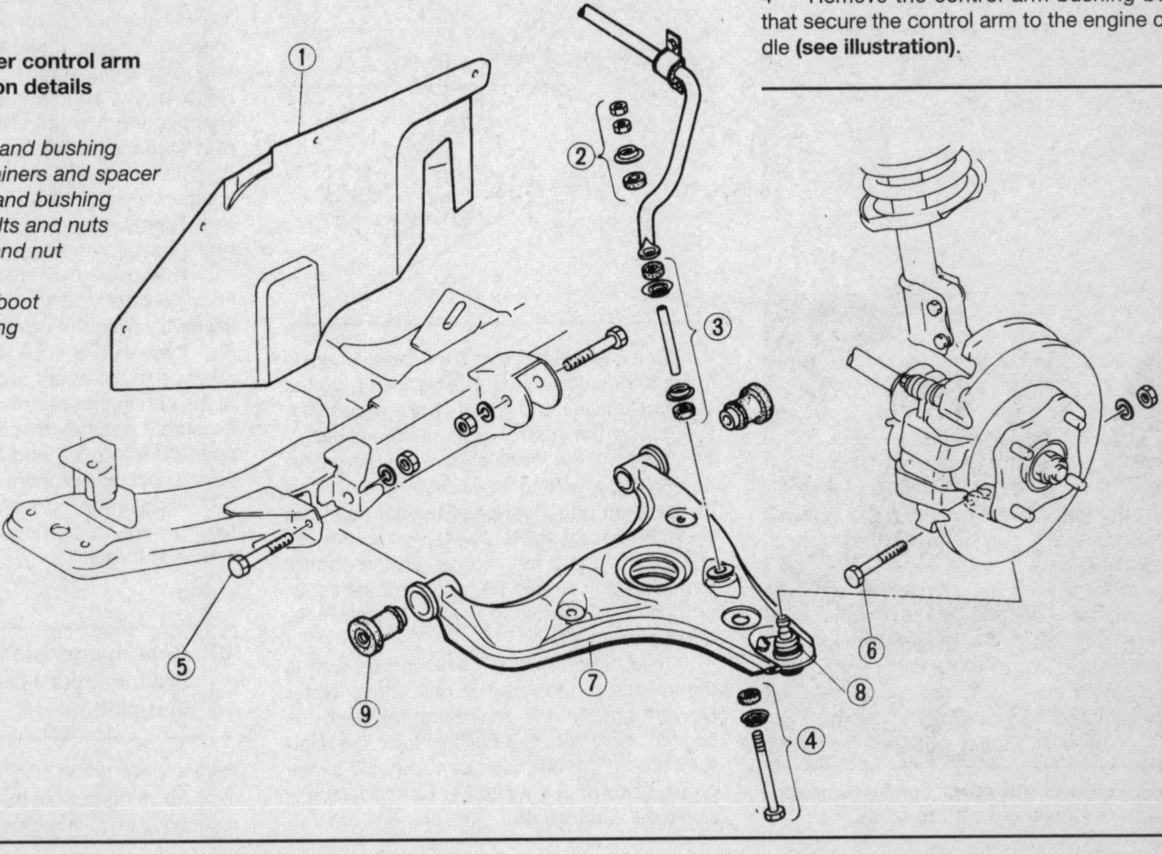

7.4 Front lower control arm installation details

1. *Splash shield*
2. *Nuts, retainer and bushing*
3. *Bushings, retainers and spacer*
4. *Bolt, retainer and bushing*
5. *Lower arm bolts and nuts*
6. *Balljoint bolt and nut*
7. *Lower arm*
8. *Balljoint dust boot*
9. *Rubber bushing*

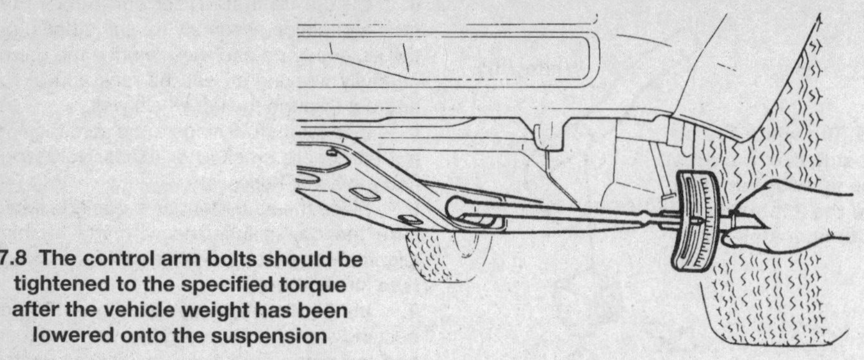

7.8 The control arm bolts should be tightened to the specified torque after the vehicle weight has been lowered onto the suspension

5 Remove the balljoint-to-steering knuckle nut and then disconnect the balljoint from the steering knuckle, using a pry bar if necessary.

6 Lower the control arm from the vehicle.

7 Inspect the control arm bushings for hardening, cracking or excessive wear and the balljoint and dust boot for damage and wear. Replacing these components requires special tools and techniques, so the control arm assembly should be taken to a dealer or properly equipped shop to have these procedures performed.

8 Installation of the lower control arm is the reverse of the removal procedure. **Note:** *Do not tighten the lower control arm-to-engine cradle bushing bolts to their specified torque until the car has been lowered to the ground and its full weight is on the suspension* **(see illustration).**

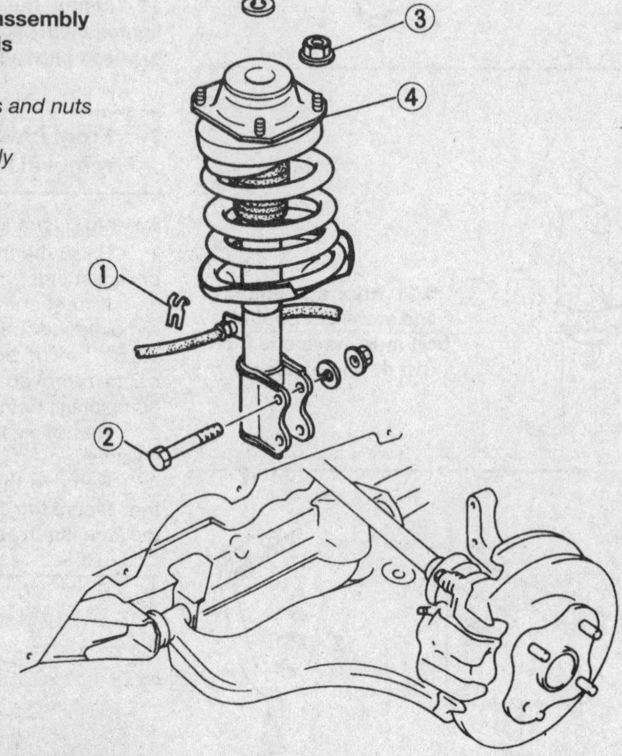

8.3 Front strut damper assembly installation details

1 *Hose clip*
2 *Steering knuckle bolts and nuts*
3 *Nuts*
4 *Strut damper assembly*

8.4 The front strut cover can be removed by pulling it off the studs

8 Front strut damper assembly - removal and installation

Refer to illustrations 8.3 and 8.4

1 Raise the front of the vehicle and support it securely on jackstands.

2 Remove the clip and disconnect the brake hose from the strut.

3 Remove the strut-to-knuckle nuts and then remove one of the nut and bolt assemblies **(see illustration)**.

4 In the engine compartment, remove the upper strut cover **(see illustration)**.

5 Remove the three way damping control switch (if equipped) (Section 11).

6 Remove the four strut damper-to-chassis stud nuts.

7 Remove the remaining strut-to-knuckle nut and bolt and lower the strut damper assembly from the vehicle.

8 Inspect the assembly for oil leakage, damage to the dust boot and rust or damage to the spring. Further disassembly of the strut requires a spring compressor and special techniques and this should be left to a dealer or a properly equipped shop.

9 Installation is the reverse of removal, taking care to tighten all fasteners to the specified torque.

9 Rear strut assembly - removal, inspection and installation

Refer to illustration 9.1

1 In the rear compartment of the car remove the rear panel for access. On three way damping control equipped models, remove the adjuster switch (Section 11). Remove the two upper strut-to-chassis stud nuts **(see illustration)**.

2 Raise the rear of the vehicle and support it securely with jackstands.

3 Remove the clip and disconnect the brake hose from the strut.

4 Remove the two strut-to-steering knuckle nuts and bolts and lower the strut assembly from the vehicle.

5 Inspect the strut for oil leaks, tears or damage to the dust boot and rust or damage of the spring. Further disassembly of the strut assembly requires a spring compressor and special techniques and this should be left to your dealer or a properly equipped shop.

6 Installation is the reverse of removal, taking care to tighten all fasteners to the specified torque.

10 Rear suspension lateral and trailing links - removal and installation

Refer to illustration 10.4

1 Raise the rear of the vehicle and support it securely on jackstands.

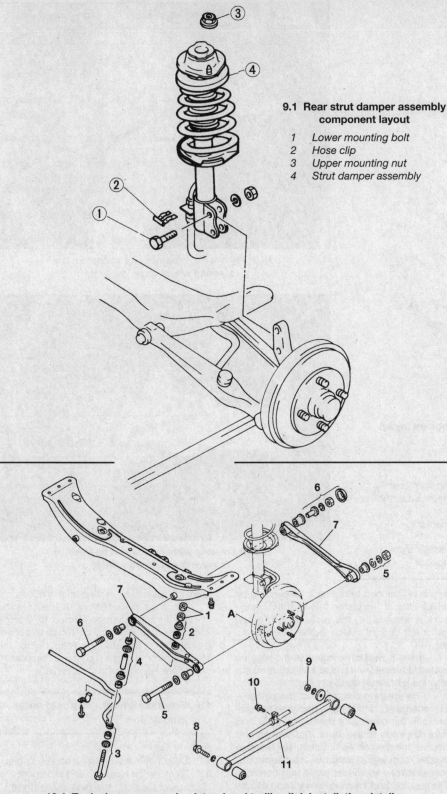

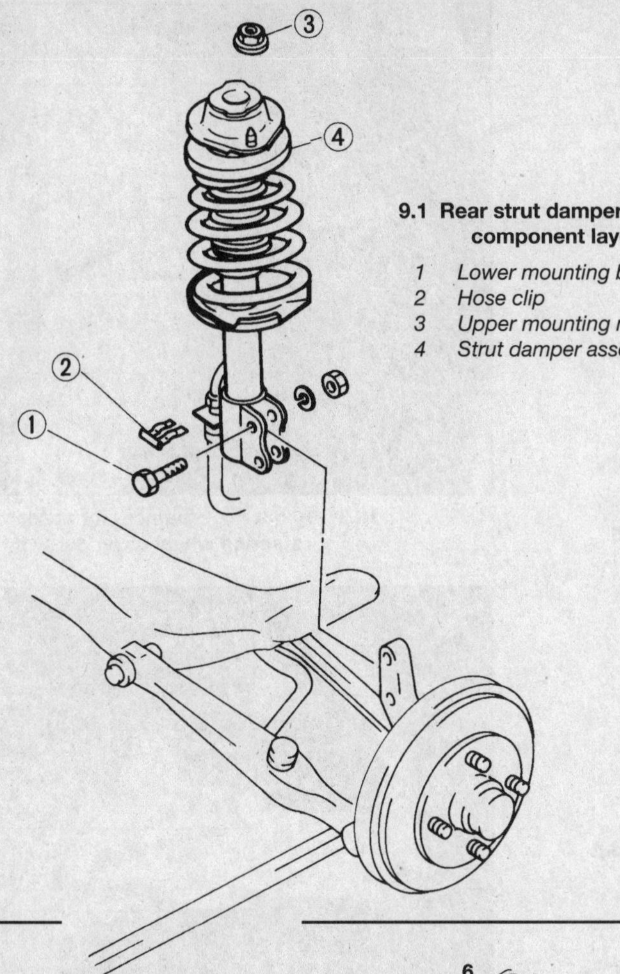

9.1 Rear strut damper assembly component layout

1. *Lower mounting bolt*
2. *Hose clip*
3. *Upper mounting nut*
4. *Strut damper assembly*

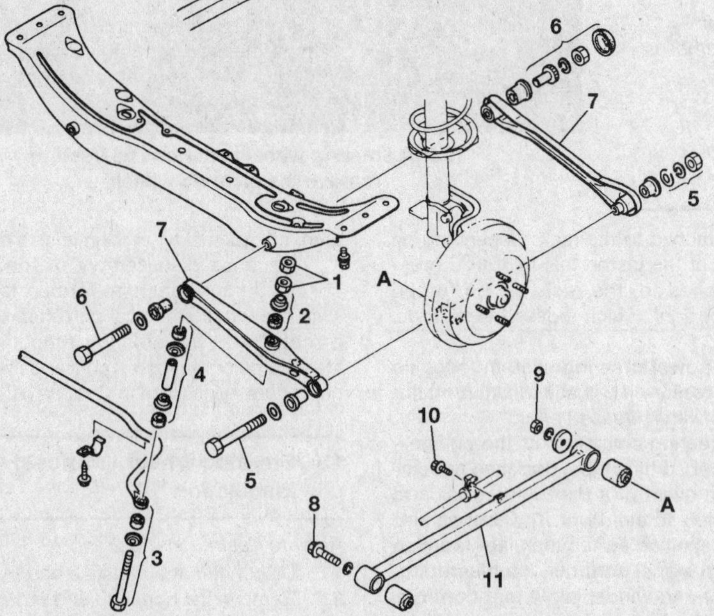

10.4 Typical rear suspension lateral and trailing link installation details

1. *Nuts*
2. *Bushing and retainer*
3. *Retainer, bushing and bolt*
4. *Retainers, bushing and spacer*
5. *Bolt and nut*
6. *Through-bolt, nut and spacer*
7. *Lateral links*
8. *Bolt*
9. *Nut*
10. *Bolt*
11. *Trailing link*

2 Remove the fuel tank (Chapter 4).

3 Mark the position of the adjustment star wheel and nut for reinstallation to the same position. Moving the nut and star wheel will affect the rear wheel toe in, so this is important.

4 Remove the lateral link-to-chassis crossmember retaining bolts, nuts and bushings and disconnect the stabilizer bar link (if equipped) **(see illustration)**.

5 Remove the lateral links from the vehicle.

6 Remove the parking brake bracket bolt.

7 Remove the through bolts and lower the trailing link from the vehicle.

8 Installation is the reverse of removal. Install all bolts temporarily and then lower the vehicle weight onto the wheels before tightening to the specified torque.

9 Have the rear wheel toe in checked by a dealer or properly equipped shop.

11 Three way damping control switches - removal and installation

Refer to illustration 11.2

1 Open the hood and remove the rubber strut cover to gain access to the front suspension switches or open the trunk or hatch and remove the rear inner panel for access to the rear suspension switches.

2 Unplug the connector, remove the two retaining screws and lift the switch from the top of the strut **(see illustration)**.

3 Installation is the reverse of removal.

12 Steering system - general information

Refer to illustration 12.1

All models are equipped with rack and pinion steering. The components making up this system are the steering wheel, steering column, intermediate shaft, rack and pinion

11.2 Removing the rear three-way damping control switch

10

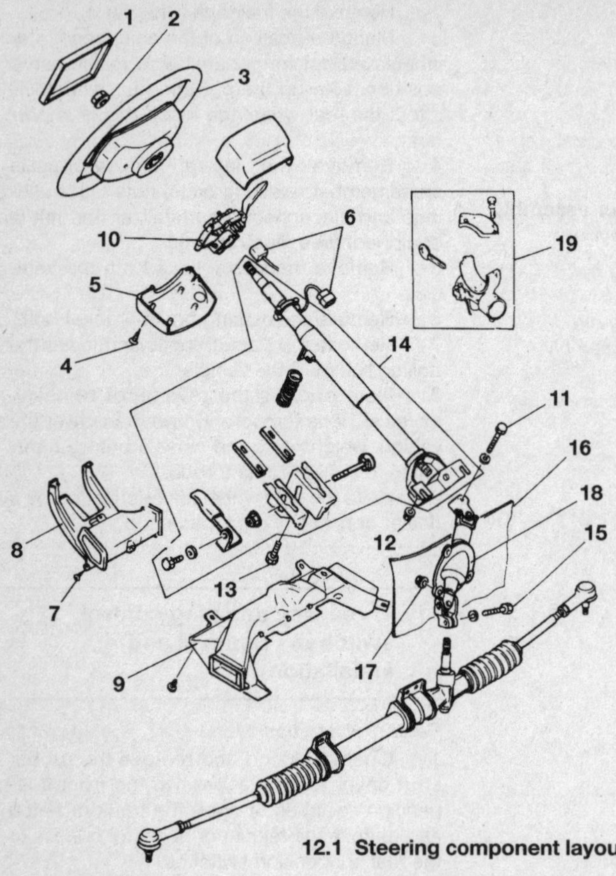

12.1 Steering component layout

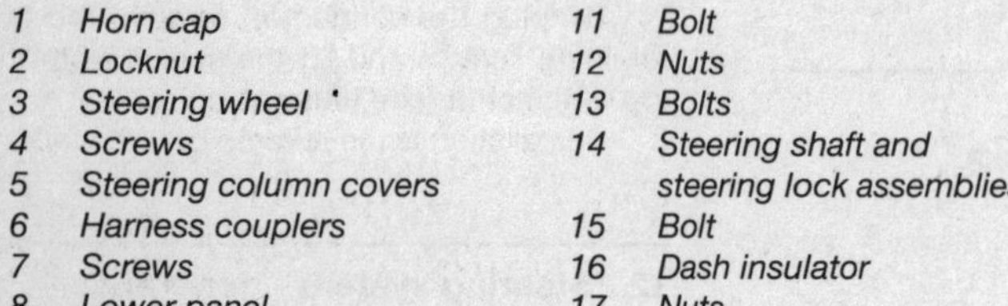

1	*Horn cap*	11	*Bolt*
2	*Locknut*	12	*Nuts*
3	*Steering wheel*	13	*Bolts*
4	*Screws*	14	*Steering shaft and steering lock assemblies*
5	*Steering column covers*	15	*Bolt*
6	*Harness couplers*	16	*Dash insulator*
7	*Screws*	17	*Nuts*
8	*Lower panel*	18	*Intermediate shaft*
9	*Air duct*	19	*Steering lock*
10	*Combination switch*		

13.2 Pry out the ornament for access to the steering wheel cover screws

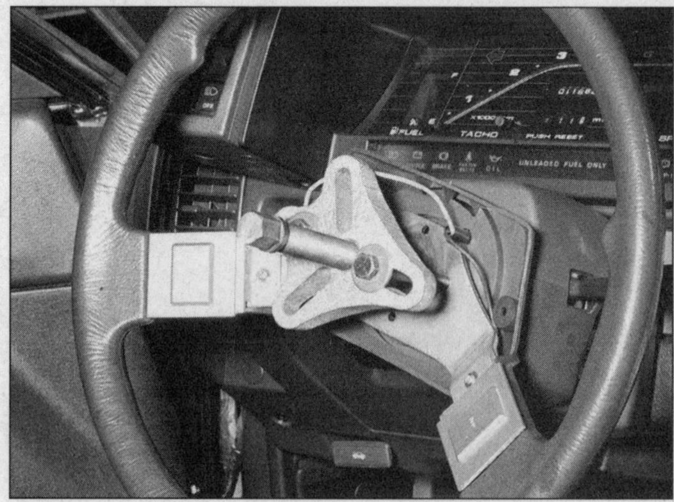

13.5 A steering wheel puller can be used to remove the steering wheel

assembly, tie rods and steering knuckles **(see illustration)**. In addition, the power steering system also uses a belt driven pump to provide hydraulic pressure.

In a manual system, the motion of turning the steering wheel is transferred through the column and intermediate shaft to the pinion shaft in the rack and pinion assembly. Teeth on the pinion shaft are meshed with teeth on the rack, so when the shaft is turned, the rack is moved left or right in the rack and pinion housing. Attached to each end of the rack are tie rods that, in turn are attached to the steering knuckles on the front wheels. This left and right movement of the rack is the direct force which turns the wheels.

The power steering system operates in essentially the same way as the manual system, except that the power rack and pinion system uses hydraulic pressure to boost the manual steering force. A rotary control valve in the rack and pinion assembly directs hydraulic fluid from the power steering pump to either side of the integral rack piston, which is attached to the rack. Depending on which side of the piston this hydraulic pressure is applied to, the rack will be forced either left or right, which moves the tie rods, etc.

If the power steering system loses its hydraulic pressure it will still function manually, though with increased effort.

The steering column is of the collapsible, energy absorbing type, designed to compress in the event of a front end collision to minimize injury to the driver. The column also houses the ignition switch lock, key warning buzzer, turn signal controls, headlight dimmer control and windshield wiper controls. The ignition and steering wheel can both be locked while the car is parked to inhibit theft.

Due to the column's collapsible design, it is important that only specified screws, bolts and nuts can be used as designated and that they be tightened to the specified torque. Other precautions particular to this design are noted in appropriate Sections.

In addition to the standard steering column, an optional tilt version is also offered.

Because disassembly of the steering column is more often performed to repair a switch or other electrical part than to correct a problem in the steering functioning, the steering column disassembly and reassembly procedure is included in Chapter 12.

13 Steering wheel - removal and installation

Refer to illustrations 13.2 and 13.5

1 Disconnect the negative battery cable.

2 Remove the horn cap and ornament and disconnect the horn wire **(see illustration)**.

3 Be sure the steering wheel is unlocked, then remove the lock nut.

4 Mark the position of the steering wheel in relation to the steering shaft.

5 Using steering wheel puller, remove the steering wheel **(see illustration)**. Caution: Under no circumstances should the end of the shaft be hammered on.

6 Installation is the reverse of the removal procedure with the following notes: Prior to installation, lightly coat the horn contact surfaces on the steering wheel hub with a moly-base grease. When installing the steering wheel on the shaft be sure the alignment marks on the steering wheel and shaft match.

14 Steering column - removal and installation

1 Disconnect the negative battery terminal.
2 Remove the steering wheel (Section 13).
3 Remove the steering column covers and unplug the harness connectors.
4 Remove the blower air duct (Chapter 11).
5 Remove the combination switch (Chapter 12).
6 Remove the steering column retaining nuts and bolts.
7 Disengage the column from the intermediate shaft and lift the column carefully from the vehicle.
8 Because of its collapsible design, the steering column is very susceptible to damage when removed from the vehicle. Be careful not to lean on or drop the column, as this could weaken the column structure and impair its performance.
9 If the car has been in an accident which resulted in frame damage, major body damage or in which the steering column was impacted, the column could be damaged or misaligned and should be checked by a qualified mechanic.
10 If disassembly of the column is necessary, refer to Chapter 12.
11 The steering column is installed by reversing the sequence of the removal operation.

15.14 Peening the hub locknut into the driveaxle groove with chisel

15 Steering knuckle/hub assembly - removal and installation

Refer to illustration 15.14

1 Raise the front of the vehicle, support it securely on jackstands and remove the front wheel.
2 Lock the hub from turning by inserting a screwdriver or similar tool through the brake caliper into the rotor and remove the front hub locknut.
3 Unbolt the brake caliper and hang it out of the way.
4 Remove the strut-to-steering knuckle mounting bolts and nuts.
5 Remove the nut that secures the tie rod to the steering knuckle.
6 Disengage the tie rod from the steering knuckle (Section 16).
7 Remove the retaining nut and bolt and disengage the balljoint from the steering knuckle.
8 Remove the steering knuckle/hub assembly from the driveaxle, using a puller tool to disengage it from the driveaxle splines if necessary, and lift it from the vehicle.
9 Inspect the knuckle for damage and corrosion and the bearings for looseness, rough turning or leaking grease. Disassembly of the hub requires a press and special techniques and this must be left to your dealer or a properly equipped shop.
10 Install the steering knuckle in position on the driveaxle and lower control arm and strut, install the retaining nuts and bolts and tighten them to the specified torque.
11 Install the tie rod and tighten the nut to the specified torque.
12 Install the brake caliper and the locknut.
13 Lock the brake rotor and tighten the locknut to the specified torque.
14 Peen the collar of the locknut into the driveaxle groove, using a punch or other blunt tool and a hammer **(see illustration)**.
15 Install the wheel and lower the vehicle.

16 Tie rod end - removal and installation

Refer to illustrations 16.3, 16.4, 16.5, 16.8a and 16.8b

1 Raise the front of the vehicle and support it with jackstands.
2 Remove the front wheel.
3 Remove the tie rod nut that secures the outer tie rod to the steering knuckle **(see illustration)**.
4 Using a suitable tool, such as a "pickle fork", disengage the tie rod from the steering knuckle **(see illustration)**.
5 Mark the relationship of the jam nut to the inner tie rod threads so similar front end alignment can be maintained upon installation **(see illustration)**.

16.3 Tie rod end and steering gear installation details

1 *Tie rod end*
2 *Jam nut*
3 *Outer boot band*
4 *Rack and pinion boot seal*
5 *Inner boot band*
6 *Tie rod nut and cotter pin*

16.4 Using a "pickle fork" tool and hammer to disengage the tie rod from the steering knuckle

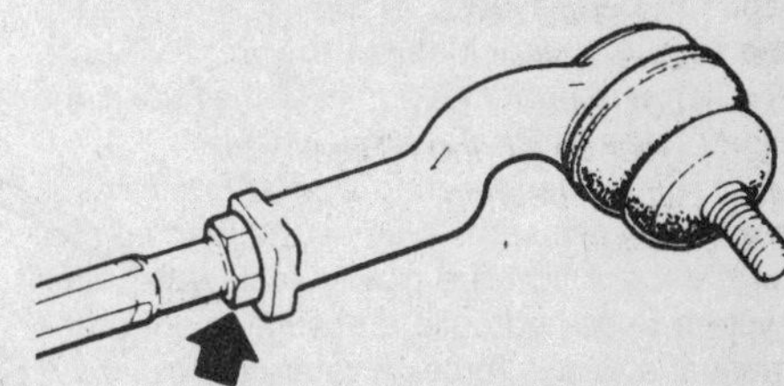

16.5 Mark the tie rod end jam nut position (arrow) before removal

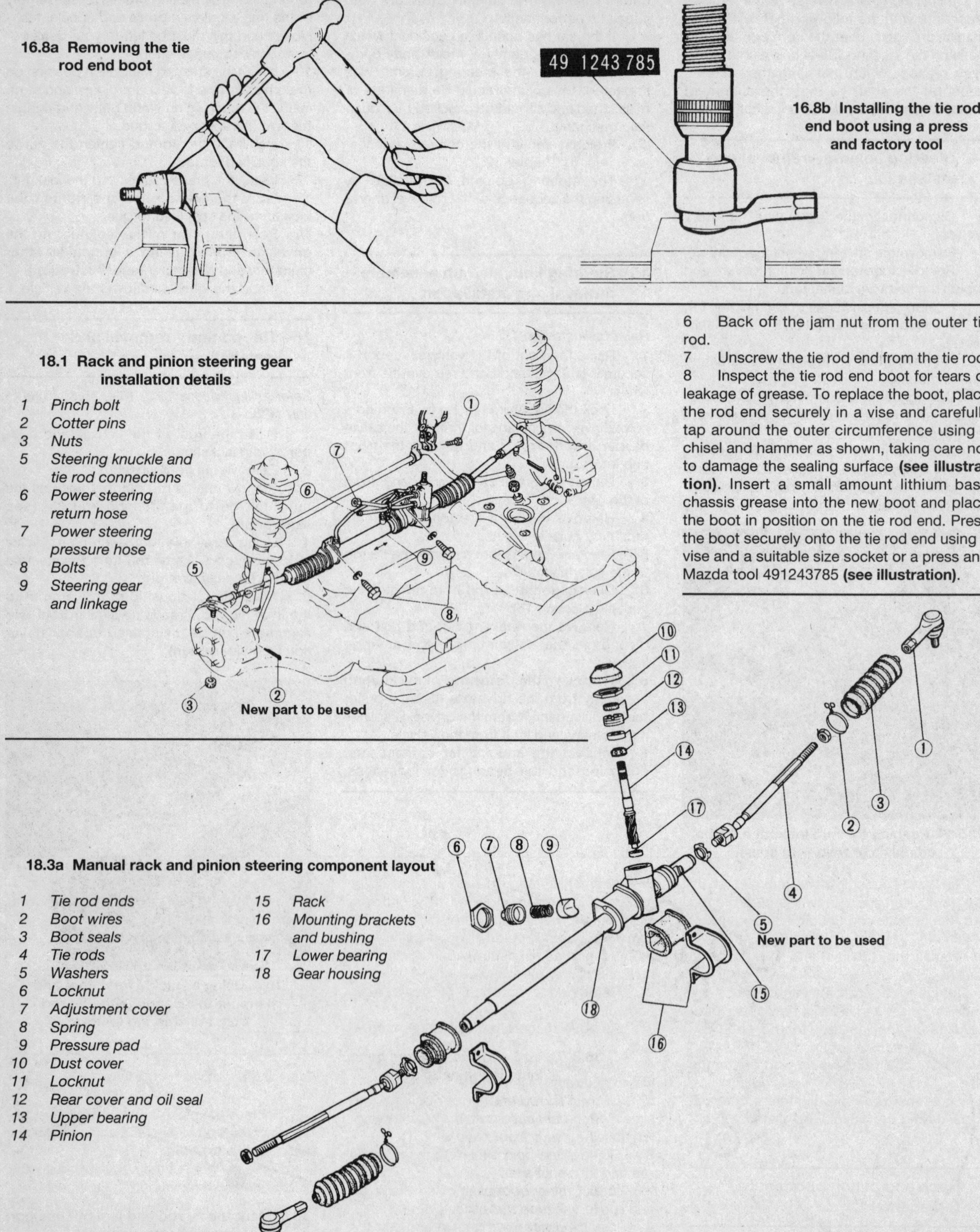

16.8a Removing the tie rod end boot

16.8b Installing the tie rod end boot using a press and factory tool

18.1 Rack and pinion steering gear installation details

1 *Pinch bolt*
2 *Cotter pins*
3 *Nuts*
5 *Steering knuckle and tie rod connections*
6 *Power steering return hose*
7 *Power steering pressure hose*
8 *Bolts*
9 *Steering gear and linkage*

18.3a Manual rack and pinion steering component layout

1 *Tie rod ends*
2 *Boot wires*
3 *Boot seals*
4 *Tie rods*
5 *Washers*
6 *Locknut*
7 *Adjustment cover*
8 *Spring*
9 *Pressure pad*
10 *Dust cover*
11 *Locknut*
12 *Rear cover and oil seal*
13 *Upper bearing*
14 *Pinion*
15 *Rack*
16 *Mounting brackets and bushing*
17 *Lower bearing*
18 *Gear housing*

6 Back off the jam nut from the outer tie rod.

7 Unscrew the tie rod end from the tie rod.

8 Inspect the tie rod end boot for tears or leakage of grease. To replace the boot, place the rod end securely in a vise and carefully tap around the outer circumference using a chisel and hammer as shown, taking care not to damage the sealing surface **(see illustration)**. Insert a small amount lithium base chassis grease into the new boot and place the boot in position on the tie rod end. Press the boot securely onto the tie rod end using a vise and a suitable size socket or a press and Mazda tool 491243785 **(see illustration)**.

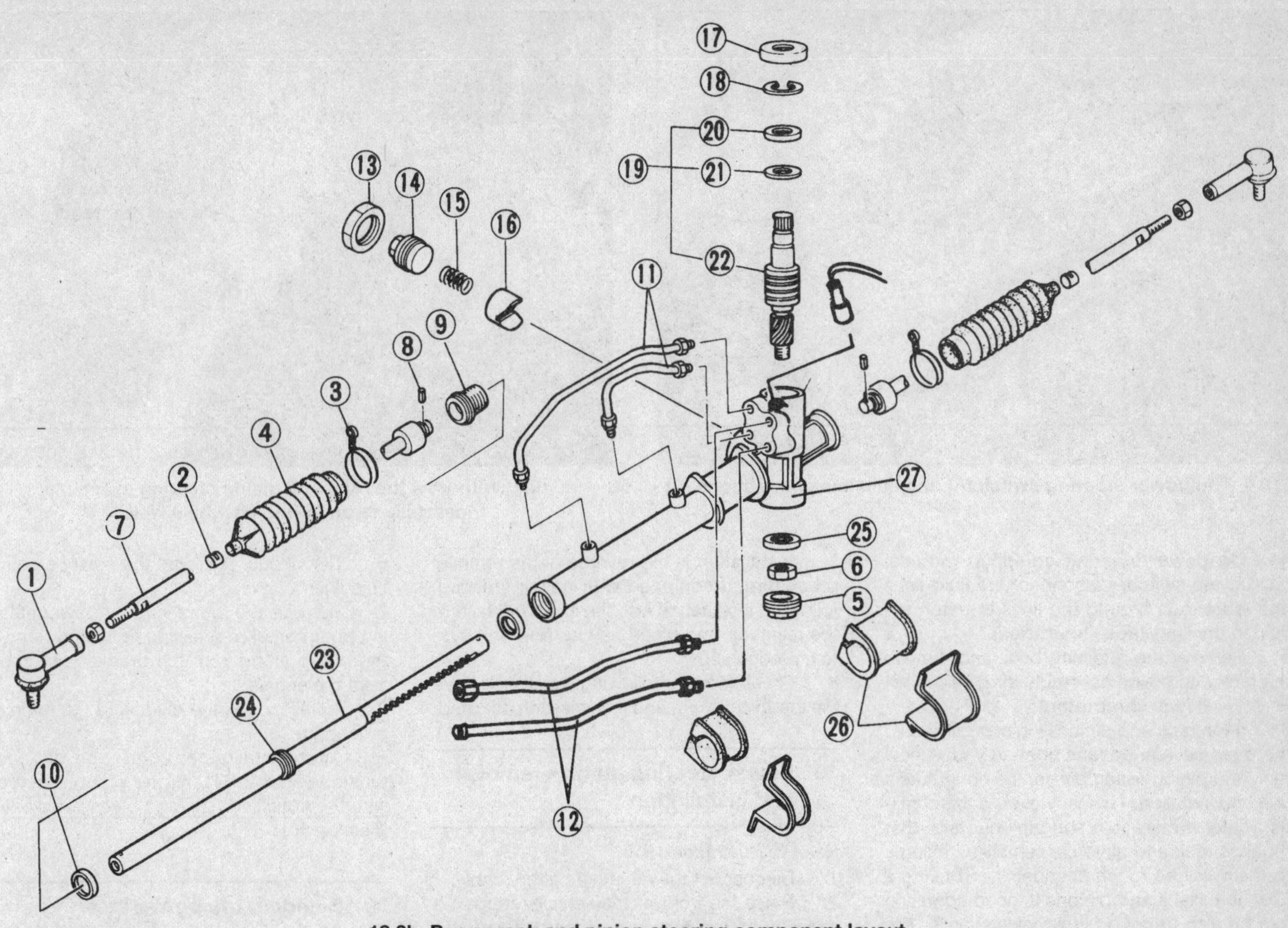

18.3b Power rack and pinion steering component layout

1 *Tie rod ends*	9 *Rack bushing assembly*	16 *Rack support*	22 *Control valve assembly*
2 *Boot bands*	10 *Oil seal*	17 *Dust cover*	23 *Rack assembly*
3 *Boot wires*	11 *Fluid pipes*	18 *Snap ring*	24 *Seal ring*
4 *Boot seals*	12 *Fluid pipes and O-rings*	19 *Control valve, oil seal and bearing assembly*	25 *Bearing*
5 *Pinion plug*	13 *Locknut*	20 *Oil seal*	26 *Mounting brackets and mounts*
6 *Lock nuts*	14 *Yoke plug*	21 *Bearing*	27 *Gear housing*
7 *Tie rods*	15 *Spring*		
8 *Spring pins*			

9 To install, position the jam nut at its mark on the threads. Screw the outer tie rod onto the inner tie rod until it is snug against the jam nut.

10 Install the tie rod into the steering knuckle.

11 Install the tie rod nut, tighten it to the specified torque and install a new cotter pin.

12 Tighten the jam nut to the specified torque.

13 Mount the front wheel and lower the vehicle.

14 Have the front end alignment checked before driving the vehicle any distance (Section 3).

17 Rack and pinion boot seals - replacement

1 The rack and pinion boot seals protect this assembly's internals from dirt and water and should be checked periodically for holes, cracking and other damage or deterioration. Damaged boots should be replaced immediately to prevent expensive damage to the rack and pinion assembly.

2 Remove the outer tie rod end (Section 16).

3 Remove the jam nut from the inner tie rod.

4 Use pliers to spread the outer boot clamp and remove it from the inner tie rod.

5 Untwist the wire inner boot clamp and slide it off the boot and onto the rack and pinion housing.

6 Remove the boot seal from the inner tie rod and the vehicle.

7 Install the new seal boot so the large end is over the rack and pinion housing lip.

8 Install the wire inner boot clamp over the large end of the boot and tighten by twisting it with pliers.

9 Install the outer boot clamp over the small end of the boot.

10 Install the jam nut and tie rod end.

18 Rack and pinion steering assembly - removal and installation

Refer to illustrations 18.1, 18.3a, 18.3b, 18.4 and 18.5

1 Remove the pinch bolt that attaches the intermediate shaft to the rack and pinion stub shaft **(see illustration)**.

2 Raise the front of the car, support it with jackstands and remove both front wheels.

3 Remove the cotter pins and nuts and separate the tie rod ends from the steering knuckles (Section 16) **(see illustrations)**.

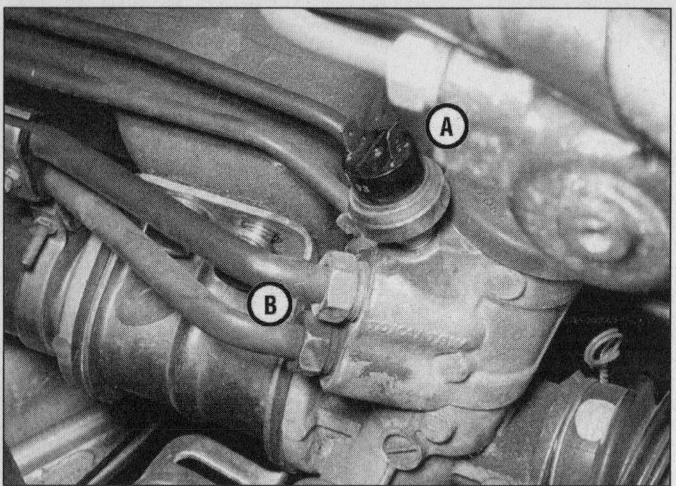

18.4 The power steering switch (A) and fluid line connections (B)

18.5 Withdraw the rack and pinion steering assembly carefully through the left wheel well

4 On power steering equipped models, unplug the switch, disconnect the fluid lines and wrap rags around the lines to catch the fluid in the lines **(see illustration)**.

5 Remove the retaining bolts and remove the rack and pinion assembly through the left wheel well **(see illustration)**.

6 If the rack and pinion is in need of repair, there are several options open to you. A new rack and pinion assembly can be bought as a unit and installed. This, however, is the costliest route. If there is a shop in your area that rebuilds rack and pinion assemblies, taking it to them will be much cheaper than buying a new unit. Rack and pinions in good condition can be also be found in wrecking yards. The final option is to rebuild the assembly yourself, though it is a somewhat difficult operation requiring the use of a press. Due to space limitations we are unable to give you a step by step procedure, but an exploded view of both racks has been included.

7 Installation is the reverse of the removal procedure. If equipped with power steering, following installation add the specified fluid to the reservoir and bleed any air from the system (Section 20).

8 On all models, following installation have the toe-in checked, and if necessary, adjusted.

19 Power steering pump - removal and installation

Refer to illustration 19.3

1 Disconnect the negative battery cable.

2 Raise the front of the vehicle, support it securely on jackstands and remove the right front wheel and splash shield.

3 Remove the power steering pump pulley bolt **(see illustration)**

4 Remove the alternator and drivebelt (Chapter 5).

5 Remove the pulley from the pump.

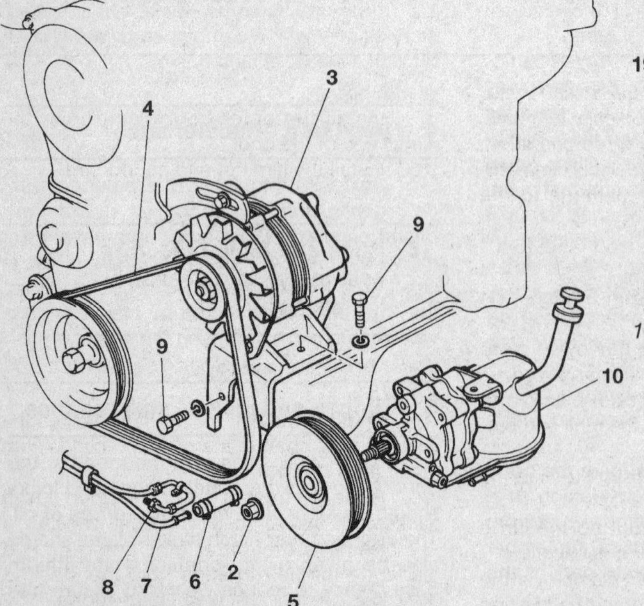

19.3 Power steering pump installation details

2 Pulley nut
3 Alternator
4 Drivebelt
5 Pulley
6 Hose band
7 Return hose
8 Pressure hose
9 Bracket bolts
10 Power steering pump

6 Disconnect and plug the power steering fluid lines.

7 Remove the four alternator/power steering pump bracket retaining bolts and remove the pump along with the bracket assembly from the engine.

8 Installation is the reverse of the removal procedure.

9 After installation, adjust the drivebelt tension (Chapter 1), fill the pump reservoir with the specified fluid and bleed the system (Section 20).

20 Bleeding the power steering system

1 Following any operation in which the power steering fluid lines have been disconnected, the power steering system must be bled of air to obtain proper steering performance.

2 Raise the front of the vehicle and support it on jackstands.

3 Turn the front wheels all the way to the left and right several times. Check the power steering fluid level and, if it has dropped, add fluid. Repeat this procedure until the fluid level on the dipstick does not drop.

4 Start the engine and allow it to run at fast idle. Recheck the fluid level and add more if necessary.

5 Bleed the system by turning the wheels from side to side without hitting the stops. This will work the air out of the system. Be careful that the reservoir does not run empty of fluid.

6 After the air is worked out of the system, return the wheels to the straight ahead position and leave the car running for several more minutes before shutting it off.

7 Road-test the car to be sure the steering system is functioning normally and is free from noise.

8 Recheck the fluid level to be sure it is up to the top arrow mark on the dipstick while the engine is at normal operating temperature and add fluid if necessary.

Chapter 11 Body

Contents

1 General information

These models are of unitized construction. The body is designed to provide vehicle rigidity so that a separate frame is not necessary. Front and rear frame side rails integral with the body support the front end sheet metal, front and rear suspension systems and other mechanical components. Due to this type of construction, it is very important that, in the event of collision damage, the underbody be thoroughly checked by a facility with the proper equipment.

Component replacement and repairs possible for the home mechanic are included in this Chapter.

2 Body - maintenance

1 The condition of your vehicle's body is very important, because it is on this that the second hand value will mainly depend. It is much more difficult to repair a neglected or damaged body than it is to repair mechanical components. The hidden areas of the body, such as the fender wells, the frame, and the engine compartment, are equally important, although obviously do not require as frequent attention as the rest of the body.

2 Once a year, or every 12,000 miles, it is a good idea to have the underside of the body and the frame steam cleaned. All traces of dirt and oil will be removed and the underside can then be inspected carefully for rust, damaged brake lines, frayed electrical wiring, damaged cables, and other problems. The front suspension components should be greased after completion of this job.

3 At the same time, clean the engine and the engine compartment using either a steam cleaner or a water soluble degreaser.

4 The fender wells should be given particular attention, as undercoating can peel away and stones and dirt thrown up by the tires can cause the paint to chip and flake, allowing rust to set in. If rust is found, clean down to the bare metal and apply an anti-rust paint.

5 The body should be washed once a week (or when dirty). Wet the vehicle thoroughly to soften the dirt, then wash it down with a soft sponge and plenty of clean soapy water. If the surplus dirt is not washed off very carefully, it will in time wear down the paint.

6 Spots of tar or asphalt coating thrown up from the road should be removed with a cloth soaked in solvent.

7 Once every six months, give the body and chrome trim a thorough waxing. If a chrome cleaner is used to remove rust from any of the vehicle's plated parts, remember that the cleaner also removes part of the chrome, so use it sparingly.

3 Upholstery and carpets - maintenance

1 Every three months remove the carpets or mats and clean the interior of the vehicle (more frequently if necessary). Vacuum the upholstery and carpets to remove loose dirt and dust.

2 If the upholstery is soiled, apply upholstery cleaner with a damp sponge and wipe it off with a clean, dry cloth.

4 Vinyl trim - maintenance

Vinyl trim should not be cleaned with detergents, caustic soaps or petroleum-based cleaners. Plain soap and water or a mild vinyl cleaner is best for stains. Test a small area for color fastness. Bubbles under the vinyl can be corrected by piercing them with a pin and then working the air out.

5 Hinges and locks - maintenance

Every 3000 miles or three months, the door, hood and rear hatch hinges and locks should be lubricated with a few drops of oil. The door and rear hatch striker plates should also be given a thin coat of white lithium base grease to reduce wear and ensure free movement.

6 Body repair - minor damage

See photo sequence

Repair of minor scratches

1 If the scratch is superficial and does not penetrate to the metal of the body, repair is very simple. Lightly rub the scratched area with a fine rubbing compound to remove loose paint and built up wax. Rinse the area with clean water.

2 Apply touch-up paint to the scratch, using a small brush. Continue to apply thin layers of paint until the surface of the paint in the scratch is level with the surrounding paint. Allow the new paint at least two weeks to harden, then blend it into the surrounding paint by rubbing with a very fine rubbing compound. Finally, apply a coat of wax to the scratch area.

3 If the scratch has penetrated the paint and exposed the metal of the body, causing the metal to rust, a different repair technique is required. Remove all loose rust from the bottom of the scratch with a pocket knife, then apply rust inhibiting paint to prevent the formation of rust in the future. Using a rubber or nylon applicator, coat the scratched area with glaze-type filler. If required, the filler can be mixed with thinner to provide a very thin paste, which is ideal for filling narrow scratches. Before the glaze filler in the scratch hardens, wrap a piece of smooth cotton cloth around the tip of a finger. Dip the cloth in thinner and then quickly wipe it along the surface of the scratch. This will ensure that the surface of the filler is slightly hollow. The scratch can now be painted over as described earlier in this section.

Repair of dents

4 When repairing dents, the first job is to pull the dent out until the affected area is as close as possible to its original shape. There is no point in trying to restore the original shape completely as the metal in the damaged area will have stretched on impact and cannot be restored to its original contours. It is better to bring the level of the dent up to a point which is about 1/8-inch below the level of the surrounding metal. In cases where the dent is very shallow, it is not worth trying to pull it out at all.

5 If the back side of the dent is accessible, it can be hammered out gently from behind using a soft-face hammer. While doing this, hold a block of wood firmly against the opposite side of the metal to absorb the hammer blows and prevent the metal from being stretched.

6 If the dent is in a section of the body which has double layers, or some other factor makes it inaccessible from behind, a different technique is required. Drill several small holes through the metal inside the damaged area, particularly in the deeper sections. Screw long, self tapping screws into the holes just enough for them to get a good grip in the metal. Now the dent can be pulled out by pulling on the protruding heads of the screws with locking pliers.

7 The next stage of repair is the removal of paint from the damaged area and from an inch or so of the surrounding metal. This is easily done with a wire brush or sanding disk in a drill motor, although it can be done just as effectively by hand with sandpaper. To complete the preparation for filling, score the surface of the bare metal with a screwdriver or the tang of a file or drill small holes in the affected area. This will provide a good grip for the filler material. To complete the repair, see the Section on filling and painting.

Repair of rust holes or gashes

8 Remove all paint from the affected area and from an inch or so of the surrounding metal using a sanding disk or wire brush mounted in a drill motor. If these are not available, a few sheets of sandpaper will do the job just as effectively.

9 With the paint removed, you will be able to determine the severity of the corrosion and decide whether to replace the whole panel, if possible, or repair the affected area. New body panels are not as expensive as most people think and it is often quicker to install a new panel than to repair large areas of rust.

10 Remove all trim pieces from the affected area except those which will act as a guide to the original shape of the damaged body, such as headlight shells, etc. Using metal snips or a hacksaw blade, remove all loose metal and any other metal that is badly affected by rust. Hammer the edges of the hole inward to create a slight depression for the filler material.

11 Wire brush the affected area to remove the powdery rust from the surface of the metal. If the back of the rusted area is accessible, treat it with rust-inhibiting paint.

12 Before filling is done, block the hole in some way. This can be done with sheet metal riveted or screwed into place, or by stuffing the hole with wire mesh.

13 Once the hole is blocked off, the affected area can be filled and painted. See the following sub-section on filling and painting.

Filling and painting

14 Many types of body fillers are available, but generally speaking, body repair kits which contain filler paste and a tube of resin hardener are best for this type of repair work. A wide, flexible plastic or nylon applicator will be necessary for imparting a smooth and contoured finish to the surface of the filler material. Mix up a small amount of filler on a clean piece of wood or cardboard (use the hardener sparingly). Follow the manufacturer's instructions on the package, otherwise the filler will set incorrectly.

15 Using the applicator, apply the filler paste to the prepared area. Draw the applicator across the surface of the filler to achieve the desired contour and to level the filler surface. As soon as a contour that approximates the original one is achieved, stop working the paste. If you continue, the paste will begin to stick to the applicator. Continue to add thin layers of paste at 20-minute intervals until the level of the filler is just above the surrounding metal.

16 Once the filler has hardened, the excess can be removed with a body file. From then on, progressively finer grades of sandpaper should be used, starting with a 180-grit paper and finishing with 600-grit wet-or-dry paper. Always wrap the sandpaper around a flat rubber or wooden block, otherwise the surface of the filler will not be completely flat. During the sanding of the filler surface, the wet-or-dry paper should be periodically rinsed in water. This will ensure that a very smooth finish is produced in the final stage.

17 At this point, the repair area should be surrounded by a ring of bare metal, which in turn should be encircled by the finely feathered edge of good paint. Rinse the repair area with clean water until all of the dust produced by the sanding operation is gone.

18 Spray the entire area with a light coat of primer. This will reveal any imperfections in the surface of the filler. Repair the imperfections with fresh filler paste or glaze filler and once more smooth the surface with sandpaper. Repeat this spray-and-repair procedure until you are satisfied that the surface of the filler and the feathered edge of the paint are perfect. Rinse the area with clean water and allow it to dry completely.

19 The repair area is now ready for painting. Spray painting must be carried out in a warm, dry, windless and dust free atmosphere. These conditions can be created if you have access to a large indoor work area, but if you are forced to work in the open, you will have to pick the day very carefully. If you are working indoors, dousing the floor in the work area with water will help settle the dust which would otherwise be in the air. If the repair area is confined to one body panel, mask off the surrounding panels. This will help minimize the effects of a slight mismatch in paint color. Trim pieces such as chrome strips, door handles, etc., will also need to be masked off or removed. Use masking tape and several thicknesses of newspaper for the masking operations.

20 Before spraying, shake the paint can thoroughly, then spray a test area until the spray painting technique is mastered. Cover the repair area with a thick coat of primer. The thickness should be built up using several thin layers of primer rather than one thick one. Using 600-grit wet-or-dry sandpaper, rub down the surface of the primer until it is very smooth. While doing this, the work area should be thoroughly rinsed with water and the wet-or-dry sandpaper periodically rinsed as well. Allow the primer to dry before spraying additional coats.

21 Spray on the top coat, again building up the thickness by using several thin layers of paint. Begin spraying in the center of the repair area and then, using a circular motion, work out until the whole repair area and about two inches of the surrounding original

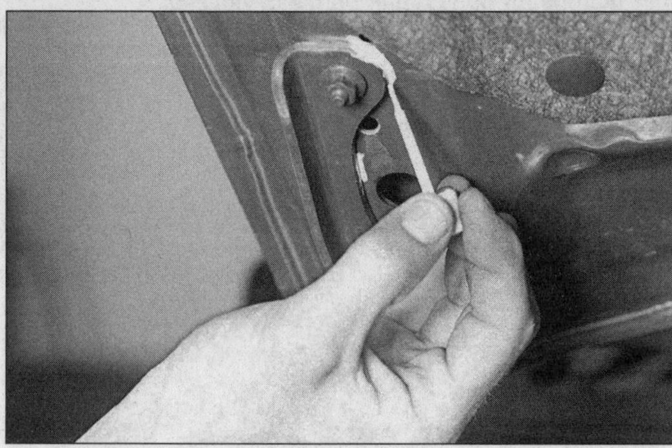
8.3 Mark the hood hinge position with paint

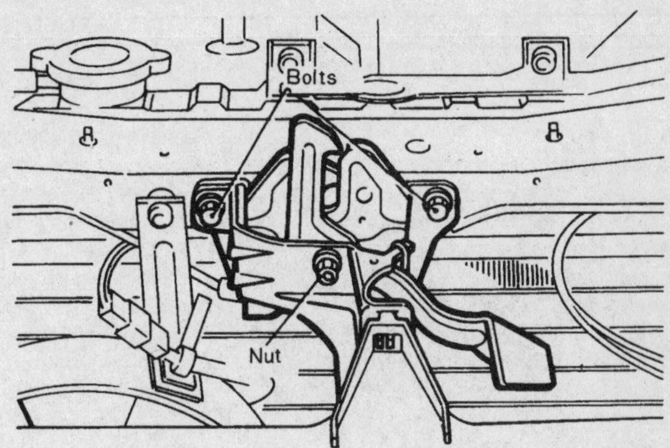

9.3 Hood lock mechanism retaining bolt and nut locations

paint is covered. Remove all masking material 10 to 15 minutes after spraying on the final coat of paint. Allow the new paint at least two weeks to harden, then use a very fine rubbing compound to blend the edges of the new paint into the existing paint. Finally, apply a coat of wax.

7 Body repair - major damage

1 Major damage must be repaired by an auto body shop specifically equipped to perform unibody repairs. These shops have available the specialized equipment required to do the job properly.
2 If the damage is extensive, the underbody must be checked for proper alignment or the vehicle's handling characteristics may be adversely affected and other components may wear at an accelerated rate.
3 Due to the fact that all of the major body components (hood, fenders, etc.) are separate and replaceable units, any seriously damaged components should be replaced rather than repaired. Sometimes these components can be found in a wrecking yard that specializes in used vehicle components, often at considerable savings over the cost of new parts.

8 Hood - removal and installation

Refer to illustration 8.3
1 Raise the hood.
2 Place protective pads along the edges of the engine compartment to prevent damage to the painted surfaces.
3 Scribe or paint lines around the mounting bracket, so the hood can be aligned quickly and accurately in the same position during installation **(see illustration)**.
4 With an assistant supporting the weight, remove the bracket bolts and remove the hood from the vehicle.
5 Installation is the reverse of removal, taking care to align the brackets and bolts with the markings made prior to removal.

9 Hood lock mechanism and release cable - removal and installation

Refer to illustration 9.3
1 Remove the front grille cover.
2 If the same hood lock mechanism is to be reinstalled, scribe or paint around the outside edge of the mechanism so that it can be quickly and easily aligned.
3 Remove the retaining nuts and bolt, disengage the release cable and remove the lock mechanism from the vehicle **(see illustration)**.
4 In the passenger compartment, loosen the release cable nut and disengage the cable from the bracket.
5 Connect string or thin wire to the end of the cable and remove it by pulling it through into the passenger compartment.
6 Installation is the reverse of removal after connecting the string or wire to the new release cable and pulling it into position.

10 Rear hatch damper - removal and installation

Refer to illustrations 10.2 and 10.3
1 Support the hatch in the fully open position.
2 Unscrew the nut retaining the damper to the hatch **(see illustration)**.
3 Remove the lower damper-to-body bolts **(see illustration)** and lift the damper from the vehicle.
4 Installation is the reverse of removal.

10.2 Use a wrench to unscrew the damper nut

10.3 The lower damper retaining bolts (arrows)

These photos illustrate a method of repairing simple dents. They are intended to supplement *Body repair - minor damage* in this Chapter and should not be used as the sole instructions for body repair on these vehicles.

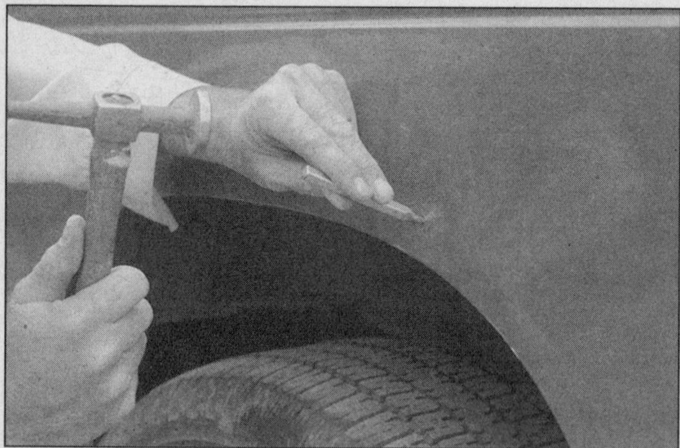

1 If you can't access the backside of the body panel to hammer out the dent, pull it out with a slide-hammer-type dent puller. In the deepest portion of the dent or along the crease line, drill or punch hole(s) at least one inch apart . . .

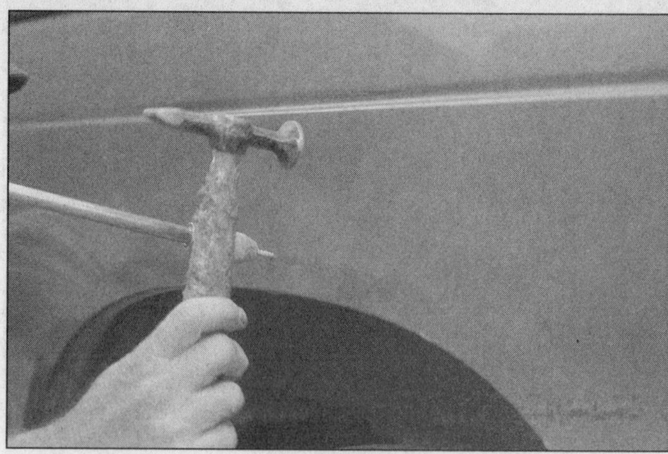

2 . . . then screw the slide-hammer into the hole and operate it. Tap with a hammer near the edge of the dent to help 'pop' the metal back to its original shape. When you're finished, the dent area should be close to its original contour and about 1/8-inch below the surface of the surrounding metal

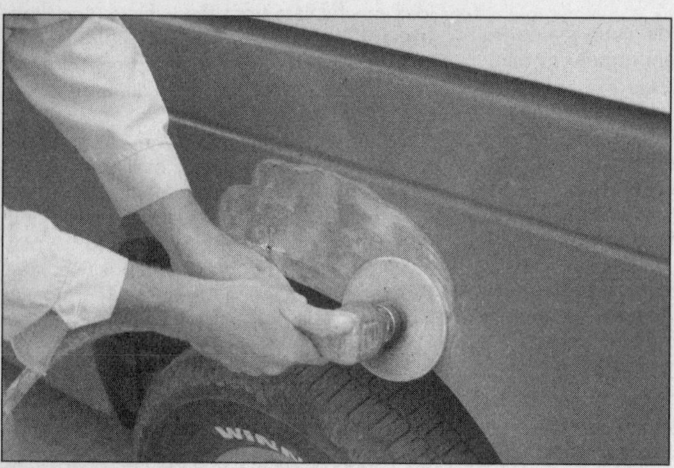

3 Using coarse-grit sandpaper, remove the paint down to the bare metal. Hand sanding works fine, but the disc sander shown here makes the job faster. Use finer (about 320-grit) sandpaper to feather-edge the paint at least one inch around the dent area

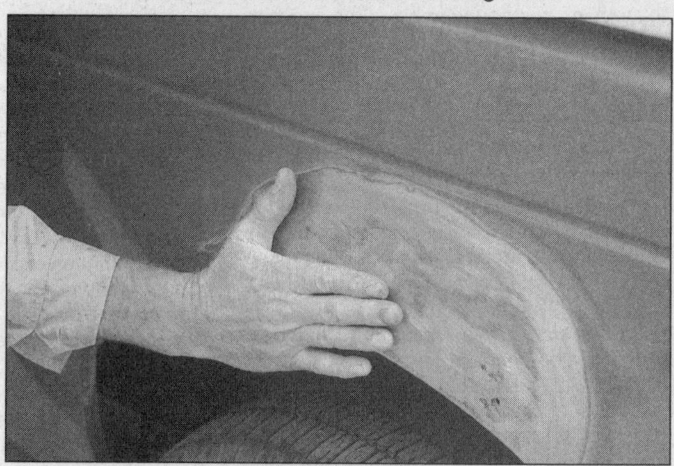

4 When the paint is removed, touch will probably be more helpful than sight for telling if the metal is straight. Hammer down the high spots or raise the low spots as necessary. Clean the repair area with wax/silicone remover

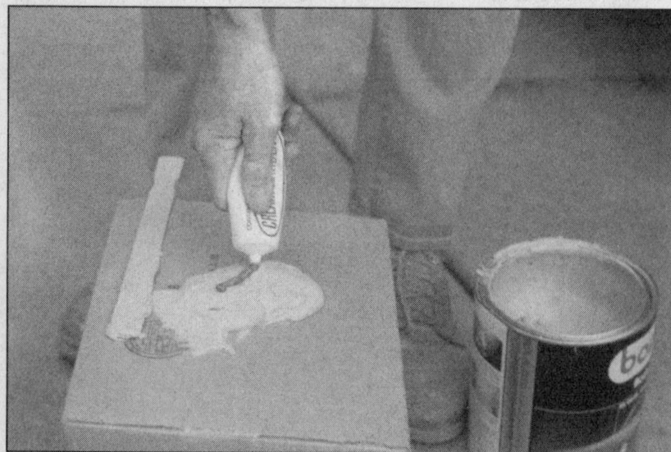

5 Following label instructions, mix up a batch of plastic filler and hardener. The ratio of filler to hardener is critical, and, if you mix it incorrectly, it will either not cure properly or cure too quickly (you won't have time to file and sand it into shape)

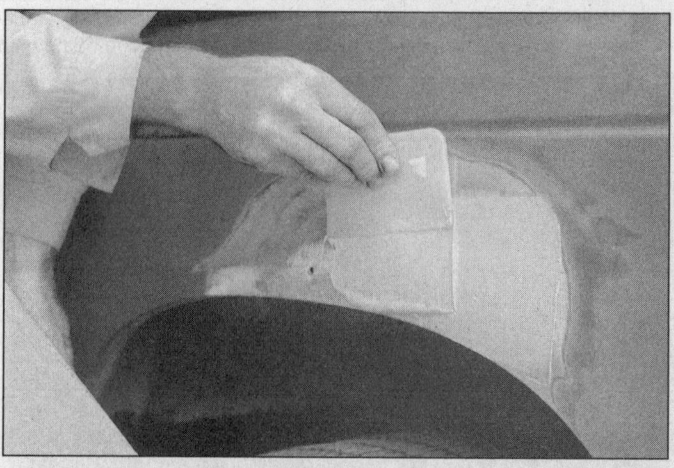

6 Working quickly so the filler doesn't harden, use a plastic applicator to press the body filler firmly into the metal, assuring it bonds completely. Work the filler until it matches the original contour and is slightly above the surrounding metal

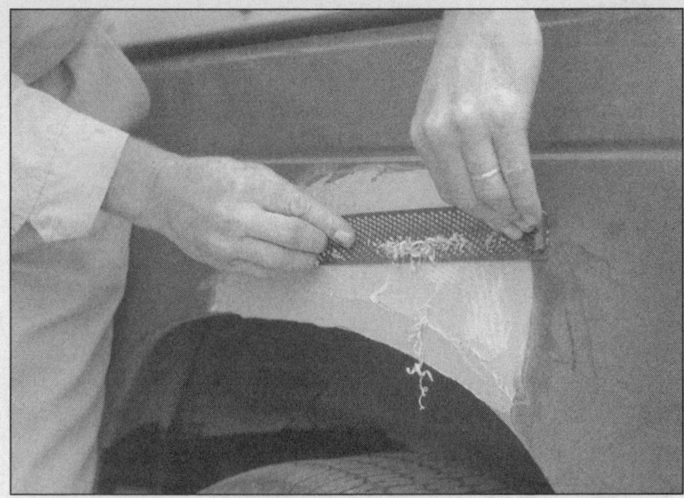

7 Let the filler harden until you can just dent it with your fingernail. Use a body file or Surform tool (shown here) to rough-shape the filler

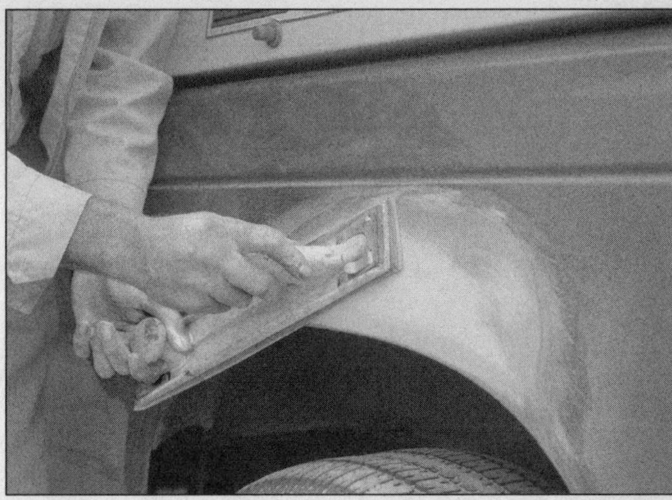

8 Use coarse-grit sandpaper and a sanding board or block to work the filler down until it's smooth and even. Work down to finer grits of sandpaper - always using a board or block - ending up with 360 or 400 grit

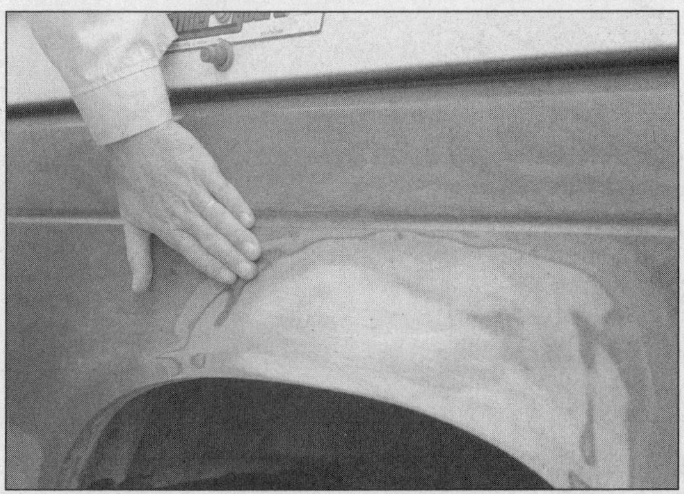

9 You shouldn't be able to feel any ridge at the transition from the filler to the bare metal or from the bare metal to the old paint. As soon as the repair is flat and uniform, remove the dust and mask off the adjacent panels or trim pieces

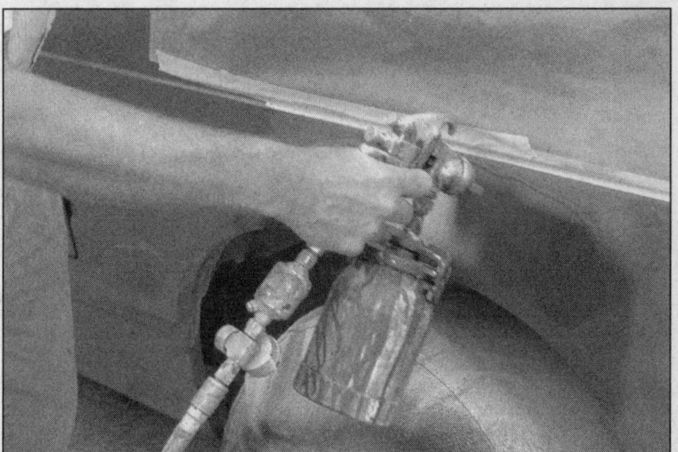

10 Apply several layers of primer to the area. Don't spray the primer on too heavy, so it sags or runs, and make sure each coat is dry before you spray on the next one. A professional-type spray gun is being used here, but aerosol spray primer is available inexpensively from auto parts stores

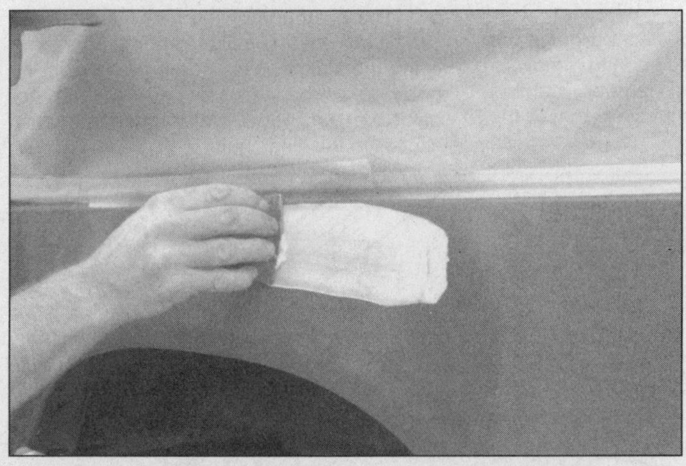

11 The primer will help reveal imperfections or scratches. Fill these with glazing compound. Follow the label instructions and sand it with 360 or 400-grit sandpaper until it's smooth. Repeat the glazing, sanding and respraying until the primer reveals a perfectly smooth surface

12 Finish sand the primer with very fine sandpaper (400 or 600-grit) to remove the primer overspray. Clean the area with water and allow it to dry. Use a tack rag to remove any dust, then apply the finish coat. Don't attempt to rub out or wax the repair area until the paint has dried completely (at least two weeks)

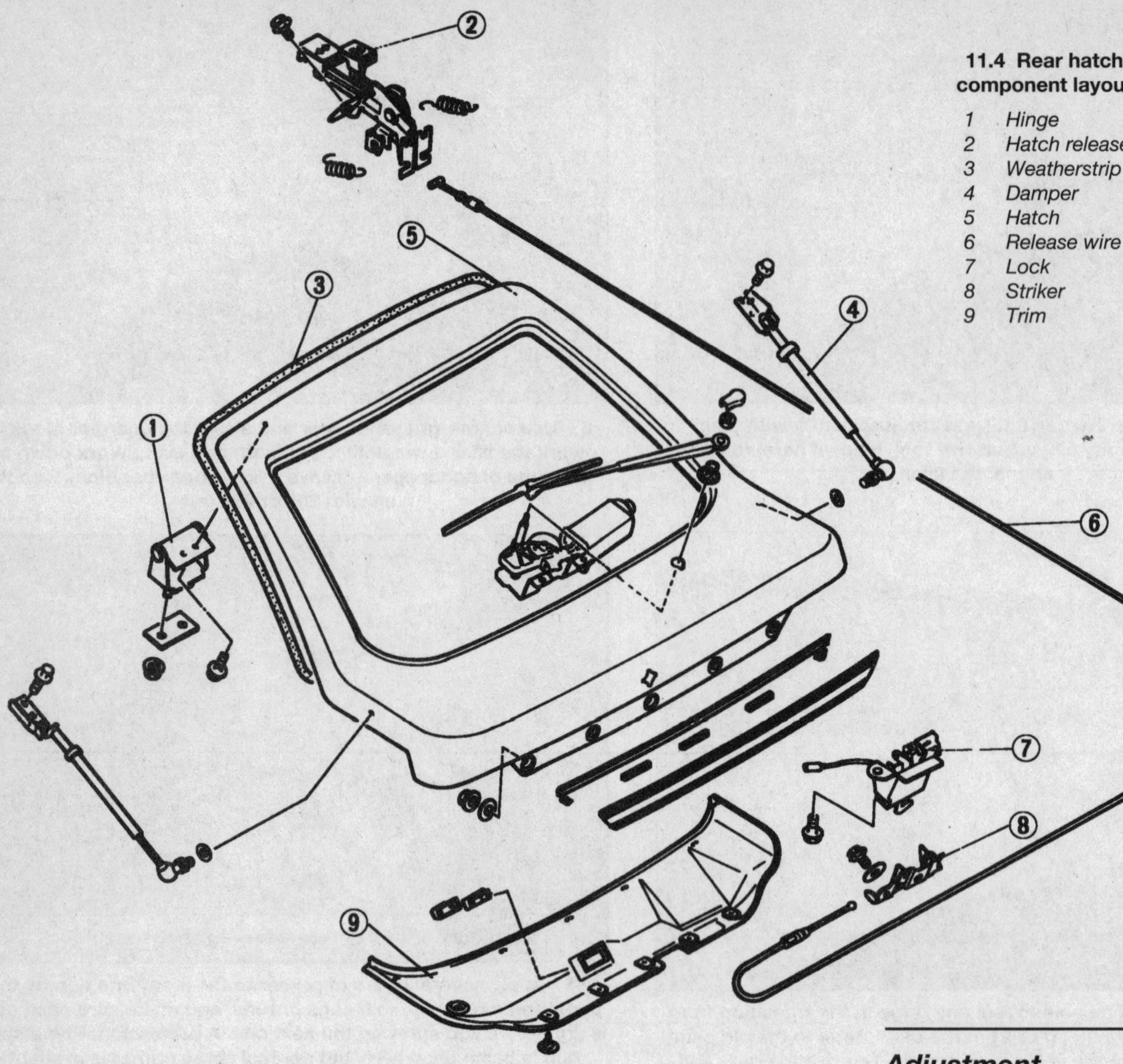

11.4 Rear hatch component layout

1 *Hinge*
2 *Hatch release*
3 *Weatherstrip*
4 *Damper*
5 *Hatch*
6 *Release wire*
7 *Lock*
8 *Striker*
9 *Trim*

11 Rear hatch - removal, installation and adjustment

Removal

Refer to illustration 11.5

1 Open the rear hatch and support it with a prop.

2 Place protective pads along the edges of the hatch opening to prevent damage to the painted surfaces while work is being performed.

3 Mark the locations of the hinges by scribing or marking with paint so they can be easily reinstalled in their original positions.

4 Unbolt the damper struts from the hatch (Section 10).

5 Disconnect any wiring harnesses which would interfere with hatch removal **(see illustration)**.

6 Remove the bolts from the hinge retaining bolts and lift the hatch from the vehicle with the help of an assistant.

Installation

7 Place the hatch in position, aligning the hinges with the marks made during removal.

8 Install the hinge and damper retaining bolts, tightening them securely. Connect the wiring harness.

Adjustment

Refer to illustrations 11.9a and 11.9b

9 The positions of the hinge and striker can be adjusted **(see illustrations)** after loosening the striker bolts and hinge nuts on the body. It will be necessary to carefully pry back the trim panel and headliner to gain access to the hinge nuts.

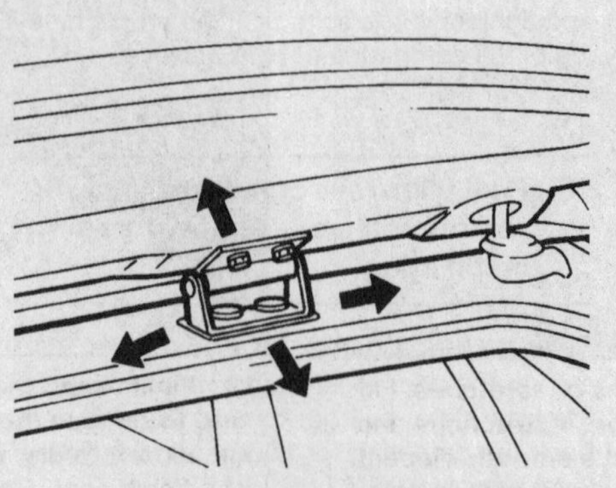

11.9a Hatch hinge adjustment

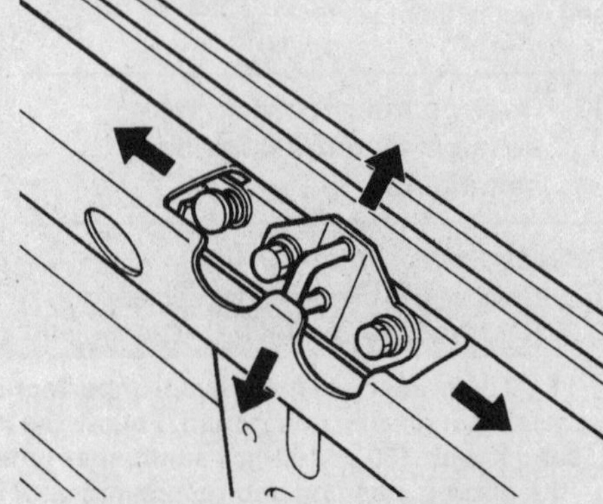

11.9b Hatch striker adjustment

13.3 Rear compartment lock installation details

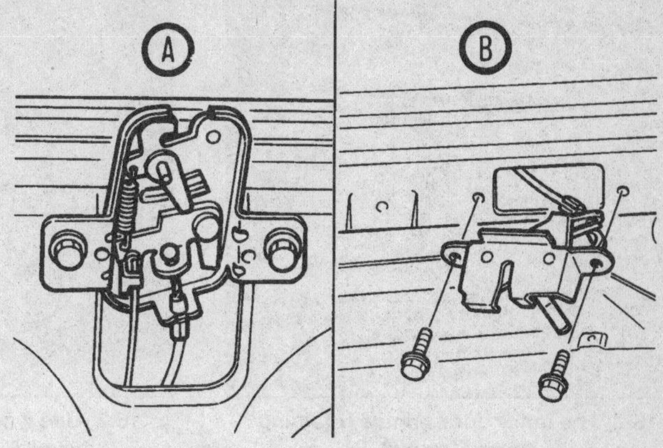

15.4 Rear compartment lock and release wire installation details

A Sedan and coupe *B Hatchback*

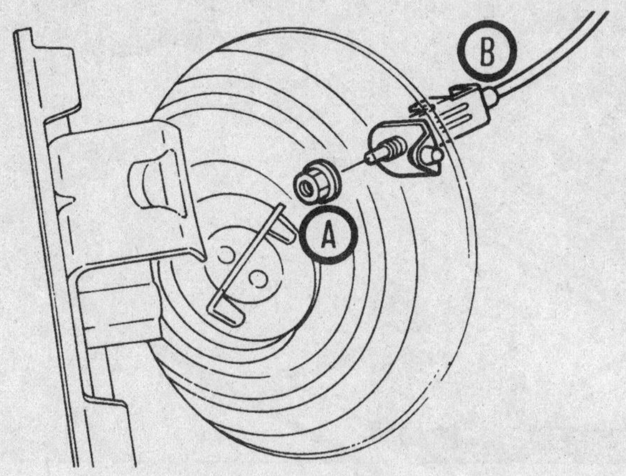

15.5 Fuel filler lid wire attachment points

A Nut *B Bracket*

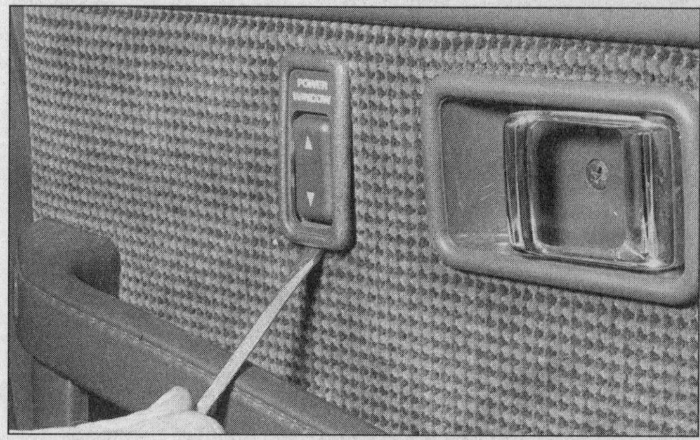

16.1 Pry off the power window switch escutcheon with a screwdriver

12 Trunk lid - removal and installation

1 Open the lid and mark the location of the nut heads by scribing around them for reinstallation to the same position.

2 With an assistant supporting the weight, remove the retaining nuts and lift the lid from the vehicle.

3 Place the lid in position, install the nuts and tighten them securely.

13 Rear compartment lid lock assembly - removal and installation

Refer to illustration 13.3

1 Remove the trim panel for access.

2 Remove the protector (sedan and coupe).

3 Remove the retaining bolts and pull the lock out for access to the release wire and rod **(see illustration)**.

4 Disconnect the release wire and rod and lift the lock from the vehicle.

5 Installation is the reverse of removal.

14 Rear compartment lid striker - removal and installation

1 Remove the trim panel for access, if necessary.

2 Mark the bolt locations.

3 Remove the bolts and lift the striker from the vehicle.

4 When installing it may be necessary to adjust the position of the striker by loosening and tightening the bolts until the proper closing of the compartment lid is achieved.

15 Fuel filler/rear compartment remote release - removal and installation

Refer to illustrations 15.4 and 15.5

1 In the passenger compartment, remove the kick plate, pull out the staples and peel back the carpeting for access to the release lever retaining bolt.

2 Remove the bolt and disconnect the wires from the lever assembly.

3 In the rear compartment, remove the trim panels for access.

4 Disconnect the wire from the rear compartment lock **(see illustration)**.

5 Disconnect the fuel filler wire from the bracket and pull on the wire to open the filler lid **(see illustration)**. Remove the nut and disconnect the wire.

6 Attach a string or thin wire to the rear compartment and/or fuel filler wire and pull the wire(s) through into the passenger compartment.

7 Installation is the reverse of removal after pulling the wires into place with the string or wire.

16 Door trim panel - removal and installation

Refer to illustrations 16.1, 16.2, 16.3, 16.4, 16.5 and 16.6

1 Remove the window regulator crank or power window switch cover **(see illustration)**.

2 Remove the inside door handle cover **(see illustration)**.

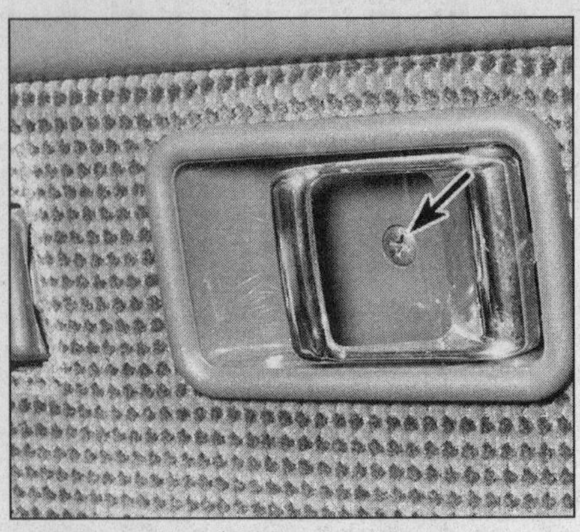

16.2 The inner door handle retaining screw (arrow)

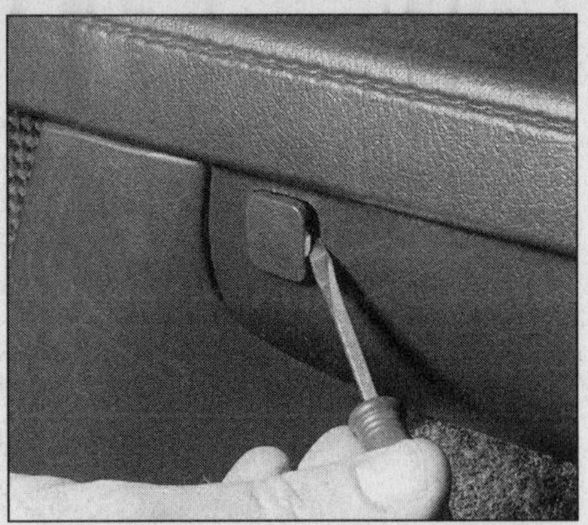

16.3 Use a screwdriver to pry off the cover for access to the arm rest retaining screw

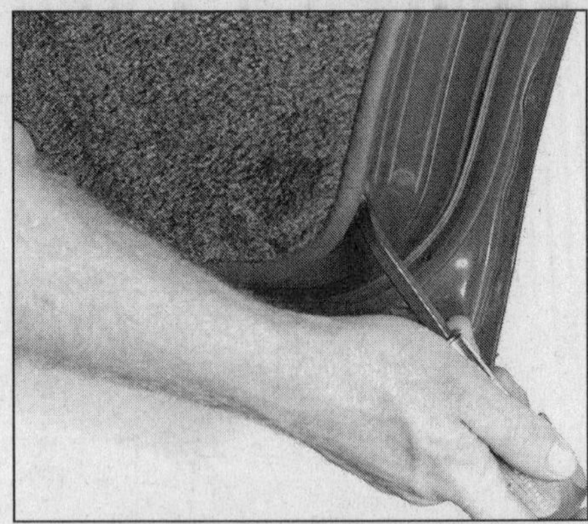

16.4 Insert a screwdriver or pry bar between the trim panel and the door and carefully disengage each clip

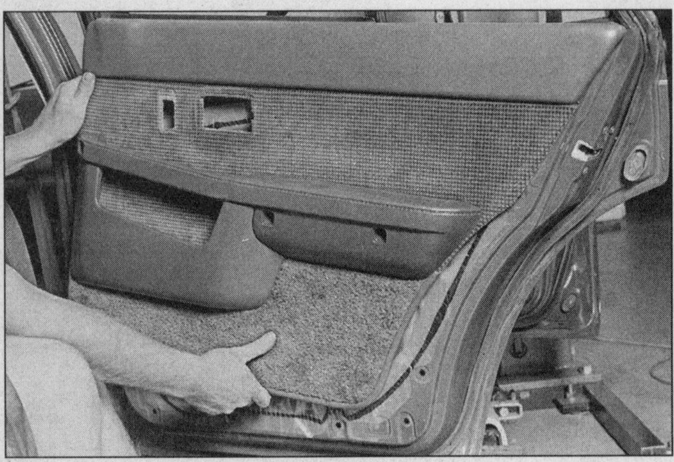

16.5 Remove the trim panel by pushing up after disengaging from the door lock

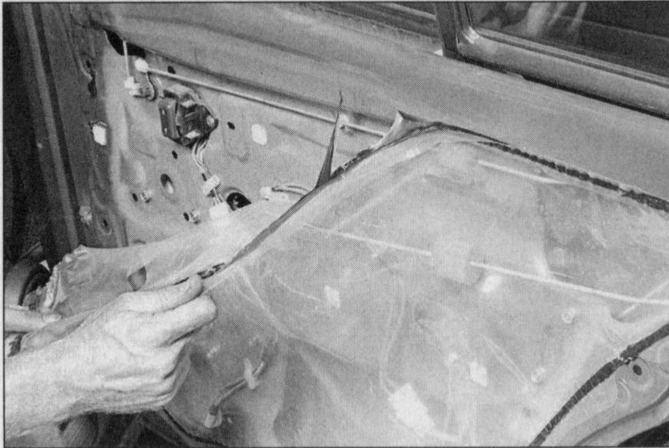

16.6 Take care when peeling the water shield off so that it is not stretched or torn

3 Remove the arm rest retaining screws **(see illustration)**.

4 Pry the trim panel loose along the bottom using a large screwdriver or pry bar to disengage the retainers. These retainers fit very tightly and care must be taken not to destroy them during removal **(see illustration)**.

5 Remove the panel by pushing up and disengaging the lock handle at the top of the door **(see illustration)**.

6 Carefully peel back the water deflector for access to the inner door panel **(see illustration)**.

7 Installation is the reverse of removal, noting the following.

8 Place the water shield carefully back in position.

9 When attaching the door trim panel to the door, locate the top of the panel over the lock handle and press down on the trim panel to engage it.

10 Position the trim panel on the inner door panel so that the panel retainers are aligned with the holes in the door panel and tap the retainers into the holes with the heel of your hand or a rubber mallet.

17 Trim fasteners - removal and installation

Refer to illustrations 17.1a and 17.1b

1 A plastic screw-type fastener is used extensively on these models. While this fastener appears to be a screw, it is actually a combination screw and clip. The base

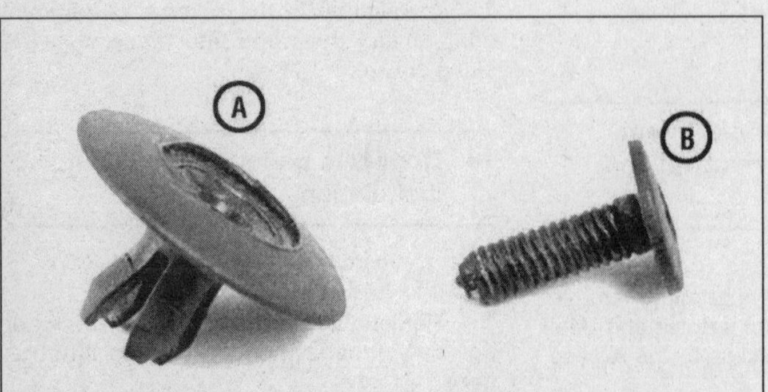

17.1a The plastic trim fastener consists of the base (A) and screw (B)

17.1b Threading the screw into the base expands and locks the base in place

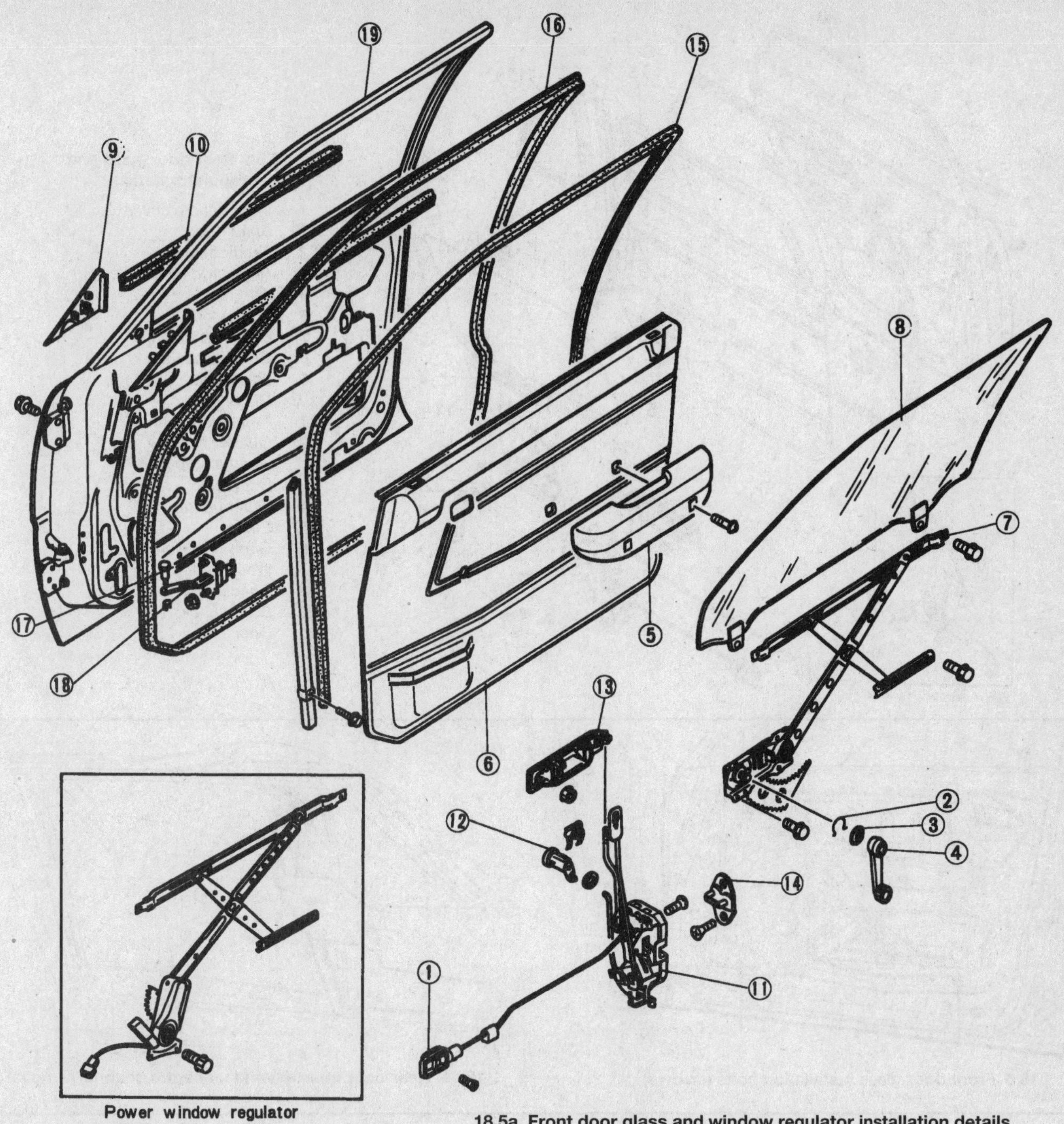

18.5a Front door glass and window regulator installation details

1	*Inner door handle cover*	6	*Door trim panel*	11	*Door lock*	16	*Weatherstrip*
2	*Snap ring*	7	*Regulator*	12	*Key cylinder*	17	*Checker pin*
3	*Escutcheon*	8	*Glass*	13	*Outer handle*	18	*Door checker*
4	*Regulator handle*	9	*Outer trim garnish*	14	*Striker*	19	*Door*
5	*Arm rest*	10	*Belt line molding*	15	*Glass channel*		

expands when the screw is threaded into it **(see illustrations)**.

2 To remove, hold the base of the screw and remove the screw from the base with a Phillips screwdriver and then pry the base out with a flat bladed screwdriver.

3 To install, snap the fastener base into position and thread the screw in with the screwdriver.

18 Door glass and window regulator - removal and installation

Refer to illustrations 18.5a, 18.5b, 18.6, 18.7a, 18.7b, 18.8a, 18.8b and 18.11

1 Lower the door glass and remove the door trim panel and water shield (Section 16).

2 On power window models, disconnect the negative battery cable.

3 On rear doors, remove the belt line molding.

4 On power window equipped models, unplug the motor connector.

5 Move the regulator position if necessary so the glass installation bolts are accessible through the service holes **(see illustrations)**.

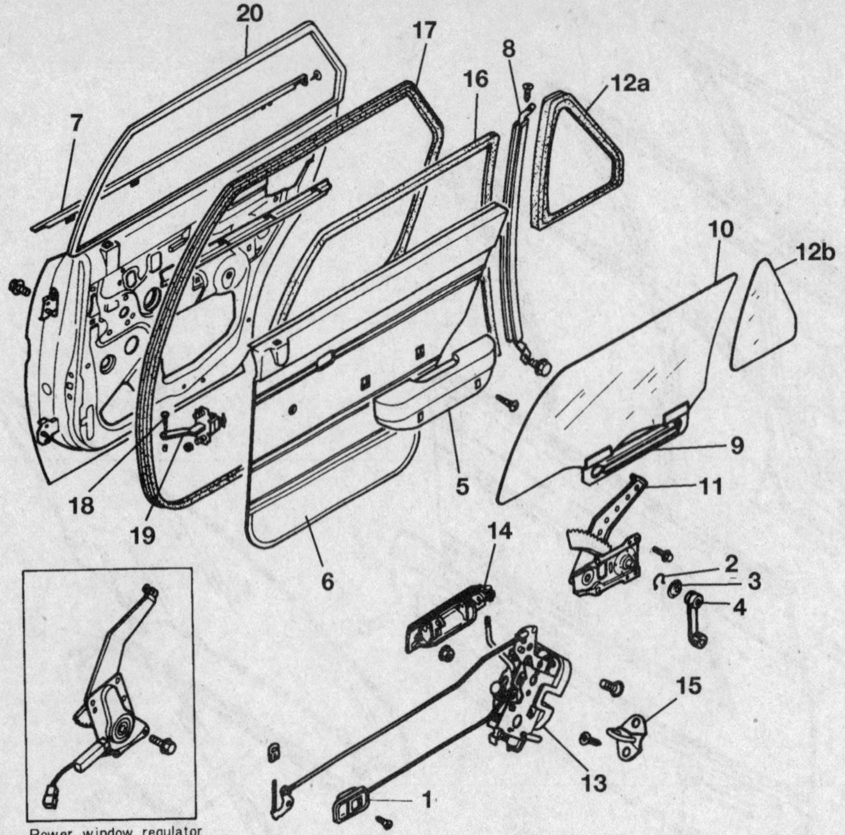

18.5b Rear door glass and regulator details

1. *Inner handle cover*
2. *Snap ring*
3. *Escutcheon*
4. *Regulator handle*
5. *Arm rest*
6. *Trim panel*
7. *Belt line molding*
8. *Center channel*
9. *Lift bracket*
10. *Glass*
11. *Regulator*
12. *Quarter window and weatherstrip*
13. *Door lock*
14. *Outer handle*
15. *Striker*
16. *Glass channel*
17. *Weatherstrip*
18. *Checker pin*
19. *Door checker*
20. *Door*

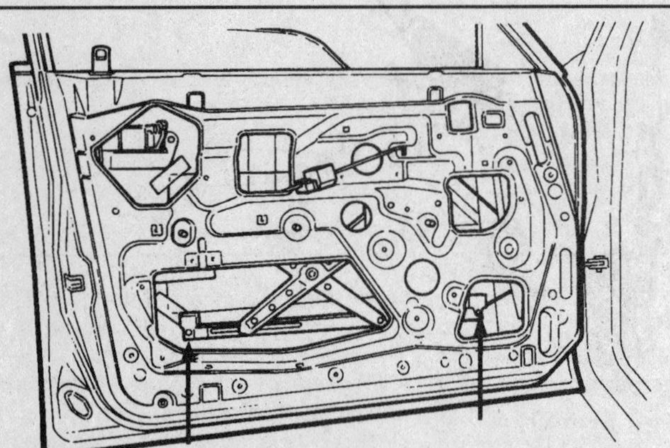

18.6 Front door glass installation bolts (arrows)

18.7a Rear door quarter window center channel removal

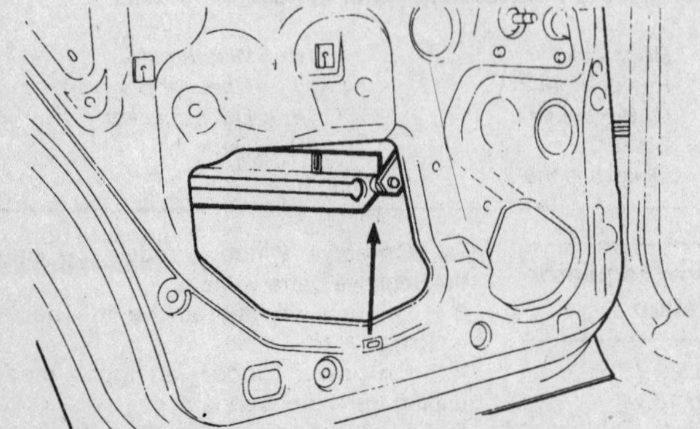

18.7b Rear door glass lift bracket and roller

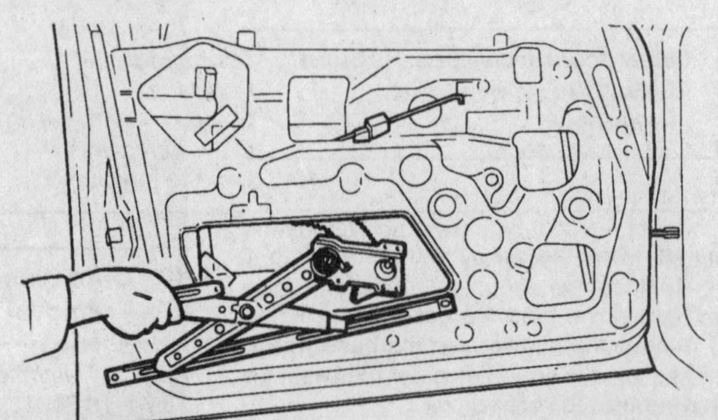

18.8a Front door window glass regulator assembly removal

18.8b Rear door window glass regulator assembly removal

18.11 Install the rear door quarter window into the channel using soapy water

6 On front doors, remove the bolts and lift the glass up and out of the door window opening **(see illustration)**.
7 On rear doors, remove the screw and bolt and lift the center channel out **(see illustration)**. Face the rear of the door glass downward, remove the lift bracket from the roller and then lift the glass up and out of the door **(see illustration)**. Remove the rear quarter glass.
8 On both front and rear doors, remove the installation bolt and lift the regulator through the service hole in the door **(see illustrations)**.
9 On power windows, unbolt the motor and remove it from the regulator. **Warning:** *Be very careful when removing the motor as the spring will be released, letting the regulator gear snap back to the Up position*.
10 Installation is the reverse of removal, paying attention to the following points.
11 Apply soapy water to the quarter window channel to ease installation **(see illustration)**.
12 On power window models, connect the battery negative cable and run the regulator to the Down position before installation of the motor.
13 After installation, run the glass up and down several times to make sure it operates lightly and smoothly, adjusting the regulator bolts as necessary.

19 Quarter window glass (coupe models) - removal and installation

Refer to illustration 19.2

1 Pry of the seat belt cover and unbolt the belt from the center pillar.
2 Remove the center pillar garnish **(see illustration)**.
3 Remove the glass installation nut, the lock installation tapping screw and then lift the glass from the vehicle.
4 Installation is the reverse of removal.

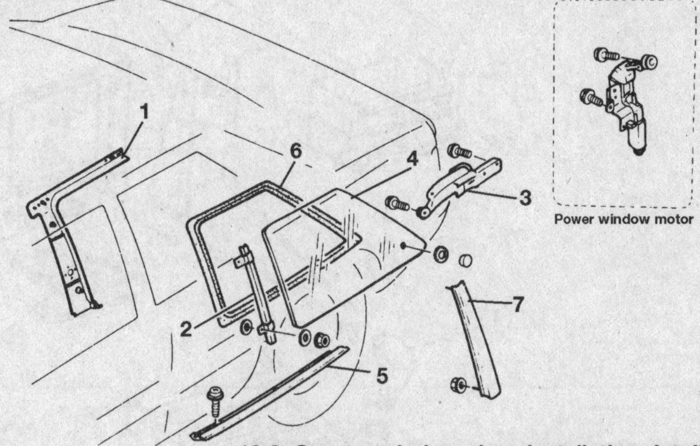

19.2 Quarter window glass installation details (coupe models)

1 *Center pillar garnish*
2 *Glass set plate*
3 *Lock*
4 *Quarter window glass*
5 *Belt line molding*
6 *Weatherstrip*
7 *Extractor grille*

20 Console - removal and installation

Refer to illustrations 20.4a and 20.4b

1 Remove the shift knob.
2 Remove the parking brake covers, the rear seat ash tray and the rear console.
3 Remove the console side walls.
4 Remove the front console and shift boot assembly **(see illustrations)**.
5 Installation is the reverse of removal.

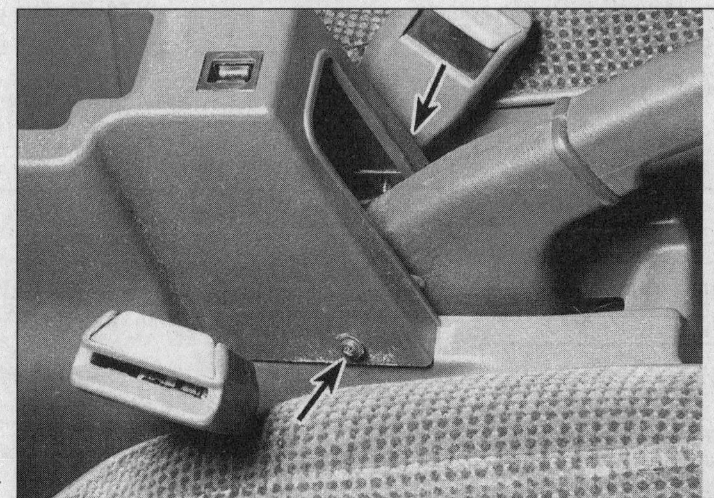

20.4a The front console bolt locations (arrows)

11

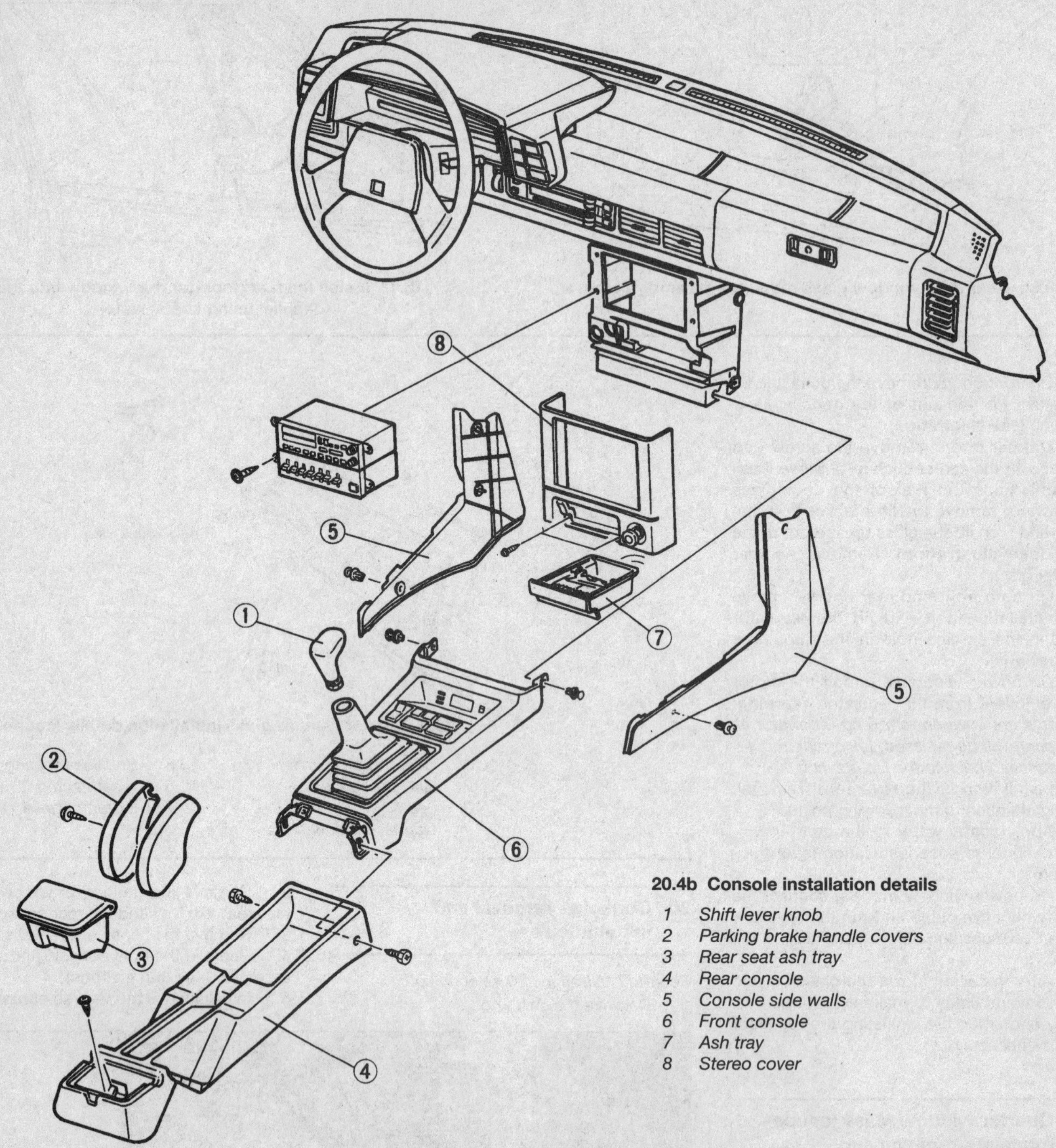

20.4b Console installation details

1 *Shift lever knob*
2 *Parking brake handle covers*
3 *Rear seat ash tray*
4 *Rear console*
5 *Console side walls*
6 *Front console*
7 *Ash tray*
8 *Stereo cover*

21 Instrument panel - removal and installation

Refer to illustrations 21.2a, 21.2b, 21.4 and 21.7

1 Disconnect the negative battery cable.
2 Remove the instrument panel meter cover and hood **(see illustrations)**.
3 Remove the meter (Chapter 12).
4 Remove the steering wheel (Chapter 10) and the upper and lower column covers **(see illustration)**.
5 Remove the lower air duct, followed by the lower panel.
6 Remove the hood release knob and dashboard undercover.
7 Remove the glove compartment **(see illustration on page 11-14)**.
8 Disconnect the heater control wire.
9 Remove the console side walls.
10 Remove the speaker and stereo covers (if equipped).
11 Remove the two front pillar trim panels.
12 Remove the retaining bolts and nuts and lift the instrument panel from the vehicle.
13 Installation is the reverse of removal.

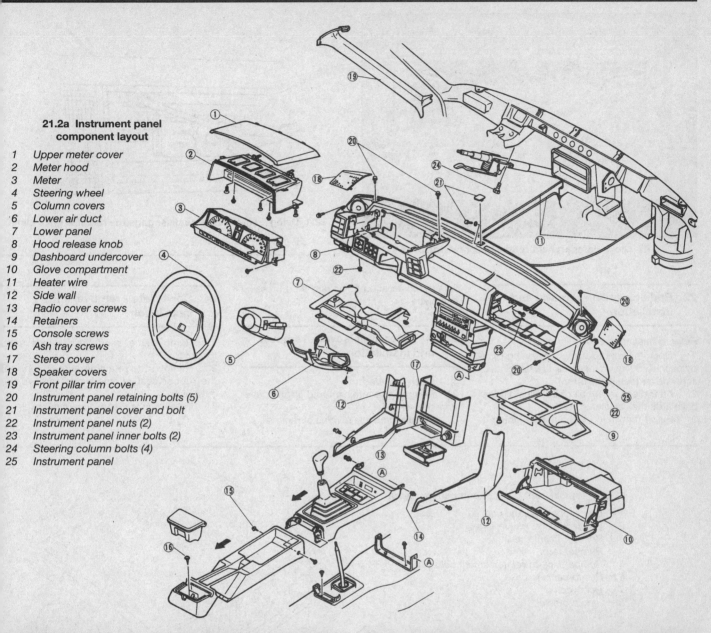

21.2a Instrument panel component layout

1 *Upper meter cover*
2 *Meter hood*
3 *Meter*
4 *Steering wheel*
5 *Column covers*
6 *Lower air duct*
7 *Lower panel*
8 *Hood release knob*
9 *Dashboard undercover*
10 *Glove compartment*
11 *Heater wire*
12 *Side wall*
13 *Radio cover screws*
14 *Retainers*
15 *Console screws*
16 *Ash tray screws*
17 *Stereo cover*
18 *Speaker covers*
19 *Front pillar trim cover*
20 *Instrument panel retaining bolts (5)*
21 *Instrument panel cover and bolt*
22 *Instrument panel nuts (2)*
23 *Instrument panel inner bolts (2)*
24 *Steering column bolts (4)*
25 *Instrument panel*

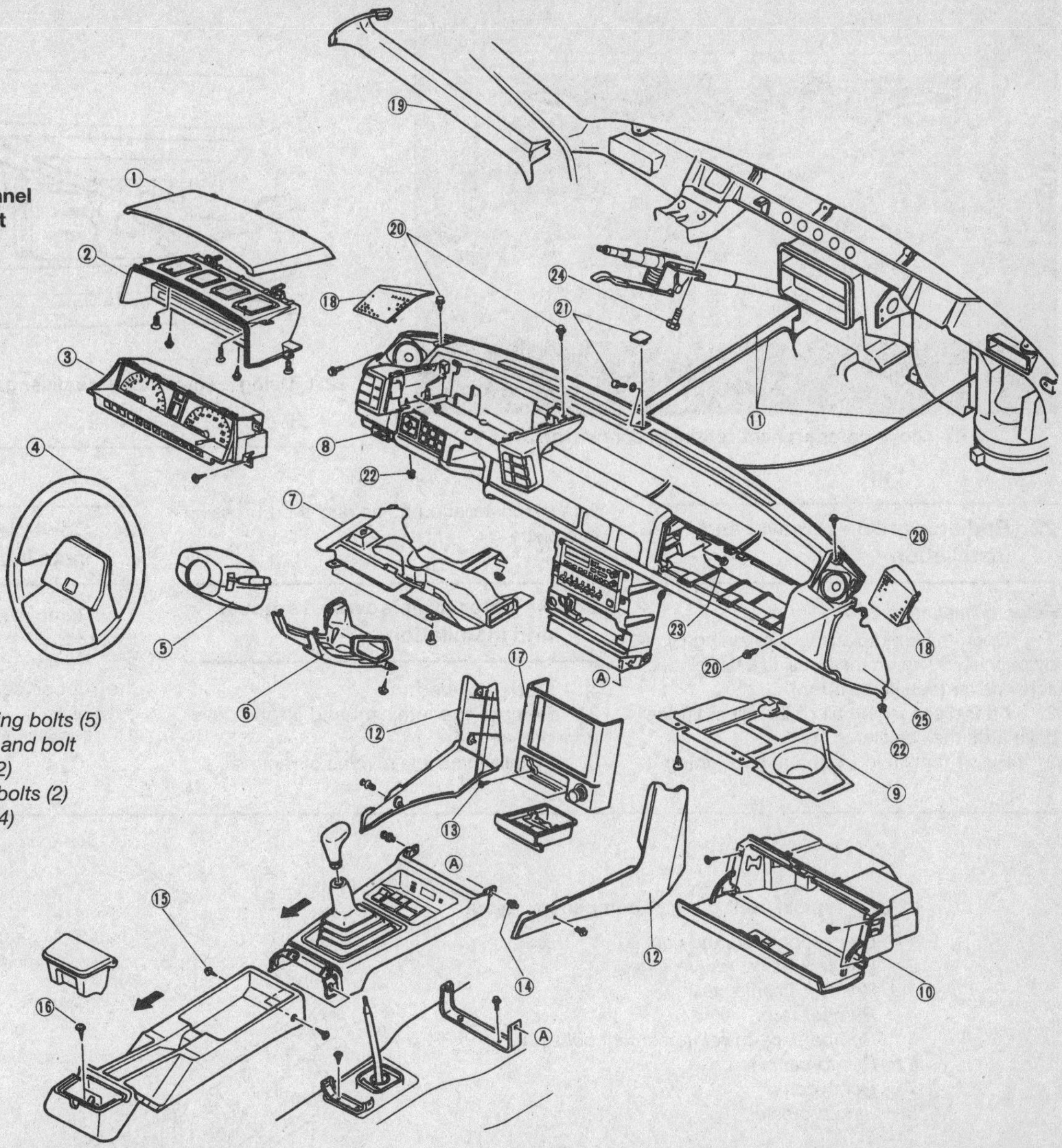

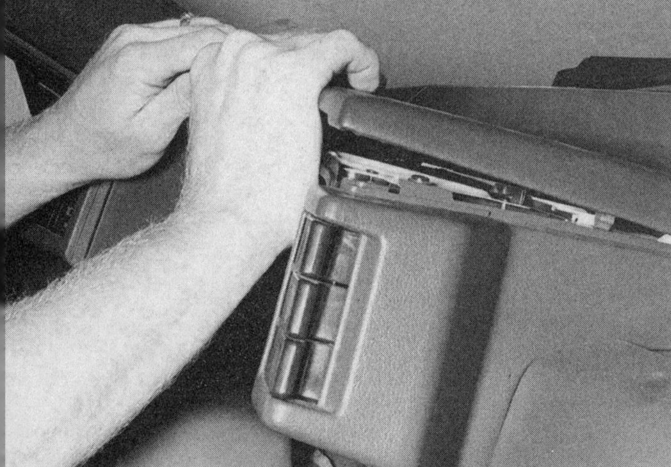

21.2b Grasp the meter top cover with both hands and snap it up to remove

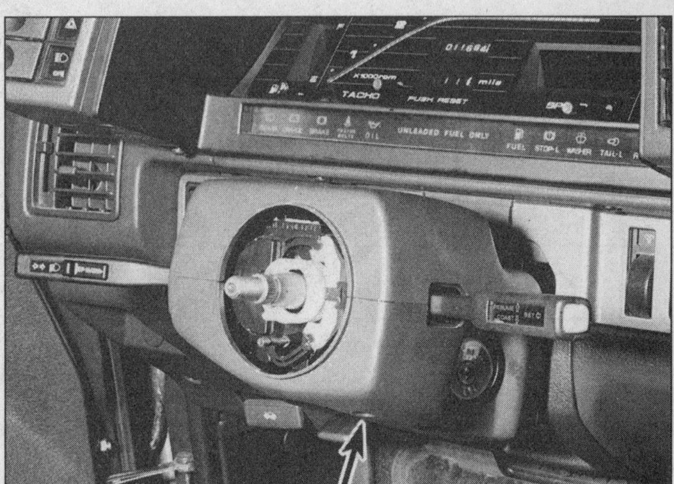

21.4 Steering column cover screw location (arrow)

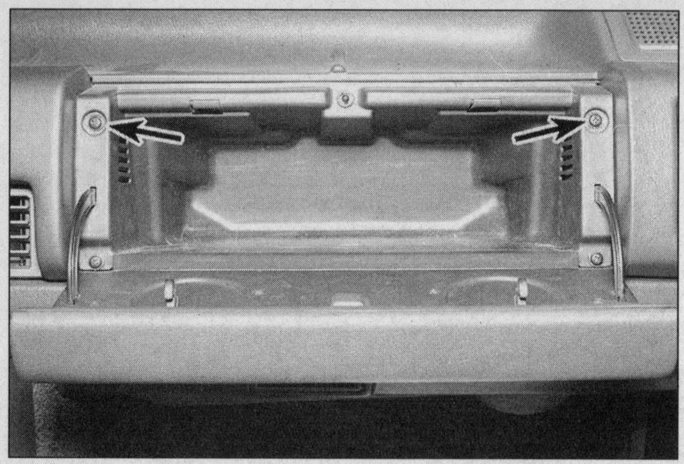

21.7 Glove compartment retaining screws (arrows)

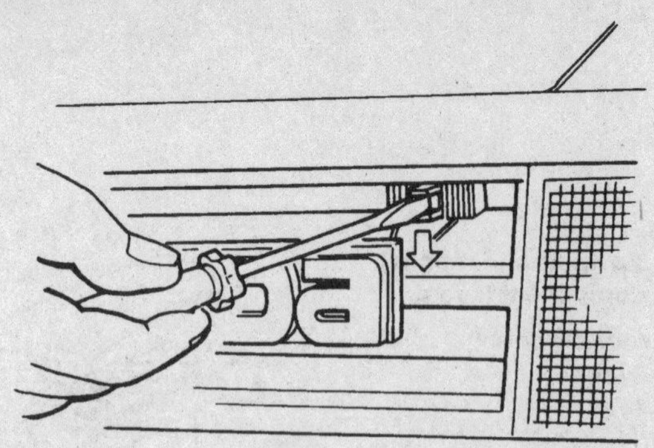

22.1 Using a screwdriver to disengage the radiator grille clips

22 Radiator grille - removal and installation

Refer to illustration 22.1

1 Open the six radiator grill retaining clips by pushing down on them, using a flat bladed screwdriver **(see illustration)**.

2 After disengaging all of the clips, lift the grille from the vehicle.

3 Place the grille in position, aligning it with the installation holes and then pressing into place.

23 Radiator grille cover - removal and installation

1 Open the hood.

2 Remove the retainers and lift the cover from the vehicle.

3 Installation is the reverse of removal.

24 Cowl plate - removal and installation

1 Remove the windshield wiper arms (Chapter 1)

2 Remove the retaining screws, pry out the rubber seal retainers and remove the cowl plate.

3 Installation is the reverse of removal.

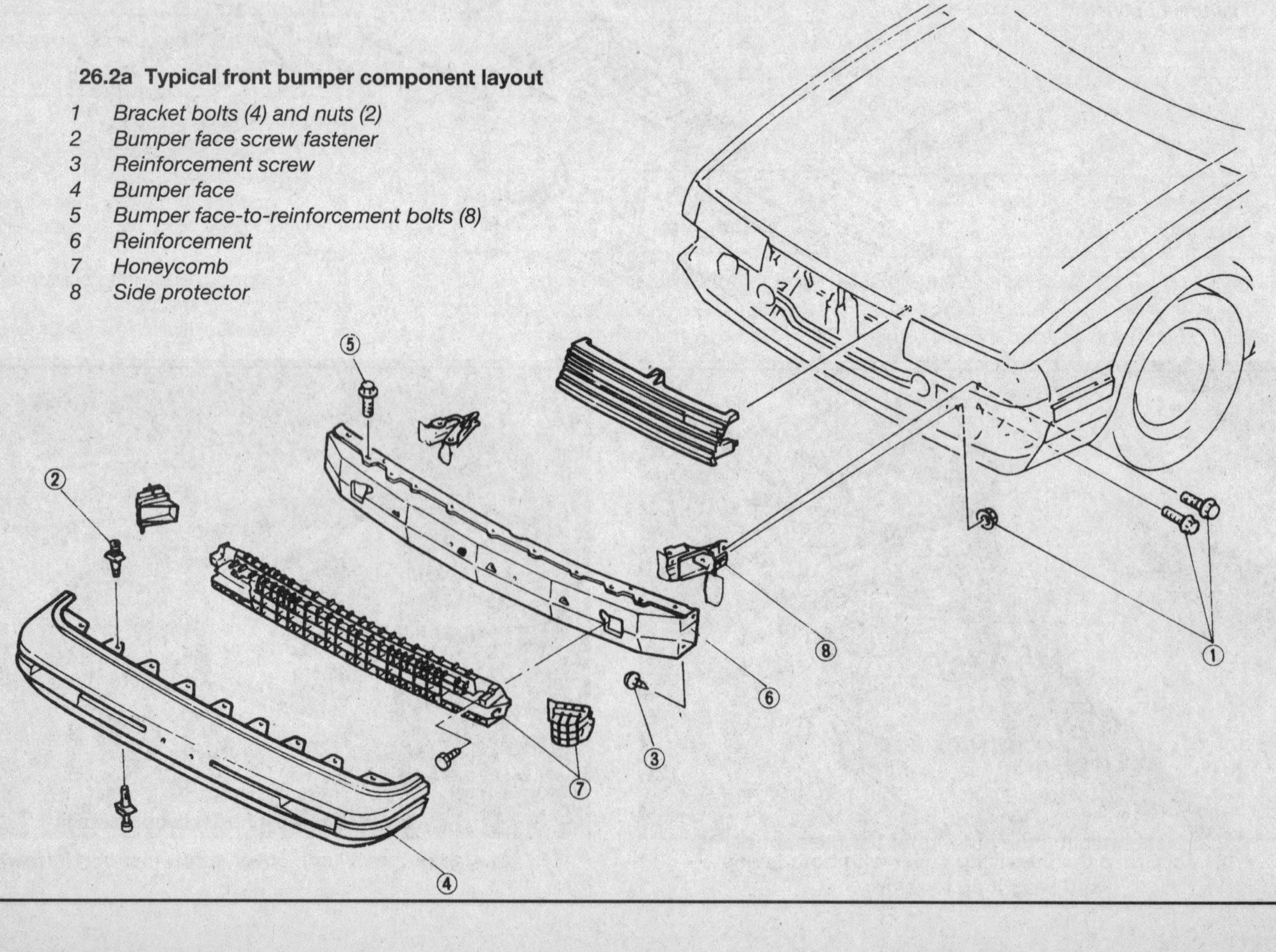

26.2a Typical front bumper component layout

1 *Bracket bolts (4) and nuts (2)*
2 *Bumper face screw fastener*
3 *Reinforcement screw*
4 *Bumper face*
5 *Bumper face-to-reinforcement bolts (8)*
6 *Reinforcement*
7 *Honeycomb*
8 *Side protector*

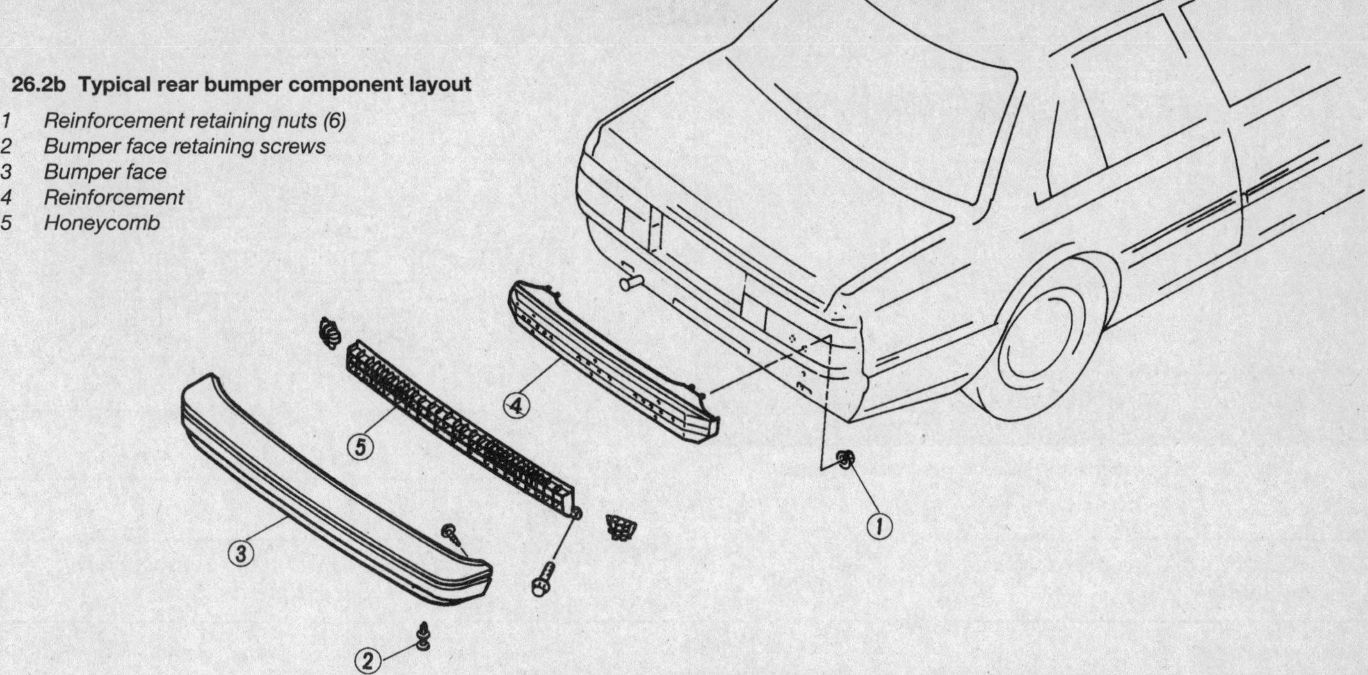

26.2b Typical rear bumper component layout

1 *Reinforcement retaining nuts (6)*
2 *Bumper face retaining screws*
3 *Bumper face*
4 *Reinforcement*
5 *Honeycomb*

25 Front skirt panel - removal and installation

1 Remove the front bumper (Section 26).
2 Remove the six retaining screws and lower the skirt from the vehicle.
3 To install, place the skirt in position and install the screws finger tight.
4 Align the skirt end with the fender and tighten the screws securely, starting at the fender line.

26 Bumpers - removal and installation

Refer to illustrations 26.2a and 26.2b

1 Remove the bumper reinforcement bracket bolts and nuts and remove the bumper assembly from the vehicle.
2 Refer to the illustrations for bumper disassembly details.
3 Installation is the reverse of removal.

27 Fixed glass replacement

Due to the requirements for special handling techniques, the fixed glass such as the windshield, rear and side glass should be replaced by a dealer or auto glass shop.

28 Door outer handle - removal and installation

Refer to illustration 28.3

1 Raise the window to the full up position.
2 Remove the trim panel and peel back the water shield (Section 13).
3 Disconnect the control rod using a flat blade screwdriver **(see illustration)**.
4 Loosen the mounting bolts and remove the outer door handle from the vehicle.
5 Installation is the reverse of removal.

29 Exterior mirror - removal and installation

Refer to illustration 29.2

1 On power window models, disconnect the negative battery cable.
2 Pry off the trim cover **(see illustration)**.
3 On power window models, unplug the connector.
4 Remove the retaining screws and lift the mirror from the vehicle.
5 Installation is the reverse of removal.

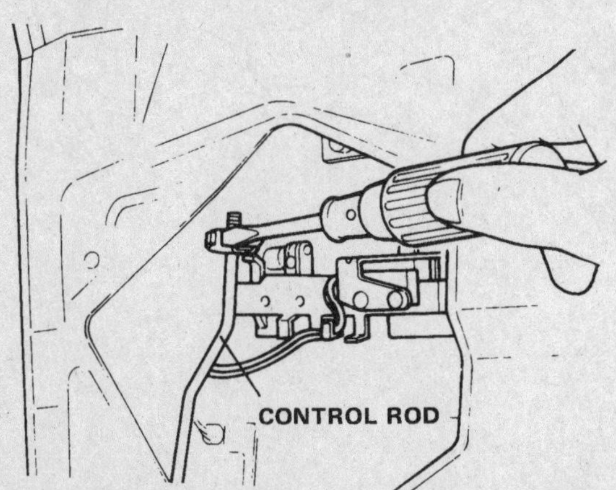

28.3 Disconnecting the outer door handle control rod

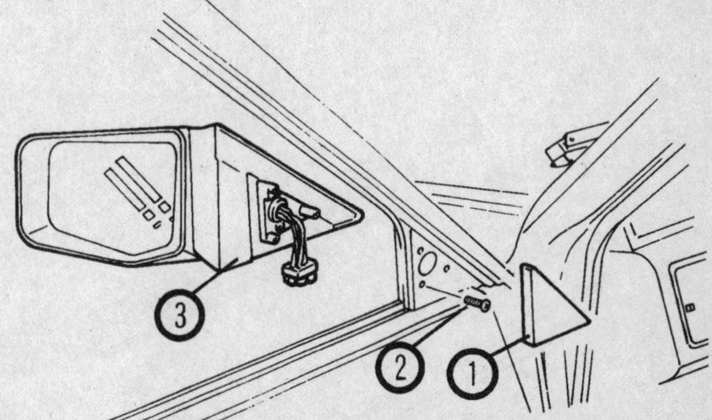

29.2 Exterior mirror installation details

1 *Trim panel* 2 *Screws (3)* 3 *Mirror*

Notes

Chapter 12
Chassis electrical system

Contents

Specifications

Bulb	**Wattage**
Front	
Headlight	
Left-hand drive	
US inner	50
US outer	35/55
European	40/45
Right-hand drive	60/65
Parking light	5/8
Front turn signal light	27
Front side marker light	3.8
Interior	
Dome light	10
Map light	5
Indicator lights	
Turn signal, hazard and fuel lights	3.4
High beam, oil pressure, alternator, stop lights, brake, parking brake, fuel, washer level, tail and seat belt lights	1.4
Illumination lights	
Automatic transaxle selector lever	3.4
Heater	3.4
Meter	1.4 and 3.4
Cigarette lighter	3.4
Radio	3.4
Rear window defroster	1.4
Rear	
Turn signal light	27
Stop and tail light	27/8
Back-up light	27
Side marker light	5
License plate light	
5-door models	6
All others	5
Luggage compartment	5 or 6

Torque specifications	**Ft-lbs**
Windshield wiper and rear wiper arm bolts	7 to 10

1 General information

The electrical system is a 12-volt, negative ground type. Power for the lights and all electrical accessories is supplied by a lead/acid battery that is charged by the alternator.

This Chapter covers repair and service procedures for the various electrical components not associated with the engine. Information on the battery, alternator, distributor and starter motor can be found in Chapter 5.

It should be noted that whenever portions of the electrical system are worked on, the negative battery cable should be disconnected to prevent electrical shorts and/or fires. **Note:** *Information concerning digital instrumentation and dash related accessories is not included in this manual. Problems involving these components should be referred to your dealer.*

2 Electrical troubleshooting - general information

A typical electrical circuit consists of an electrical component, any switches, relays, motors, fuses, fusible links or circuit breakers related to that component and the wiring and connectors that link the component to both the battery and the chassis. To help you pinpoint an electrical circuit problem, wiring diagrams are included at the end of this Chapter.

Before tackling any troublesome electrical circuit, first study the appropriate wiring diagrams to get a complete understanding of what makes up that individual circuit. Noting if other components related to the circuit are operating properly, for instance, can often narrow trouble spots, down. If several components or circuits fail at one time, chances are the problem is in a fuse or ground connection, because several circuits are often routed through the same fuse and ground connections.

Electrical problems usually stem from simple causes, such as loose or corroded connections, a blown fuse, a melted fusible link or a failed relay. Visually inspect the condition of all fuses, wires and connections in a problem circuit before troubleshooting the circuit.

If test equipment and instruments are going to be utilized, use the diagrams to plan ahead of time where you will make the necessary connections in order to accurately pinpoint the trouble spot.

The basic tools needed for electrical troubleshooting include a circuit tester or voltmeter (a 12-volt bulb with a set of test leads can also be used), a continuity tester, that includes a bulb, a battery and set of test leads, and a jumper wire, preferably with a circuit breaker incorporated, which can be used to bypass electrical components. Before attempting to locate a problem with test instruments, use the wiring diagram(s) to decide where to make the connections.

Voltage checks

Voltage checks should be performed if a circuit is not functioning properly. Connect one lead of a circuit tester to either the negative battery terminal or a known good ground. Connect the other lead to a connector in the circuit being tested, preferably nearest to the battery or fuse. If the bulb of the tester lights, voltage is present, which means that the part of the circuit between the connector and the battery is problem free. Continue checking the rest of the circuit in the same fashion. When you reach a point at which no voltage is present, the problem lies between that point and the last test point with voltage. Most of the time the problem can be traced to a loose connection. **Note:** *Keep in mind that some circuits receive voltage only when the ignition key is in the Accessory or Run position.*

Finding a short

One method of finding shorts in a circuit is to remove the fuse and connect a test light or voltmeter in place of the fuse terminals. There should be no voltage present in the circuit. Move the wiring harness from side-to-side while watching the test light. If the bulb goes on, there is a short to ground somewhere in that area, probably where the insulation has rubbed through. The same test can be performed on each component in the circuit, even a switch.

Ground check

Perform a ground test to check whether a component is properly grounded. Disconnect the battery and connect one lead of a self-powered test light, known as a continuity tester, to a known good ground. Connect the other lead to the wire or ground connection being tested. If the bulb goes on, the ground is good. If the bulb does not go on, the ground is not good.

Continuity check

A continuity check is done to determine if there are any breaks in a circuit - if it is passing electricity properly. With the circuit off (no power in the circuit), a self-powered continuity tester can be used to check the circuit. Connect the test leads to both ends of the circuit (or to the "power" end and a good ground), and if the test light comes on the circuit is passing current properly. If the light doesn't come on, there is a break somewhere in the circuit. The same procedure can be used to test a switch, by connecting the continuity tester to the switch terminals. With the switch turned On, the test light should come on.

Finding an open circuit

When diagnosing for possible open circuits, it is often difficult to locate them by sight because oxidation or terminal misalignment are hidden by the connectors. Merely wiggling a connector on a sensor or in the wiring harness may correct the open circuit condition. Remember this when an open circuit is indicated when troubleshooting a circuit. Intermittent problems may also be caused by oxidized or loose connections.

Electrical troubleshooting is simple if you keep in mind that all electrical circuits are basically electricity running from the battery, through the wires, switches, relays, fuses and fusible links to each electrical component (light bulb, motor, etc.) and to ground, from which it is passed back to the battery. Any electrical problem is an interruption in the flow of electricity to and from the battery.

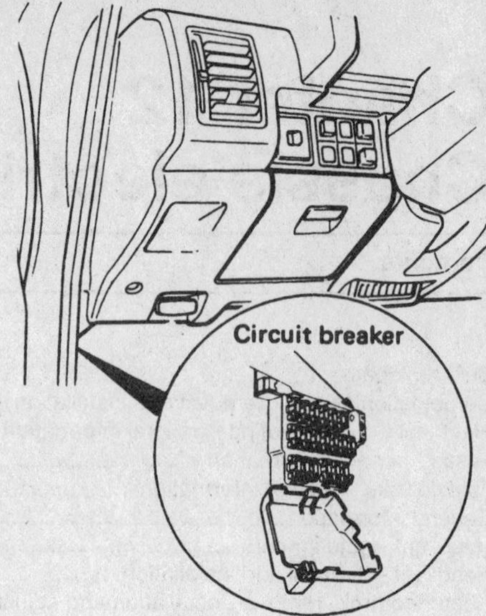

3.1a Fuse box and circuit breaker location

3 Fuses - general information

Refer to illustrations 3.1a, 3.1b, 3.2a and 3.2b

The electrical circuits of the vehicle are protected by a combination of fuses, circuit breakers and fusible links. The fuse box unit combines the fuse box, circuit breakers, harnesses and their connectors and is located on the kick panel under the dash on the driver's side **(see illustrations)**.

Each of the fuses is designed to protect a specific circuit and the various circuits are identified on the fuse panel itself **(see illustrations)**. Miniaturized fuses of blade terminal design are employed in the fuse block.

If an electrical component fails, your first check should be the fuse. Inspecting the element inside the clear plastic body can easily identify a fuse that has blown. Also, the blade terminal tips are exposed in the fuse body, allowing for continuity checks.

It is important that the correct fuse be installed. The different electrical circuits need varying amounts of protection, indicated by the amperage rating molded in bold, color coded numbers on the fuse body and marked on the fuse box cover.

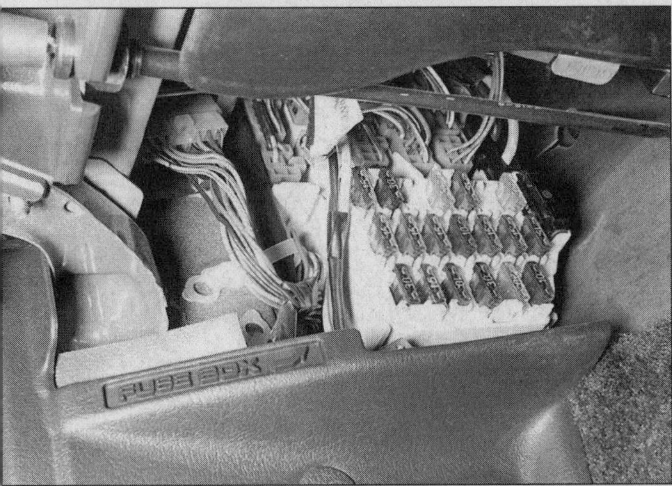

3.1b The fuses are accessible after removing the fuse box cover

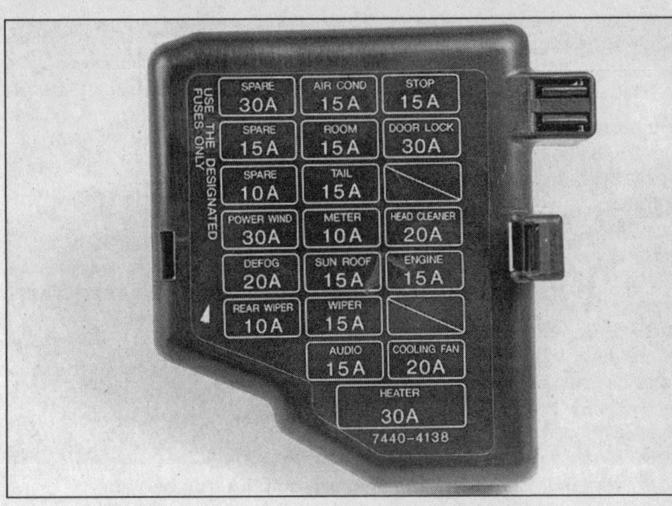

3.2a The fuse location and type information can be found on the fuse box cover

If the replacement fuse immediately fails, do not replace it again until the cause of the problem is isolated and corrected. In most cases, this will be a short circuit in the wiring caused by a broken or deteriorated wire.

The heater and air conditioner consume a lot of power and the fuse box contains a circuit breaker to protect their circuits. If the circuit is broken by the circuit breaker, turn off the air conditioner and heater before pushing the circuit breaker reset button.

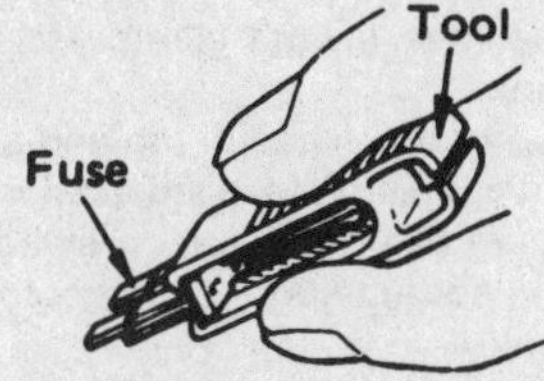

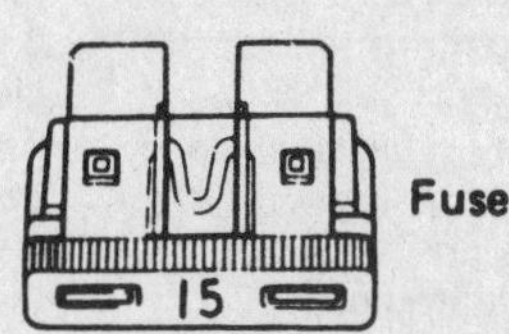

3.2b Fuse type and replacement procedure

4 Fusible links - general information

Refer to illustration 4.2

In addition to fuses, the wiring is protected by fusible links. These links are used in circuits not ordinarily fused, such as the ignition circuit.

The fusible links used on these models consist of special wires that plug into a fusible link block located on the inner fender panel adjacent to the battery. The location of other fusible links on your particular vehicle may be determined by referring to the wiring diagrams at the end of this book. The fusible links cannot be repaired, but a new link of the same size wire (available at your dealer) can be put in its place. The procedure is as follows:

a) *Turn the ignition switch Off.*
b) *Pull the fusible link straight out of the block.*
c) *Push a new fusible link securely into the block* **(see illustration)**.

5 Three way adjustable suspension damper actuator - testing

Refer to illustration 5.2

1 Remove the damper actuator cover and unplug the connector (Chapter 10).

2 Use an ohmmeter to measure the resistance across the Sport (L to B) and Normal (W to B) terminals **(see illustration)**. The resistance should between 2.8 and 3.3 ohms.

4.2 Fusible link replacement

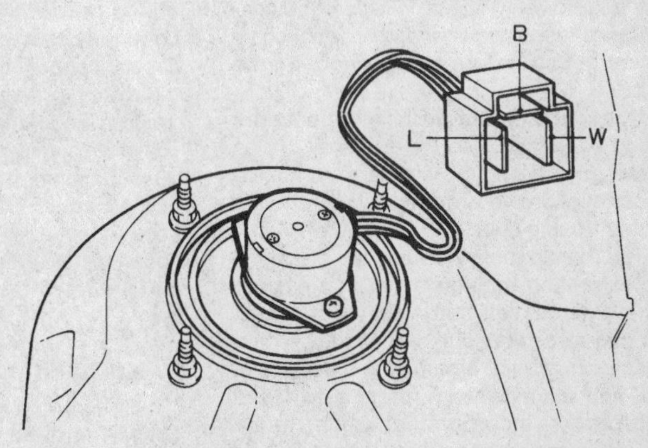

5.2 Three-way adjustable suspension actuator connector

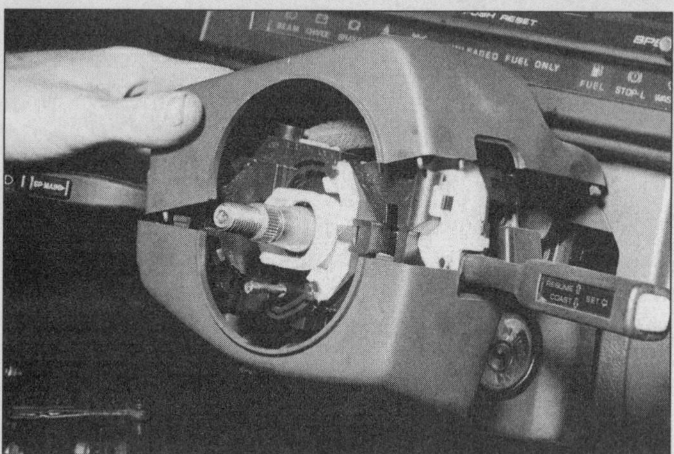

6.3 Removing the steering column trim halves

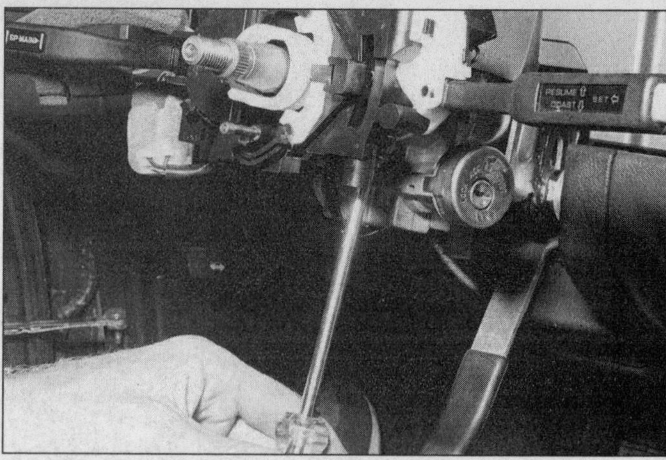

6.6 Loosening the combination switch screw

6 Combination switch - removal and installation

Refer to illustrations 6.3, 6.6, 6.7 and 6.8

1 Disconnect the battery negative cable.
2 Remove the steering wheel (Chapter 10).
3 Remove the screws and separate the column trim halves **(see illustration).**
4 Pull the ignition switch lock ring off.

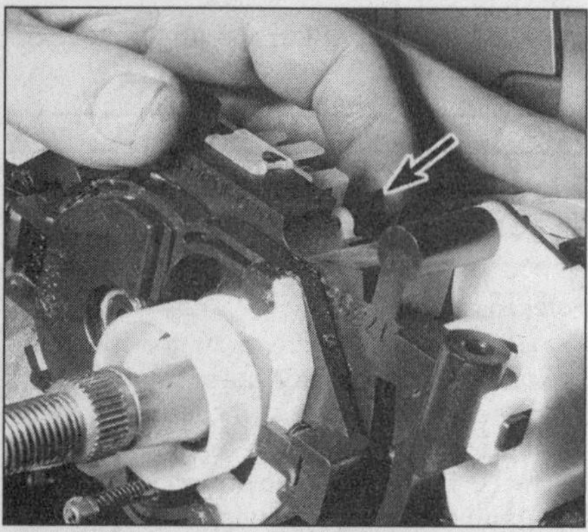

6.7 Press up on the combination switch locating tab (arrow) to release it, then slide the switch out of the column

5 Remove the ignition switch illumination bulb and (if equipped) lower the column tilt lever.
6 Loosen the switch clamp screw **(see illustration).**
7 Lift up on the locating tab and slide the switch off the column **(see illustration).**
8 Remove the combination switch from the column and unplug the connectors **(see illustration).**
9 Installation is the reverse of removal.

7 Ignition switch - removal and installation

Refer to illustration 7.2

1 Remove the steering wheel (Chapter 11) and the combination switch (Section 6) to provide access to the ignition switch.
2 Drill out the ignition switch retaining bolts **(see illustration).**
3 Remove the switch from the steering column and unplug the connector.
4 To install, place the switch in position, install the bolts and tighten them until the heads break off.
5 Install the combination switch and steering wheel.

8 Headlight - removal and installation

1 Remove the radiator grille cover (if equipped) and grille assembly (Chapter 11).
2 Disconnect the negative battery cable.

Sealed beam-type

Refer to illustrations 8.3 and 8.4

3 Remove the headlight bezel and combination light assembly **(see illustration).**
4 Remove the four screws which secure the retaining ring and withdraw the ring. Support the sealed beam unit as this is done, unplug the connector and remove it from the vehicle **(see illustration).**
5 Position the new unit close enough to connect the wires and install the retaining ring and mounting screws.
6 Install the bezel and check for proper operation. If the adjusting screws were not turned, the headlight should not require adjustment.

Bulb-type

Refer to illustration 8.8

7 Remove the front side light assembly.

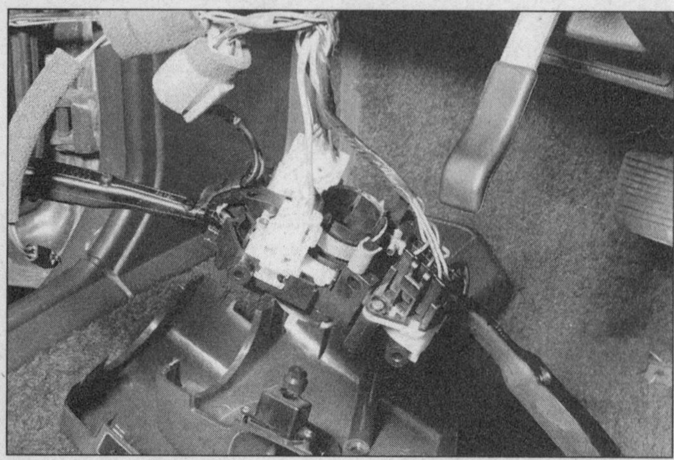

6.8 With the switch removed from the column, the connectors can be easily unplugged

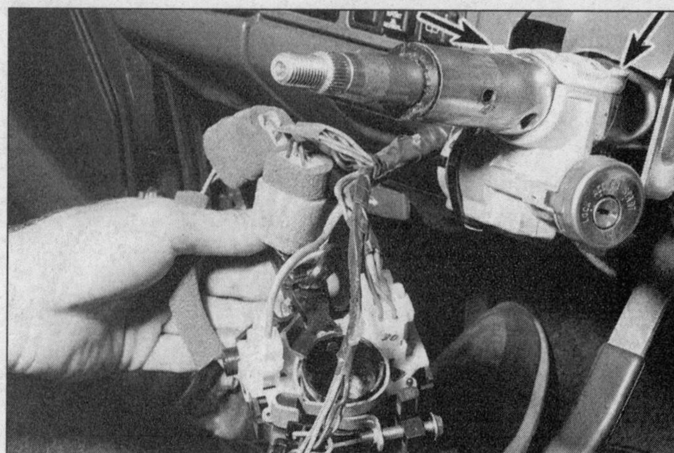

7.2 The heads of the ignition switch retaining bolts (arrows) must be drilled out to remove the switch

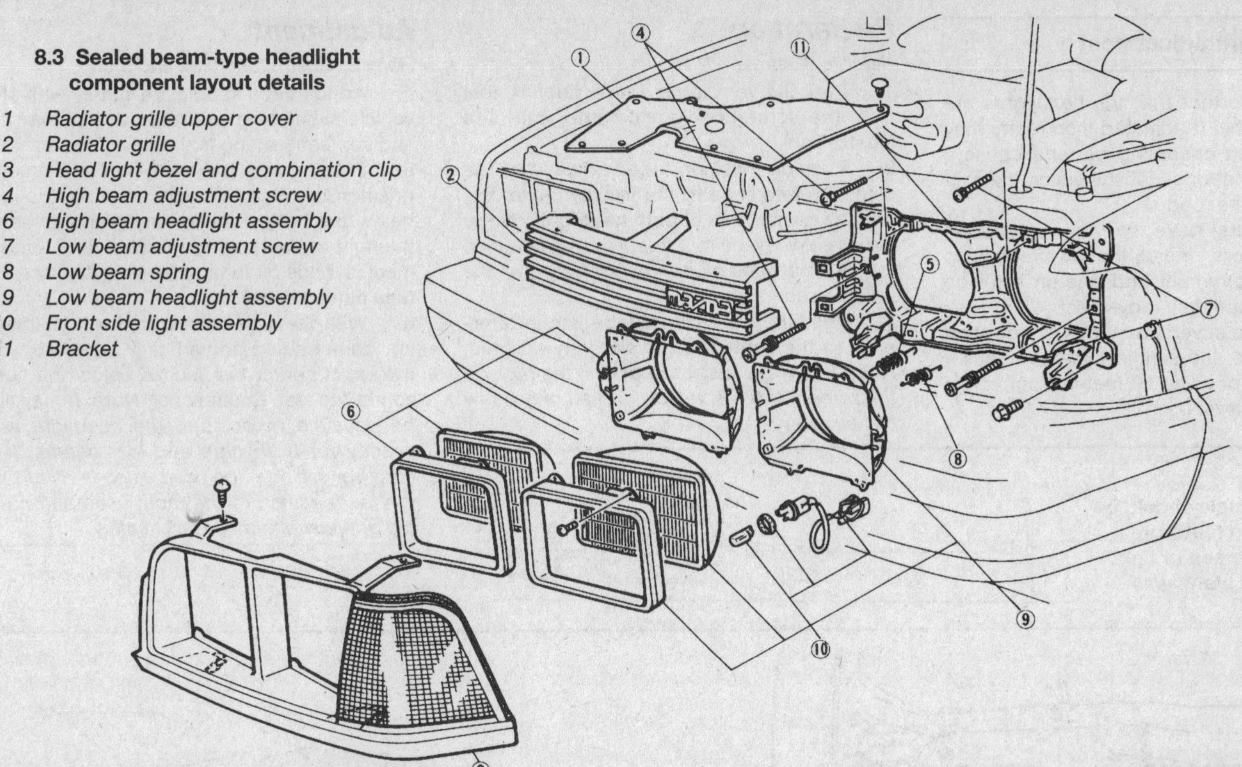

8.3 Sealed beam-type headlight component layout details

1 *Radiator grille upper cover*
2 *Radiator grille*
3 *Head light bezel and combination clip*
4 *High beam adjustment screw*
6 *High beam headlight assembly*
7 *Low beam adjustment screw*
8 *Low beam spring*
9 *Low beam headlight assembly*
10 *Front side light assembly*
11 *Bracket*

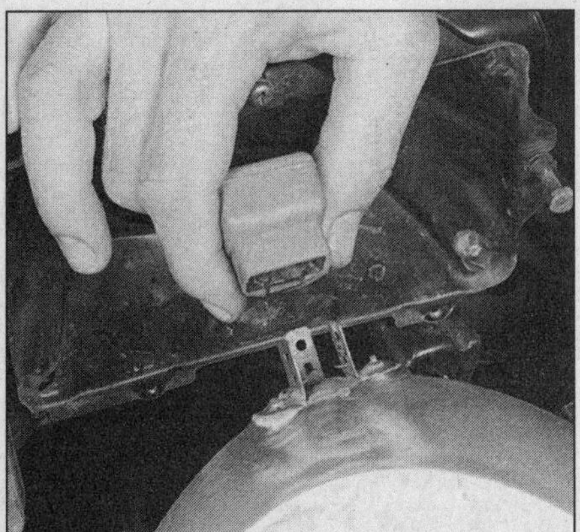

8.4 Support the headlight while unplugging the connector

8 Remove the headlight assembly cover, disconnect the spring and remove the bulb **(see illustration)**.

9 Installation is the reverse of removal. On halogen bulbs, take care not to touch the bulb with your bare fingers as oil from your fingers could cause damage when the bulb is turned on. Clean the bulb with rubbing alcohol after installation if you do touch it.

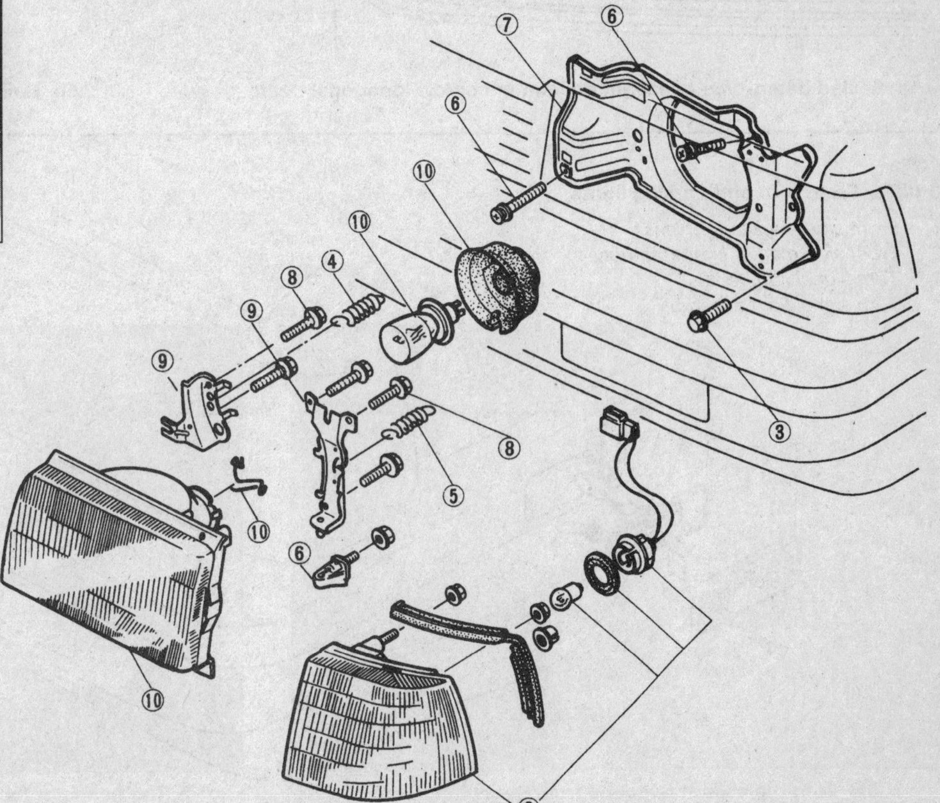

8.8 Bulb-type headlight installation details

2 *Front side light assembly*
3 *Bolts*
4 *Inner spring*
5 *Outer spring*
6 *Headlight adjustment screw*
7 *Bracket*
8 *Bolts*
9 *Bracket*
10 *Headlight assembly (cover, spring, lens, bulb and holder)*

9 Headlight adjustment

It is important that the headlights are aimed correctly. If adjusted incorrectly they could blind an oncoming car and cause a serious accident or seriously reduce the your ability to see the road.

Headlights have two spring loaded adjusting screws, one on the top affecting up and down movement and one on the side affecting left and right movement.

There are several methods of adjusting the headlights, the simplest method uses a screen or empty wall 10 feet in front of the vehicle and a level floor.

Preparation

Refer to illustration 9.1

1 Park the vehicle on a level floor 10 feet from the screen or light colored wall **(see illustration)**.

2 Position masking tape vertically on the screen in reference to the vehicle center line and the center lines of both headlights. **Note:** *If the vehicle has a four headlight system then four vertical lines plus the vehicle center line will be used.*

3 Position a horizontal tape line in reference to the center line of all the headlights. **Note:** *It may be easier to position the tape on the screen with the vehicle parked only a few inches away.*

Adjustment

Refer to illustrations 9.5a and 9.5b

4 Adjustment should be made with the vehicle sitting level and the gas tank half full and someone sitting in the driver's seat.

5 Starting with the low beam adjustment, position the high intensity zone so it is just below the horizontal line and two inches to the right of the headlight vertical line. Adjustment is made by turning the adjusting screws **(see illustrations)**.

6 With the high beams on, the high intensity zone should be vertically centered with the exact center two inches below the horizontal line (see illustrations). **Note:** *It may not be possible to position the headlight aim exactly for both high and low beams. If a compromise must be used, keep in mind that the low beams are the most used and have the greatest effect on driver safety.*

9.1 The vehicle should be placed ten feet from a vertical screen or light colored blank wall

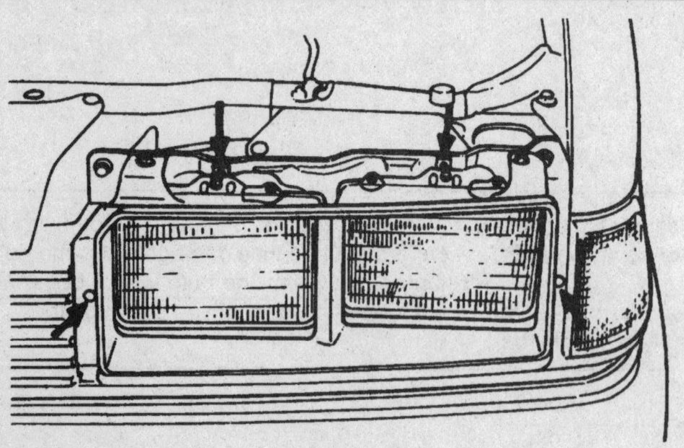

9.5a Sealed beam-type headlight adjustment screw locations

9.5b Bulb-type headlight adjustment

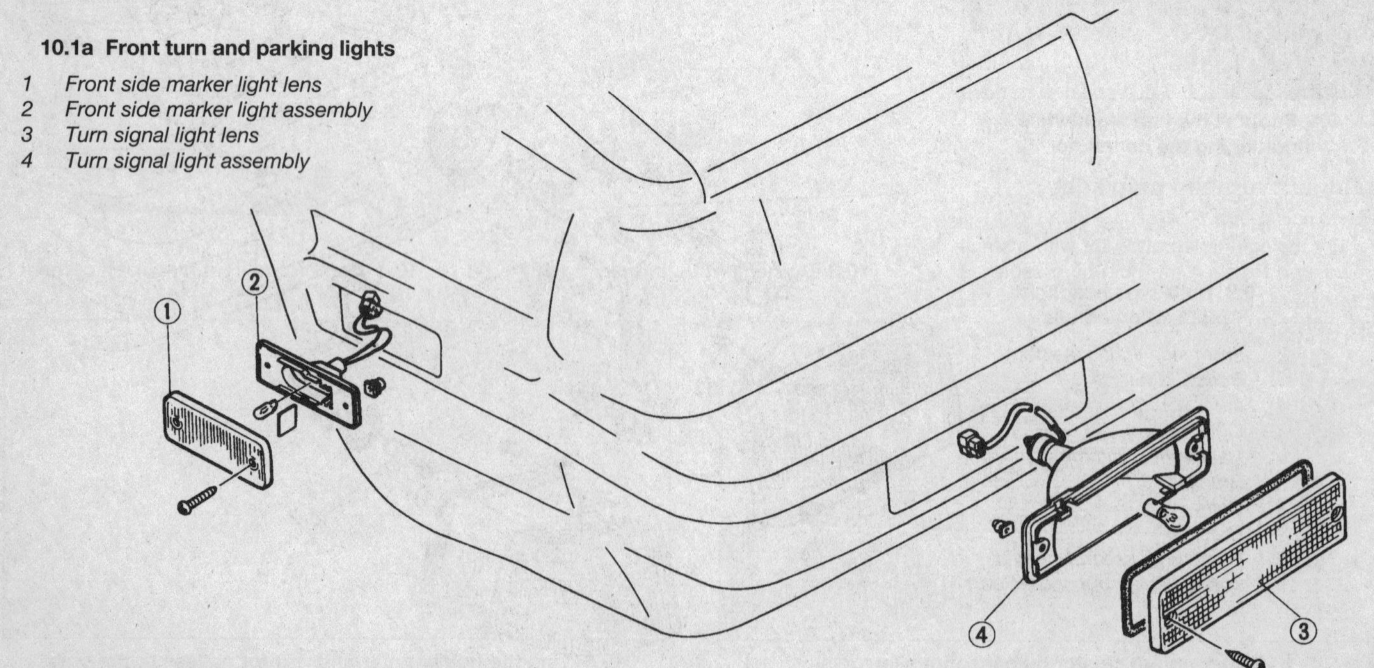

10.1a Front turn and parking lights

1 *Front side marker light lens*
2 *Front side marker light assembly*
3 *Turn signal light lens*
4 *Turn signal light assembly*

10.1b The side marker bulbs insert straight into the socket

10.1c The turn signal bulb is installed or removed by pushing in and rotating

10 Bulb replacement

Front end

Turn signal and side marker lights

Refer to illustrations 10.1a, 10.1b and 10.1c

1 The turn signal and side marker light bulb can be replaced after removing the screws and lenses. Grasp the bulb and pull it from the socket (side marker) or press in and rotate the bulb counterclockwise (turn signal) **(see illustrations)**.

Interior

Ignition switch light

Refer to illustration

2 Remove the steering column cover for access. Pull the bulb from the socket and press the new one into place.

Dome/map light

Refer to illustration 10.3

3 Grasp the lens and pull down to remove it. Remove the bulb by pulling it straight down **(see illustration)**.

Optional overhead map light

Refer to illustration 10.4

4 Pry the light lens/button off with a small screwdriver. Replace the bulb by grasping it and pulling it out of the socket **(see illustration)**.

Instrument panel lights

Refer to illustrations 10.5 and 10.6

5 The instrument panel bulbs can be replaced after removal of the instrument cluster (Section 12) **(see illustration)**.

6 Rotate the holder, withdraw it from the panel and remove the bulb from the holder **(see illustration)**.

Radio illumination

7 The radio illumination bulb is located in a twist-in holder and is accessible after removing the radio (Section 11).

Rear end

Luggage compartment light

8 Pry off the lens, grasp the bulb and pull it from the socket.

License plate light

Refer to illustration 10.9

9 Remove the license plate housing screws and housing for access to the bulb **(see illustration on next page)**.

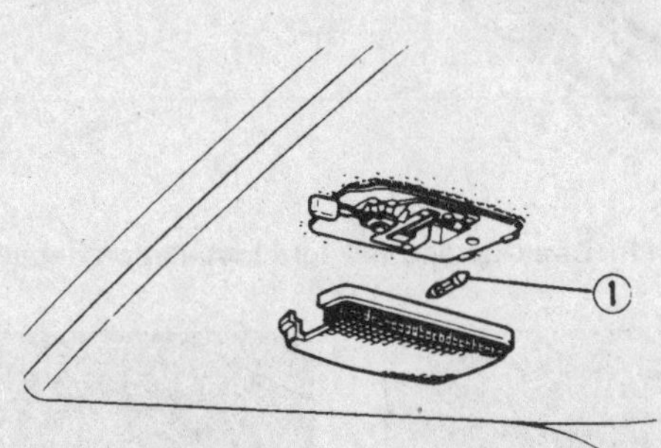

10.3 Dome light bulb replacement

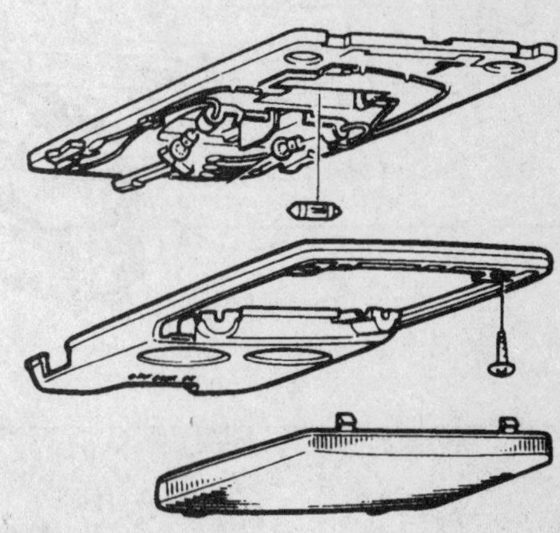

10.4 Dome/map light bulb replacement

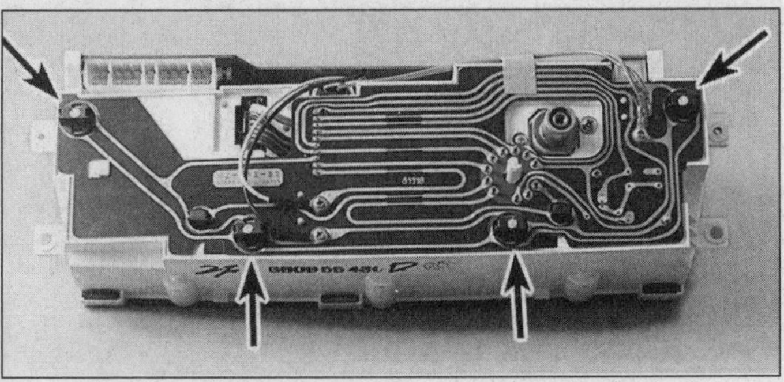

10.5 Instrument cluster bulb locations (arrows)

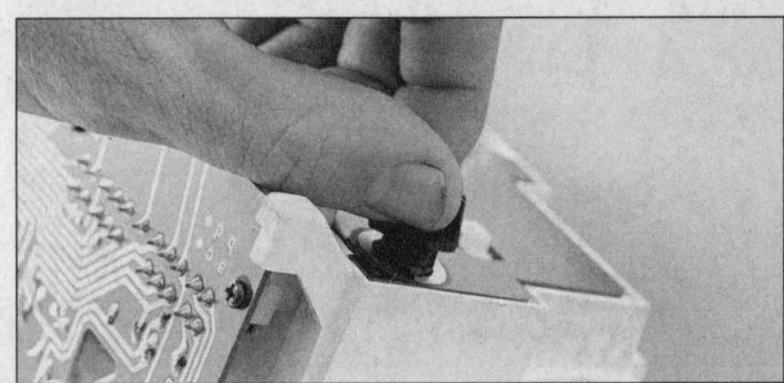

10.6 Turn the holder and remove it for access to the bulb

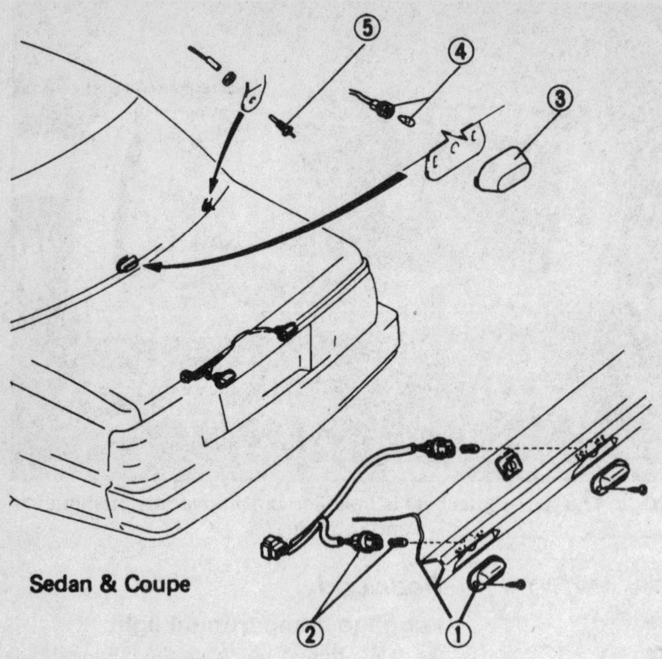

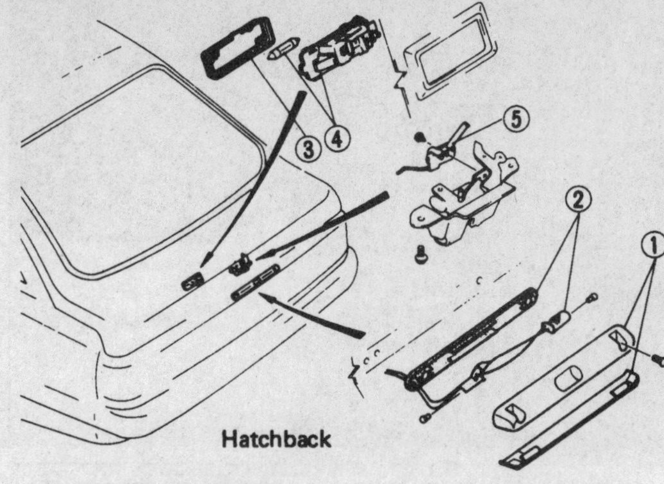

10.9 License plate and tail light component layout

1. *License plate light lens*
2. *License plate bulb*
3. *Luggage compartment light lens*
4. *Luggage compartment light bulb and holder*
5. *Switch*

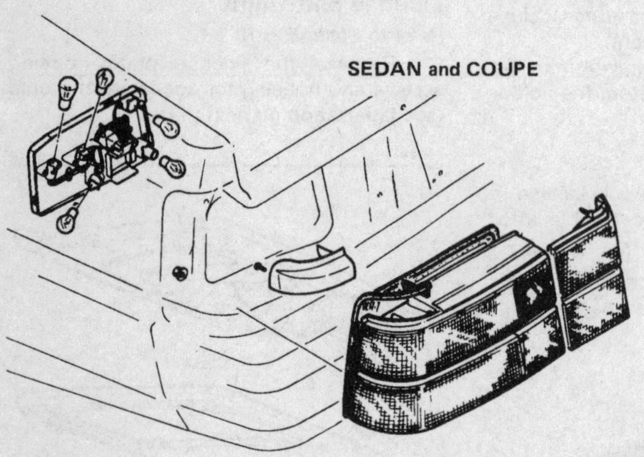

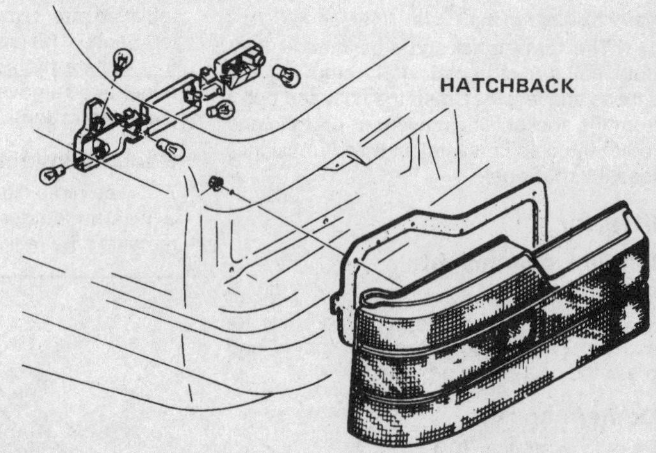

10.11a Back-up and tail light installation details

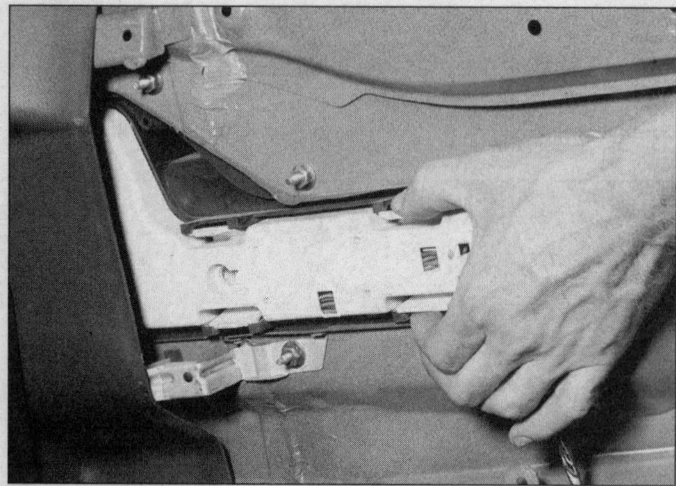

10.11b Depress the tabs and lift off the housing

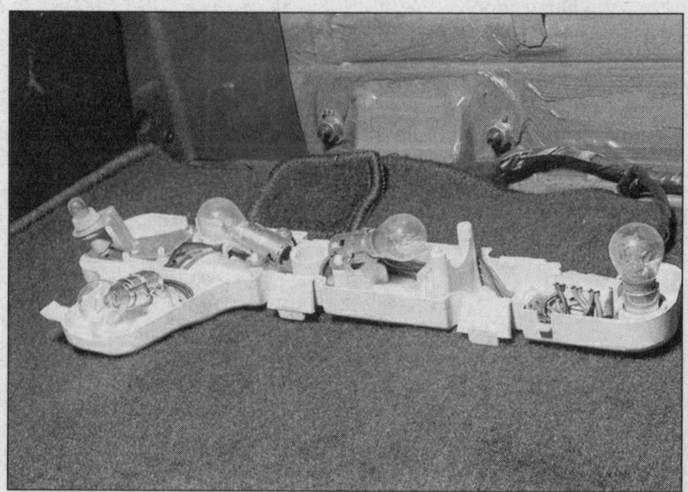

10.11c With the housing removed, the bulbs can be easily replaced

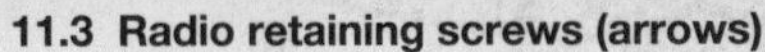
11.3 Radio retaining screws (arrows)

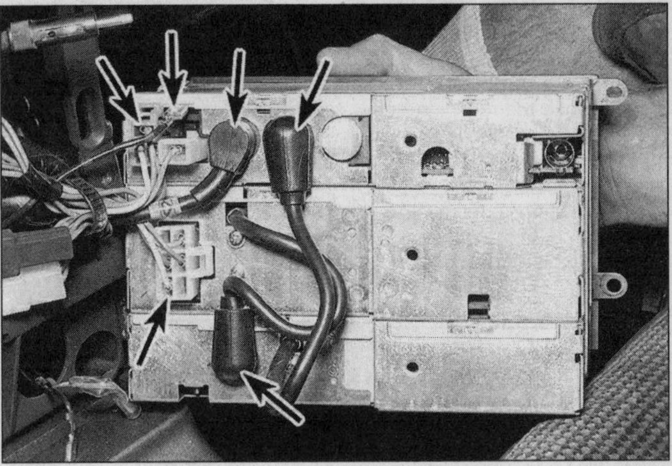
11.4 Radio electrical connections (arrows)

Rear lights

Refer to illustrations 10.11a, 10.11b and 10.11c

10 Remove the inner trim panel.

11 Depress the tabs and remove the light housing for access to the tail, back up, rear marker and parking light bulbs (see illustrations). When installing, make sure the tabs snap into position when the housing is pressed into place.

11 Radio and speakers - removal and installation

Radio

Refer to illustrations 11.3 and 11.4

1 Disconnect the negative battery cable.

2 Remove the instrument panel side walls (Chapter 11).

3 Remove the radio retaining screws **(see illustration)**.

4 Pull the radio out and unplug the electrical connectors **(see illustration)**.

5 Lift the radio from the dash.

6 Installation is the reverse of removal.

Speakers

Refer to illustration 11.7

7 Locate the speaker **(see illustration)**.

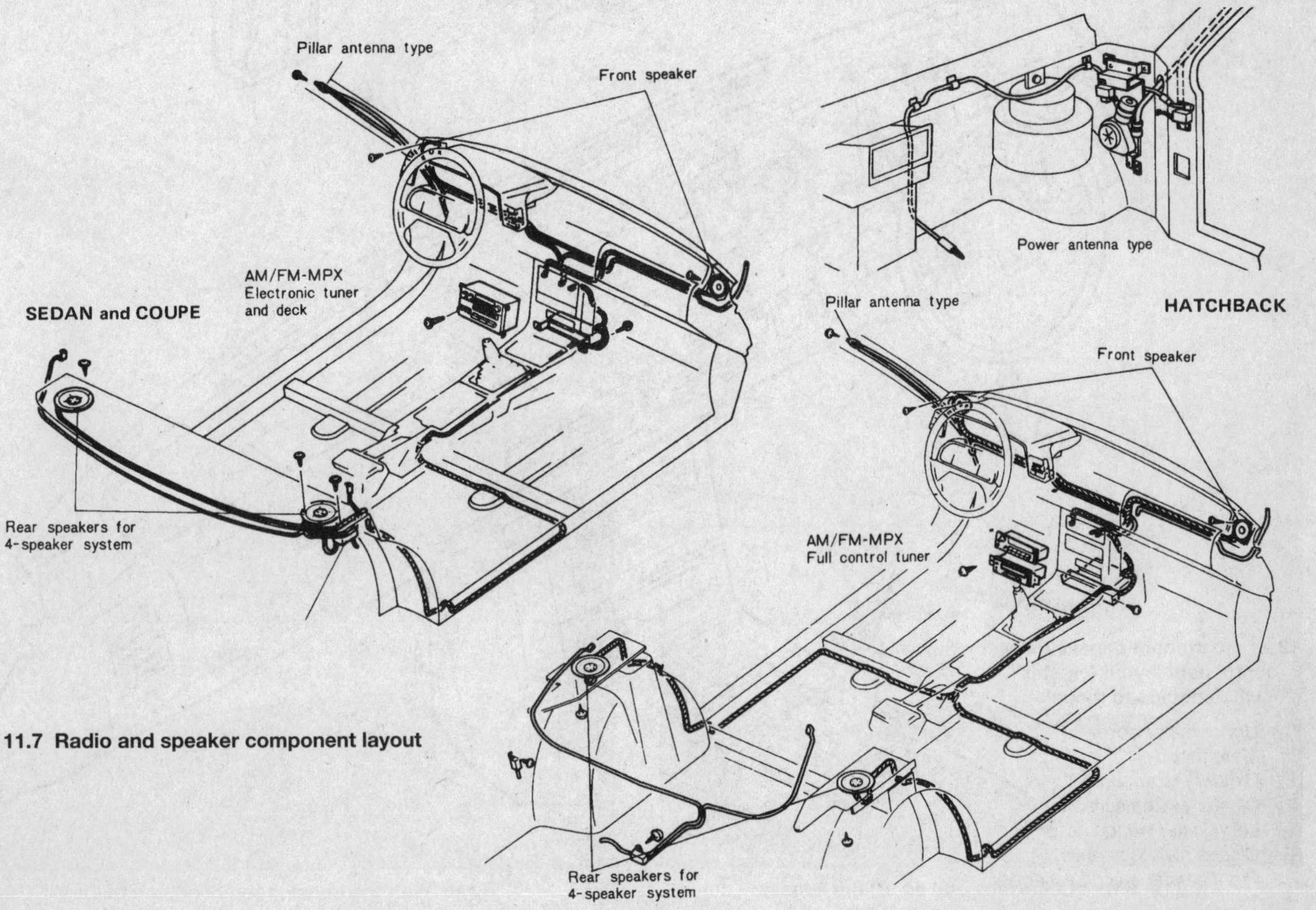

Pillar antenna type
Front speaker
AM/FM-MPX Electronic tuner and deck
SEDAN and COUPE
Rear speakers for 4-speaker system
Power antenna type
Pillar antenna type
HATCHBACK
Front speaker
AM/FM-MPX Full control tuner
Rear speakers for 4-speaker system

11.7 Radio and speaker component layout

8 Rear speakers are accessible after opening the trunk or hatch. On front speakers it will be necessary to pry off the speaker cover.

9 Remove the retaining screws, withdraw the speaker sufficiently to allow the connector to be unplugged and remove the speaker from the vehicle.

10 Installation is the reverse of removal.

12 Instrument panel cluster - removal and installation

Refer to illustrations 12.2a, 12.2b, 12.3 and 12.5

1 Disconnect the battery negative cable and lower the adjustable (if equipped) steering wheel.

2 Remove the cluster upper cover screws and meter hood **(see illustrations)**.

3 Remove the cluster retaining screws **(see illustration)**.

4 Disconnect the speedometer cable.

5 Pull the cluster out, disconnect the wiring and remove the cluster and (if equipped) switch assemblies from the instrument panel **(see illustration)**.

6 Installation is the reverse of removal.

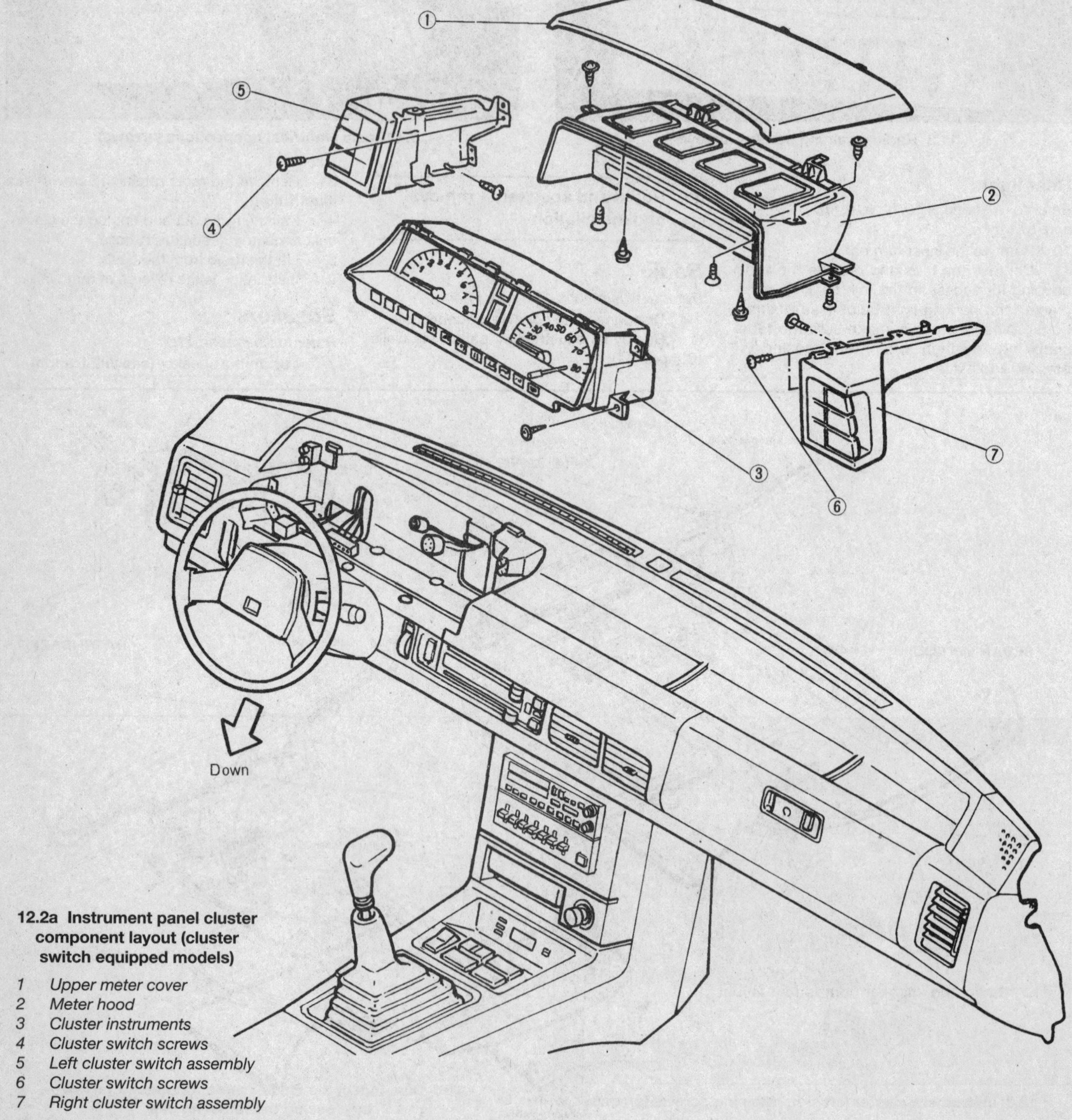

12.2a Instrument panel cluster component layout (cluster switch equipped models)

1 *Upper meter cover*
2 *Meter hood*
3 *Cluster instruments*
4 *Cluster switch screws*
5 *Left cluster switch assembly*
6 *Cluster switch screws*
7 *Right cluster switch assembly*

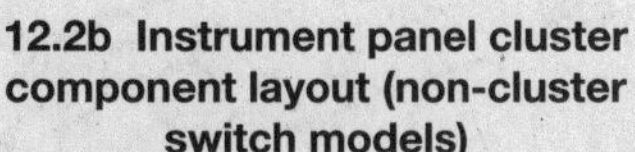

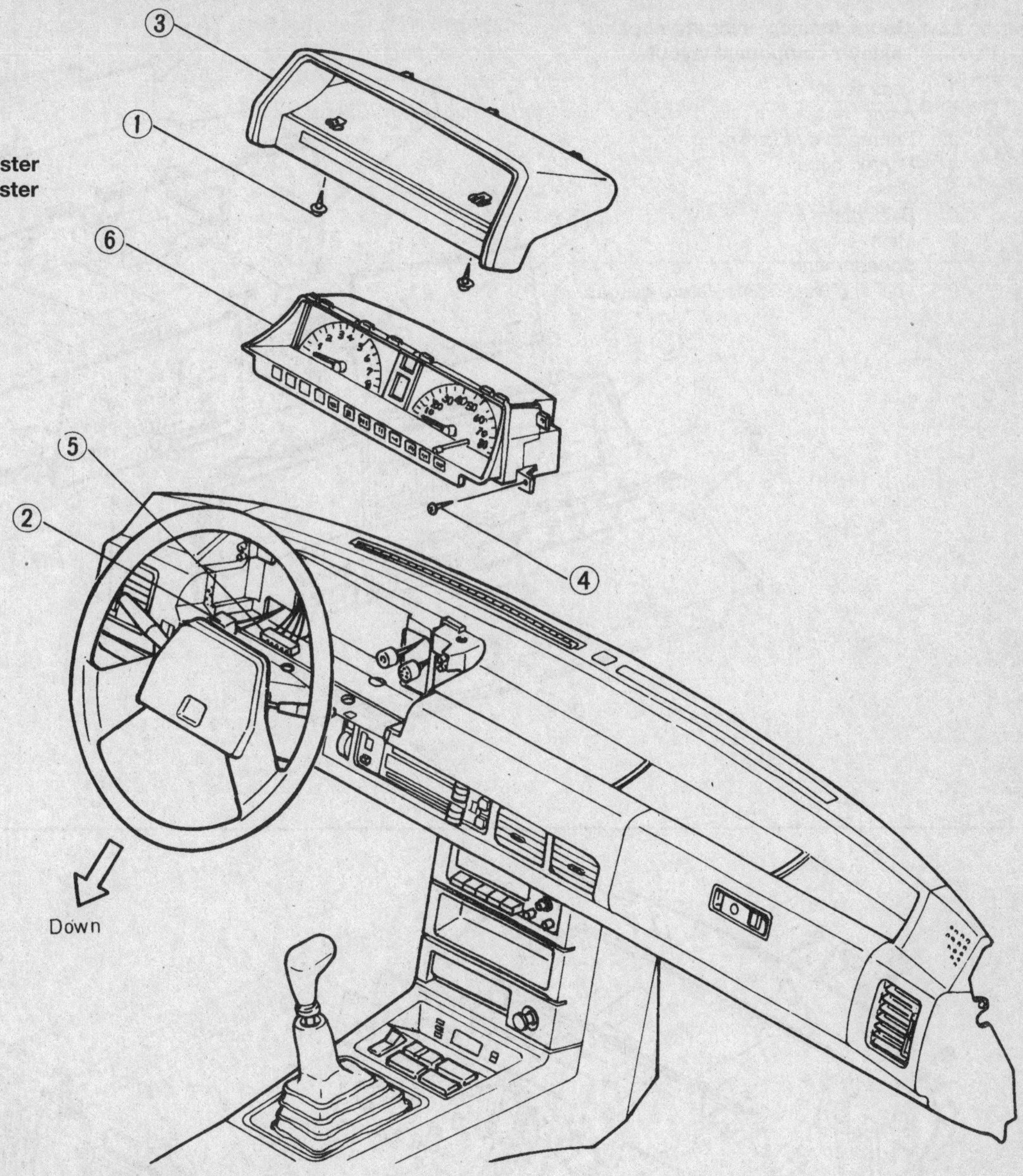

12.2b Instrument panel cluster component layout (non-cluster switch models)

1. *Screws*
2. *Illumination light*
3. *Meter cover*
4. *Screws*
5. *Electrical connectors*
6. *Cluster instruments*

Down

12.3 Instrument cluster left side retaining screws (arrows)

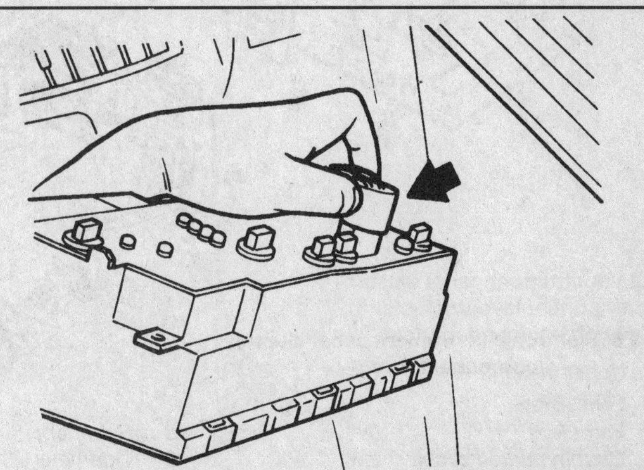

12.5 Disconnect the cluster meter connector (arrow) by pressing the retaining clip

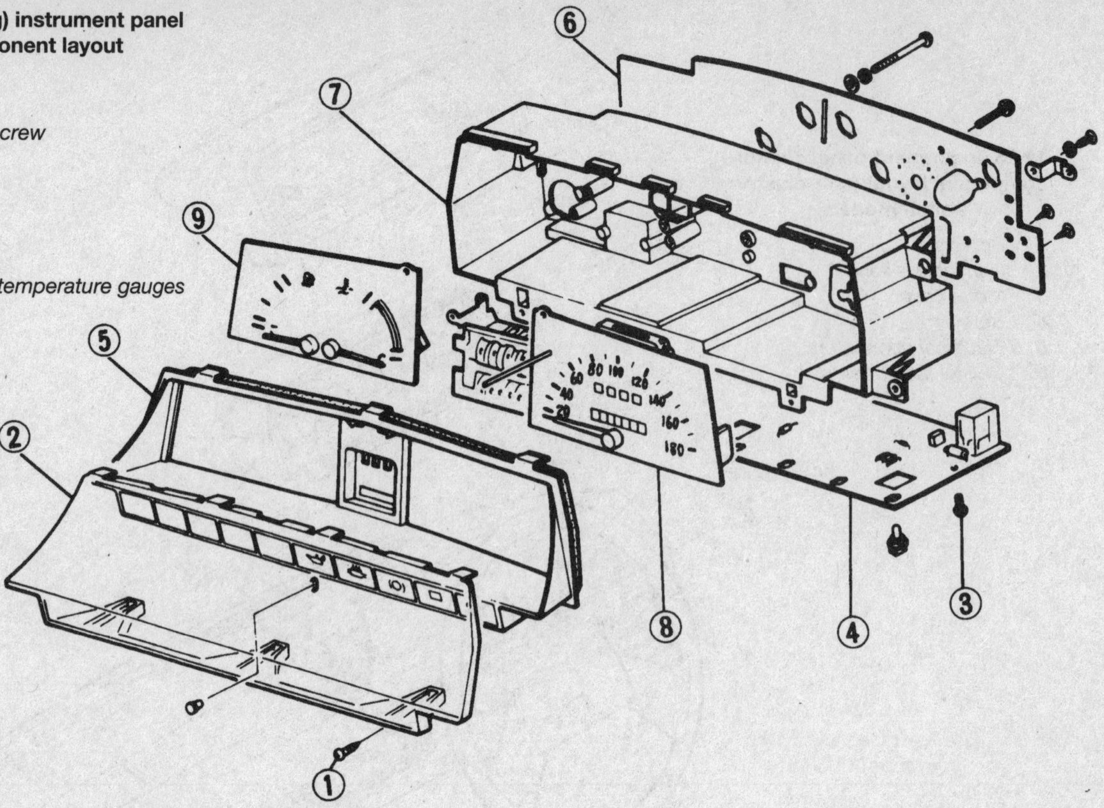

13.3 Gauge (analog) instrument panel cluster component layout

1 *Lens screw*
2 *Front Lens*
3 *Printed circuit screw*
4 *Printed circuit*
5 *Plate*
6 *Back plate*
7 *Meter case*
8 *Speedometer*
9 *Fuel and water temperature gauges*

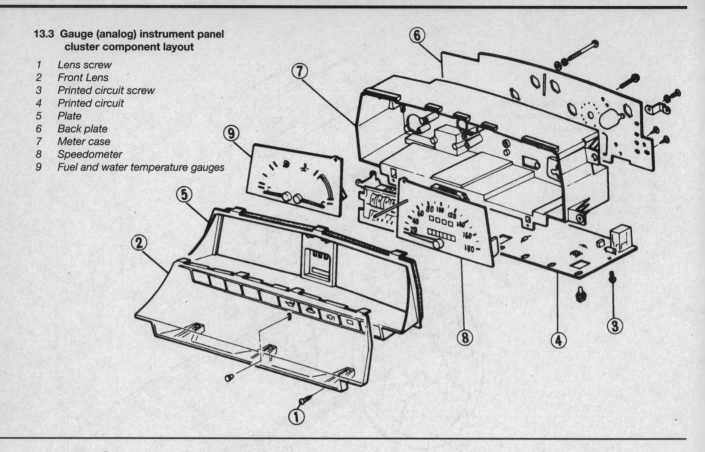

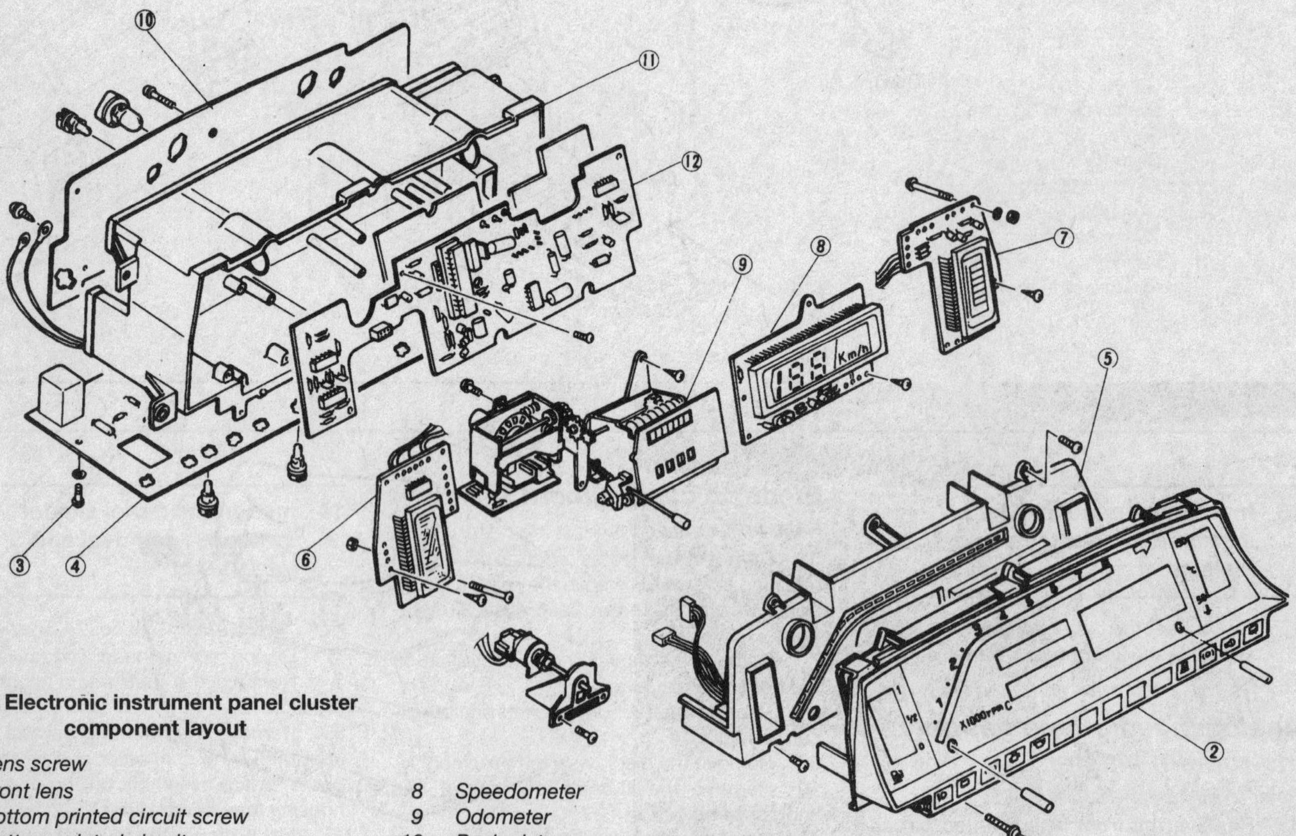

13.6 Electronic instrument panel cluster component layout

1 *Lens screw*
2 *Front lens*
3 *Bottom printed circuit screw*
5 *Bottom printed circuit*
6 *Fuel gauge*
7 *Water temperature gauge*
8 *Speedometer*
9 *Odometer*
10 *Back plate*
11 *Meter case*
12 *Printed circuit*

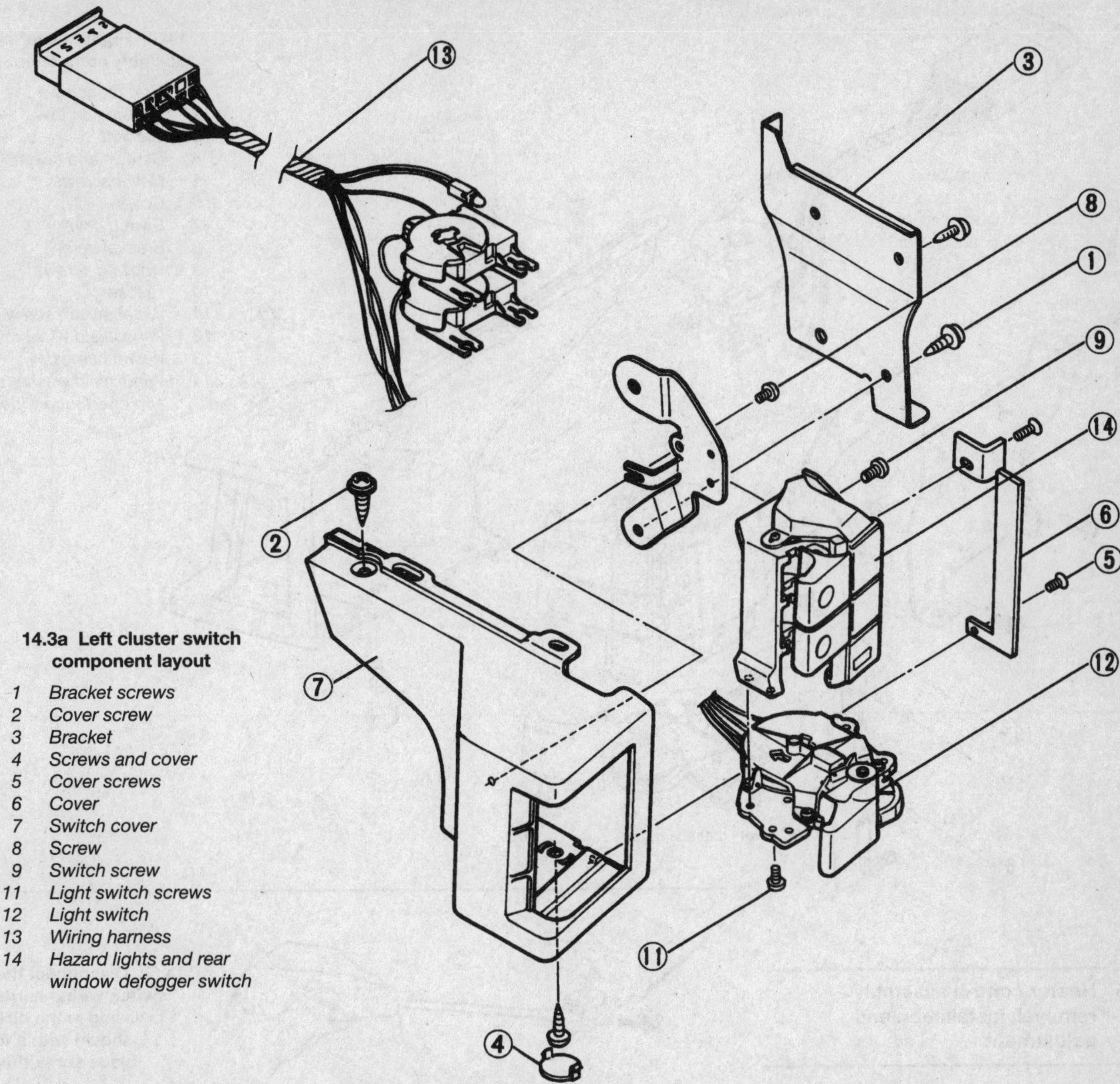

14.3a Left cluster switch component layout

1 *Bracket screws*
2 *Cover screw*
3 *Bracket*
4 *Screws and cover*
5 *Cover screws*
6 *Cover*
7 *Switch cover*
8 *Screw*
9 *Switch screw*
11 *Light switch screws*
12 *Light switch*
13 *Wiring harness*
14 *Hazard lights and rear window defogger switch*

13 Instrument panel cluster instruments - removal and installation

1 Disconnect the battery negative cable.

2 Remove the instrument panel cluster (Section 12).

Analog (needle-type gauges) instrument cluster

Refer to illustration 13.3

3 Remove the front lens, printed circuit and plate **(see illustration).**

4 Remove the retaining bolts and lift the instruments from the cluster.

5 Installation is the reverse of removal.

Electronic instrument panel

Refer to illustration 13.6

6 Remove the bulbs and sockets and retaining screws to remove the printed circuit boards from the meter case **(see illustration).**

7 Remove the retaining screws and lift off the front lens plate.

8 Remove the tachometer and printed circuit assembly.

9 Remove the display switch assembly.

10 Remove the illumination control and knob assembly.

11 Remove the retaining screws and unplug the speedometer, fuel and temperature meters from the case.

12 Installation is the reverse of removal.

14 Instrument panel cluster switches - removal and installation

Refer to illustrations 14.3a, 14.3b and 14.3c

1 Disconnect the battery negative cable.

2 Remove the instrument cluster panel (Section 12).

3 Remove the retaining screws, disconnect the wiring connector and lift the appropriate switch assembly off the cluster meter housing **(see illustrations).**

4 Installation is the reversal of removal.

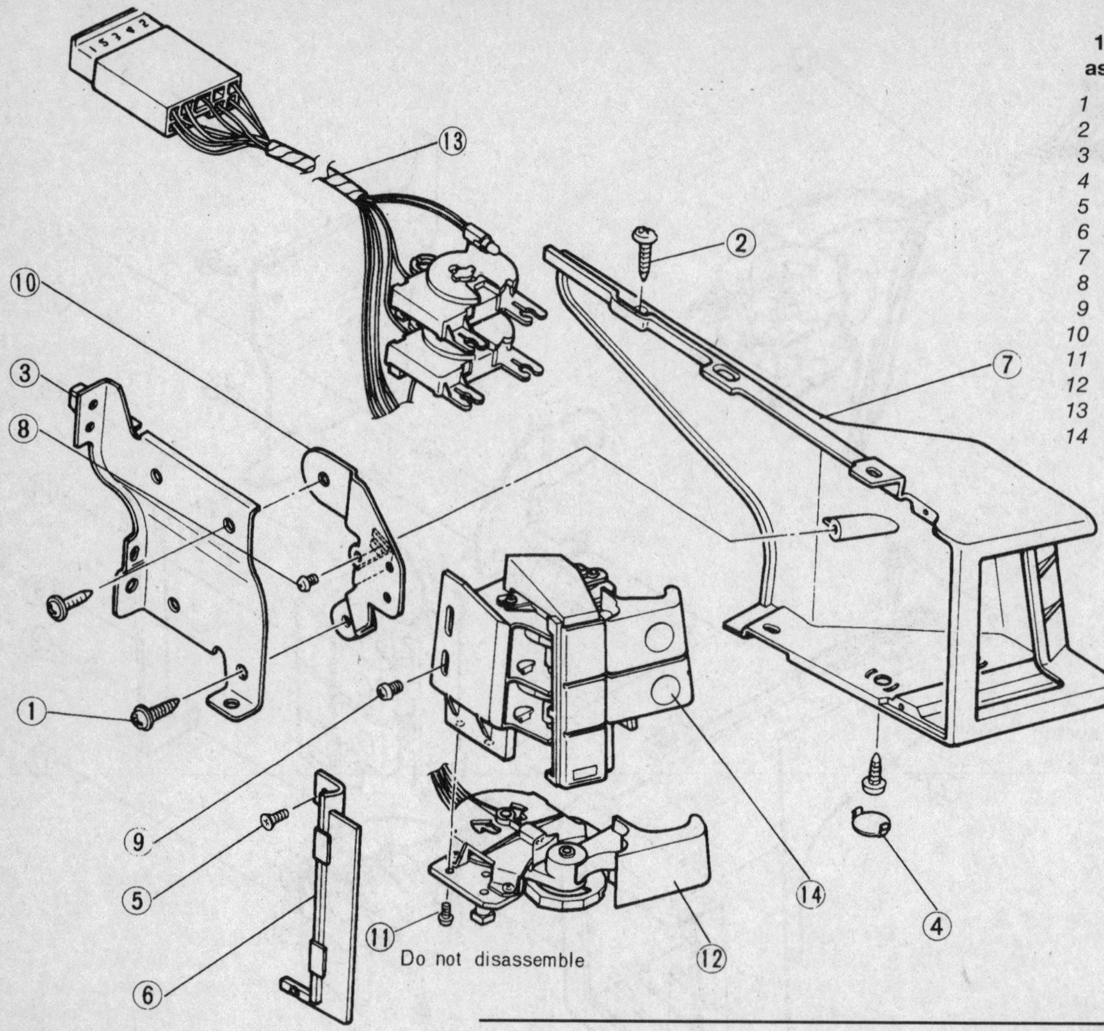

Do not disassemble

14.3b Right cluster switch assembly component layout

1. *Bracket screws*
2. *Housing screws*
3. *Bracket*
4. *Screws and covers*
5. *Cover screws*
6. *Cover*
7. *Switch cover*
8. *Bracket screw*
9. *Housing screws*
10. *Bracket*
11. *Wiper switch screws*
12. *Windshield wiper switch*
13. *Wiring harness*
14. *Windshield washer switch and one-touch wiper switch*

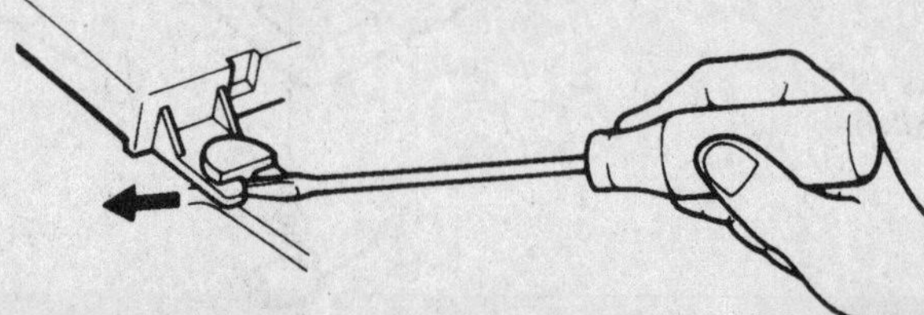

14.3c Disconnect the cluster switch wiring harness by pressing in the direction shown with a flat blade screwdriver

15 Heater control assembly - removal, installation and adjustment

Refer to illustrations 15.2a, 15.2b, 15.2c, 15.3 and 15.5

1 Disconnect the battery negative cable.

2 Pry off the air conditioner switch and the swing louver assembly and disconnect them for access to the control assembly retaining screws **(see illustrations).** On 1998 and later models, remove the radio and the center trim panel to access the heater control assembly screws.

3 Remove the control assembly retaining screws and remove it from the instrument panel **(see illustration).**

4 Unplug the electrical connector from the control unit.

5 Disconnect the control wires **(see illustration).**

6 Installation is the reverse of removal except for connection and adjustment of the control wires described below.

15.2a Pry the air conditioner switch off with a screwdriver for access to the screws

15.2B Squeeze the connector and unplug it from the swing louver

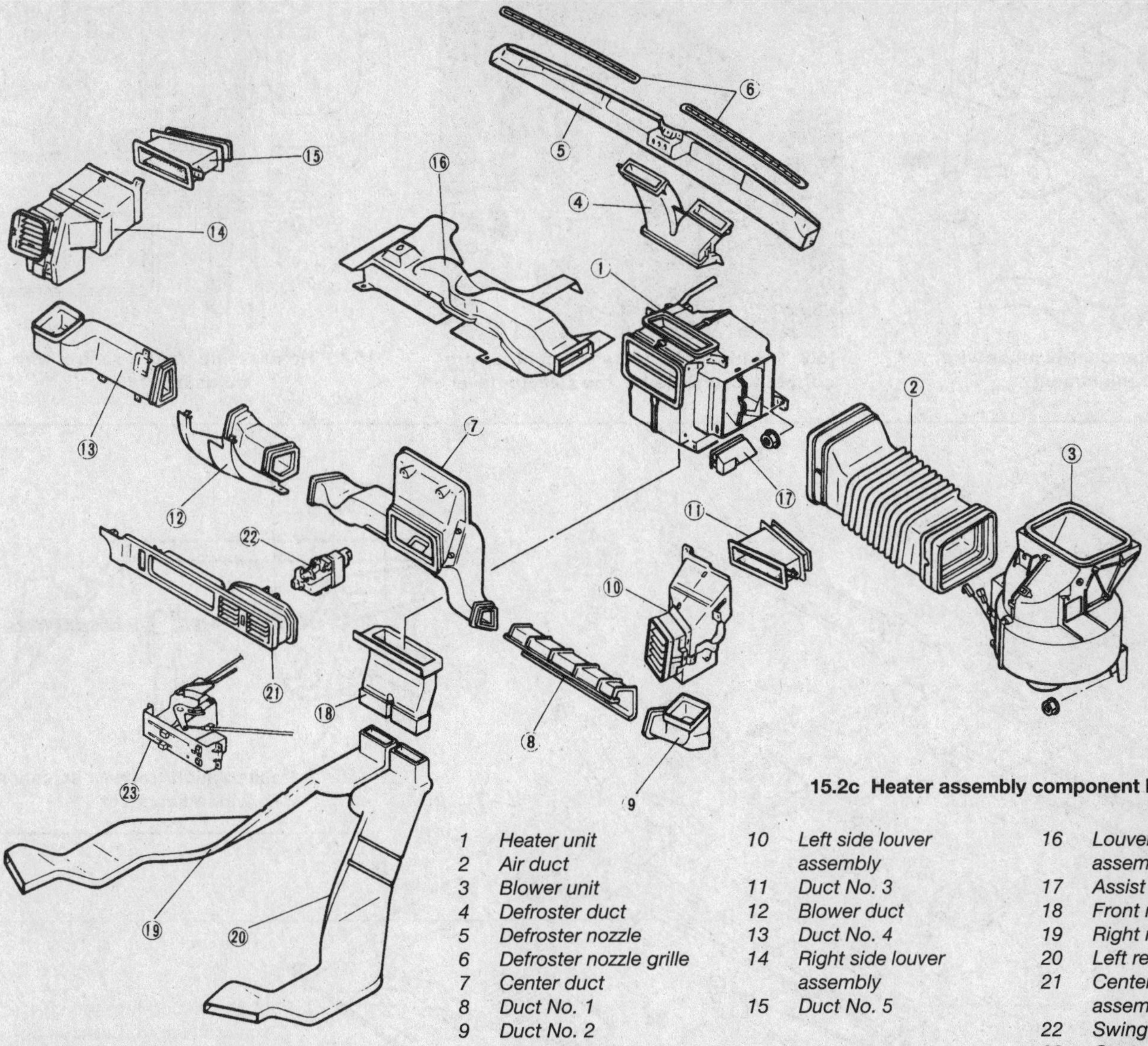

15.2c Heater assembly component layout

1 *Heater unit*
2 *Air duct*
3 *Blower unit*
4 *Defroster duct*
5 *Defroster nozzle*
6 *Defroster nozzle grille*
7 *Center duct*
8 *Duct No. 1*
9 *Duct No. 2*
10 *Left side louver assembly*
11 *Duct No. 3*
12 *Blower duct*
13 *Duct No. 4*
14 *Right side louver assembly*
15 *Duct No. 5*
16 *Louver panel assembly*
17 *Assist side duct*
18 *Front rear heater duct*
19 *Right rear heater duct*
20 *Left rear heater duct*
21 *Center louver assembly*
22 *Swing louver*
23 *Control assembly*

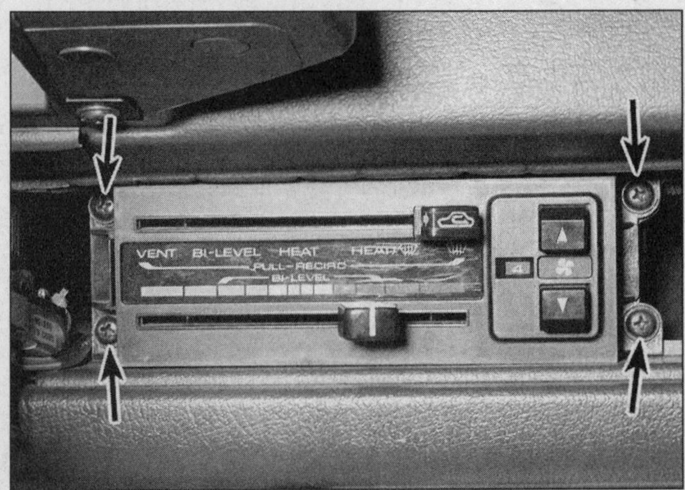

15.3 Heater control retaining screw locations (arrows)

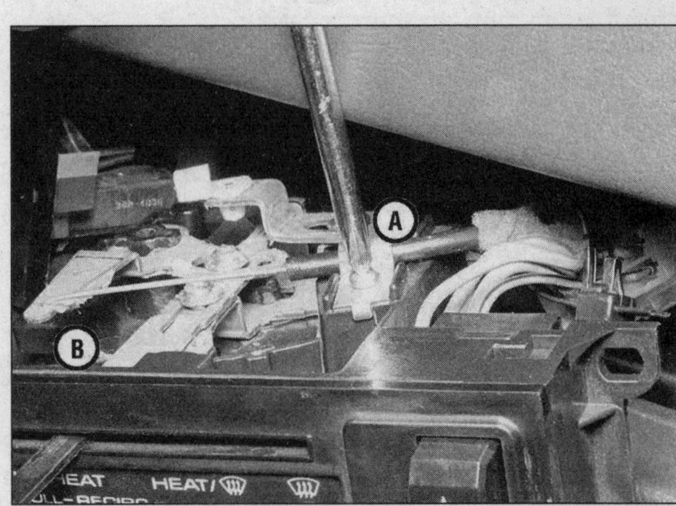

15.5 Disconnect the heater control wires by removing the clamp (A) and unhooking the end (B)

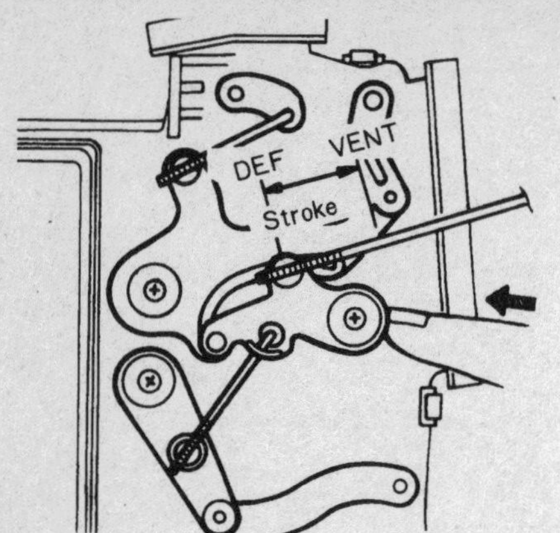

15.7 Heater control mode wire adjustment

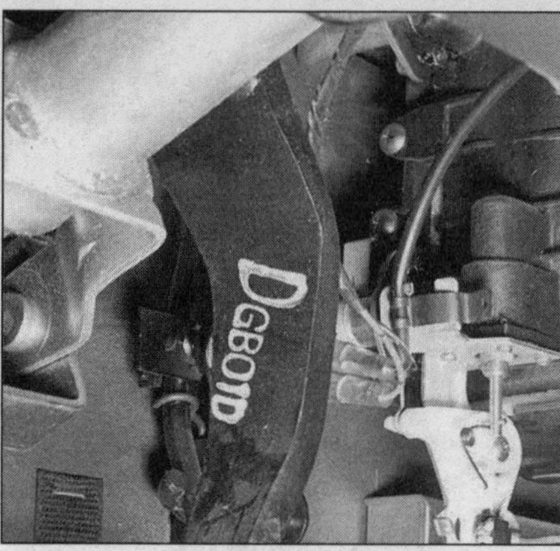

15.9 The heater temperature control wire correctly connected to the selector lever

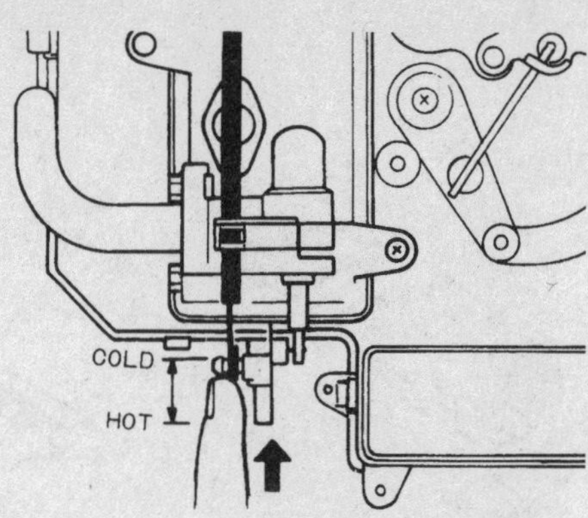

15.10 Heater temperature control wire adjustment

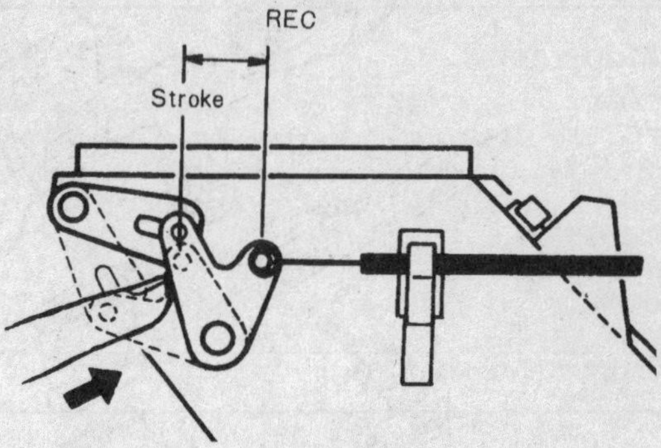

15.12 Recirculation/fresh air selection wire adjustment

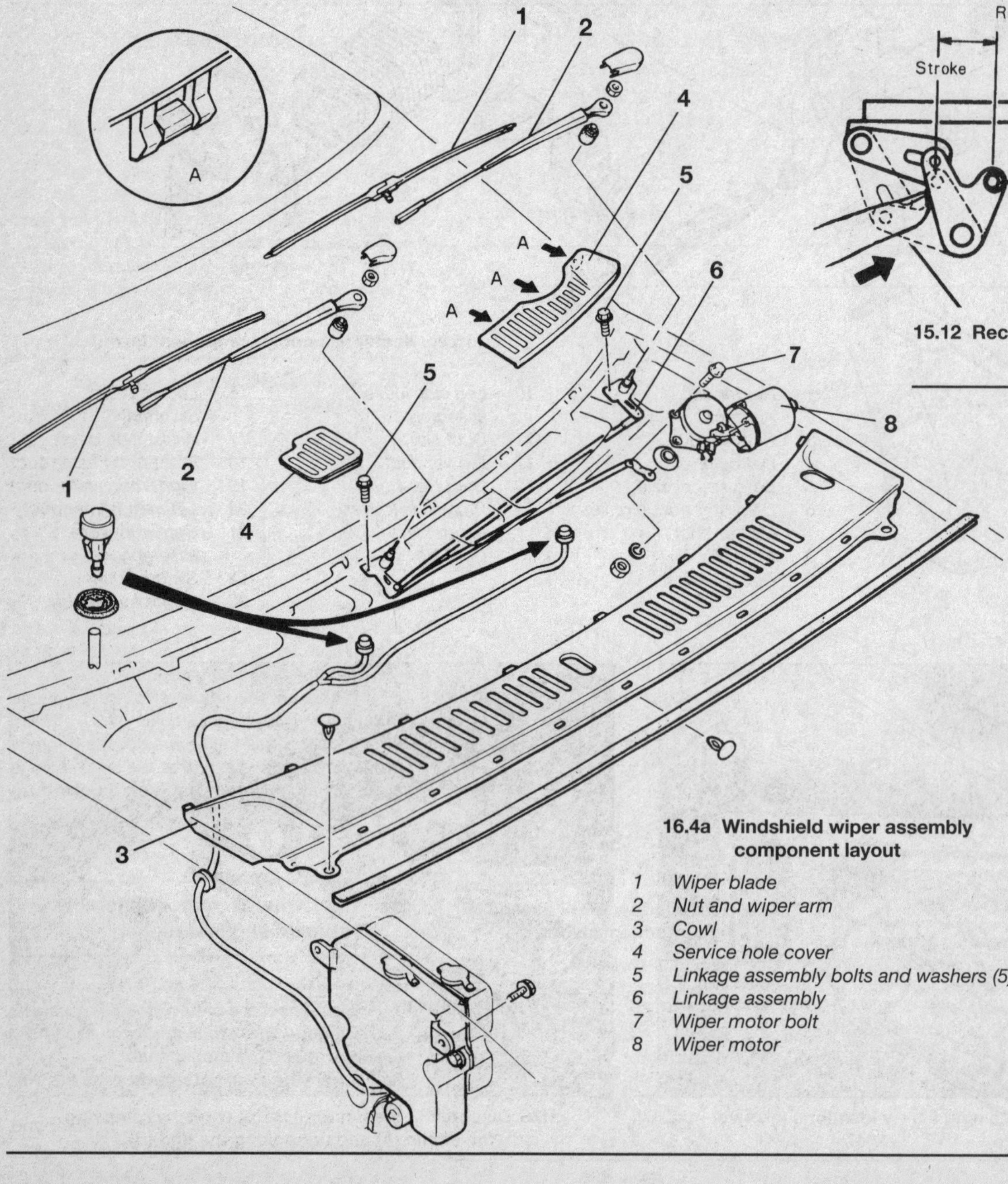

16.4a Windshield wiper assembly component layout

1. *Wiper blade*
2. *Nut and wiper arm*
3. *Cowl*
4. *Service hole cover*
5. *Linkage assembly bolts and washers (5)*
6. *Linkage assembly*
7. *Wiper motor bolt*
8. *Wiper motor*

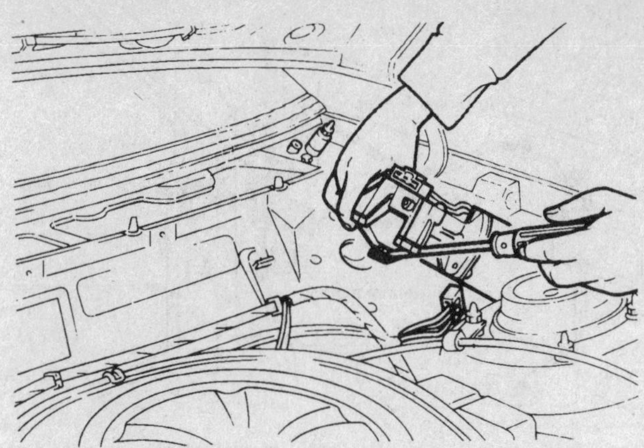

16.4b Separating the wiper motor from the linkage with a screwdriver

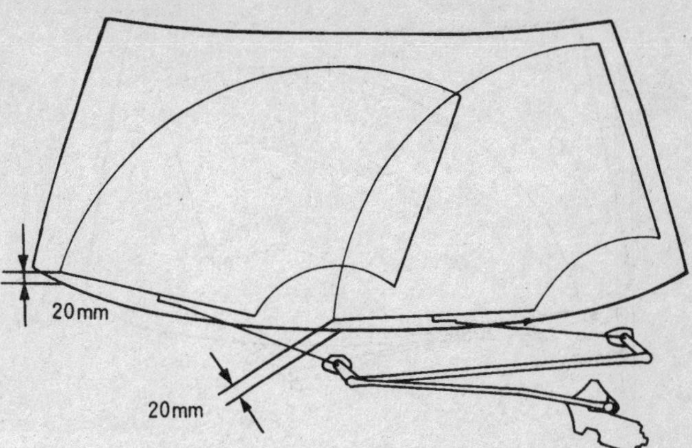

16.6 Windshield wiper pattern adjustment

Mode wire

Refer to illustration 15.7

7 With the control knob set to Defrost and the mode lever pushed all the way forward, connect the wire and install the clamp **(see illustration)**.

8 Connect the battery cable, turn the blower switch to the 4 position and make sure there are no air leaks from the center and floor area outlets.

Temperature control wire

Refer to illustrations 15.9 and 15.10

9 Set the temperature control knob to Cold and push the heat/cool selection lever all the way up to the Cold position and connect the wire and clamp **(see illustration)**.

10 The selection lever must move all the way from Cold to Hot **(see illustration)**.

Recirculated/fresh air selection wire

Refer to illustration 15.12

11 Pull the mode control knob fully outward.

12 With the recirculated/fresh air selection wire pulled out all the way to the Rec position, connect the wire and install the clamp **(see illustration)**.

13 Check for proper operation by pulling the control knob in and out several times.

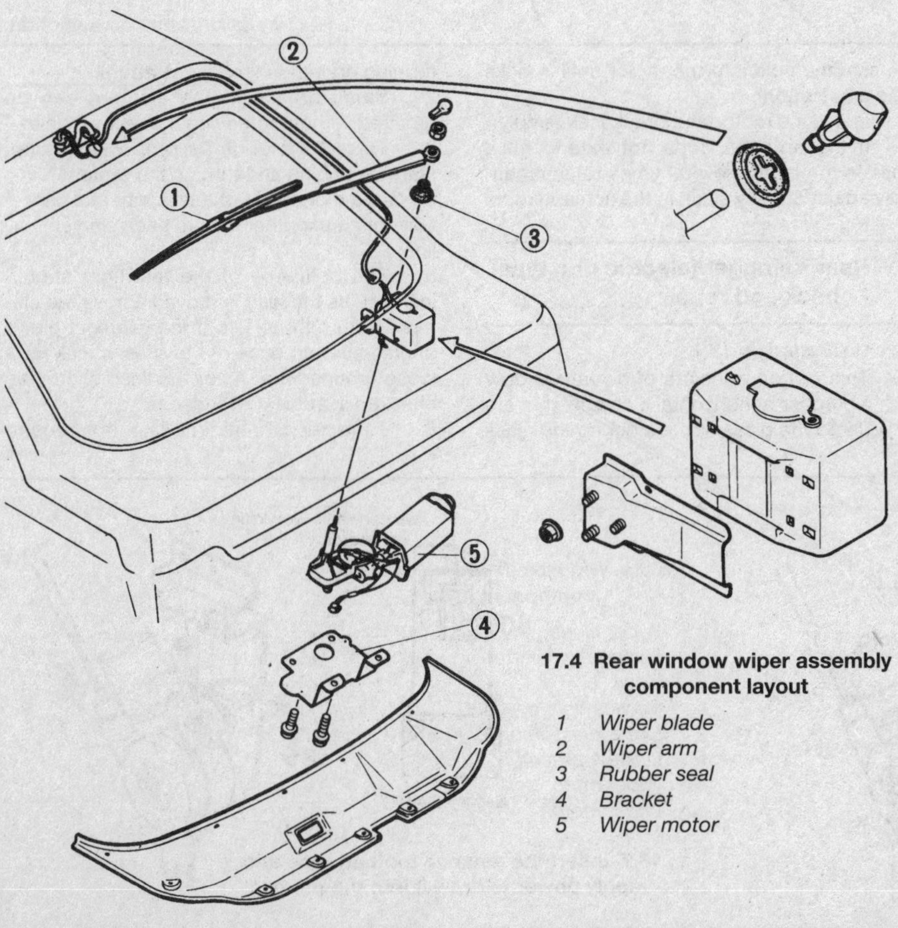

16 Windshield wiper motor and linkage assembly - removal and installation

Refer to illustrations 16.4a, 16.4b and 16.6

1 Disconnect the negative battery cable.

2 Remove the wiper arms (Chapter 1).

3 Remove the cowl and service hole cover.

4 Remove the linkage and motor retaining bolts, unplug the electrical connector and disengage the motor from the linkage as shown in the **(see illustrations)**.

5 Withdraw the linkage from the vehicle through the body access hole.

6 Installation is the reverse of the removal procedure, making sure that the arm height is adjusted as shown in the **(see illustration)** illustration.

17.4 Rear window wiper assembly component layout

1 *Wiper blade*
2 *Wiper arm*
3 *Rubber seal*
4 *Bracket*
5 *Wiper motor*

17 Rear window wiper assembly - removal and installation

Refer to illustrations 17.4 and 17.5

1 Disconnect the battery negative cable.

2 Remove the wiper and arm assembly (Chapter 1) and the rubber seal.

3 Open the rear hatch and remove trim panel.

4 Remove the retaining bolts, bracket and wiper motor **(see illustration)**.

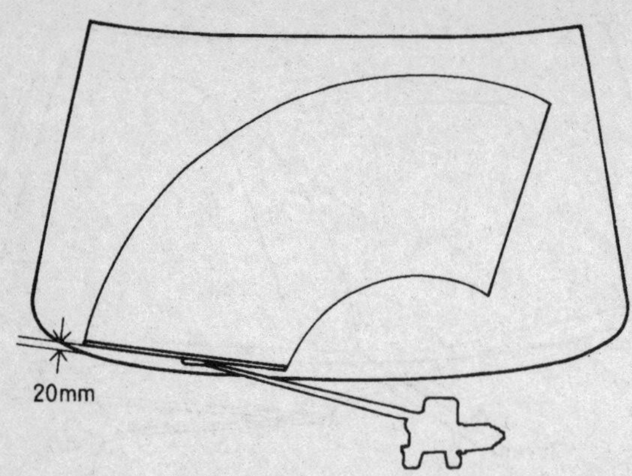

17.5 Rear window wiper pattern

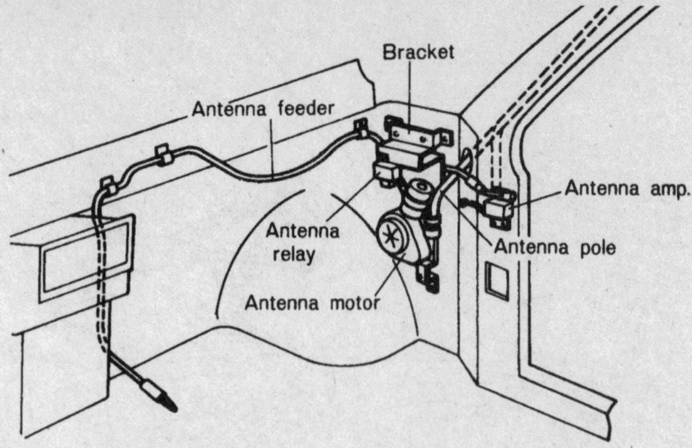

18.3 Power radio antenna installation details

5 Installation is the reverse of removal, making sure to check the wiper arm height adjustment **(see illustration)**.

18 Power radio antenna and motor - removal and installation

Refer to illustrations 18.3, 18.4, 18.5 and 18.7

1 Remove the dash under panel, glove compartment, and the heater air duct and blower unit.
2 Remove the side trim and disconnect the antenna feed, but not the power.
3 Remove the antenna motor bracket with the motor and antenna pole **(see illustration)**.
4 To remove the antenna, first insert a flat blade screwdriver into the slot in the antenna pole and pull the antenna out approximately 1/2-inch **(see illustration)**.
5 Apply battery power to the B and BG terminals of the connector and pull the antenna out of the motor as shown **(see illustration)**.
6 Loosen the two antenna-to-pillar screws and remove the antenna pole from the body.
7 Install the antenna to the body and insert the toothed end of the antenna rope into the motor. Apply battery power as shown to draw the antenna into the motor and push the antenna pole into the motor until it locks **(see illustration)**.
8 Install the motor and bracket assembly.
9 If the antenna does not extend fully, operate the motor several times to automatically adjust out any slack in the antenna rope.

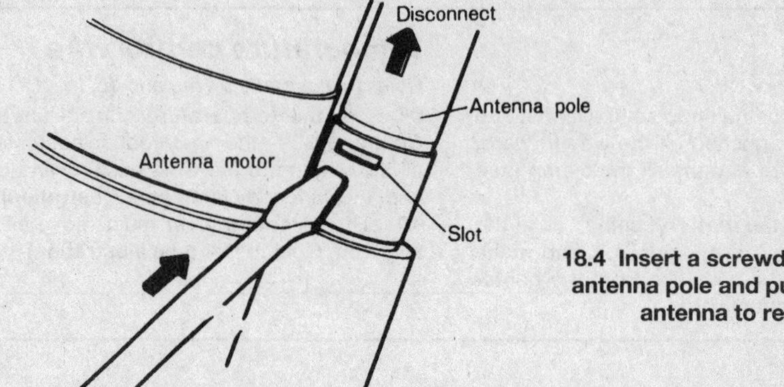

18.4 Insert a screwdriver into the antenna pole and pull up on the antenna to remove

19 Rear defogger (electric grid type) - check and repair

Refer to illustration 19.1

1 This option consists of a rear window with a number of horizontal elements that are baked into the glass surface during the glass forming operation **(see illustration)**.
2 Small breaks in the element can be repaired without removing the rear window.
3 To test the grids for proper operation, start the engine and turn on the system.
4 Ground one lead of a test light and carefully touch the other lead to each element line.
5 The brilliance of the test light should increase as the lead is moved across the element from right to left. If the test light glows brightly at both ends of the lines, check for a loose ground wire. All of the lines should be checked in at least two places.
6 To repair a break in a line, it is recom-

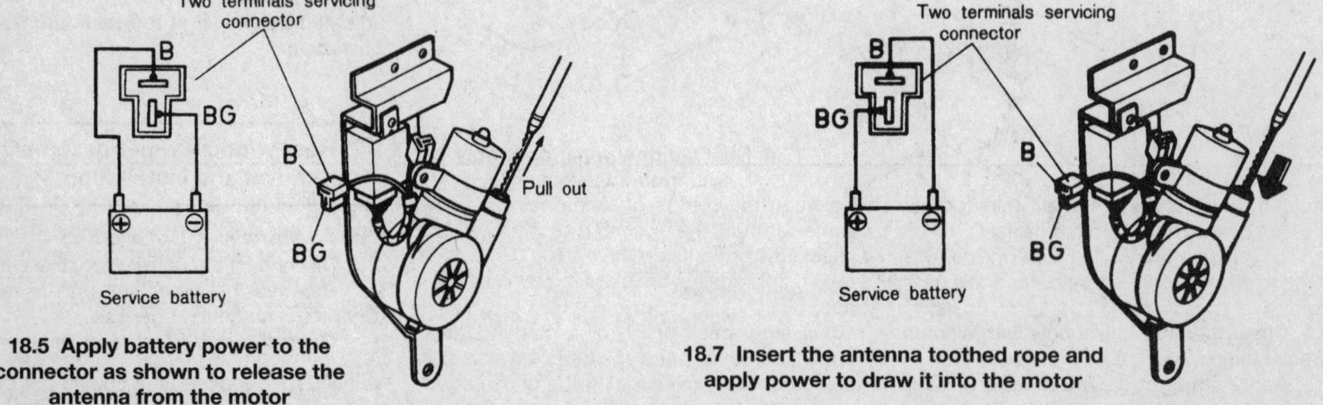

18.5 Apply battery power to the connector as shown to release the antenna from the motor

18.7 Insert the antenna toothed rope and apply power to draw it into the motor

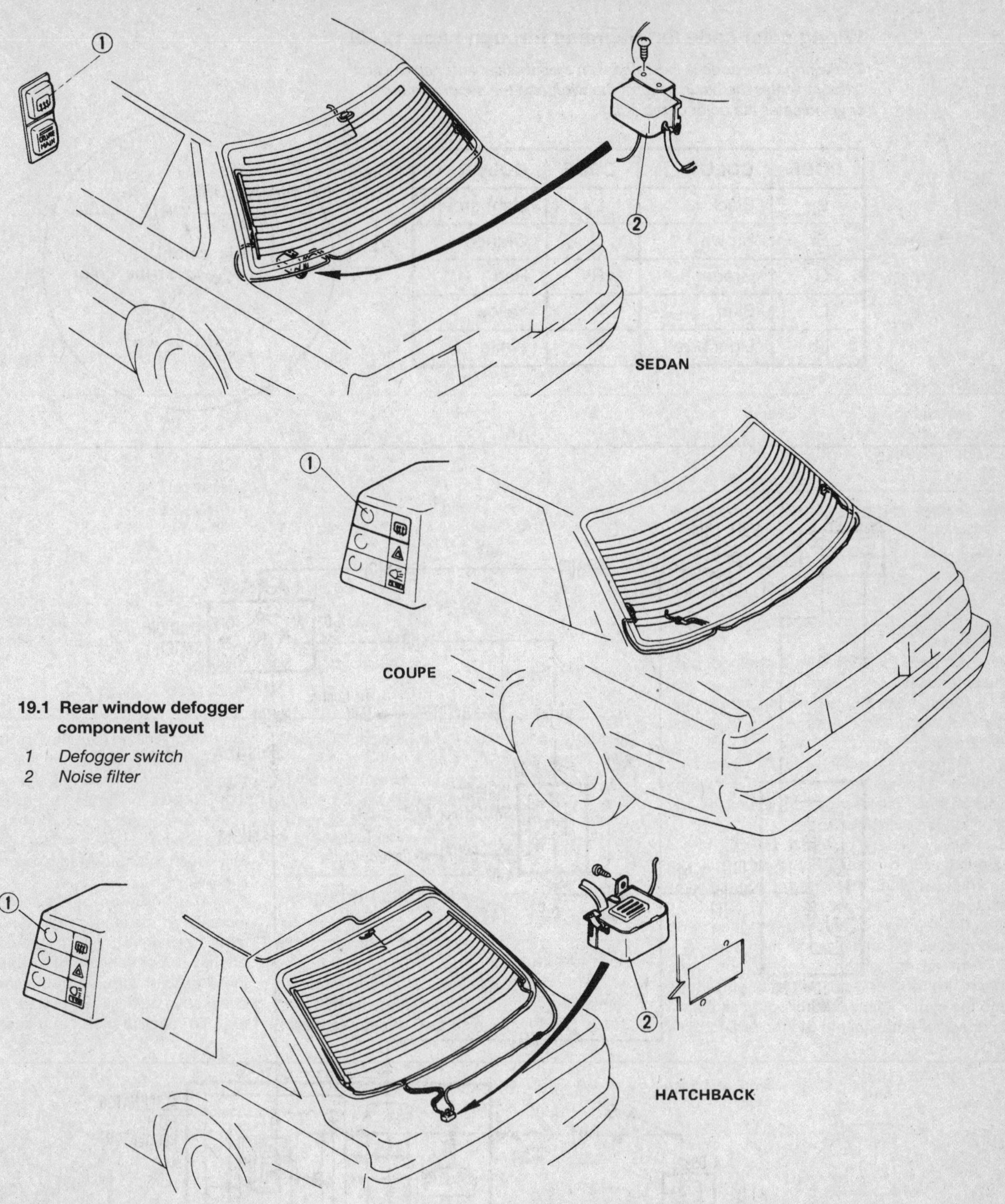

19.1 Rear window defogger component layout

1 Defogger switch
2 Noise filter

mended that a repair kit specifically for this purpose be purchased from a dealer.

7 To repair a break, first turn off the system and allow it to de-energize for a few minutes.

8 Clean the area thoroughly with alcohol or paint thinner.

9 Apply strips of electrical tape to both sides of the area to be repaired. The space between the pieces of tape should be the same width as the existing lines. This can be checked from outside the vehicle. Press the tape tightly against the glass to prevent seepage.

10 Using small brush or a marking pen, apply the silver paint mixture between the pieces of tape, overlapping the undamaged area slightly on either end.

11 Allow the repair to set for 24 hours or apply a constant stream of hot air directly to the repaired area. A heat gun set at 500 to 700 degrees Fahrenheit is recommended. Hold the gun about one inch from the glass for one to two minutes.

12 Although the defogger is now fully operational, the repaired area should not be disturbed for at least 24 hours.

Wiring color code for diagrams through page 12-38

The wiring color code is indicated with alphabetical letter(s). the first letter indicates the basic color of the wire, and the second letter (if any) indicates the color of the stripe.

CODE	COLOR	CODE	COLOR
B	Black	Lg	Light green
Br	Brown	O	Orange
G	Green	R	Red
L	Blue	Y	Yellow
Lb	Light blue	W	White

MAIN FUSE
WR[F]
Basic color
Stripe color

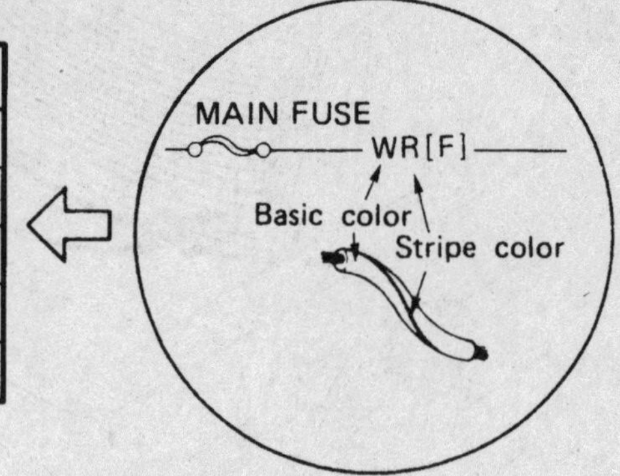

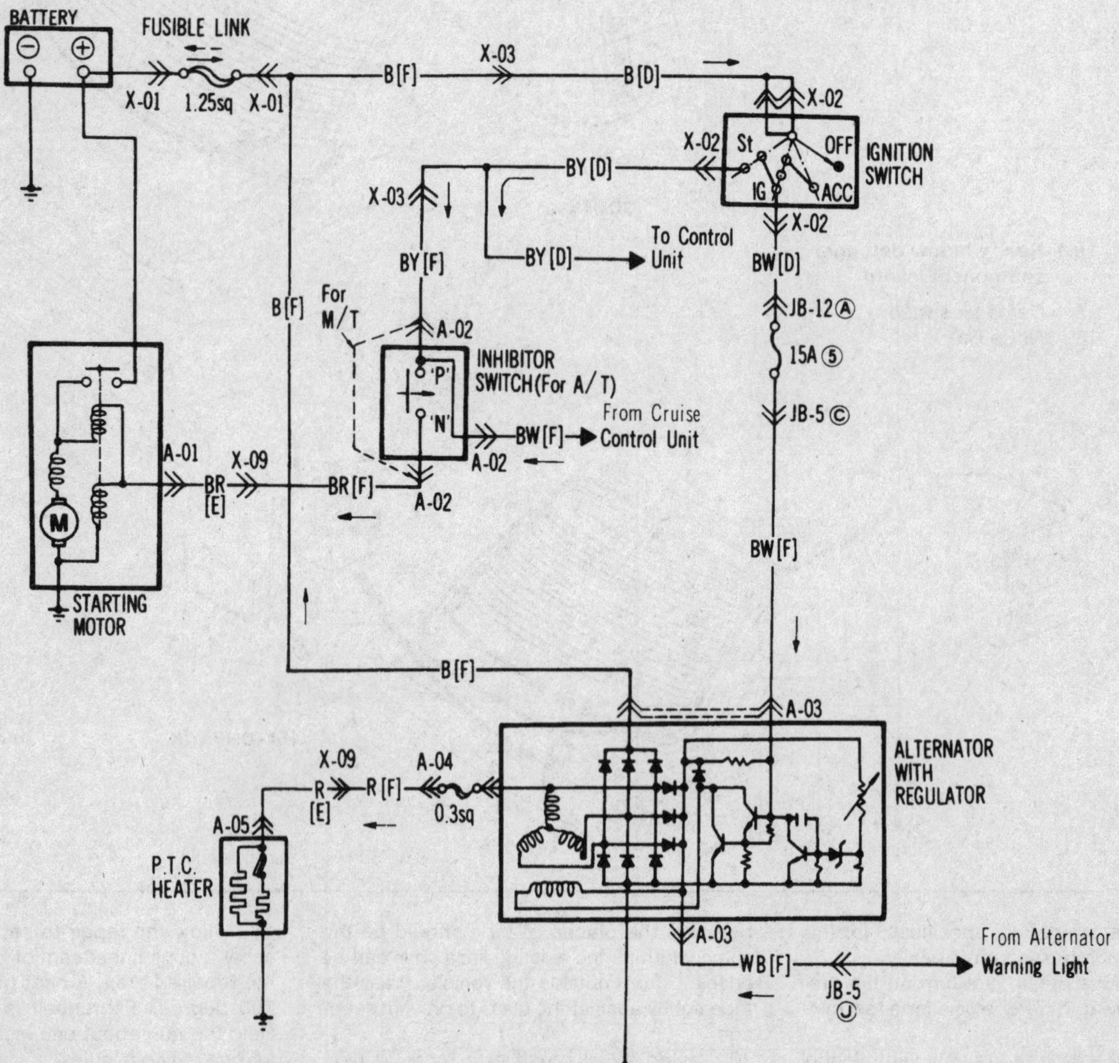

BATTERY
FUSIBLE LINK
X-01
1.25sq
X-01
B[F]
X-03
B[D]
X-02
X-02
St
OFF
IG
ACC
IGNITION SWITCH
BY[D]
X-03
BY[F]
BY[D]
To Control Unit
X-02
BW[D]
B[F]
For M/T
A-02
INHIBITOR SWITCH(For A/T)
'P'
'N'
BW[F]
From Cruise Control Unit
A-02
JB-12 Ⓐ
15A ⑤
JB-5 Ⓒ
A-01
X-09
BR [E]
BR[F]
A-02
M
STARTING MOTOR
BW[F]
B[F]
A-03
X-09
A-04
R [E]
R[F]
0.3sq
A-05
P.T.C. HEATER
ALTERNATOR WITH REGULATOR
A-03
WB[F]
JB-5 Ⓙ
From Alternator
Warning Light

Charging and starting system wiring diagram

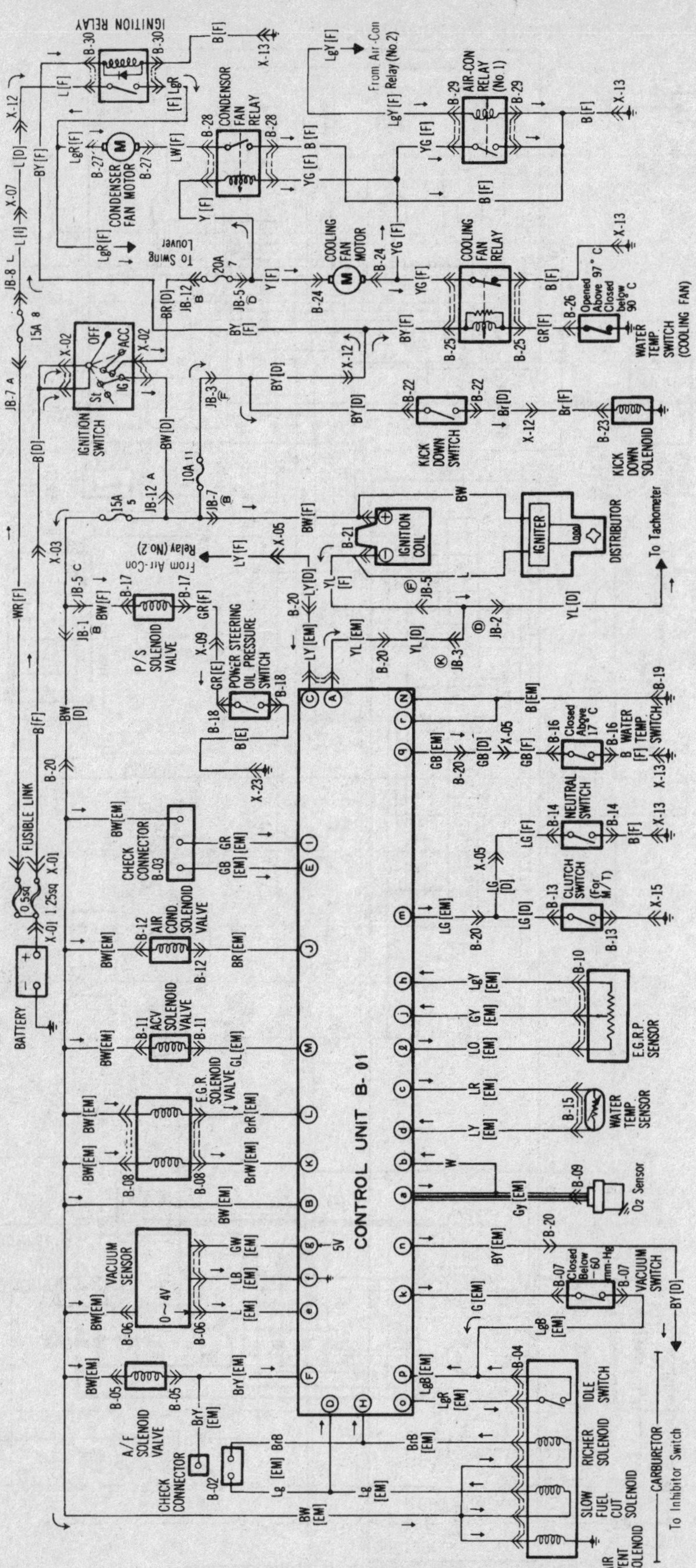

Emission control, ignition, cooling fan systems and automatic transaxle kickdown solenoid wiring diagram (1985 and earlier models)

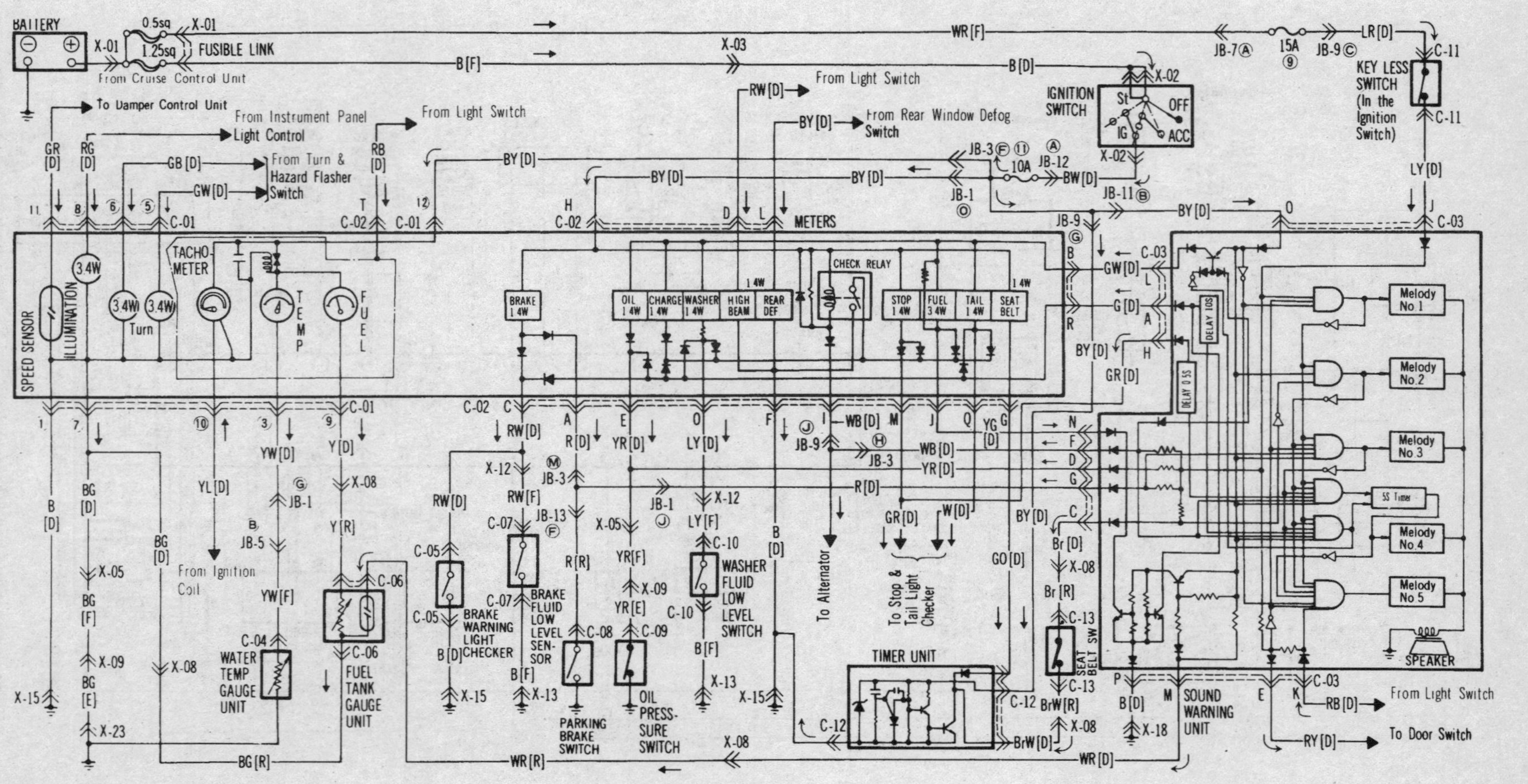

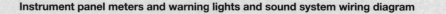

Instrument panel meters and warning lights and sound system wiring diagram

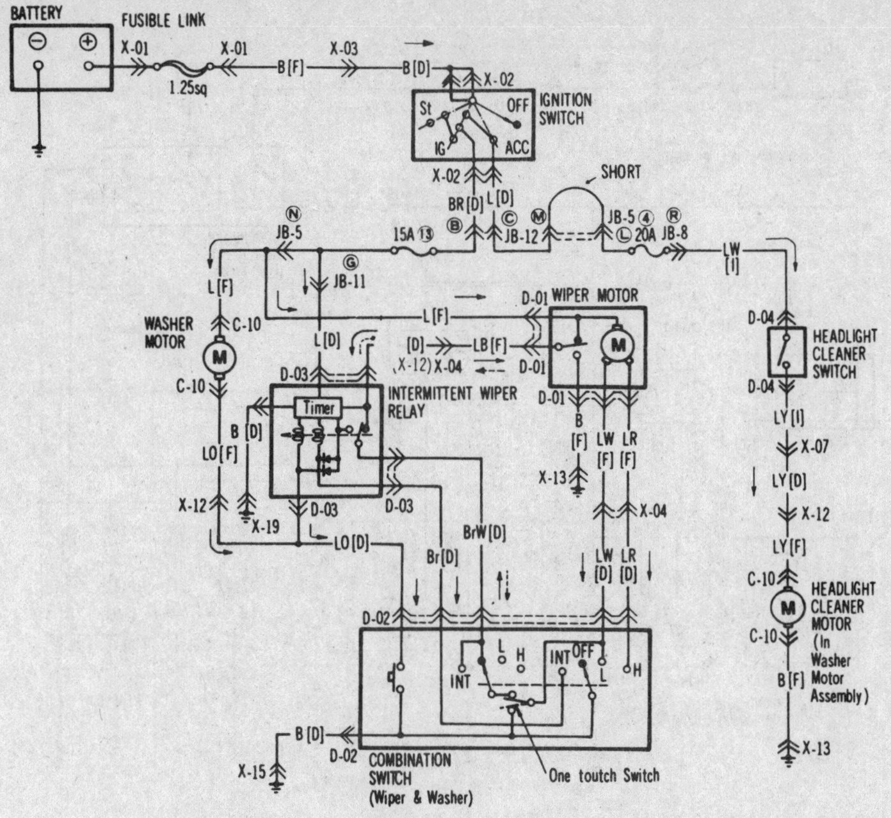

Wiper/washer and headlight washer (4-door models) wiring diagram

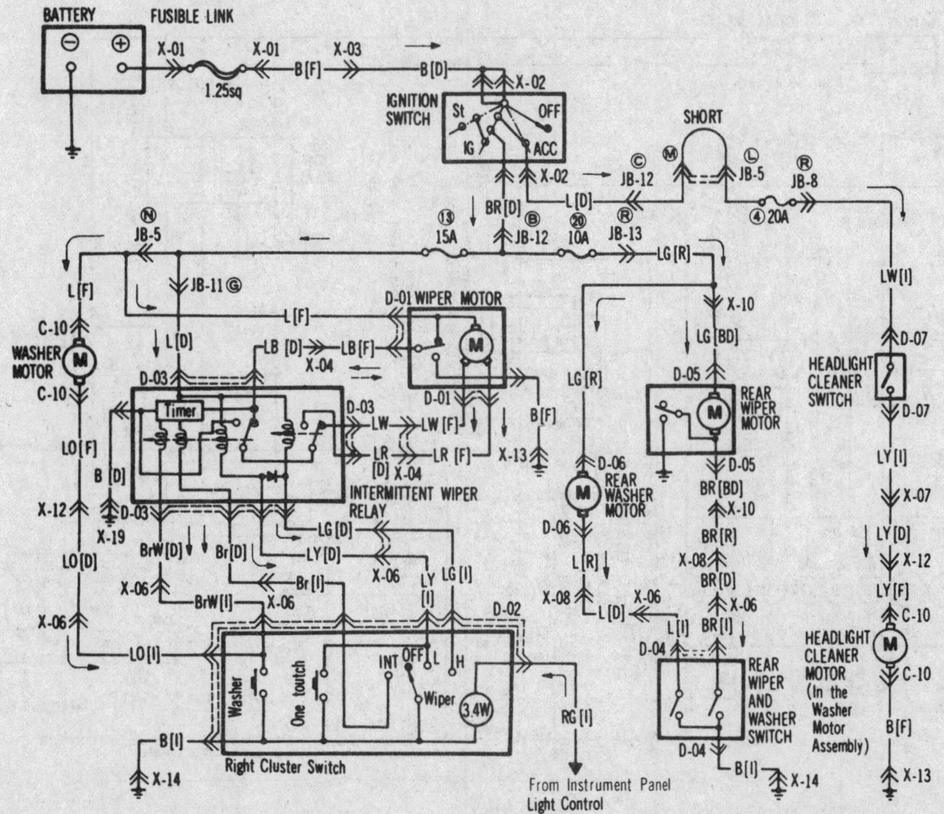

Wiper/washer and headlight washer (2- and 5-door models) wiring diagram

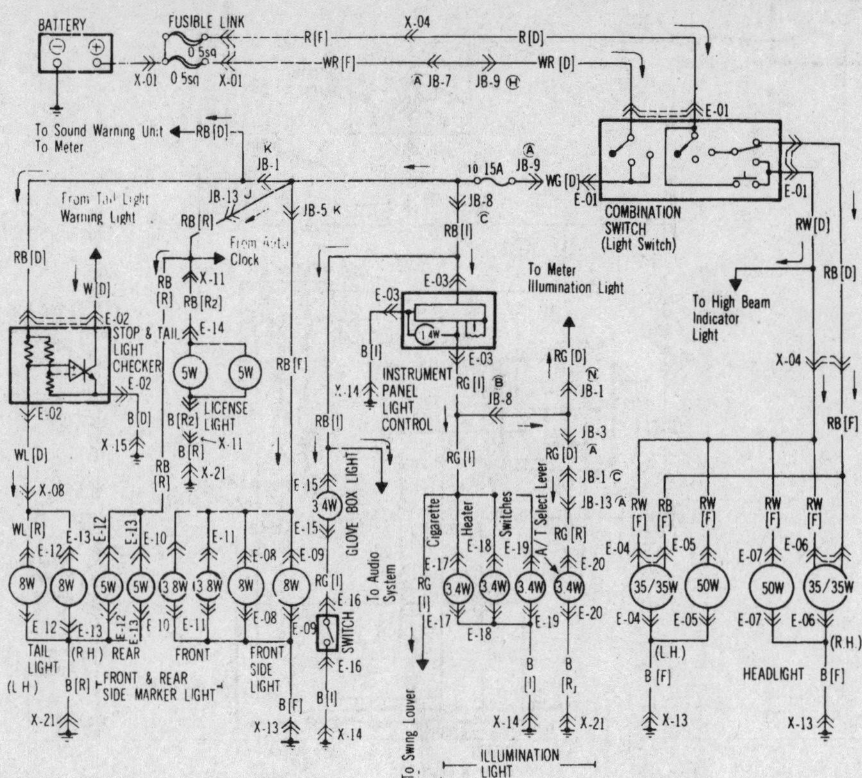

Headlight, tail, front side, front and rear marker, license and illumination lights (4-door models) wiring diagram

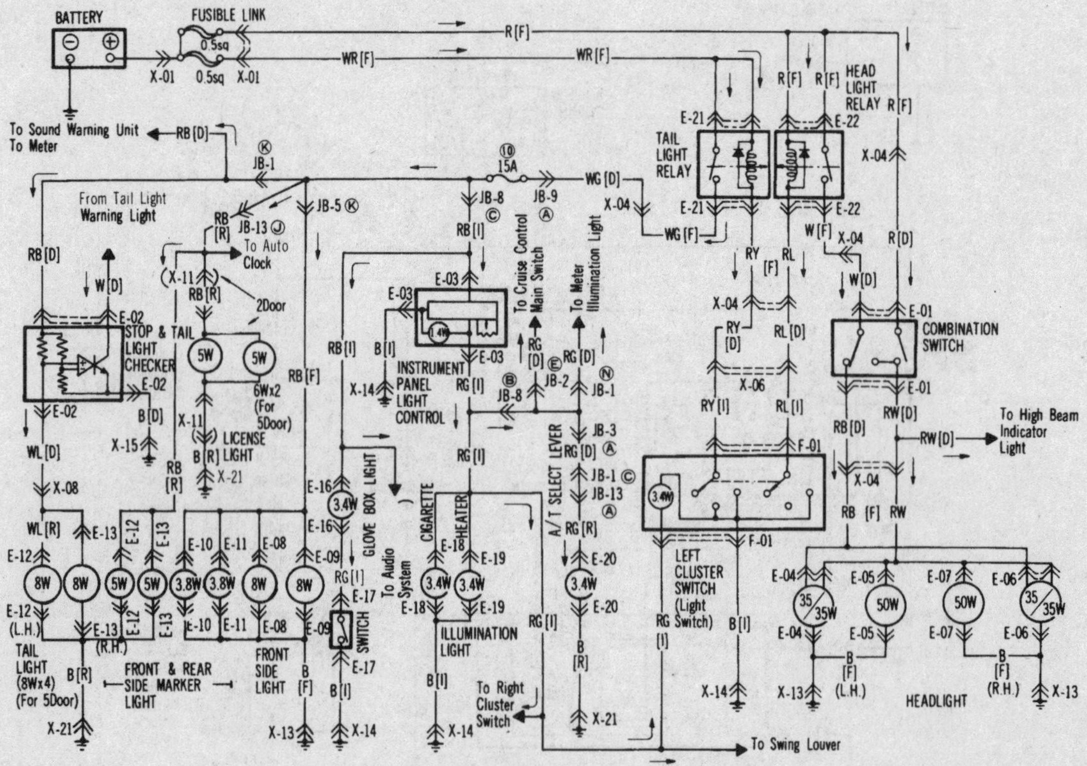

Headlight, tail, front side, front and rear marker, license and illumination lights (2- and 4-door models) wiring diagram

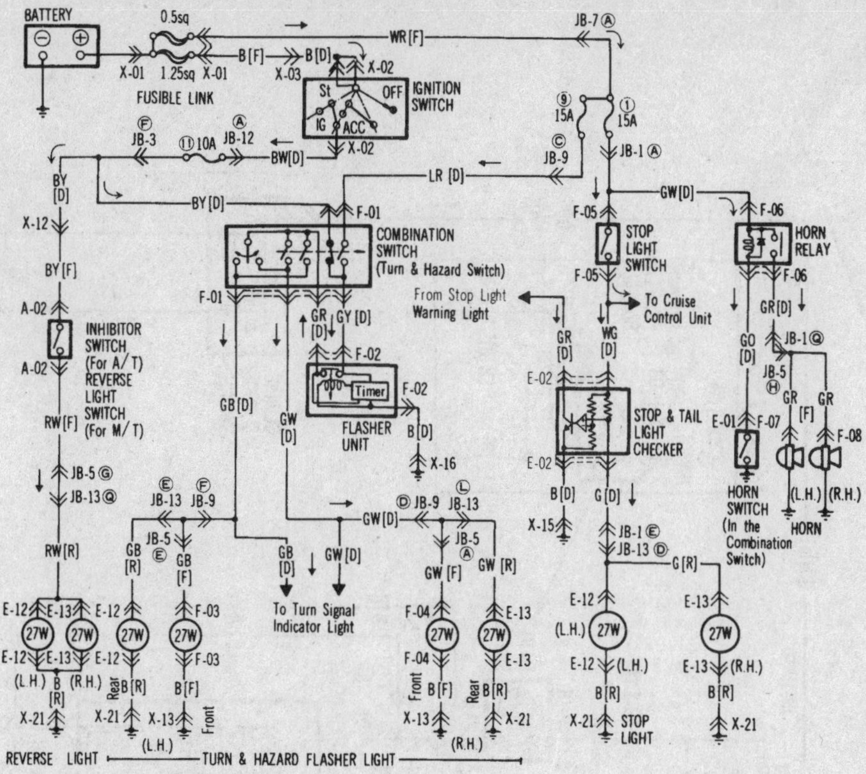

Turn and hazard flasher lights, horn, stop lights, backup light wiring diagram

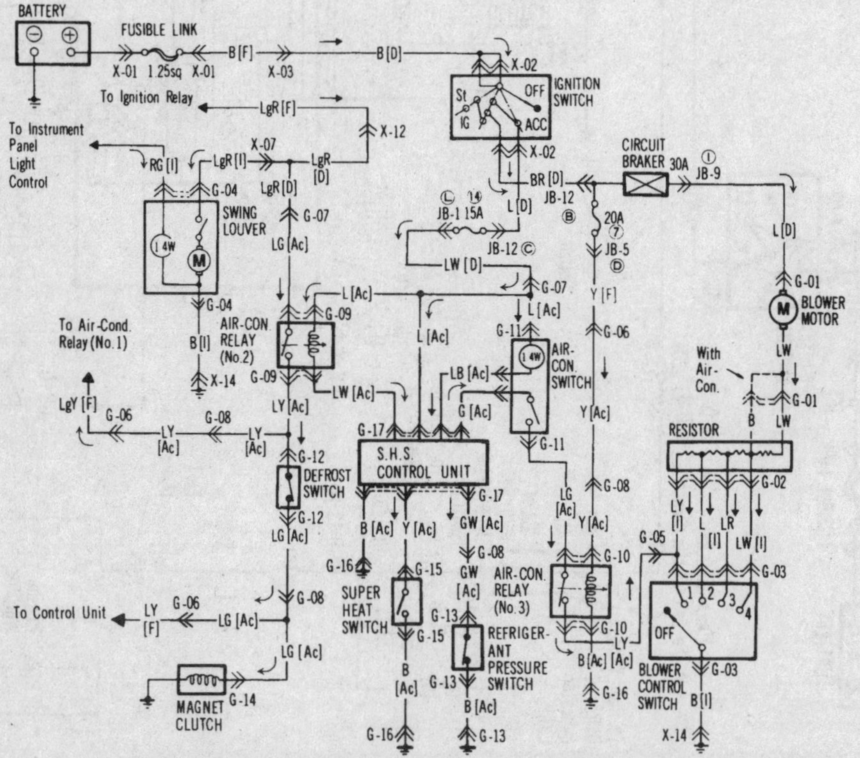

Air conditioning and swing louver fan motor wiring diagram

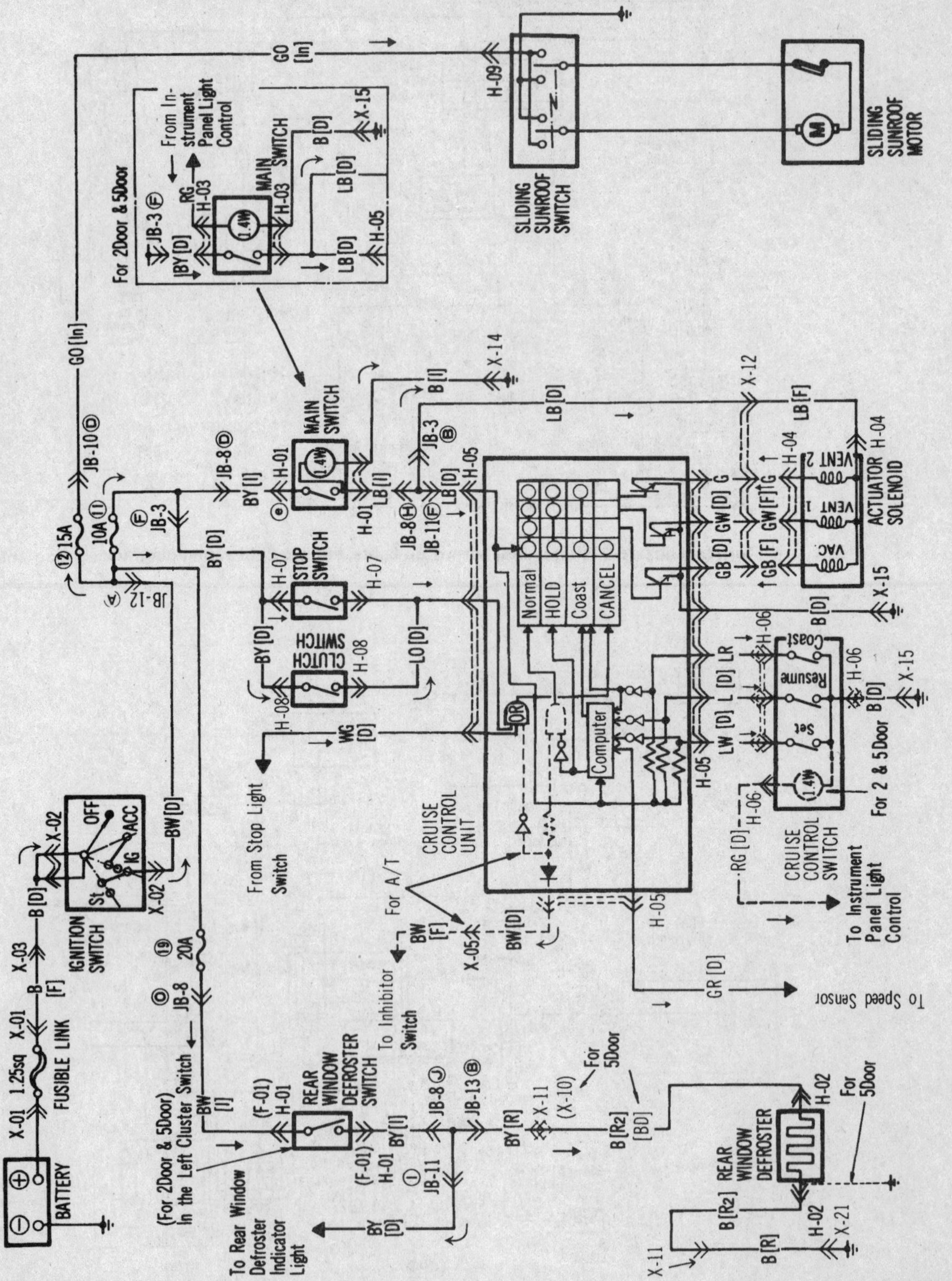

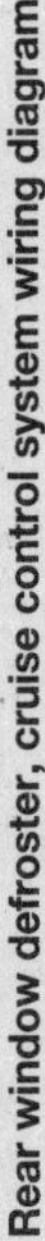

Rear window defroster, cruise control system wiring diagram

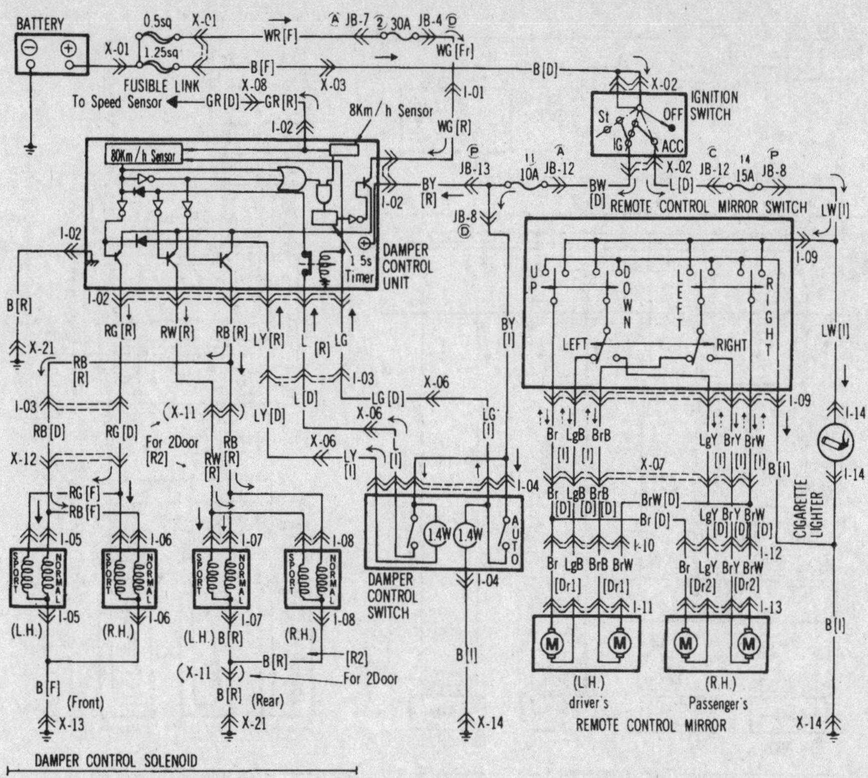

Three-way adjustable suspension damping system, power mirror and cigarette lighter wiring diagram

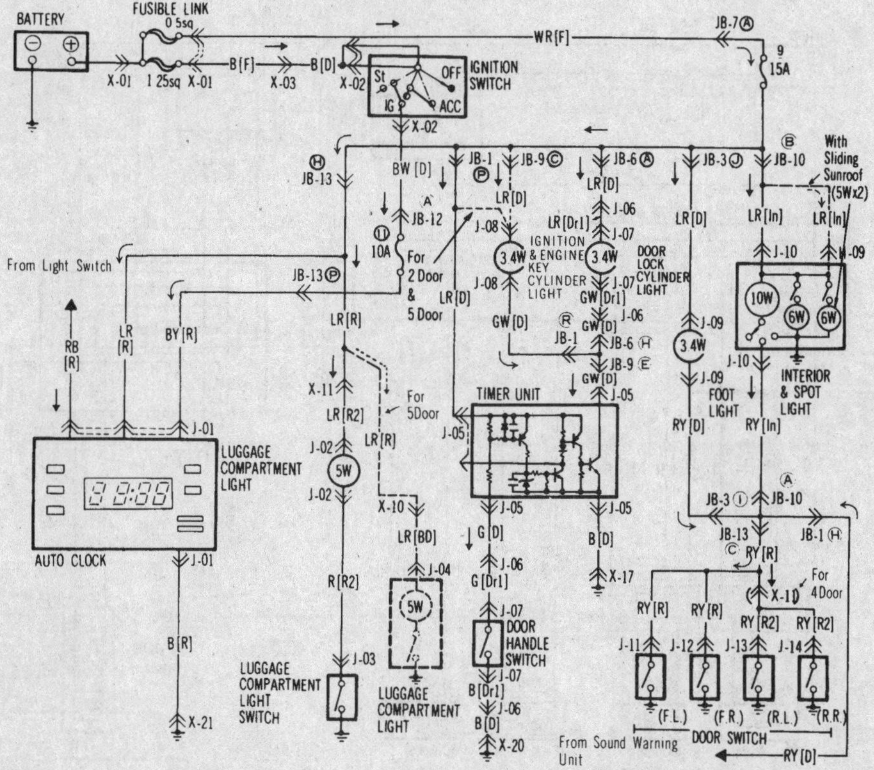

Digital clock, luggage and interior light wiring diagram

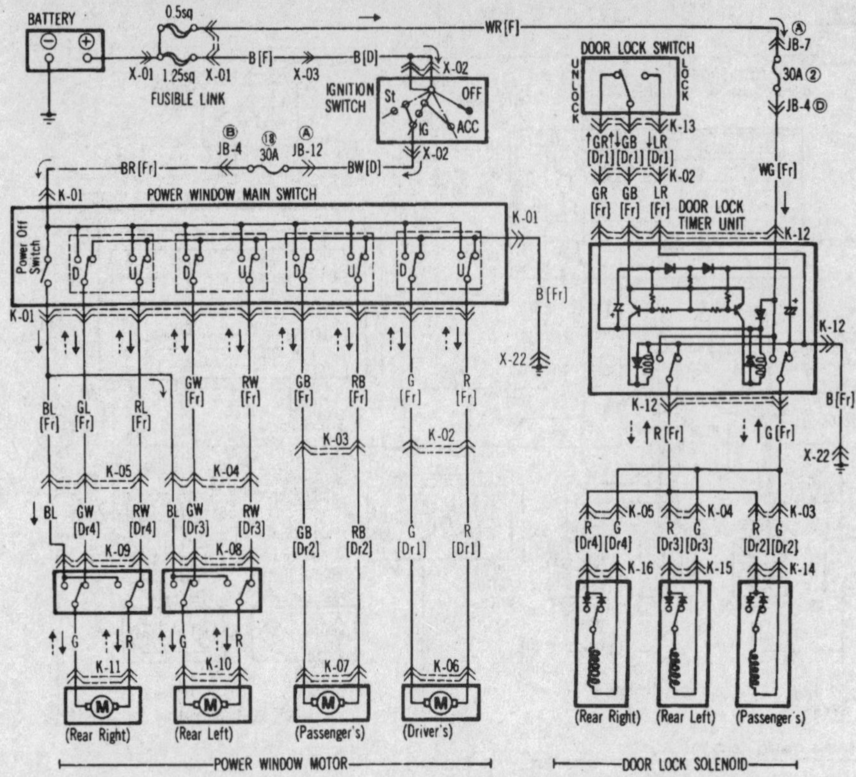

Power window and door lock (4- and 5-speed models) wiring diagram

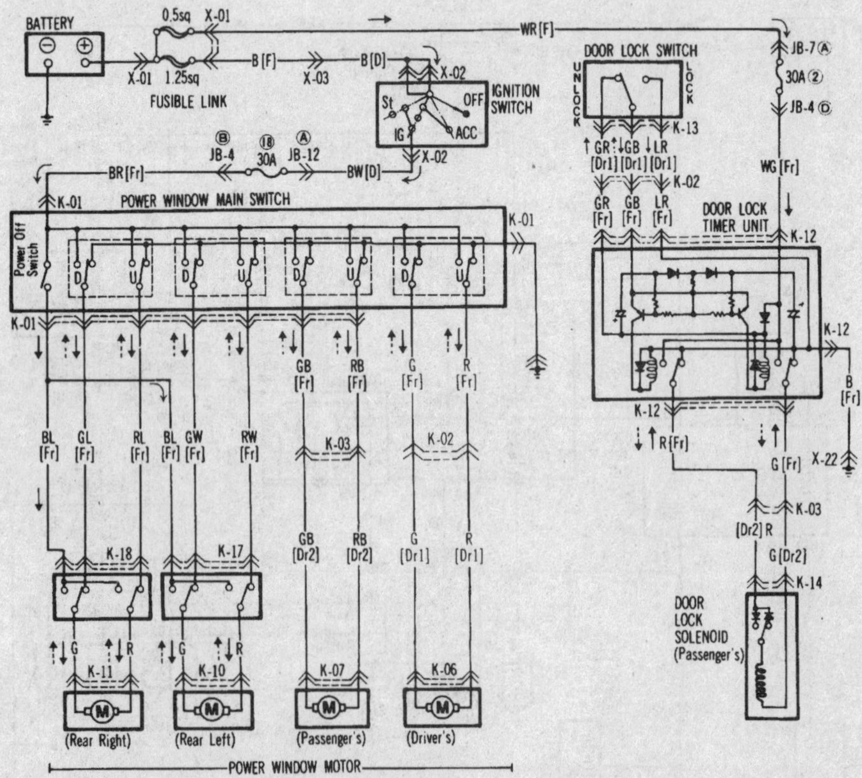

Power window and door lock (2-door models) wiring diagram

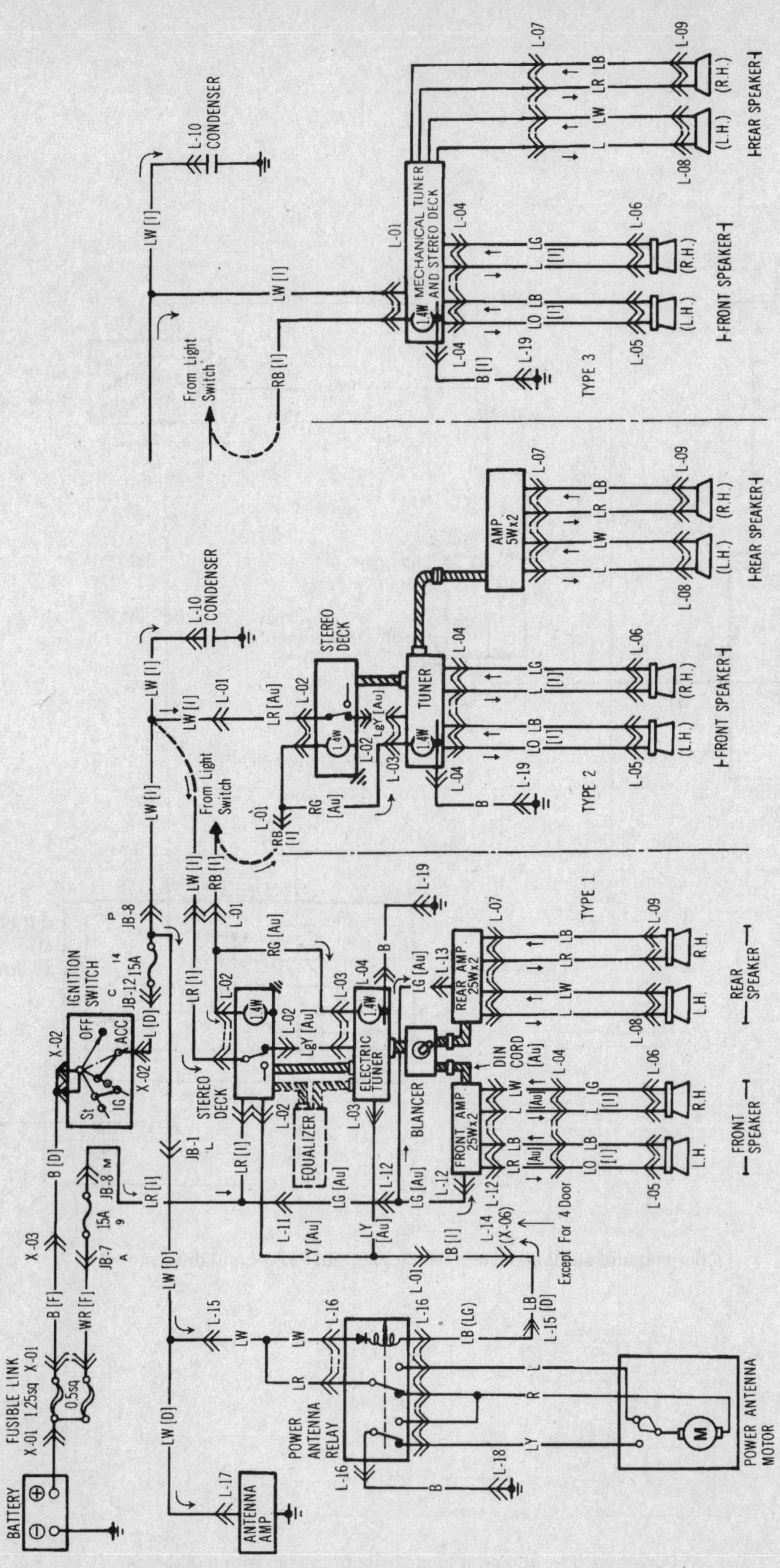

Audio system and power antenna wiring diagram

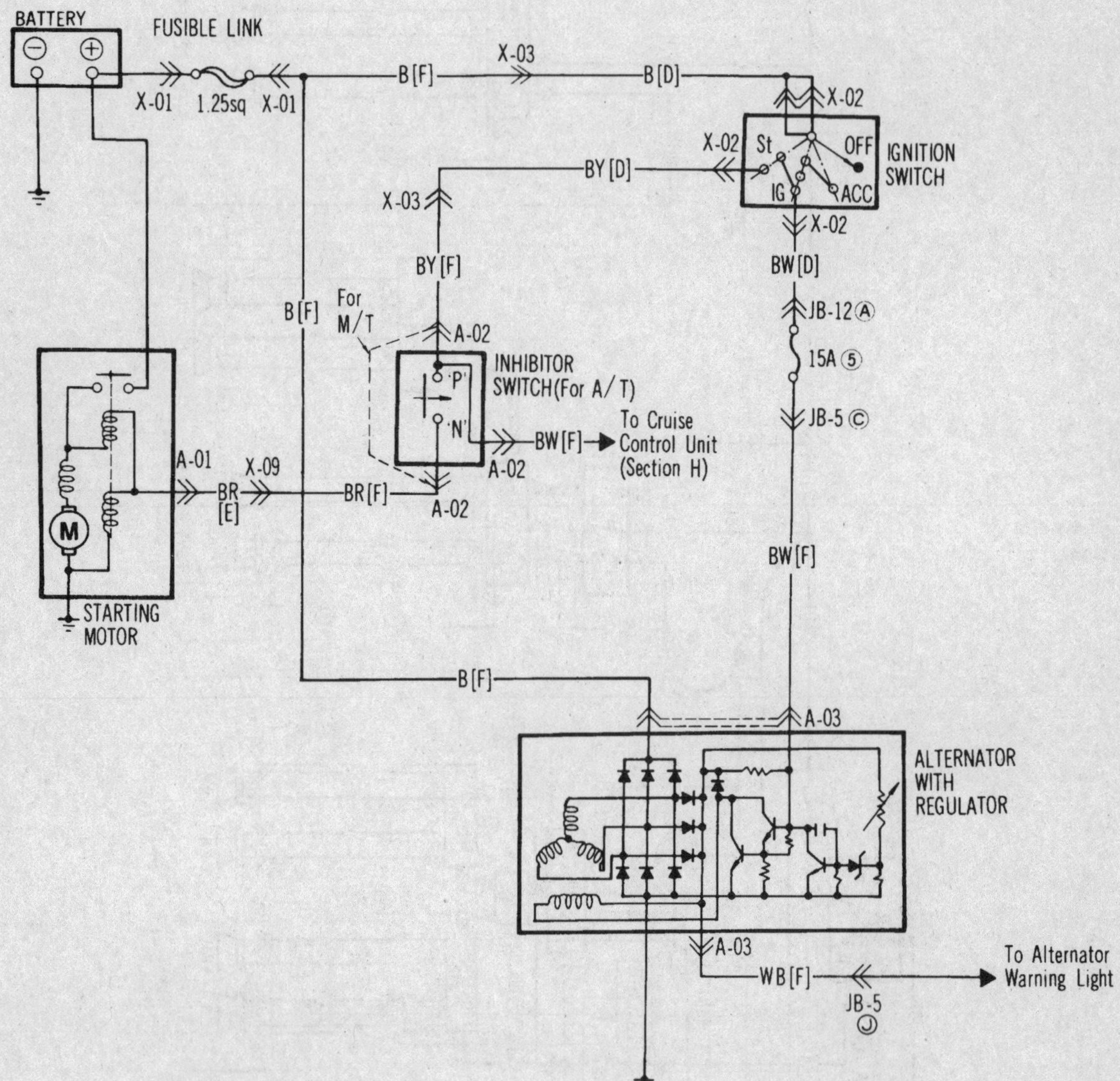

Charging and starting system wiring diagram (right-hand drive models)

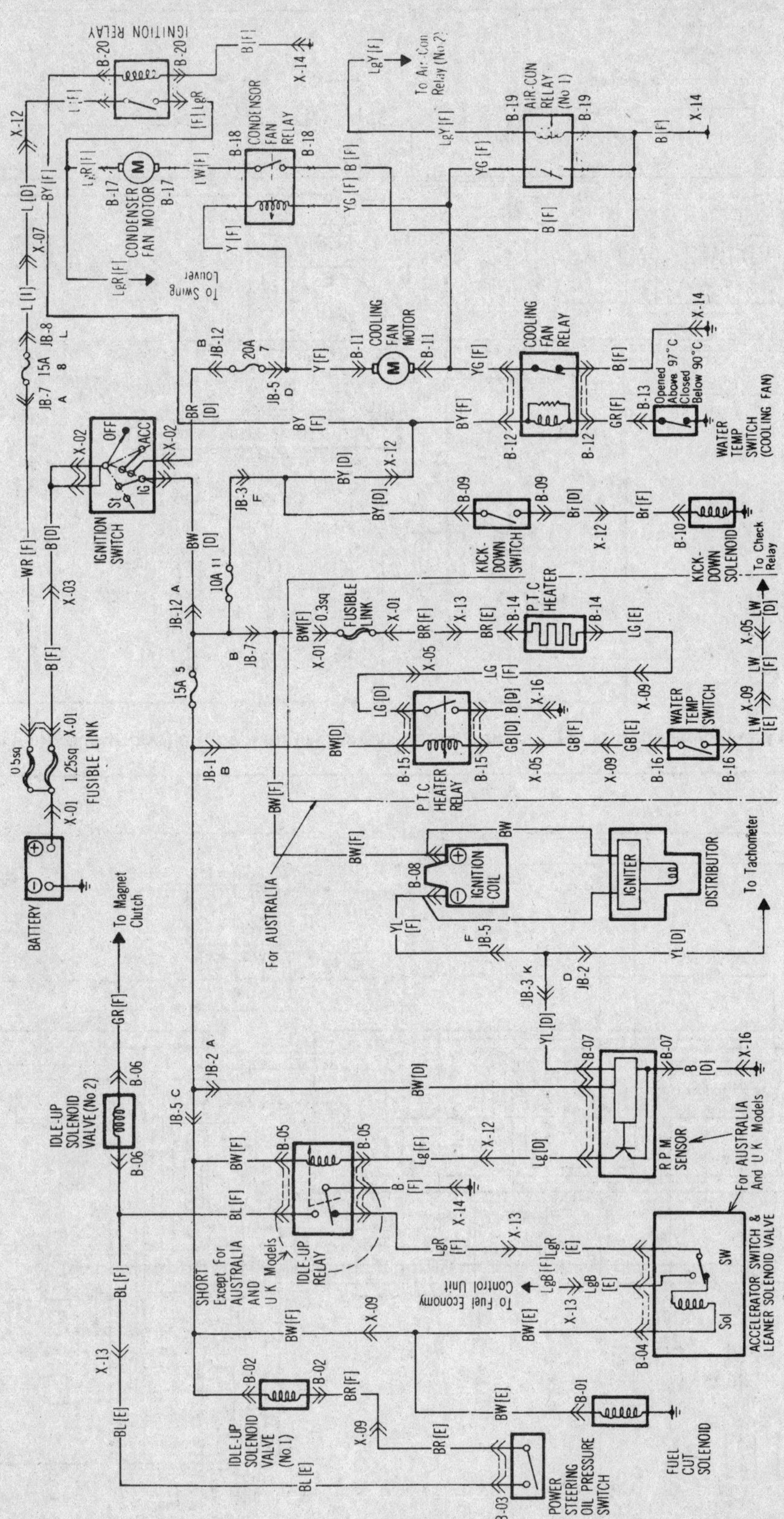

Engine control wiring system wiring diagram (1985 and earlier right-hand drive models)

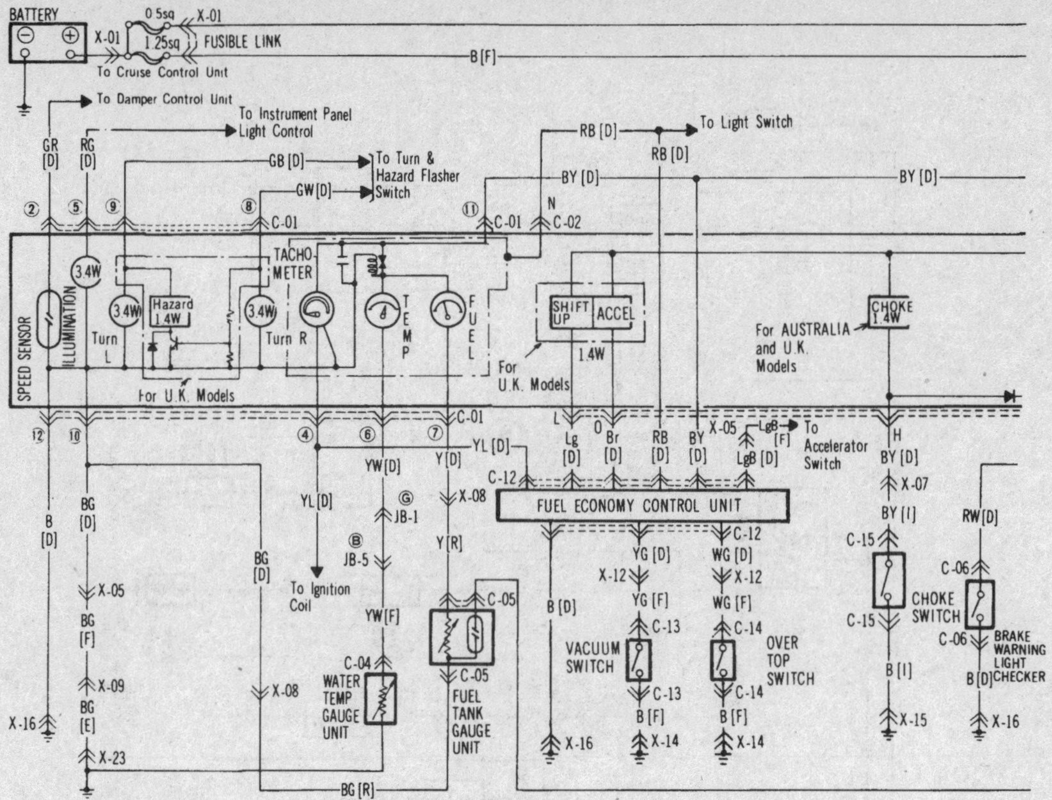

Instrument panel cluster warning lights and sound system wiring diagram (right-hand drive models)

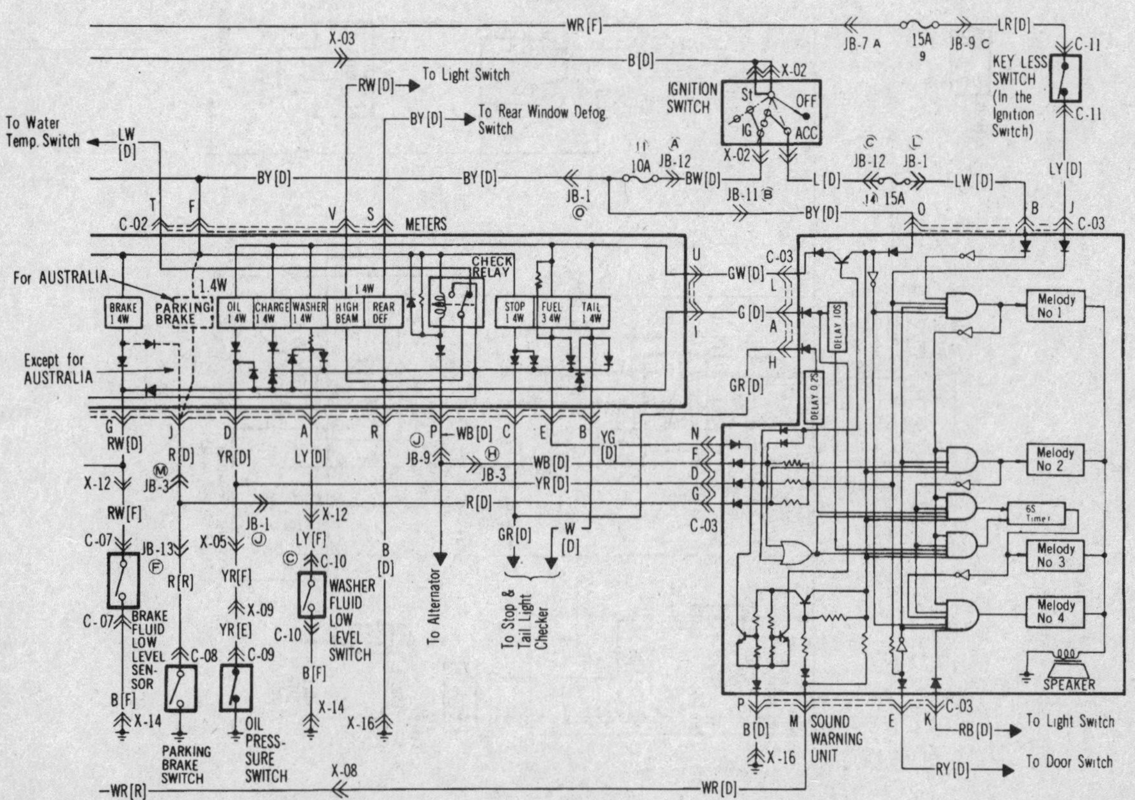

Instrument panel cluster, warning lights and sound system wiring diagram (right-hand drive models) (continued)

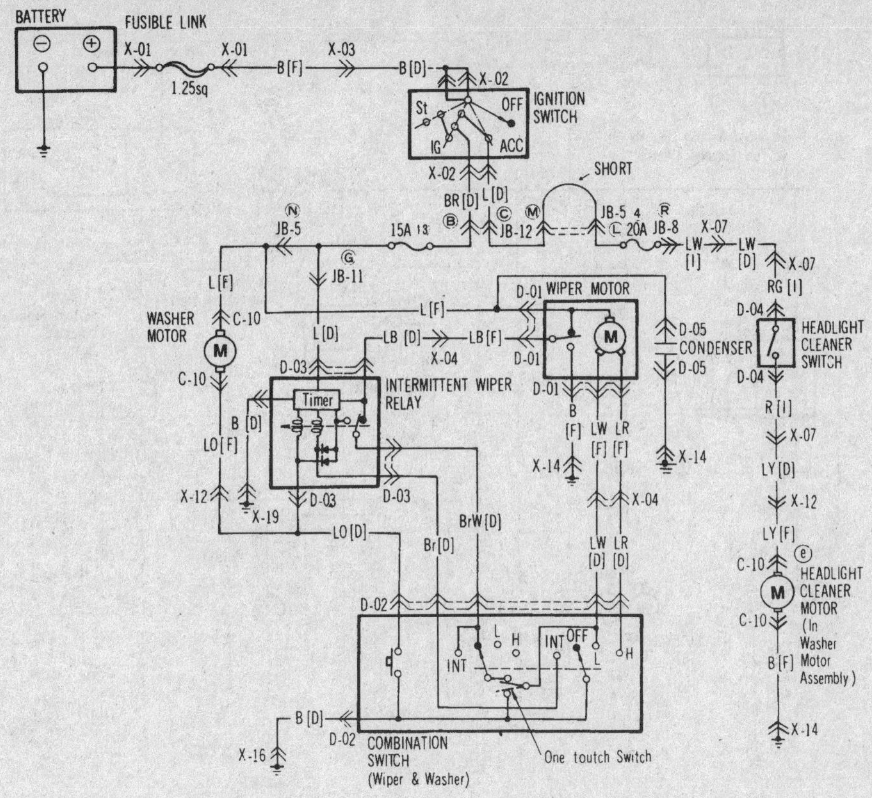

Windshield wiper/washer (except 5-door models) wiring diagram (right-hand drive models)

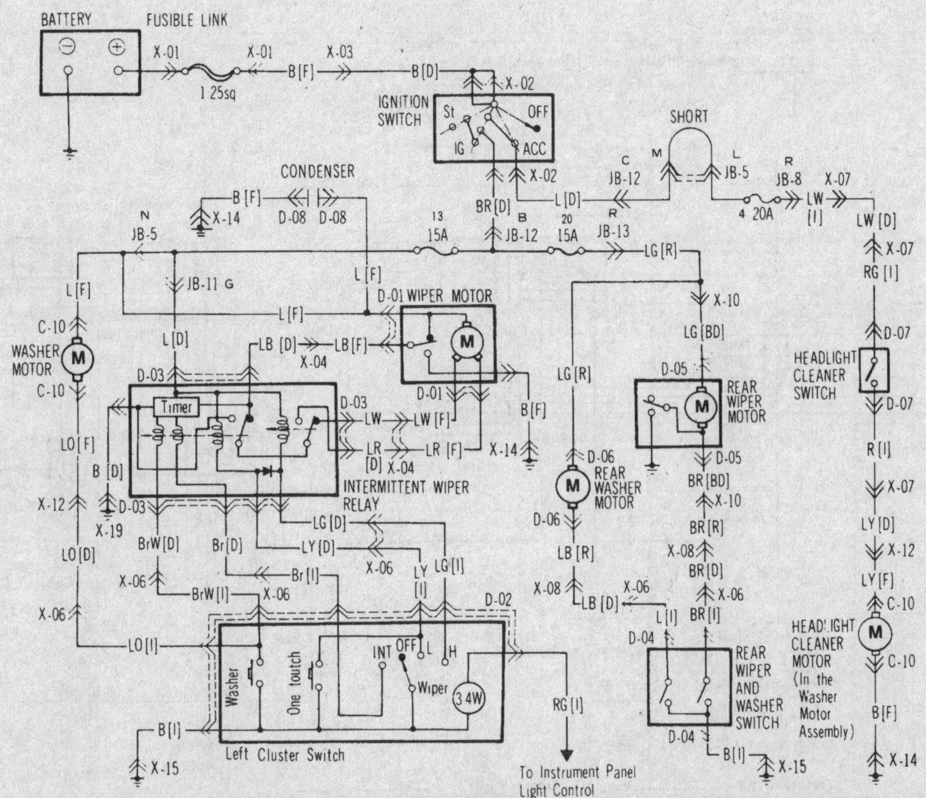

Windshield wiper/washer (5-door models) wiring diagram (right-hand drive models)

12

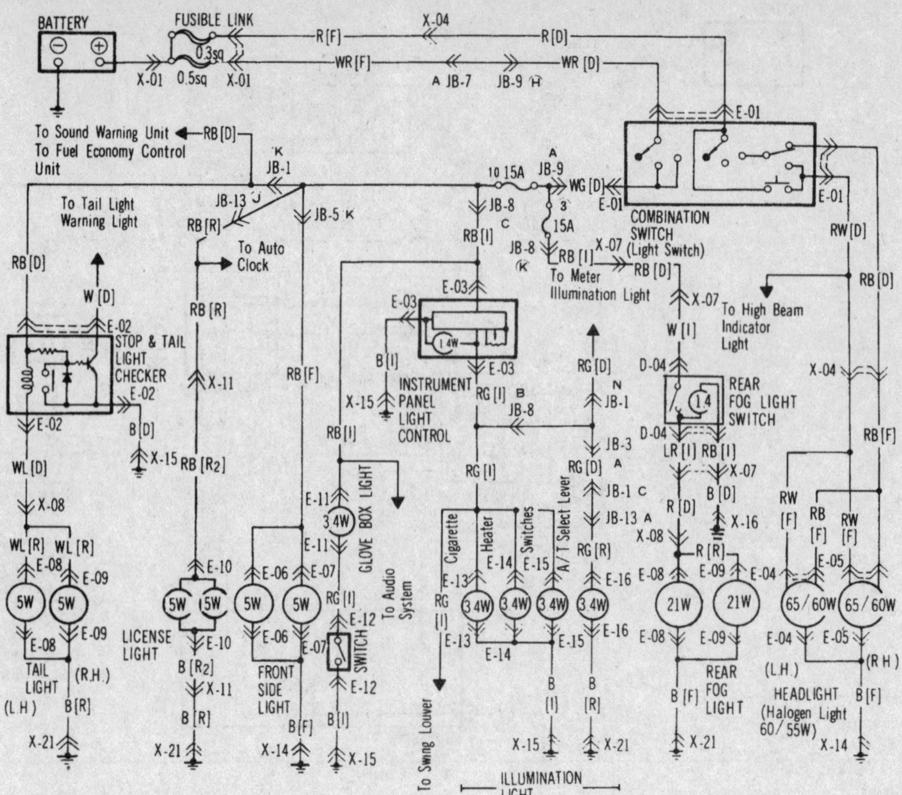

Headlight, tail, front side, front and rear marker, license and illumination lights wiring diagram (right-hand drive models)

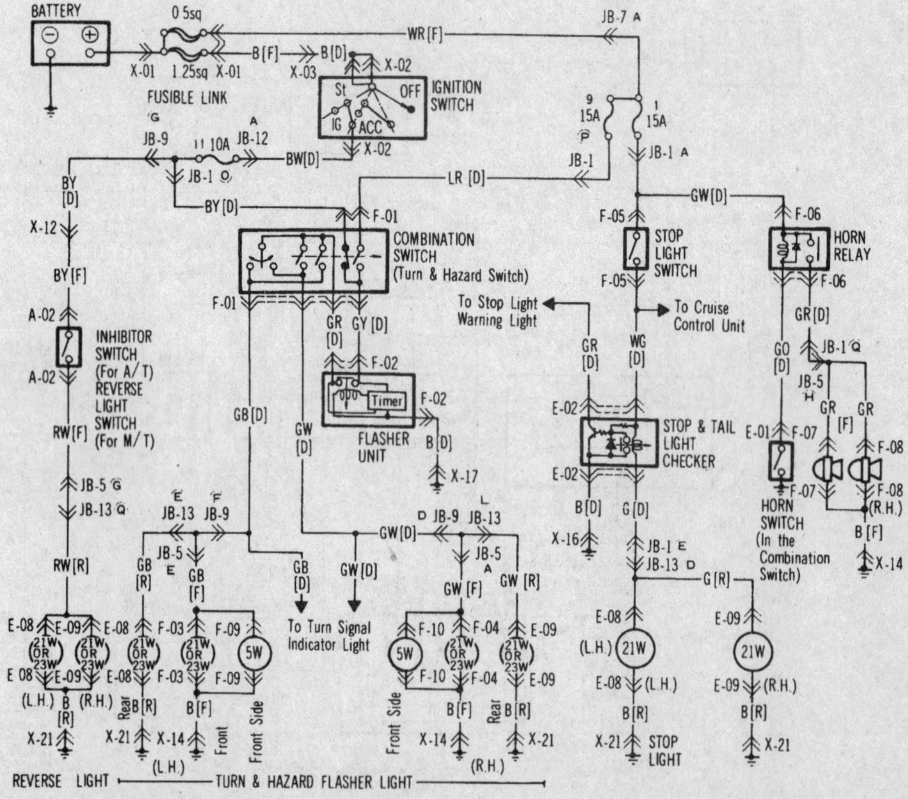

Turn and hazard flashers, stop and backup light lights and horn wiring diagram (right-hand drive models)

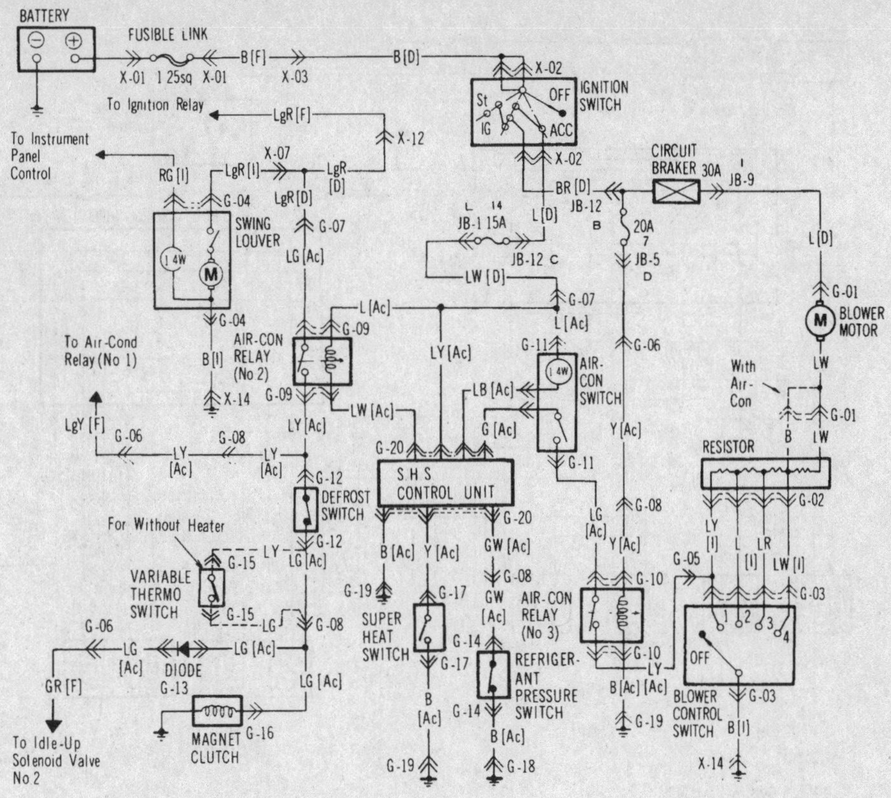

Air conditioning and swing louver fan motor wiring diagram (right-hand drive models)

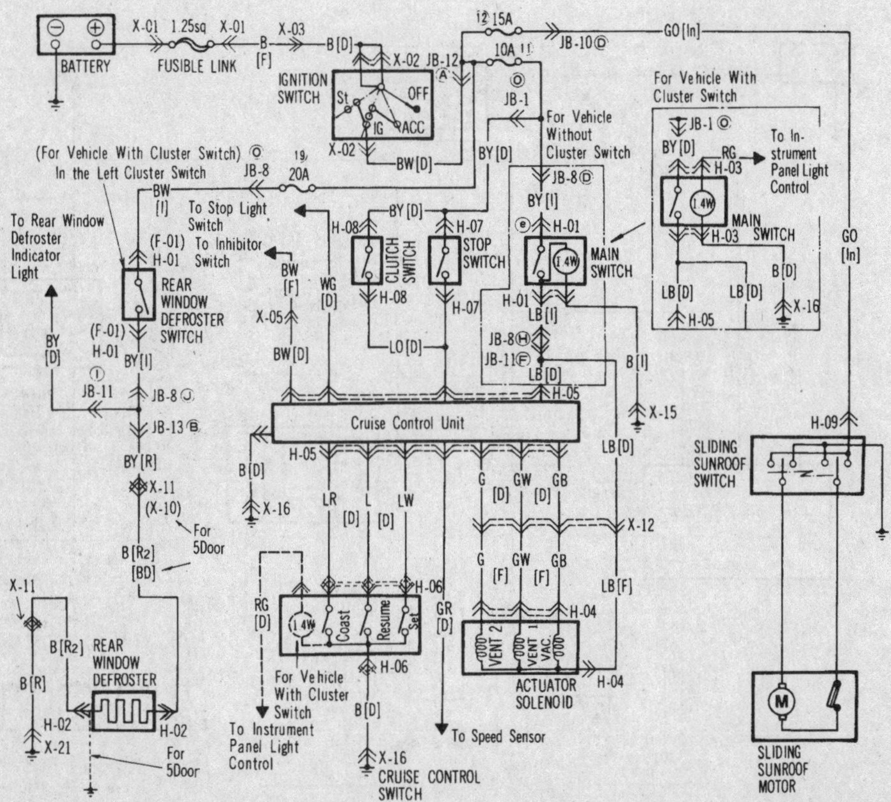

Rear window defroster, cruise control system wiring diagram (right-hand drive models)

12

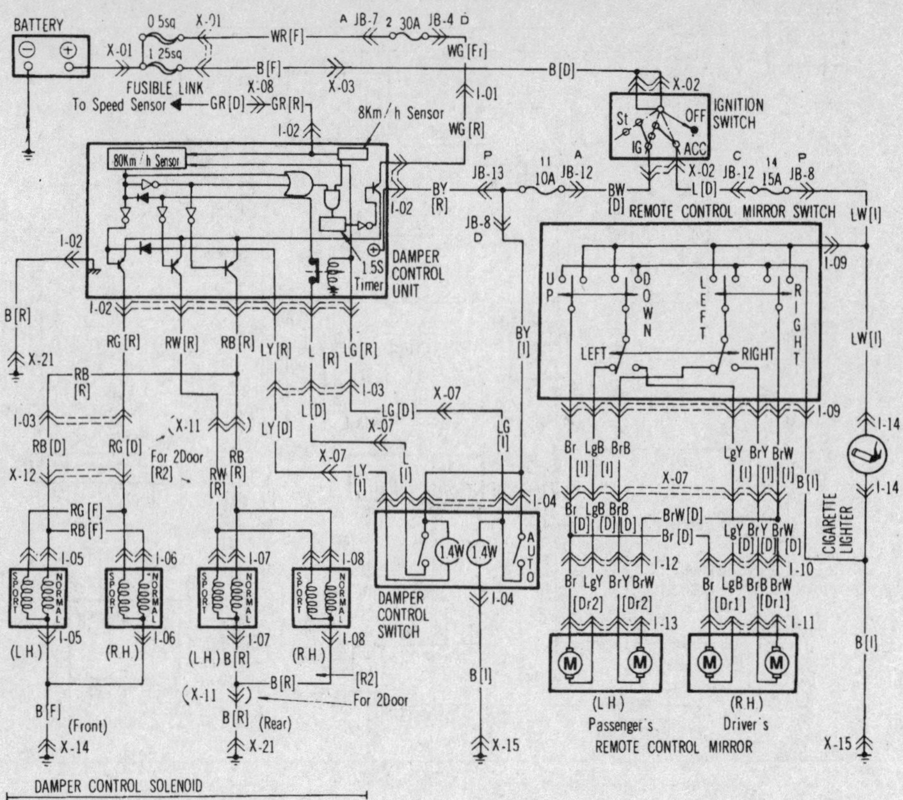

Three-way adjustable suspension damping system, power mirror and cigarette lighter wiring diagram (right-hand drive models)

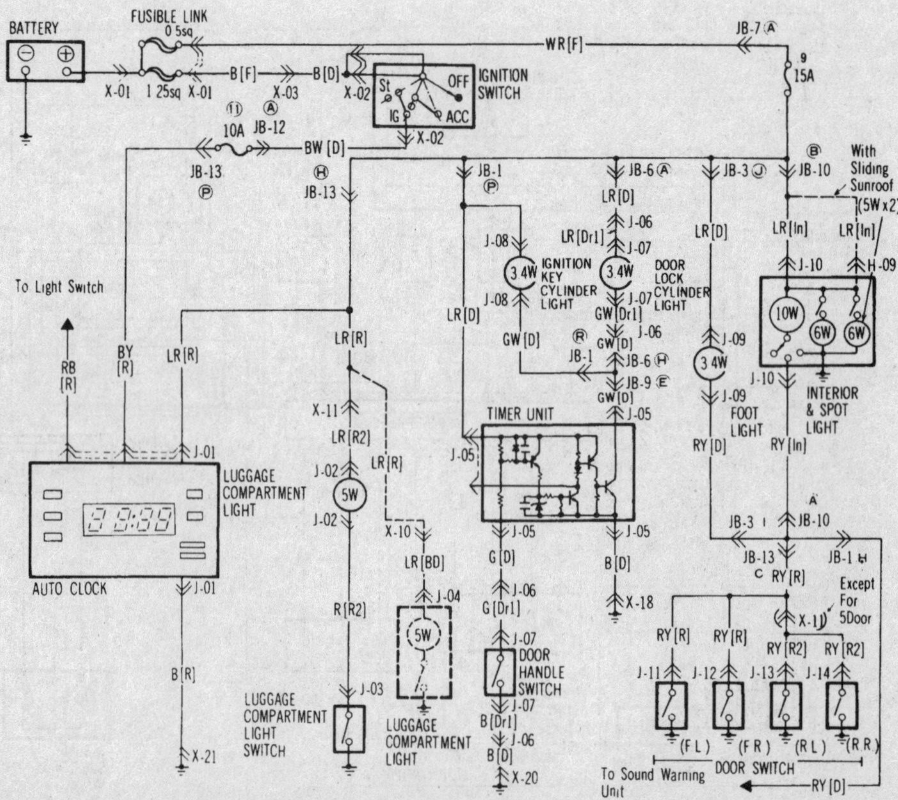

Digital clock, luggage compartment, ignition key, door lock, interior, spot and foot light wiring diagram (right-hand drive models)

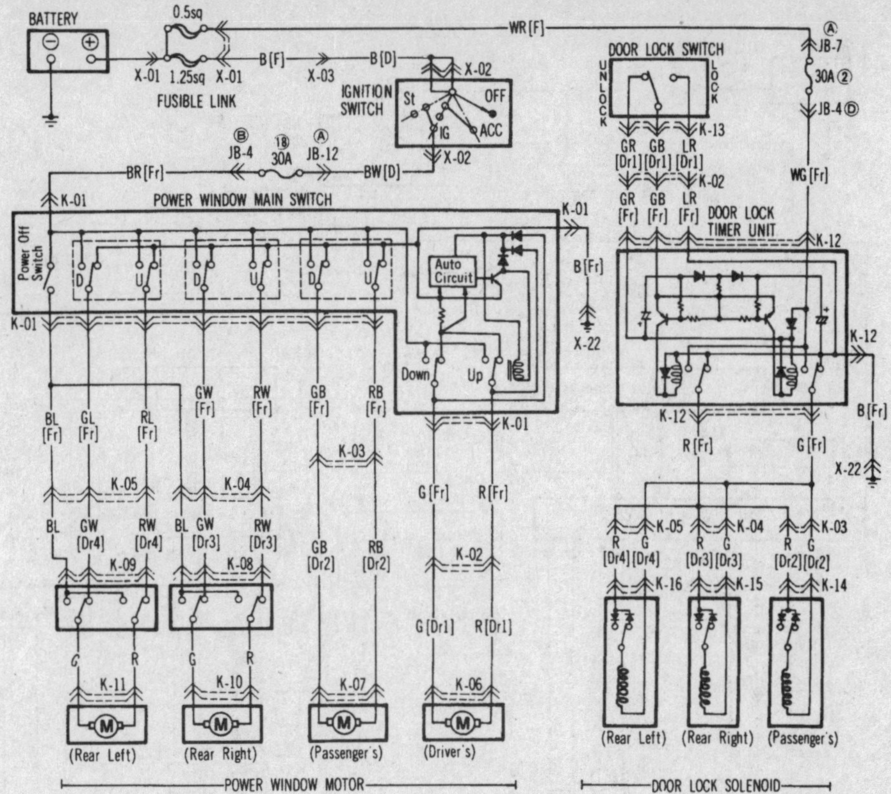

Power window and door lock (4- and 5-door models) wiring diagram (right-hand drive models)

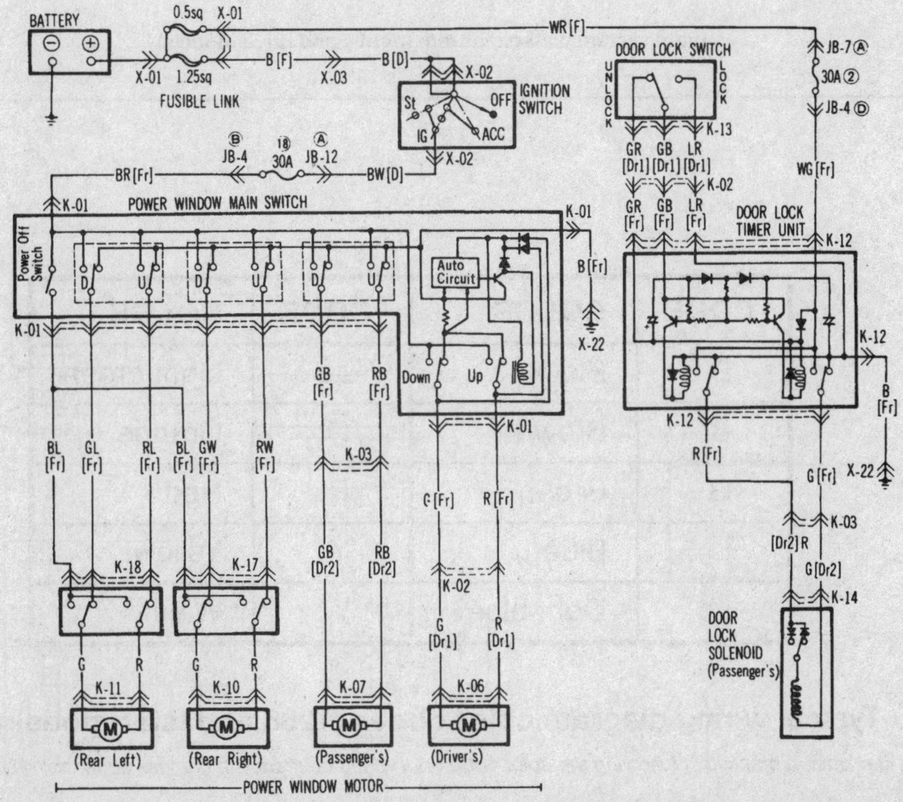

Power window and door lock (2-door models) wiring diagram (right-hand drive models)

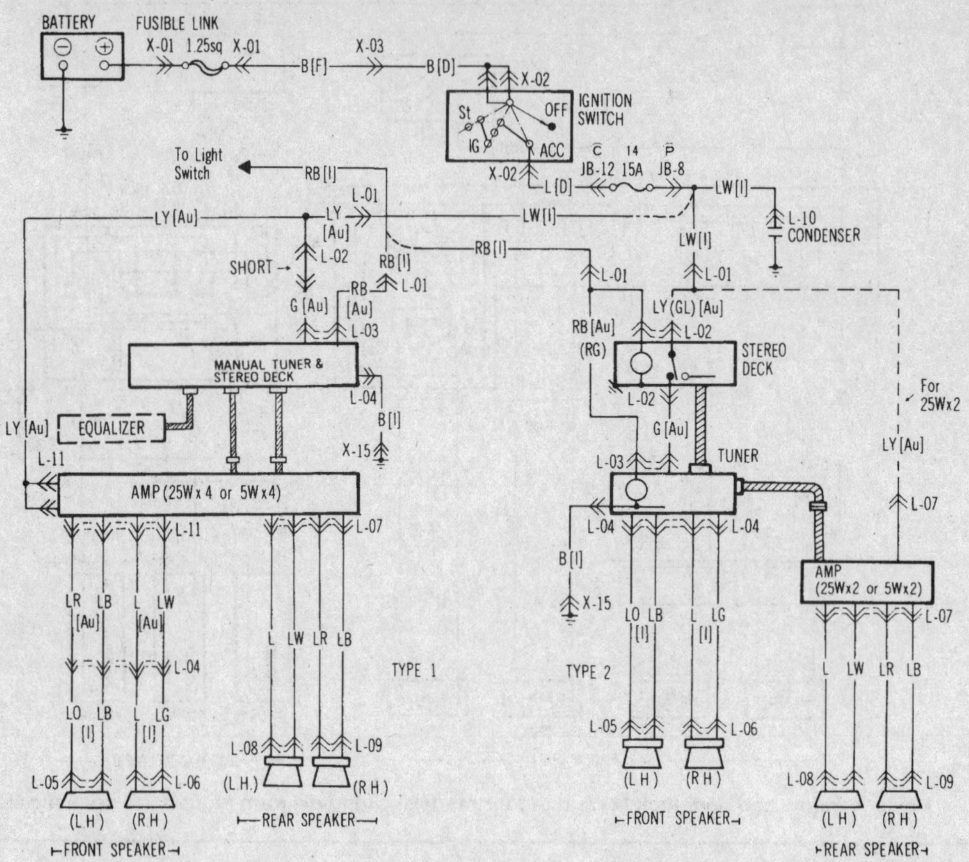

Audio system wiring diagram (right-hand drive models)

CODE	COLOR	CODE	COLOR
B	Black	Lg	Light green
Br	Brown	O	Orange
G	Green	R	Red
L	Blue	Y	Yellow
Lb	Light blue	W	White

Typical wiring diagram color codes (1986 and later models)

(Note: the letter in brackets[ ] following the color code on a wiring diagram is a harness code, not a color code

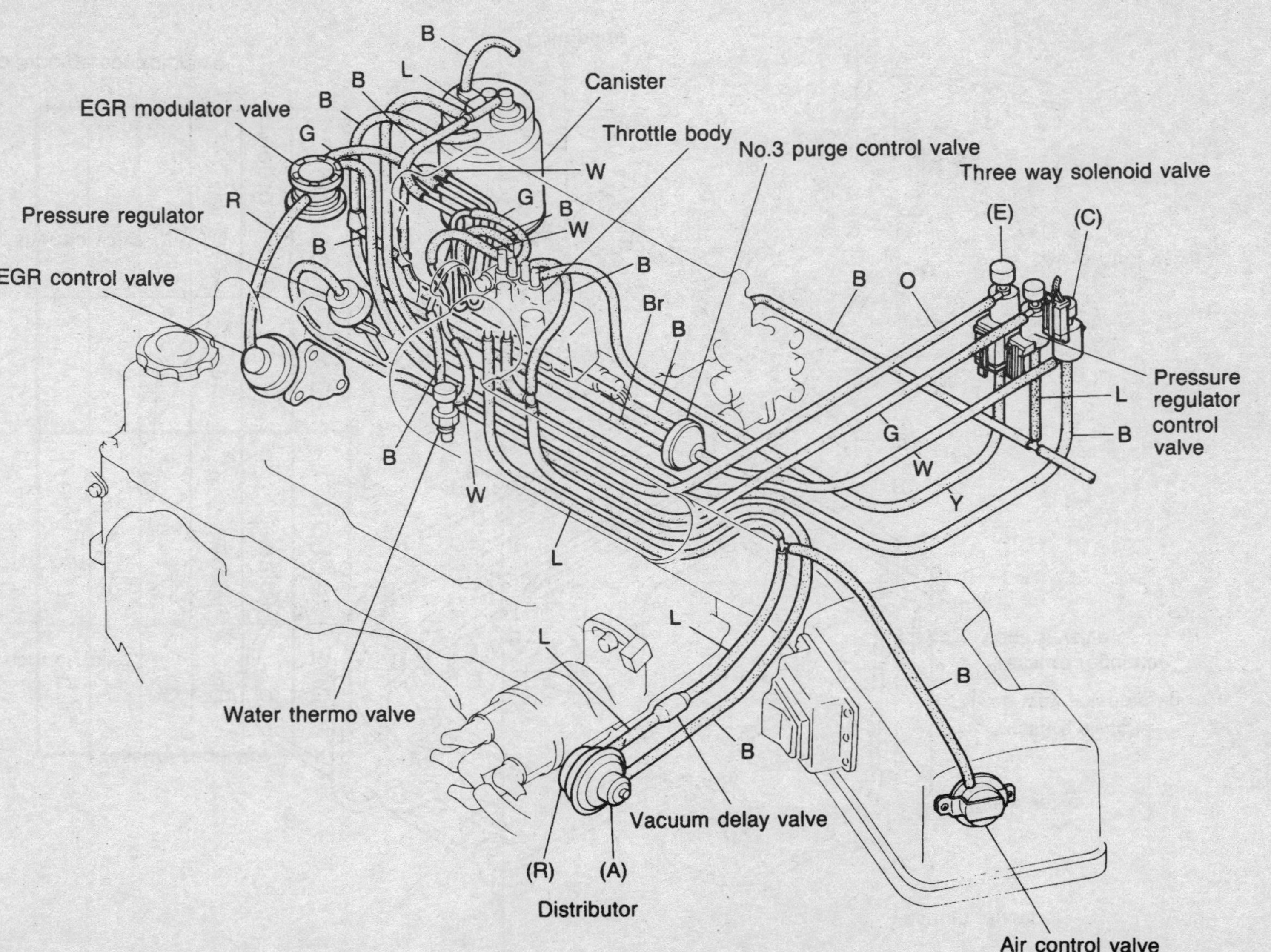

Normally aspirated engine vacuum hose routing diagram (1986 and later models)

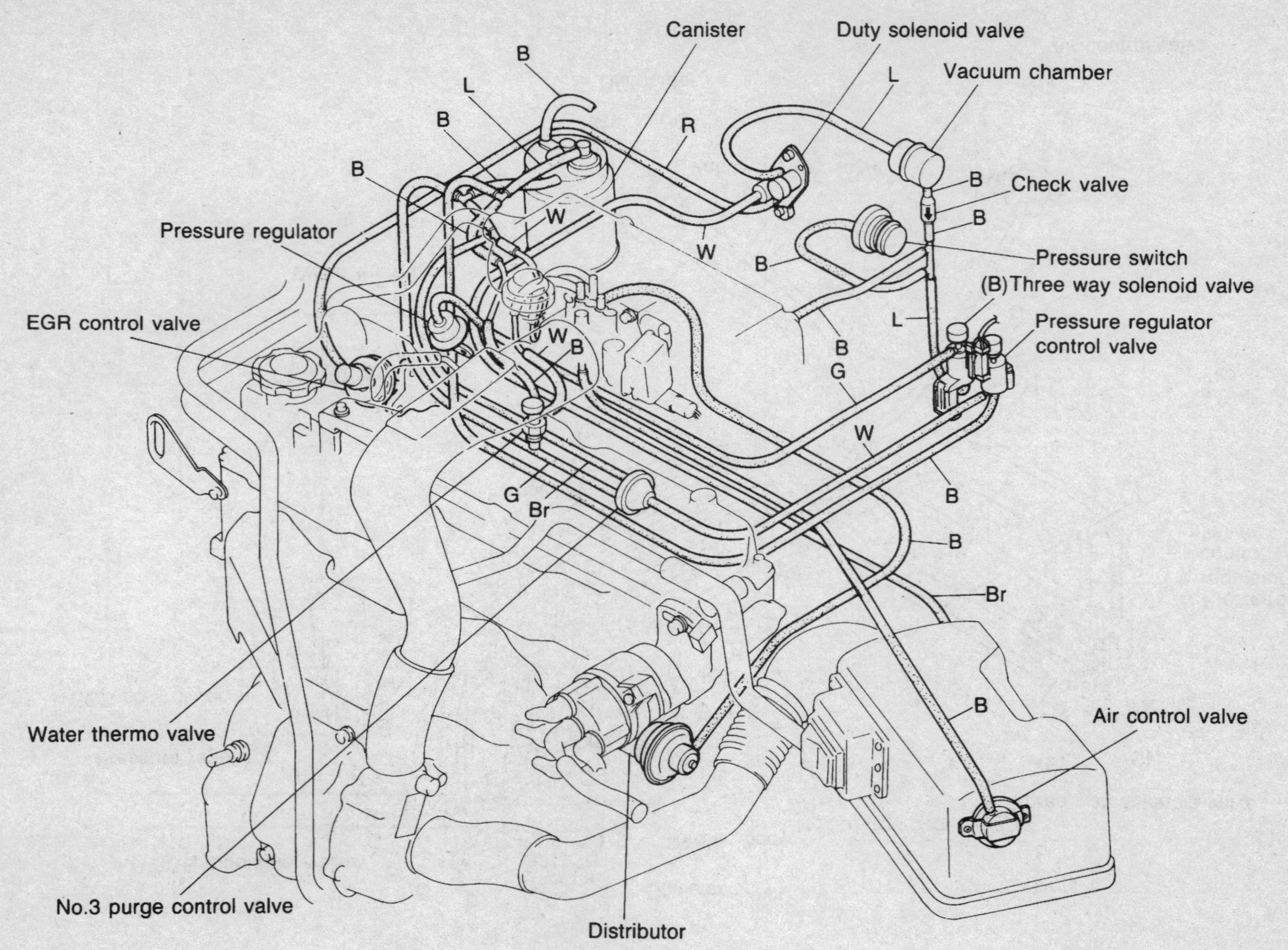

Turbocharged engine vacuum hose routing diagram (1986 and later models)

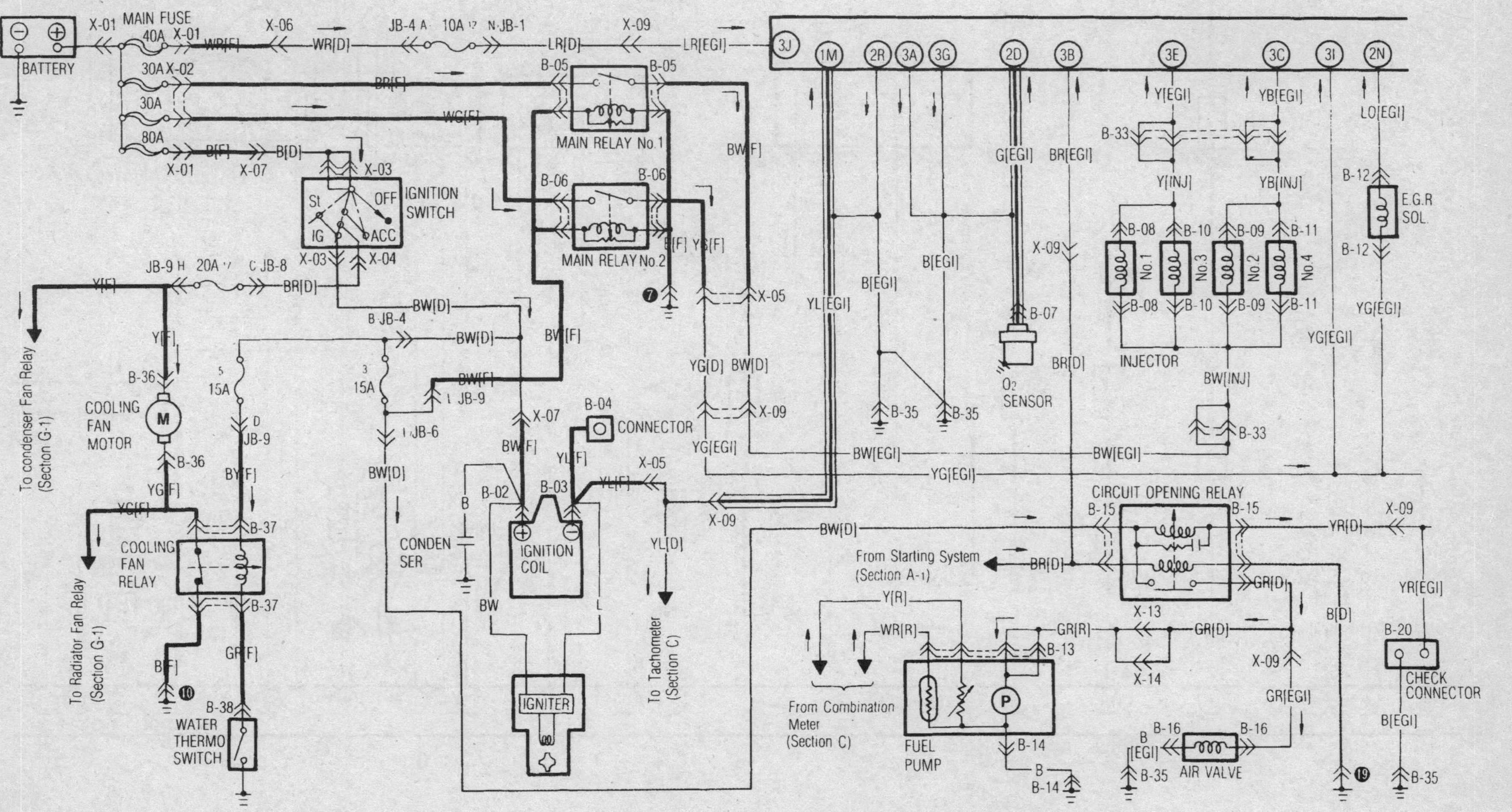

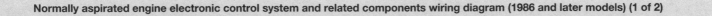

Normally aspirated engine electronic control system and related components wiring diagram (1986 and later models) (1 of 2)

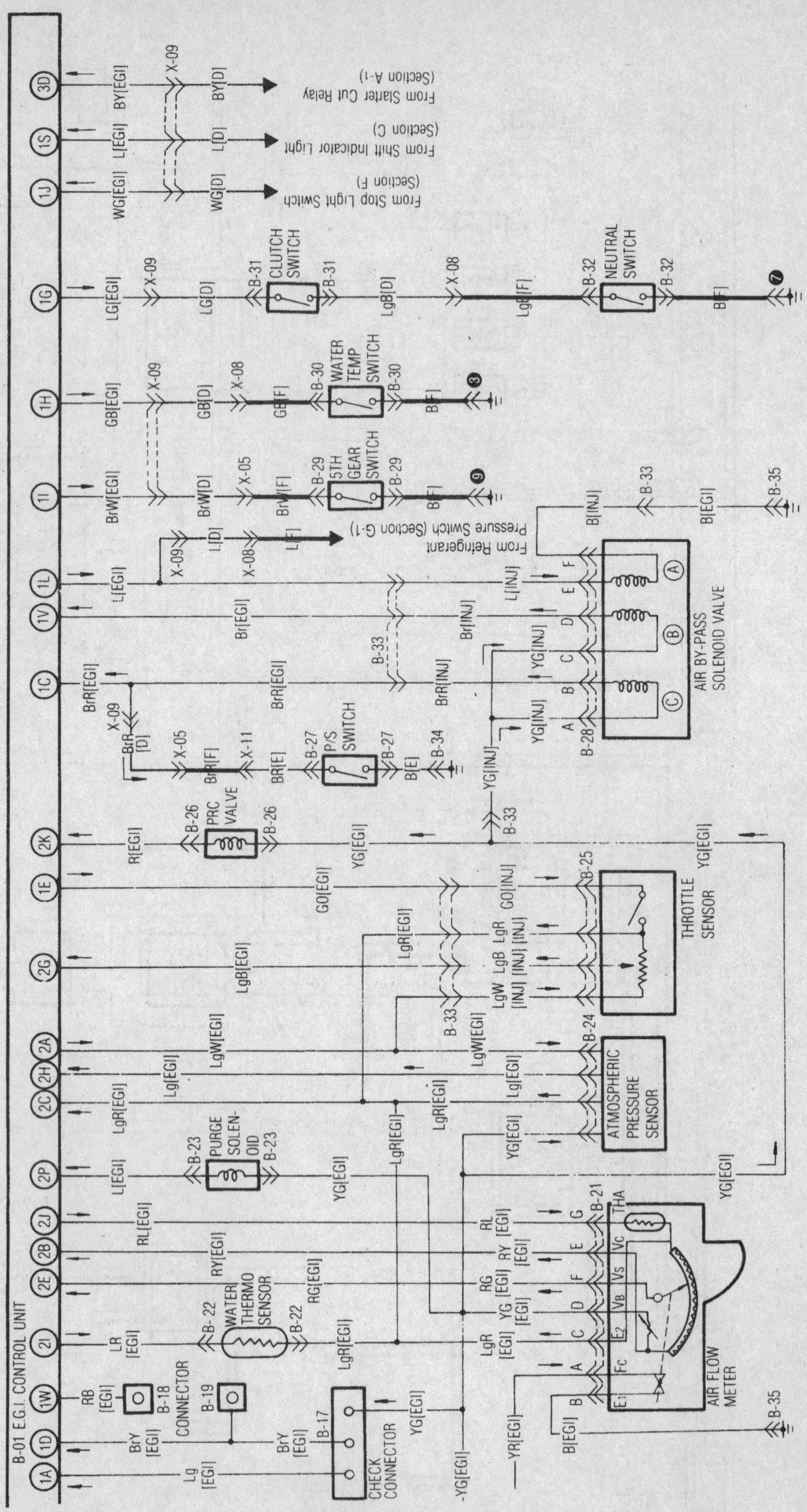

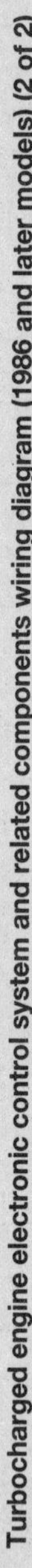

Turbocharged engine electronic control system and related components wiring diagram (1986 and later models) (2 of 2)

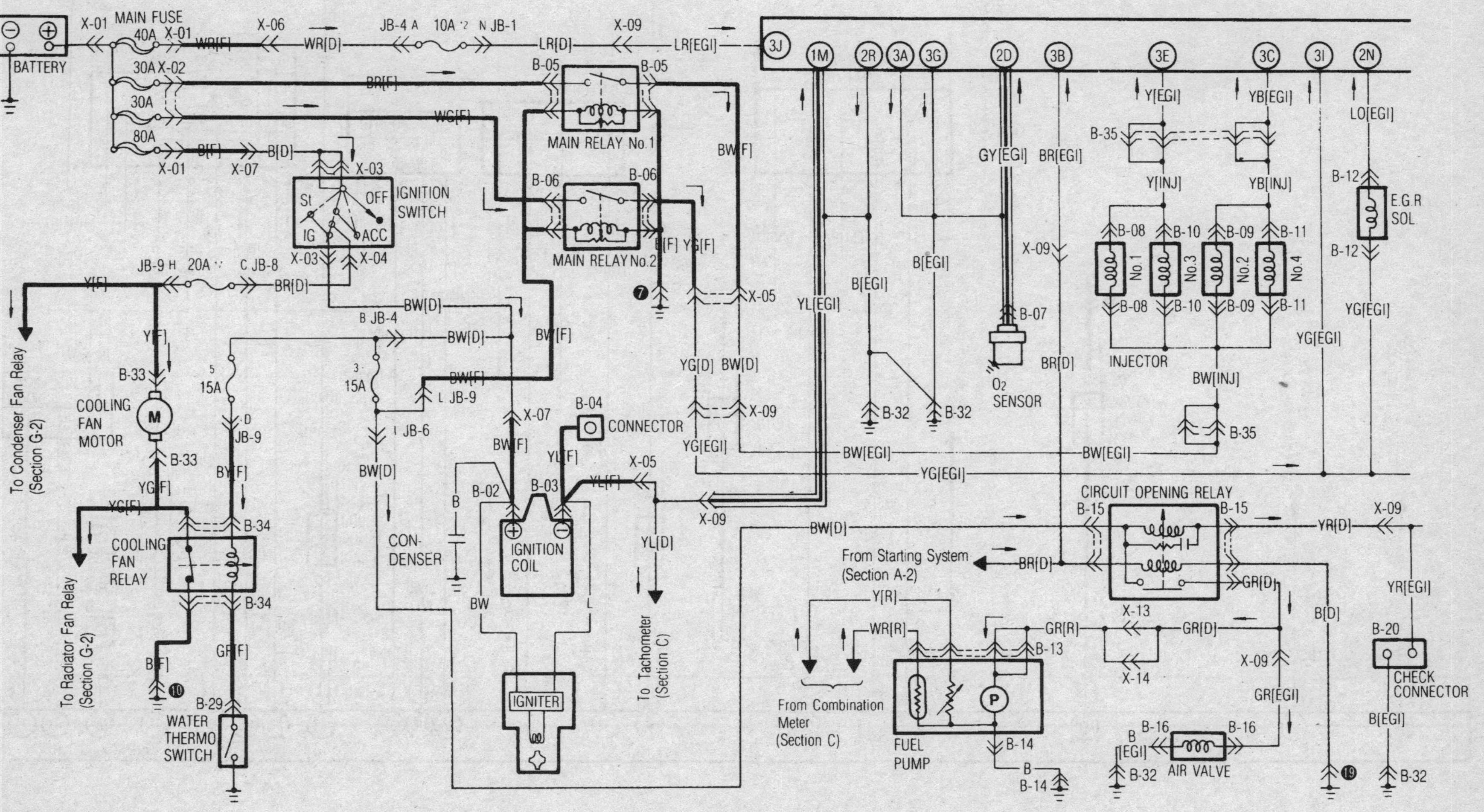

Normally aspirated engine with automatic transaxle electronic control system and related components wiring diagram (1986 and later models) (1 of 2)

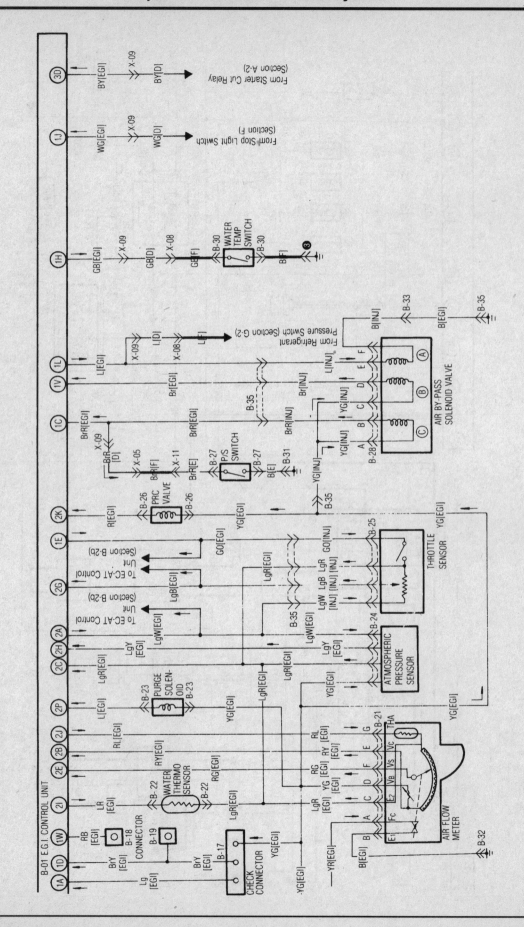

Normally aspirated engine with automatic transaxle electronic control system and related components wiring diagram (1986 and later models) (2 of 2)

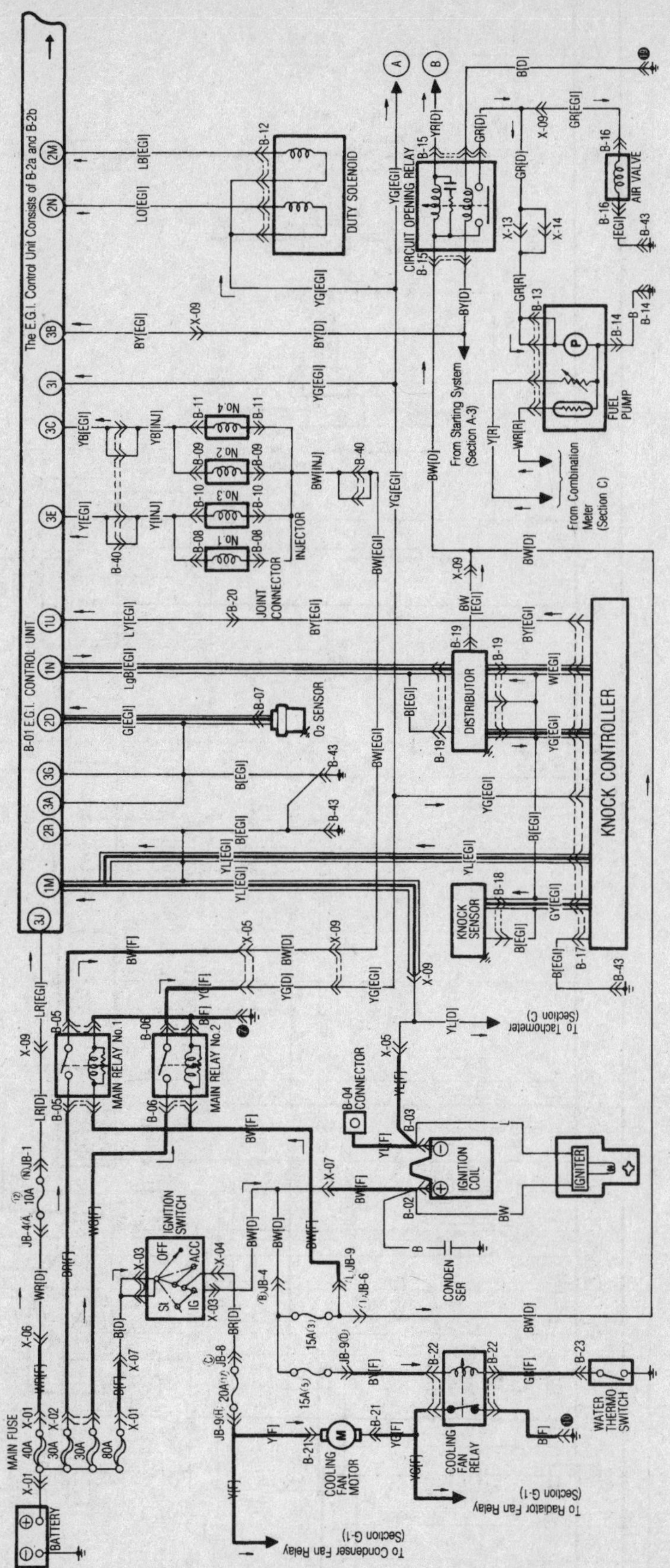

Turbocharged engine electronic control system and related components wiring diagram (1986 and later models) (1 of 2)

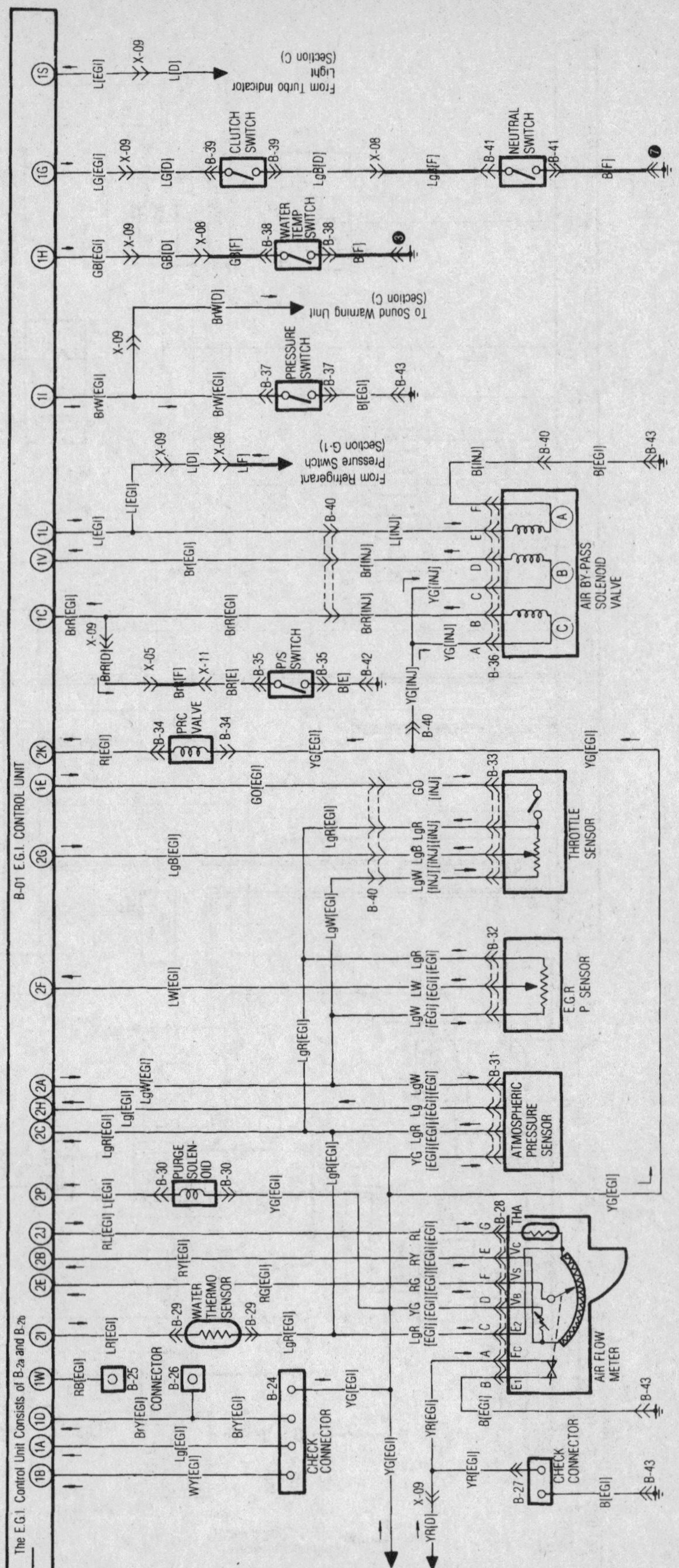

Turbocharged engine electronic control system and related components wiring diagram (1986 and later models) (2 of 2)

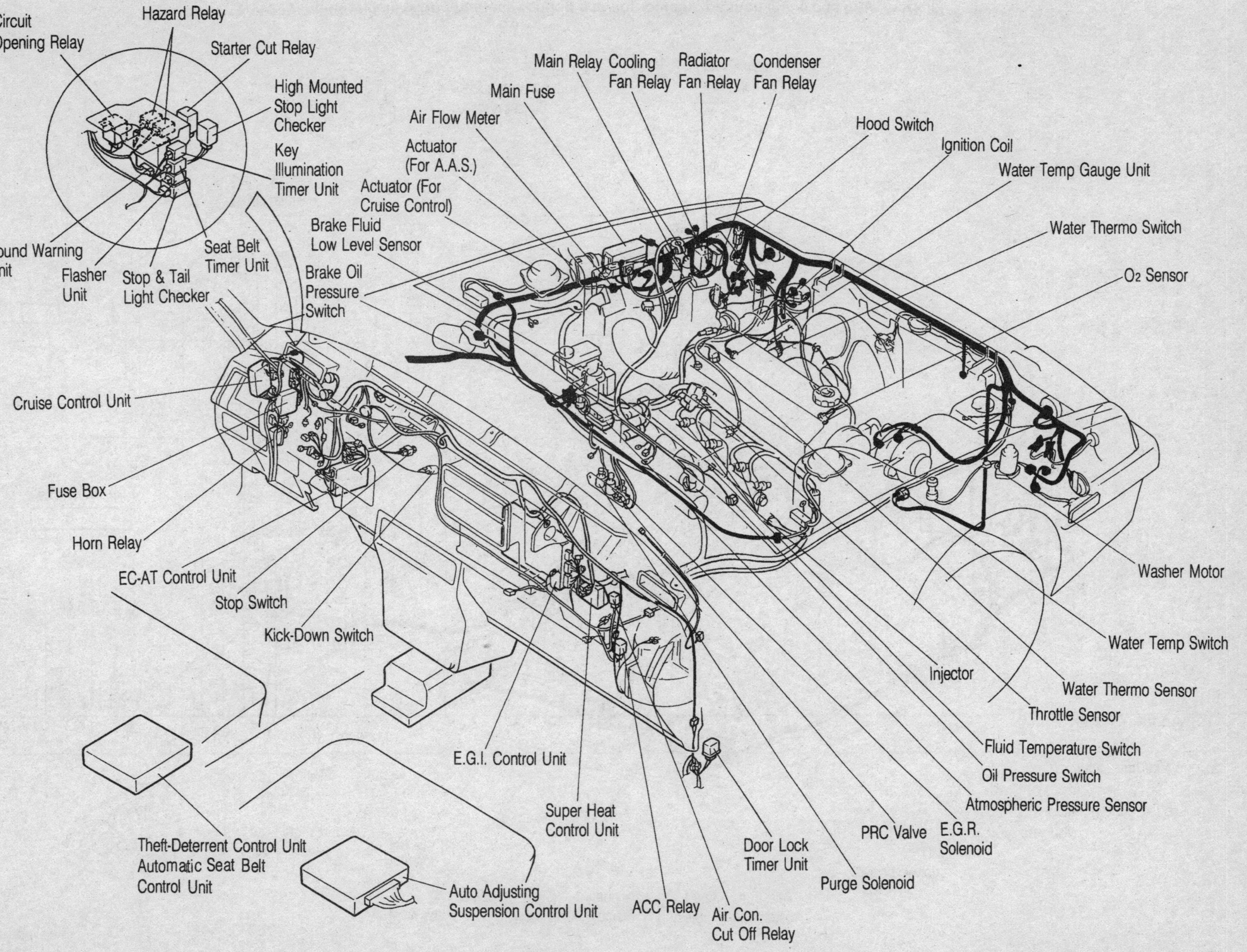

Normally aspirated engine wiring harness routing and component location (1986 and later models)

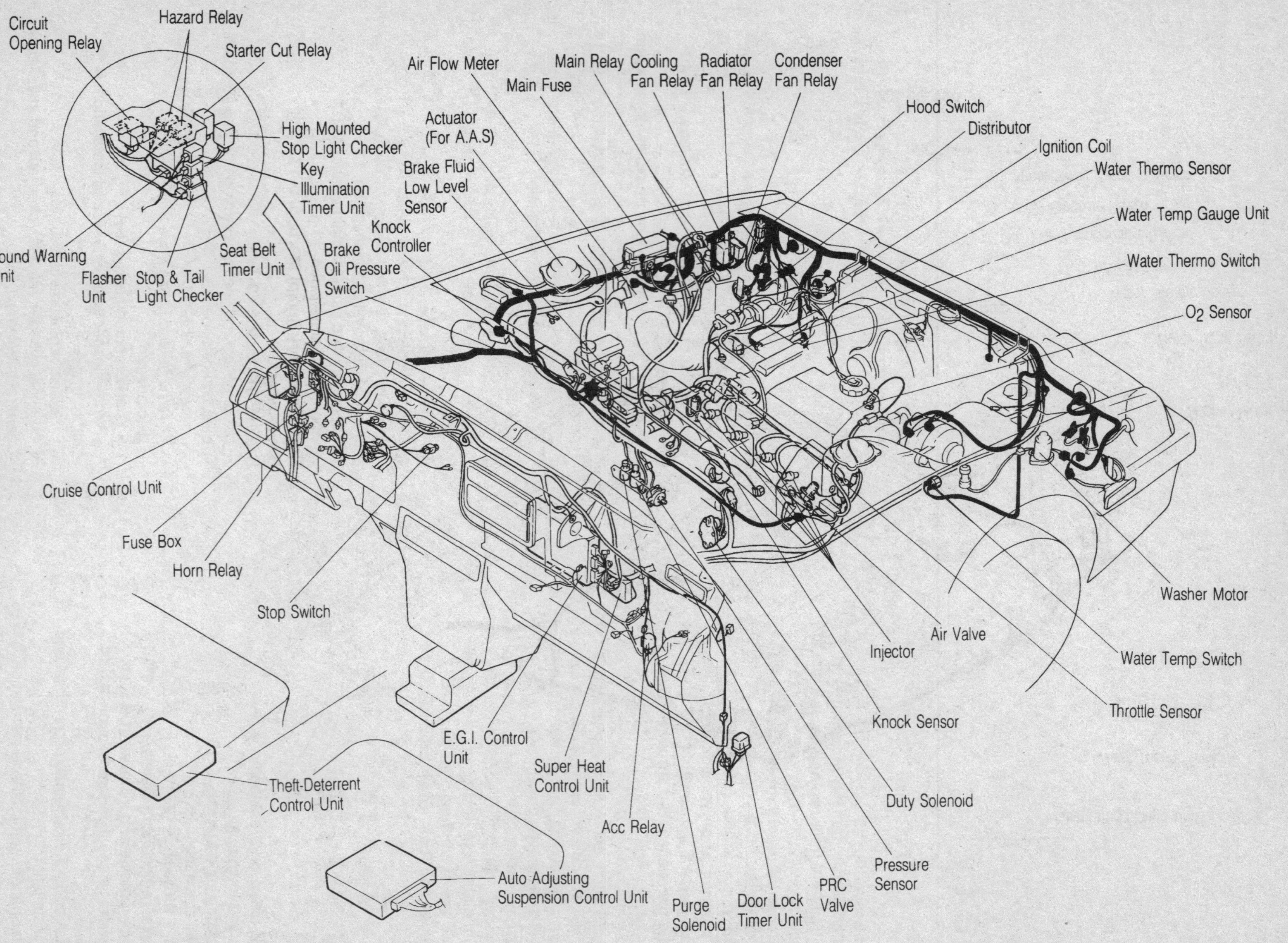

Turbocharged engine wiring harness routing and component location (1986 and later models)

Index

C

D

E

F

O

P

Q

R

S

Haynes Automotive Manuals

NOTE: New manuals are added to this list on a periodic basis. If you do not see a listing for your vehicle, consult your local Haynes dealer for the latest product information.

ACURA

- 12020 **Integra** '86 thru '89 **& Legend** '86 thru '90
- 12021 **Integra** '90 thru '93 **& Legend** '91 thru '95

AMC

- **Jeep CJ** - *see JEEP (50020)*
- 14020 **Mid-size models** '70 thru '83
- 14025 **(Renault) Alliance & Encore** '83 thru '87

AUDI

- 15020 **4000** all models '80 thru '87
- 15025 **5000** all models '77 thru '83
- 15026 **5000** all models '84 thru '88

AUSTIN-HEALEY

- **Sprite** - *see MG Midget (66015)*

BMW

- *18020 **3/5 Series** not including diesel or all-wheel drive models '82 thru '92
- 18021 **3-Series** incl. Z3 models '92 thru '98
- 18025 **320i** all 4 cyl models '75 thru '83
- 18050 **1500 thru 2002** except Turbo '59 thru '77

BUICK

- *19010 **Buick Century** '97 thru '02
- **Century (front-wheel drive)** - *see GM (38005)*
- *19020 **Buick, Oldsmobile & Pontiac Full-size (Front-wheel drive)** '85 thru '02 **Buick** Electra, LeSabre and Park Avenue; **Oldsmobile** Delta 88 Royale, Ninety Eight and Regency; **Pontiac** Bonneville
- 19025 **Buick Oldsmobile & Pontiac Full-size (Rear wheel drive)** **Buick** Estate '70 thru '90, Electra'70 thru '84, LeSabre '70 thru '85, Limited '74 thru '79 **Oldsmobile** Custom Cruiser '70 thru '90, Delta 88 '70 thru '85,Ninety-eight '70 thru '84 **Pontiac** Bonneville '70 thru '81, Catalina '70 thru '81, Grandville '70 thru '75, Parisienne '83 thru '86
- 19030 **Mid-size Regal & Century** all rear-drive models with V6, V8 and Turbo '74 thru '87
- **Regal** - *see GENERAL MOTORS (38010)*
- **Riviera** - *see GENERAL MOTORS (38030)*
- **Roadmaster** - *see CHEVROLET (24046)*
- **Skyhawk** - *see GENERAL MOTORS (38015)*
- **Skylark** - *see GM (38020, 38025)*
- **Somerset** - *see GENERAL MOTORS (38025)*

CADILLAC

- 21030 **Cadillac Rear Wheel Drive** all gasoline models '70 thru '93
- **Cimarron** - *see GENERAL MOTORS (38015)*
- **DeVille** - *see GM (38031 & 38032)*
- **Eldorado** - *see GM (38030 & 38031)*
- **Fleetwood** - *see GM (38031)*
- **Seville** - *see GM (38030, 38031 & 38032)*

CHEVROLET

- *24010 **Astro & GMC Safari Mini-vans** '85 thru '02
- 24015 **Camaro V8** all models '70 thru '81
- 24016 **Camaro** all models '82 thru '92
- 24017 **Camaro & Firebird** '93 thru '00
- **Cavalier** - *see GENERAL MOTORS (38016)*
- **Celebrity** - *see GENERAL MOTORS (38005)*
- 24020 **Chevelle, Malibu & El Camino** '69 thru '87
- 24024 **Chevette & Pontiac T1000** '76 thru '87
- **Citation** - *see GENERAL MOTORS (38020)*
- 24032 **Corsica/Beretta** all models '87 thru '96
- 24040 **Corvette** all V8 models '68 thru '82
- 24041 **Corvette** all models '84 thru '96
- 10305 **Chevrolet Engine Overhaul Manual**
- 24045 **Full-size Sedans** Caprice, Impala, Biscayne, Bel Air & Wagons '69 thru '90
- 24046 **Impala SS & Caprice and Buick Roadmaster** '91 thru '96
- **Impala** - *see LUMINA (24048)*
- **Lumina '90 thru '94** - *see GM (38010)*
- *24048 **Lumina & Monte Carlo** '95 thru '01
- **Lumina APV** - *see GM (38035)*
- 24050 **Luv Pick-up** all 2WD & 4WD '72 thru '82
- **Malibu '97 thru '00** - *see GM (38026)*
- 24055 **Monte Carlo** all models '70 thru '88
- **Monte Carlo** '95 thru '01 - *see LUMINA (24048)*
- 24059 **Nova** all V8 models '69 thru '79
- 24060 **Nova and Geo Prizm** '85 thru '92
- 24064 **Pick-ups '67 thru '87** - Chevrolet & GMC, all V8 & in-line 6 cyl, 2WD & 4WD '67 thru '87; Suburbans, Blazers & Jimmys '67 thru '91
- 24065 **Pick-ups '88 thru '98** - Chevrolet & GMC, full-size pick-ups '88 thru '98, C/K Classic '99 & '00, Blazer & Jimmy '92 thru '94; Suburban '92 thru '99; Tahoe & Yukon '95 thru '99
- *24066 **Pick-ups '99 thru '01** - Chevrolet Silverado & GMC Sierra full-size pick-ups '99 thru '01, Suburban/Tahoe/Yukon/Yukon XL '00 thru '01
- 24070 **S-10 & S-15 Pick-ups** '82 thru '93, **Blazer & Jimmy** '83 thru '94,
- *24071 **S-10 & S-15 Pick-ups** '94 thru '01, **Blazer & Jimmy** '95 thru '01, **Hombre** '96 thru '01
- 24075 **Sprint** '85 thru '88 **& Geo Metro** '89 thru '01
- 24080 **Vans - Chevrolet & GMC** '68 thru '96

CHRYSLER

- 25015 **Chrysler Cirrus, Dodge Stratus, Plymouth Breeze** '95 thru '00
- 10310 **Chrysler Engine Overhaul Manual**
- 25020 **Full-size Front-Wheel Drive** '88 thru '93
- **K-Cars** - *see DODGE Aries (30008)*
- **Laser** - *see DODGE Daytona (30030)*
- 25025 **Chrysler LHS, Concorde, New Yorker, Dodge** Intrepid, **Eagle** Vision, '93 thru '97
- *25026 **Chrysler LHS, Concorde, 300M, Dodge** Intrepid, '98 thru '03
- 25030 **Chrysler & Plymouth Mid-size** front wheel drive '82 thru '95
- **Rear-wheel Drive** - *see Dodge (30050)*
- *25035 **PT Cruiser** all models '01 thru '03
- *25040 **Chrysler** Sebring, **Dodge** Avenger '95 thru '02

DATSUN

- 28005 **200SX** all models '80 thru '83
- 28007 **B-210** all models '73 thru '78
- 28009 **210** all models '79 thru '82
- 28012 **240Z, 260Z & 280Z** Coupe '70 thru '78
- 28014 **280ZX** Coupe & 2+2 '79 thru '83
- **300ZX** - *see NISSAN (72010)*
- 28016 **310** all models '78 thru '82
- 28018 **510 & PL521 Pick-up** '68 thru '73
- 28020 **510** all models '78 thru '81
- 28022 **620 Series Pick-up** all models '73 thru '79
- **720 Series Pick-up** - *see NISSAN (72030)*
- 28025 **810/Maxima** all gasoline models, '77 thru '84

DODGE

- **400 & 600** - *see CHRYSLER (25030)*
- 30008 **Aries & Plymouth Reliant** '81 thru '89
- 30010 **Caravan & Plymouth Voyager** '84 thru '95
- *30011 **Caravan & Plymouth Voyager** '96 thru '02
- 30012 **Challenger/Plymouth Saporro** '78 thru '83
- 30016 **Colt & Plymouth Champ** '78 thru '87
- 30020 **Dakota Pick-ups** all models '87 thru '96
- *30021 **Durango** '98 & '99, **Dakota** '97 thru '99
- 30025 **Dart, Demon, Plymouth Barracuda, Duster & Valiant** 6 cyl models '67 thru '76
- 30030 **Daytona & Chrysler Laser** '84 thru '89
- **Intrepid** - *see CHRYSLER (25025, 25026)*
- *30034 **Neon** all models '95 thru '99
- 30035 **Omni & Plymouth Horizon** '78 thru '90
- 30040 **Pick-ups** all full-size models '74 thru '93
- *30041 **Pick-ups** all full-size models '94 thru '01
- 30045 **Ram 50/D50 Pick-ups & Raider and Plymouth Arrow Pick-ups** '79 thru '93
- 30050 **Dodge/Plymouth/Chrysler** RWD '71 thru '89
- 30055 **Shadow & Plymouth Sundance** '87 thru '94
- 30060 **Spirit & Plymouth Acclaim** '89 thru '95
- *30065 **Vans - Dodge & Plymouth** '71 thru '03

EAGLE

- **Talon** - *see MITSUBISHI (68030, 68031)*
- **Vision** - *see CHRYSLER (25025)*

FIAT

- 34010 **124 Sport Coupe & Spider** '68 thru '78
- 34025 **X1/9** all models '74 thru '80

FORD

- 10355 **Ford Automatic Transmission Overhaul**
- 36004 **Aerostar Mini-vans** all models '86 thru '97
- 36006 **Contour & Mercury Mystique** '95 thru '00
- 36008 **Courier Pick-up** all models '72 thru '82
- *36012 **Crown Victoria & Mercury Grand Marquis** '88 thru '00
- 10320 **Ford Engine Overhaul Manual**
- 36016 **Escort/Mercury Lynx** all models '81 thru '90
- 36020 **Escort/Mercury Tracer** '91 thru '00
- 36024 **Explorer & Mazda Navajo** '91 thru '01
- 36028 **Fairmont & Mercury Zephyr** '78 thru '83
- 36030 **Festiva & Aspire** '88 thru '97
- 36032 **Fiesta** all models '77 thru '80
- *36034 **Focus** all models '00 and '01
- 36036 **Ford & Mercury Full-size** '75 thru '87
- 36040 **Granada & Mercury Monarch** '75 thru '80
- 36044 **Ford & Mercury Mid-size** '75 thru '86
- 36048 **Mustang V8** all models '64-1/2 thru '73
- 36049 **Mustang II** 4 cyl, V6 & V8 models '74 thru '78
- 36050 **Mustang & Mercury Capri** all models Mustang, '79 thru '93; Capri, '79 thru '86
- *36051 **Mustang** all models '94 thru '03
- 36054 **Pick-ups & Bronco** '73 thru '79
- 36058 **Pick-ups & Bronco** '80 thru '96
- *36059 **F-150 & Expedition** '97 thru '02, **F-250** '97 thru '99 **& Lincoln Navigator** '98 thru '02
- *36060 **Super Duty Pick-ups, Excursion** '97 thru '02
- 36062 **Pinto & Mercury Bobcat** '75 thru '80
- 36066 **Probe** all models '89 thru '92
- 36070 **Ranger/Bronco II** gasoline models '83 thru '92
- *36071 **Ranger** '93 thru '00 & **Mazda Pick-ups** '94 thru '00
- 36074 **Taurus & Mercury Sable** '86 thru '95
- *36075 **Taurus & Mercury Sable** '96 thru '01
- 36078 **Tempo & Mercury Topaz** '84 thru '94
- 36082 **Thunderbird/Mercury Cougar** '83 thru '88
- 36086 **Thunderbird/Mercury Cougar** '89 and '97
- 36090 **Vans** all V8 Econoline models '69 thru '91
- *36094 **Vans** full size '92 thru '01
- *36097 **Windstar Mini-van** '95 thru '03

GENERAL MOTORS

- 10360 **GM Automatic Transmission Overhaul**
- 38005 **Buick Century, Chevrolet Celebrity, Oldsmobile Cutlass Ciera & Pontiac 6000** all models '82 thru '96
- *38010 **Buick Regal, Chevrolet Lumina, Oldsmobile Cutlass Supreme & Pontiac Grand Prix** (FWD) '88 thru '02
- 38015 **Buick Skyhawk, Cadillac Cimarron, Chevrolet Cavalier, Oldsmobile Firenza & Pontiac J-2000 & Sunbird** '82 thru '94
- *38016 **Chevrolet Cavalier & Pontiac Sunfire** '95 thru '01
- 38020 **Buick Skylark, Chevrolet Citation, Olds Omega, Pontiac Phoenix** '80 thru '85
- 38025 **Buick Skylark & Somerset, Oldsmobile Achieva & Calais and Pontiac Grand Am** all models '85 thru '98
- *38026 **Chevrolet Malibu, Olds Alero & Cutlass, Pontiac Grand Am** '97 thru '00
- 38030 **Cadillac Eldorado** '71 thru '85, **Seville** '80 thru '85, **Oldsmobile Toronado** '71 thru '85, **Buick Riviera** '79 thru '85
- *38031 **Cadillac Eldorado & Seville** '86 thru '91, **DeVille** '86 thru '93, **Fleetwood & Olds Toronado** '86 thru '92, **Buick Riviera** '86 thru '93
- 38032 **Cadillac DeVille** '94 thru '02 **& Seville** - '92 thru '02
- 38035 **Chevrolet Lumina APV, Olds Silhouette & Pontiac Trans Sport** all models '90 thru '96
- *38036 **Chevrolet Venture, Olds Silhouette, Pontiac Trans Sport & Montana** '97 thru '01
- **General Motors Full-size Rear-wheel Drive** - see BUICK (19025)

GEO

- **Metro** - *see CHEVROLET Sprint (24075)*
- **Prizm** - *'85 thru '92 see CHEVY (24060), '93 thru '02 see TOYOTA Corolla (92036)*

(Continued on other side)

** Listings shown with an asterisk (*) indicate model coverage as of this printing. These titles will be periodically updated to include later model years - consult your Haynes dealer for more information.*

Haynes Automotive Manuals (continued)

NOTE: New manuals are added to this list on a periodic basis. If you do not see a listing for your vehicle, consult your local Haynes dealer for the latest product information.

40030 **Storm** all models '90 thru '93
Tracker - *see SUZUKI Samurai (90010)*

GMC
Vans & Pick-ups - *see CHEVROLET*

HONDA
42010 **Accord CVCC** all models '76 thru '83
42011 **Accord** all models '84 thru '89
42012 **Accord** all models '90 thru '93
42013 **Accord** all models '94 thru '97
*42014 **Accord** all models '98 and '99
42020 **Civic 1200** all models '73 thru '79
42021 **Civic 1300 & 1500 CVCC** '80 thru '83
42022 **Civic 1500 CVCC** all models '75 thru '79
42023 **Civic** all models '84 thru '91
42024 **Civic & del Sol** '92 thru '95
*42025 **Civic** '96 thru '00, **CR-V** '97 thru '00, **Acura Integra** '94 thru '00
42040 **Prelude CVCC** all models '79 thru '89

HYUNDAI
*43010 **Elantra** all models '96 thru '01
43015 **Excel & Accent** all models '86 thru '98

ISUZU
Hombre - *see CHEVROLET S-10 (24071)*
*47017 **Rodeo** '91 thru '02; **Amigo** '89 thru '94 and '98 thru '02; **Honda Passport** '95 thru '02
47020 **Trooper & Pick-up** '81 thru '93

JAGUAR
49010 **XJ6** all 6 cyl models '68 thru '86
49011 **XJ6** all models '88 thru '94
49015 **XJ12 & XJS** all 12 cyl models '72 thru '85

JEEP
50010 **Cherokee, Comanche & Wagoneer Limited** all models '84 thru '00
50020 **CJ** all models '49 thru '86
*50025 **Grand Cherokee** all models '93 thru '00
50029 **Grand Wagoneer & Pick-up** '72 thru '91 Grand Wagoneer '84 thru '91, Cherokee & Wagoneer '72 thru '83, Pick-up '72 thru '88
*50030 **Wrangler** all models '87 thru '00

LEXUS
ES 300 - *see TOYOTA Camry (92007)*

LINCOLN
Navigator - *see FORD Pick-up (36059)*
*59010 **Rear-Wheel Drive** all models '70 thru '01

MAZDA
61010 **GLC Hatchback (rear-wheel drive)** '77 thru '83
61011 **GLC (front-wheel drive)** '81 thru '85
61015 **323 & Protogé** '90 thru '00
*61016 **MX-5 Miata** '90 thru '97
61020 **MPV** all models '89 thru '94
Navajo - *see Ford Explorer (36024)*
61030 **Pick-ups** '72 thru '93
Pick-ups '94 thru '00 - *see Ford Ranger (36071)*
61035 **RX-7** all models '79 thru '85
61036 **RX-7** all models '86 thru '91
61040 **626** (rear-wheel drive) all models '79 thru '82
61041 **626/MX-6 (front-wheel drive)** '83 thru '91
61042 **626** '93 thru '01, **MX-6/Ford Probe** '93 thru '97

MERCEDES-BENZ
63012 **123 Series Diesel** '76 thru '85
63015 **190 Series** four-cyl gas models, '84 thru '88
63020 **230/250/280** 6 cyl sohc models '68 thru '72
63025 **280 123 Series** gasoline models '77 thru '81
63030 **350 & 450** all models '71 thru '80

MERCURY
64200 **Villager & Nissan Quest** '93 thru '01
All other titles, see FORD Listing.

MG
66010 **MGB** Roadster & GT Coupe '62 thru '80
66015 **MG Midget, Austin Healey Sprite** '58 thru '80

MITSUBISHI
68020 **Cordia, Tredia, Galant, Precis & Mirage** '83 thru '93
68030 **Eclipse, Eagle Talon & Ply. Laser** '90 thru '94
*68031 **Eclipse** '95 thru '01, **Eagle Talon** '95 thru '98
68040 **Pick-up** '83 thru '96 **& Montero** '83 thru '93

NISSAN
72010 **300ZX** all models including Turbo '84 thru '89
72015 **Altima** all models '93 thru '01
72020 **Maxima** all models '85 thru '92
*72021 **Maxima** all models '93 thru '01
72030 **Pick-ups** '80 thru '97 **Pathfinder** '87 thru '95
*72031 **Frontier Pick-up** '98 thru '01, **Xterra** '00 & '01, **Pathfinder** '96 thru '01
72040 **Pulsar** all models '83 thru '86
Quest - *see MERCURY Villager (64200)*
72050 **Sentra** all models '82 thru '94
72051 **Sentra & 200SX** all models '95 thru '99
72060 **Stanza** all models '82 thru '90

OLDSMOBILE
73015 **Cutlass** V6 & V8 gas models '74 thru '88
For other OLDSMOBILE titles, see BUICK, CHEVROLET or GENERAL MOTORS listing.

PLYMOUTH
For PLYMOUTH titles, see DC DGE listing.

PONTIAC
79008 **Fiero** all models '84 thru '88
79018 **Firebird** V8 models except Turbo '70 thru '81
79019 **Firebird** all models '82 thru '92
79040 **Mid-size Rear-wheel Drive** '7 thru '87
For other PONTIAC titles, see BUICK, CHEVROLET or GENERAL MOTORS listing.

PORSCHE
80020 **911** except Turbo & Carrera 4 '65 thru '89
80025 **914** all 4 cyl models '69 thru '76
80030 **924** all models including Turbo ... '82
80035 **944** all models including Turbo ... '89

RENAULT
Alliance & Encore - *see AMC (14*

SAAB
*84010 **900** all models including Turbo '79 ... '88

SATURN
*87010 **Saturn** all models '91 thru '02

SUBARU
89002 **1100, 1300, 1400 & 1** ... 71 thr
89003 **1600 & 1800** 2WD & 4W ... 30 thru

SUZUKI
90010 **Samurai/Sidekick & Geo Tracker** '86 ... 01

TOYOTA
92005 **Camry** all models '83 thru '91
92006 **Camry** all models '92 thru '96
*92007 **Camry, Avalon, Solara, Lexus ES 300** '97 thru '01
92015 **Celica Rear Wheel Drive** '71 thru '85
92020 [illegible]
92025 [illegible]
92030 [illegible]
92032 [illegible]
92035 [illegible]
92036 [illegible]
92040 [illegible]
92045 [illegible]
92050 [illegible]
92055 [illegible]
92056 [illegible]
92065 [illegible]
92070 [illegible]
92075 [illegible]
*92076 [illegible]
*92078 [illegible]
92080 **Previa** all models '91 thru '95
*92082 **RAV4** all models '96 thru '02
92085 **Tercel** all models '87 thru '94

TRIUMPH
94007 **Spitfire** all models '62 thru '81
94010 **TR7** all models '75 thru '81

VW
96008 **Beetle & Karmann Ghia** '54 thru '79
*96009 **New Beetle** '98 thru '00
96016 **Rabbit, Jetta, Scirocco & Pick-up** gas models '74 thru '91 & Convertible '80 thru '92
96017 **Golf, GTI & Jetta** '93 thru '98 **& Cabrio** '95 thru '98
*96018 **Golf, GTI, Jetta & Cabrio** '99 thru '02
96020 **Rabbit, Jetta & Pick-up** diesel '77 thru '84
96023 **Passat** '98 thru '01, **Audi A4** '96 thru '01
96030 **Transporter 1600** all models '68 thru '79
96035 **Transporter 1700, 1800 & 2000** '72 thru '79
96040 **Type 3 1500 & 1600** all models '63 thru '73
96045 **Vanagon** all air-cooled models '80 thru '83

VOLVO
97010 **120, 130 Series & 1800 Sports** '61 thru '73
97015 **140 Series** all models '66 thru '74
97020 **240 Series** all models '76 thru '93
97040 **740 & 760 Series** all models '82 thru '88
97050 **850 Series** all models '93 thru '97

TECHBOOK MANUALS
10205 **Automotive Computer Codes**
10210 **Automotive Emissions Control Manual**
10215 **Fuel Injection Manual, 1978 thru 1985**
10220 **Fuel Injection Manual, 1986 thru 1999**
10225 **Holley Carburetor Manual**
10230 **Rochester Carburetor Manual**
10240 **Weber/Zenith/Stromberg/SU Carburetors**
10305 **Chevrolet Engine Overhaul Manual**
10310 **Chrysler Engine Overhaul Manual**
10320 **Ford Engine Overhaul Manual**
10330 **GM and Ford Diesel Engine Repair Manual**
10340 **Small Engine Repair Manual,** 5 HP & Less
10341 **Small Engine Repair Manual,** 5.5 - 20 HP
10345 **Suspension, Steering & Driveline Manual**
10355 **Ford Automatic Transmission Overhaul**
10360 **GM Automatic Transmission Overhaul**
10405 **Automotive Body Repair & Painting**
10410 **Automotive Brake Manual**
10411 **Automotive Anti-lock Brake (ABS) Systems**
10415 **Automotive Detaiing Manual**
10420 **Automotive Eelectrical Manual**
10425 **Automotive Heating & Air Conditioning**
10430 **Automotive Reference Manual & Dictionary**
10435 **Automotive Tools Manual**
10440 **Used Car Buying Guide**
10445 **Welding Manual**
10450 **ATV Basics**

SPANISH MANUALS
98903 **Reparación de Carrocería & Pintura**
98905 **Códigos Automotrices de la Computadora**
98910 **Frenos Automotriz**
98915 **Inyección de Combustible 1986 al 1999**
99040 **Chevrolet & GMC Camionetas** '67 al '87 Incluye Suburban, Blazer & Jimmy '67 al '91
99041 **Chevrolet & GMC Camionetas** '88 al '98 Incluye Suburban '92 al '98, Blazer & Jimmy '92 al '94, Tahoe y Yukon '95 al '98
99042 **Chevrolet & GMC Camionetas Cerradas** '68 al '95
99055 **Dodge Caravan & Plymouth Voyager** '84 al '95
99075 **Ford Camionetas y Bronco** '80 al '94
99077 **Ford Camionetas Cerradas** '69 al '91
99083 **Ford Modelos de Tamaño Grande** '75 al '87
99088 **Ford Modelos de Tamaño Mediano** '75 al '86
99091 **Ford Taurus & Mercury Sable** '86 al '95
99095 **GM Modelos de Tamaño Grande** '70 al '90
99100 **GM Modelos de Tamaño Mediano** '70 al '88
99110 **Nissan Camioneta** '80 al '96, **Pathfinder** '87 al '95
99118 **Nissan Sentra** '82 al '94
99125 **Toyota Camionetas y 4Runner** '79 al '95

** Listings shown with an asterisk (*) indicate model coverage as of this printing. These titles will b... ...ally updated to include later model years - consult your Haynes dealer for more informatio*

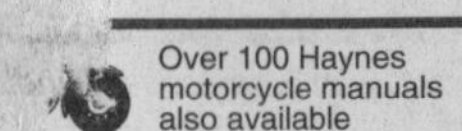